Fact and Fancy

in Television Regulation

Fact and Fancy in Television Regulation

An Economic Study of
Policy Alternatives

HARVEY J. LEVIN

Russell Sage Foundation　　　　　*New York*

PUBLICATIONS OF *Russell Sage Foundation*

This material was prepared with the support of the National Science Foundation Grant No. DAR 75–22336. However, any opinions, findings, conclusions, and/or recommendations expressed herein are those of the author(s) and do not necessarily reflect the views of NSF.

Library of Congress Catalog Number: 79–90148
Standard Book Number: 0–87154–531–4

To my parents

and

N. A. R. K. D. T.

Contents

PART I

Basic Framework

PART III
Assessment of Selected Alternatives

Tables

Acknowledgments

THIS STUDY was initiated in 1970 and since then has been mainly supported by the National Science Foundation and the Augustus B. Weller Chair in Economics at Hofstra University. A supplemental grant from the Russell Sage Foundation during the summer and fall of 1978 permitted major substantive revision of the final draft. I want to thank all three organizations for the extensive resources without which the inquiry could never have occurred, and in particular Aaron Wildavsky, then President of Russell Sage, and other foundation officers; Chuck Brownstein, Al Shinn, and Tom Sparrow at NSF; and, at Hofstra, colleagues and officials too numerous to name.

An advanced version of all or much of my final draft was thoroughly critiqued by Stanley Besen (Rice), Douglas Ginsburg (Harvard), Merton Peck (Yale), Geoffrey Shepherd (Michigan), and William Vickrey (Columbia). In addition to their helpful written comments, I very much benefited from many illuminating discussions about the work and from numerous specific suggestions.

Prior drafts of many chapters were also invaluably reviewed by Robert Crandall, Douglas Webbink, and John Peterman and, on a few special problems, by David Colander, Kenneth Jones, and Oliver Williamson. Beyond that I am deeply indebted to Richard Caves and Marc Roberts for incidentally helping me clarify important conceptual points in their excellent review of a paper I contributed to their book, *Regulating the Product* (1975). Thanks are further due to the Interuniversity Committee on Public Utility Economics for a chance to re-examine my methodology in a paper for their Sixth Annual Conference that year.

Earlier still, advanced planning for the full inquiry was much abetted by perceptive critiques of a detailed Interim Report, for which grateful thanks are especially due to Kenneth Jones, Henry Geller, Robert Crandall, and Leland Johnson. At the very outset, finally, initial planning was also aided by conference presentations for the American Economic Association in 1971, and the University of Chicago Business School in 1972, and by discussions at Stanford, Massachusetts Institute of Technology, and Harvard.

In Washington I was consistently helped to stay abreast of issues, data, and policy alternatives, first by Federal Communications Commissioner Nicholas Johnson, Robert Thorpe, Tracy Westen, Frank Lloyd, and Kenneth Cox, and later by Commissioner Glen Robinson, who also extensively critiqued my Interim Report and discussed many aspects at length, as well as by Alex Korn and Larry Eads. I am also grateful to Robert Blau for generous cooperation throughout and for many helpful observations. In addition, I must acknowledge valuable materials, criticisms, and insights from Stephen Barnett, John Barton, William Baxter, Michael Botein, Charles Firestone, Ed Greenberg, Ed Kuhlman, William Melody, Jesse Markham, John McGowan, Bridger Mitchell, Dick Moore, Bill Niskanen, Roger Noll, Bruce Owen, Ed Park, Edwin Parker, and Jim Rosse. I am further indebted to the American Research Bureau and the A. C. Nielsen Company for providing and explaining extensive audience and programming data; to the publishers of *TV Guide* for a full set of regional issues and related coding materials at the outset; to the program departments of the national television networks for classificatory information; to the Standard Rates and Data Service for information needed to complete complex compilations of usable rates data; and to John Dimling (N.A.B.) and Dave Blank (C.B.S.) for various industry studies and testimony.

For many editorial suggestions and important help in locating key research personnel, I owe a special debt to my good friend Natalie Allon. Special thanks are due also to Jacob Weissman, Departmental Chair, for sustained support throughout, and to Alice Gargiulo for office management beyond the call.

During the last five years of my investigation I worked in close collaboration with Jacob Merriwether, a Columbia Business School econometrician who developed the statistical design, provided continuing advisement on model specification and computer runs, and reviewed advanced drafts of all chapters. Jacob Merriwether's countless analytic memoranda and lucid commentary were invaluable in executing this study, and he personally confirmed all statistical results. Throughout he was assiduously aided by Jefferson Latham, my chief computer programmer and director of statistical analysis, who further assumed massive responsibilities in data base management. Under Latham's careful supervision, the complex data compilations were themselves painstakingly organized and cross-checked by several Hofstra research assistants—mainly Joe Bass, Marion Lord, Chere Latham, Steven Levitt, Glen Powell, and David Tedesco. In addition, two Hofstra law students—Jerome Harris and Louis Shoichet—helped me codify and assess copious docket materials; whereas Ted Woodruff, a Columbia doctoral economics fellow, ably reviewed cogent literature on the effects of direct regulation, as it pertained to my methodological framework.

This, then, was the "team" that produced the study. I alone, however, am fully responsible for the final results, for factual accuracy, and for the many interpretative details. In no case do my conclusions necessarily represent those of the National Science Foundation, the Russell Sage Foundation, or Hofstra University.

H. J. L.
Garden City, New York
December 1979

Fact and Fancy

in Television Regulation

Chapter 1

Scope and Method

THIS BOOK examines the licensing of television stations. In particular, it addresses the stated objectives and actual results of the licensing policy and practices of the Federal Communications Commission. The inquiry, then, is a case study in regulatory effects and policy alternatives. My procedure will be, first, to identify the relevant regulatory goals, at least those that frequently appear in regulatory, legislative, and judicial pronouncements, though not necessarily reflected in sustained FCC policies; second, and most important, to measure the divergence of these stated goals from actual licensee performance; third, to explain these divergences; and fourth, to consider alternative ways to narrow or eliminate them.

Briefly, I shall measure the impact of federal licensing and allocation on TV station profitability, program diversity, and prime-time program composition. The question is whether the long-standing policy of license limitation acts to raise profitability, and if so, whether higher diversity levels and cultural-informational programming also result. If profits and scarcity rents do rise, but with no offsetting enhancement of program composition, the further task is to assess the principal techniques often proposed to rectify the situation. To the extent that the FCC has been successful in diverting *potential* profits into public service before they materialize, however, one might well *observe* no relationship between the two variables. The stated goals of regulation would then converge with results, and the need for further remedial action would diminish, upon the assumption that the stated goals are worthwhile objectives.

In this study, franchise values, economic rents, and supernormal station profitability are assumed to be the formally unintended and, initially, unexpected consequences of federal licensing. At the least, the professed goals of broadcast regulation do not include private gain but emphasize instead the public interest, convenience, and necessity. My reading of broadcast regulatory doctrine reveals its principal stated goal, from the earliest period, to be diversity of ideas, standards, and values in program content even if such a mix were on that account less remunerative than otherwise. In the early rhetoric, too, there was generally special emphasis on news, public affairs, and an electorate-informing service. A second goal is localism, that is, a program service responsive to local tastes, interests, and needs supplied, insofar as feasible, through locally owned stations limited by rule in the amount of nationally originated programs they may carry overall. Related to these is a third goal, the wide geographic availability of service even in markets too weak to attract it without regulatory implementation, and where possible provided by stations in each locality. Finally, if the ultimate goal is maximum program choice—diversity with cultural-informational programming, from local as well as national sources—then the proximate goal is competition consistent with public service responsibilities.

Objectives versus Results in
Regulatory Assessment

My assumption throughout this inquiry is that the stated purposes of federal broadcast licensing (as of regulation elsewhere) can quite properly serve as a major yardstick by which to evaluate its end results; so, too, can those coincidental side effects that are not initially mandated by Congress and the courts. Indeed, recognition of regulatory effects as such already abounds in the economic literature. However, the principal focus is often on *unanticipated* results and far less on the formally mandated purposes.

Professed purposes are not always neglected in practice. Nor are the many studies of (unexpected) effects devoid of their own important insights. But one misses a critical dimension of regulatory assessment by not looking as closely at "purposes"—the formal or legitimate mandate —as at results. My principal concern is therefore this: Are the formal purposes of broadcast licensing furthered at all? By how much? Or are they essentially a façade to mask or legitimatize the side effects? And what would change if alternative regulatory policies were adopted?

In broadcasting, as elsewhere, many regulatory goals are noneconomic, and the possible price of their furtherance could, though not necessarily, be a loss in economic efficiency and a reduction in pecuniary measures of consumer welfare. Accurate predictions and wide public divulgence of this price are important lest policymakers wrongly reject one or more goals, or lack adequate incentives to devise ways to further them at lower costs in forgone efficiency.

There is nothing new about such a multidimensional approach to federal regulation. A number of studies have by now included administrative standards in their appraisal of structure and conduct in the regulated industries. In addition to price-cost efficiency, such studies consider product diversity, quality, safety, reliability, innovative performance, military security, and so forth. These multidimensional assessments permit the simultaneous appraisal of industry and regulatory performance alike. In applying orthodox industry-study methodology to regulated industries, such studies underscore the need to determine the consistency of explicit regulatory priorities with other, more familiar market performance considerations.

In that general spirit I propose to distinguish here between regulatory goals (intentions) and regulatory results (realizations). I shall further assume that economic efficiency is not necessarily the same as *regulatory* efficiency; that regulatory efficiency exists when results accord with goals (in a least-cost manner), whereas a widening divergence between them represents "regulatory failure" or something tantamount to "regulatory fraud." The element of fraud inheres in the fact that the public promises remain largely unrealized, while, in addition, unwanted side effects raise further doubts whether the initial rules, regulations, and laws would have been enacted at all had their multiple consequences been fully grasped at the outset. Moreover, even if regulation's formal objectives are in some fashion realized, there may still be unanticipated or unauthorized consequences, failures that impair public confidence in its efficacy and integrity. In both cases a fraud is seemingly perpetrated more by the collective process of regulation as a whole than by any conscious intent of individual regulators.[1] To say that many regulatory policies are rationalized by political statements where agencies are simply trying to safeguard their budgetary security in the appropriations process in no way alters the element of fraud as herein conceived. In the final analysis, publicly nurtured expectations remain unmet. My conception may be obscured where intended goals such as diversity are obtained but where there are *also* unintended results, such as economic rents earned. But there, too, the public may in a real sense have had to pay more than anticipated for "benefits" received.[2]

By the same token, such failures or regulatory fraud could be rectified by devising techniques, policies, or institutional arrangements that act to (1) narrow the divergence between stated intentions and results; (2) eliminate the unauthorized effects of regulation without upsetting any in-

1. The economic literature in which the distinctions drawn in this paragraph emerge is reviewed in my "Unanticipated Consequences under Direct Regulation," in *Salvaging Public Utility Regulation,* ed. Werner Sichel (Lexington, Mass.: D. C. Heath, Lexington Books, 1976), especially pp. 117–32, 140–46.
2. See Charles A. Reich, "The New Property," *Yale Law Journal* (April 1964): 733–87.

tended effects; or (3) facilitate more intended results without more unwanted economic side effects.[3] Then, and only then, may regulators in
fact achieve what they purport to achieve. Only then, indeed, can we embark upon the more basic task of economic regulation—to formulate appropriate substantive standards, without which no implementing policy
can be meaningful.

Some observers may, of course, argue that the effects designated here
as unintended (such as rents, franchise values, or supernormal profits)
are very much the regulator's major preoccupation—indeed, his true objective. For such observers, the stated or reputed goals serve only as a
ceremonial smokescreen of little import. I disagree. If the side effects
are indeed what regulation is all about, and the stated goals only a distraction or side show, one might properly ask whether the techniques
in use should be tolerated *at all,* or whether their impropriety is not
inherent in stated goals that largely serve to mask regulation's consciously restrictive value-creating function.[4]

In broadcasting, for example, restrictive entry controls have never
been, and clearly could not publicly nor politically be, justified for creating economic rents and valuable private privileges. The rents simply
arise as coincidental side effects of regulatory control of marginal signal
interference and, within those constraints, of the pursuit of localism and
diversity. In that specific sense the rents are clearly not formally mandated or legitimate results of regulation but rather unintended consequences that arise in the regulator's pursuit of particular public goals.
True, these formally illegitimate side effects have been tacitly sanctioned
(and acquiesced to) by inaction. There may even be problems in taking
away monopoly rents once they have been earned, or in recapturing
franchise values that new companies have already paid for. Nevertheless,
the FCC is nowhere instructed to create or subsequently to sanction
such private economic advantages, and has long been subject to sharp
criticism for having done so.

Be this as it may, my approach explicitly recognizes the importance
of (1) using dependent variables not limited to economic efficiency; (2)
the distinction between intentions and results in terms of these variables;
(3) removing effects due to major control factors; and (4) evaluating
policy alternatives within such a framework. In so doing, we necessarily
distinguish between what a commission says it *wants* to do and the actual
consequences that follow, whether or not consistent with those pronouncements.

3. This framework would clearly permit me to assess current proposals for deregulation. Deregulation in the form of an easing of entry restrictions and program
regulations could in principle be justified under any one of these three yardsticks. To
determine which is most appropriate is a matter of empirical analysis, a task that much
of this book will undertake.
4. For a classic statement about such growing governmental largess, see Charles A.
Reich, "The New Property."

In the Sixth Report and Order released in 1952, for example, the FCC stated its intentions in the form of five allocational objectives. In order of priority, these goals were: (1) to provide at least one TV service to all parts of the nation; (2) to provide each community with at least one TV station; (3) to provide a choice of at least two TV services to all parts of the nation; (4) to provide each community with at least two TV stations; and (5) to assign to various communities any channels that remain unassigned under the preceding priorities, according to community size, geographical location, and the number of TV services available to such communities from TV stations located in other communities.[5] In using these goals for purposes of regulatory assessment, one might first determine the degree to which any or all have been *realized* over the ensuing twenty-five years. Next, one might consider the trade-offs or conflicts among the goals as, for example, between wide-area service and local community stations; big-city outlets and service to smaller communities or rural areas; localism and competing stations or services. One would also consider whether these or related conflicts could be reconciled or reduced by reliance on alternative institutional or financial arrangements, which might include pay-cable grids linked nationally by satellites as a vehicle for reconciling, say, localism with wide-area service and competition.

Still another distinction is also pertinent that is, between the *resources* that regulators expend to implement their stated goals, and what they *claim* to be doing. Not all "unanticipated" side effects are due exclusively to poor regulatory analysis and prediction: the regulatory effort may simply be deficient. Nevertheless, this latter distinction is largely ignored in this study on at least two counts. First, to ascertain the extent to which a commission "seriously" pursues a stated objective would require far more research and analysis than any mere cataloging of regulatory statements of intent. If only for those practical reasons the question of intensity of commission effort must be ignored in what follows. Second, regulation's true resolve is largely beside the point for present purposes. Suffice it to note only that if regulation *purports* to pursue, say, product safety, reliability, diversity, localism, or wide geographic service, its success or failure in doing so both can and ought to be assessed and constitutes important knowledge which, when injected into the decisional process, can well lead to changes in legislative oversight and reform. Whether the commission's true objectives and reputed goals fully coincide may, of course, come to light in any thoroughgoing investigation. However, neither the stability nor the consistency of such regulatory preferences is by any means self-evident and must be clearly established in each case.

5. See Federal Communications Commission, Sixth Report and Order in re: Amendment of 47 CFR par. 3.606, FCC Docket No. 8736, 17 Fed. Reg. 3905, 3906, 3912 (1952).

For the present purpose, any such determination seems beyond my available resources. I therefore propose instead to work with public pronouncements and statements of intent.[6] I do, of course, recognize that the empirical relevance of such pronouncements is often discounted by those who contend that the latter tells us more about what regulation purports to do than about actual intentions. Rather than accept such a façade, economists are increasingly invited to undertake quantitative studies of regulatory impact.

Yet this latter approach leaves some vital questions unanswered: Which consequences shall we examine, and how shall they be assessed? Whose standards shall we use, which dependent variables? One could of course select indicators of regulatory impact by "intuition." But it seems imprudent to rule out at least some attention to stated objectives. With only modest changes, most studies of regulation could in fact take explicit account of such objectives. In so doing, one must presumably review the legal-administrative materials directly, lest one be unduly influenced by the often vague norms that public agencies invoke. The resultant allocation of professional energy between intentions and results will no doubt vary from case to case.

Methodologically, then, the stated mandate or purpose of regulation can quite properly serve as an *additional* yardstick with which to evaluate end results. Estimates of regulatory effects already abound in the economic literature, but most attention has been focused on internal and allocative efficiency, and far less on the formally mandated, putative purposes. I propose to modify this practice here by casting my entire assessment in terms of intentions and results.

Broadcast Regulatory Criteria
as Standards for Evaluation

The appropriate standards for evaluating television are clearly not economic efficiency and technical progress alone but also include such frequently asserted goals as: diversified station ownership and program sources as instrumental to content diversity; unencumbered access to limited broadcast facilities by a broad spectrum of groups, and fairness in

6. There does remain the possibility of testing empirical techniques to ascertain "true" regulatory preferences on specific policy issues. The problems in using that approach are illustrated in F. Nelson and R. Noll, "In Search of Scientific Regulation—The UHF Allocation Experiment," a paper for the Sixth Annual Telecommunications Policy Research Conference at Airlie, Virginia, May 10–13, 1978. Nelson and Noll apply a survey instrument they developed as consultants to the FCC's UHF Task Force during the fall and winter of 1977.

their use; a wide geographic diffusion of facilities and service; and above all, a programming responsive to minority as well as to majority tastes, to local as well as to national interests.[7]

The Commitment to Localism, Information, Diversity, and Competition

The FCC has explicitly stated its commitment to local and informational service, as well as to the economic capabilities and know-how of licensees to provide them adequately. In determining what constitutes substantial service in television, the commission singles out local, news, and public affairs programming "designed to contribute to an informed electorate." It states:

> The Congressional scheme of TV allocations is based on local outlets. . . . If a television station does not serve in a substantial manner as a local outlet—if it is, in effect, a network spigot or mere purveyor of nonlocal film programming, it is clearly not meeting its crucial role. Similarly, we have stated that the reason we have allotted so much spectrum space to broadcasting is because of the contribution which it can make to an informed electorate. . . . If a broadcaster does not make such a contribution in a substantial fashion, he is again undermining the basic allocations scheme.[8]

Beyond this stated concern with the local and informational elements of program composition, the commission has further underscored the importance of "maximum competition among broadcasters and the greatest possible diversity of programming sources and viewpoints." [9] These "twin

7. I do not imply that economic efficiency is unrelated to content diversity or minority interest programming under existing or conceivable structures. It is, however, only loosely linked, and there are important trade-offs and inconsistencies. For an illuminating analysis of such issues, see M. Spence and B. Owen, "Television Programming, Monopolistic Competition and Welfare," *Quarterly Journal of Economics* (February 1977):103–26. The writers demonstrate that with or without unlimited entry, advertiser-supported and pay-TV systems both "contain biases against certain kinds of programs," in particular against "minority taste programs, and those that are expensive to produce" (p. 122). The authors further note that "no legitimate welfare considerations follow from [their] analysis, unless one values variety for its own sake" (p. 106). However, they also conclude that, with unlimited entry (cable TV), pay TV will result in more programs than supported by advertising, with "a desirable effect on viewer welfare, quite aside from [any] reduction in the [aforementioned] bias" (p. 125). My own assumptions in this book appear in some measure consistent with Spence and Owen. I presume only that under the present largely limited-entry, advertiser-supported framework, the policies used (or needed) to safeguard program diversity and special interest or minority service need at best not maximize viewer preferences or price-cost efficiency generally. Perhaps the most one can say is that the welfare loss due to alternative content diversifying strategies will vary with the cost and demand characteristics of the particular TV program in question.

8. Federal Communications Commission, Notice of Inquiry in Docket No. 19154 (Comparative Renewal Applicants), February 23, 1971, par. 3.

9. Federal Communications Commission, Report and Order in Docket No. 16068 (Group Ownership Rules), February 1969, par. 1. See also FCC, Notice of Inquiry in Docket No. 18449, February 8, 1969, par. 5.

goals of diversity and economic competition," however, are not always fully consistent; and where this is so, diversity is said to prevail:

> As to competition in particular, the national public policy (expressed in antitrust laws and elsewhere) in favor of competition . . . finds a reflection in the actions of the Commission. Sometimes, this policy will yield, however, to the even higher goals of diversity and the delivery of quality broadcasting. . . . This is a vitally important matter, for it is essential to a democracy that its electorate be informed and have access to divergent viewpoints on controversial issues. Needless to say, thought [has] to be given to how much diversity to seek in terms of providing the best practicable service to the American public.[10]

The vital importance of a diversity of sources as a condition of a diversity of viewpoints expressed, has also been frequently asserted:

> Diversification of control is a public good in a free society, and is additionally desirable where a government licensing system limits access by the public to the use of radio and television facilities. . . . As the Supreme Court has stated, the First Amendment . . . "rests on the assumption that the widest possible dissemination of information from diverse and antagonistic sources is essential to the welfare of the public." . . . That radio and television broadcast stations play an important role in providing news and opinion is obvious. That it is important in a free society to prevent a concentration of control of the sources of news and opinion and, particularly, that government should not create such a concentration, is equally apparent, and well established. . . .[11]

And again, more recently:

> Basic to our form of government is the belief that . . . "right conclusions are more likely to be gathered out of a multitude of tongues, than through any kind of authoritative selection." Thus our Constitution rests upon the ground that "the ultimate good desired is better reached by free trade in ideas—that the best test of truth is the power of the thought to get itself accepted in the competition of the market." These principles . . . are the wellspring . . . of the Commission's policy of diversifying control of [broadcast ownership]. For, centralization of control over the media . . . is, like monopolization of economic power, per se undesirable. The power to control what the public hears and sees over the airwaves matters, whatever the degree of self-restraint which may withhold its arbitrary use.[12]

Nor is the monitoring of licensee *conduct* in any case an adequate substitute for *structural* diversity as a guarantee of diversity in the viewpoints to which viewers have access:

10. Federal Communications Commission, Second Report and Order in Docket No. 18110 (Cross-Ownership Inquiry), January 31, 1975, par. 99 and n. 20.
11. Policy Statement on Comparative Broadcast Hearings, FCC–65–689 71120, July 28, 1965, p. 2.
12. Federal Communications Commission, First Report and Order in Docket No. 18110, April 6, 1970, pars. 16–17.

It is true that section 315 of the Communications Act, the . . . Fairness Doctrine, and . . . rules relating to personal attacks and station editorials . . . all contribute substantially toward insuring that, whatever a station's ownership, and the view of the licensee, each station will present conflicting viewpoints on controversial issues. However, this is not enough. . . . For . . . the key to the question is the public interest in acquiring information from diverse and antagonistic sources, and "news communicated to the public is subject to selection and, through selection, to editing, and . . . in addition there may be diversity in methods, manner and emphasis of presentation." This is true not only with respect to news programs, but also the entire range of a station's treatment of programs dealing with public affairs.[13]

To cite such stated recent commitments to localism, diversity, and information as useful standards for regulatory assessment does not imply that the goals of the Communications Act are fixed and immutable. I fully recognize that these purposes may change over time (as interpreted by the commission and the courts); that the act is highly plastic; and that the philosophies of individual commissioners are varied. Therefore, I do not suggest any rigid consistency of purpose from the outset of broadcast regulation in 1927.[14] Regulatory objectives admittedly emerge in a dynamic interplay of political, economic, social, and technological forces.

Nevertheless, we know that certain standards *have* survived these changes and the commission's periodic attempts at codification. Nor is there any question that the FCC's current commitments to localism, diversity, information, and competition (whatever their origins and changing character over time) *are* an appropriate yardstick for assessment and reform *today*.

Comparative Broadcast Licensing

With regard to licensing criteria more narrowly viewed, there appear to have developed two levels of licensing standards: minimum and maximum, the latter exacted at comparative proceedings. Thus an applicant may secure a license if uncontested where he has certain basic legal, technical, and financial qualifications, and meets standards of good engineering practice, and where his program plans do not violate existing rules on, say, obscenity or give-away shows. Nor may he already own the maximum number of stations permissible under the Multiple Owner-

13. Ibid., pars. 19–20; see also Second Report and Order, January 31, 1975, par. 110, where the commission states as its primary concern "diversity in ownership as a means of enhancing diversity in programming service to the public. . . ."

14. In radio's early days, for example, and again with the advent of television, cursory review of the legal literature suggests that the FCC apparently believed that some degree of economic concentration was justified to finance rapid development of the industry. Only much later did it start to question the *extent* of "needed" concentration, and its potential for abuse.

ship Rules, or propose to serve substantially the same area or areas contiguous to one in which he already holds a license. Besides this, sections 326(a) and 316 of the Communications Act require all licensees to refrain from obscenity and lotteries;[15] section 315 requires stations giving time to one political candidate to give equivalent time to all other candidates.

These minimum standards must ostensibly be met by all candidates and would thus appear to "stand on their own feet." But beyond this, according to the FCC's formal litany, at joint hearings of mutually exclusive applicants with equal technical, legal, and financial qualifications, it appears to prefer local residents to outsiders, and corporate applicants with highly integrated stock ownership where owners propose active participation in management to those with widely dispersed stock where responsibility is delegated. Also according to the litany, the commission has often said it prefers applicants with no broadcast interests elsewhere to those with such interests, nonnewspaper candidates to newspapers, applicants from underserved areas to those from well-served areas. Finally, the FCC often states a preference for applicants who propose "superior" programming in local live shows and "balanced" discussion of controversial questions to otherwise satisfactory rivals.[16]

In sum, the formal litany invoked at comparative hearings appears to be premised on a theory that the "public interest" will best be served by a licensee who knows his community's tastes and needs; spends full time on the job; shows initiative in contacting local, civic, cultural, and other groups; makes sincere attempts to activate whatever local talent is available; provides a "balanced" program service including some unspecified but "reasonable" number of sustaining programs as well as commercial ones, local live shows as well as network, recorded or wire service ones, and fair, thorough, and balanced discussion of public issues as well as entertainment.

Nevertheless, public critics find that the criteria formally "approved" by the FCC often diverge from its *actual* touchstones in particular decisions.[17] There is even some quantitative evidence to document this well-known proposition. In one study (1952–59) of 180 applicants in 65

15. Applicable also is Title 18 U.S. Code Annotated (St. Paul, Minn.: West Publishing Co., 1966), 1301 (lotteries), 1343 (fraud), 1464 (obscenity).

16. For an extensive review of comparative cases and proposals for simplification, see Robert Anthony, "Towards Simplicity and Rationally in Broadcast Licensing Proceedings," *Stanford Law Review* (November 1971), pp. 1–115. The commission's policy was codified in FCC, Policy Statement on Comparative Broadcast Hearings, FCC–65–689 71120, July 28, 1965, and its Policy Statement on Comparative Hearings Involving Regular Renewal Applicants, FCC–70–62 40869, January 15, 1970. However, this was overruled in Citizens Communication Center v. FCC, 447 F.2d 1201 (1971).

17. For a classic legal critique, see Henry J. Friendly, *The Federal Administrative Agencies* (Cambridge, Mass.: Harvard University Press, 1962), chap. 4. See also James M. Landis, Report on Regulatory Agencies to the President-Elect, Washington, D.C.: December 1960, pp. 53–54.

contested licensing cases, the FCC was shown to have overridden its stated criteria almost as often as it approved them.[18] In a more recent study (1967–70), of 16 contests involving 45 applicants, locally owned candidates offering more news, public affairs, and local originations were found to have *less* chance for success despite the FCC's formal preference for those attributes. On the other hand, available resources and total proposed programming may have heightened the chances for success regardless of the formal *demerit* of ties with other broadcast media.[19]

Nor are such inconsistencies without their own possible rationale: one observer has shown, for example, that a seemingly contradictory application of the newspaper ownership criterion is in many cases perfectly consistent with *political* considerations.[20] Other theories of regulatory behavior *imply* that the costly, interminable comparative TV licensing proceedings may essentially be mechanisms to find a conflict-avoiding compromise among competing special interests. For those observers, regulators want to maximize administrative discretion the better to safeguard their own personal welfare, future job status in the industry, and, above all, the agency's survival and growth. Avoidance of direct confrontations with powerful special interests is said to further those goals.[21] One could argue in that context that the sheer multiplicity of "approved" comparative licensing criteria permits the FCC to make almost *anything* look reasonable, particular sets of inconsistencies notwithstanding.

In spite of a divergence between the FCC's stated commitments and the actual criteria that ensure success in any given contest, my proposed use of agency goals for purposes of regulatory assessment is nonetheless valid. The commission's *actual* licensing decisions may raise questions about the degree of any sustained commitment to policy goals it has *professed*; but its codified standards remain.[22] Therefore, licensing

18. See Harvey Levin, "Regulatory Efficiency, Reform, and the FCC," *Georgetown Law Journal* (Fall 1961), nn. 91–92 and associated text.

19. See Roger Noll, Merton J. Peck, and John J. McGowan, *Economic Aspects of Television Regulation* (Washington, D.C.: The Brookings Institution, 1973), pp. 112–15.

20. See Bernard Schwartz, "Comparative Television and the Chancellor's Foot," *Georgetown Law Journal* (Summer 1959), pp. 655–99. Notwithstanding similar qualifications in many cases, during the Eisenhower administration "some nine Democratic newspapers [were] denied television licenses, while eight papers which [were] Republican or Eisenhower Democrats [were] awarded channels" (p. 693).

21. See Noll, Peck, and McGowan, *Economic Aspects of Television Regulation*, pp. 120–28, and especially Roger Noll, "The Behavior of Regulator Agencies," *Review of Social Economy* (March 1971), pp. 15–19. A very similar thesis is documented somewhat differently in George W. Hilton, "Basic Behavior of Regulatory Commissions," *American Economic Review* (May 1972), pp. 47–54.

22. The long criticized inconsistencies in FCC licensing behavior may indeed have been exaggerated. A sophisticated analysis of comparative licensing criteria published after galleys for this chapter were set concludes that, while the FCC's decision process has many economic and administrative shortcomings, "its outcomes appear less capricious than they were charged as being before the (1965) Policy Statement. Indeed, the Policy Statement appears to have refined the decision criteria, and the

behavior notwithstanding, we can still quite properly ask what the impact of policies based on the FCC's *stated* standards *would* be if they were now applied more rigorously, and consistently. Later chapters will attempt to determine just that, mainly by measuring regulatory impact on local and informational programming and program diversity generally—the stated areas of agency concern—as well as on economic performance, a measure of unintended side effects.

Postulated Agency Objectives

With regard to regulatory preferences as to programming, Professor Kenneth Jones of Columbia Law School has cautiously summarized the present state of affairs as follows:

> There are frequent references to FCC preferences for some types of programming over others. As to some of these preferences, one could show that, in *some* contexts, at *some* time, *some* members of the Commission expressed a preference for particular types of programs. In terms of sustained policy, however, it is doubtful that a demonstration could be made which went beyond these limited propositions:
> (a)   Some degree of [locally] oriented programming is desirable (but without any quantitative measure).
> (b)   Some significant attention to news and public affairs is desirable (but without any quantitative measure).
> (c)   Increased diversity in program offerings is desirable (but without clear articulation as to what "diversity" encompasses and how it is to be measured).
> At no point has any optimum figure for any category been developed. Even as to the items mentioned, it would seem inappropriate to suggest that increased local offerings and increased news and public affairs programming are to be favored without regard to the magnitudes already reached in existing offerings. "Diversity" may be more open-ended and the optimum may be infinite; but that may depend on the definition and context.[23]

I return to these and related issues in chapter 3; but meanwhile, suffice it to say that I want to avoid any semblance of a scientific use of "regulatory preferences" or formal priorities in assessing agency or industry performance. I agree with Kenneth Jones that it is probably more accurate simply to say that, *if* one were interested in furthering, say, diversity, as defined and measured in some convincing fashion, then it

---

FCC seems to be operating within its guidelines." Margaret Barton, "Conditional Logit Analysis of FCC Decisionmaking," *Bell Journal*, Autumn 1979, pp. 409–10. In particular, the FCC is shown to have applied its stated preferences for local ownership as reflected in integration of ownership with management, diversification of mass media ownership, and total hours broadcast, more consistently than often contended by scholarly investigators. Ibid., pp. 399–411.

23. From a private communication with William K. Jones.

is possible and useful to test for the impact of a number of structural and ownership policies on that yardstick. I also agree that it is possible to test any number of other touchstones that regulators pay frequent lip service to in their decisions (localism, wide-area service) for consistency with each other and with diversity, as well as with economic efficiency. We would then leave the legislator or regulator to decide what to do with our new factual knowledge about trade-offs. In other words, it seems sounder to let the reader use the evidence as he sees fit than to couch our results in an overly rigid manner as any definitive assessment in terms of a fixed, coherent set of regulatory preferences.[24]

Nevertheless, my entire quantitative analysis of programming here is set in terms of performance dimensions very close to those widely recognized by public officials, opinion leaders, and academic investigators. Specifically, my policy assessment mainly relates to regulatory impact on the diversity of program types and of options within types, and on the mix of cultural, informational, or serious programming aimed at minority audiences, on one hand, and light entertainment or standard fare geared to majority audiences, on the other hand.[25] In this I have actually undertaken to assess program service in terms of such well-known criticisms of television as what one widely read study has called its failure "to exploit its potential . . . for educating, informing, and elevating tastes"; its further neglect of minority audiences and emphasis on mass entertainment; its additional failure to provide variety within conventional commercial program series; and finally, the power of a few organizations and persons in that industry to "exert an enormous influence on political opinions and cultural standards." [26]

I am of course aware that the Federal Communications Commission largely focuses on informational and local programming, not on narrower distinctions between serious or light drama, fine arts or mass entertainment, and so forth; [27] that its diversity goal is at best vague and ill-defined; and that even using the industry's own self-classification of programs, it is hard to avoid subjective overtones.

Nevertheless, even accepting Jones's strictures, we could still quite properly say that, if one wanted to further cultural or informational

24. A recent empirical technique to ascertain such preference was cited in note 6.
25. Our selection of these variables for intensive analysis was arrived at independently of the attention they receive in passing in Noll, Peck, and McGowan, *Economic Aspects of Television Regulation*, pp. 267–70. Furthermore, I fully recognize that available measures of program type diversity and program composition among major informational and entertainment categories entirely ignore the issue of quality. I have not attempted to distinguish low-cost and possibly low-quality from high-cost and possibly high-quality programs. Readers are therefore alerted to the absence of quality weights in all quantitative measures in this study.
26. Ibid., pp. 1–2.
27. The composition of programming among major entertainment and informational categories is more explicitly examined in chapters 3 and 5 and in Part II generally.

service, or specifically fine arts including drama, then it is possible to quantify the relevant variables and test for the relative impact of different licensing policies on them.

My practical strategy has been to treat the regulatory authority as if it sought to further the indicated program service or diversity levels generally. Although I will not presume to have demonstrated that such goals *are* consistently or systematically always sought by regulators, my proposed methodology is not seriously impaired. After all, anyone who is *not* interested in, say, "full employment" may prefer not to spend much time reading the work of John Maynard Keynes. However, anyone who *is* interested can obviously learn a lot from his work or from discussions of it without worrying about how far and when the goal of full employment, let alone its accurate and unambiguous definition and measurement, became an integral part of national priorities in the United States. Likewise, I address policies and policy goals that have doubtless been espoused in certain contexts, at certain times, by at least some members of the FCC, of legislative oversight committees, or of the judiciary, and by opinion leaders more generally. And I do so without presuming to have scientific knowledge of their true preferences.

And though the FCC has a stated goal of substantial service in local and informational programming, this is not open-ended in that "more is not necessarily better." [28] Therefore, to imply, as I shall, that more diversity, more information, or more cultural and fine arts programming are better than less, is a mere working assumption herein, and no reflection of any demonstrable FCC policy.

Nevertheless, many policymakers and other readers *are* concerned with diversity levels and program composition, in particular with the mix of so-called fine arts and mass entertainment programs, the adequacy of news, public affairs, and other information. It is to these readers that this book is mainly addressed. However, others who are not personally or officially concerned with those dimensions of television programming may also want to consider the effects on our several program indicators of actions to pursue *other* policy objectives—say, those of competition or the wide diffusion of economic and political power.

Evidence on the trade-offs between the latter regulatory policies and our programming variables could at least help clarify the price of any single policy goal in terms of other goals that its furtherance might impair or abet. Such factual knowledge would thereby help regulators to better determine the consistency of their competing policy objectives, under existing and alternative arrangements. Properly injected into the arena of decision, such evidence could also help discipline the regulator to deliver more of what he promises. One reason that an agency's rhetoric

28. Further Notice of Inquiry in Docket No. 19154 (Comparative Renewal Applicants), 20 August 1971, par. 4, n. 2.

and rationalizations so often diverge from what it actually does may be that public coalitions are not formed with the power or the influence to reconcile utterance and deed. Short of gross abuse, quantitative assessment alone may fail to evoke the public outrage that activates such coalitions; yet it is a step in the right direction.

The Economic Theory
of Regulation

One recent criticism of my method derives from the so-called economic theory of regulation.[29] According to that theory at least, the economic power determinants of regulation are so powerful that virtually nothing economists can do in the present political framework could possibly change it. Most regulation is essentially deemed to further the economic interests of groups that have the power and the resources to "buy" what they want. We are told that there is little evidence that the "true" purposes of regulation are public interest goals, but that attempts to attain these goals have backfired; or that the agency's alleged lack of resources, or deficient planning capabilities, or mismanagement, have forced the unwanted response.[30] The seemingly perverse or unanticipated side effects are explained as due mainly to the power of the benefiting groups.[31]

To resign oneself to these "realities" of power seems unduly defeatist. True, proponents of the economic theory may simply have wearied of fruitless attempts to ground proposals for regulatory reform (that nobody heeds) on a massive measurement of effects. They particularly deplore the frequency of regulations with no beneficial impact at all, intended or unintended. Economists are urged here, too, to discover exactly who is benefiting from existing policies, at whose expense. A massive new application of positive economics is called for to trace the economic beneficiaries of in-place controls.

But must we really stop there and abstain from policy studies en-

29. This theory is set forth most systematically in George Stigler. "Theory of Economic Regulation," *Bell Journal of Economics and Management Science* (Spring 1971); Richard Posner, "Theories of Economic Regulation," *Bell Journal of Economics and Management Science* (Autumn 1974). See also Stigler, "The Source of Economic Legislation," revised September 4, 1973, paper presented at Regulated Utilities Seminar, Graduate School of Business, University of Chicago, June 1974.

30. Ibid., "Theories of Economic Regulation," pp. 337–39.

31. Ibid.; see also Stigler, "Sources of Economic Legislation," pp. 1–5.

tirely? Or can we not at least inject the results of our independent audits of effects (especially of their asymmetrical shape) back into the decision process and let the chips fall where they may? Respect for power in designing and evaluating our policy proposals will admittedly help keep an investigator from "baying at the moon." But this is surely a far cry from advising economists to abdicate their policy-formulating role entirely, leaving that function to government or industry officials, lawyers, and other consultants.

It can indeed be argued that (1) measuring and divulging the divergence between intentions and results may act to galvanize potential political coalitions to capitalize on the "regulatory failure" this divulgence dramatizes. This is particularly arguable if (2) specific policy alternatives are offered to rectify the failure. It is also more plausibly arguable if (3) the particular groups that benefit and lose from the reform can be identified and their costs and gains quantified accordingly.[32]

In that regard, the insights of the economic theory of regulation could actually help us refine our analysis of unanticipated consequences; that is, by injecting his quantitative assessment of intentions and results back into the decision-making arena, an investigator could conceivably *alter* the existing power configuration. What is unworkable and impractical one day may become less so on the next, at least once knowledge of regulatory effects has been more widely diffused.

Suppose, for example, that we were to rank our policy proposals according to the degree to which some groups would gain a lot from a given reform, while others would lose but little. Suppose, moreover, that for whatever losses the latter would suffer due to reform, they could be fully compensated out of the gains now enjoyed by the former. Or, better still, suppose that gainers could win without imposing losses on others. And lastly, suppose that factual evidence on the preceding policy alternatives was widely diffused and amply dramatized. Would it not be more likely that policy options high in this ranking might be politically acceptable *notwithstanding* the existing distribution of power and benefits of regulation?

Surely the sheer public embarrassment of voracious entrenched interests who adamantly oppose changes that would impair their position but little, while greatly improving that of potential gainers, could have far-reaching political and institutional consequences. The main lesson from the economic theory of regulation is probably that it is simply not enough to identify and measure regulatory goals, results, and their divergence. We must also identify the beneficiaries of current regulation and quantify their benefits. And we must, finally, estimate the probable size and incidence of gains and losses due to specific alternatives in reform.

32. See comments in Levin, "Unanticipated Consequences under Direct Regulation," pp. 132–34.

My current study has been able to undertake the second and third tasks only peripherally. However, the measurement and divulgence of divergent intentions and results remain an all-important first step in assessing current regulations and alternatives. I shall, therefore, devote my principal efforts to this initial task in what must be a continuing process of regulatory evaluation.

Meanwhile, it suffices to note that economists increasingly recognize unintended consequences as a proper subject for analysis, though they remain reluctant to do much with reputed regulatory goals as such. In broadcast regulation, the divergence of intentions and results flows from the asymmetrical impact of FCC licensing-allocation policies. Economic rents and franchise values are quite clearly created by license limitation here as elsewhere. But in broadcasting, the common property character of spectrum makes such rents in some sense inevitable insofar as efficient resource use virtually requires entry controls of some sort to control or mitigate the costly external effects of spectrum utilization.[33]

True, rents would exist regardless of the nature of the resource if there were restrictions on entry for other reasons. But in broadcasting, the simple fact is that the character of the resource may be at issue, and the alternatives to present entry controls seem far less practical on technical or political grounds than in, say, motor or air transport.[34] Finally, the rents are necessarily bolstered also by government's massive role in telecommunications research and development, which has extended the intensive and extensive margins of spectrum and has thus enhanced the value of broadcast frequencies to next-best nonbroadcast users.[35]

33. Nor would development of a property rights system for subsequent transfers alter the existence of rents in any *initial* license grant; it would alter only their distribution afterward.

34. See Harvey Levin, "Externalities, Common Property Pricing, and the Management of TV Broadcast Rents," in *New Dimensions in Public Utility Pricing*, ed. Harry Trebing (East Lansing: Michigan State University Press, 1976), pp. 85–90.

35. The government's extensive security-related R&D programs, first in radar, and then in booster and orbital technology, and so forth, sequentially opened up the microwave spectrum both for terrestrial and later for space satellite usage. Mobile radio use of the UHF spectrum was also a by-product of the government's wartime technical breakthroughs in communications. Clearly, the economic value of TV licenses necessarily rose when the number and the productivity of next-best nonbroadcast users of TV spectrum also rose—in the wake of the government-induced advances in spectrum utilization. That is, the opportunity costs of TV's occupancy of spectrum, and the implicit rents occupancy represents, vary directly with the value output which next-best (nonbroadcast) users could optimally derive from the same frequencies. On the government's historical role in telecommunications development, see Harvey Levin, *The Invisible Resource* (Baltimore: Johns Hopkins University Press, 1971), chap. 9. On the resultant impact of the rising marginal value of spectrum to broadcast and common carrier users, see also pp. 167–69, 173–74, 201–02, 206, 230, 275–76, 333. Finally, some issues posed by attempts to recover "in kind" the nation's equity in spectrum development, are examined in my paper on franchise values and merit programming, in *Regulating the Product—Quality and Variety*, eds. Richard Caves and Marc Roberts (Cambridge, Mass.: Ballinger, 1975), pp. 234–38.

Scope of This Study

In our ensuing policy studies I propose to examine several devices to reconcile stated objectives with results. In organizing my research I consider three sets of questions:

1. Do restrictive licensing and allocation or ownership concentration significantly bolster licensee profits, rents, and franchise values, notwithstanding the absence of any explicit formal mandate (or stated intention) of so doing?
2. If so, are there commensurate offsetting public benefits in diversity and informational-cultural programming? That is, are these benefits sufficient to justify the rents regulation creates?
3. If not, with what alternatives to restrictive licensing now available may TV regulators try to narrow the gap between unanticipated or formally unintended economic side effects, and the diversified programming being sought? Specifically, what other policy options could better divert economic rents and supernormal profits into diversity and merit programming, at a price in allocative inefficiency or economic retardation so small as to constitute no persuasive case against many of the latest proposals for decontrol?[36] In view of the poor record of restrictive regulation and cross-subsidization as vehicles to further public goals elsewhere, and of the basic theoretical case against such arrangements, how likely are they to succeed in diverting rents into merit programs and diversity in television?

But before proceeding to the first two questions in Part II, and to the third set in Part III, Part I presents the key elements of our basic framework, its concepts, measurement techniques, and so forth. Thus because neither the economic or programming performance nor the impact of TV regulation can be understood without reference to the licensee's linkage with advertisers, national network companies, interconnection facilities, and program suppliers, I describe and analyze these components and interrelations briefly in chapter 2. Then in chapter 3 I argue that the FCC's loosely conceived concept of diversity, rarely measured seriously to date, can offer a suggestive starting point for an assessment of current policies and alternatives. Important differences can and must be drawn between viewer response to individual programs and separate program types. But what I view as the major *unintended* side effects of restrictive licensing-allocation policies today are the economic advantages they confer on different classes of licensee. In chapter 4

36. See, for example, the proposed Communications Act of 1978 (HR 13015), secs. 414c (random selection of competing applicants for new TV grants), 420 (no regulation of program content), 431 (indefinite licenses for radio stations at once, and after ten years, for TV), 434b (no regulatory procedures for licensee ascertainment of community needs or interests), 437a (no consideration of competing applications in renewal actions).

I show such policies themselves to be necessitated by the marginal signal interference effects of radio spectrum utilization. In chapter 5 I contend that regulatory objectives can be identified sufficiently for purposes of assessment, and the entire inquiry is further sketched there as grounded essentially in a comprehensive analysis of regulatory impact on several diversity measures, on program composition with special reference to cultural-informational service, and, lastly, on station rates, income, revenue, time sales, and sales prices.

Such an approach will indeed permit us to consider in Part II any asymmetry between the economic and programming effects of the nation's major television policies. There I focus mainly on the stated objectives and the likely consequences of owner diversity (chapters 6 and 7), structural diversity (chapter 8), and proposals to "pare back" network power in prime time (chapters 9, 10, and 11). Then in Part III I conclude by reviewing a few recurrent initiatives to institute alternatives to present licensing practice. In particular, I turn to quantitative renewal requirements (chapter 13) and to a tax on economic rents to fund public broadcasting (chapter 14).

PART ONE

Basic Framework

Chapter 2

Economic Structure

and Regulatory

Framework

THE U.S. broadcast system is composed of several related segments. Hardware companies manufacture the receivers, set owners watch the programs and buy the products advertised, and stations transmit the programming. National or specialized network companies, independent program producers, and the stations supply the programs. Advertisers provide the basic support for programs, buying time for commercial announcements, to reach specified markets, or over chains of stations. Network companies integrate stations into nationwide systems, mainly through leasing the microwave and cable links from the American Telephone and Telegraph Company in order to tie together their affiliates. Periodicals and newspapers supply information regarding programs and personalities involved, while ratings companies evaluate audience response. Finally, the FCC allocates spectrum to the several broadcast services and licenses stations under criteria designed to reconcile a varied program mix with acceptable signal quality.

To promote program diversity, broadcast regulation purports to free individual stations from the control of networks and advertisers. In theory, the objective is to widen audience choices both by diversifying program sources and by inducing licensees to subsidize cultural, informational, and educational programming.

The Stations

Broadcast stations operate under three-year licenses granted by the FCC to applicants whose technical, legal, and financial qualifications, program plans, past experience, and involvement in the community appear to qualify them for service in the public interest. Under the Communications Act, licensees are expected to provide informational and instructional media and serve as disseminators of entertainment and advertising. Although the networks are not licensed directly, the commission influences their operations by requirements imposed on affiliated stations and by decisions regarding rates paid for program transmission.

Broadcast stations discharge their widely reputed responsibilities to provide a diversified (albeit not profit-maximizing) mix of information and entertainment programming, mainly through decisions on content, format, and scheduling. Affiliation contracts with a national network company provide one source of programming. However, broadcast stations can also deal directly with independent program producers, film syndicators, and local or national spot advertisers. Only some one hundred commercial TV stations lack a network tie today, with just ten of these stations outside the fifty largest markets. In the smaller markets, where the number of available network affiliations exceeds the number of stations, stations may gain relative bargaining power in securing a preferred network tie.

A major question in later chapters is whether the licensing-allocation function is an efficient mechanism for widening and enriching program choices between local and national service, between majority and minority tastes, and among entertainment, news, and information. A second question is whether any advances in program diversity obtained are associated with significant losses in competition and the creation of sizable economic rents.[1] If so, we must ask whether some more radical alternative to the present licensing system may not be in order, one that recovers the rents from commercial licensees directly or diverts them instead to an alternate source of public service programming.

Under the present TV Allocation Plan, only some twelve hundred commercial assignments could be made today on the eighty-two channels that the FCC initially laid out in 492 MHz of TV broadcast spectrum.[2]

1. My working assumption throughout this book is that the FCC pays at least lip service to the goals stated in this paragraph. See chapter 1 notes 5 through 13, and associated text. Whether the FCC or any other federal body *ought* to promote such goals directly is open to debate. My position is that it is quite proper for the government to create a framework of indirect *structural incentives* to correct present economic and technical restrictions on diversity, localism, merit programming, and information.

2. This number of assignments could of course be increased by any authorization of short-spaced VHF stations, so-called "drop-ins" accommodated by relaxing geographic separations criteria.

Controlled access to markets therein is the major source of supernormal profits and rents. However, the principal *disparities* in earnings follow from channel type differences, and the disparate signal power, receiver quality, and service range still associated with them.

Aside from channel type, market size, and competitors, TV stations can be further classified by ownership (or affiliation) ties. Most stations are affiliated with one of three national television networks, and many of these are owned by a large number of "groups" that operate more than one TV station across geographically separate markets. A smaller number of stations are owned by daily newspapers located in the same market, or are owned singly.

For the year 1972, I examined 632 (of 693) commercial television stations then on the air for which comprehensive economic and programming data could be compiled.[3] Almost nine-tenths of the stations studied had a network affiliation, three-fourths a VHF license, and three-fifths a nonnetwork group owner tie. However, only one-seventh had a newspaper tie in the same market, and less than one-tenth a joint newspaper group tie (see table 2.1). The 558 network affiliates studied had relatively more VHF licenses, nonnetwork group ties, and newspaper ties than the 74 independents did.

TABLE 2.1
Distribution of Network-Affiliated and Independent Television Stations by Channel Type and Owner Attribute, 1972
(N = 632)

Type/Owner	Total Stations		Network		Independents	
	Number	Percent	Number	Percent	Number	Percent
Total	632	100.0	558[a]	100.0	74	100.0
VHF stations	471	74.5	450[a]	80.6	21	28.4
Group owned[b]	396	62.7	356	63.8	40	54.0
Newspaper owned[c]	83	13.1	77	13.8	6	8.1
Joint newspaper and group owned[d]	54	8.5	49	8.8	5	6.8

SOURCE: Derived from station directories in *Broadcasting Yearbook, 1973* and *Television Factbook, no. 43* (1973-74).
[a]Includes 15 network-owned stations.
[b]Excludes network-owned stations.
[c]In-town newspaper owners only, whether or not group-owned.
[d]As specified in the preceding two footnotes.

Of special interest are the fifteen VHF stations owned and operated by the national television networks. In 1976, fourteen of these stations operated in the ten largest markets, and nine in the three top markets—

3. I started with the whole population of 693 stations in 1972, eventually analyzing the 632 for which data were available for all matching variables in my regressions.

New York, Los Angeles, and Chicago. Each five-station network group reached some 22 percent of all TV homes through the stations it owned outright, separate and distinct from the still larger audiences delivered via all of its *affiliates*.[4]

The National Network Companies

The networks have traditionally performed a middleman or brokerage function, producing or buying programs and reselling them to national advertisers along with the air time of their station affiliates. But they have also financed the industry's technical development, launched vital program experimentation before sets were in wide use, and created the physical means to provide advertisers with geographically dispersed mass audiences simultaneously.

Basic Function

In a classic statement thirty years ago, Peter Steiner defined the networks' functions as those of a middleman:

> They wholesale time of stations to advertisers or their agents, they provide and/or distribute programs to advertisers for widespread simultaneous broadcast over many interconnected stations, and they provide, through lease from AT&T, . . . wires that provide the interconnection. . . . In practice they are more than middlemen; they sell their services not to any station but to a chosen station in a given area. They act and to some extent think of themselves as principals and stations as distribution points in an integrated enterprise for program presentation.[5]

More recently Robert Crandall has spelled out the entrepreneurial risk-bearing function of the TV networks mainly in terms of "program brokerage," although he, too, sees a network as ". . . more than a mere broker of programs for it provides investment capital for program development and commits itself to procurement of programs in advance of sales to advertisers."[6]

From the outset, the network companies have provided all affiliates with programs too expensive to produce locally, have borne the costs of delivering them on coaxial cable and microwave facilities, and have paid commissions to advertising agencies. In early years, they also granted

4. See FCC, Notice of Inquiry in Docket No. 21049 (Commercial TV Network Practices), January 14, 1977, par. 9 (hereafter called Network Inquiry).

5. Peter Steiner, *Workable Competition in Radiobroadcasting* (Ann Arbor, Mich.: University Microfilms, 1949), p. 32.

6. Robert Crandall, "The Economic Effect of Television Network Program 'Ownership,'" *Journal of Law and Economics* (October 1971), p. 389.

their affiliates first option on all network shows for a seventy-two-hour period before releasing them to other stations in the same market. They further provided simultaneous nationwide transmissions for advertisers who sought national coverage. The distribution of network programming was facilitated by contractual arrangements [7] that designated an affiliate's network time rate and its compensation for carrying network commercial program; the number of unsponsored programs the network would provide gratis; the "free" hours during which stations promised to carry network commercial shows without charge; and the affiliate's willingness to accept all shows the network might want to "clear" (air) during specified option time periods.

By "option privileges," the FCC referred to any agreement preventing network affiliates "from scheduling programs before the network agrees to utilize the time during which the programs are scheduled. . . ." Originally, all stations retained the right to reject network programs, to receive at least fifty-six days' notice on option programs, to limit such clearances to three hours within each of four time segments (twelve hours in all), and to refrain from granting option privileges that ban or displace other networks. The networks' option time practice found analogous to "block-booking," in 1958, was condemned as a violation of the Sherman Act (sec. 1) in United States v. Paramount Pictures Inc., 334 U.S. 131 (1958), and was subsequently abolished.[8]

Today no television or radio station may serve as an *exclusive* affiliate to any network. Exclusivity was prohibited following the FCC's chain broadcasting investigation in 1941. One form of prohibited exclusivity prevented a station from transmitting the programs of a rival network, whereas territorial exclusivity entailed the network's refusal to release any program to an unaffiliated station in any affiliate's market, even on a delayed basis, and even if the affiliate had rejected it or its signal had failed to reach people in remote parts of the market.[9]

Primary affiliation is still permissible, however, and this may well tie up a station's prime-time hours for one network, leaving any rival network with less choice hours and more limited audiences. Primary affiliation is allowed on the theory that only with an affiliate in each key market can a network secure the program clearances to facilitate ef-

7. For details see Harlan Blake and Jack Blum, "Network Television Rate Practices: A Study in the Failure of Social Control of Price Discrimination," *Yale Law Journal* (July 1965), pp. 1343–46; John Peterman, "The Structure of National Times Rates in the Television Broadcast Industry," *Journal of Law and Economics* (October 1965), pp. 83–92; House Commerce Committee, *Report on Network Broadcasting* (Washington, D.C.: U.S. Government Printing Office, 1958), pp. 40–44; and Stanley Besen and Ronald Soligo, "The Economics of the Network-Affiliate Relationship in the Television Broadcasting Industry," *American Economic Review* (June 1973), pp. 259–68.

8. See the antitrust critique in House Commerce Committee, *Report on Network Broadcasting*, pp. 379–89.

9. See Federal Communications Commission, *Report on Chain Broadcasting* (Washington, D.C.: U.S. Government Printing Office, 1941), chaps. 6–7.

fective competition. R. E. Park estimates that a successful new network operation in TV would require at least potential access to 90 percent of all U.S. television homes.[10]

One major recent development is the American Broadcasting Company's success in "equalizing" its competitive position vis-à-vis CBS and NBC,[11] a matter to which I return in chapter 10. Here it is sufficient to note simply that ABC's growing economic strength may in part reflect: (1) the weakening of historic ties and loyalties between the networks and their affiliated stations; (2) the ability of an erstwhile minor network (or a newcomer) with popular programs to wrest prime-time program clearances from primary affiliates of a major network in markets that lack enough affiliations to "go around"; (3) the further chances for a minor network to compete for primary affiliations in such markets.[12]

In recent years, the relationship between networks, advertisers, and program producers has in any event changed notably. However, the broadcaster still finds a network contract invaluable because of the great popularity of many network shows, the compensation he receives for carrying them, and the expense he is spared by not having to prepare or buy his own programming to fill unfilled parts of the broadcast day. Network affiliation is valuable, finally, for helping affiliates meet their public service responsibilities by providing each station with diversified programs that include news, public affairs, and costly public events specials.

There is also the alleged value of "audience flow," whereby popular network shows enhance the value of adjacent time spots for commercial announcements, although this may have been exaggerated (see chapter 9). More important, doubtless, are advantages that affiliates enjoy insofar as the networks must set the compensation rates paid them sufficiently high to keep them (the stations) from seeking more of their programs from independent programmers and syndicators. Underlying all this are several crucial ways in which the networks act to reduce the costs of their packagers, advertisers, and station affiliates.[13]

10. See citations and associated text in chap. 10, note 15.
11. Ibid., note 22.
12. See *Proposed Findings of Fact by Justice Department* in FCC Docket No. 16828 (ABC-ITT Merger), May 22, 1967, pars. 6.8, 6.12, 6.13, 6.15, 6.27. In 1960 ABC accounted for only 87 network affiliates compared with 244 for NBC and 195 for CBS—further compared, in 1977, with 190 (ABC), 212 (NBC), and 210 (CBS). Of special further interest, while 28 former CBS and NBC affiliates switched to ABC, 1968–77, only 15 ABC affiliates switched the other way, leaving ABC with a net gain of 13 stations and its rivals each with a net loss to ABC. Finally, of the 46 stations changing their affiliations, 28 were located in the smallest 100 markets, and in the top 50 and second 50 markets, only 10 and 8 respectively. (FCC Network Inquiry Special Staff, *An Analysis of the Network-Affiliate Relationship in Television* [preliminary], October 1979, chap. 2, pp. 48–53).
13. See R. Noll, M. Peck, and J. McGowan, *Economic Aspects of Television Regulation* (Washington, D.C.: The Brookings Institution, 1973), pp. 59–61. See also the textual discussion associated with notes 11–13 in chap. 9.

Network Television Interconnection

During the past decade or so, the three television networks spent an average of $54,530,200 annually for inter- and intracity relay circuits to deliver their programs nationally.[14] Although this sum has declined by 20 percent since 1970, it still stood at $17,200,000 per network in 1977. How valuable such outlays are to the many station affiliates served thereby is a question to which we shall now turn.

Comparative Costs of Electronic and Conventional Systems for "Live" or Simultaneous Delivery. A major reason for the present system of interconnection over electronic microwave links is the need to accommodate live national programming. No system based on conventional shipment by mail could obviously provide such a service.

But, then, are the networks on that count becoming obsolete? Clearly, simultaneous transmissions made eminent sense in the 1950s when over four-fifths of NBC and CBS programming and one-half of ABC's was live (see table 2.2). But a decade later this proportion had dropped to about one-third for NBC and CBS, respectively, and one-seventh for ABC. Indeed, live programming dropped further still in the years that followed. By 1973, it accounted for less than one-fifth of the network "feed," whereas film accounted for almost one-third, and videotape for almost half.

Nevertheless, the availability of live capabilities (however infrequently used), is the *sine qua non* of a network-interconnected electronic delivery system. Furthermore, most live programming today is sports programming and special events, for which the live element and simultaneity across time zones are both essential. Simultaneous transmission of other videotape or film (*within* time zones) could be facilitated by conventional mail. However, the cost would be prohibitive, and electronic delivery over nationwide circuits is therefore favored. Indeed if such tape networks were more efficient than electronic delivery, TV stations and program syndicators would have discovered this fact by now. A direct assessment of comparative costs is needed, however, to determine if the networks have somehow managed to induce their affiliates to remain interconnected (through implicitly coercive tactics), so as to protect themselves against new programmer entry.[15]

The justification for network interconnection probably never depended exclusively on the technical requirements of live transmission. In addition, film costs in television's early days were much higher than costs for live or tape shows. Even in 1964, for instance, network-produced

14. Derived from expense data published in the FCC's annual financial reports for the TV Broadcast Service, 1970–77.
15. Comparative systems costs are briefly illustrated in the appendix to this chapter. Except for live sports or special events, simultaneous transmission of taped or filmed programs occur only *within* (not across) different time zones.

TABLE 2.2

Film, Tape, and Live Programs on Air: Weekly Hours, Minutes, and Percentage Distribution by National TV Network, 1953-73

Total Time of Three Networks	Three Network Totals							
	Film	Percent	Video-tape	Percent	Live Programs	Percent	Time for All Programs	Percent
1972-73	91:55	35.6	117:58	45.7	47:22	18.7	257:15	100
1962-63	76:00	33.9	88:02	39.2	60:34	26.9	224:36	100
1958	49:45	24.0	12:30	6.0	144:30	70.0	206:45	100
1953	34:05	21.8	–	–	122:40	78.2	156:45	100
Percentage Change								
1953-73		+132.4		–		−57.5		+59.2
1958-73		+59.3		+852.0		−63.6		+21.7

	Individual Networks								
	ABC			CBS			NBC		
Year	Film	Video-tape	Live Programs	Film	Video-tape	Live Programs	Film	Video-tape	Live Programs
Network Weekly Time									
1972-73	30:53	38:00	6:38	40:02	36:45	17:26	21:00	43:13	23:18
1962-63	26:45	23:48	8:30	23:58	28:53	26:53	25:18	35:21	25:11
1958	17:30	3:00	21:00	14:15	4:45	57:15	18:00	4:45	65:00
1953	13:45	–	15:00	8:00	–	52:00	12:20	–	55:40
*Percentage of Each Network's Weekly Time**									
1972-73	40.4	50.8	9.3	42.5	39.1	18.5	24.0	49.4	28.6
1962-63	45.2	40.5	14.4	30.1	36.3	33.7	29.6	41.4	29.4
1958	42.1	7.2	50.6	18.7	6.2	75.1	20.5	5.1	74.1
1953	47.8	–	52.2	13.3	–	86.7	18.1	–	81.9

SOURCE: *Broadcasting Yearbook*, selected volumes, 1953-74.
*Percentages are of each network's total weekly hours during each year reported, for all three categories—film, tape, and live programs—but due to rounding, totals may not equal 100 percent.

half-hour, film-only episodes cost $62,234 as compared to $54,038 for live or tape-only shows—about 15 percent more. In 1963, the comparable costs of packager licensed episodes were $54,378 and $46,000, eighteen percent more for film.[16] But in 1960, half-hour filmed episodes in network entertainment series cost more than double the cost of live or taped shows rerun in subsequent years.[17] Before 1958 and the advent of videotape (which was much easier to edit and correct than film; hence its costs were substantially lower), the disparity between the costs of live programs and film prints was probably even larger, and the cost advantages of electronic delivery undoubtedly substantial.

The high proportion of live programming in 1953 would necessarily require network interconnection (via AT&T) to spread program investment costs over large national audiences. Once the interconnection circuits were leased, of course, film programs could also be delivered that way, and later videotapes. Bear in mind that AT&T circuits were then leased on a fixed-charge, 24-hour-a-day basis. There was, therefore, a more powerful inducement for networks to use AT&T to deliver *all* their programming, than if, say, the diversion of film prints to shipment by mail would have resulted in significant reductions in AT&T's annual interconnection charges.[18]

There were occasional advantages also in the networks delivering TV programs to their affiliates beforehand, enabling the latter to record, store, and subsequently rebroadcast at will. Aside from greater flexibility for stations in local scheduling, the networks themselves could avoid the need to check film prints frequently for wear, and the risk of outright loss.

Public Relations Value. The present system is favored because the industry appears to believe that simultaneous telecasts (whether live, videotape, or film), may have special public relations value. Specifically, many industry leaders believe that larger aggregate audiences (and hence greater advertiser income) can be generated by simultaneous telecasts of first-run videotapes than by a series of discrete shipments (of tape or film) to separate groups of affiliates, for delayed transmission at their discretion.

I have not been able to assess that thesis here. However, it would especially hold where preliminary promotion of the program in other media is entailed. In addition, any TV program's newsworthiness or feature story value for local newspaper readers would appear to decline as the program is rerun in subsequent seasons, or even broadcast after a delay (as with so-called bicycled tape networks).[19] Also, the size and composition of audience any advertisement will reach can be more readily pre-

16. *Television Program Production, Procurement and Syndication*, vol. 2 (Cambridge, Mass.: Arthur D. Little, 1966), table 23.

17. Ibid., table 24.

18. The availability of so-called occasional rates for selective part-time usage years later presumably altered the networks' incentive structure.

19. Those configurations are delineated in the appendix to this chapter.

dicted if it appears on a given program at the same time in different markets (within the same time zone at least). In principle, finally, simultaneous transmission might further be expected to optimize audience flow across the network schedule.

Emerging Patterns in Network Program Production, Procurement, and Distribution

The suppliers of television programming today include advertisers, independent program producers (the creative agent), packagers (the companies that hire them), and the networks themselves.[20]

Advertisers normally acquire (but no longer produce) their own program series from an independent producer or packager for exhibition by a network. Together the producer and the advertiser share the risks and the rewards of these program ventures, and the network participates only as a time sales agent for its interconnected station affiliates.

However, networks also deal directly with independent producers, or with the program supply companies (packagers) that hire them. Here the network "licenses" from the packager programs that now constitute the bulk of the prime-time network "feed." The networks often provide significant venture capital for these packager-licensed programs, and share in the subsequent revenues. Advertisers, too, may buy time slots in many such programs instead of providing their own to the network. Networks also produce their own entertainment and public affairs programs.

Twenty years ago, advertisers produced or bought over one-half of the programs which the networks carried, whereas today the networks acquire (from packagers or producers) or produce themselves three-fifths of these programs. Between 1957 and 1968, the percentage of entertainment program hours the networks produced declined from 23.9 to 4.8 percent, those supplied (whether or not produced) by advertisers fell from 36.1 to 3.4 percent, while the share of packager-licensed programs rose from 39.3 to 91.2 percent. The shifts for all regularly scheduled network series were very similar, the network share declining from 29.5 to 15.7 percent, the advertiser's share from 33.4 to 3.0 percent, and the packager's share rising from 36.4 to 80.7 percent.[21]

Because advertisers supply and networks produce far fewer entertainment programs themselves, the networks have increasingly dealt directly with program producers and packagers, in many of whose shows the advertiser also buys commercial minutes. As a consequence, the percentage of network entertainment program hours with only one advertiser has also declined, from 42.1 percent of all their entertainment hours

20. For a lucid description of this program supply industry, see Robert Crandall, "Economic Effects of Television Network Program Ownership," *Journal of Law and Economics* (October 1971), pp. 387–89.

21. *Television Program Production, Procurement, Distribution and Scheduling* (Cambridge, Mass.: Arthur D. Little, 1969), tables 1(1), 2(2).

in 1957 to 2.8 percent in 1967. In contrast, the percentage with six or more advertisers rose from 2.9 to 88.3 percent of all such program hours. Advertisers have clearly preferred to participate fractionally rather than exclusively, a pattern further reflected in the declining portion willing to sponsor any program fully, from 34.7 percent of all network advertisers in 1957 to a mere 1.3 percent in 1967 (see table 2.3).

TABLE 2.3

Program Hours by Number of Advertisers
per Program Series: All Series, 1957-67
(6-11 P.M.)

Number of Advertisers	Percentage of Total Hours	
	1957	1967
One advertiser	42.1	2.8
Three or more	15.0	93.1
Six or more	2.9	88.3
Twenty-five or more	0.0	50.2

SOURCE: Arthur D. Little, *Television Program Production, Procurement, Distribution and Scheduling* (Cambridge, Mass.: Arthur D. Little, 1969), table 8(11).
NOTE: Data refer to the number of advertisers over the whole series, not per program.

In sum, the shift has been from single to multiple sponsorships, and from few to many programs per advertiser.[22] In addition, the relative portion of either network-produced or advertiser-supplied entertainment hours has declined dramatically at a time when the packagers' share more than doubled. Nevertheless, one other critical detail must be noted. In absolute and relative terms, the shows *licensed* by the networks directly from the packagers have grown substantially in number, while the shows that *packagers* place independently on the *affiliates'* schedule have actually declined (see table 2.4). Looking at all series in section B (including news and public affairs), the networks produced 28.7 percent in 1957 and only 16.3 percent in 1968. However, when combined with programs produced by others but licensed to *networks*, the network share clearly rose from 67.2 to 96.7 percent. In contrast, the share of series packagers provided directly to the affiliates or the advertisers was

22. This trend reflects in part the network's new interest in breaking into the small advertisers' market. That is, advertisers too small to afford solo sponsorship can now increasingly share in multiple sponsorship on prime-time television, while the networks have improved their competitive position in the national spot market. In addition to accommodating more multiple sponsorship from 1957–68, the networks have more recently switched from 60-second to 30-second spot announcements and, hence, become more directly competitive with the national station (spot) representatives (see chapter 9, discussion associated with note 17).

TABLE 2.4
Analysis of Network Programs by Source and Network, 1957-68
(percentages)

	ABC		CBS		NBC		All Three Networks	
	1957	1968	1957	1968	1957	1968	1957	1968
A. Evening Network Entertainment Programs								
Network produced	5.4	0.0	38.8	4.2	15.2	8.2	21.1	4.1
Network licensed from								
packager	62.2	97.9	26.5	92.7	45.6	85.7	43.2	92.1
Subtotal	67.6	97.9	65.3	96.9	60.8	93.9	64.4	96.2
Independently supplied	32.4	2.1	34.7	3.1	39.2	6.1	35.6	3.8
B. All Evening Network Programs[a]								
Network produced	19.7	11.1	43.9	17.8	21.4	19.6	28.7	16.3
Network licensed from								
packager	51.7	87.0	24.3	79.5	40.8	75.0	38.5	80.4
Subtotal	71.4	98.1	68.2	97.3	62.2	94.6	67.2	96.7
Independently supplied	28.6	1.9	31.8	2.7	37.8	5.4	32.8	3.3

SOURCE: FCC, Report and Order in Docket No. 12782, May 4, 1970, pp. 11-12.
[a]Includes all entertainment and nonentertainment programs, such as news and public affairs.

32.8 percent in 1957 but only 3.3 percent in 1968. The figures for entertainment-only (section A) are very similar, with the networks' total share (produced and licensed) rising from 64.4 to 96.2 percent and the independent packagers' share declining from 35.6 to 3.8 percent. The economic and regulatory significance of this decline in independent packagers selling directly to affiliates and of the growing magnitude of packaged shows licensed directly to the networks, has been debated widely. I will return to it in chapters 9 through 11.

It is important to note here that those who oppose an excess of network-licensed shows appear mainly concerned about the networks' acquisition of proprietary rights in independently produced programs. Through such rights, the networks are alleged to exact disproportionate earnings from the independent producers, rendering them increasingly dependent upon the networks for initial risk capital and subsequent access to station air time. The declining access to prime-time television without going through the networks is further believed to strengthen the networks' dominance in program decision making, and to reduce the viability and magnitude of alternative sources of nonnetwork programming. That is, with growing network economic control through proprietary interests in independent shows, and the competitive disadvantage of packagers in winning prime-time clearances on their own, the viewing public is deemed increasingly dependent upon the program development and scheduling decisions of three major companies.[23]

On the other hand, the networks contend that they provide vital venture capital in program development. They further contend that even compulsory access by independent producers and syndicators to network distribution facilities will mean little if the public does not watch the often less popular nonnetwork programming. For the network companies, the viewer is the ultimate arbiter of what he sees. Furthermore, the packager is said to be able to gain prime-time access directly and readily with shows of comparable quality and popularity.

What remains unresolved is how far the network proprietary interests operate to insure prime-time access for shows which are otherwise comparable to packager shows that *fail* to gain such access. Glen Robinson has indeed questioned whether, if networks exacted disproportionate profit shares from nonnetwork suppliers, the latter would, in fact, return "with new series year after year—strange behavior for sophisticated profit maximizing firms who are being 'forced' to accept nonremunerative prices." [24] Robinson further concludes that "the ultimate practical effect of [prohibiting network acquisition of proprietary interests in nonnetwork programming] has not been to reduce network power or to strengthen independent producers—as was intended—but simply to increase the dominant position of major Hollywood film producers, those large enough to possess the risk capital to invest in programming without network support." [25]

Independent Program Producers and
the Nonnetwork System

There have traditionally been two systems of program production and distribution in the United States: one integrated by the national network companies; the other by advertisers or their agencies "shopping around" for programs and time clearances, or by syndicators who produced or bought feature films, TV series, and specials. Like the networks, most syndicators purchased programs from independent producers (packagers) for subsequent resale to advertisers for placement on stations with which, however, the syndicator has no special ties. In the distribution

23. See FCC, Report & Order in Docket No. 12782, May 4, 1970, pars. 1–21; Report & Order in Docket No. 19622, January 23, 1974, pars. 8–10, 12–16.

24. See Dissenting Opinion of Commissioner Glen O. Robinson, Second Report & Order in Docket No. 19622 (Prime-Time Access Rule), January 17, 1975, p. 3 footnote).

25. Ibid.

process, the syndicator might work through a spot representative, or sell to a local station, though he would obviously prefer to deal directly with the advertiser, leaving *him* to arrange for his own clearances.[26]

During the past decade, this pattern has started to change. Now, increasingly, the local stations, not the syndicators or agencies, are the entrepreneurs of the nonnetwork system. The packagers sell programs directly to the stations which, however, sell the advertisers mainly time for spot announcements, not programs or program time. These latter constitute only a small fraction of what the advertiser and his agencies actually buy.

The economics of syndication superficially resembles that of networking in that both services need about the same number of market clearances to be profitable. Syndicators have a seeming advantage in being spared the large program production overhead of a packager or a network news/public affairs department, and the fixed interconnection charges for simultaneous transmission. Network interconnection may contribute to significant distribution economies even if videotape is used and local transmission delayed. However, the syndicator may achieve his own distribution economies by simply rerunning films in different markets at different times.

The key advantage that networks do retain is in getting high rates of clearance (simultaneous or delayed) for the popular programming they supply to their affiliates, and in knowing definitely about this beforehand. That is, the affiliates will clear time slots for the networks in advance, leaving advertisers or syndicators with a serious residual risk of failing to get their programs aired.

Syndicators encounter problems because network affiliates fear that the clearance of too much syndicated material may jeopardize their network contracts and because an affiliate's profits are on the average higher on the network programs it carries. Although an affiliate would presumably like to run every syndicated show that is more profitable than the best available network alternative, it will not risk its affiliation (and the *general* profitability of *other* network shows) to do so. "Affiliates are affiliates," according to Owen, Beebe, and Manning, "because the network supply of programming *as a whole* [emphasis added] is more profitable than syndicated material." The fact is that an affiliate "could show network and some syndicated fare, while . . . an independent . . . could show only syndicated programming." [27] On balance, affiliates prefer not to run the risk of losing their affiliation and the *net* economic advantages that result.

26. See *Report on Network Broadcasting*, pp. 38–40, 45–49; also Robert Crandall, "The Economic Effects of Television Network Program 'Ownership,'" pp. 386–91.

27. Bruce Owen, Jack Beebe, and Willard Manning, *Television Economics* (Lexington, Mass.: Lexington Books, 1974), p. 95. For the facts on the network and syndicated program supply market see also pp. 17–35.

Nevertheless, the nonnetwork system continues to provide a major source of programming and revenues for the roughly one hundred independent TV stations now on the air, and for network affiliates that reject a network show [28] or choose to carry a nonnetwork program during "station time," when no network show is available.

Although national nonnetwork (spot) and local television advertising have grown at changing rates since 1950, together they now account for one-half or more of all television advertising (see table 2.5). National spot advertising actually soared forty-eight-fold since 1950, compared to a growth in national network advertising at half that rate and in local advertising at somewhat less. This occurred during a period when all U.S. advertising grew fourfold. Since 1960, moreover, when national spot and network advertising each rose somewhat less than threefold, local advertising grew more rapidly than each, by over four times. Indeed, this growth rate from 1960 to 1975 is probably the more relevant here because the number of stations did not really start to grow until the mid-1950s.

Briefly, television accounts for a full 10 percent of *local* advertising on all media today, while *national spot* takes over 12 percent of all *national* advertising, almost as much as the network share of national. Any advertising medium with a growth record like that of local and spot television—the core of the nonnetwork system—cannot be dismissed lightly.

The Advertiser

A review of the advertiser's role will enable us to sum up the discussion so far. Most big national advertisers buy through the network companies and, in television, they must still agree to spend a minimum total on the whole network, though it is no longer necessary to order any specific *list* of stations.[29] In addition to network coverage, some advertisers

28. According to a *Thirty-Market Nielsen Survey*, affiliates rejected a total of 141 weekly hours of network programs in November 1968, compared with 93.5 hours in November 1962—a rise of almost 51 percent. See Arthur D. Little, *Television Program Production, Procurement, Distribution and Scheduling*, table 71.

29. At one time CBS and NBC placed about fifty-five of their radio-TV affiliates on a "must buy" list. Although the practice was dropped voluntarily a decade ago, advertisers are still required to spend a minimum amount on the whole network ("minimum buy"). The antitrust aspects of the original must buy practice are examined in House Commerce Committee, *Report on Network Broadcasting*, pp. 503–22. An analogy is drawn with tying contracts found *per se* illegal in *Times Picayune* 345 U.S. 594 (1953) and Northern Pacific Railroad 142F. Suppl. 679 (1956); and with "block booking," condemned in Paramount Pictures 334 U.S. 131 (1948). On the additional problems posed by minimum buy, see Blake and Blum, note 7, pp. 1347–62.

TABLE 2.5
Annual Advertising Expenditures in the United States, 1950-75

| | Expenditures (millions of dollars) | | | | Percentage | | | | | | | | | | | |
| | 1950 | 1960 | 1970 | 1975 | Medium | | | | National or Local | | | | Grand Total | | | |
					1950	1960	1970	1975	1950	1960	1970	1975	1950	1960	1970	1975
Television																
National network	85	783	1658	2325	49.7	49.2	46.1	43.7	2.6	10.7	15.2	15.1	1.5	6.6	9.1	8.2
National spot	31	527	1234	1645	18.7	33.1	34.3	30.9	1.0	7.2	11.3	10.7	0.5	4.4	6.8	5.8
Local	55	281	704	1355	32.2	17.7	19.6	25.4	2.2	6.1	9.7	10.5	1.0	2.4	3.9	4.8
Total	171	1591	3596	5325	100.0	100.0	100.0	100.0					3.0	13.3	19.8	18.8
Radio																
National network	196	47	63	80	32.4	6.8	5.3	4.0	6.0	0.6	0.6	0.5	3.4	0.4	0.3	0.3
National spot	136	222	360	440	22.5	32.1	30.3	21.8	4.2	3.0	3.3	2.9	2.4	1.9	2.0	1.5
Local	273	428	767	1500	45.1	61.1	64.4	74.2	11.1	9.2	10.6	11.6	4.8	3.6	4.2	5.3
Total	605	692	1190	2020	100.0	100.0	100.0	100.0					10.6	5.8	6.6	7.1
Newspapers																
National	533	836	990	1200	25.7	22.6	18.8	14.2	16.4	11.5	9.1	7.8	9.3	7.0	5.5	4.2
Local	1542	2867	4275	7250	74.3	77.4	81.2	85.8	62.9	61.8	59.0	56.0	27.0	24.0	23.6	25.6
Total	2076	3703	5265	8450	100.0	100.0	100.0	100.0					36.4	31.0	29.0	29.8
Total																
National	3257	7296	10883	15380					100.0	100.0	100.0	100.0	57.0	61.1	60.0	54.3
Local	2453	4636	7244	12940					100.0	100.0	100.0	100.0	43.0	38.9	40.0	45.7
Grand Total*	5710	11932	18127	28320									100.0	100.0	100.0	100.0

SOURCE: McCann Erickson Inc., and Bureau of the Census estimates, as cited in Statistical Abstracts of the United States for 1950, 1960, 1970, and 1975 (Washington, D.C.: U.S. Government Printing Office).

*Includes magazines, farm publications, direct mail, outdoor, business papers, and miscellaneous, as well as television, radio, and newspapers.

sometimes prefer selective market (spot) coverage, handled by national station representatives, to concentrate better on a few key regions, or because there are no network affiliates in a desired place. Several hundred national advertisers buy network time on television today, several thousand buy spot time, and the one hundred largest account for the bulk of both kinds of expenditures.

The Demand for Programs

As noted earlier, advertisers are the proximate consumers whose demand prices influence the organization and pattern of program production from the industry's supply side. They have traditionally bought time *and* programs to secure access to large audiences with their commercial announcements. In arranging for the *programs* needed to attract these and to sell products, the advertiser has traditionally had four choices.

First, he might produce his own programs, which he formerly did in great number but rarely does any longer. Using this option, he would supply the program himself and pay the network a time rate for access to interconnected affiliates where he and the packager (but not the network) would share the financial risks and the potential rewards. (Today the advertiser increasingly prefers to spread his risks over more stations and more time slots to increase the cost-effectiveness of his total expenditures, buying both programs and time from a national network company and sharing the sponsorship with other advertisers in the process.)

Second, he might buy a network-produced show for transmission over the network, paying alike for program and program time on the affiliates that carried it. Here, the network bore the whole cost and risk of program development, and enjoyed the whole resultant gain or loss. This too is quite rare today except for public affairs, special events, or cultural programs.

Third, the advertiser might deal directly with an independent supplier or syndicator, buying the show and arranging for its transmission over time bought from a local station, from a station representative over selected stations, or from a network company for extensive nationwide clearances.

Fourth and last, the advertiser might agree to sponsor a show the network bought in whole or part from an independent packager or syndicator. Often, he will participate with a group of advertisers in sponsoring the program. In either case, the network provides at least some venture capital and reaps large potential gains or sustains losses.

For all intents and purposes, there are really only two effective choices in buying programs: to buy them from a network company, or directly from one of hundreds of independent packagers and syndicators. Buying from the former, the advertiser might enjoy the convenience of arranging for his nationwide program clearances at the same time. Buying from the latter, he would have to arrange for his own clearances, possibly through a network company, though more likely through a spot representative or local station sales staff.

The Demand for Time

Of greater relevance is the advertiser's demand for *time* (see table 2.5). Once again, he has normally had two choices: he could buy time for national advertising, or for local. If national, he might buy from a network (securing his programming in one of the ways just mentioned, though probably buying that from the network too). Or he could buy time from a national station representative for selective market (spot) coverage, and acquire his program from an independent packager or film syndicator. Finally, he might buy local time directly from a local station, also buying his program from a packager, or from the station itself. The only exception is that when the advertiser or agency is located in the same market as a station, the local sales staff would handle national spot business too, and this might be significant in markets like New York, Chicago, Los Angeles, and so on.

As noted, advertisers tend no longer to buy whole time periods for transmission of particular programs, with commercial messages interspersed. Instead they will more frequently participate with others, thus bearing only a fraction of the program or time costs; or they increasingly elect to buy time for spot announcements in so-called "adjacencies," the time spots located between different programs. In such transactions they may deal with a network, a spot representative, or a local station sales staff.[30]

According to informed industry executives, the factor that still favors the networks as preferred choice is the advertiser's advantage in spreading his spot announcements (participations) widely over the whole network schedule. He will normally purchase a package of commercial minutes long before needed, using them afterward on different programs over the year. He thereby hopes to hedge his bets better in light of past (and expected) ratios of successes to failures, leaving networks to bear the risks of acceptable audience delivery. Superficially he could do the same with national spot, but this would be more costly to transact (with numerous stations separately), and a less reliable way to reach the desired audience circulation. The growing caution in advertiser outlook is, in any case, said to have become gradually built into the time rate structure.

30. The market for time is usefully described in Peterman, "Structure of National Time Rates," note 7, especially pp. 77–93.

The Demand for Circulation

The markets for time and programs, though separate in principle, are still linked closely in fact. What the advertiser really buys is "audience circulation"—a number of people reached by a given commercial message (unduplicated), adjusted by probable enthusiasm for the program sponsored or for the preceding one, or by any knowledge of the special tastes and habits of the audience reached.[31] The network service enables the advertiser to buy both elements conveniently, at a single point, and thus to plan more effectively on a nationwide scale; yet allows him, in theory, the choice over both variables—time and programs. As suggested, the advertiser's main alternative is to deal with the nonnetwork system of stations, station representatives, independent packagers, and film syndicators.

This would all change if a magazine format were more fully and widely instituted. In that event, if the advertiser wanted a certain time slot he would virtually have to accept the program which the broadcaster had *already* scheduled, not, as in the past, when advertisers often produced or bought their own programs first, and sought particular time slots afterwards. At that time, a TV schedule would mainly emerge in negotiations between networks and stations which sold time, and advertisers who wanted to place their own shows in preferred slots. With a magazine format, the program schedule is fixed and confronts the advertiser as a datum, not a variable. He could in no way select programs and time slots simultaneously. This would, indeed, approximate the current British situation where a magazine concept has been in force for some time. True, American advertisers increasingly reduce their risks by buying time spots widely over the network schedule rather than whole time periods, with or without specific programs. Therefore, the de facto differences from Great Britain may be less important than imagined. Nevertheless, there is a difference, and American broadcasters remain visibly sensitive to it.

The Federal Communications Commission

A final word on the FCC's broadcast licensing-allocation function is in order. No one can own or operate a broadcast station without a license, and the commission's licensing power operates in new grants, renewals,

---

31. Compare Peterman with Blake and Blum, "Network Television Rate Practices," pp. 1347–48. The linkage between the markets for time, programs, and circulation is not always made explicit, nor is the interaction therein of advertisers, networks, independent programmers, and station representatives.

and transfers. Licensees must secure permission to enter the industry, as well as to continue therein. New licenses are distributed to qualified sole applicants (on a first come, first served basis) or to the best among qualified competing applicants.

Because only the broadcast station is licensed there is no really direct control of the industry's two major sources of power, the network company and the advertiser.[32] However, the commission can influence the behavior of each through the rules and regulations it imposes on licensee conduct.

The FCC's television licensing function purports, first and foremost, to provide for diversified programming responsive to local as well as national interests, minority as well as majority taste groups, and balanced between information and entertainment. The commission pursues this "basic" goal in large part by attempting to: (1) free each station licensee from undue restraints by networks, advertisers, or, in some cases, group or newspaper parents; (2) impose certain, albeit vague, program service responsibilities on all stations (relating, for example, to fairness, over-commercialism, news and public affairs, and so forth); and (3) encourage competition in internetwork, interstation, and network-station relations.[33]

The Basic Goal of Program Diversity and Balance

To sustain this goal of basic diversity as conceived herein, and the public service responsibilities associated with it, nonremunerative merit programming subsidized from earnings on popular entertainment is required. How much of such programming occurs, in fact, is a matter to be reviewed in later chapters. Here it should simply be noted that not all public service or merit programs are necessarily unprofitable. Some, such as the network evening news, appear to be an important source of network profits, and no FCC policy is needed to induce licensees to carry them.

On the other hand, one important constraint on the FCC in promoting merit programming of the other sort—the unprofitable kind—may literally be the wrath of the viewers themselves. Clearly, millions of viewers may well feel "worse off" when networks are required (or induced) to substitute public affairs programs or documentaries for popular entertainment shows having double the audience size. At the time the policy on public service programming was instituted, no one could predict how

32. One exception relates to the Prime-Time Access Rule and its exemptions for network news, public affairs, and children's programming (see chap. 11).

33. The doctrinal grounding of these dual functions of broadcast regulations is described at length in *Second Interim Report on TV Network Program Procurement*, Part II (1965), in Docket No. 12782, chaps. 1–3; see also Ibid., *Report on Network Broadcasting*, chap. 3.

large the audiences for mass entertainment programs would be or therefore, how costly the merit programs.

Nevertheless, the FCC has instituted some public service and diversity policies that could impair station profitability. These policies relate to the length, frequency, and loudness of commercials; [34] to children's programming and related advertising; to the magnitude and scheduling of public affairs and cultural programs, local live service, and rural programs; and to program balance and diversity on individual stations.

The question in each case is whether short-run profit maximization has in any fashion been sacrificed to date in order to meet the commission's admittedly vague exhortations. Industry spokesmen frequently complain about the magnitude of this sacrifice, as well as about the arbitrariness and free speech threats of regulatory program requirements. The latter allegations lie beyond our scope in this book, though the former will be examined in some detail.

Of paramount importance throughout, in any event, is a three-way categorization of merit programs that warrants brief mention at this point.[35] The cultural elitist view is that even if people want comedy/variety shows, we should give them Shakespeare, which they may never come to like or watch in the face of alternatives, but which will make them "better people" when they do (gratifying our elitists in the process). At the extreme, viewers would be compelled to watch what is "good for them" by depriving them of what is not.

My analysis in this book has very little to do with cultural elitism, though a second, infant industry argument is germane, namely, that when exposed to merit programs, people will eventually develop a taste for them, making the programs viable and the people "better." [36] Merit programs of that sort are part of the diversified program mix that constitutes our principal standard of assessment in what follows.

However, my main focus will be on a third category of so-called minority-audience programming, directed to limited ethnic, intellectual, social, or cultural groups. In certain cases, of course, the line between all three categories is very slim. Just as not all merit programs need be uneconomic (network evening news, Watergate hearings), so not all minority-audience programs need be merit goods.[37] Minority tastes be-

34. Mention should be made also of the propriety of commercials on personal products, liquor, firearms, and betting (issues which the commission does not actually address publicly), where the broadcaster's apparent desire to forestall administrative intrusions from outside has led him to impose his own profit qualifying constraints through the NAB's Television Code.

35. Merton J. Peck suggested the following distinctions in a private communication.

36. Contrariwise, if left to the unregulated market entirely, unqualified profit-maximizers are believed likely to "take the line of least resistance," and act in ways that reduce standards of taste, morals, and culture.

37. Nor do I contend that no entertainment program ever brings about reputedly desirable changes in basic social attitudes. I recognize that any distinction between

come a public interest to be protected because there are so few stations catering to them, and because there is no widely used pay mechanism to register the viewer's intensity of desire and consumer surplus.

Safeguarding Licensee Discretion

A major instrumental policy to further the commission's basic goal of diversity and public service is to encourage a multiplicity of program suppliers and advertisers for licensees to choose from in selecting and scheduling their programs, and to safeguard their discretion in doing so, consistent with fulfillment of their public service responsibilities. One good example of the commission's long-concern with this issue is the abolition of so-called "option time" in 1958 (see preceding note 8 and associated text). A second example is the commission's controversial action in reducing the number of hours, weekly, to which the network may have access so as to permit freer licensee choice, such as between network and nonnetwork programs. A third example is the FCC's past consideration of the above-mentioned magazine concept to weaken earlier advertiser control over content and scheduling.

By scrutinizing network practices in particular, the FCC has sought to prevent the network-affiliate relation from foreclosing access to key evening markets by nonnetwork advertisers and independent nonnetwork program suppliers.[38] Thereby, the commission has sought to equalize the network and nonnetwork system of program production and distribution. It has further required the networks to provide more advanced knowledge of program content to licensees (to end blind buying), and has also required licensees to seek out more complete knowledge of community needs, interests, and resources.

Finally, the commission's policy of owner diversification is geared to maintain a competitive local interstation and intermedia structure, and to increase the number of separate media voices (owners) in each market.

---

entertainment and cultural-informational merit programs is necessarily subjective. However, I simply could not weight the number of minutes individual programs devote to "serious" cultural or informational issues by size of audience reached.

38. At least the commission's assumptions and stated objectives are perfectly clear. The factual question requiring further resolution is whether the "adjacencies,"—that is, station breaks available to nonnetwork advertisers—are as good a product as network time. Are the prices of each, that is, proportional to their respective costs per thousand people delivered per unit of time in question? Only if the network price for adjacencies and station breaks is "too high" *relative to their sales productivity*, would this constitute exclusion in fact. But in assessing the evidence, published cost-per-thousand data must be adjusted for de facto discounts, as well as for differences in age, sex, income, attentiveness of viewer and so on.

Conclusion

The above interrelations of television's several major components and the FCC's principal licensing policies provide the framework within which some of those policies will be assessed in this book. The policies on owner diversity, structural diversity, and network-affiliate relations, will command special attention in Part II. Before proceeding to this extended empirical assessment, however, we must consider, in the remainder of Part I, two concepts utilized through the entire study. Reference is made to program diversity as the basic goal of regulation (chapter 3), economic rents as a major unintended consequence (chapter 4), and the divergence of the two, as a broad index of regulatory failure (chapter 5).

Appendix 2A: Alternative Costs for
TV Program Delivery Systems

This appendix will briefly compare some illustrative cost estimates for distributing television programs by present-day interconnected electronic delivery and by videotape networks using conventional shipment. Several configurations will be specified, and some trade-offs examined. The result is that TV program delivery costs appear to vary with (1) the level of reliability desired (via protection circuits), (2) the availability of special common carrier links, (3) simultaneity requirements, and (4) the permissible delay associated with alternative "bicycled" relays, systems which could also deliver TV programs nationally.

The implications for TV broadcast structure are first, that electronic interconnection costs, however, calculated, are no serious barrier to the entry of a fourth television network; second, that this is particularly true with the advent of specialized common carriers (and, though not examined here, of satellite relay systems too); third, that modified seminetworks tailored for delayed transmission of videotapes through bicycled networks using conventional shipment, would lower the entry costs even more, although normally associated with national nonnetwork programmers.

All estimates in table 2.6 are derived from facts in Robert Crandall's suggestive study of the economics of live pay television from Lincoln Center.[39] In passing, Crandall addresses the cost of interconnecting two

39. Robert Crandall, *The Economic Prospects for A "Live from Lincoln Center" Pay Television Service* (Cambridge, Mass.: Center for Policy Alternatives, 1975).

hundred local cable systems within designated geographic areas, either by (1) AT&T common carrier circuits; (2) specialized common carriage; (3) community antenna relay carriers (CARS); or (4) physical shipment of duplicated videotapes. Crandall does not directly compare the cost of interconnected over-the-air broadcast and alternative tape networks under item (4). Nevertheless, the crude estimates we derive from his numbers facilitate an assessment of sorts.

In regard to the results in table 2.6, note in particular that Crandall assumes the cost of tapes for a videotape network to be $50 per two-hour program (including $5 for shipment), doubling which (to $100) will provide a spare tape to ensure against loss, wear and tear, and so on.[40] Consider next our own estimate that each TV network carried an average of 450 programs for six months in 1974 (table 3.2), and 900 programs for the full year, that count being derived from A. C. Nielsen data for the period 7 to 11 P.M. Because that portion of prime time entails 1,456 program hours for the year, the average effective program length would be 1 hour 40 minutes, roughly in line with Crandall's assumed 2-hour program length.

Next, at $100 per program (including a spare tape for security), 900 programs could be shipped at $90,000 per station affiliate of any television network. The capacity for simultaneous transmission via shipment, then, would come to $18,180,000 for, say, all 202 affiliates served by NBC in 1974. This distribution cost is roughly double that of the single-tape network, and the security provided by the extra tape makes the proper comparison with costs for a "protected" electronic delivery system. In table 2.6, then, we must compare the $18,000,000 estimate for System C, Model 1, with the actual $14,600,000 cost of AT&T's protected common carrier links for each TV network in 1974 (System A, Model 1), and the $8,611,000 cost we derive from this for protected circuits of hypothetical specialized common carriers (System B, Model 1).

By the same token, the cost of acquiring, duplicating, and shipping a single tape to all 202 affiliates (with no backup tape), would be about $9,000,000 under System C, Model 2, best compared with delivery costs via an "unprotected" specialized common carrier whose rates we estimate as roughly $388 per mile per year, compared to AT&T's at $980 per mile per year.[41] On these assumptions at least, unprotected delivery costs via a specialized carrier in 1974 would hypothetically have been $14,600,000 × 39.6 percent or $5,717,000 (System B, Model 2), not quite two-thirds of the comparable cost of a single-tape (unprotected) videotape network under System C, Model 2.

Special attention must, however, be given signal quality, reliability, and the possibility of live transmission, which remains available with

40. Ibid., pp. 45–46.
41. Ibid., pp. 69–70. See also derivation in table 2.6.

TABLE 2.6

Average TV Program Delivery Costs for AT&T, Specialized Carriers, and Videotape Networks Using Conventional Transportation for One National TV Network, 1974

Model No.	No. of Affilia- tions	Pro- tection	Microwave Interconnection		Videotape Network		
			System A AT&T	System B Specialized Carriers	System C Simultaneous Distribution & Airing	System D One "Bicycle" Relay	System E Two "Bicycle" Relay
1	200	yes	$14,546,000	$8,611,000	$18,000,000	$9,000,000	$6,000,000
2	200	no	–	$5,717,000	$ 9,000,000	$4,500,000	$3,000,000

SOURCE:

System A, Model 1   See FCC, 1974 Financial Report for Television Broadcasting, table VI, schedule 2, line 22.

System B, Model 1   See Robert Crandall, *The Economic Prospects for a "Live from Lincoln Center" Pay Television Service* (Cambridge, Mass.: Center for Policy Alternatives 1975), p. 69; app. III, p. A-16. Crandall estimates fully protected AT&T microwave charges at $980 per mile per year for a number of cable network alternatives, compared to specialized common carrier rates (with protection) at $580 per mile per year without stereo charges. (The specialized carrier costs were actually $40 per mile per month plus $500 per local loop/60 miles, which equals $48.30 per mile per month, or $580 per mile per year.) Accordingly, specialized carrier rates for protected circuits are 580/980, or 59.2 percent of AT&T's rates. Costs of System B, Model 1 would therefore total about $14,546,000 X 59.2% or $8,611,000.

System B, Model 2   Ibid., app. III, p. A-16. Crandall further reports for a "mixed" system (in twenty-seven states using specialized carriers where available, and AT&T where not), all microwave charges are at $24 per mile per month plus $300 or $500 local connection charges per month. For $500 local connections at $24 per mile per month plus $500/60 miles, this totals $32.30 X 12 months or $388 per mile per year. The mixed system annual charges are therefore 388 ÷ 988, or 39.3 percent of AT&T's rates. Hence System B, Model 2, largely unprotected, would cost $14,546,000 X 39.3% or $5,717,000.

System C, Model 2   Ibid., p. 45 and app. A, p. 17. Crandall further assumes $45 to acquire and duplicate each two-hour videotape, and $5 for shipment costs. Using that estimate, we estimate that the 900 prime-time programs each network carried in 1974 (see table 3.2), at an average length of 1 hour 42 minutes, would have cost $450,000 to copy and ship to a single affiliate. All two hundred affiliates (for a typical broadcast network) could have had their programs available for simultaneous transmission (with say, ten-day shipment time) at $9,000,000. The cost of an extra tape (as insurance against wear and tear, loss, or damage), would raise the costs to $18,000,000 (System C, Model 1).

System D, Model 1   Ibid., pp. 45-46. By arranging for each affiliate to ship any given tape to one other affiliate, the tape cost could be halved, with shipment cost constant, and the average delay rising from ten to fifteen days per program. Specifically, two groups of one hundred affiliates each could be given 450 tapes at a given time, with instructions to ship to a partner in the other group after a specified period. Here System B, Model 4 would cost 450 X $100 (2 tapes) X 100 (affiliates), or $4,500,000 per affiliate group. Without the extra tape for insurance, again, the cost could be roughly halved. (System D, Model 2).

System E, Model 1   Ibid. By dividing the two hundred affiliates into three equal groups, only 300 tapes need be sent to each group of sixty-six to sixty-seven stations. Tape costs would thus be further reduced to 300 programs times $100 (2 tapes) times 67 stations equals $2,010,000 times 3 groups of affiliates, or $6,030,000 in all.

System E, Model 2   The unprotected equivalent of System E, Model 1, using one tape of each program only, would be 300 X $50 X 67 = $1,005,000 X 3 groups = $3,015,000.

electronic delivery but not with conventional shipment.[42] Thus the main difference between the fully protected circuits under System A, Model 1 (at $14,600,000 in 1974), and a two-tape (protected) videotape network under System C, Model 1 (at $18,000,00), is that System A, Model 1 permits live shows, whereas System C, Model 1 does not (its minimum delay being roughly 7–10 days for any full distribution).[43] Furthermore, System A, Model 1 has superior technical capabilities for high quality signal, whereas System C, Model 1 is more dependent on lower quality videotape equipment and transmissions.[44]

Note, finally, that the $9,000,000 single-tape (unprotected) network using conventional shipment (System C, Model 2), still costs 50 percent more than a comparable specialized carrier that also uses no protection circuits (System B, Model 2). Nor does System C, Model 2 (the single-tape unprotected network) cost any less than System B, Model 1, the protected delivery circuits of a specialized carrier. Yet System C, Model 2 offers no live service capabilities whatever, and at best lower signal quality.

Only under Systems D and E, where tapes are bicycled to a second or third station, do the "shipment-plus-tape-costs" decline dramatically; the greater the average delay before any tape is broadcast over all 200 affiliates, the lower the aggregate delivery cost.[45] Consider three possibilities. First, with no bicycling of tapes, for simultaneous delivery, fully 900-tape cassettes must hypothetically be shipped directly to 200 affiliates with, say, 7–10 days for certain delivery, at $50 per tape including a $5 shipment cost, for a total cost of $9,000,000 for 180,000 cassettes in all, or double that sum with a spare tape to insure against loss, wear and tear, and so on. Second, with two groups of 100 affiliates each, only 90,000 cassettes would be needed since all 900 programs need be sent initially to only 100 stations, which would subsequently ship them to the second group of stations. Bicycling in this manner would reduce tape costs by one-half, but leave shipment costs constant and double shipment time from 7–10 days to 14–20 days. Third, dividing the 200 affiliates into three groups of roughly 66 each would further reduce needed cassettes to 60,000 and costs by another one-third.[46] But again, shipment costs remain constant, while time delays before all affiliates air all programs would rise from 7–10 to 14–20 to 21–30 days. Finally, this assumes that all broadcasts occur on the day the tape is received, or that tapes are

42. Crandall, *The Economic Prospects,* pp. x, 41, 46, 106.
43. This is the time needed to ship tapes to all two hundred affiliates for a hypothetical simultaneous showing.
44. Crandall, *The Economic Prospects,* pp. x, 5, 106.
45. Ibid., pp. x, 45, 46.
46. My assumptions are documented in the preceding notes and in table 2.6. Costs would be further reduced by any reuse of tapes for new programs (after erasure), depending, of course, on the breakdown in cost between cost of the tape itself and cost of the duplication process.

copied and the master shipped at once to the next station. If, instead, the stations retain the master for one week to capitalize on any superior technical quality for a number of replays, this would further lengthen the period before tapes were aired by all affiliates, on the preceding assumptions, to 28 to 34 days for a two-group system and to 42 to 51 days for one with three groups. Here, then, any cost advantage in a bicycled videotape network quite clearly comes at the expense of simultaneity, live transmission capabilities, and sheer signal quality. Such a system, though far removed from national network service today, does seem usable by nonnetwork program producers. However, the promotional advantages of simultaneous transmission may be very hard to retain, even within the same time zones.

Chapter 3

The Concept and

Measurement of

Diversity

PROGRAM DIVERSITY, loosely defined, has long been a professed objective of federal broadcast regulation. It is, accordingly, a cogent yardstick by which to evaluate current or proposed regulatory policies. However, diversity is often conceived ambiguously, and rarely measured empirically.[1]

The purpose of this chapter is therefore twofold: first, to specify and distinguish several kinds of diversity—in program options, program types, and sources; second, and foremost, to measure the relative impact of options diversity and types diversity on aggregate audience behavior. Briefly, the task is to determine whether the typology used in this book to measure type diversity is entirely producer-related, and unrelated to diversity as *viewers* perceive it. My evidence questions the validity of this undocumented assumption.

---

1. For that reason some students have questioned the concept's usefulness for regulatory purposes at all. See, for example, Bruce Owen, "The Economics of Diversity in Broadcasting," unpublished paper presented at the Fourth Annual Conference on Telecommunications Policy Research, Airlie, Virginia, April 1976. A more affirmative view appears in Stanley Besen and Bridger Mitchell, *Watergate and Television: An Economic Analysis* (Santa Monica, Calif.: Rand Corporation, May 1975), pp. 1–12, reprinted in *Communication Research*, vol. 3, July 1976, pp. 243–60. The Besen and Mitchell view is that if "program types" and "diversity" are to be meaningful concepts, they must be based on actual viewer behavior. See further threefold distinction between program options, types, and tone drawn by Roger Noll, Merton Peck, and John McGowan, *Economic Aspects of Television Regulation* (Washington, D.C.: Brookings Institution, 1973), pp. 8–13, 49–57. The latter distinctions resemble concepts developed in this chapter.

Toward a Working Concept
of Program Diversity

Program diversity can in the first instance be defined as the number of different programs available to viewers across all stations in the market at any point in time. A more diverse program mix is one that simply offers the viewer more choices (options) at any moment, and where any single program must therefore compete against more numerous substitutes than in a less diverse mix. It is true but of no clear conceptual consequence here that where a larger set of choices does not include a smaller set, viewers may prefer the smaller set (for its preferred options) to the larger set though the former was less diversified.

Diversity, then, can be thought of either relative to the viewers who perceive differences among the available programs, or relative to the packagers, stations, or networks that make the programs available. Admittedly, one empirical and conceptual problem is that most programming data are now compiled and organized only within a variety of categories specified in terms related to producers. These data simply do not take account of *viewer* perceptions of intracategory differences. To develop useful viewer-related concepts and measures, we must somehow analyze viewer response to program variations within as well as between producer-related categories.[2]

Alternative Kinds of Diversity [3]

All programs can in some basic sense be considered unique, from an audience viewpoint at least. In the absence of unattainable information on program costs and demand schedules, some observers imply that we had best treat each program as if unique for viewers. Yet this really need not preclude meaningful distinctions among different classes of programs (that is, program types). The relative importance of differences within and between these program types then becomes an empirical question, albeit not an easy one to answer. Putting aside viewer preferences and percep-

2. These distinctions have been usefully spelled out by Edward Greenberg and Harold Barnett, "Television Program Diversity—New Evidence and Old Theories," *American Economic Review*, May 1971, 89–93. They are further endorsed in Noll, Peck, and McGowan, *Economic Aspects*, pp. 8–9.

3. The forms of diversity discussed in this chapter are briefly defined in table 3.1.

TABLE 3.1
Illustrative Forms of Diversity in Television

Sources Diversity	Relates to the number of separately owned stations in market—sometimes further classified by network status and channel type, each station representing a source of program content, as well as a proxy for the number of programs available, and sources diversity thus subdividing into (1) sources number diversity, (2) sources class diversity, and (3) number of sources and their distribution over classes, for example, number of network VHF, network UHF, independent VHF, independent UHF stations.
Program Diversity	
Types diversity	Number of program types offered within a given horizontal or vertical time slot. (Intertype diversity.)
horizontal	Number of types available in a market at a point in time, for example, totaled, for example, for each 15-minute period during a sample week, 6 P.M. to 11 P.M.
vertical	Average number of different types carried in a day by any station, or class of station, namely, diversity on a station, over time, a vertical time slot being each 15-minute period, 6 P.M. to 11 P.M., each day of week.
Options diversity	Number of different programs in a vertical or horizontal slot. (Intratype diversity.)
horizontal	Number of different programs or program options available in a market at a point in time, represented by a simple count of the number of stations there.
vertical	Average number of different programs or program options carried by a station over the broadcast day, 6 P.M. to 11 P.M., not examined here due to insufficient variation among stations.

tions temporarily, reference will be made first to producer-related concepts and measures (see table 3.1).

Options Diversity

Two polar bounds here are perfect equidistance, where each pair of programs is assumed to differ by just as much as any other pair, and perfect options duplication, where each program is assumed to duplicate all others. With perfect equidistance, the greater the number of programs available to viewers in any market, at any time, the closer they can come to satisfying their preferences. If programs are indeed all equidistant, then the number of stations in any market provides a suitable proxy for program diversity, and the term options diversity makes eminent sense. Under these assumptions, much of the debate over diversity would probably disappear. The controversy arises when public policy proposes to raise not merely the number of stations-cum-program options for viewers, but also to determine how widely dispersed the types of programs or stations are.[4]

In implementing a concern for such dispersion, the assumption is that options within given classes of programs (or generated by a particular station class) are perceived as significantly closer substitutes for one another than for options within some other program class. It is therefore deemed insufficient for public policy to attempt to maximize the number of program options alone, program type diversity being conceived of at least equal importance.[5]

Program Type Diversity

Use of the program type diversity concept assumes that individual programs can be usefully subclassified among a set of program categories such that programs across classes (types) are perceived by viewers as offering poorer substitutes than do programs within the same class. The principal categories are normally defined by program packagers, ratings services, and station owners to include news, public affairs (with documentaries), cultural, comedy, variety, mystery-suspense, and so on (see table 3.2).

Useful distinctions can also be made between vertical diversity (type differences throughout the average broadcast day) and horizontal diversity (type differences across all stations in the market at designated times). To these we turn presently below, and, in far greater detail, in subsequent chapters. Table 3.2 presents a set of program categories devised by A. C. Nielsen, Inc., in cooperation with the three national television networks. These categories differ in certain regards from those analyzed in this book, but the tabulation does illustrate the kind of typology now widely used by television broadcasters, and hence the ingredients of a quantitative measure of program type diversity.

4. This point has now been frequently emphasized in the literature. See, especially, Noll, Peck, and McGowan, *Economic Aspects*, note 1, pp. 8–13, 269; John McGowan and Merton Peck, "Television: Theories, Facts and Policies—Discussion," *American Economic Review*, May 1971, pp. 96–98; also, more generally, Greenberg and Barnett, "Television Program Diversity," note 2; and Owen, "Economics of Diversity."

5. Even those who reject the diversity concept or question its measurability across separate program types or station formats, openly recognize the empirical requirements that could in principle permit valid classifications. See Bruce Owen, *Economics and Freedom of Expression* (Cambridge, Mass.: Ballinger, 1975), p. 21. Others, who caution against any undiscriminating use of type diversity as a basis for regulatory policy, themselves frequently distinguish between program options and program types in their own policy-related work. See Noll, Peck, and McGowan, *Economic Aspects*, pp. 8–13. Greenberg and Barnett, too, while critically assessing past attempts to measure type diversity, nonetheless suggest the empirical requirements of the needed typology ("Television Program Diversity," pp. 90–93). Gary Bowman and J. U. Farley have indeed experimented with a related methodology toward the same end. See Bowman and Farley, "TV Viewing: Applications of a Formal Choice Model," *Applied Economics*, December 1972.

TABLE 3.2

Selected Evening Network Television Program Types and Their Audiences, 1974 (7-11 P.M.)

1	2	3	4	5	
	No. of Programs	Mean Audience (millions)	Standard Deviation	95% Confidence Interval for Mean (millions)	
Award ceremonies	6	17.6	1.4	16.1-19.2	
Musical drama	1	16.7	0.0		
Situation comedy	321	14.7	4.2	14.3-15.2	
Evening animated	21	13.9	3.9	12.2-15.8	
General variety	23	13.8	2.9	12.5-15.1	
Private detective	96	13.6	2.7	13.0-14.1	
Comedy variety	68	13.2	3.3	12.3-13.9	
Western drama	58	13.1	3.4	12.2-14.0	
Official police	188	13.0	2.7	12.6-13.4	
Feature film	240	12.8	3.1	12.4-13.2	
General drama	197	12.7	3.6	12.2-13.2	
Sports event	19	12.4	4.1	10.4-14.4	
Suspense mystery*	32	12.1	2.4	11.2-12.9	
Popular music, contemporary	14	11.6	2.7	10.0-13.1	
General documentary	20	11.3	4.9	9.0-13.6	
Adventure	19	10.9	1.4	10.2-11.5	
Sports commentary	3	10.7	1.9	5.8-15.6	
Science fiction	10	9.8	1.4	8.8-10.7	
News	2	9.4	3.6	-23.0-41.8	
Children's, evening	2	8.6	0.9	.6-16.6	
News documentary	18	7.8	2.9	6.3- 9.2	
Total	1358	13.2	3.6	13.0-13.4	

F = 5.836, P = 0.0001 (DF = 29,1328)

SOURCE: All data derived from A.C. Nielsen Inc., Nielsen Television Index (NTI) Reports for January-March, October-December 1974. The network schedule normally started at 7 P.M., and we therefore excluded the preceding hour of prime time, mainly filled by local and syndicated programs. Some of the 7-8 P.M. period was also programmed by nonnetwork producers under different versions of the Prime Time Access Rule during 1974 (see pp. 324-25).
*Except official police and private detective.

For each of the twenty-one categories listed in the first column, four items of information are reported. In the second column, the number of programs Nielsen assigned to each category from among all network evening shows aired during the first three and last three months of 1974 are presented. In the third column, the average audience for all programs within each program category is shown; in the fourth column, that audience's dispersion in standard deviations. In the fifth column, a 95 percent confidence interval around each mean audience is given; that is, this column reports the range within which the true mean would fall —specifically, 95 percent of the mean audiences of successive samples of programs drawn from the full population of programs. Hence, the fifth column indicates which types have audiences of significantly different sizes (at the .05 confidence level),[6] assuming independence of the types. I shall have more to say about this table presently.

Source Diversity

Midway between options and types diversity in the above sense is diversity of program sources, defined here as numbers within different station classes for which there is a station in a given market. One conceivable measure of sources diversity would be the number of network-affiliated and of independent VHF or UHF stations.[7]

Strictly speaking, this four-way breakdown of program sources refers to stations and not to small program producers; the former locally produce only a small fraction (10 percent) of all programming they carry. Nevertheless, the different classes of stations each have quite different financial capabilities, and hence potential program resources. This measure of sources diversity assumes that programs generated by stations

6. Any comparison of a pair of program types wherein the upper end of one confidence interval lies below the lower end of another, reveals a statistically significant difference between the mean audience of the two program types, at the .05 confidence level. Examples here are situation comedy versus comedy variety versus adventure versus western drama, and so on. Beyond this, differences which at least approach significance and merit closer scrutiny can also be readily recognized. These cases are pairs whose confidence intervals overlap to a very limited degree—for example, news documentary versus general documentary, adventure versus science fiction. Note, finally, that an overall analysis of variance reveals that, for all twenty-one categories, between-type variability exceeds within-type variability significantly, at a better than .001 confidence level ($F = 5.836$, $DF = 29,1328$). This further suggests that the program typology as a whole may represent a meaningful set of categories for the viewing public. To confirm these results, however, more detailed analysis is needed of data normalized for other influences on viewers, as we do later.

7. This fourfold classification of "sources diversity" as a form of "options diversity" seems close to the latter's treatment in Noll, Peck, and McGowan, *Economic Aspects*, pp. 49–53. Their regression analysis of the audiences of sixty-five network affiliates actually specifies each affiliate's channel type and network tie, as well as the number of competing affiliates and independents in its market (p. 59). See also Owen, *Freedom of Expression*, pp. 21–22.

located in different station classes will tend to be more dissimilar than programs aired by stations within any given station class.

One further refinement of sources diversity would be to distinguish between the total time stations in each class devoted, for example, to entertainment and information. In that case, not simply the number of stations in each station class, but the number of entertainment and information minutes they carry, could become still another ingredient in the program mix available to viewers in any market. However, limitations of time and resources prevented the exploration of such possibilities.

Producer- and Audience-Related Concepts

Before proceeding, note, finally, the principal ambiguities that mark all three kinds of diversity, namely, whether the differences which audiences perceive among programs within each program type, source, or station option are in fact significantly smaller than the differences perceived across these types, sources, and station options. If not, the above classifications, at best producer-related, will have little bearing on audience satisfaction or consumer welfare. But if the impact on aggregate viewing of having more categories represented is substantial, and significantly larger than the impact of having more stations within a category, then mere options diversity will not suffice as a policy desideratum.[8] Each program, from an audience viewpoint, will then not in fact be unique.

The main empirical question, to which I will shortly return, is this: does the mere number of available programs (option diversity) have more or less impact on aggregate viewing in any market than (1) the number of program type differences across all stations in the market (horizontal types diversity); or (2) the number of stations in different station classes along with their associated programming differences (sources diversity)?

I will address this matter at length later in this chapter, but a further word first about the concept of type diversity and some problems in measuring it.

8. A still more fundamental question is whether types diversity, or sources diversity, will add significantly to economic value. The absence of direct demand prices for TV programs makes this very hard to answer, though we return to it in chapters 10 and 13. Aggregate viewing is, in any case, only one attribute or index of value.

Type Diversity—The Concept and Its Measurement

Horizontal versus Vertical Program Type Diversity [9]

Let us define vertical diversity as the average number of prime-time television program types available during any given day, on any given station, during the sample week. In contrast, let horizontal diversity be the total number of types available across all stations in the market, for each fifteen-minute prime-time program period throughout the week. Thus in a two-station market, if each station carried a different program type from the other during all twenty quarter-hour slots nightly, from 6 P.M. to 11 P.M., the maximum number of types available to viewers on a given night, in any market, must be 40. However, treating types that reappear on other nights on one station as "different" if aired when the second station carries some other type would imply a maximum of 280 different types during the whole week.

Before considering these concepts further, note first that both diversity measures are valid proxies for stated regulatory goals in television. Thus vertical diversity is precisely what the commission has long had in mind in its efforts to impose program balance on individual licensees—balance and diversity among the several program types—news, documentary, instructional, comedy/variety, drama, and so on, though with heavier weights on informational than on entertainment categories. The classic statement of this policy appears in the commission's "bluebook," *Public Service Responsibilities of Broadcast Licensees,* 1946. The commitment to vertical diversity harks back to the very outset of broadcast regulation in the 1930s, when most markets had few outlets. At that time, the commission's attempts to induce individual licensees to diversify their programming may have made sense. Licensees were expected to internally subsidize certain less popular (merit) program types so as to produce the desired, diversified program mix over the broadcast day.

In contrast, the newer "community balance" concept reveals a growing commitment to horizontal diversity in an age of multichannel broadcast and cable capabilities. The commitment to multistation and multiservice markets in the TV and FM allocation plans is also geared to horizontal diversity. So, too, are the so-called Barrow Report and a more recent proceeding on TV network trade practices that focus on reducing network power to sustain the growth of a viable nonnetwork alternative comprised of independent programmers, stations, and advertisers. Such a non-

9. My distinctions here were first systematized for a Regulated Utilities Conference at the University of Chicago, June 1972, and in a related paper, "Program Duplication, Diversity and Effective Viewer Choices," *American Economic Review,* May 1971, pp. 81–88.

network system, or even a new network entrant, is expected to differentiate its product from the existing networks and thereby produce greater horizontal diversity. One can in any case test the impact of resultant changes in diversity—horizontal or vertical—on the level of aggregate viewing.

Aggregate viewing is by no means my sole index of industry performance. In subsequent chapters, I also examine major economic indicators, and focus as well on my two diversity measures directly. My concern throughout is with trade-offs between a number of programming and economic variables. Nevertheless, analysis of the impact of diversity on aggregate viewing provides a useful way to infer the viewer's perception of diversity, and the satisfaction he may or may not derive from it. Presumably, there is a simultaneous determination of total audience, program composition, audience distribution among stations, diversity, and so on, which the market is grinding out all the time. About all we can do here is to focus on a few of these measures and relationships in order to get a better feel of the underlying process.

In sum, a vertical approach to diversity at the station level relates as much to a producer as to a consumer viewpoint. The vertical programming diversity of broadcast licensees is clearly one yardstick by which to appraise the performance of the Federal Communications Commission.[10] To consider consumer welfare implications, however, one must examine horizontal as well as vertical diversity. Only the horizontal approach, in fact, looks at diversity across all stations in the market. True, the less time-bound a viewer is, the more program alternatives he may enjoy, vertically. Nevertheless, actual time constraints make the prime evening hours especially attractive, and underscore the need to study diversity horizontally.

Thus for the mass of the working population, daytime and nighttime programs are not good substitutes for each other. Even within the prime evening hours—6 P.M. to 11 P.M.—viewers cannot switch freely among alternative time slots. We know, for example, that the later a program is aired (during prime time), the smaller its audience. This is also true after taking account of day-of-the-week differences, network source, program length, and program type (see table 3.3). By the same token, programs aired on different days (again taking account of the above factors), usually have audiences of significantly different sizes, the most visible being the larger followings on Sunday and Monday. Such evidence quite clearly underscores the importance of time constraints on viewer behavior, and hence the conclusion that horizontal

10. Yet note that vertical diversity refers only to the average *number* of different categories aired daily. Rising levels of vertical (or horizontal) diversity need not necessarily imply greater access to so-called merit programming, an issue that we treat separately later.

diversity of program options, types, and sources (across all stations in the market), during major time periods, captures one crucial dimension of effective viewer choice.[11]

For expository convenience I start with twenty well-known program types: dramatic adventure, cartoons, children's, situation comedy, drama, quiz or game, popular music, fine arts, sports events, serials, variety, feature film, news, instruction (light), instruction (heavy), interview, discussion & debate, political, documentary & news specials, religious.[12] The assumption is that diversity across these several program types provides more basic choices for viewers than a multiplicity of programs within types. This assumption does need greater empirical verification that could conceivably produce a more relevant set of categories, but the twenty-point coding is a good place to start.

Station Class and Sources Diversity

There is further useful linkage between program composition, source diversity, and options diversity. Basic station classes (network, independent, VHF, UHF) have well-known differences in economic and programming performance. These differences, sketched briefly in chapter 2, are confirmed more fully in later chapters.

Midway between the extremes of treating each program as unique in the consumer's eyes, and collapsing whole groups of programs into a more limited (and arbitrary) set of types, lies the possibility of defining the number of entertainment and information minutes broadcast by at least four basic classes of stations, namely, network VHF, network UHF, independent VHF, and independent UHF. The resulting measure would combine data on the number of competing stations (as program sources) with the simplest treatment of program composition, as between entertainment and information shows. I encourage other investigators to probe these and other conceivable diversity measures, but now can only assess from a consumer viewpoint a few of the simpler operational concepts set forth earlier.

11. Without interaction between, say, day-of-week and time-of-night on one hand, and network source and program type on the other, we cannot tell just how time-bound the viewer really is. A proper test would require such interactions to hold constant other major influences. Short of that, we have at least accounted for these other factors.

12. The distinction between "light" and "heavy" instructional programs is adapted from Gary Steiner, *The People Look at Television*, (New York: Knopf, 1963), chaps. 5–6, and appendix C, tables 10–11. All other categories correspond to those used by Herman Land Associates, *Television and the Wired City* (Washington, D.C.: National Association of Broadcasters, 1968), pp. 56–58. However, our data base was far more extensive than Land's, and, in any case, compiled separately from his, and earlier. See my "Program Duplication," pp. 81–85.

Program Options, Types Diversity,
and Aggregate Market Viewing

Let us next consider how aggregate viewing responds to changing numbers of program options and program types when cogent control factors are held constant. We also wish to know if the amount of extra viewing added by another option versus another type is itself significant.

The number of program types is derived from a coding of prime-time program logs for 486 codable TV stations reported in *TV Guide* for 25 February through 3 March 1967. The measure of options utilized will vary with the specific tests, and includes: (1) the number of commercial stations in the market; (2) the separate number of VHF and UHF television stations; and (3) the number of network and independent VHF and UHF stations.

Intratype versus Intertype Diversity

The question to be investigated is whether options *or* types diversity, or both, have significant effects on viewing. Answers to this question are of critical importance in evaluating the three hypotheses, that (1) programs, as seen by viewers, are essentially unique; that (2) as many or more differences are perceived *within* broad program types, as *among* (or across) different types; and that therefore, (3) some actions to increase program type diversity could reduce consumer welfare (viewer satisfaction).[13] If programs are all unique, such policies will deprive some viewers of particular programs they prefer to those which remain.

This brings us to a number of criticisms of the typology in question. If intratype diversity impacts significantly on aggregate viewing but intertype diversity does not, the typology might to some degree be considered arbitrary. While able to help explain producer behavior, has it any relevance to types differences from a *consumer* viewpoint? [14] If not, even analyzing policy effects on types diversity could be misleading, and the task for this chapter is to establish the sheer *existence* of such diversity. If our diversity measure were, as often asserted, entirely producer-related, its policy relevance to the FCC would obviously be cast into quite a different light.

13. A more rigorous standard by which to test these hypotheses is that the impact of options diversity on viewing is significantly greater than that of types diversity. If this holds true, our three hypotheses are most clearly confirmed, whereas if *types* diversity has greater impact, the hypotheses are rejected. Nevertheless, the link between options and types diversity means that the test is more complex than simply to measure which effect is greater.

14. This question is raised by Edward Greenberg and Harold Barnett, "Television Program Diversity—New Evidence and Old Theories," *American Economic Review,* May 1971, pp. 89–93.

An invaluable starting point in this determination lies in the separate set of Nielsen network program data summarized in table 3.2, and then briefly discussed. Unlike our *TV Guide* listings of individual station programs, the Nielsen data contain the actual audience size of each of the network programs coded there, across twenty-one types, for six months during 1974. In determining how operational this typology is we must ask whether the national network audience sizes of successive pairs of the twenty-one Nielsen program types are significantly different from one another. That determination for national network television, below, will further help clarify the validity of a similar twenty-category *TV Guide* typology employed throughout most of this book. (The latter was used to generate data on the program mix of each of 486 individual stations, as well as across all stations in major television markets.)

Pairwise Differences in Program Type Impact on National Network Audience Size

In table 3.2, for some pairwise comparisons, the 95-percent confidence intervals for mean audience size of each of the twenty-one program categories did *not* overlap. Such evidence suggested the existence of types diversity, namely of significant differences among programs from a consumer viewpoint (see note 6).

Toward an Estimation of National TV Network Audiences. Because the data in table 3.2 had not first been normalized to correct for extraneous influences on viewing, however, only tentative conclusions could be drawn regarding program type diversity in television. In what follows, we have now controlled for network source of program, program length in minutes, and the day of week and time of night each program was broadcast. In addition, we simultaneously considered the audience size of all twenty-one program types studied, for all conceivable (four hundred) pairwise comparisons.

Preliminary variance analysis and regressions soon revealed that network source and program type were the two principal determinants of a program's audience size among the factors examined. In both cases, between-class variability significantly exceeded within-class variability at the .01 level.

Our estimating equation is reported in table 3.3. In interpreting those results (as well as the grid of pairwise comparisons in table 3.4), bear in mind that:

1. The impact of each program type is estimated by the use of twenty dummy variables, relative to the situation comedy base, chosen on the basis of its being the most popular type after excluding musical drama and award ceremonies as having too few observations to provide a reasonably stable base.

2. The impact of each of the two early segments of prime time

TABLE 3.3
Estimating Equation for National TV Network Audience Size, 1974
(8-11 P.M.)

Line	Variable Name	Coefficient	t-value	Line
1	Constant	15.993	76.980	1
2	Program length (hours)	0.311	2.500	2
3	Network dummies (vs. CBS base)*			3
4	NBC	−1.176	−10.660	4
5	ABC	−2.971	−27.440	5
6	Day-of-week dummies (vs. Monday base)*			6
7	Tuesday	−0.424	−2.600	7
8	Wednesday	−0.710	−4.360	8
9	Thursday	−0.876	−5.400	9
10	Friday	−1.649	−10.030	10
11	Saturday	−1.477	−9.040	11
12	Sunday	0.158	0.880	12
13	Time-of-night dummies (vs. 10-10:59 P.M. base)†			13
14	8-8:59 P.M.	0.797	6.830	14
15	9-9:59 P.M.	0.568	5.350	15
16	Program type dummies (vs. situation comedy base)*			16
17	Adventure	−5.031	−12.530	17
18	Award ceremony	2.803	4.500	18
19	Child's evening	−4.695	−3.050	19
20	Comedy variety	−1.649	−6.930	20
21	Documentary, general	−2.193	−5.780	21
22	Documentary, news	−6.691	−16.510	22
23	Evening animated	−1.035	−2.290	23
24	Evening western	−1.681	−6.530	24
25	Feature film	−1.948	−8.210	25
26	General drama	−2.003	−10.300	26
27	General variety	−1.025	−2.920	27
28	Musical drama	0.159	0.160	28
29	News	−4.467	−4.080	29
30	Popular music, contemporary	−2.637	−5.680	30
31	Private detective	−1.819	−7.960	31
32	Official police	−1.250	−6.440	32
33	Sports commentary	−3.390	−1.920	33
34	Sports event	−1.608	−3.860	34
35	Science fiction	−5.697	−11.100	35
36	Suspense/mystery	−0.818	−2.660	36

Dep. var. = viewing households
Sample mean = 13.065 × 1,000,000
Sample size = 5,222 15-minute program units
R^2 = 0.23658
Adj. R^2 = 0.23240

SOURCE: All data derived from A.C. Nielsen, Inc., NTI Reports for January-March, October-December 1974. Under the Prime Time Access Rule, varying portions of the 7-8 P.M. were filled by nonnetwork programs (see pp. 324-25). By limiting our sample here to 8-11 P.M. only, we insured against including cases where one network's program may have faced a nonnetwork program on either or both of its rivals.

*Labeled attribute for all dummy variables = 1, 0 for designated base.

†Time-of-night dummies include programs starting on the hour, the quarter hour, half hour, and three-quarter hour.

(shows that start anywhere from 8 to 8:59 P.M. or from 9 to
9:59 P.M.) is estimated (again with dummy variables), relative
to that of the latest segment starting time of 10 to 10:59 P.M.

3.   Network impact, using dummy variables for NBC and ABC, is
actually measured relative to CBS (which had the largest audiences).

4.   Day-of-the-week impact, using six dummy veriables, is measured
relative to Monday night (comparable in prime time audience
size to Sunday night, though with a more typical program mix).

5.   The impact of program length, a continuous variable, is estimated
for additional minutes of length.

To ensure the reliability of our final fully specified equation, we developed the results sequentially, running the equation first with two
network and twenty program type dummies only. Then we added program length and two time-of-night dummy variables. Third, we added
six day-of-the-week dummies, for a total of thirty-two independent
variables. For one final check we removed the time-of-night and program
length dummies (whose impacts were smallest), and reran a fourth equation with network, day-of-week, and program type dummies only.

The stability of coefficients and t-values across all four equations is
striking. Also, we consistently pick up explained variance adjusted for
degrees of freedom, which rose from .1969 for equation 1, to .2324 for
equation 3, our fullest specification (reported here).

In table 3.3, taking into account network source, day-of-week, time-
of-night differences, and program length, our program type coefficients
denote impacts on levels of national viewing compared to levels commanded by situation comedy. With one minor exception (the one musical drama in our deck), all pairwise comparisons with situation comedy,
cet. par., reveal statistically significant differences in audience size (normally at the .01 confidence level). That is, significantly more households
watch situation comedy than any other program type coded. It follows, then, that in nineteen out of twenty tests performed, the net differences in viewers indicate that the pairs of program types examined
are, on balance, perceived as different at least by those who obviously
do not watch both.

No Evidence on Program Homogeneity. But suppose there had been
no statistically significant difference in the size of audiences watching
any two types? Even then we could not be sure that those types were
homogeneous. Entirely different sets of viewers could have been watching the two program types—our data simply permit no certain conclusion on this matter. The basic point is that, if significantly more viewers
watch one program than another, then, assuming equal opportunity to
watch both programs, there have to be some people who watched one
but not the other. For those people (the minimum number being the
difference in audience sizes for the two programs), we contend that the
programs are statistically different. At no point in our research, however,

TABLE 3.4

Pairwise Differences in Program Type Impacts on National TV Network Audience Size, 1974
(Sample Mean = 13.06522 × 1,000,000 Households)

Type No.	No. of Programs	Name of Type		1	2	3	4	5	6	7	8	9
1	321	Situation comedy	B		−5.0[a]	2.8[a]	−4.7[a]	−1.7[a]	−2.2[a]	−6.7[a]	−1.0[b]	−1.7[a]
			%		−38.3	21.4	−36.0	−13.0	−16.8	−51.3	−7.7	−13.0
2	19	Adventure	B			−7.8[a]	−.3	−3.4[a]	−2.8[a]	1.7[a]	−4.0[a]	−3.4[a]
			%			−60.0	−2.6	−25.9	−21.7	12.7	−30.6	−25.6
3	6	Award ceremonies	B				7.5[a]	4.5[a]	5.0[a]	9.5[a]	3.8[a]	4.5[a]
			%				57.4	34.1	38.2	72.7	29.4	34.3
4	2	Child's evening	B					−3.1[b]	−2.5[d]	2.0[d]	−3.7[b]	−3.0[c]
			%					−23.3	−19.2	15.3	−28.0	−23.1
5	68	Comedy variety	B						.5[d]	5.0[a]	−.6[d]	.0
			%						4.2	38.6	−4.7	.2
6	20	Documentary, general	B							4.5[a]	−1.2[b]	.5[d]
			%							34.4	−8.9	−3.9
7	18	Documentary, news	B								−5.7[a]	−5.0[a]
			%								−43.3	−38.3
8	21	Evening animated (cartoons)	B									.7[d]
			%									4.9
9	58	Evening western	B									
			%									
10	240	Feature film	B									
			%									
11	197	General drama	B									
			%									
12	23	General variety	B									
			%									
13	1	Musical drama	B									
			%									
14	2	News	B									
			%									
15	14	Pop. music, contemporary	B									
			%									
16	96	Private detective	B									
			%									
17	188	Official police	B									
			%									
18	3	Sports commentary	B									
			%									
19	19	Sports event	B									
			%									
20	10	Science fiction	B									
			%									
21	32	Suspense/mystery (except OP and PD)	B									
			%									

SOURCE: Derived from estimating equation in table 3.3, with all program type dummy variables defined as therein. B, denotes regression coefficient and %, denotes unit change in dependent variable as percent of sample mean (PCDV). Superscripts denote statistical significance (two-tailed test), as: a = 1 percent confidence level; b = 5 percent; c = 10 percent; d = t-value exceeds 1 but less than 1.645, at 10 percent level.

10	11	12	13	14	15	16	17	18	19	20	21	Type No.
-1.9[a]	-2.0[a]	-1.0[a]	.2	-4.5[a]	-2.6[a]	-1.8	-1.3[a]	-3.4[b]	-1.6[a]	-5.7[a]	-.8[a]	1
-14.5	-15.3	-7.7	1.2	-34.4	-19.9	-13.8	-10.0	-26.0	-12.2	-43.6	-6.3	
-3.1[a]	-3.0[a]	-4.0[a]	-5.2[a]	-.6	-2.4[a]	-3.2[a]	-3.8[a]	-1.6	-3.4[a]	.7[d]	-4.2[a]	2
-23.6	-23.2	-30.7	-39.7	-4.3	-18.3	-24.6	-28.9	-12.6	-26.2	5.1	-32.2	
4.8[a]	4.8[a]	3.8[a]	2.6[b]	7.3[a]	5.4[a]	4.6[a]	4.1[a]	6.2[a]	4.4[a]	8.5[a]	3.6[a]	3
36.4	36.8	29.3	20.2	55.6	41.6	35.4	31.0	47.4	33.8	65.1	27.7	
-2.8[c]	-2.7[c]	-3.7[b]	-4.9[a]	-.2	-2.1[d]	-2.9[c]	-3.5[b]	-1.3	-3.1[b]	1.0	-3.9[b]	4
-21.0	-20.6	-28.1	-37.2	-1.8	-15.8	-22.0	-26.4	-10.0	-23.6	7.7	-29.7	
.3[d]	.4[d]	-.6[c]	-1.8[c]	2.8	1.0[b]	.2	-.4[c]	1.7	-.0	4.0[a]	-.8[b]	5
2.3	2.7	-4.8	-13.8	21.6	7.6	1.3	-3.0	13.3	-.3	31.0	-6.4	
-.2	-.2	-1.2[b]	-2.4[b]	2.3[b]	.4	-.4	-7.2[a]	1.2	-.6[d]	3.5[a]	-1.4[a]	6
-1.9	-1.5	-8.9	-18.0	17.4	3.4	-2.9	-7.6	9.2	-4.5	26.8	-10.5	
-4.7[a]	-4.7[a]	-5.7[a]	-6.9[a]	-2.2[b]	-4.1[a]	-4.9[a]	-5.4[a]	-3.3[c]	-5.1[a]	-1.0[d]	-5.9[a]	7
-36.3	-35.9	-43.4	-52.4	-17.0	-31.0	-37.3	-41.6	-25.3	-38.9	-7.6	-44.9	
.9[c]	1.0[b]	-.0	-1.2[d]	3.4[a]	1.6[a]	.8[c]	.2	2.4[d]	.6[d]	4.7[a]	-.2	8
7.0	7.4	-.1	-9.1	26.3	12.3	6.0	1.6	18.0	4.4	35.7	-1.7	
.3[d]	.3[d]	-.7[c]	-1.8[c]	2.8[b]	1.0[c]	.1	-.4[c]	1.7	-.1	4.0[a]	-.9[b]	9
2.1	2.5	-5.0	-14.1	21.3	7.3	1.1	-3.3	13.1	-.6	30.7	-6.6	
	.1	-.9[a]	-2.1[b]	2.5[b]	.7[d]	-.1	-.7[a]	1.4	-.3[d]	3.8[a]	-1.1[a]	10
	.4	-7.1	-16.1	19.3	5.3	-1.0	-5.3	11.0	-2.6	28.7	-8.6	
		-1.0[a]	-2.2[b]	2.5[b]	.6[d]	-.2	-.8[a]	1.4	-.4[d]	3.7[a]	-1.2[a]	11
		-7.5	-16.5	18.9	4.9	-1.4	-5.8	10.6	3.0	28.3	-9.1	
			-1.2[d]	3.4[a]	1.6[a]	.8[b]	.2	2.4[d]	.6[d]	4.7[a]	-.2	12
			-9.1	26.3	12.3	6.1	1.7	18.1	4.5	35.8	-1.6	
				4.6[a]	2.8[a]	2.0[b]	1.4[d]	3.5[c]	1.8[c]	5.9[a]	1.0	13
				35.4	21.4	15.1	10.8	27.2	13.5	44.8	7.5	
					-1.8[d]	-2.6[b]	-3.2[a]	-1.1	-2.9[b]	1.2[d]	-3.6[a]	14
					-14.0	-20.3	-24.6	-8.2	-21.9	9.4	-27.9	
						-.8[c]	-1.4[a]	.8	-1.0[c]	3.1[a]	-1.8[a]	15
						-6.3	-10.6	5.8	-7.9	23.4	-13.9	
							-.6[a]	1.6	-.2	3.9[a]	-1.0[a]	16
							-4.4	12.0	-1.6	29.7	-7.7	
								2.1[d]	.4	4.4[a]	-.4[d]	17
								16.4	2.7	34.0	-3.3	
									-1.8	2.3[d]	-2.6[d]	18
									-13.6	17.7	-19.7	
										4.1[a]	-.8[c]	19
										31.3	-6.0	
											-4.9[a]	20
											-37.3	
												21

TABLE 3.5
*A Summary of Pairwise Program Type Differences Ranked in
Descending Order of Significant Test Results*
(N = 21)

Program Type	No. of Programs	No. of Significant Pairwise Tests (at .05 level and better)	Proportion of 20 Tests Which Were Significant	Rank of Proportion
Award ceremonies	6	20	100	1
Situation comedy	321	18	90	2.5
Documentary, news	18	18	90	2.5
Adventure	19	16	80	4
Musical drama	1	15	75	6
News	2	15	75	6
Science fiction	10	15	75	6
General variety	23	14	70	9.5
Popular music, contemporary	14	14	70	9.5
Official police	188	14	70	9.5
Suspense/mystery	32	14	70	9.5
Child's, evening	2	13	65	12
Evening western	58	12	60	14
General drama	197	12	60	14
Private detective	96	12	60	14
Comedy variety	68	11	55	17.5
Documentary, general	20	11	55	17.5
Evening animated	21	11	55	17.5
Feature film	240	11	55	17.5
Sports event	19	10	50	20
Sports commentary	3	4	20	21

SOURCE: Table 3.4.

do we conclude that two programs are homogeneous simply because their audience sizes do *not* differ significantly.[15]

A Grid of Pairwise Comparisons. Turning to our full grid of four hundred pairwise comparisons in table 3.4, we can draw a number of conclusions. Those complete results of all conceivable type comparisons are more briefly synopsized for present purposes in table 3.5. That table ranks our twenty-one program types according to the proportion of pairwise comparisons that yield statistically significant differences in au-

15. Our inability to trace directly who is watching what precludes our commenting on homogeneity except where we *do* have significant audience differences. However, even then, the aggregate nature of our data prevents us from identifying audience flows unambiguously (see Appendix 3A).

dience size. We also report the number of observations for each type analyzed.[16]

Our summary statistics indicate:

1. Seven out of twenty-one types had significant differences from types in fifteen to twenty pairwise comparisons (out of the twenty tests run per type), that is, in 75 to 100 percent of the basic comparisons made.

2. Another eight out of twenty-one types had significant differences from other types in twelve to fourteen comparisons, or 60 to 70 percent of each set of twenty test runs.

3. In only one case (sports commentary) were fewer than 50 percent of the comparisons statistically significant at the .10 confidence level.

Actually these significant impacts constitute conservative estimates of program type differences because, as noted, even where the differences are insignificant, different viewers may be watching any pair of types. Therefore, as summarized in table 3.5, the coefficients in 3.4 indicate important program type differences from a consumer viewpoint. As conceived here, then, type diversity is a lower-bound estimate of such differences; it could be higher, perhaps much higher.

Using our conservative yardstick only, the program types that reveal the most frequent differences from *other* program types, are:

Award ceremonies
Situation comedy
News documentary
Adventure
Musical drama
News
Science fiction

Next come:

General variety
Popular music
Official police
Suspense/mystery

At the bottom of the list are:

Sports commentary
Sports events

Illustrative of the importance of type diversity to TV viewers gen-

16. The test is essentially one that indicates whether, for viewers as a whole, program *types* are good substitutes. If they are, audiences should be equal. However, we learn nothing about within-category heterogeneity.

erally[17] are the magnitude and significance of differences between such
seemingly related program type pairs as:

Impact of	Minus	Impact of	Difference (in millions of viewers)
News documentary		General documentary	−4.5[a]
		News	−2.2[b]
General variety		Popular music	1.6[a]
		Comedy variety	.62[c]
		Award ceremonies	−3.83[a]
Official police		Mystery/suspense	−.43
		Private detective	.57[a]
Evening animated (cartoons)		Children's	3.66[b]
Adventure		Science fiction	.67[d]
		Children's	−.34
		Cartoons	−3.99[a]
General drama		Evening western	−.32[d]

minimum viewing = 3,570,000
mean viewing = 13,065,220
maximum viewing = 26,990,000

SOURCE: Table 3.4. (Superscripts a, b, c, d, denote different levels
of statistical significance, as indicated in Table 3.4).

Confidence Intervals around the Mean Audiences of Nielsen Program Types: Problems of Interpretation

So much for the evidence on diversity across major Nielsen program
types. The results suggest that type diversity does in fact matter to television audiences. However, critical readers may object to my use of the
confidence interval of the mean (as in table 3.2) and to the related
evidence in tables 3.3 and 3.4. It could indeed be argued that while an
interval of 14.3 to 15.2 million delimits the range of the true mean for
situation comedies in 1974, this does not imply that the audiences of
all situation comedies fell within that narrow range. Rather, that is indicated by the standard deviation which, in this case, denotes that, assuming a normal distribution, 97 percent of situation comedies would
have audiences plus or minus two standard deviations, or 6.3 to 23.1
million.

A *Possible Qualification*. Following this argument, every program
type in table 3.1 would have a mean better than the *worst* of the
situation comedies, which may be why the network shows other programs too. If the *best* of each program type does indeed do better than

17. Along lines qualified earlier in notes 15 and 16 and the associated text.

many of the *weaker* situation comedies, the evidence in tables 3.2, 3.3, and 3.4 must be reinterpreted. Audience overlap would then seem much greater than we have contended there, and the existence of program type differences would start to break down.

Nevertheless, the mean is generally accepted as the best point estimate of a category and the confidence interval about the mean denotes the reliability of that point estimate. Therefore, although extremes exist, the mean of a category is the best *single* estimate of how a particular type of program will do, and when these confidence intervals do not overlap we can be quite sure that the odds are that the long-run or average audiences will be statistically different in size.

Restatement of Findings on Types Diversity

In light of these considerations, our modified interpretation of the results reported in tables 3.2, 3.3, and 3.4 is as follows:

1. The chances, *cet. par.*, of any network pulling significantly more viewers with a situation comedy (whose true mean statistically exceeds the true mean of every other program type in table 3.2), are clearly greater than for any other type.

2. Nevertheless, several factors could help offset the handicap of running a type (say, news documentary) which, on the average, does more poorly than situation comedy. The network's task is to estimate the chances of doing as well as the very best of news documentaries (or adventure, science fiction, or mystery), on one hand, or as poorly as the worst of the situation comedies. In a sense, the magnitude of the handicap varies directly with the distance between the confidence intervals in table 3.2, for the mean of any pair of program types.

3. In answering the above question a broadcaster must ideally consider factors beyond those we were able to introduce into our equations in table 3.3. That equation explained only 23 percent of the variance in the program audiences studied. Such additional factors as these may affect a network's chances of doing much better (or worse) than the average audience of a given type, that is, of ranking high (or low) in the dispersion of programs within any type: (a) talent available, namely, presence of an established star; (b) competitive programs scheduled on other networks at the same time; (c) format or content of particular programs within any type (for instance, broad national issue versus a narrow provincial one); (d) available resources for program development; (e) existing program mix in the network schedule (another situation comedy could be too much of a good thing).

4. In short, our results in tables 3.2, 3.3, and 3.4 do not imply that every program in a designated type must do significantly better (or worse) than those in a type whose true mean is significantly different. Rather, the chances for such a divergence are greater, *cet. par.*, the greater the distance between the confidence intervals about the mean for any pair of types.

Types Diversity as One Program Attribute Among Many. The upshot is that program type differences do matter to viewers, but that audiences also respond (positively and negatively) to other attributes of individual programs within types. This may indeed explain why the dispersion around the mean is as large as it is in some cases. Types diversity does appear to be operational, that is, viewers in some crude sense "perceive" it, and on that score the typology appears meaningful. But how important type differences alone are to viewers cannot be inferred from our analysis of the means (in tables 3.3 and 3.4), even when considering network origin, day of week, time of night, or program length.

Perhaps the most prudent implication is that, in chapters 5 through 8 in particular, my analysis of types diversity relates to one among many program attributes of demonstrable importance to viewers, as well as to the FCC, to the networks, and to advertisers. This may sound like a rather small finding, but it has been widely questioned.

On any number of (albeit neglected) counts, the finding should actually not be surprising. Douglas Ginsburg of Harvard Law School says:

> [The Nielsen typology] would in fact use categories that viewers would agree are discrete. They would do so in part because of the need for non-overlapping categories of reference[.] . . . [Furthermore,] the categorizers and the viewers are drawn from the same cultural milieu, and . . . the categorizers have a business incentive to devise categories that will appeal to their audiences' sense of differences. If, for example, *TV Guide* classified programs by some criterion that we as viewers considered arbitrary, such as the ratio of male to female actors in the show, we would find its system of trivial usefulness in deciding what to watch. Simply, it is not too surprising if communication within the industry and between the industry and its audience employs a functional vocabulary.
>
> Second, . . . is the possibility that the congruence between popular and industry perception of discrete categories results itself from the fact that the audience has adopted the industry's typology. Some one from another culture, first exposed to American television, might, after all, group programs in an equally sensible but quite different matter. For example, they might, in the language of a morality or passion play, group detective or western shows together on the ground that morality or at least authority is vindicated over evil. . . . [I]t is (by no means) tautological or trivial to demonstrate that the categories used in the industry are indeed considered important in the behavior of viewers. . . .[18]

In line with Ginsburg's observations one might usefully reflect on the problems in selecting a proper categorical system to test in the first place. One could, for example, elaborate on the reasons Ginsburg states for thinking that the Nielsen typology would in fact tend to differentiate among TV programs the same way viewers do, as inferred from audience behavior, although time and space limitations preclude such an elaboration.

I do not in any case imply that type diversity can or ought to be pursued at *any* price from a consumer viewpoint. If all stations were told to

18. From a private communication with Douglas Ginsburg.

raise the number of program types by, say, 50 percent per day, the drain on available resources, restrictions on suitable talent, and so forth, could well limit the audiences that actually result.

With the above in mind, let us turn to the impact of options and types diversity on both aggregate national network viewing, and the proportion of households that watch. If the types differences identified in table 3.4 do indeed matter to viewers, one would expect significant effects also when types differ horizontally, across all stations in the market, and vertically, on stations over the broadcast day.

Options Diversity, Types Diversity, and Marketwide Viewing in Television—Some New Evidence

To estimate the relative impact of changes in types diversity and options diversity on aggregate viewing in 133 leading markets, we specified and ran a number of equations, the detailed considerations for which are summarized at length in Appendix II (pp. 476–86). Suffice it to note only that the hypothesis underlying our estimates of aggregate viewing in table 3.6 (and proportions of tuned-in households in table 3.7), is that, other things being equal, the number of program options and of program types across all stations in the market, both have significant effects.

Specification of Key Equations. Leaving the reader to review the full account of my preliminary experiments and major specifications in Appendix II, let us next turn to the "best" equations as reported in tables 3.6, 3.7, and 3.8.*

Specification of Options and Types. Our final specification of program options in tables 3.6 and 3.7 utilized a four-way breakdown of stations —number of network VHFs, network UHFs, independent VHFs, and independent UHFs. Our assumption here was that the program mix on network affiliates and independent stations was quite different, as were the economic resources available to enrich it. So, too, were there significant economic differences between VHF and UHF stations, grounded on differences in signal quality and range.

Therefore, the four-way breakdown of stations sought to distinguish between the major sources of programs, in terms of each class of station's capabilities and incentives and the likely program mix that results. The chances that significant impacts of program options on viewing would be revealed will presumably be greater when the above attributes are explicitly specified (see Appendix II, pp. 483–84).

In specifying program types, on the other hand, I simply summed the number of different types carried across all commercial stations in

---

* As elsewhere in the book, note that most estimating equations in this section (e.g., tables 3.7 and 3.8) appear close to the impact coefficients derived from them (cf. 3.7A, 3.8A). This seemed best even though the two measures are necessarily discussed separately, that is, at different points in the text.

TABLE 3.6
Estimating Equation for Aggregate Quarter-Hour
Viewing in 133 Television Markets, 1967
(Sample mean = 21.804 × 10,000 Average quarter-hour homes)

Independent Variables	Regression Coefficient	t-value
Constant	−0.375	
Percent homes with less than $3,000 income	+0.777[d]	1.390
January mean temperature	−0.086[a]	2.510
Percent multiset homes	+20.350[a]	3.430
Central time zone dummy	+2.376[a]	3.620
Number of program types in market	−0.037[a]	3.530
Program types × TV homes in market	+0.002[a]	34.380
Log (No. of network VHF station + 1)	+12.802[b]	2.270
Log (No. of network UHF station +1)	+14.339[b]	2.160
Log (No. of independent VHF + 1)	+26.415[a]	5.040
Log (No. of independent UHF + 1)	+12.700[b]	2.030
Log (No. network UHF + 1) × (TV homes)	−0.384[b]	2.260
Log (No. independent VHF + 1) × (TV homes)	−0.600[a]	15.650
Log (No. independent UHF + 1) × (TV homes)	−0.411[a]	8.030

Adj. R−square = .9922

SOURCE: The following data were derived from *Broadcasting Yearbook*, 1973, and *Television Factbook* No. 43, 1973-74: number of stations within the American Research Bureau's Area of Dominant Influence markets, by channel type and network tie; percentage of homes with more than one TV set; time zone location of each market. Additional sources include: U.S. Bureau of the Census, Population Reports for 1967, for percentage of families earning less than $3,000 income; Statistical Abstract of the U.S. (1967), for January mean temperature of market. Number of program types derived from *TV Guide*, February 25-March 3, 1967, and Broadcast Measurement Bureau, *Series, Serials, and Packages—A Film Source Book*, vol. 6, issue #2 (1965-66) and issue #2S (Fall 1966). Statistical significance (two-tailed test) is: a = 1 percent; b = 5 percent; c = 10 percent; d = t-value exceeds 1 but less than 1.645, the 10 percent confidence level.

each of the 133 ADI markets where more than one station operated in 1967 (see earlier discussion of horizontal diversity). Note further that program type differences were first coded according to a standard twenty-category classification whose validity was just confirmed by analysis of a related Nielsen typology in connection with tables 3.2, 3.3, and 3.4.

Logarithmic Form and Interactions with TV Homes. Two other decisions must also be mentioned: first, to cast the number of options into a log form, and second, to interact options, and types, separately with TV homes.

The log form for number of stations captured the element of nonlinearity in the relationship between that variable and the level (and proportion) of tuned-in TV households. In tables 3.6 and 3.7, too, non-linearity was present due to the declining percentage increase repre-

TABLE 3.7

Estimating Equation for Proportions of
Tuned-In Households in 133 TV Markets, 1967*
(Based on Market Data)
(Sample Mean = .5396 × 100 percent ADI Homes)

Independent Variables	Regression Coefficient	t-value
Constant	0.251	5.88
Percent homes with less than $3,000 income	0.008	0.70
January mean temperature	−0.001	−1.60
Percent multiset in market	0.255	2.07
Central time zone dummy	0.036	2.70
Number of program types in market	0.001	2.75
Program types × TV homes	**	
No. of TV homes in market	−0.002	−0.50
Log (no. of network VHF stations + 1) in market	0.128	1.12
Log (no. of network UFH stations + 1)	0.100	0.75
Log (no. of independent VHF stations + 1)	−0.145	−1.38
Log (no. of independent UHF stations + 1)	−0.030	−0.24
Log (no. of network VHF + 1) × (TV homes)	**	
Log (no. of network UHF + 1) × (TV homes)	−0.059	1.71
Log (no. of independent VHF + 1) × (TV homes)	0.003	0.54
Log (no. of independent UHF + 1) × (TV homes)	−0.005	−0.61

SOURCE: All data sources as for table 3.6.
Adj. R^2 = .408
*Dependent Variable = percentage of TV homes which tune in some designated amount of time weekly, as estimated by the American Research Bureau for its "Areas of Dominant Influence."
**Not calculable due to collinearity.

sented by one more station of any class, and due also, in table 3.6 at least, to the far-ranging distribution of our dependent variable.

As for interactions with TV homes, my hypothesis for the two equations (in tables 3.6 and 3.7) was that the number of options and the number of types have different effects on viewing in different-sized markets. Such divergent effects are assumed due both to the different economic resources potentially available, and to differences in degrees of urbanization and kinds of lifestyle therein (Appendix II, pp. 478–84).

Exogenous Variables. To improve the reliability of our derived options and types coefficients, I further introduced several exogenous control factors. Though these factors are known to influence TV viewing, they are themselves neither a function nor determinants of options and types—our principal policy-related variables. Access to unpublished Nielsen Survey data for 1971 helped me select from among a number of likely candidates for inclusion in our final equations. Thus the Nielsen Survey data quite clearly revealed that viewing per household is greater where there

TABLE 3.7A

*Impact of Horizontal Program Diversity on Proportions of Tuned-in
TV Households, 1967* (Based on Market Data)
(Sample Mean = .5396 × 100 percent ADI Homes)

Postulated Change in Independent Variable	Impact	t-value	Unit Change in Dependent Variables Percent Sample Mean (PCDV)
Add one percentage point multi-set homes in market	.255	2.07	47.3
Add first network VHF to market	.039	1.12	7.2
Switch to Central Time Zone	.036	2.70	6.7
Add second network VHF to market	.023	1.12	4.2
Add twenty-one program types in market	.021	2.75	3.9
Add third network VHF to market	.016	1.12	3.0
Add fourteen program types in market	.014	2.75	2.6
Add one percentage point of homes with less than $3,000 annual income	.008	0.70	1.5
Add seven program types in market	.007	2.75	1.3
Add one program type in market	.001	2.75	0.2
Add one degree January mean temperature in market	−.001	1.60	−0.2
Add third independent UHF	−.006	0.47	−1.1
Add second independent UHF	−.009	0.47	−1.6
Add first independent UHF	−.015	0.47	−2.8
Add third network UHF	−.015	1.44	−2.8
Add third independent VHF	−.017	1.37	−3.1
Add second network UHF	−.022	1.44	−4.0
Add second independent VHF	−.024	1.37	−4.4
Add first network UHF	−.037	1.44	−6.8
Add first independent VHF	−.040	1.37	−7.5

SOURCE: Derived from regression equation in table that precedes, according to a method described in Appendix 3B. All impact coefficients for additional stations calculated at the mean of TV homes, except those for network VHFs which, in the equation above, we could not interact with homes due to multicollinearity.

are: (1) more than one TV set in a home; (2) more than one person in the household; (3) access to color sets; and also where (4) families earn less than $5000; (5) viewers are at least fifty years of age; (6) viewers are female rather than male; (7) viewing occurs during the winter rather than summer months.

After a good many experiments, those exogenous variables were ultimately selected which appeared to be the most germane *a priori*, and in terms of statistical impact. (See Appendix II, pp. 478–82.) As is readily apparent in table 3.6, 3.7, and 3.7A, my equations include: the percentage of TV homes earning less than $3000 annually (the Census data closest to Nielsen's income discriminant); January mean temperature of the market (as a proxy for lifestyle, in terms of the likely importance of indoor versus outdoor recreational activity); the percentage of homes with more than one TV set. Then a Central Time Zone dummy was added (to take account of the different times that East and West Coast programs are received in the central states). The significance of each of these factors in tables 3.6 and 3.7, in contrast with the insignificance of other exogenous factors in a number of early experiments, confirms the validity of my final specification in that regard.

One last exogenous variable was TV homes in the market. There my assumption was that viewing levels would be higher, *cet. par.*, where TV homes or multiset families (and hence potential viewers) were also higher. In all early experiments run on level aggregate viewing, TV homes was indeed consistently the strongest independent variable, with or without multiset families in the equation.

Proportion of Households Tuned In versus Level Aggregate Viewing as Alternative Dependent Variables. In table 3.6, I estimated the impact of horizontal diversity on level aggregate viewing across all stations in the American Research Bureau's ADI market. Yet it is known that there are both more stations and more homes, relatively, in the larger TV markets. Lest the collinearity of these two variables render my observed impacts misleading, I have controlled for market size in two ways—first, by introducing TV homes as an independent variable, and second, by interacting TV homes with number of stations and number of program types. These two variables would largely correct for any tendency of added stations to serve as an unintended proxy for market size in the analysis of diversity's impact on viewing.

Nevertheless, there is still a better way to correct for such distortion, namely by using "proportion of TV homes which view" as the dependent variable. This is what I did indeed analyze in table 3.7, albeit with the identical set of independent variables as for table 3.6 (due to difficult time and resource limitations). (See Appendix II, pp. 485–86.)

Replication of Results at the Station Level. In table 3.8, I further tested for our hypothesized impact of types diversity on viewing at the station level, first, by specifying the former as "vertical diversity," and the latter as "proportion of tuned-in TV households" (based on stations rather than market data, as for table 3.7). I could not introduce our exogenous variables into the station equations at all. However, I did improve the reliability of our types coefficients by specifying a number of stations variable and market attributes (network tie, channel type, TV homes, competition), and again, by interacting stations with market size.

So much for some high points of my principal equation specifications to estimate the impact of diversity on viewing, as reported in tables 3.6, 3.7, and 3.8. We turn next to major findings—the derived results in 3.7A, 3.8A, and 3.9—and to their implication for the theories of viewer behavior.

The Major Findings. As several times noted, this chapter attempts to determine first, whether options diversity and types diversity *each* impact significantly on TV viewing measured in absolute levels, or as proportions

TABLE 3.8

Estimating Equations for Proportions of Tuned-In TV Households, 1967
(Based on Station Data)

Independent Variables	Dependent Variables		
	ADI Rating	Metro Rating	Metro Share
Constant	1.267	.178	.305
	(5.8)	(5.2)	(5.7)
Av. no. of program types daily	.290	.028	.043
	(3.8)	(5.0)	(4.9)
TV homes	.008	*	*
	(2.0)		
Network dummy†	.108	.114	.164
	(.4)	(6.3)	(5.8)
VHF dummy†	−.630	.017	.028
	(2.2)	(.9)	(.9)
Log (no. VHF stations + 1) in market	−3.81	−.359	−.594
	(10.8)	(11.0)	(11.4)
Network dummy × VHF dummy	1.111	.029	.052
	(3.7)	(1.4)	(1.6)
Network dummy × TV homes	−.001	−.0001	−.0002
	(.5)	(1.5)	(1.8)
No. Program types × TV homes	−.001	−.0001	−.0002
	(1.6)	(3.4)	(3.8)
Log. (No. stations + 1) × TV homes	*	.001	.001
		(4.2)	(4.6)
Adj. R^2	.428	.616	.622
Sample size (stations)	466	399	399
Sample mean	2.102×10	$.214 \times 100$	$.330 \times 100$

*Not calculable due to collinearity.
†Labeled attribute equals 1 ; 0 otherwise.

NOTE: "Ratings" are percentages of TV homes in market that tune in designated stations specified amounts of time weekly, as estimated by the American Research Bureau. "Shares" are percentages of tuned-in audiences in each market that watch designated stations. ADI markets are "areas of dominant influence" as defined by ARB, whereas metro areas (narrower than ADI markets) are core metropolitan market areas therein.

Upper number in each cell is a regression coefficient, and lower number in parentheses is a t-value denoting statistical significance.

TABLE 3.8A

Impact of Station Vertical Diversity on Proportions of Tuned-In TV Households, 1967
(Based on Station Data)

	1	2	3	4	5	6	7	8
Row No.	Type of Station	Postulated Change Independent Variable	ADI Rating	PCDV (%)	Metro Rating	PCDV (%)	Metro Share	PCDV (%)
1	Unrestricted[1]	Add one program type	.245[a] (3.6)	11.7	.021[a] (4.3)	9.9	.031[a] (4.0)	9.4
		Switch from						
2	UHF	Independent to network affiliate	.087 (.37)	4.1	.109[a] (6.3)	50.8	.154[a] (5.7)	46.6
3	VHF	Independent to network affiliate	1.196[a] (5.6)	56.9	.138[a] (9.1)	64.3	.206[a] (8.8)	62.6
4	Unrestricted[1]	Independent to network affiliate	.566[b] (2.5)	26.9	.155[a] (9.6)	72.4	.235[a] (9.3)	71.2
5	Unrestricted[1]	Add second station	−.671[a]* (10.8)	−31.9	−.056[a] (9.5)	−26.2	−.092[a] (10.0)	−27.9
		Add third station	−.476[a]* (10.8)	−22.7	−.040[a] (9.5)	−18.6	−.065[a] (10.0)	−19.8
		Add fourth station	−.369[a]* (10.8)	−17.6	−.031[a] (9.5)	−14.4	−.051[a] (10.0)	−15.4

[1] "Unrestricted" denotes switch from average of all stations without differentiation, to average of station with specified attributes. That is, for all stations in row 1, adding one program type will raise ADI ratings by .245 percentage points. Where, however, station type *is* given, switch is from average of those stations only, to average of stations with attributes specified in column 2. For example, in row 2, for UHF stations only, a switch from independent to network stations raises ratings by .087 percentage points.

*All coefficients interacted at sample mean of TV homes in designated equations, except for coefficients marked by asterisk, where collinearity prevented necessary calculations.

NOTE: Upper number in each cell in columns 3, 5 and 7 is impact coefficient derived from estimating equation in Table 3.8, according to method described in Appendix 3B. Lower number in parentheses is t-value denoting statistical significance, further indicated by superscripts (two-tailed test) as follows: a = 1 percent confidence level, b = 5 percent level, c = 10 percent level. PCDVs, in columns 4, 6 and 8, denote unit change in dependent variable as percent of sample mean.

of tuned-in households; and second, whether types diversity ranks *equally* with options diversity in those impacts on viewing.

Interrelatedness of Options and Types. One major specification problem inheres in the fact that options and types diversity are intertwined. Adding a station gives the viewer (1) more options at any time; (2) more diversity within any program type; and (3) more types of programs. I do not claim to have disentangled those three effects but believe a useful start was made by taking account of types when postulating an increase of options (specified as a four-way breakdown of stations), and vice versa.

The problem is that added options and added types are hard to compare in an entirely objective fashion, unlike the comparisons elsewhere of the relative impact of two dummy variables on a common dependent variable (see tables 4.9, 4.10 6.10, and 6.11). At issue here is the fact that types are more nearly a continuous variable, whereas options (number of stations) are discrete and lumpy, with big jumps in the data.

Postulated Increases in Number of Program Types. In later chapters I attempted to handle this problem by specifying a variety of market dummies (see tables 4.11 and 5.4). In early experiments here, however, to ascertain the relative impact of options and types diversity (in tables 3.7A, 3.9, and 3.10), I initially postulated an increase of 66, then 88, and finally, 110 program types. These postulated types increments were an admittedly crude attempt to examine the impact of an increment comparable to that of one more station of any class.[19]

I subsequently concluded, however, that to postulate such large increments in those tables would produce evidence at best unrealistic, and at worst misleading. That is, a postulated increase of 88, 110, or 66 types probably lay beyond the threshold of reasonableness within which the coefficients could be properly used, or meaningfully interpreted. At best, those increments were unrealistic and far from real-world possibilities. To postulate them, for example, clearly implied many other changed conditions for my other independent variables, and in particular, the addition of another station (something my equations explicitly precluded).

It seemed less misleading to consider smaller types increments (at the margin), and to compare the impact of *those* increments to that of one more station. Toward that end I recast tables 3.7A, 3.9, and 3.10, using increments of one, seven, fourteen, and twenty-one program types, for reasons to be noted momentarily. In table 3.9, these more reasonable hypothesized increments yielded impacts expressed as percentages of the sample mean (PCDVs), of about .1 percent, .8 percent, 1.6 percent, and 2.4 percent, compared to 10.3 percent for a second network VHF,

19. An increase of 88 types was the average of types increments as we move across all market classes, from one-station markets incrementally up to eight-station markets. An increase of 110 types, and of 66 types, were for illustrative purposes set at levels 25 percent above, and 25 percent below, the sample mean of types increments— namely 88.

TABLE 3.9

Sensitivity of Average Aggregate Quarter-Hour Viewing in 133 Television Markets to Specified Changes in the Number of Program Options and Program Types, 1967
(Sample mean = 21.804 × 10,000 average quarter-hour homes)

Postulated Change in Independent Variable	Impact	t-value	Unit Change in Dependent Variable as Percent Sample Mean (PCDV)
Add first network VHF to market	3.854	2.27	17.7
Switch to Central Time Zone	2.376	3.62	10.9
Add second network VHF to market	2.254	2.27	10.3
Add third network VHF to market	1.560	2.27	7.2
Add first independent VHF to market	1.161	0.80	5.3
Add 1 percentage point of homes with less than $3,000 annual income	0.777	1.39	3.6
Add second independent VHF to market	0.679	0.80	3.1
Add twenty-one program types in market	0.514	2.46	2.4
Add third independent VHF to market	0.482	0.80	2.2
Add fourteen program types in market	0.343	2.46	1.6
Add 1 percentage point multiset homes in market	0.204	3.43	0.9
Add seven program types in market	0.171	2.46	0.8
Add one program type in market	0.024	2.46	0.1
Add third network UHF to market	−0.015	−0.03	−0.1
Add second network UHF to market	−0.021	−0.03	−0.1
Add first network UHF to market	−0.036	−0.03	−0.2
Add one degree January mean temperature in market	−0.086	−2.51	−0.4
Add third independent UHF to market	−0.345	−0.53	−1.6
Add second independent UHF to market	−0.487	−0.53	−2.2
Add first independent UHF to market	−0.832	−0.53	−3.8

SOURCE: Derived from regression equation in table 3.6 using computation method outlined in Appendix 3B to this chapter. All impact coefficients for additional stations are calculated at the mean of TV homes, except those for network VHF stations which, in table 3.6, we were unable to interact with homes due to insufficient variance.

7.2 percent for a third network VHF, and 3.1 percent for a second independent VHF. These comparative results are much closer than those of my earlier experiments to the view of those who contend that a second or third network VHF, by bringing the second or third network service into a market, will act to raise viewing (and possibly consumer welfare) far more than any reasonable postulated increase in program types carried across all stations in that market *before* the second or third VHF affiliate is assumed to be added.

The hypothesized additions of one, seven, fourteen, and twenty-one types (in tables 3.7A, 3.9, and 3.10) are admittedly "arbitrary" but do gibe with common-sense possibilities. Thus we start by postulating that each station in any market introduces one program type weekly (or nightly) that is not already being carried by other stations there at the same time. Our

TABLE 3.10

Relative Impact on Average Aggregate Quarter-Hour Viewing of Specified Additional Numbers of Program Options and Program Types in 133 TV Markets, 1967: Alternative Second-Order Tests

(Sample mean = 21.804 × 10,000 average quarter-hour homes)

1	2	3	4	5	6	7	8
				Second-order Tests			
Change in First Attribute	Impact	Change in Second Attribute	Impact	Impact of +1 Type minus column 4	Impact of +7 Types minus column 4	Impact of +14 Types minus column 4	Impact of +21 Types minus column 4
Add twenty-one program types	.514[b]	Add first network VHF	3.854[b]	−3.830[b]	−3.682[b]	−3.511[c]	−3.340[c]
Add fourteen program types	.343[b]	Add second network VHF	2.254[b]	−2.230[b]	−2.083[b]	−1.912[c]	−1.740[d]
Add seven program types	.171[b]	Add third network VHF	1.560[b]	−1.536[b]	−1.389[c]	−1.257[d]	−1.046[d]
Add one program type	.024[b]	Add first independent VHF	1.161	−1.137	−0.990	−0.818	−0.647
		Add second independent VHF	0.679	−0.655	−0.508	−0.336	−0.165
		Add third independent VHF	0.482	−0.457	−0.311	−0.139	−0.032
		Add first network UHF	−0.036	0.061	0.208	0.379	0.550
		Add second network UHF	−0.021	0.046	0.193	0.364	0.535
		Add third network UHF	−0.015	0.040	0.186	0.358	0.529
		Add first independent UHF	−0.832	0.857	1.004	1.175	1.346
		Add second independent UHF	−0.487	0.511	0.658	0.830	1.001
		Add third independent UHF	−0.345	0.370	0.517	0.688	0.860[d]

SOURCE: The impacts reported in columns 1 and 4 are taken from table 3.9, in turn derived from the equation in table 3.6, using computation procedures outlined in Appendix 3B. Second-order impact coefficients in columns 5-8 are derived from the absolute differences between the impact of the additional station options and program types postulated. Statistical significance (two-tailed test) is: a = 1 percent level; b = 5 percent; c = 10 percent; d = t-value is at least 1 but less than 1.645. Column 4 impacts are all calculated at the mean of TV homes except those for network VHFs (which we were unable to interact with homes in table 3.6 due to insufficient variance). Minor discrepancies in columns 5-8 due to rounding errors.

assumption is eased also in that the same "new" type can be rerun each night of the week (under the stated conditions), thereby counting as seven new types. If two stations meet the condition, we have fourteen new types, and if three stations do so, we have twenty-one types.[20]

Options versus Types Impacts. The revised second-order tests in table 3.10 quite clearly indicate that, with one minor exception, the impact of one more, seven more, or fourteen more types is indeed significantly smaller than that of a first, second, or third VHF affiliate in the market. Comparable conclusions are at least suggested by the point estimates and signs for the differences between the absolute impact on viewing of twenty-one more types, and that of additional network VHFs.[21]

Discrete versus Continuous Data: A Possible Source of Bias. In assessing the preceding findings (in tables 3.6, 3.7, 3.9, and 3.10), the reader must still be cautioned about one other factor that may bias the estimated types impact upward and my options impact downward. Briefly, I do not know how large the interactive effect of the number of stations and types is, nor precisely what portion is properly allocated to either variable in estimating its impact on viewing. Part of the problem reflects my failure to interact the number of stations with the number of types. That failure was in turn due mainly to a primary concern with interacting both these variables, as well as the ownership dummies, with TV homes. In addition, I explored numerous interactions of owner dummies with channel type (only network affiliation times channel type survived).

There were good reasons for exploring these interactions with market size (discussed earlier, and in Appendix II, pp. 484–87), and a limit to which we could simultaneously consider other interesting interactions. Hindsight may suggest the usefulness of other experiments, but the reported coefficients in tables 3.6 to 3.10 reflect our best judgment at the time.

The final problem here is that the categorical (discrete or lumpy) data (number of stations) are presumably allocated *less* of these interacted effects, and the continuous (types) data, a larger share than is truly the case. All we actually know here is that the number of stations got less than 50 percent of the interacted impact, and the number of types more than 50 percent.

Impact of Diversity on Aggregate Viewing Levels: Summary. The upshot would appear to be as follows:

20. Note that two-thirds of commercial stations in 1967 operated in markets with three or more stations, the mean number of stations per market being three. As a working convenience, therefore, the small incremental changes which my postulated additions of 1 to 21 types represent, contrast with a maximum of 20 possible types in twenty quarter-hour periods, per station, per night, summing to a maximum of 140 types weekly.

21. Note, however, that though the computed t-values here are 1.78, 1.49, and 1.23, only the first is statistically significant at the .10 level.

1.   Additional types and network VHF options *both* impact significantly
      on viewing in tables 3.6 and 3.9; however, additional independent
      VHF or UHF options do not, and neither do additional network
      UHF options.
2.   The impact of another VHF affiliate in table 3.10, clearly swamps
      that of one more type weekly, or nightly (tantamount to one,
      seven, or fourteen more types weekly).
3.   Further supportive of the prior conclusion is the probable upward
      bias of the types impact (and downward bias of stations impact),
      due to the respective share of the interactive effect each picks up.
4.   Nonetheless, the first conclusion still holds. Putting to one side the
      relative importance of types and options impacts, the data strongly
      suggest that viewers do perceive significant differences among
      many of my program types. The typology is on that score, too, and
      not just from the viewpoint of regulatory semantics or adver-
      tiser/broadcaster convenience, one useful basis on which to assess
      the FCC's impact on diversity.

It follows, then, that viewers perceive differences both in added network VHF options *and* added program types, but that the former appear
to yield significantly more program choices than the latter, and hence
more opportunities, relatively, for the viewer to find a preferred program option. On the other hand, viewers perceive, in added types and
added UHF (or independent VHF) options, only statistically *comparable*
opportunities to improve their position, no great surprise in light at least
of UHF's inferior signal quality and service range, and the further fact
that network UHFs often retransmit what network VHFs had carried
elsewhere, earlier.

Analysis of Proportions of Households That Tune In. Two supportive
afterthoughts are reported next in tables 3.7 and 3.8. Both those estimates focus on a possibly more revealing dependent variable, that is,
proportions of tuned-in TV households, in the first case estimating the
impact of horizontal diversity, and secondly, of vertical diversity using
station rather than market data.

The extension of my analysis into these two new areas was in response
to earlier perceptive critiques. However, limited time and resources at
that advanced stage permitted, at the very most, only a crude attempt
to replicate the findings in tables 3.6, 3.9, and 3.10, with the new dependent variable (proportions of tuned-in TV households). I was in effect constrained to do so mainly by using, or adapting, equations I had
already developed.

The principal question in table 3.7 was whether the types impact (no
one ever debates options impact) would continue to stimulate viewing
when cast in terms of proportions of households that tune in. For a
quick, rough look the equation in table 3.6 was used, but with the alternate
dependent variable. The types impact was indeed clearly confirmed, and
this even though I once again controlled for market size, and, gratui-
tously perhaps, again interacted the number of options and types with TV

homes.[22] The lack of significant impact of another VHF affiliate despite a large positive point estimate, and a t-value of 1.1, may in part reflect an overcorrection due to the log form of the stations variable now that the dependent variable, cast as a proportion, is made more linear on that account.

I would also have expected as strong a positive impact of VHF affiliates on the proportion of households tuning in (table 3.7), as on the level of viewing (table 3.6), though the opposite was found. The fact is that the log (number of network VHFs + 1) variable has a stronger simple correlation with the proportion than the level of viewing, whereas the three other types of stations—network UHF, independent VHF, independent UHF—have less correlation with the proportion (as one would expect for all four types). This higher simple correlation for network VHFs in the proportion equation (table 3.7) would, in the absence of multicollinearity, have led one at least to expect a more significant, positive coefficient in the proportion than in the audience level equation (table 3.6). The fact that this was not found to be so is further evidence that something like multicollinearity must be affecting the results of table 3.7.[23]

Replication of Results at the Station Level. Turning next to table 3.8, my question was somewhat different: could I replicate the results at the station level where, for convenience and economy at a late stage of work, I adapted the equation reported in table 6.4? Once again, additional types (vertical diversity) impacted significantly on the station's ADI ratings, metro ratings, and metro share, measures of the proportion of households that tune it in. Here, too, the initial evidence of types impact in table 3.6 is further confirmed at the station level, with substantial sample size, and t-values of 3.8, 5.0, and 4.9 respectively.

As expected, added stations in table 3.8 impact negatively on viewing proportions at the station level. With the number of TV homes and program diversity both constant, the percentage of homes watching a marginal entrant must decline as stations are added. True, a new station's negative impact on all station ratings may be mitigated by attracting new viewers into the market. However, the equation in table 3.8 does

22. The use of proportions of tuned-in households would tend to eliminate any danger that types or options impact was really a proxy for the larger number of TV homes in larger markets, and it would do so *without* further explicit controls for market size. However, I did so control in table 3.7 as in 3.6, where controlling for market size in this way *was* crucial for the analysis.

23. My associates and I did indeed conclude that it was the relatively small sample (N = 133), together with the limited variation found in the proportion dependent variable, that prevented us from registering significance for the network VHF variable:

Table	Dependent Variable	Variance	Variance/Mean	Coefficient of Variation
3.6	Audience	1493.2	68.48	1.77
3.7	Audience/TV Homes	0.00817	0.01514	0.17

not permit us to estimate new viewers here in the way suggested by the analysis in tables 3.6 and 3.9, for aggregate viewing across all stations in the market.

Problems of Overlapping Signals. One final implication of tables 3.8 and 3.8A relates to the existence of market overlap, namely the problem in measuring aggregate viewing accurately where stations deliver sizable audiences in neighboring markets which are not included in trade source estimates of that market's viewers. This so-called overlap problem is considered at length by Park et al., and earlier by Crandall,[24] both of whom report separate tests on county data to correct for it. The use of data from the smaller county area is believed to minimize possible overlap in station signal contours within the larger ADI market perimeter.

For present purposes we have taken advantage of our separate ratings data for the larger ADI market and the more narrowly defined metro area within it. The latter is by no means as small as the county units Park and Crandall utilized. However, the smaller metro central areas should also reduce any distorting effects of overlapping signals caused by stations located outside the ADI, which viewers near the latter's outer perimeter may watch, and which may in turn exaggerate the impact of local station options (or types diversity) on reported ADI viewing. That is, if the difference between impacts on ADI and metro ratings had been large, then the overlap problem could be serious, but here the largely similar results suggest no serious distortion.

True, the metro area is by no means so far from the ADIs outer perimeter as to eliminate all effects of stations located beyond it. Nevertheless, some of these signals are doubtless excluded, as is clear from a cursory review of ADI and metro area maps in *Television Factbook.*[25] If interpreted with caution, a comparison of types diversity impacts on metro and ADI ratings is at least suggestive of the degree of market overlap.

In effect, I find the impacts in both equations to be statistically significant. However, no (second order) tests of the significance of the differences between them are possible because both types coefficients come from different equations. Yet simple inspection indicates that the reduction of impact on audience ratings when we move from ADI to metro contours is very small indeed.[26] For types diversity at least, the problem of market overlap appears unimportant.

What of options diversity? Here, too, added stations have significant

24. See R. Park, L. Johnson, and B. Fishman, *Projecting the Growth of Television Broadcasting: The Implications for Spectrum Use* (Santa Monica, Calif.: Rand Corporation, 1976), appendix B; R. Crandall, "The Economic Case for a Fourth Commercial Television Network," *Public Policy* (Fall 1974), pp. 521–22.

25. *Television Factbook* (Washington, D.C.: Television Digest, Inc., 1977).

26. The sample means reported below the estimating equations indicate that proper comparisons of ADI and metro ratings coefficients require that decimal points for the latter be moved one place to the right.

negative effects on viewing proportions in both ADI and metro areas. The metro area effects, again, are smaller than is true for the type impacts just described. Whether the difference between these metro and ADI area impacts of added station options is in fact significant cannot be determined here with certainty. More important is that the conclusion on options and types diversity impacts drawn in our earlier discussion of tables 3.6 to 3.10, remains virtually the same regardless of the market area analyzed. Whatever the actual degree of overlap, then, its consequences should not be exaggerated here.

Implications for Theories of Viewer Behavior

A significant positive impact on viewing of the number of options, of types, or of both, can be explained in terms of several different theories of viewer behavior. Thus the seminal Steiner theory presumes that viewers watch their first preference only, or else switch off.[27] In the Steiner model, successive station entrants into a market will continue to duplicate the program types carried by existing rivals, until the audience for all is so fractionated that a marginal entrant finds it profitable to introduce a "new" program type, not then available anywhere. According to that theory it can be argued that, to attract new viewers into the market (and thus raise aggregate viewing levels), a larger number of stations must enter than can normally be accommodated under current channel allocations, especially in the VHF band.[28]

The so-called passive theory of viewer behavior, on the other hand, assumes that viewers will always prefer *some* viewing to no viewing, however low the program on their preference scale.[29] According to Owen, Beebe, and Manning, for example, "the total audience for all three networks combined seems to be determined almost completely by exogenous factors, such as seasonal patterns of family entertainment." [30] Total viewing is indeed said to have remained stable "despite drastic changes in the kinds and qualities of programs offered, the advent of

27. See Peter Steiner, "Program Patterns and Preferences, and the Workability of Competition in Radio Broadcasting," *Quarterly Journal of Economics*, May 1952, and systematic assessment in Jack Beebe, "Institutional Structure and Program Choice in Television and Cable Markets," *Quarterly Journal of Economics*, February 1977.

28. Stanley Besen and Bridger Mitchell, *Watergate and Television: An Economic Analysis* (Santa Monica, Calif.: Rand Corporation, 1975), pp. 3–4.

29. Bruce Owen, Jack Beebe, and Will Manning, *Television Economics* (Lexington, Mass.: Lexington Books, 1974), pp. 95–96; Leo Bogart, *Age of Television* (New York: Frederick Ungar, 1972), pp. 84–85.

30. Owen et al., *Television Economics*, pp. 95–96.

color, the fact that April is now . . . occupied (though not in earlier years) almost entirely by re-run programming, and . . . TV homes [have] increased. . . ." [31] Although highly passive viewers are believed to "[switch] channels only [due to] extreme provocation," they may indeed switch among programs to gain preferred options, when program availability changes.

According to the Rand Corporation theory, viewers "will watch a second or low choice program but . . . will become non-viewers if the available viewing alternatives are sufficiently poor." [32] That is, "Rand" viewers will watch options that are *not* first preference, though, unlike passive viewers, they will at *some* point prefer nonviewing to watching less preferred options.[33]

According to Wiles, finally, viewers have second-level as well as first-level viewing preferences. Unlike Steiner, Wiles contends that viewers may indeed be willing to watch mass-audience (or common denominator) programming when their first preference options are not available. This is often preferable for Wiles viewers to not watching television at all. However, they will switch to first preference options whcn they become available. Finally, they may in some cases (rarer than Rand viewers?) prefer nonviewing to mass-audience options where first options are not available.[34]

A positive, significant (horizontal) options or types diversity impact on aggregate viewing clearly implies that increased diversity causes at least some nonviewers to switch on. In principle, this appears to occur if (1) some Steiner nonviewers may find their first preference; [35] if (2) some Rand nonviewers find *something* worth watching, though not necessarily their first preference; or if (3) even Wiles nonviewers find first preference (or mass-audience) programs hitherto not available.[36] A positive response of viewing to increased diversity is inconsistent only with the passive theory, since the latter assumes viewers always prefer watching to not watching, whatever programs are available.

31. Ibid.
32. Besen and Mitchell, *Watergate and Television*, p. 29.
33. Ibid., pp. 29–31. A lucid review of all four theories appears on pp. 1–14. Rand viewers are ordinary economic men, other viewers being special cases of them.
34. Peter Wiles, "Pilkington and the Theory of Value," *Economic Journal*, June 1963, pp. 183–94. Actually Wiles viewers are Rand viewers, but with a particular assumption about the nature of their preference. Also, in the Wiles model, as the number of stations increases, some previously shown programs may be eliminated. This does not happen in the Steiner model.
35. Without relaxing Steiner's assumptions, however, there is a question of how realistic it is to expect the addition of a mere second or third network VHF to so fractionate the TV audience as to increase types diversity and then bring in nonviewers.
36. Here I define options and types "horizontally," as programs or types available in each fifteen-minute segment during prime evening hours, across all stations in the market. Options or types could however also be defined "vertically," on each station throughout prime hours. Any viewer's likelihood of finding his first preference program, et cetera, must be assessed relative to this horizontal or vertical configuration.

This does not mean that positive options or types diversity coefficients only imply more viewing. In addition, some prior viewers may now switch among programs (or types) to watch *preferred* programs or types not hitherto available. Such behavior is consistent with the passive, Rand, and even Wiles theories, but not with the extreme Steiner model.

One must of course be cautious in relating these few empirical results to the theories of viewer behavior. In this chapter, I have essentially found that additional program types, taking options into account, do, at the margin, appear to bring in significant numbers of nonviewers, and hence to swell aggregate net viewing. So, too, does the addition of network VHF options, taking types into account. In those cases, for reasons stated, the tentative implication is that Rand nonviewers, or Wiles nonviewers, may switch on under our postulated conditions. It is, however, will watch a second, third, but not an nth preference before tuning off; less clear whether Steiner nonviewers will do so without a more detailed specification of the relative size of the preference groups in question.

None of the above implications, however, further denies the possibility that *existing* viewers may also switch from their present to a preferred option in the face of (1) additional options of any sort, or of (2) additional types. Nor that such switchers could be (3) passive viewers who prefer to watch almost anything rather than nothing, and may well have hitherto settled for a lesser preference; (4) Rand-style viewers, who and even (5) Wiles viewers, who may discover, in an added type or option, a preferred mass-audience program preferable to what they have hitherto watched, or even a first-level preference. Without significant increases in aggregate net viewing, however, the Steiner viewer alone is ruled out as a potential switcher from a present to a preferred option. By definition, he has either already found his first-preference program, or will remain among the ranks of nonviewers until he does. He, as the nonviewer, has better things to do with his time.

What about an added UHF or independent VHF option? In no case did I find significant effects on viewing. But neither did I find that the significant types impact resulted in additional viewing statistically greater than the point estimates of changes in viewing levels due to another network UHF, independent UHF, or independent VHF. Nor, in any case, have I been able to isolate the link between additional options and additional types which, if accurately measured, could (though need not) yield significant effects due to these other classes of options too.[37]

On these limited facts, therefore, the most that can be prudently con-

37. There is no requirement in my equations that the independent variables have no causal relationships among themselves. Therefore, station options may indeed impact on types. Yet even after accounting for the effects of types, I do not unambiguously segregate out all possible effects of options on viewing (including those that operate through the addition of new program types).

cluded is that the more limited resources of independent stations generally, and of UHF outlets whether network or independent, may simply result in a quality and mix of programming unable to attract sufficient new viewers to raise viewing levels significantly. It would follow, then, that the options offered by such stations do not appear to impact on Steiner, Rand, or Wiles viewers the way additional network VHF options do. Without more refined analysis, we can be sure only that the network VHFs have a large and significant impact.

Conclusion

Program diversity is a principal yardstick by which broadcast regulation will be assessed in this study. I have therefore taken special pains to examine it here and, while important issues require additional analysis, there is ample evidence that the diversity concept is one meaningful basis on which to appraise industry and commission performance. Subsequent chapters will therefore undertake a regulatory assessment in programming as well as economic performance terms.

Diversity has been conceived here, first, as the number of program options, and second, of program types (classes of options), horizontally available across all stations in the market, at a given time. Type diversity has also been conceived of vertically, as the average number of different program categories appearing daily on each station, over the broadcast day, and the broadcast week. Still another concept related diversity to program sources, that is, to the *kind* of station that carries a program, whether network VHF, independent VHF, or the like. In this book I normally refer to options (and types) diversity only, in that, while the station source provides the program, the resulting program option (or type) is what really matters to the viewer.

Options diversity is in any case simply measured by the number of stations in the market, one assumption being that every program broadcast at a given time, on any station, offers a separate and potentially unique option to the deliverable audience. But these individual options can be further collapsed into broader classes or types of programs, wherein intracategory differences are assumed to be less important than intercategory ones, from a producer viewpoint at least. Because program types are in the first instance defined by the program supply industry and ratings services, there was an open question as to how homogeneous they were from a consumer viewpoint. We therefore devised tests to clarify the matter.

First, and most important for this study, is the simple finding that type differences *do* appear to matter for the viewer. This conclusion emerges from my analysis of horizontal diversity across all stations in the market, as it impacts, *cet. par.,* on the level of aggregate viewing therein, and as further replicated on the proportion of households that tune in at all. It is confirmed also by a final replication of our results at the station level. In both our market equations, moreover, a number of exogenous control factors were specified, whereas stations and types impacts were estimated conditional upon market size.

However, I also found that additional network VHF options had a significantly larger impact on viewing levels (and on proportions of households viewing), than increases in viewing due to the addition of one to twenty-one program types (postulated increments deemed realistic in light of the actual distribution of stations by market size), though the program options provided by any other kind of station did *not*.

In sum, though crude, the program typology employed in this book, is basically sound for current purposes, both from a producer and a consumer viewpoint. However, this does not imply that, without program cost and price information not now in the analysis, one can draw any categorical conclusions as to the *consumer welfare aspects* of higher diversity levels.[38] I have deliberately stopped short of such inferences here, and the assessment in Part II will be couched in simple terms of regulation's dual impact, both on economic performance and on types diversity.

Appendix 3A. The Case of
Monday Night Football

The purpose of this appendix is to further probe the existence of diversity within and across major program types in television. Using the Nielsen data on national network viewing for 1358 programs, I examine one broad program type—network entertainment—and another, more specific nonentertainment type, ABC's recurrent sports special "Monday Night Football." The latter was aired regularly during the fall of 1974 in the face of CBS and NBC entertainment shows that remained largely the same as on Monday nights without ABC football.

I conducted statistical tests of the significance of changes in each net-

38. Because we have been unable to take account of the *intensity* with which viewers may prefer *particular* programs within a given category, we have no really scientific basis, later, for choosing among FCC policies to promote diversity. Nevertheless, the yardsticks developed here do permit us to evaluate the FCC's principal policy choices meaningfully, concretizing much that the Commission implies but has never systematically analyzed.

work's program ratings, audience size, and shares associated with "Monday Night Football," and in aggregate audience indicators for all three networks together. Bear in mind that ABC's major entertainment shows had substantially lower audiences, ratings, and shares in 1974 than those of its rivals. (See table 3.11.) The recurrent football special would understandably have been considered an alternative to popular CBS and NBC entertainment programs, worth trying just because ABC's overall entertainment showing was a poor third. True, the mean indicators of ABC's Monday night entertainment shows appear somewhat stronger than for its entertainment programs generally. Nevertheless, Monday nights would be a likely time to experiment because viewing then is normally higher than on any other night but Sunday.[39] (See table 3.3.)

The following evidence suggests that types diversity does in fact exist from a consumer viewpoint. However, the data are only in part illustrative of the information I would really like to have had but was unable to generate. Specifically, a significant increase in estimated total viewing (including nonnetwork), in response to the postulated change in program scheduling would appear consistent with the hypothesis that "Monday Night Football" induces new viewers to switch on, reduces the number of nonviewers thereby, and constitutes a different and distinct program type from the consumer viewpoint.

The problem is that we can only measure net, not gross flows of viewers among the three networks. That is, we cannot decompose our audience flow data sufficiently to determine how many viewers actually switch among the affiliated and independent stations, when ABC does not carry "Monday Night Football." Nevertheless, the discussion helps illustrate the kind of additional work that could more completely confirm the existence of types diversity which we reported in the text of this chapter.

The Watergate Study

Of special interest at this point is the aforementioned Besen and Mitchell study of television's Watergate hearings coverage and the type diversity this arguably represented. The authors postulated that the hearings and all other network shows normally run at the same time (soap operas), were perceived by viewers as two quite different program types.[40] Their evidence shows that the hearings coverage attracted large numbers of potential TV viewers who had either watched inde-

---

39. This statement must be qualified in the light of national football game schedules. The National Football League might have refused any other night than one adjacent to Sunday because to have one game more than one day after the others might place too much of a disadvantage on the teams playing off the regular schedule. They would have less time to prepare for their game the next Sunday.

40. Besen and Mitchell, *Watergate and Television*, pp. 13–14.

TABLE 3.11

Average Audiences, Ratings, and Shares for Programs in Selected Categories, by Network, 1974

	ABC				CBS				NBC			
	N	Mean Audience (Millions)	Mean Ratings	Mean Shares	N	Mean Audience (Millions)	Mean Ratings	Mean Shares	N	Mean Audience (Millions)	Mean Ratings	Mean Shares
Situation comedy	84	10.6	15.8	24.7	178	16.5	24.5	38.5	59	15.2	22.6	36.6
Comedy variety	13	9.3	13.6	21.5	31	14.6	21.9	35.9	24	13.3	20.0	32.0
Evening animated	6	10.2	14.9	24.3	12	16.1	23.7	37.2	3	13.1	19.1	28.7
Evening western	21	9.9	14.9	23.7	27	14.2	21.1	32.0	10	16.8	24.6	37.8
Contemporary music	3	9.2	13.6	20.7	2	16.3	24.7	38.0	9	11.3	22.3	28.2
Private detective	16	9.9	18.3	26.0	71	14.2	21.0	33.6	9	15.3	18.4	37.9
Official police	75	12.3	12.4	29.5	36	15.9	23.6	36.2	77	12.4	17.2	29.5
Feature film	93	12.3	18.3	28.4	48	12.6	18.7	31.3	99	13.5	20.1	31.4
General documentary	9	9.0	13.7	21.6	5	17.2	25.8	39.0	6	9.7	14.4	22.7
News documentary	5	7.2	10.5	16.6	7	7.3	10.8	19.0	6	8.8	13.2	22.8
News sustainers	12		18.1	30.7	9		17.7	31.3				
Other	118				95				116			
Total programs	455				521				418			

SOURCE: All data derived from A. C. Nielsen NTI Reports for January-March, October-December 1974. Ratings are percentages of all U.S. TV homes watching a given network program, and shares, the program's portion of TV homes then watching all available network and nonnetwork shows.

pendent stations or none at all at that time of day.[41] In short, the distinctive character of Watergate coverage was deemed to constitute type diversity for television viewers, distinguishing that programming from options which the networks had normally carried in its place.[42]

At one point the authors conclude that virtually *any* recurrent live special might provide a similar opportunity to examine the thesis that between-type diversity exceeds within-type diversity in the consumer's eyes.[43] To test the validity of this speculation, at their suggestion we sought to study ABC's "Monday Night Football" as an illustrative case in point. In particular, I examined each television network's program ratings, shares, and audiences for a six-month period in 1974, on all Monday nights when ABC did and did not carry football.

From this review of Monday night data I sought to make two determinations: first, whether total mean television audiences (with and without nonnetwork viewing included) are significantly different when ABC carries "Monday Night Football"; second, whether anything can be deduced from such results regarding the diversity that ABC football did or did not represent for viewers who normally watch no television at all on Monday nights, or at least do not watch any network affiliate.

The Findings on Monday Night Football

The findings in table 3.12 quite clearly suggest that "Monday Night Football" is associated with: (1) significantly higher mean ratings, shares, and audiences for the entertainment programs CBS and NBC chose to run against ABC football, compared with those they broadcast on Monday nights without football; and (2) significantly *lower* mean ratings and audiences for ABC football (with audience shares relatively stable) compared with ABC's record on Monday nights without football. However, we also found (3) significantly larger *three-network totals* of mean program audiences, ratings, and shares with than without "Monday Night Football."

What bearing have these results on an hypothesis that the 12,920,000 ABC football viewers (table 3.12) include many "new" viewers who would not otherwise have watched network television on Monday nights? We obviously cannot prove that thesis with the data now available, but we surely can defend it in the following manner.

First, note that the CBS plus NBC Monday night viewers increase significantly when ABC carries football, from 26,377,000 to 30,163,000, or by 3,770,000 (14.2 percent). Clearly, day-of-the-week variations cannot explain this substantial increase, given that our entire subsample is limited to Monday nights. Neither do variations in program length ex-

41. Ibid., pp. 17–29.
42. Ibid., pp. 29–31.
43. Ibid., pp. 39–40.

TABLE 3.12

Network Mean Audiences, Ratings, and Shares, with and without "Monday Night Football," 1974

	Monday Nights, without ABC Football				
Network	No. of 15-Minute Units	Mean Audiences	Mean Ratings (percent)	No. of 15-Minute Units	Mean Audience Shares (percent)
CBS	188	14,791,000	22.085	188	33.399
NBC	183	11,586,000	17.342	187	26.316
ABC	184	13,616,000	20.275	188	31.005
Total of three-network averages		39,993,000	59.702		90.720

	Monday Nights, with ABC Football				
Network	No. of 15-Minute Units	Mean Audiences	Mean Ratings (percent)	No. of 15-Minute Units	Mean Audience Shares (percent)
CBS	80	16,469,000[a]	24.042[a]	80	37.300[a]
NBC	75	13,694,000[a]	20.124[a]	80	31.012[a]
ABC	80	12,920,000[b]	18.860[a]	80	32.200[c]
Total of three-network averages		43,083,000[a]	63.026[a]		100.512[a]

SOURCE: All data derived from A. C. Nielsen NTI Reports for January-March, and October-December 1974.

EXPLANATION: Average audiences for designated network entertainment programming and for football. Average ratings are mean percentages of all U.S. TV homes which watch each network program studied. Average shares relate to the proportion of *all* viewers (including nonnetwork) watching television at a given time, who in fact watch a given network program. Shares totaling to over 100 reflect rounding errors in part, but more important, the higher level of multiset usage in response to the football special. Specifically, although each network's audience swells due to multiset usage, Nielsen calculates its share of total viewing (including nonnetwork) as a simple fraction of total *homes* watching (each home counting only once). Shares approaching 100 due to multiset usage clearly imply that substantial numbers of nonviewers tune in when ABC carries football. Statistical significance (two-tailed test) is: a = 1 percent; b = 5 percent; c = 10 percent. Thus CBS mean entertainment audiences on Monday nights without ABC football are 14,791,000 but 16,469,000 with ABC football, the difference being significantly greater than zero at the .01 confidence level.

plain the observed changes in that such effects are extremely small (though significant).[44] Neither, finally, are seasonal influences important here in that both subsamples (with and without ABC football) are derived from the period of greatest television viewing, the first and last three months of 1974.

From where then do these additional 3,770,000 CBS and NBC entertainment viewers come? It seems unlikely that many of them were watching independent stations in the *absence* of "Monday Night Football." After all, any nonnetwork viewer *could* have switched to CBS or NBC at that time and clearly did not. Without some far-reaching change in major network or nonnetwork programming (of which we have no evidence), there is simply no reason to assume that many of the new CBS or NBC viewers were prior nonnetwork viewers. Nor, indeed, is it likely that they were former *non*viewers, since the latter, too, by definition chose not to watch CBS or NBC before ABC switched to football. It therefore follows that most of the 3,770,000 new CBS and NBC viewers must have been former ABC entertainment viewers who, when deprived of those ABC programs, preferred similar shows on the other two networks to watching ABC football, or to not watching television at all.

For argument's sake, let us assume that all 3,770,000 new CBS and NBC viewers switched from ABC when that network put on football. In table 3.12, this would leave 9,846,000 ABC viewers (that is, 13,616,000 minus 3,770,000) who chose *not* to switch to another network and were thereby free to watch ABC football, or turn to an independent station, or switch off their set. The maximum number of nonviewers which ABC football must have activated is clearly the 12,920,000 who watched it, minus the 9,846,000 of ABC's nonfootball viewers who did not switch to CBS or NBC when ABC put on football, that is, 3,074,000 nonviewers.

However, some of these viewers could previously have watched independents or public television, a fact which might reduce the estimated number of nonviewers activated by ABC football. Football is so different from network entertainment that it seems difficult not to consider it also different from nonnetwork programs. Assuming it *were* indeed so viewed, there seems no reason why there could not be a flow of viewers from ABC to nonnetwork (and PTV) as well as to CBS and NBC entertainment. It is, however, true that the latters' entertainment programs are probably better substitutes for ABC entertainment than nonnetwork shows would be (ABC viewers had clearly failed to select that option over ABC entertainment). Nevertheless, it could be argued that any increase in total network viewing (as in table 3.12) may well be due to an influx of nonnetwork viewers as well as nonviewers.

In that regard, consider table 3.13, which reports three estimates of

44. For every 15-minutes longer, *cet. par.*, a program would attract only 77,000 (or .589 percent of the mean) more viewers (see table 3.3).

nonnetwork viewing, one for Monday nights without football (row 1, column 1), and two others derived from data for all programs in the full Nielsen data deck (rows 2–3, column 2). Note that my estimate of non-network viewing in row 1, column 2 is derived directly by (1) dividing the combined three-network audience (39,993,000) by (2) the three-network audience shares in table 3.13 (90.720), to estimate total viewing as 44,084,000, and, by subtraction, nonnetwork viewing as 4,091,000.

TABLE 3.13

Estimated Total Viewing and Non-Viewing
with and without Monday Night Football, 1974

	Monday Nights	N	1 Combined 3-Network Audience	2 Estimated Nonnetwork Audience	3 (1 + 2) Estimated Total Viewers	4* Estimated Nonviewers
1	Without Football	555	39,993,000	4,091,000	44,084,000	24,416,000
2	With Football (A)	235	43,083,000[a]	3,628,000 (A)	46,711,000[a]	21,789,000[a]
3	With Football (B)	235	43,083,000[a]	4,438,000 (B)	47,521,000[a]	20,979,000[a]

SOURCE: Same as for table 3.12.
*Nonviewers estimated by subtracting estimated total viewers in column 3 from the American Research Bureau's estimate of 68,500,000 TV homes in 1974.
EXPLANATION: Nonnetwork viewers are estimated as follows:
    A = mean of nonnetwork viewers for nineteen postulated network schedules where (1) mean of combined network audiences estimated directly, (2) total viewers then derived by dividing combined network audiences by total of combined network audience shares, and (3) nonnetwork viewers further calculated as mean of estimated total viewers for the nineteen schedules minus the mean of combined network audiences, or 3,628,000.
    B = nonnetwork viewers calculated as same percentage of combined network audiences as on Monday nights without football, that is, as 43,083,000 × 10.3 percent = 4,437,549.
[a]Denotes that all three estimates for total Monday night viewers are significantly greater at 1 percent confidence level when ABC carries football than when it does not; also, that estimated *non*viewers are significantly fewer when ABC carries football.

On the other hand, in table 3.13 one estimate of nonnetwork viewing *with* ABC football (row 2), is derived from a set of nineteen separate network program schedules through a procedure like that just described. Estimated nonnetwork viewing for all nineteen postulated schedules average out to 3,628,000 which I use as estimate A in that table. (See explanatory note there.)

Finally, estimate B of nonnetwork viewing in table 3.13 is calculated, as indicated therein, simply as the same percentage of combined network audiences for Monday nights with football as we found to be true for Monday nights *without* football, namely, as 43,083,000 × 10.3 percent = 4,437,549.

The upshot is that in column 4 our two residual estimates of nonviewers who tune in ABC football are (A) 24,416,000 − 21,789,000, or

2,627,000, and (B) 24,416,000 – 20,979,000, or 3,437,000. Both of these figures are significantly larger than zero. So, too, are the equivalent differences between total viewing with and without ABC football (column 3). Note, finally, how close these estimates of new viewers are to my initial estimate of 3,074,000 (in discussing table 3.12). In table 3.13, my two estimates of nonviewers who tune in "Monday Night Football" average out to 3,032,000. By the same token, the alternative estimates of nonnetwork viewing therein—3,628,000 and 4,438,000—average out to 4,033,000, again very close to my direct estimate of 4,091,000. An assumption of "constant nonnetwork viewing" when ABC carries "Monday Night Football" may not be so far from the mark after all.

Nevertheless, suppose that some former nonnetwork viewers did in fact switch to ABC football, a choice they previously had not had. This might reduce the number of former nonviewers who also did so to below the 3,074,000 minimum we have estimated. Yet if we postulate such a redistribution of nonnetwork viewers despite the evidence just cited to the contrary, we must surely allow for a possible shift the *other* way too, of some former ABC entertainment viewers to nonnetwork or, indeed, to nonviewing. The fact is that all we can really measure are net flows, not gross flows.

Finally, any sizable diversion of the 9,846,000 ABC entertainment viewers (who did not turn to its rivals) to nonnetwork or nonviewing, would imply that ABC entertainment was more distinctive than its program ratings, shares, and audiences suggest (table 3.11). Any such diversion must, in any case, be made up by a still larger shift the other way, from nonnetwork and nonviewing to ABC, to generate the 12,920,000 known mean audiences of ABC football.

Conclusion

Accordingly, I conclude with three comparable estimates of nonviewers who tune in ABC football. In table 3.13, I derived an upper bound estimate of 3,437,000 and a lower bound estimate of 2,627,000, whereas in table 3.12, a separate third estimate was calculated directly and came in somewhere in the middle at 3,074,000 new viewers of "Monday Night Football." As at the outset, the reader is again cautioned in his or her use of these results. Except for the impact of ABC football on total network viewing, the reported estimates are at best very crude. The main problem is in estimating nonnetwork viewing, with or without ABC football. Nevertheless, without individual household diaries, the data just presented are at least suggestive of what more definitive in-depth study of fully decomposed audience flows might show, and, like findings of the chapter proper, do seem consistent with a positive impact of types diversity on aggregate viewing.

Appendix 3B. Computation Procedure
for Interacted Impacts

The purpose of this appendix is to demonstrate how I derived the impacts reported in several text tables from the estimating equation associated with them. The presence of interaction coefficients in each equation prevents us from reading the variable impact right off the table (as with simple linear equations such as in table 5.2).

For illustrative purposes I shall therefore consider how to get from the main equation in table 3.6 to the derived results reported in 3.9. The basic concept is that, if we are focusing on the effect of a change in one attribute (say, of the log of number of network VHFs in the market), then only those variables which involve (reflect) that attribute can be involved in the calculation. In table 3.6, where nondummy variables are combined, we will generally find that all variables that *can* be involved in the calculation *will* be involved. This is not true for comparable interacted *station* equations, at least where we interact dummy variables only. (See Appendix to chapter 4, table 4.11.)

Bear in mind the distinction between coefficients and variables. When we change an attribute (say, going from one to two network VHFs in the market), a variable is changing or, if that attribute is interacted, perhaps several variables. In table 3.6, for example, the number of network VHFs was not successfully interacted with TV homes (due to collinearity), and thus appears in only one variable, whereas the number of independent VHFs, independent UHFs, and network UHFs, *were* interacted with TV homes and hence appear in two variables, namely the basic (log—no. of independent VHFs + 1, and so on) variable, plus the interactive term (log—no. of IV + 1) × (TV homes).

Therefore, when we want to determine the impact of the change in an attribute, we must first consider in which variables in the equation that attribute appears in some form. Our computations will at most involve those variables and their coefficients. Briefly, the impact of the change in an attribute is the sum of the corresponding change in each affected variable, each multiplied by its coefficient. In the simplest case there is only one variable, and therefore one coefficient involved.

Let us consider a few simple computations and then work up to the more difficult ones. For a start, how do we derive the estimated impact on quarter-hour viewing of an added 7 program types across all stations in the market, reported in table 3.9 as +.17139 × 10,000, or 1,714 homes?

First, we see that types and TV homes are both affected, and that we must therefore select a level of TV homes at which to estimate (that is, interact) the types impact. We shall interact here at the mean of TV homes, or 37.6 × 10,000—namely 376,000 homes.

Second, by how much do the affected variables change when types increase by 7? Types increase by the same 7 units, but the interactive variable will change by 37.6 times the change in types, or 37.6 × 7, or 263.3.

Third, the impact of an added 7 units of types is the sum of the changes in each affected variable, each multiplied by its coefficient, reported in table 3.6. The coefficient of types is –.0365144, and of types × TV homes, .00162175 × 37.61308.[45] Therefore the change in average quarter-hour viewing is:

= (−.0365144 × 7)	+	.00162175	×	(37.61308 × 7)
coefficient of types	change in types	coefficient of types × TV homes		TV homes × change in types
= −.2556008	+	.00162175	×	263.29156
−.2556008	+	.4269799		
= .1713791				

A second example will calculate the impact of a third network VHF. Note that only the log (#VHF + 1) stations variable is affected because we were unable to interact it with TV homes (due to collinearity). Assuming, then, that there are already two network VHFs in the market, adding a third means that #VHFs changes from 2 to 3, while #VHF + 1 (a correction to eliminate uncalculable zero log values), rises from 3 to 4.[46] Therefore, log(#network VHF + 1) will change from log(3) to log(4). From a log table we can determine that log(3) = .47712, and log (4) = .60206, the difference between the two being .12494.

Hence the impact on quarter-hour viewing is the *change* in log(#network VHF + 1), .12494, multiplied by its coefficient, which is +12.802 (in table 3.6)—namely, .12494 × 12.802 = 1.5995. (The discrepancy from our reported impact in table 3.9, as noted, is due to rounding errors.)

45. The computer carries all coefficients to 8 decimal points and using them in this computation permits us to replicate the computer-derived impact of +7 types reported in table 3.9. The correct procedure is thereby demonstrated. However, all coefficients in this table (and elsewhere in our study) are, for convenience, normally reported only to three decimal places. Due to rounding errors, therefore, the reader may be unable to replicate reported impacts anywhere in the book except roughly. Indeed the discrepancies may in some cases be rather large as a consequence. Nevertheless, the computer works with the true coefficients and the reported impacts are therefore correct.

46. On the problems posed by zero log values, see Appendix I, pp. 422–25.

For a third and final example let us estimate the impact of a second independent VHF. Now two variables are affected, log #independent VHF + 1 (whose coefficient = +26.415 in table 3.6), and the interactive variable, log #VHF + 1 × TV homes (whose coefficient = −.600). We calculate the impact of a second independent VHF as follows:

1. When #independent VHF changes from 1 to 2, #independent VHF+1 changes from 2 to 3, and the log #independent VHF+1 will therefore rise from log (2) to log (3).
2. From a log table we can determine that log (2) = .30103 and log (3) = .47712, the difference being .17609.
3. The impact on quarter-hour viewing is made up of two components: (*a*) change in log #independent VHF+1 (.17609), multiplied by its coefficient (+26.415), or 4.6514; plus (*b*) change in log #independent VHF+1 × TV homes, or (−.600 × .17609) (37.61308), or −(.105654) (37.61308). Summing the two components, we replicate the reported impact as: 4.6514 (+) −3.9739723, or .6774.

Interacted coefficients in tables 3.7 and 3.7A, in log form and otherwise, can be computed in precisely the same way. As noted, the three steps are these: first, to determine which variables are affected by the changing attribute; second, for each affected variable, to determine how each is affected, that is, by how much it changes when the attribute changes; third, to sum the products of each change in a variable times its coefficient.

Chapter 4

Origin and Incidence

of Economic Rents

in Broadcasting

BY "rents" we refer to payments to any factor of production in excess of the "minimum earnings necessary to induce the particular unit of it to do its work"—that portion of the payment made for use of a unit of a resource, over and beyond the amount necessary to ensure its utilization for the class of purposes at hand. Rents arise because of artificial limits on access to, or scarcity of, resources, or both. That is, one must distinguish between natural physical or technical limitations on one hand, and, on the other, limitations due to law, administration, or to controlling complementary resources which are themselves limited in supply (port facilities, riparian access, and so on).

In general, a principal factor determining *spectral* rents is the nation's system of centralized licensing and allocation—a set of regulations instituted, in theory at least, to maintain efficient utilization of radio frequencies with due allowance for their potential marginal signal interference effects. *Broadcast* rents derive from spectral rents, but also from concentrated control by TV network companies and talent unions of unique talent and programming sources, themselves a limited-supply complementary resource for frequency utilization.

In probing the origin of rents here, I shall first consider the common property character of radio frequencies and the entry control techniques long utilized to prevent their potentially costly external effects. The use of entry controls will indeed be shown to be the direct proximate cause of rents, and the absence of station price or time rate controls or significant license charges is the reason these rents accrue to private parties.

This will be followed by two pieces of quantitative evidence: the first, some estimates of aggregate franchise value in television broadcasting, derived from a large set of sales price data, and from published income and revenue statistics; the second, a regression analysis of the determinants and incidence of implicit economic rents with special reference to such factors as restrictive licensing, allocation policy, network, group, and newspaper affiliations.

I estimate aggregate private economic rents for VHF television for the year 1975 to range between $371,000,000 and $417,000,000, or some $753,000 to $847,000 per VHF station on the air, a sum equal to 35 to 40 percent of average station intangibles (sales price minus original cost) for a sample of 323 transfers, 1949–70. The major determinants of private economic rents implicit in TV sales prices appear to be license limitation and, to some extent, age of station and channel type differences. The additional impact of network ties is itself further reflective of channel allocations, and their resultant restrictions on new station and new network entry. Of special import is the incidence of implicit rents among stations classified by owner type of seller and buyer.

In what follows I do not imply that economic rents need distort allocative efficiency, or that recovering them for the whole community, in TV broadcasting, is free of its own dangers for efficiency and incentives. There are, however, three overriding reasons why rents do matter for the regulator and why in this book I deem them indicative of some sort of regulatory failure.

First, there is the familiar distributional issue. Given the public, common property character of spectrum, is it fair to permit private users to retain spectral rents that really belong to the whole community? Equity, if not efficiency, underlies the political urgency of recovering the spectral rents in some form, cash or public service, for the public at large.

Second, and equally pertinent, large rents virtually create television's incentives and wherewithal to attempt to impede the introduction of new entry-opening technologies like cable television, pay-TV, and satellite broadcasting. Such impediments necessarily restrict the widening of effective program choices. Hence, even if one disagrees on the optimal *disposition* of the rents, there is no question that their existence tends to induce action aimed at their preservation by inhibiting the emergence of a more competitive and viewer-responsive system of broadcasting.

Third and last, rents are by no means a legitimate, formally mandated result of the present regulatory framework. Rather they are an unintended side effect whose very existence attests to a divergence between formal regulatory goals and end results, to regulatory failure.

The Radio Spectrum as Common Property

To define and defend exclusive use rights in the radio spectrum poses a complex and expensive task. Other common property resources—say, land—pose far simpler and less costly requirements, because of two marked differences from the spectrum. First, the ability of one hold-out to disrupt an entire transaction between hypothetical buyers and sellers of use rights is greater in the spectrum case just because pervasive external effects necessarily require agreement among far more users of spectrum than of land in the land case. For similar reasons, the extent to which given rights to congest the common resource are jointly held by different parties, is also greater for spectrum than for land. On both counts, unambiguous rights definition and enforcement are particularly difficult in radio spectrum utilization.

Externalities and Signal Interference Effects

Utilization restrictions for spectrum assignments are required in order to prevent licensees from adopting patterns of use that raise the costs to others and so create substantial social cost. This is mainly because it is impractical to try to hold a user accountable for the costs he imposes on others—that is, for his complex and hard-to-trace patterns of signal interference.

Because the required restrictions were never put in the form of clearly drawn, exclusive property rights, licensees have had an incentive to expand their use of spectrum such that the resultant interference would leave no one with usable frequencies for broadcasting purposes. The common resource would thereby be overused but for public or private intervention to prevent this.

Users of the radio spectrum have had three effective options: (1) to enter and waste the potential net productivity of the common resource by disorganized use; (2) to seek private collaborative agreements to give uncluttered use; or (3) to seek direct public control of the spectrum. In this, the users of spectrum are basically no different from users of other environmental resources, oil pools, or ocean fisheries. In each case, the users must presume that failure to prevent any single user from capturing or despoiling units of the resources from the common pool will leave him with an incentive to do just that, at everyone else's expense.

In cases of common resources generally, as an alternative to attempting to preempt private use "rights" by dint of occupancy (that is, squatters' rights), by sole ownership of the entire common resource, or by interuser cooperative agreements, recourse is frequently made to direct governmental control of entry and output. Such entry control is normally sanctioned to reduce congestion, overuse, overcapacity, and inefficiency generally. The centralized allocation and licensing of TV broadcast stations in this country is a classic example of this approach.

Direct Control of Entry to Internalize the Externalities

To limit costly marginal signal interference, congestion, and inefficiency, regulatory authorities have since 1927 controlled the number of
spectrum users in given geographical areas. Limits are also set on the
power, frequencies, and time periods of operation. The need for such
centralized licensing and allocation arises from the intangible and hard-
to-trace nature of the far-flung external effects which makes it extremely
difficult to define, enforce, or exchange clear unambiguous rights in
spectrum.

The principal problem is that spectrum rights cannot now be exchanged
in a market unless their spatial, spectral, and temporal contours are at
least minimally predictable. Yet no user can now predict the signal interference he himself will suffer (or create) unless he knows everyone else's
transmission inputs. An adequately detailed specification of inputs would
so increase the cost of "internalizing the externalities" of spectrum use as
to eliminate any net economic gains from the exchange of rights to use
radio frequencies, while too little input specification would result in considerable uncertainty as to spatial and temporal contours of rights.

Still, spectrum output rights have not yet been defined with such clarity, or signal interference effects on others so delimited, that the costs of
exchanging and enforcing emission rights will remain low enough to
make market transactions worthwhile. On the other hand, even an arbitrary definition (and control) of permissible spectrum *inputs* will suffice
to define user rights for allocational purposes. Each user's allowable signal power, polarization, antenna heights, directivity, and so forth—its
input rights—can be specified. But output rights—rights to occupy some
specified, predictable multidimensional volume of spectrum space—have
so far been conceived in ways that would make subsequent free market
exchanges among individual right holders too cumbersome and costly to
be economic.[1]

Furthermore, even if these economic and technical/physical factors
posed far fewer problems than at present, there are well-known *political*
obstacles to creating a full-fledged spectrum market today. These have
been spelled out at length elsewhere and need not be repeated.[2] Suffice
it to note only that restrictive licensing and allocation over several dec-

1. See, generally, Harvey Levin, *The Invisible Resource* (Baltimore: Johns Hopkins
University Press, 1971), pp. 91–97; also Levin, "Spectrum Allocation Without Markets," *American Economic Review Papers & Proceedings* (May 1970), pp. 210–12.
2. Levin, *The Invisible Resource*, pp. 104–15; Levin, "Spectrum Allocation," pp.
212–13.

ades must inevitably have created broadcast rents *unless* (1) broadcast station sales prices had been regulated directly from the outset; (2) licensees were subject to a lump-sum franchise tax; (3) stations were charged annual fees for their licenses at levels much closer to "value to recipient"; or, at the least, (4) were taxed substantially when transferred or sold to recapture the rents at that time.[3]

The absence of any of these devices necessarily leaves the bulk of industry rents intact. This presents the following policy questions: What compensating public service can or ought broadcasters be made to perform in return for the valuable exclusive access to the nation's spectrum resource they now enjoy? And how can this *quid pro quo,* or indeed the costs and benefits of the entire transaction, be convincingly measured? How, finally, would different regulatory alternatives affect the character of the transaction?

These questions are the subjects of inquiry in later chapters. Here I shall note only why, in the absence of appropriate economic policy—sizable license fees or direct control of sales price—substantial rents must necessarily occur.[4] And why the resultant rents must necessarily pose regulatory problems of their own.

Entry Control without License Charges or a Franchise Tax

Restrictive control of entry in fields like television, without license charges or a franchise tax, must confer rents on all original entrants. But proposals to induce an optimal level of entry through such charges or taxes raise difficult additional problems. To use such levies where a spectral region is *already* overcongested will presumably encounter intense political resistance by anyone forced to withdraw, and a levy high enough to force such withdrawal will exceed the gains from reduced congestion for those who remain, so that they too will resist. Also, the information costs of determining a "correct" tax or charge are high. However, even if this were not the case, there are important administrative rigidities in making desired changes afterward, when spectrum users have already invested (perhaps substantially) in equipment designed according to predetermined specifications. (Initial allocations are obviously not subject to such rigidities.)

---

3. Strictly speaking, these ancillary regulations would not have eliminated the rents, only prevented their capitalization and resale. Licensees would still have "collected" rents in their annual salaries, dividends, and retained earnings.

4. While license fees could operate to eliminate all or some of the rents, the control of sales prices would presumably only prevent, or limit, transfer of the rents to others. Such implicit transfer of rents would be conceivable under price control if, say, (1) the licensee invested his annual rents in improved equipment or other physical assets; and (2) the station's sales price was limited to the current replacement cost of those "improved" assets.

One could of course reduce the number of licensees gradually, and take steps later to recapture the resultant rents. In land-mobile radio, and parts of AM broadcasting, it is often said there is already too much congestion. If this were so, limited term licenses could be sold to the highest bidder, though with a prior public announcement that the number of licenses would subsequently be reduced. To optimize spectrum congestion in the above situation, a number of incumbents must doubtless be made to withdraw. But phasing in restrictive licensing as just described could help minimize unduly harsh inequities. Auction bids would also reflect the bidder's estimation of incremental franchise values due to the diminution of firms over time.

To date such economic incentives have nowhere been introduced among users of spectrum—neither in such apparently congested services as AM broadcasting or land-mobile radio, where they seem particularly germane, nor in TV, where a preengineered, congestion-free allocation table may superficially appear to make them less applicable. However, license fees or a franchise tax could have been combined in still another way in TV broadcasting too. The TV broadcast rights could have been sold to the highest bidder. One goal there would be to recapture the rents for the whole community; another would be to keep auction price incentives consistent with social and allocational priorities. (We return to both these issues in chapter 14.) Finally, such an auction scheme could be combined with a system of annual license charges, or a lump-sum franchise tax.

Nevertheless, the failure to make progress with a number of such past proposals appears mainly due to several (debatable) assumptions widely held by influential regulatory and industrial groups. These groups contend that such schemes would: (1) price small business out of the market and accentuate the concentration of broadcast facilities in the large, populous urban centers; (2) deter new venture capital by raising the costs of entry still higher than they are now; (3) give broadcast licensees equitable claims they do not now have, thereby undermining the FCC's power to regulate in the public interest; (4) saddle the licensee with additional capital costs and thus induce him to reduce the amount of public service programming and otherwise to compromise quality.

There is little reason to accept the validity of such assumptions out of hand (and telling arguments to the contrary).[5] Yet there is little doubt that they represent major roadblocks to instituting substantial license charges or a franchise tax in television, nor that, in the absence of such charges, restrictive licensing and centralized allocation necessarily create tremendous economic rents.

5. See, for example, Levin, "Federal Control of Entry in the Broadcast Industry," *Journal of Law and Economics* (October 1962), pp. 56–64; Levin, "Regulatory Efficiency, Reform and the FCC," *Georgetown Law Journal* (Fall 1961), pp. 31–33.

Entry Control Without Direct Control
of Advertising Rates or Station Sales Price

Had entry control in broadcasting been accompanied by ceilings on
maximum advertising rates and rates of return, there is no question that
rents accruing to broadcast stations would be smaller today, and the
controversy over their utilization far less important. However, the rents
and the allocation problem would have shifted to advertiser access to the
spectrum. Thus, had commercial time rates been controlled, price would
not have rationed the amount that advertisers demand. To make up for
lower per unit revenues, stations, with fixed total capacity, would have
devoted more time to commercials, and less to programming. Without
strict controls on this growing number and length of commercials, the
quality of service would decline. However, an upsurge of commercials
might well elicit rigorous regulatory limits on the number of time spots
for sale, as well as additional controls on loudness and good taste, so as
to reduce earnings to an "allowable" level.[6]

The Communications Act of 1934 explicitly deems broadcasting not
to be a common carrier (section 3[h]), and therefore not subject to direct regulation of its rates and returns. Accordingly, competition in
broadcasting was left where regulation found it, though subject to the
entry controls on spectrum allocation. Nowhere in the regulatory history
of broadcasting does one find serious proposals to regulate rates or profits directly by amending section 3(h). Nor is there evidence that the
special problems posed by applying such public-utility-type rate regulation to an industry subject to the technical constraints on aggregate output that characterize broadcasting were fully grasped or adequately
assessed.

In contrast, there have been proposals to control or otherwise weigh
station prices at the time of sale. Historically, these proposals have been
grounded on four long-debated assumptions. First, unregulated sales
prices were believed to permit the licensee to sell at prices so high as to
incorporate within them a payment for the license itself. Yet licenses to
use public spectrum were clearly public privileges, not the broadcaster's
to sell. Sale at inflated prices far above original cost was deemed a
wrongful appropriation of valuable public property. Second, to permit
licensees to acquire licenses for early resale was deemed inimical to the
selection of public-spirited, civic-minded licensees willing to bear the

6. It is usually possible to expand the capacity of a public utility to satisfy demand,
whereas a TV station's capacity is fairly strictly limited. Therefore, the goal in utility
regulation is, quite properly, to reduce price and increase output (as well as improve
service) until monopoly profits disappear. In broadcasting, any comparable regulation
of advertising rates and service standards would require rationing of time to advertisers
and transfer of rents to the selected advertisers, unless program quality were so debased, or station time sales and commercials so increased, that the resultant lower
quality of service would lead viewers to turn elsewhere and the demand and supply
of advertising were thereby balanced.

high costs and risks of program innovation, balance, and diversity. Third, sales prices must be kept from rising so high as to compel buyers later to reduce public service or quality, to increase the frequency and length of commercials, or more generally, to strengthen their resistance to non-price regulation (relating to public affairs coverage, etc.), in order to obtain a reasonable return on the purchase price and complementary investments. Finally, it was assumed that unregulated buying and selling might aggravate ownership concentration of broadcast facilities, as well as geographic bunching in large urban centers at the expense of service in remote rural areas.

None of these assumptions seems convincing. Surely high sales prices simply reflect the high profits the purchaser expects. Nor was there any reason why concentration of ownership and geographic bunching could not be handled more directly (which, of course, is precisely what the FCC subsequently did). Nor, even assuming the propriety of a government agency's trying to sustain program quality or the amount of public service, is it clear that this could not be done without reference to station purchase (or sale) prices, say, by defining minimal air time requirements for local or public affairs programming. Nevertheless, the assumptions do illustrate the major concerns about station transfers that preoccupied Congress and the commission throughout a long period in regulatory history, and do identify a number of still sensitive problems in federal regulation today.

Despite considerable debate over such issues, no action was ever taken that effectively controlled transfer prices in broadcasting.[7] There appear to be two main reasons for this. First, there was wide recognition of the conceptual and practical difficulties of allocating franchise value between a broadcaster's ingenuity, enterprise, and risk-bearing on one hand, and a federal licensing system that protects him against competition, on the other. There was heavy reliance instead on careful screening and regulation of station buyers in an attempt to recover in public service something comparable to the franchise value the *seller* had "wrongfully" appropriated.[8] Thus the price at which a station could be sold has never been directly controlled, or with it, the licensee's ability

7. There were several attempts to do so, starting as early as 1926 in the legislative history of the Federal Radio Act of 1927. On the FCC's early abandonment of the effort, see W. Jones, *Regulated Industries* (Mineola, N.Y.: Foundation Press, 1967), p. 1071, in regard to Pacific Radio Corp. 5 FCC 427 (1938), and Selma Seitz, 7 FCC 315, 318 (1939). On congressional abandonment, see citations in H. Levin, "Federal Control of Entry," n. 24.

8. Suppose the seller got only one-half the capitalized total rents when he sold in the bilateral negotiation that ensued, and the buyer got the remainder. Assume further that no changes occurred afterward in technology, tastes, or income distribution, so that the buyer's rents were entirely a riskless transfer from the seller. Clearly, then, seller's portion would go with him when he left the industry, whereas buyer's portion would in theory be "fair game" for the FCC. That indeed is the sense in which this statement describes what has implicitly long been the thrust of broadcast licensing in this country.

to recover his rents at the time of sale. But the *subsequent* service of station buyers has been (and is) closely regulated. In so doing, the FCC has at least paid lip service to recovering (some of) their expected rents *in kind,* and thus limiting the willingness of potential buyers to offer high prices, and the ability of sellers to capture the discounted value of these future rents (or even to retain past rents). That is, the commission has apparently expected to be able to exact from the new buyer, in kind, what it had failed first time round to recover from the *seller,* either in cash or in kind. Where the seller of a station had somehow managed to avoid diverting his economic rents into nonremunerative informational or cultural programming during his own tenure, there were presumably two remedial options. Either the FCC could collect the rents for the whole community through a transfer tax on the seller, *or* it could "try again" afterward, to recover from the buyer in kind.

Second, there was fear that the vital inflow of venture capital for sustained industry growth would be impeded by the mere complexity of the comparative proceedings required to weigh sales price properly as a factor in transfer decisions. Such proceedings, even short of outright control of the sales price, would inevitably impede *exit* and hence deter *entry* by firms unwilling to risk being forced to remain in an industry longer than they found economic. Direct control of transfer price would further exacerbate this problem by reducing the long-run capital gains a new entrant could reasonably expect, and hence his willingness to invest.

In sum, the unregulated sale of valuable federal licenses was sanctioned largely because of (1) the difficulty of pricing the license correctly; (2) a belief that wrongly appropriated franchise values could somehow be at least partly recovered in service; and (3) a fear that any "cure" might be worse than the disease. But what we do not know for sure is whether public officials realized that if transfer price regulation effectively kept licensees from selling at prices that covered all their economic rents, it might *also* discourage them from even *trying* to sell most of their TV properties. Accordingly, the rents would remain intact, and pressures on regulators to divert them into nonremunerative programming would be at least as intense as today. Also, the incumbent's incentives to inhibit the introduction of new entry-opening technology would remain as strong as at present. Regulatory public service programming requirements could in principle continue to deplete licensee rents, for example, until the lowest admissible transfer price included a volume of rents just greater than that which program requirements left untouched.

So much for a brief conceptual analysis of the origin of rents in broadcasting. We turn next to two pieces of quantitative evidence regarding their magnitude and incidence.[9]

9. Our empirical work focuses on television and, though the situation differs in radio, nevertheless very similar problems arise there too with regard to the most valuable

The Magnitude of TV Broadcast Rents

The magnitude of monopoly rents in television broadcasting will be derived and interpreted in three ways: first, from a direct estimation of station intangibles from a sample of sales price and cost data, 1949–70; second, from the estimation of supernormal earnings of all stations in 1975; and third, from a derivation of the rate of return on total assets for all VHF stations—with special reference to the cost of capital in television—in 1973. Data imperfections and measurement problems will be examined in passing, and an attempt will be made to fit the three approaches together.

Estimation of Average Station Intangibles for Stations Sold, 1949–70

Our first study revealed an average price of $3,201,000 for 323 stations sold, 1949–70 (see table 4.1). A gross estimate of the upper bounds of the rents could be derived from the spread between that price and the average original plant cost of all TV stations on the air in those years (excluding the network-owned stations, which do not appear in our sample). In one sense at least, virtually the whole spread can be ascribed to the TV license: no one can operate a television station in this country without a federal license. However, the *average* spread between price and cost does not take accurate account of the true spread for each individual case, and in table 4.1 this could bias our estimate of intangibles upward.

Yet this is no really serious cause of concern here. First, the estimates of current original costs in table 4.1, our best proxy for replacement costs, for reasons stated above tend to be well above initial plant costs generally (especially in light of inflation and market growth). The difference between mean costs and mean prices in any single year would therefore tend to understate the true spread.

Second, the "countervailing" effect of duplicate sales (not revealed in our crude estimate of average intangibles), could be serious only if the duplicate sales were quite numerous, and the absence of rents frequent. There is evidence, however, that duplicate sales are relatively infrequent in our sample,[10] and hence, any distortion very small. One can

---

class-time-power designations of AM broadcast licenses. Indeed the differences in economic values associated with different classes of AM and FM stations, operating with different power, antenna heights, and permissible broadcast hours, under varying levels of permissible competition, not only confirm the existence of rents, but also clarify the incidence of their distribution.

10. In 1966, for instance, we know only that 95 (16 percent) of 592 stations on the air had been sold more than once, whereas in 1956 a scant 7 (1.5 percent) of 457

TABLE 4.1

Derivation of Estimated Average Margins between Sales Price and Current Original Cost in 323 Station Sales, 1949-70

Year	(A) Mean Sales Price ($1000s)	(B) Number of Sales	(C) Original Cost of TV Stations[1] ($1000s)	(D) Number of Stations on Air Excl. O & Os	(E) Cost Per Station ($1000s) (C/D)	(F) Mean Sales Price Minus Mean Original Cost ($1000s) (A minus E)
1949	375	1	36,791	85	433	−58
1950	905	3	44,756	93	481	424
1951	1877	3	(54,433)	(93)	(585)	(1,292)
1952	1633	3	63,110	93	679	954
1953	3304	7	161,512	309	523	2,781
1954	2644	16	(213,463)	(359)	(595)	(2,049)
1955	1139	14	(265,414)	(409)	(649)	(490)
1956	1869	24	317,366	459	691	1,178
1957	3244	26	422,725	485	872	2,372
1958	3001	22	386,669	495	797	2,204
1959	2691	21	423,085	504	840	1,852
1960	2743	16	452,298	515	878	1,865
1961	3862	18	494,898	525	943	2,919
1962	4162	19	530,522	539	984	3,178
1963	6981	14	567,291	550	1,031	5,950
1964	6737	30	616,232	560	1,100	5,637
1965	3849	6	692,967	573	1,209	2,640
1966	2071	12	808,882	593	1,364	707
1967	5215	21	947,123	597	1,587	3,629
1968	3692	18	1,050,235	642	1,636	2,056
1969	3322	13	1,444,916	658	2,196	1,126
1970	5104	16	1,201,064	671	1,790	3,314

SOURCE: Sales prices compiled from lists of all TV transfers published annually in *Broadcasting Yearbook* and *Television Factbook*. Original cost data derived from FCC's Annual Financial Reports for Television Broadcasting.
( ) Denotes straight-line interpolation for data not available.
[1] For whole industry excluding the networks and their owned stations.

Summary

	Average, 1949-70
1: Mean sales price each year	$3,201,000
2: Current original cost per station each year (Col. E/22)	$ 994,000
3: Sales price minus original cost (Col. F/22)	$2,207,000

indeed argue that the rent is an attribute of the property, while who gets it is a separate issue. A second selling price for the same station will then reflect discounted future earnings, just as did the first. Double counting would be a problem only if one were trying to measure the total amount which transferors had extracted from television, something we are not doing here.

We have so far assumed that virtually the whole margin between sales price and current original cost can be ascribed to the TV license. Furthermore, we have concluded that our sample (an approximation of the full universe of major sales over time), underestimates the value of TV properties today, and of the licenses to operate them. However, we also know that some part of total station intangibles reflects going concern value, good will, working capital, and network or talent contracts.[11]

Estimation of Supernormal Earnings in VHF Television

One crude estimate of the share of station intangibles allocatable to goodwill, and so forth, may be approached through another route, by reference to the FCC's annual grouped data on pretax profits and revenues, by revenue class and profit class of stations, and by number of stations therein. For illustrative purposes I shall assume, for argument's sake, that dollar TV economic rents in each revenue class are equal to all income in excess of double that needed to produce the average annual manufacturing profit margin after tax. This assumption is on the low side in that, in 1975, total manufacturing profits before tax were only 7.5 percent of sales, well below a doubling of that sector's 4.6 percent margin after tax as reported by the Federal Trade Commission and Securities Exchange Commission.[12]

---

stations were in that category (see United Research Inc., *The Implications of Limiting Multiple Ownership of Television Stations*, in FCC Docket No. 16068, 1 October 1966, vol. II, appendix table A-9). Furthermore, though 80 (84.2 percent) of the 95 stations on the air in 1966 that were sold more than once were group-owned, only 142 (44 percent) of 323 buyers in our sample were group-owned, and only 232 (71.8 percent) of 323 sellers. Thus our sample includes a smaller percentage of both group buyers and group sellers than the percentage of group-owned stations on the air in 1966 that had been sold more than once.

11. We define "intangibles" here as I = V − K, where V = market values (sales price) of all stations properties when sold, and K = invested tangible capital, that is, original cost of tangible physical assets. One question is how much of the intangibles includes talent defined as human capital of a semi-idiosyncratic (low-mobility) sort. But whether the value of talent or network contracts really determines the magnitude of the station intangibles, is not entirely clear. Restrictive licensing presumably creates a pool of aggregate rents from which scarce, complementary talent (administrative, legal, artistic) can exact its own share. Without a sizable initial pool of such rents, talent scarcities would appear able to exact little beyond their earning capacity outside of broadcasting. Their prices can therefore be properly considered as much rent-determined as rent-determining factors, from a regulatory viewpoint at least.

12. See U.S. Bureau of the Census, *Statistical Abstract of the United States: 1976* (Washington, D.C.: U.S. Government Printing Office, 1976), p. 523.

Nor do profit margins in manufacturing diverge substantially from those for "creative" industries, recognized as the most comparable to broadcasting. Margins for printing and publishing were remarkably close to those for all manufacturing in 1965–75,[13] whereas earlier studies show motion pictures, newspapers, and magazines to have generally lower margins than those for all manufacturing.[14] Using the latter margins as a benchmark could result in higher estimates of "excess revenues" for television. Finally, students of broadcasting have preferred the profit margin to returns on tangible property as a measure of television's profitability, and often compare TV's margins on revenues with margins in manufacturing.[15]

As summarized in table 4.2, our procedure was as follows: using FCC's grouped financial data for 1975, I first identified all groups of stations whose profit margin on revenues was at least 9 percent (roughly double the after-tax margin for all manufacturing corporations). In 1975, 352 of 398 profitable VHF stations earned the required 9 percent on revenues, and 61 of 86 profitable UHFs also did so. Second, I tabulated the aggregate estimated revenues of all profitable classes of stations as the midpoint of the narrow range for which each revenue class is reported, $4 to $5 million being $4.5 million, and so forth. Third, I calculated each station class's "excess margin" as its gross profit margin minus 9 percent (a crude proxy for a competitive profit margin). Fourth, this excess margin was multiplied by the aggregate revenue for each station class and we then summed all excess revenues for all 352 stations earning them. This totaled $416,900,000, our crude approximation of gross economic rents, or that portion of total station revenues in excess of the amount necessary to attract the station's needed capital and labor inputs. These rents were actually retained, in this example, out of the $1,643,950,000 in revenues of our 352 profitable VHFs. Thus, my estimated rents constituted 25.3 percent of aggregate revenues, and were also equal to 80 percent of the stations' estimated profits of $519,930,000.

A similar calculation for UHF stations was of $5,500,000 excess margins out of $91,300,000 total revenues, for 61 UHF stations which also earned more than 9 percent on revenues.

In short, gross average VHF monopoly rents in 1975 in this example would be some $1,200,000 per station for 352 stations whose profit margins exceeded 9 percent, and average UHF rents some $90,000 for 61 comparable UHF stations. The average rents for *all* 492 VHFs on the air,

13. Ibid.
14. See Levin, "Economic Effects of Broadcast Licensing," *Journal of Political Economics* (April 1964), pp. 153–55; Levin, *Invisible Resource*, pp. 368–69.
15. See Roger Noll, Merton Peck, and John McGowan, *Economic Aspects of Television Regulation* (Washington, D.C.: Brookings Institution, 1973), pp. 16–17. See also CBS testimony in Senate Commerce Committee, *Television Inquiry*, part IV, 86th Congress, 2d sess., pp. 2017–33; and statement by David Blank, in FCC Docket No. 12285, attachments and discussion therein.

TABLE 4.2

*Illustrative Estimation of TV Station Rents in 1975
from Grouped Income and Revenue Data*

		VHF Stations	UHF Stations
A.	Number of Profitable Stations	398	86
B.	All Stations Reporting	462	166
C.	All Stations On Air	492	177
D.	Number of profitable stations earning at least 9% on revenues	352	61
E.	Aggregate revenue of all stations in D	$1,643,950,000	$91,300,000
F.	Aggregate profits of all stations in D	$519,930,000	$12,300,000
G.	Estimated Rents*	$416,900,000	$5,470,000
H.	Estimated rents per Station (1) Earning rents (row G/row D) (2) All stations (row G/row C)	$1,184,000 $847,000	$90,000 $31,000

SOURCE: Derived from FCC, *Financial Report for TV Broadcasting—
1975*, table 8; 1976 Statistical Abstract of the U.S., tables 858-59, p. 523.
*Aggregate revenue for each station class in E times its excess margin, or
gross profit margin minus 9 percent.

and all 177 UHF stations, were $847,000 and $31,000 per station, respectively. Comparable figures for 308 profitable VHF in 1965 estimated
the same way as above, imply excess returns of about $887,000 per station
that year. As so defined, VHF rents over the decade were relatively stable, rising by 35 percent with a 48 percent rise in income, a 114 percent
rise in revenue, and a 56 percent rise in wholesale prices.

One could of course argue that the highly profitable VHF stations simply belong to licensees with valuable talent and network contracts and
who are themselves "talented." Nevertheless, the FCC's profit and expense data by revenue class of station provide no information on interest
charges. Inclusion of the latter would have resulted in still higher VHF
returns on revenues than those utilized in table 4.2. Furthermore, my
profit data are *net* of all talent, film, license fees, royalties, and administrative costs. Such costs are particularly high for VHF stations, especially
for the largest revenue classes of stations, and undoubtedly include
sizable scarcity rents of their own. Finally, my profit data also exclude
the cost of maintaining fixed capital intact, and hence clearly report
"pure" profit. On all three counts, the estimation of aggregate rents in
table 4.2 would appear to be a lower-bound estimate.[16]

Superficially, these estimates (and those in table 4.1) appear to imply
that over one-half of total intangible assets of VHF stations sold between

16. See generally, *Federal Communications Commission, Television Broadcast Financial Data for 1975* (Washington, D.C., 1976), table 11–12.

1949 and 1970 may be capitalized as pure economic rent. However, a more suggestive comparison would be for estimated rents and intangibles in, say, the years 1963–70, or for an even shorter time period, 1964–66. The proportion of intangibles seemingly capitalized as pure rents in those more limited periods would be somewhat smaller, about 38 percent and 29 percent, respectively.

Nevertheless, such comparisons could be misleading and must be interpreted with care. First, though there is strictly speaking no reason why we cannot compare income flows and capital stock (here, intangibles), estimated supernormal earnings for 1975 should more properly be compared to intangibles for stations sold *that* year, not with an average of intangibles for 323 sales over a twenty-two-year period characterized by inflation and market growth. Second, the composition of my two sets of data is quite disparate. Thus the estimates in table 4.2 are derived from data for all 628 stations reporting in 1975, whereas table 4.1 tabulates data for only one-half that number of station sales (323), from 1949 to 1970. Indeed, the largest number of sales in any single year in table 4.1 was thirty (for 1964), only one-nineteenth of the 560 stations on the air then. Nor is my sample representative of the full universe of sales since 1949, let alone reflective of the value of stations during the period that were never sold.

Any comparison of estimates derived from sample data so different in their composition may be misleading, wholly aside from distortions due to inflation and market growth.

Estimation of an Excess Rate of Return on Total VHF Assets over the Cost of Capital

The main problem with my estimation in the preceding section is that it does not take account of the special risks in broadcasting. It has been frequently stated that creative industries like television are much riskier than manufacturing generally, and have capital turnover, operating ratios, and intangible assets closer in relative size to one another's than to manufacturing's.[17] In addition, the networks appear to face, in some ways, larger risks than their station affiliates.[18] Therefore, I will now take explicit account of the risk factors by utilizing an alternative procedure.

Toward this end I estimate the rate of return on total assets for VHF television in 1975, and compare it with a recent estimate of television's cost of capital in 1973. The difference between the two—a measure of

17. See CBS testimony in Senate Commerce Committee, *Television Inquiry*, pp. 2017–27; Levin, "Economic Effects of Broadcast Licensing," pp. 154–55; Levin, "Economic Structure and the Regulation of Television," *Quarterly Journal of Economics* (August 1958), pp. 445–46; and Douglas Webbink, "The Value of the Frequency Spectrum Allocated to Specific Users," *IEEE Transactions of Electromagnetic Compatibility* (August 1977), p. 346.

18. Levin, "Economic Effects of Broadcast Licensing," pp. 155–57.

the supernormal returns that industry enjoyed in 1975—can be multiplied by total VHF assets that year to generate a rough measure of economic rents. In this case, however, unlike the estimation procedure for table 4.2, I do in fact take television's riskiness into account.

Let us first derive alternative rates of return in table 4.3. Pretax income for all VHF stations in 1975 (including network-owned stations) was $561,900,000, to which the industry's interest payments of $28,600,000 have been added. The combined return of $590,500,000 is then applied to two estimates of total assets, one assuming that intangibles are 30 percent of total assets, the other, that they are only 20 percent.[19] The resultant rates of return are 67.2 percent and 76.8 percent, respectively.

But what of the cost of capital in TV broadcasting? Here I have used Crandall's estimate that this was about 25 percent in 1973.[20] The excess rate of return actually earned in VHF television in 1975, over this minimal cost of capital, would be 42.2 percent (assuming intangibles to be 30 percent of total assets), and 51.8 percent (with intangibles 20 percent). Finally, in the former case, estimated rents would be $370,600,000 for 477 VHF stations, and in the latter case, some $398,100,000 (see table 4.4, estimates A and B).

A Further Comparison of the Results

Even when applying a cruder yardstick of supernormal profits (as in estimate C), the results are very similar. Thus, taking from the pretax profit margin on sales for all VHF stations in 1975 (27.4 percent) the margin for all manufacturing corporations (8.8 percent), and multiplying the difference (of 18.6 percent) by aggregate net VHF revenues of $2,157,800,000, I estimate $401,351,000 as revenues in excess of those needed to attract the industry's necessary investment inputs that year.

19. The second estimate is taken from Robert Crandall's examination of the balance sheets of five group-owned broadcasters, 1975–76. See his "Regulation of Television Broadcasting—How Costly Is the Public Interest?" *Regulation* (January/February 1978), p. 33, note 5. The first estimate is based on my own study of ten group owner balance sheets, where intangibles, film licenses or contracts, franchise rights, and so on, are itemized. Intangibles averaged 27 percent of total assets for these companies, whereas intangibles plus film rights, and so forth, averaged 33 percent. In estimating total assets on that assumption, we simply divided the depreciated cost of tangible physical property by .7.

20. Crandall derived this as follows: first, he calculated a measure (beta) of systematic risk for the average broadcasting stock listed in the New York Stock Exchange, 1973, at roughly 1.7. Second, he estimated the after-tax cost of equity capital as the return on risk free investments of 7 percent; plus 1.7 times the expected risk premium (of 6 percent) on the entire portfolio of risky assets available to investors that year, or a total of 7 percent plus 1.7 times 6 percent, or 17.2 percent. He further estimated the before-tax cost of equity as no more than 33 percent. Third, he noted that broadcasters paid some 9 percent on debt in 1973 and were levered at a 1:2 debt-equity ratio. Therefore, Crandall concluded that the before-tax cost of capital for broadcasting was equal to (2/3) times 33 percent plus (1/3) times 9 percent, or a 25 percent rate of return on assets. (These more detailed computations appear in a prepublished version of the paper cited above in note 19, and are set forth here with the author's permission.)

TABLE 4.3

Derivation of Rates of Return on Total Assets, Profit Margins, and Capital Turnover Ratios for VHF Television Stations and All Manufacturing Corporations, 1975

		All VHF Stations (including network-owned) ($ millions)	All Manufacturing Corporations ($ billions)
(1)	Pretax income	561.9	79.8
(2)	Interest	28.6	(14.3)
(3)	Return on total invested capital (1 + 2)	590.5	(94.1)
(4)	Depr. cost net tangible assets	614.8	811.5
(5)	Estimated Total Assets where VHF Tangible Assets =		
(6)	(a) 70% total assets (TA/.7)	878.3	
(7)	(b) 80% total assets (TA/.8)	768.5	
(8)	Net revenue	2157.8	1066.7
(9)	Total return/revenue (3/8)	27.4%	8.8%
(10)	Revenue/total assets		1.31
(11)	(a) where total assets = (6)	2.46	
(12)	(b) where total assets = (7)	2.81	
(13)	Total return/total assets		11.6%
(14)	(a) where total assets = (6)	67.2%	
(15)	(b) where total assets = (7)	76.8%	

SOURCE: Television data mainly from Federal Communications Commission, *Report on Television Broadcast Financial Data for 1975* (Washington, D.C., 1976). However, line 6 derived in part from Moody's Industrials, 1976-77, and line 7 in part from R. Crandall, "Regulation of Television Broadcasting—How Costly Is the Public Interest?" *Regulation* (January/February 1978).

Manufacturing data, with one exception, from U.S. Bureau of the Census, *Statistical Abstract of the United States:* 1975 (Washington, D.C.: U.S. Government Printing Office, 1975). Interest was, however, estimated as follows: first we calculated the ratio of interest to debt (defined as total assets minus net worth) in 1972, for the Internal Revenue Service, *Statistics of Income for 1972—Corporation Income Tax Returns* (Washington, D.C.: U.S. Government Printing Office, 1977). Then we applied this ratio to a comparable estimate of debt for 1975. The product was a crude projection of interest for that year.

Placing the initial estimate of rents (by revenue class of stations) of $416,900,000 at one extreme (estimate D), my additional estimates range down to a low of $370,600,000 (estimate A) and include two alternate estimates in between (estimates B and C).

We note here that the better measure of income plus interest yields a more accurate rate of return and profit margin than the initial estimate, though the latter is better able to capture the varied earnings experience of different classes of stations than crude industry-wide aggregates can. Taking risks into account in estimates A and B, the main question is whether I assume intangibles to be 30 percent or 20 percent of total assets. I found intangibles to be somewhat larger than Crandall. However, the number of group broadcasters whose balance sheets were sufficiently detailed to make this evaluation was very small (only ten in my study, and five in his). Nevertheless, I recognize that stations will normally have smaller intangibles than networks. At any rate, my second

TABLE 4.4

Alternative Estimates of Economic Rents for VHF Television Stations, 1975
(including network-owned stations)

Part A

	(1)	(2)	(3)	(4)
	Assets or Revenues (in $ 000,000s)	Supernormal Rate of Return or Profit Margin	Estimated Aggregate Rents ($ millions) (Col. 1 × 2)	Estimated Rents per Station ($ millions) (Col. 3/492)
Estimate Total assets for 492 VHF stations = tangible assets				
A 70% total assets	878.3	42.2%	370.6	.753
B 80% total assets	768.5	51.8%	398.1	.809
C Total revenues for 492 VHF stations	2157.8	18.8%	401.4	.785
D Total revenues for 352 VHF stations earning over 9% on sales by revenue class of station	1643.9		416.9	.847

Part B: Derivation of Part A, Column 2

	(1)	(2)	(3)	(4)	(5)	(6)
	VHF Rate of Return	VHF Cost of Capital	Supernormal Rate of Return (Col. 1 minus Col. 2)	VHF Profit Margin	All Mfg. Corp. Profit Margin	Supernormal Profit Margin (Col. 4 minus Col. 5)
Estimate A	67.2%	25%	42.2%			
Estimate B	76.8%	25%	51.8%			
Estimate C				27.4%	8.8%	18.6%
Estimate D	Estimated by revenue class of station—see table 4.2.					

SOURCE: Table 4.3.

rents estimate ($398,100,000), and the midpoint between the first two ($384,400,000), are both quite close to estimate C ($401,400,000), itself derived from estimated supernormal profit margins on sales.

Of particular interest, then, is the closeness of all three estimates. That is, whether or not risks are explicitly taken into account (estimates A and B), or a comparison made between VHF profit margins and margins for all manufacturing (estimates C, D), aggregate estimated rents vary relatively little. Estimate D, derived from revenue class of station data for profitable VHFs only, is of course somewhat higher on that score.

TABLE 4.5
Number, Sales Prices, and Economic Attributes of TV Stations
Sold in 277 Homogeneous Markets, 1949-70

Market Type		Number of Stations in Market						All Market Sizes
		1	2	3	4	5	7	
VHF-only markets	Mean price (in $1000s)	1791	2161	5768	4506	5183	3815	3661
	Number	73	60	95	25	3	5	261
UHF-only markets	Mean price (in $1000s)	514	3419	2306	–	1941	–	1909
	Number	5	3	6		2		16
VHF-only markets	Mean TV homes (in 1000s)	157	187	384	529	732	2759	337
	Number	72	60	95	25	2	5	259
UHF-only markets	Mean TV homes (in 1000s)	158	296	214	–	336	–	227
	Number	5	3	6		2		16
VHF-only markets	Mean hourly rate ($)	313	422	779	872	1200	1525	600
	Number	57	53	81	23	2	4	220
UHF-only markets	Mean hourly rate ($)	195	517	367	–	475	–	352
	Number	5	3	3		2		13
VHF-only markets	Mean visual power (in kilowatts)	1050	1597	1479	1806	3160	1129	1430
	Number	73	60	95	25	3	5	261
UHF-only markets	Mean visual power (in kilowatts)	2289	1620	1873	–	1077	–	1856
	Number	5	3	6		2		16

SOURCE: See table 4.1.

Regulatory Impact versus Owner Attributes
as Determinants of Implicit Rents

Because these industry aggregates and simple averages hide important differences in the rents associated with major rent-yielding station attributes, I have tabulated more detailed price data in tables 4.5 and 4.6. Thus, in table 4.5, compare the prices of stations sold in markets where all stations operated on the same class of channel, VHF *or* UHF. There, regardless of number of stations in the market, VHF prices appear consistently higher than UHF. These price differences may indeed reflect VHF's substantially higher hourly rates (and associated earnings record), and the more numerous TV homes normally available to it, but not any advantage in authorized signal power.

Next, table 4.6 reports estimates for mean TV homes, visual power, highest hourly rates and sales prices, and does so by channel type and age of station. Note, first, that mean prices decline as licensees operate higher in the spectrum, a pattern which may in part reflect the fact that: (1) the lowest VHF channels provide the clearest signal with the least visual or aural power; (2) the higher VHFs offer the next-best signal quality, though with much higher power requirements; and (3) the UHFs offer lowest quality with the highest power requirements.[21] Note secondly, that the oldest stations, whether located on low or high VHF frequencies, were generally sold in the largest markets. (The sole exception is that the older, low-channel VHF sales took place in markets no larger than those where the "new" UHF sales occurred.)

In sum, the economic advantages associated with different classes of TV licenses appear to vary considerably, and with them presumably also the magnitude of any *quid pro quo* regulators, or legislators, can hope to recover for the public as a whole.

In further analysis of the key determinants of aggregate rents now extracted by broadcast licensees, special account must be taken of a host of policy variables and owner affiliations, including but not limited to those just cited. My hypothesis is that the price of a TV station will vary, other things being equal, with the size of market to which regulation permits entry. But price depends also on still other, more explicit policy variables—the number of stations permitted to enter any market, their assigned channel type, signal power, and age relative to the administrative hiatus in all TV licensing, 1948–52. Finally, I want to compare the relative importance of each of these several policy variables, and their

21. For greater precision, one should really know the variation in cost per kilowatt of effective antenna power as a function of frequency, something I have been unable to determine.

TABLE 4.6

Number, Sales, Prices, and Economic Attributes of TV Stations Sold, 1949-70, by Age and Channel Type of Station, for 323 Sales

Channel Type	Age of Station		TV Homes in Market (in 1000s)	Highest Network Hourly Rate before Sale ($)	Visual Power (kilowatts)	Sales Price (in $1000s)
Low VHF (channels 2-7)	Total	Mean value	314	624	891	4206
		Number of stations	139	118	140	140
	Old (pre-52)	Mean value	511	1025	635	6845
		Number of stations	29	22	30	30
	New (post-52)	Mean value	262	532	960	3486
		Number of stations	110	96	110	110
High VHF (channels 8-13)	Total	Mean value	415	651	2056	3527
		Number of stations	149	130	151	151
	Old (pre-52)	Mean value	385	1579	1768	6389
		Number of stations	17	12	17	17
	New (post-52)	Mean value	290	557	2093	3164
		Number of stations	132	118	134	134
UHF (channels 14+)	Total	Mean value	560	358	2195	2078
		Number of stations	32	27	32	32
	Old (pre-52)	Mean value	–	–	–	–
		Number of stations	–	–	–	–
	New (post-52)	Mean value	560	358	2195	2078
		Number of stations	32	27	32	32
All channels (VHF + UHF)	Total	Mean value	386	611	1565	3678
		Number of stations	320	275	323	323
	Old (pre-52)	Mean value	834	1220	1045	6680
		Number of stations	46	34	47	47
	New (post-52)	Mean value	311	525	1653	3166
		Number of stations	274	241	276	276

SOURCE: See table 4.1.

structural consequences, with those of each station seller's (and buyer's) major owner affiliations (network, group, and newspaper).[22] However, most of that discussion must be reserved for chapter 6.

I propose to explore these related questions here, and in chapter 6, using an interactive regression methodology described in Appendix I.

Estimated Impacts of Alternative Policy Factors

Let us now turn to table 4.7 and the changes in sales price (adjusted for inflation) due to changes in alternative policy variables. The reported coefficients actually record dollar changes in sales price due to changes in the independent factors listed in columns 1 and 2, when all other factors are held constant. The statistical significance of each coefficient is further designated by superscripts, my major focus being on significance at the 1 percent, 5 percent, or 10 percent confidence levels.

Clearly, a restrictive licensing policy will have a significant bolstering impact on the price of any TV station whose competitors are subject to it. Thus reducing the number of VHFs in the market, say, from four to three, other things being equal, will raise sales price by $3,627,000, an amount statistically greater than zero at the .01 confidence level. In contrast, a regulatory decision to raise video power by even as much as 900 KW (three-fifths of the sample mean of power) will raise price by only $168,638 \times 3 = $505,900, about 10 percent of the mean price. This small absolute impact on price seemingly reflects the FCC's deliberate attempt to equalize each station's geographic service range regardless of topography or channel type.

Additionally relevant here are the impact of age of station and channel type (see table 4.8). In regard to age, a license granted before the administrative hiatus in TV licensing from 1948 to 1952 confers significantly more economic value than one granted afterward. Indeed my test simultaneously considers the impact of pre-1952 enfranchisement (the policy variable) and age in months at the time of sale. Older stations, regardless of when licensed, are known to have preferred advertiser, network, and talent contracts, superior expertise and community contacts. Finally, in some measure I corrected for the effect on price of date of sale, first by deflating price data by an implicit GNP price deflator, and second, by coding all independent variables over the 1949–70 period studied, at the time of each sale in the sample. (See Appendix II, p. 457.)

My tabulated findings on age can be illustrated very simply as follows. On the average, a station licensed in 1950 (pre-1952) and sold in 1953, would have commanded $1,487,000 more had it remained on the air

22. Buyer and seller dummies permit us to estimate the impact of switching from one type of buyer (and seller) to another, on station sales price. The price reflects the buyer's future earnings expectations (and hence expected rents), and it also determines the seller's realized rents at the time of sale.

TABLE 4.7
Sensitivity of TV Station Sales Prices to Changes in Regulatory Policy Variables, 1949-70*

(1)	(2)	(3)
Class of Station in Test	Postulated Change in Independent Variable	Unit Increase in Price (× $1000)
All UHF	Switch from independent to network	7318[a] (2.68)
All independent	Switch from UHF to VHF	6827[a] (2.58)
All stations	Reduce from 4 to 3 VHF in market	3267[a] (4.82)
All stations licensed before 1952	Increase age by 200%	1487[a] (3.49)
All VHF	Switch from independent to network	1103 (0.79)
All network affiliates	Switch from UHF to VHF	613 (0.47)
All stations licensed after 1952	Increase age by 200%	455 (1.18)
All stations	Increase visual power by 300 KW	169[b] (2.18)

Mean price = $5,110 × $1000
Sample size = 310

*The upper number in each cell in column 3 is a regression coefficient denoting the absolute dollar impact of the change postulated in column 2, for the station class indicated in column 1. Station attributes in column 1 are "given" where attributes in column 2 are interacted with other variables in equation. For the basic equation on which the table is based, and derivation of sample interacted coefficients, see equation 1 in Appendix to this chapter. Parenthetical numbers in column 3 are t-values which denote statistical significance, further designated by superscripts to coefficients there, as follows (two-tailed test): a = 1 percent confidence level; b = 5 percent level; c = 10 percent level. All price data are in 1958 dollars as adjusted by implicit price deflators for total GNP, 1949-70 (1958 = 100). See Economic Report to the President (January 1972), Appendix table B-3.
    INTERPRETATION: For UHF stations in row 1, a switch from independent to network status acts to raise price by $7,317,800, taking all other factors into account. That amount, in column 3, is significantly greater than zero at the 1 percent confidence level. Other results subject to similar interpretation.

three times longer after licensed ($3 \times 3 = 9$) and been sold in 1959. Similarly, a station licensed in 1953 (post-1952) and sold in 1955 would have commanded $455,000 more had it been sold instead six years after licensing ($2 \times 3 = 6$), again in 1959. Age enhances the price of both these stations, but appears to favor the pre-1952 (and hence VHF) licensee more than the other, even after taking account of channel type. Is the difference between the absolute impacts in these two cases significant?

To answer this question I must refer to the second order coefficients in table 4.8, column 5. That coefficient indicates the size of the absolute

TABLE 4.8
Sales Price Impact of Station Age, 1949-70*

(1)	(2)	(3)	(4)	(5)
Station Licensed before 1952	Price Increase (× $1,000)	Station Licensed after 1952	Price Increase (× $1,000)	Difference between columns 2 and 4 (× $1,000)
Increase age by 200%	1487[a] (3.49)	Increase age by 200%	455 (1.18)	1032[a] (4.25)

Sample mean price = $5,110 × $1,000
Sample size = 310

*Coefficients and t-values reported as in table 4.7. derived from table 4.11 estimating equation 1 in Appendix 4A, with all price data again adjusted for inflation.
[a]Denotes statistical significance at 1 percent confidence level.

INTERPRETATION: For stations licensed before 1952, a tripling of their age before sale, other things equal, will raise price by $1,487,000 (column 2), but only by $455,000 for stations licensed after 1952 (column 4). The difference in these impacts, of $1,032,000 (column 5), is itself statistically significant. Therefore, age has a statistically greater impact for older stations (column 1) than newer stations (column 3).

difference between the impact of the two age variables on sales price, with and without the presence of other factors. Here the absolute difference in the impact on price of the assumed tripling of the number of months that the two classes of stations (those licensed before and after 1952) remained on the air before being sold, would be $1,032,300. This sum is significantly greater than zero at the .01 level, and I therefore conclude that the cessation of all licensing during the years 1948–52, while the initial TV Allocation Plan was being instituted, has had a significant differential impact on the price (and implicit economic rents) of stations licensed before and after that period. This regulatory impact is indeed significant regardless of age of station more generally, or of market size, number of competitors, channel type, network, group, or newspaper affiliations.

But what of channel type itself? Does that factor too have the magnitude of economic impact so often ascribed to it?

Impact of Channel Allocations and Network Affiliation

The nation's Allocation Plan has produced significant differences between the current value of VHF and UHF stations today. By providing for relatively few homogeneous markets (those with at least four VHF or four UHF stations), moreover, the Plan has necessarily also impeded new network entry. This has further perpetuated the earnings disparity between network affiliates (who enjoy the benefits of large-scale program distribution and national advertiser income), and independents (who normally do not).

These several impacts of channel allocation are clearly suggested by the coefficients in tables 4.7 and 4.9. Thus the performance of UHF outlets is so poor, relatively, and that of VHF so strong, that the bolstering effect of a network contract for UHF ($7,317,500) is significantly larger than for a VHF ($1,103,760).[23] In contrast, a VHF license raises the (relatively weak) independent's price by $6,826,960 over the price of a UHF independent, though only $613,200 over a UHF when both are (relatively prosperous) network affiliates.

The relative VHF advantage over UHF for any independent is presumably greater than when both are affiliates for four reasons. First, independents cluster in the top fifty markets, whereas affiliates are distributed among all two hundred. Second, VHF signal power appears to vary with population density for otherwise comparable geographic market areas (see table 4.5). Therefore, the audiences which VHF transmitters can technically reach will be larger for independents than for affiliates as a whole. Third, the inferior UHF signals can reach the inner market areas comparably for all size markets, but their more limited penetration of the outer perimeter (than VHF) results in a greater relative loss of potential audience in the more populous markets. Fourth, though we include market size in our regression equations, we were unable to interact our channel type dummy with TV homes in calculating the relative VHF impact on independent and affiliate sales prices. This was due to problems of collinearity, time and resource limitations, and the many other interactions we sought to pursue.[24]

All in all, given the serious technical differences between VHF and UHF, the intermixture of both channel types in most markets has clearly bolstered the current value of VHF grants, and lowered UHF values. The related failure to go to an all-UHF or all-VHF system, as urged by a number of proponents, has necessarily had a similar effect. Accordingly, the FCC's effective allocation of UHF and VHF channels nationally has had a substantial differential impact on the capitalized earnings expectations of licensees operating on either. Finally, any licensee lacking both a network contract and a VHF grant will be very hard pressed indeed, and either attribute will have considerable value to him. But once having one of these attributes, possession of the second appears to add little additional benefit. This is most vividly apparent in table 4.9, when I compare the impact of being *both* network and VHF over being neither (+$7,931,160), with the impact of network affiliation for a UHF (+$7,317,520), or of VHF for an independent (+$6,826,960).[25]

23. The absolute difference in price here is $6,214,000, significantly greater than zero at the .05 confidence level.

24. See Appendix II, pp. 462–66, and more generally, Appendix I, p. 420. To evaluate my textual exercises, finally, see Appendix 4A in particular for computation procedures and estimating equations.

25. None of these three dollar impacts is significantly different from either of the other two.

TABLE 4.9

Sensitivity of TV Station Sales Prices to Changes in Network Status and Channel Type, 1949-70*

(1) Station Class	(2) Change in Independent Variable	(3) Price Increase (× $1,000)	(4) Station Class	(5) Change in Independent Variable	(6) Price Increase (× $1,000)	(7) Difference between columns 3 and 6
All UHF	Switch from independent to network	7318[a] (2.68)	All independent	Switch from UHF to VHF	6827[a] (2.58)	491 (0.26)
			All VHF	Switch from independent to network	1104 (0.79)	6214[b] (2.15)
			All network	Switch from UHF to VHF	613 (0.47)	6705[c] (1.94)
All independent	Switch from UHF to VHF	6827[a] (2.58)	All VHF	Switch from independent to network	1104 (0.79)	5723[c] (1.68)
			All network	Switch from UHF to VHF	613 (0.47)	6214[b] (2.15)
All stations	Switch from independent UHF to network VHF	7931[a] (3.16)	All UHF	Switch from independent to network	7318[a] (2.68)	613 (0.47)
			All independent	Switch from UHF to VHF	6827[a] (2.58)	1104 (0.79)

Sample mean price = $5,110 × $1,000
Sample size = 310

*The results here are essentially similar to those in table 4.7, with coefficients and T-values recorded (here in columns 3 and 6), for postulated changes in independent variables (in columns 2 and 5), for "given" classes of stations (columns 1 and 4). The main additional information appears in column 7, which records the difference between the absolute impact of a postulated change in column 2, and one in column 5. For estimating equation and derivation of interacted coefficients, see Appendix 4A, equation 1 in table 4.11.

INTERPRETATION: By way of illustration (at row 1), for UHF stations a switch from independent to network status, holding other factors constant, will raise price by $7,318,000, significant at the 1 percent confidence level (column 3). This impact can then be compared to impacts in column 5 where, say, at row 2, we see that for VHF stations, a comparable switch from independent to network status raises price by only $1,104,000, and where the difference between these impacts, $6,214,000 (in column 7), is itself statistically significant. Therefore, a network tie has a significantly larger impact on price for UHF than for VHF stations.

Incidence of Rents among Alternative Classes of Network Affiliates

The incidence of rents among network affiliates, group, and newspaper grantees will be more fully discussed in chapter 6. Here it suffices only to synopsize my major findings.

Note first, that the results in table 4.10 depict the response of sales price to a postulated change in market size for network affiliates by channel type of license, when all other factors in the equation are held constant. The number of competitors are of course taken into account *within* each market class, in markets with respectively 250,000, 388,000, and 1,000,000 TV homes.[26] Therefore, the change in homes from 250,000 to 1,000,000 as such does not reflect license limitation. But we also know that TV homes rise more rapidly than the number of stations as we switch from the smallest to the largest markets.[27] For that reason at least, the postulated quadrupling of homes (from 250,000 to 1,000,000) in table 4.10 does serve as a proxy for license limitation.

Bearing this in mind, it is of interest that, for every market examined, (1) the value of a network tie is significantly larger for a UHF than a VHF station (for reasons explained earlier); but that (2) the impact of switching from 250,000 to 1,000,000 TV homes is relatively greater for a network VHF than a network UHF.[28] Stated otherwise, the impoverished UHFs derive relatively more benefit from a national network than the wealthier VHFs, but network VHFs better improve their relative ability to extract rents when the size of market in which they operate is assumed to rise. Specifically, the impact of network affiliation on a VHF price is only +$434,400 at 250,000 homes but a full +$4,701,400 at 1,000,000 homes, a more than ten-fold increase, whereas the comparable increase for UHF is only about double, from $3,725,400 to $7,997,500. In short, the network VHFs appear considerably better able than net-

26. These three rounded levels of TV homes, selected for expository convenience, are well within the actual range of my sample. Note also that the spread between 250,000 and 1,000,000 is just short of one standard deviation in my data, whereas 388,000 is the actual sample mean of TV homes. Thus my postulated small-market level, 250,000, is set about two-thirds of the mean value of homes, and my big-market level, 1,000,000, about three times the mean. These outer bounds are convenient and entirely reasonable numbers.

27. See my paper in R. Caves and M. Roberts. eds., *Regulating the Product—Quality and Variety* (Cambridge, Mass.: Ballinger, 1975), pp. 224–25; also Levin, *The Invisible Resource*, pp. 340–41.

28. "Large" and "small" markets may both have comparable geographic areas, but their population density varies considerably, and hence the chances for the (technically superior) VHF signal to reach more viewers for advertisers than UHF signals can. With potential VHF power the same across different-sized markets, the superior VHF signal is underutilized where population is in fact less dense. UHF signals, on the other hand, could more reliably reach viewers within the community of license than those at the market's outer perimeter. Therefore, while UHF's absolute audience potential is greater in larger than in smaller markets, its relative access to viewers (compared to VHF) would be smaller in those larger markets.

TABLE 4.10

Impact on TV Station Sales Price of Changes in Market Size for Stations with Designated Network Status and Channel Type, 1949-70*

(1) Station Class	(2) Change in Independent Variable	(3) First-level TV Homes (× 1,000)	(4) Price Increase (× $1,000)	(5) Station Class	(6) Second-level TV Homes (× 1,000)	(7) Price Increase (× $1,000)	(8) Difference between columns 4 and 7
	Switch from:						
UHF	Independent to network	1,000	7,998[a] (3.04)	UHF	388	4,885[c] (1.65)	3,513[a] (3.93)
VHF	Independent to network	1,000	4,701[a] (3.05)	VHF	388	1,191 (0.88)	3,510[a] (3.93)
UHF	Independent to network	388	4,885[c] (1.65)	UHF	250	3,725 (1.35)	760[a] (3.93)
Independent	UHF to VHF		4,170 (1.61)	Network		874 (0.69)	3,291 (1.16)
UHF	Independent to network	250	3,725 (1.35)	UHF	1,000	7,998[a] (3.05)	-4,272[a] (3.93)
VHF	Independent to network	388	1,191 (0.88)	VHF	250	434 (0.31)	757[a] (3.93)
VHF	Independent to network	250	434 (0.31)	VHF	1,000	4,701[a] (3.05)	-4,267[a] (3.93)
UHF	Independent to network	1,000	7,998[a] (3.04)	VHF	1,000	4,701[a] (3.05)	3,297 (1.16)
UHF	Independent to network	388	4,485[c] (1.65)	VHF	388	1,191 (0.88)	3,294 (1.16)
UHF	Independent to network	250	3,725 (1.35)	VHF	250	434 (0.31)	3,291 (1.16)

Sample mean price = $5110 × $1000
Sample size = 310

*With two exceptions, the results reported are similar to those in table 4.9. Coefficients and t-values are again recorded (here in columns 4 and 7), for postulated changes in independent variables (column 2), for given classes of stations (columns 1 and 5). The additional information includes, in columns 3 and 6, the TV homes levels at which the coefficients are interacted and, in column 8, a set of second order coefficients. As in table 4.9, all price data adjusted for inflation.

INTERPRETATION: By way of illustration (at row 1), for UHF stations a switch from independent to network status will raise price by $7,998,000 when TV homes equal 1,000,000, but by only $4,885,000 when homes equal 388,000. The first impact is statistically greater than zero at the 1 percent level, and the second impact at the 10 percent level. Finally, the dollar difference between these two impacts in column 8 ($3,513,000), is also statistically significant. Therefore, the absolute impact on price of a switch from independent to network is significantly larger at the 1,000,000 homes level than at the 388,000 homes level. For estimating equation and derivation of interacted coefficients again see equation 3 in table 4.11.

work UHFs to improve their share of economic rents in the switch from small to large markets, although the absolute increments in both cases remain almost the same, around $4,000,000.

Incidence of Rents among Group and Newspaper Licensees

The distribution of rents will be delineated still another way in chapter 6 (table 6.11), where we have calculated the impact of adding 100,000 TV homes on the prices of stations with and without designated owner attributes and network ties.[29] In every case studied, stations with any two (or all three) designated attributes (newspaper, group, or network), are seen to enjoy significantly larger price increases from additional homes than stations without such attributes. All of this implies that the incidence of rents among stations appears to favor the affiliated classes; that is, newspaper, group, and network affiliates appear to be in a better position than stations not so linked to extract benefits from the restraints imposed by restrictive licensing.

Appendix 4A. Estimating Equations and Computation Procedures for Interacted Impacts

This appendix will demonstrate how I derived the impacts reported in several text tables above, and again in chapter 6. Such computational exercises should enable the reader to replicate similar impacts involving regression analysis of station data reported elsewhere in the book. In each case reference will be made to a particular estimating equation, and the demonstration will mainly show how an impact can be derived from so-called interacted coefficients, those composed of two or more separate components.

I have of course already gone through such an exercise in chapter 3 in regard to impacts derived from interacted coefficients in a major market equation. Nevertheless, the four station equations reported below encompass different sorts of variable specifications and functional forms and a separate demonstration is in order. As in chapter 3, here,

29. Of greatest interest there are my second-order tests to determine the significance of differences in absolute impact of more homes on the prices of stations with and without (1) newspaper sellers and group buyers; (2) newspaper and group sellers; (3) network-affiliated newspaper sellers and group buyers; (4) network-affiliated newspaper and group sellers. Because the number of stations is held constant in each equation, my postulated increase in TV homes is now a direct proxy for license limitation. An increase in homes served by the same number of stations is equivalent to a reduction of stations with homes constant.

too, the reader is further directed to Appendix I for a more general discussion of my statistical method.[30]

The Four Estimating Equations for Sales Prices

For the reader's convenience table 4.11 shows the four estimating equations utilized in my sales price analysis in this chapter, and again in chapter 6. Much of the discussion in both chapters relates to the impacts derived from equation 1, and most of the computational exercises here focus on table 4.7. Nevertheless, it will be useful to derive another class of results as reported in table 4.10, and derived from equation 3. All four equations later figure in the derivation of table 6.11.

It should also be emphasized that equation 1 was my major specification and emerged from a very lengthy set of experiments. Those experiments entailed extensive exploratory interactions of major variables in my initial equation, as well as alternative functional forms (see Appendix II, on pp. 462–69). The many lessons of that detailed inquiry for equations with other dependent variables elsewhere justified a relatively large investment of resources for specification and subsequent analysis.

Essentially, tables 4.7 and 4.9 are fully derived from equation 1 (as are table 6.10 and part A of table 6.11). In the other three equations I first removed two variables with particularly low t-values (Pb, our newspaper buyer dummy, and HPb, its interaction with TV homes). This permitted me to explore the impact of other important factors on sales price. In equation 2, for example, I added HG, or group seller × TV homes; and in equation 3, HGb and HN, or group buyer × TV homes, and network affiliate × TV homes. Finally, equation 4 includes HG and HN, that is, group seller × TV homes *and* network affiliate × TV homes. Thus table 4.10 derives from equation 3, and table 6.11 from all four equations.

I can of course be criticized for introducing these additional interactions one or two at a time, which admittedly weakens my conclusions but was the best procedure under the circumstances. Very simply, sufficient independent observations for each interactive term were lacking, along with the kind of impact needed to get significance notwithstanding multicollinearity among the interacted variables.[31] Some of these

30. The appendix on pp. 416–19 distinguishes between the simpler additive model utilized extensively at the outset of our inquiry (reported at length in chapter 5, and parts of chapters 8 and 10), and the more detailed interactive methodology applied elsewhere (mainly in chapters 3, 4, 6, 13).

31. The basic and related interactive variables are often too similar and hence collinear, to yield significant separate impacts on our dependent variable. For example, network affiliates (N) are almost always VHF (V). If all Ns were in fact Vs, then the basic variable, N, would be identical to the interactive term, NV, and one of them would have to be removed. Short of that extreme situation here, the distribution of both components of my interactives often results in such collinearity as to preclude significant impacts of either.

TABLE 4.11

Four Estimating Equations for Television Station Sales Prices, 1949-70

	Equation 1		Equation 2		Equation 3		Equation 4	
	Sales Price		Sales Price		Sales Price		Sales Price	
	Coefficient	t-value	Coefficient	t-value	Coefficient	t-value	Coefficient	t-value
Constant	−104.950	1.99	−83.158	1.63	−59.745	1.18	−55.471	1.11
TV homes in market	5.053	5.70	3.647	3.96	1.704	1.57	1.798	1.70
Nonnetwork group seller	11.878	1.77	−5.856	.76	12.403	1.92	−.545	.07
In-town newspaper seller	25.939	1.68	31.509	2.11	29.843	2.03	32.583	2.22
Nonnetwork group buyer	16.934	2.31	16.419	2.41	8.021	1.02	15.079	2.25
In-town newspaper buyer	−12.354	.50	n.i.		n.i.		n.i.	
No. of VHF stations in market	.413	.06	.501	.07	−.191	.03	.107	.01
Visual power	.566	2.18	.493	1.96	.418	1.67	.427	1.72
Network affiliate	73.205	2.69	54.965	2.05	23.048	.79	17.034	.59
VHF channel	68.291	2.59	45.698	1.76	41.711	1.61	33.074	1.28
Markets with 3+ VHF	129.425	5.27	112.875	4.72	80.139	3.10	78.319	3.06
Log no. months on air when sold	9.538	1.84	11.618	1.49	11.644	1.50	13.475	1.76
No. of VHF × market dummy	−33.080	3.36	−28.866	3.03	−19.346	1.95	−18.922	1.93
Newspaper seller × TV homes	3.023	1.81	2.371	1.47	1.078	.65	1.384	.86
Newspaper-group seller	−63.669	3.08	−76.552	3.80	−64.282	3.24	−76.083	3.84
Network affiliate × VHF channel	−62.177	2.15	−39.350	1.39	−32.952	1.17	−24.612	.87
Newspaper buyer × TV homes	3.480	.61	n.i.		n.i.		n.i.	
Newspaper-group buyer	57.062	1.88	64.392	2.99	59.681	2.80	63.399	2.99
Age dummy × log age	21.646	4.25	19.903	4.04	19.249	3.93	18.818	3.88
Group seller × TV homes	n.i.		5.534	4.27	n.i.		3.945	2.91
Group buyer × TV homes	n.i.		n.i.		2.038	1.80	n.i.	
Network affiliate × TV homes	n.i.		n.i.		5.693	3.93	4.961	3.38
Adjusted R-square	.3890		.4264		.4364		.4461	
Sample size	310		310		310		310	
Sample mean (in $100,000s)	51.1023		51.1023		51.1023		51.1023	

SOURCE: Most data compiled from issues of *Television Factbook* (Washington, D.C.: Television Digest, Inc.), and *Broadcasting Yearbook* (Washington, D.C.: Broadcasting Publications, Inc.). For derivation of equations, see Appendix II, pp. 456-69.

n.i. = Not included in equation for design purposes.

Notation	Variable Definition
K	constant
H	TV homes, that is, number of homes with one or more TV sets with market areas of dominant influence (ADI) as defined by the American Research Bureau, in thousands
G or Gs	For nonnetwork group *seller* = 1, O otherwise (not network-owned)
P or Ps	For colocated newspaper *seller* = 1, O otherwise
Gb	For nonnetwork group buyer = 1, O otherwise (not network-owned)
Pb	For colocated newspaper buyer = 1, O otherwise
#VHF	Number of VHF stations in metropolitan area market
Vis. Pw:.	Visual (video) power in hundreds of kilowatts
N	For network-affiliated seller = 1, O otherwise
O	For network owner = 1, O otherwise
V	For VHF channel = 1, UHF = O
M	Market dummy, 1 = 3 or more VHF stations in market, O otherwise
logAge	Log of station's age in months at time of sale
A	Age dummy, 1 = licensed 1951 or before, O = licensed 1952 or after
A × logAge	Age dummy × logAge: for stations licensed before $1952 - \text{logAge}$, O otherwise
#VHFM	Number of VHFs in market × market dummy: for markets with 3 or more VHF = #VHF, O otherwise
HP	Newspaper seller dummy × TV homes: for newspaper seller = H, O otherwise
PG	For newspaper-group seller = 1, O otherwise
NV	For network affiliated VHF seller = 1, O otherwise
HPb	Newspaper buyer dummy × TV homes: for newspaper buyer = H, O otherwise
PG[b]	For newspaper-group buyer = 1, O otherwise
HG	Group seller dummy × TV homes: group seller = H, O otherwise
HN	Network affiliate dummy × TV homes: for network affiliate = H, O otherwise
HGb	Group buyer dummy × TV homes: for group buyer = H, O otherwise
$\bar{R}^2$	Adjusted R-square
$\bar{Y}$	Mean of dependent variable

interactive terms are doubtless proxies for others not included in an equation. But I simply could not get them all in simultaneously, despite extensive experimentation with many more than these variable combinations. With still more resources and time, I might have improved on the final specification. Short of that, tables 4.10 and 6.11 offer the additional evidence derived from my other three equations (#2 through #4). The basic stability of the major coefficients, across all four equations, attests to the value of reporting those additional results in table 4.11. So does the bearing of the latter's clear pattern on the hypotheses under scrutiny.

Estimation Procedures and Special Notation

My estimation procedures for the coefficients of interacted variables, and the notation used in some of this discussion (see list of variable definitions), can best be explained with a few examples. (Coefficients for noninteracted variables can be read off the regression equation directly.)

By way of illustration, in table 4.7, consider the postulated change in the number of VHF stations in the market from four to three, reported to result, other things being equal, in a $3,265,000 increase in sales price. How is this coefficient calculated? Following the steps outlined in Appendix 3B, the variables affected by the postulated attribute change in table 4.7, are: #VHF (number of VHF stations in the market), M (market dummy, which equals 1 for markets with three or more VHFs), and #VHFM (number of VHF times market dummy). In measuring each affected variable, it is convenient to tabulate its value before and after the change:

	Column 1 Before			Column 2 After			Column 3 Change		
Test	#VHFs	M	#VHFM	#VHFs	M	#VHFM	#VHFs	M	#VHFM
4 to 3 VHFs	4	1	4	3	1	3	−1	0	−1

The magnitude of change due to each affected variable is then estimated by simply multiplying the coefficients of #VHFs, M, and #VHFM, respectively, by the postulated change in its value (in column 3). Thus in table 4.11, equation 1:

$$\text{Sales Price} = \overset{\#\text{VHF}}{0.4130\,(-1)} + \overset{M}{129.425\,(0)} - \overset{\#\text{VHFM}}{33.080\,(-1)}$$
$$= -0.4130 + 0 + 33.080 = 32.667 \times \$100,000.$$

Dividing by the sample mean, the unreported PCDV is 32.667/51.102, or 63.9 percent.

For a second example, also in table 4.7, consider the impact for all VHF stations of a switch from independent to network status. The af-

fected variables now include Network (N), VHF (V), and Network ×
VHF (NV), and our tabulation is:

Test	Column 1 Before			Column 2 After			Column 3 Change		
VHF (Network)	N	V	NV	N	V	NV	N	V	NV
	0	1	0	1	1	1	+1	0	+1

Once again, we multiply the coefficients of N, V, and NV, respectively,
by the postulated change in its value in column 3 as follows:

$$\text{Sales price} = 73.205\ (+1) + 68.29\ (0) - 62.177\ (+1)$$
$$= 73.205 + 0 - 62.177 = 11.028 \times \$100,000.$$

In sum, for a VHF station in our sample a network affiliate's sale price,
other things being equal, is $1,103,000 higher than an independent's.

For still another and somewhat different case, again drawn from table
4.7, consider further the postulated tripling of the age (when sold) of a
station licensed before 1952. As explained in the text, such stations enjoyed blockaded market entry during the hiatus in licensing, 1948–52. In
addition, older stations are, *cet. par.*, more likely to have better ties
with advertisers, talent agencies, and networks, and more loyal audiences.

The variables affected here are log age of a station in months at the
time of sale, and an interactive variable equal to log of age times an
age dummy equal to one for stations licensed before 1952, and zero
otherwise. What impact on price would a tripling of age have on stations licensed before 1952? The difference in the logs of two numbers,
one of which is three times the other, is simply the log of 3, which is
.47716. Therefore, in going from the sale of a station licensed before
1952, to sale of another such station three times older, the logarithm of
age and the interactive age dummy (dummy × log of age), both increase by .47716.

In effect, multiplying the coefficients of log of age and the interactive
age variable by .47716, we estimate the change in sales price to be
(see equation 1, table 4.11) = 9.538 (.44716) + 21.646 (.47716), or 14.8798 ×
$100,000, as reported in table 4.7. For a station licensed after 1952 the
age dummy (A) is zero, so that the interactive variable (A × log of age)
is equal to zero time log of age, or zero, before and after the age change.
Therefore, that computation would simply be .47716 times the coefficient
of log of age (9.538), or 4.551 × $100,000, again as reported in table
4.7.

For a fourth and final example let us now turn to table 4.10 (and
equation 3). Consider, in 4.10, the top row of results which report that,
for UHF stations in the sample, *cet. par.*, a switch from independent to
network status will raise sales price by $7,998,000, assuming there are
1,000,000 TV homes in the market, but only by $4,485,000 if there are
only 383,000 homes (sample mean).

How are these two derived impacts calculated?[32] Again, consider the variables affected by our postulated attribute changes: network, VHF, network × VHF, and network × TV homes (HN). Our tabulation is as follows:

		Column 1 Before					Column 2 After					Column 3 Change			
Test		N	V	NV	HN	H	N	V	NV	HN	H	N	V	NV	HN
A	N(U, H = 1000)	0	0	0	0	1000	1	0	0	1000	1000	+1	0	0	+1000
B	N(U, H = 383)	0	0	0	0	383	1	0	0	383	383	+1	0	0	+383

Multiplying the relevant values by the respective coefficients for N, V, NV, HN, H (see list of variable definitions), we may first calculate the postulated impact on price at a 1,000,000-homes level as follows =

$$\underline{A}\ \overset{N}{(23.048)}\ \overset{V}{(\$100,000)(+1)} + \overset{NV}{41.711(0)(+)} - \overset{HN}{32.952(0)} =$$

$$\overset{H}{(5.693)(1,000,000)(+1)} + (1.704)(1,000,000)(0) =$$

$$\underline{A} \qquad \$2,304,800 \qquad \qquad +0 \qquad \qquad -0$$
$$+\$5,693,000 + 0 \qquad \qquad = \$7,997,800$$

We may also calculate the comparable impact on price at a 383,000-homes level, as follows =

$$\underline{B}\ \overset{N}{(23.048)}\ \overset{V}{(\$100,000)(+1)} + \overset{NV}{41.711(0)(+)} - \overset{HN}{32.952(0)} +$$

$$\overset{H}{(5.693)(383,000)(+1)} + 1.704(383,000)(0) =$$

$$\underline{B} \qquad \$2,304,800 \qquad \qquad +0 \qquad \qquad -0$$
$$+ \$2,180,419 + 0 \qquad \qquad = \$4,485,219$$

So much for the four estimating equations, our computational procedure, and abbreviated notation. For the major experiments in developing our final variable specifications, the reader should turn to Appendix II, on pp. 462–69.

32. I will not attempt to demonstrate how, in col. 8 of table 4.10, the difference between these two absolute impacts, $3,510,000, is itself significantly greater than zero (t = 3.93). This entails rather intricate analysis of the respective covariances of the first order impacts of our postulated attribute changes, readily handled by our computer program.

Chapter 5

Objectives versus Results in Federal Broadcast Regulation

I HAVE now laid out two concepts, the diversity goal and the economic consequences of license limitation, which constitute the principal components of regulatory assessment in this book. Before turning to that task in later chapters, I first offer here a broad overview of the degree to which regulatory objectives and results converge. I do so fully mindful of the complexities encountered in defining and measuring the diversity goal in chapter 3, and economic rents as regulatory side effects, in chapter 4.

From the very outset a major stated objective of broadcast regulation has been to sustain a diversified and balanced program service through licensing-allocation policies designed to affect industry structure and conduct. Balance refers to the industry's product mix as between local, national, and regional programming, or as between entertainment, advertising, news, public affairs, and other program types. Diversity refers to the variety of participating program sources and suppliers of talent as well as to the range of program options which result. It has long been regulatory practice to demand from licensees, in return for free access to a valuable resource, the radio frequency spectrum, a public service contribution which they themselves subsidize. Whether or not more than lip service is paid to this commitment, the goal is in fact rationalized in this way.

Much of this book undertakes to measure the terms of the above transaction. New measures have been devised, and new data compiled and analyzed, on the private economic advantages conferred on broadcast licensees, and the character of the public service they provide in return. Subsequent chapters will assess these dual effects of particular licensing policies, but first a profile of regulatory impact in economic and programming terms needs to be presented.

An Overall Quantitative Assessment

My statistical analysis will now distinguish between the measurable consequences of regulatory policies distinctive to the FCC, and procompetitive policies. For present purposes, "distinctive" regulations are defined as those which aim to sustain meritorious program service and diversity. These so-called "qualitative" policies may influence licensee conduct directly in ways that impinge on overall industry performance, specifically on the range, variety, and quality of available program options. Competitive policies, on the other hand, relate to so-called "quantitative licensing" and "structural diversity," our main proxies for which are the policies which govern new station entry and the size and affluence of markets to which access is granted. But special attention is given also to policies which relate to channel type and channel spacing as factors affecting the level of entry barriers. Indeed still another set of policies (on owner affiliation) also impinges on licensee size and viability. However, the expectations which policymakers have of affiliated licensees derive in part from the latter's allegedly greater economic resources for diversity and merit service. In that sense the policies which relate to ownership can be viewed as a form of qualitative regulation.

But how effective are any of these policies? Do they realize such basic stated goals as program diversity, or do they simply enhance the profitability of those able to obtain a license? How can current policies be modified or replaced to correct these unwanted side effects, or improved to further the formal stated goals? If the price in unwanted effects is too high, and the possible remedies too awkward, the goals may of course have to be reexamined. However, a prior step would be to consider conceivable modifications in existing policies (as I do in Part II), and the more promising regulatory alternatives (as in Part III).

The Variables Analyzed and the Data Utilized

The three policies around which most of my research in Part II is organized pertain to ownership diversification, new commercial entry, and regulation of network-affiliate relations. In testing hypotheses regarding the probable effects of such regulatory options, two sets of data have been developed, one of which incorporates aggregate market statistics for 1967, and the other more detailed station information, for both 1967 and 1972.

Because of legal rules of confidentiality, the earnings of broadcast licensees are divulged only by station class and market size, on a grouped basis. Those aggregate financial statistics do, however, provide a useful basis on which to test a number of hypotheses. They are particularly valuable given the very limited amount of information made available for detailed individual station analysis. They are valuable, also, because of the limited usefulness of consolidated income and balance sheet data on publicly-held corporations published by Moody's, Standard and Poor's, and the Securities and Exchange Commission.

My market-level information includes, moreover, separate compilations from trade sources of data, described in chapter 3, relating to a measure of horizontal program type diversity, namely a summation of program type differences across all stations in the market during each quarter-hour throughout any sample week.

My first broad assessment of regulatory impact on economic and programming performance, then, has for important practical reasons been based on market-wide information. Analysis of such data appeared to be a good place to start, notwithstanding the limited conclusions one can draw from market averages without knowing the distribution of individual observations therein.

My individual station deck then permitted a more refined analysis of selected program variables such as news, public affairs, and fine arts, and vertical diversity measured as the average daily number of program types per station, by station class, during a sample week. Moreover, despite the absence of published FCC station financial data, the station deck includes copious compiled rates statistics, with and without implicit discounts. Finally, station audience and ratings data provide still another economic proxy variable, whereas TV station sales prices were particularly helpful (in chapters 4 and 6) in estimating the unanticipated effects of licensing on economic rents and franchise values.

On a practical level, then, so many different economic dependent variables are analyzed mainly to insure the reliability of overall results in the face of widely divergent data sources and of compilation problems. Conceptually, moreover, my economic indicators usefully supplement each other.

Thus spot rates are offer prices which stations quote and some advertisers presumably pay, depending on audience size measured in absolute terms or by "ratings"—that is, percentages of all TV homes tuning in any station. The latter data are abundantly available in standard trade sources, and permit us to estimate station audience size. Market averages of realized income, revenue, and time sales pertain to closed transactions which determine the sums that stations in any market actually earn, on the average, given the rates they charge, the audiences they deliver, and hence the advertiser's effective demand for their time.

On all counts, it was prudent to seek confirmation of estimated impacts on major economic indicators (say, rates), by replicating the results on alternate measures.

With these facts and hypotheses in mind, we may now take a brief initial look, in table 5.1, at the economic and programming performance of major classes of television licensees. The reader should, however, bear in mind that this table presents only simple descriptive data for a few key variables and fails to take account of many important interrelations among them as well as of still other determinants of program composition. These factors are considered later in the chapter.

The question here, however, is whether the most profitable station classes carry the most (presumably nonremunerative) information, news, public affairs, or local programming generally.[1] An overall look at the ten and fifty largest markets shows quite clearly that VHF stations as a whole are both more profitable than UHF and carry more information, news, public affairs, local news, and apparently more locally produced programs as such. Similarly, network affiliates are not only distinctly more prosperous than independents as a class, but also carry substantially more news, public affairs, local news, and, in the top ten markets at least, more local [2] programs overall. Even combining channel type and network tie, with one or two exceptions the more affluent network VHFs carry substantially more news, public affairs, local news, local programs generally, and even local public affairs than the less affluent network UHFs. The same pattern holds also for independent VHFs and

1. Although local news has accounted for a large share of TV station profits in large markets in recent years, news documentaries commanded by far the smallest audience of any program category listed in table 3.2, and far smaller than the leading entertainment types. Nor are stations which carry more nonlocal news (or more local public affairs) apparently as attractive to advertisers as those carrying more local news (or more nonlocal public affairs). [See tables 10.7 and 10.8, and related discussion in Appendix 10A.] On those counts at least, informational programming may well be less profitable than entertainment and better carried by stations with the wherewithal to do so.

2. This may follow from the classification here which is limited to actual local productions, both live and taped, and exclusive of syndicated materials produced elsewhere, or network reruns.

independent UHFs. In short, the gross indications in table 5.1 are that greater profitability is associated with more informational and local programming.

Yet even in this broad-brush compilation there is evidence that a more refined analysis of the interrelation of licensee classes may uncover a somewhat different pattern. Thus, for local programs as a whole and local public affairs, the less affluent independents show greater relative strength over affiliates, at least if the comparison is of stations of the *same* channel type—that is, independent VHFs with affiliated VHFs, and so on. All this holds true, finally, despite the high costs of such programming and the independents' further dependency on syndicated fare. In short, the relationship between profitability and informational service appears to break down at the local service level for independents and affiliates using the same channel type.

A somewhat similar gross (positive) relationship to that observed earlier between profitability and programming also appears to exist between newspaper and nonnewspaper stations and between group and nongroup. However, the pattern there is noticeably weaker and less revealing in the absence of cross-classifications for network tie and channel type.

A more definitive analysis of these relationships required consideration of many more determinants of program composition, as well as tests of statistical significance. Turning to those requirements next, my data base permits scrutiny of the issues from a slightly different viewpoint. Does license limitation significantly bolster licensee profitability? If so, are there commensurate offsetting public benefits in diversity and cultural-informational programming? Do licensees affiliated with newspaper, group or network companies enjoy special economic advantages on that account, and are there compensating benefits once again in public service rendered?

The statistical technique used here will simplify the interactive methodology of earlier chapters by turning to a less complex additive regression model.[3] One new requirement is to give the reader a better "feel" of the relative impact of the many independent (policy) variables on each of several dependent variables: what, for example, is the relative impact of channel type, or removing one station from the market, or newspaper ownership on station rates, revenues, audiences on one hand, and local news and local public affairs on the other?

To make the answers to such questions meaningful, a mere reporting

3. In that statistical model a large number of independent variables are each analyzed for their individual impacts on a given dependent variable, taking into account all other independent variables. The process is then repeated for additional dependent variables. This additive regression model is by no means optimal but was necessitated here by time constraints, the broad range of issues I scrutinize, expositional clarity, and the best use of limited budgetary resources. See Appendix I, pp. 413–19, and Appendix II, pp. 435–38.

TABLE 5.1

Economic and Programming Indicators by Station Class and Market Size, 1972
(total stations and means of variables, 6 P.M.-11 P.M.)

	Number of Stations	30-Second Spot Rate $	Per-cent**	Number of Stations	Estimated Station Revenue $000s	Per-cent**	Number of Stations	Station Audience 000s	Per-cent**
Top Ten Markets									
VHF*	26	942	175	27	11424	133	27	212	132
UHF	23	84	16	12	2209	26	11	37	23
Network*	18	1061	197	16	14044	164	16	260	162
Independent	31	237	44	23	4794	56	22	90	56
Network VHF*	16	1186	220	16	14044	164	16	260	162
Network UHF	2	58	11	–	–	–	–	–	–
Independent VHF	10	553	103	11	7614	89	11	144	89
Independent UHF	21	86	16	12	2209	26	11	37	23
Newspaper	8	970	180	9	9617	112	9	183	114
Nonnewspaper*	41	456	85	30	8280	96	29	155	96
Group (nonnetwork)	35	660	122	35	8333	97	34	163	101
Nongroup*	14	238	44	4	10826	126	4	153	95
Network Owned VHF	13	2697	500	14	28206	328	14	547	340
Top Fifty Markets									
VHF*	141	473	130	147	6160	121	146	117	122
UHF	56	89	25	46	1600	32	47	30	31
Network*	135	457	126	142	5851	115	141	113	118
Independent	62	158	43	51	2904	57	52	51	53
Network VHF*	121	497	137	128	6313	124	126	121	126
Network UHF	14	121	33	14	1633	32	15	40	42
Independent VHF	20	330	91	19	5129	101	20	92	96
Independent UHF	42	77	21	32	1583	31	32	25	26
Newspaper	37	532	146	39	6658	131	39	127	132
Nonnewspaper*	160	325	89	154	4671	92	154	88	92
Group (nonnetwork)	142	425	117	150	5411	107	146	105	109
Nongroup*	55	205	56	43	3890	77	47	67	70
Network Owned VHF	14	2576	708	15	26891	530	15	523	545

SOURCE: Station attributes derived from *Broadcasting Yearbook-1973* (Washington, D.C.: Broadcasting Publications Inc., 1974) and *Television Factbook No. 43, 1973-74* (Washington, D.C., Television Digest Inc., 1974). Spot rates derived from *Spot Television Rates and Data-1972* (Skokie, Ill.: Standard Rates and Data Service Inc., 1972). Station revenue estimates derived from market revenue data in FCC Financial Report on Television Broadcast Service for 1972, and station metro shares in American Research Bureau, *Day-Part Audience Summary* (New York: American Research Bureau, 1972). Thus each station's metro share for all stations in sample was first multiplied by the aggregate revenues reported for its market in 1972. These estimates of individual station revenue were then averaged by station class, first for all stations in the top ten, and then top fifty markets. Station audience data from American Research Bureau, ibid. Programming data from FCC, *Annual Programming Report for Commercial Television Stations—1973* (Washington, D.C.: Federal Communications Commission, 1973), in minutes of air time, 6 P.M.-11 P.M., during composite week for 1972-73.

*Excludes network-owned stations.

**Class means as percent of respective subsample means, first for top 10, and then for top 50 markets.

					Minutes of Program Time						
Number of Stations	All News	Percent**	All Public Affairs	Percent**	Local News	Percent**	Local Public Affairs	Percent**	Number of Stations	All Local Programs (included entire)	Percent**
Top Ten Markets											
28	292	159	134	141	202	155	49	123	21	268	147
28	76	41	55	58	58	45	31	78	28	118	65
21	316	172	141	148	180	139	37	93	17	208	114
35	104	57	67	71	100	77	42	105	32	168	92
18	441	240	153	161	199	153	44	110	14	237	130
3	209	114	66	70	62	48	0	0	3	72	40
10	215	117	99	104	207	159	58	145	7	330	181
25	60	33	54	57	57	44	35	88	25	123	68
10	236	128	105	111	153	118	46	115	8	196	108
46	173	94	92	97	125	96	39	98	41	179	98
41	207	113	106	112	153	118	49	123	34	205	113
15	122	66	64	67	67	52	16	40	15	130	71
14	346	188	130	137	229	176	28	70	11	258	142
Top Fifty Markets											
146	278	127	116	114	162	129	35	106	128	199	122
66	90	41	70	69	46	37	29	88	65	139	85
145	280	128	124	122	146	116	30	91	129	178	109
67	89	41	54	53	81	64	34	103	64	179	110
128	292	133	122	120	160	127	31	94	113	193	118
17	195	89	137	134	43	34	25	76	16	74	45
18	182	83	73	72	175	139	47	142	15	243	149
49	54	25	46	45	46	37	30	91	49	160	98
40	294	134	109	107	176	140	33	100	33	223	137
172	203	93	98	96	114	91	31	94	160	170	104
155	240	110	108	106	139	110	34	103	139	184	113
57	163	74	82	80	89	71	24	73	54	166	102
15	350	160	135	132	231	183	28	85	12	262	161

of absolute impacts and significance levels will not suffice. It will at least facilitate the discussion to express all regression coefficients—that is, unit changes in our dependent variables due to postulated changes in various independent variables—as percentages of the former's sample mean (PCDV).[4] This does not permit us to test for the significance of the difference between the absolute impact of any single independent variable on any two dependent variables, but does provide a general feel of the relative magnitude of this impact.[5]

Since our task in this chapter is essentially to determine the relative degree to which licensee profitability and informational programming, or diversity, respond to changes in each of several policy variables (and control factors), even a crude quasi-elasticity, or PCDV, that cuts across a whole gamut of equations is better than a more refined and possibly more accurate measure that does not.

Economic and Programming Effects of License Limitation

The origin, rationale, and certain economic consequences of restrictive licensing were spelled out at length in chapter 4. However, the survey that follows will draw on a much wider range of economic indicators, now including market as well as station data; and data on rates, ratings, audiences, income, revenues, and time sales, as well as on station sales prices. Furthermore, the effect of license limitation on program composition and diversity will also be assessed.

Thus the private advantages that limited licensing confers, and the programming benefits derived, can be readily contrasted in tables 5.2 and 5.3 which, together, provide a convenient audit of the impact of regulatory control of entry in 1967, well after the TV Allocation Plan was instituted. Under that plan in 1952, VHF and UHF outlets were assigned to the same markets, according to designated social priorities.[6]

In working out trade-offs and compromises among conflicts in these priorities the commission proceeded as follows. Once every community could receive at least one signal (service), the Allocation Table struck a balance between multiservice areas and local community stations. To safeguard the former goal, the FCC sometimes had to refrain from allocating local channels to particular communities. Next, additional chan-

4. We refer to this measure throughout as a "PCDV"—that is, a percentage change of dependent variable.
5. See Appendix I, pp. 430–31.
6. See FCC, Sixth Report and Order in re: Amendment of 47 CFR par. 3.606, FCC Docket No. 8736, 17 Fed. Reg. 3905, 3906, 3912.

TABLE 5.2

Sensitivity of Television Market Income, Net Revenue, and Program Diversity in Relation to Rent-Yielding Market Variables, 1967[1]

(based on commercial data only)

Independent Variables	Averages			Commercial Diversity: No. of Program Types per Market (6-11 P.M.)	
	Income per Station[3]	Revenue per Station[3]	Time Sales per Station[3]	Per Commercial Station	Total
Number of 15-minute	−1.65[b]	−.89[b]	−1.42[a]	−.32[a]	.66[a]
program units in market[2]	(2.4)	(2.4)	(4.2)	(9.0)	(16.0)
TV homes in market	.83[a]	.62[a]	.49[a]	.02[a]	.01
	(6.9)	(9.4)	(8.3)	(2.7)	(1.1)
Proportion of Stations With:					
Network affiliation	1.25	−1.34[b]	−.89	−.19[b]	−.13
	(1.2)	(2.3)	(1.7)	(2.5)	(1.5)
VHF license	.35[c]	.31[a]	.19[b]	.01	.01
	(1.9)	(3.0)	(2.0)	(.4)	(.5)
Network owner	.22[a]	.13[a]	.95[a]	.001	.001
	(6.4)	(6.9)	(5.5)	(.4)	(.3)
Nonnetwork group owner	.35[c]	.16	.14	−.01	.002
	(1.9)	(1.6)	(1.6)	(.2)	(.1)
Outside newspaper owner	.03	.02	.005	.003	.01
	(.4)	(.7)	(.2)	(.6)	(1.2)
In-town newspaper owner	.12[c]	.05	.05	.003	.01
	(1.7)	(1.3)	(1.5)	(.6)	(1.2)

[1] Upper number in each cell is an elasticity calculated at the mean: percentage change in the dependent variable per 1 percent change in the independent variable. Lower number (in parentheses) is t-value of regression coefficient, with statistical significance (two-tailed test) indicated by superscripts, a = 1 percent confidence level, b = 5 percent, c = 10 percent.

[2] Results report the number of 15-minute commercial program units. This scaling permits me to calculate more informative elasticities than with the actual number of stations. However, in the estimating equations which appear below I report station coefficients proper. These two variables are directly proportional and scaling differences do not alter elasticities reported here.

[3] Per station figures derived by dividing market data by number of stations in market.

Estimating Equations for Table 5.2
(coefficients)

Independent Variable	Income per Station $100,000's	Revenue per Station $100,000's	Time Sales per Station $100,000's	Commercial Diversity: Number of Program Types per Market	
				Per Commercial Station	Total
Constant	14.862	50.386	11.509	121.962	138.68
No. of commercial					
stations in market[4]	−3.696[b]	−6.986[b]	−2.114[a]	−11.760[a]	71.862[a]
100,000's TV homes	.774[a]	2.014[a]	.301[a]	.406[a]	.536
Proportion of Stations With:					
Network affiliation	−9.996	−37.512[b]	−4.675	21.644[b]	−43.749
VHF license	3.217[c]	10.093[a]	1.144[b]	1.092	4.463
Network owner	58.511[a]	120.412[a]	16.429[a]	2.968	14.385
Nonnetwork group owner	4.037[c]	6.581	1.080	−1.078	1.047
Outside newspaper owner	1.207	3.703	.151	2.184	14.821
In-town newspaper owner	5.324	7.657	1.563	2.450	15.729
Adj. R^2	.764	.855	.744	.435	.872
Sample size (markets)	101	101	101	143	143
Sample mean	7.4	26.0	4.9	111.0	325.5

[4] See note 2 above.

TABLE 5.3

Sensitivity of Station's Share of Viewers, Advertising Rates, Prime-Time Program Diversity, and Composition of Prime-Time Programs to Changes in Rent-Yielding Market Variables[1]

Change in Independent Variable	Station's Share of Viewers		20-Second Prime Rate	Vertical Diversity: Average Number of Program Types Nightly	Type of Prime-Time Programming						
	ADI Ratings	Metro Ratings			Local	All Non-network	News	Public Affairs	Fine Arts and Drama	Mass Entertainment	Feature Film
Remove one commercial station	10.58^a (4.6)	8.67^a (4.9)	13.08^a (3.3)	1.17^c (1.9)	-2.95 (1.1)	-1.72 (1.2)	.14 (.1)	11.3 (.4)	2.83 (.6)	.0037 (.001)	-2.15 (.8)
Add 100,000 TV homes	-.16 (.6)	-.18 (1.0)	9.14^a (17.5)	.14^c (1.8)	-.58^c (1.8)	-.25 (1.3)	-.26 (.9)	-.01 (.02)	-.15 (.2)	.17^b (2.1)	-.22 (.6)
Switch from UHF to VHF	21.37^a (4.6)	23.85^a (7.1)	47.45^a (5.5)	2.96^b (2.2)	-3.27 (.6)	.45 (.1)	5.24 (1.1)	-11.68 (1.6)	-17.17 (1.6)	3.12^b (2.4)	3.66 (.7)
Switch nongroup to network group	24.90^b (2.2)	10.59 (1.3)	220.87^a (9.8)	-3.96 (1.1)	10.75 (.7)	-11.42 (1.4)	32.14^a (2.6)	31.16^c (1.6)	10.70 (.4)	-8.66^b (2.5)	12.02 (.8)
nonnetwork group	6.24^c (1.7)	2.22 (.8)	7.05 (1.0)	.19 (.2)	3.60 (.8)	5.74^b (2.3)	8.66^b (2.3)	6.55 (1.1)	-6.83 (.8)	-.15 (.1)	1.43 (.3)
Switch nonnewspaper to outside newspaper	-.48 (.1)	-1.46 (.4)	-5.12 (.5)	-1.18 (.8)	-5.48 (.9)	-.97 (.3)	-4.03 (.8)	3.88 (.5)	2.54 (.2)	1.17 (.8)	.44 (.1)
in-town newspaper	8.06^c (1.8)	9.34^a (2.8)	9.74 (1.1)	3.57^b (2.5)	-1.94 (.3)	.94 (.3)	4.40 (.9)	20.77^a (2.7)	-3.89 (.3)	-1.72 (1.2)	-7.82 (1.3)
Switch independent to CBS	39.14^a (4.6)	63.40^a (10.9)	109.45^a (7.2)	7.19^a (3.0)	-131.03^a (13.2)	-208.63^a (37.0)	60.04^a (7.1)	-55.87^a (4.3)	-127.53^a (6.6)	5.78^b (2.4)	-38.81^a (3.9)
NBC	33.47^a (3.9)	60.26^a (10.2)	111.38^a (7.4)	-4.79^b (2.0)	-142.20^a (14.3)	-223.54^a (39.7)	70.73^a (8.3)	-106.51^a (8.2)	26.50 (1.4)	2.82 (1.2)	-58.66^a (5.8)
ABC	16.69^c (1.9)	43.67^a (7.5)	100.08^a (6.6)	-7.52^a (3.1)	-130.88^a (13.2)	-198.83^a (35.3)	5.99 (.7)	-71.86^a (5.5)	-11.61 (.6)	12.94^a (5.4)	-13.38 (1.3)
CBS-ABC	60.41^a (5.3)	87.10^a (10.8)	98.47^a (4.9)	4.54 (1.5)	-133.18^a (10.4)	-219.71^a (30.0)	40.96^a (3.7)	-59.31^a (3.6)	-98.99^a (4.0)	7.33^b (2.4)	-42.95^a (3.3)
NBC-ABC	49.18^a (4.5)	74.55^a (9.4)	86.86^a (4.5)	-4.44 (1.4)	-140.55^a (11.1)	-225.77^a (31.3)	55.75^a (5.1)	-94.83^a (5.7)	7.89 (.3)	4.27 (1.4)	-60.37^a (4.8)
CBS-NBC	40.63^a (2.7)	65.64^a (6.2)	86.46^a (3.2)	-3.68 (.9)	-121.77^a (6.9)	-211.59^a (21.3)	59.70^a (4.0)	-103.52^a (4.5)	-87.62^b (2.6)	7.51^c (1.8)	-52.37^a (2.9)
CBS-NBC-ABC	75.53^a (6.4)	79.61^a (8.8)	101.30^a (5.0)	2.33 (.7)	-147.26^a (10.9)	-226.62^a (29.7)	44.72^a (3.9)	-93.05^a (5.3)	-38.32 (1.5)	8.95^a (2.8)	-50.48^a (3.7)

[1] Upper number in each cell denotes percentage change in dependent variable (column heading) due to change specified in independent variable. Lower number (in parentheses) is t-value of regression coefficient, with statistical significance (two-tailed test) indicated by superscripts, as follows: a = 1 percent confidence level, b = 5 percent, c = 10 percent. The estimating equation for each dependent variable appears below.

Estimating Equations for Table 5.3
(coefficients)

Independent Variables	Station's Share of Viewers		20-Second Prime Rate ($)	Average Number of Program Types Nightly	Type of Prime-Time Programming (in 15-minute units)						
	ADI Ratings (%)	Metro Ratings (%)			Local	All Non-network	News	Public Affairs	Fine Arts and Drama	Mass Entertainment	Feature Film
Constant	16.094	10.950	-386.14	3.364	98.089	123.912	5.723	16.084	7.548	92.831	88.258
Number of commercial stations	-2.229[c]	-1.838[a]	32.619[a]	-.049[c]	.954	.769	-.027	-.095	-.095	-.004	.528
100,000s TV homes	-.035	-.039	22.802[a]	.006[c]	-.187[c]	-.112	-.050	-.001	-.005	.181[b]	-.053
Dummy variables:[2]											
VHF channel	4.502[a]	5.057[a]	118.371[a]	.123[b]	-1.060	.200	-.981	-.876	-.577	3.379[b]	.899
Network group owner (0 & 0)	5.244[b]	2.246	550.983[a]	-.165	3.479	-5.116	6.022[a]	2.335[c]	.360	-9.388[b]	2.951
Nonnetwork group owner	1.313[c]	.470	17.592	.008	1.166	2.570[b]	1.623[b]	.491	-.230	-.159	.350
Outside newspaper owner	-.102	-.309	-12.762	-.050	-1.772	-.436	-.755	.291	.085	1.263	.108
In-town newspaper owner	1.697[c]	1.980[a]	24.303	.149[b]	-.629	.423	.824	1.557[a]	-.131	-1.859	-1.920
CBS affiliation	8.243[a]	13.443[a]	273.040[a]	.301[a]	-42.409[a]	-93.490[a]	11.252[a]	-4.187[a]	-4.288[a]	6.268[b]	-9.530[b]
NBC affiliation	7.050[a]	12.777[a]	277.852[a]	-.200[b]	-46.025[a]	-100.167[a]	13.254[a]	-7.981[a]	.891	3.053	-14.404[a]
ABC affiliation	3.432[c]	9.259[a]	249.652[a]	-.314[a]	-42.360[a]	-89.097[a]	1.122	-5.385[a]	-.391	14.023[a]	-3.285
CBS-ABC affiliation	12.724[a]	18.468[a]	245.636[a]	.190	-43.104[a]	-98.451[a]	7.676[a]	-4.445[a]	-3.328[a]	7.945[b]	-10.544[a]
NBC-ABC affiliation	10.358[a]	15.806[a]	216.687[a]	-.185	-45.489[a]	-101.170[a]	10.447[a]	-7.107[a]	.265	4.630	-15.069[a]
CBS-NBC affiliation	8.558[a]	13.918[a]	215.688[a]	13.918	-39.413[a]	-94.814[a]	11.187[a]	-7.758[a]	-2.946[b]	8.140[c]	-12.859[a]
CBS-NBC-ABC affiliation	15.908[a]	16.880[a]	252.708[a]	16.880	-47.664[a]	-101.547[a]	8.380[a]	-6.973[a]	-1.288	9.702[a]	-12.394[a]
Adj. R²	.432	.636	.769	.226	.393	.839	.346	.185	.302	.122	.158
Sample size (stations)	445	408	452	486	486	486	486	486	486	486	486
Sample mean	21.1	21.2	249.5	4.2	32.4	44.8	18.4	7.5	3.4	108.4	74.6

[2]Labeled attribute equals one, zero otherwise.

nels were allocated on a population basis. However, ceilings had to be imposed in the big city markets to safeguard the availability of services and stations elsewhere, in smaller communities generally, and in contiguous regions "overshadowed" by big city stations. In the final analysis, the commission had to pay a price in fewer competing services for more local assignments; and a price in fewer big city stations for a more equitable geographic dispersion of facilities elsewhere. And a price, finally, in slower commercial entry to ensure long-run educational use.

The three variables analyzed below which most directly derive from aspects of the commission's Allocation Plan that we have called quantitative licensing, are channel type, competitors, and TV homes. In tables 5.2 and 5.3, each of those variables impinges significantly on private economic benefits as reflected in market averages of income, revenue, and time sales; and station rates, audiences, and sales prices. However, we find few compensating public benefits in greater market diversity or informational programming.

Analysis of Market Aggregates

In table 5.2, for instance, the true market elasticities (not PCDVs) show quite clearly that a 1 percent *reduction* of commercial quarter-hour program units (a refined proxy for number of stations), would have raised the market averages of income, revenues, and time sales per station, respectively, by 1.7 percent, .9 percent, and 1.4 percent.[7] In contrast, horizontal diversity per station would have risen only .3 percent, and the absolute level of horizontal diversity across all stations in the market would actually have declined substantially, by .7 percent.

Similarly, a 1 percent rise in TV homes—an equally valid proxy for license limitation, given that the number of stations is held constant [8]— would have raised the market averages in question by .8 percent, .6 percent and .5 percent respectively, again with only token effects on diversity per station (+.02 percent), and no effect at all on absolute diversity. It must also be noted that these elasticities are estimated after accounting for effects of the other variables in the equation, like market size, and proportions of stations with designated attributes. Note finally the impact of channel type—every 1 percent increase in the proportion of all stations in the market which have VHF grants will also raise per sta-

---

7. If the stations in any market could conspire to restrict their aggregate output, of course, this, too, would act to raise average station profitability in the market. However, such interfirm agreements would violate the antitrust laws. In contrast, the FCC's limitist licensing policy in some ways performs the same restrictive function, without the antitrust risks, though with similar economic results.

8. With number of stations in the equation, a postulated increase in TV homes, *cet. par.*, implies more TV homes per station. This is tantamount to reducing the number of stations in the market with TV homes constant. Hence both postulated changes can be used to capture the impact of restrictive licensing on market economic and programming dependent variables.

tion income, revenues, and time sales, though by less than would the postulated changes in stations and TV homes—that is, by +.4 percent, +.3 percent and +.2 percent respectively. But again, our so-called VHF proportion
has no significant effects on absolute diversity or on diversity per station.

Analysis of Station Behavior

Further corroboration appears in table 5.3, which pertains to individual
stations only. Here, removing one station from the market, taking account of other factors, will raise the proportion of TV homes which
watch any remaining station by 2.2 percentage points or +10.6 percent
of the sample mean of ADI ratings. Similarly, with stations constant, a
rise in TV homes of 100,000 (a proxy for license limitation) impacts
significantly on twenty-second prime rates (+9 percent),[9] though not on
audience ratings, whereas the affirmative impact on vertical program
diversity [10] is very small (+.1 percent). Furthermore, program composition is sometimes affected adversely from the commission's viewpoint,
with, for instance, a 3 percent decline in local service.

As with the market elasticities, full account has been taken of effects
due to channel type and owner affiliations. Together, therefore, these
results seriously question any presumption that license limitation generates programming benefits commensurate with its effect on station
profits.

Lastly, the advantages enjoyed by VHF licensees under the current
allocation plan are even clearer in table 5.3 than in table 5.2. The VHF
audience ratings (in table 5.3) are 21 to 24 percent higher than the
average of all VHF and UHF stations in the sample, their twenty-second
prime rates some 47 percent higher. In contrast, they carry only a token
of .123 more program types per evening than UHF stations do, a mere

9. The expected negative impact on rates of *adding* one station to the market does
not occur, however, possibly because TV homes, and per station income, revenues and
time sales rise much more rapidly in markets whose stations exceed three. That is, in
the larger markets, those economic indicators grow more swiftly than the number of
operating stations, deliberately constrained to insure a more equitable geographic distribution of facilities. These divergent growth rates are indeed one reason for interacting TV homes with number of stations (as in chapter 6), and our failure to do so
here may mean that our simpler equation does not adequately take these factors into
account. Furthermore, adjacent and cochannel interference, per square mile, is the
same in big as in small markets, though the former's population density is much greater,
so that effective entry barriers will also be higher there. Thus, if few applicants hypothetically tried to enter any populous market, marginal signal interference effects there
would be smaller, and the technical barriers to entry lower, than if numerous applicants appeared. Hence another reason for the higher spot rates in these more populous
markets may be that there are actually fewer station competitors per 1,000 homes
there than in the less densely populated rural markets.

10. Vertical diversity was defined in chapter 3 as the average number of different
program types which appear, nightly, on any class of station during the sample week,
and was distinguished there from horizontal or market diversity of programming across
all stations in the market.

3 percent of the sample mean of types. Nor do they have advantages in any other program variable except mass entertainment (+3 percent). However, this does not take into account possible quality differences for any given program type.

Effects of Owner Affiliation

If the interstation structure associated with the Television Allocation Plan has markedly different effects on rates, profitability, diversity, and program composition, what about the impact of colocated cross-ownership? Multiple station ownership across geographically separate markets? Various network-affiliations? That is, when account is taken of competitors, homes, and channel type, what are the relative effects of different ownership affiliations and how do they compare with the effects of interstation structure?

I shall now consider these questions in regard, first, to station profitability; second, to advertising rates; and third, to programming. Before proceeding, however, technical readers may want to turn to Appendix 5A which explores why, if at all, newspaper-owned TV stations, for one, should be expected to charge higher rates, attract larger audiences, or earn more than otherwise comparable stations without such links.

Profitability

Again the tables tell a revealing story. As for profitability, newspaper and group ownership have only weakly significant effects in table 5.2 on the market averages of income, none on revenue and time sales. For newspapers, the income elasticity is barely significant at the 1.0 level (t = 1.71), and even then is only +.1 percent compared to −1.7 percent for program units in the market, and +.8 percent for TV homes. True, the hypothesis being tested is very strong, namely, that colocated newspaper-TV stations have sufficiently higher profits, revenues, or time sales to raise the market averages in question significantly. It also abstracts from possible anticompetitive effects vis-à-vis the newspaper industry. Furthermore, though failing this market-average test two times out of three, colocated newspaper- and group-owned stations, for one, could conceivably enjoy higher income or rates than nonnewspaper stations, *at the station level*.

Nevertheless, the market proportion of stations in a market owned by the TV networks does pass my test with flying colors. So, too, does the proportion of VHF stations. Therefore, the absence of almost any significant newspaper or group owner effects suggests that such stations may earn no more than those without such ties.[11]

Note further, in table 5.3, the absence of any significant newspaper owner superiority in prime rates, the limited advantages in audience ratings (+8 percent to 9 percent of the sample mean), in contrast with decisive rate and audience advantages for network-owned stations (+220 percent, +25 percent), and of advantages up to 87 percent for network affiliates.

Further Analysis of Advertising Rates

By way of further review of economic effects let us turn next to table 5.4 and its alternate equations for advertising rates. There I sought first to take account of special restrictive conditions in the larger, more densely populated markets, due to the greater demand for spectrum therein, per 1000 TV homes. This I did by introducing a new dummy variable which had a value of 1.0 for markets with four or more stations, zero otherwise.[12] Once I include that variable in table 5.4, I find that an additional 100,000 TV homes will raise the level of one-time rates roughly 6 to 7 percent of the sample mean, depending on the sample analyzed.[13] In addition, note that VHF stations charge rates 29 percent of the sample mean higher than UHF stations. This fact further indicates the special benefits that favored classes of stations still derive from the current allocation structure.

The same pattern holds, incidentally, for discounted five-time rates, which are probably a better measure of station viability. There too, an additional 100,000 TV homes will raise five-time rates comparable to one-time rates (5.2 percent of sample mean), whereas VHF rates will be 31 percent of the sample mean higher than UHF rates.

Recall next the insignificant newspaper- and group-owner impacts on one-time rates which table 5.3 reports. It is at least conceivable that the high network owner impacts there may have obscured the impact of

11. True, the network-owned stations are concentrated in the largest markets and their absence elsewhere may obscure any estimated impact due to changes in the proportion of stations with other attributes. Nevertheless, my tests do not assume independence of control factors among themselves. I simply calculate each factor's impact on the dependent variables after accounting for the impact of all others, each *impact* being assumed independent. Lastly, I find significant effects due to many of these control variables, notwithstanding the collinearity that exists among them. Furthermore, any distortion due to the bunching of network-owned stations would be minimized by having controlled for market size, the principal determinant of potential profit and diversity. This procedure clearly heightens the reliability of all reported impact elasticities in table 5.2, virtually regardless of the distribution of different stations throughout the sample markets.

12. See Appendix II, pp. 444, 463–64.

13. The PCDVs in column 1 (section A of table 5.4), pertain to the full sample of one-time rates ($N = 426$), whereas column 2 figures pertain to a modified sample, adjusted for comparability to the five-time rates ($N = 296$).

TABLE 5.4

Sensitivity of Twenty-Second Prime Rates in Relation to Rent-Yielding Market Variables, 1967—Alternate Formulations[1]

Change in Independent Variable	(A) TV Homes in Equation			(B) Delivered Audience in Equation		
	20-Second One-Time Rate	20-Second One-Time Rate	20-Second Five-Time Rate	20-Second One-Time Rate	20-Second One-Time Rate	20-Second Five-Time Rate
Add 100,000 TV homes to potential audience	7.39[a] (17.1)	5.87[a] (10.0)	5.15[a] (10.7)	n.i.	n.i.	n.i.
Add 100,000 TV homes delivered	n.i.	n.i.	n.i.	59.18[a] (21.8)	55.10[a] (13.3)	51.71[a] (15.0)
Add $100 to median city income	.49 (1.3)	.16 (.3)	.21 (.5)	.54 (1.6)	.10 (.2)	.19 (.5)
Switch from 1-3 station to 4+ station markets	109.22[a] (11.0)	136.41[a] (11.6)	178.18[a] (16.0)	97.97[a] (11.0)	117.85[a] (10.8)	143.31[a] (13.6)
Switch from UHF to VHF	28.98[a] (3.7)	28.70[a] (2.9)	30.75[a] (3.7)	9.01 (1.3)	20.25[b] (2.3)	23.53[a] (3.2)
Switch nongroup to:						
network group owner	193.10[a] (9.8)	n.i.	n.a.	131.04[a] (7.1)	n.i.	n.a.
nonnetwork group owner	3.94 (.6)	6.22 (.9)	10.59[c] (1.7)	6.52 (1.2)	8.75 (1.3)	12.44[b] (2.3)
Switch nonnewspaper to:						
outside newspaper owner	−3.28 (.4)	.64 (.1)	−.72 (.1)	−13.20[c] (1.7)	−13.77 (1.6)	−13.61[c] (1.9)
in-town newspaper owner	9.29 (1.2)	14.51 (1.5)	19.98[b] (2.5)	−6.00 (.9)	6.51 (.8)	13.44[c] (1.9)
Switch independent to:						
CBS affiliate	89.58[a] (6.7)	72.92[a] (4.0)	97.39[a] (6.2)	−42.25[a] (3.8)	−61.22[a] (4.3)	−24.38[b] (2.1)
NBC affiliate	87.57[a] (6.6)	67.76[a] (3.8)	95.14[a] (6.2)	−37.00[a] (3.4)	−58.40[a] (4.3)	−19.70[c] (1.7)
ABC affiliate	79.68[a] (6.1)	70.25[a] (3.9)	93.95[a] (6.0)	−37.57[a] (3.4)	−54.09[a] (3.9)	−18.13 (1.6)
CBS-ABC affiliate	77.70[a] (4.6)	50.44[b] (2.2)	64.29[a] (3.2)	−44.73[a] (3.1)	−80.11[a] (4.3)	−53.56[a] (3.4)
NBC-ABC affiliate	73.31[a] (4.4)	51.20[b] (2.4)	70.06[a] (3.8)	−56.26[a] (4.0)	−91.92 (5.1)	−60.73[a] (4.1)
CBS-NBC affiliate	76.53[a] (3.3)	54.78[c] (1.9)	76.24[a] (3.1)	−64.28[a] (3.2)	−111.85[a] (4.3)	−77.13[a] (3.6)
CBS-NBC-ABC affiliate	73.27[a] (4.1)	48.84[b] (2.1)	65.97[a] (3.2)	−48.05[a] (3.1)	−73.00[a] (3.8)	−43.77[a] (2.7)

n.i. = Not included in equation for design purposes.
n.a. = Data not available.
[1]Upper number in each cell denotes percentage change in dependent variable (column heading) due to change specified in independent variable. Lower number (in parentheses) is t-value of underlying regression coefficient, with statistical significance (two-tailed test) indicated by superscripts, as follows: a = 1 percent confidence level, b = 5 percent, c = 10 percent. Estimating equations appear below.

Estimating Equations for Table 5.4
(coefficients)

Independent Variables	TV Homes in Equation			Audience Delivered in Equation		
	20-Second One-Time Rate	20-Second One-Time Rate	20-Second Five-Time Rate	20-Second One-Time Rate	20-Second One-Time Rate	20-Second Five-Time Rate
	($100s)	($100s)	($100s)	($100s)	($100s)	($100s)
Constant	−4.152	−0.690	−1.221	0.111	1.209	−7.869
100,000s TV homes in market	.193[a]	.134[a]	.097[a]	n.i.	n.i.	n.i.
100,000s TV homes delivered	n.i.	n.i.	n.i.	1.543[a]	1.259[a]	.978[a]
Median city income in $100s	.013	.004	.004	.014	.002	.004
Dummy variables:[2]						
4+ more stations in market	2.847[a]	3.117[a]	3.368[a]	2.554[a]	2.693[a]	2.709[a]
VHF channel	.756[a]	.656[a]	.581[a]	.235	.463[b]	.445[a]
Network owner	5.034[a]	n.i.	n.a.	3.416[a]	n.i.	n.a.
Nonnetwork group owner	.103	.142	.200[c]	.170	.200	.235[b]
Outside newspaper owner	−.085	.015	−.014	−.344[c]	−.315	−.257[c]
In-town newspaper owner	.242	.332	.378[b]	−.156	.149	.254[c]
CBS affiliation	2.335[a]	1.666[a]	.184[a]	−1.101[a]	−1.399[a]	−.461[b]
NBC affiliation	2.283[a]	1.548[a]	1.799[a]	−.965[a]	−1.334[a]	−.373[c]
ABC affiliation	2.077[a]	1.605[a]	1.776[a]	−.979[a]	−1.236[a]	−.343
CBS-ABC affiliation	2.026[a]	1.152[b]	1.215[a]	−1.166[a]	−1.830[a]	−1.013[a]
NBC-ABC affiliation	1.911[a]	1.170[b]	1.324[a]	−1.467[a]	−2.100	−1.148[a]
CBS-NBC affiliation	1.995[a]	1.252[c]	1.441[a]	−1.676[a]	−2.555[a]	−1.458[a]
CBS-NBC-ABC affiliation	1.910[a]	1.116[b]	1.247[a]	−1.253[a]	−1.668[a]	−.828[a]
Adj. R^2	.817	.684	.734	.855	.737	.792
Sample size (stations)	426	296	296	426	296	296
Sample mean	2.607	2.285	1.890	2.607	2.285	1.890

n.i. = Not included in equation for design purposes.
n.a. = Data not available.
[2] Labeled attribute equals one, zero otherwise.

other owner attributes. After all, in table 5.4 newspaper ownership does impact significantly on five-time rates in the absence of network owner-ship data, and group ownership is also weakly significant. When full ac-count is taken of homes, channel type, median income, competitors, and network affiliations, that is, in-town newspaper stations have five-time rates 20 percent higher than the sample mean, and nonnetwork groups, 10.6 percent higher.

Nevertheless, to check further I removed the network owner values from my full sample of one-time rates, and otherwise made that sam-ple comparable to the smaller sample of five-time rates. Once again, the adjusted R^2 is substantial, .684 (table 5.4). However, the group and in-town newspaper coefficients remain insignificant for this adjusted sam-ple (as for the full sample), though their t-values are now larger. In table 5.4, then, newspaper and group stations do reveal greater power than unaffiliated stations to withhold the cost-savings implicit in their five-time rates, but appear unable to charge higher undiscounted (i.e., one-time) rates. (This apparent anomaly is discussed in Appendix 5A.)

Programming

Given this pattern of private benefits (substantial for network-owned stations and affiliates, much less for nonnetwork groups and in-town newspaper owners), what about public benefits? How do newspaper, group, and network ties impact on diversity and program composition?

In regard to program diversity in table 5.2, quite clearly the presence of even network-owned stations, let alone of newspaper owners or non-network groups, has virtually no effect. This holds true for both absolute commercial diversity and for diversity per station. Thus, while analysis of the market averages reveals at least limited economic benefits, there is virtually no compensatory programming contribution.

At the station level (table 5.3) the picture changes a little. The network-owned stations, with franchises of greatest value, clearly excel in the volume of news and public affairs carried and, in particular, carry more network public affairs than the nongroup stations, and probably also than the nonnetwork groups. However, my four ownership dummies impact significantly on programming or diversity, even at the permissive 10 percent level, in only seven out of thirty-two calculated coefficients. Note, for example, that nonnetwork groups like Westinghouse carry more news than stations without such group owners (8.7 percent of the sam-ple mean), and more nonnetwork programs (5.7 percent), but they have no other significant impact.[14] Neither does out-of-town newspaper

14. More nonnetwork programs on the groups, in any case, are not necessarily an unmitigated blessing, given that they "make their own." The groups' vertical linkage with program production, for example, could operate to the competitive detriment of other program producers who sell to the networks. However, it could also provide in-

ownership. Even in-town newspaper licensees—with 21 percent of the sample mean more public affairs and slightly more vertical diversity than nonnewspapers (3.6 percent)—perform no differently than the latter in fine arts or mass entertainment, feature film, news, local or nonnetwork.

Likewise, network affiliation—*the* single decisive determinant of audience size and advertising rates—has only mixed effects on vertical diversity, and decisively negative effects on local and nonnetwork programming, fine arts, and public affairs. Only in regard to news do affiliates substantially outproduce the independents. However, they also show far fewer feature films than the independents (probably because of carrying more network series), though more mass entertainment generally.

Summary

The bolstering economic impact of network affiliation appears considerably larger than that due to license limitation, or even channel type. But the compensating effects on programming are mixed. There is little or no contribution to vertical diversity, indeed some negative impact there, and, contrary to FCC goals, decisively less local and nonnetwork programs than on independents; relatively more mass entertainment and less fine arts; and decisively less public affairs. However, the affiliates do carry significantly more news and less feature film. This contrasts with the frequently insignificant economic effects of group and newspaper ownership, though it resembles the latter's spotty programming contributions. Perhaps only the network-owned stations perform comparably on *both* sides of the ledger—in their higher rates *and* higher public affairs and news, but lower mass entertainment record.

Conclusion

This initial review shows that the effects of TV regulation are clearly asymmetrical. The commission's procompetitive function has neither dissipated the industry's substantial rents nor, with one important exception, decisively promoted diversity and merit programming.

Specifically, license limitation, preferred channel assignments, network affiliation, and especially network ownership, all have substantial

dependent packagers with an additional source of expensive programming, and otherwise offset the networks' dominance in prime-time broadcasting. Furthermore, our main textual point remains—namely that, overall, the groups' impact on programming is even less apparent than it is on station and market economics. That is, there is far less evidence of any offsetting public contribution here than for the network-owned stations, which carry considerably more news, public affairs, and apparently, cultural-educational shows, than the nonnetwork groups.

bolstering effects on station audiences, rates, and market averages of per-station income and revenue. However, ownership by nonnetwork groups or colocated newspapers apparently does not.[15] As for programming, license limitation has virtually no effects whatever on program composition, whereas it clearly does act to reduce horizontal diversity (with little offsetting enhancement of vertical diversity). The divergence of public and private advantage is therefore unmistakable.

On the other hand, network affiliates appear to combine some of their economic advantages with superior performance in the amount of (admittedly profitable) network news, and, for the affiliates, less reliance on feature film. But the independents carry more fine arts, public affairs, local and nonnetwork programs than the affiliates, and less mass entertainment, although their economic standing is considerably weaker. Thus profits and merit service or diversity continue to diverge here for affiliates, at many though not all points. A balance between both variables is more apparent for network-owned stations, where greater profits are matched by more news, more public affairs, and less mass entertainment than on nongroup stations. In contrast, the far more meager economic advantages of newspaper- and group-owned stations are also offset by only meager or spotty informational contributions.

So much for this broad preliminary look at objectives and results in federal broadcast regulation. In Part II, I turn to closer scrutiny of three principal policy approaches—namely those that pertain to owner diversity, structural diversity, and network-affiliate relations.

Appendix 5A. The Owen, the Peterman, and the Lago Rate Studies

The purpose of this note is to consider why, if at all, one should expect TV stations affiliated with in-town newspaper owners to charge higher advertising rates, attract larger audiences, or earn more than otherwise comparable stations without such links. This question can be considered by reference to a single criterion, namely the newspaper-owned licensee's power to set its own advertising rates.[16]

15. A major confirmation of these initial results appears in chapter 6. Why, notwithstanding the absence of significant economic advantages, newspapers, for one, should seek and retain TV subsidiaries, is a matter to which we return in chapters 6 and 7.

16. Monopoly rates, if such exist, will presumably operate to generate monopoly income, revenue, and time sales, which would, in turn, result in significantly higher station sales prices than for nonnewspaper-owned stations. Furthermore, the larger income enjoyed by a newspaper-owned facility might permit it to create more attractive programming, and thereby contribute to some superiority in audience size.

There appear to be three hypotheses. First, newspaper owners could in theory charge higher TV time rates than nonnewspaper TV licensees if they dominated the market for newspaper advertising and could thereby compel advertisers to buy TV time at premium rates as a condition for access to their newspaper space. Newspaper space would in this case be the so-called tying product, and TV time the tied product. The issue is how much leverage a newspaper owner could derive from its market position in the tying product, and how much of a premium TV time rate it could thereby exact.

Second, and closely related to the first thesis, suppose that the joint newspaper-TV enterprise commands a very large share of total advertising on all newspapers and TV stations within its market, and that other media are poor substitutes. In such a case, too, the joint enterprise might have greater combined market power that would lead to higher profit-maximizing rates on both ends of the enterprise. On the TV end, this would presumably show up as a time rate significantly higher than that charged by otherwise comparable nonnewspaper owners.[17]

According to a third hypothesis, the newspaper-owned stations cannot only charge more than a nonnewspaper-owned station would for the above reasons, they may also set an umbrella price which permits nonnewspaper owners who compete with any newspaper-owned station to charge more than they otherwise could, and more than they in fact do in markets without newspaper-owned stations. However, studies with otherwise different conclusions generally agree that the umbrella effect is not statistically significant, and we will not consider it here.

In regard to the first two hypotheses, Peterman (also Lago) and Owen do indeed come to quite different conclusions, in large part apparently due to their different variable specifications.[18] Of major importance is Owen's deliberate exclusion of audience size from his equation on technical-econometric grounds,[19] leaving as control factors only channel

17. See citations in footnote 18.
18. See B. Owen, *Empirical Results on the Price Effect of Joint Ownership in the Mass Media,* Memorandum 93, Research Center in Economic Growth, Stanford University (November 1969), and a revised version, "Newspaper and Television Station Joint Ownership," *Antitrust Bulletin* (Winter 1973), pp. 787–807. Owen's first statement was filed in FCC Docket No. 18110 as an appendix to Rosse, Owen, and Grey, *Economic Issues in Joint Ownership of Newspaper and TV Media,* Memorandum No. 97, Research Center in Economic Growth, Stanford University, 1 June 1970. The Owen study was followed by J. Peterman, "Concentration of Control and the Price of Television Time," *American Economic Review* (May 1971), pp. 74–80; Lago and Osborne, *A Quantitative Analysis of the Price Effects of Joint Mass Communication Media Ownership,* filed 9 March 1971, in FCC Docket No. 18110 for the National Association of Broadcasters; restated in Lago, "The Price Effects of Joint Mass Communications Media Ownership," *Antitrust Bulletin* (Winter 1971), pp. 789–813; and "Comments of the National Association of Broadcasters," in Docket 18110, appendix D, filed 18 August 1971.
19. There are some technical-economic arguments over whether Owen or other researchers have used the correct specification. See especially Rosse's detailed rebuttal of Owen's critics, in *Credible and Incredible Economic Evidence,* Memorandum No.

type, median income, degree of local competition, and network tie. Briefly, he found that in 1968 newspaper-owned stations charged 15 percent higher network hourly rates than nonnewspapers, a premium charge significantly greater than zero. On the other hand, Peterman and Lago did include audience size in their equations and, contrarily, found no significant impact of newspaper ownership.

My own control factors in table 5.4 appear to be somewhat more complete than Owen's, and my dependent variable—twenty-second prime rates—a better proxy for station revenues than his network hourly rates. Finally, my combined use of TV homes and median income may be a better measure of advertising potential than income alone.

Nevertheless, my significant in-town newspaper coefficients on the (discounted) five-time rates are clearly consistent with Owen's results, though the same coefficients on (undiscounted) one-time rates are *not* (table 5.4). Overall, these mixed results suggest that nonnewspaper licensees are more likely than colocated newspaper licensees to set five-time rates that are lower than one-time rates (conceivably reflecting quantity discounts), but that neither type of owner systematically sets lower one-time rates than the other.[20]

Nor does the substitution of audience size for TV homes in my equations change these contrasting results very much (see section B of table 5.4). Therefore this analysis has special interest in trying to reconcile the divergent findings of rate studies by Owen, Peterman, Lago, and the National Association of Broadcasters.[21] Once again, in-town newspaper and nonnetwork group coefficients are insignificant at the 10 percent level for one-time rates, even with the O&Os out of the sample. However, with five-time rates, even with audience circulation in, the colocated newspaper coefficient is positive and weakly significant ($t = 1.86$), whereas the nonnetwork group owner coefficient is significant at the 5-percent level.

As for network affiliation, virtually all network coefficients are significant for both one-time and five-time rates, in all equations reported. However, with TV homes in the equation, the sign of these coefficients is

109, Research Center in Economic Growth, Stanford University, filed in Docket No. 19110, 29 April 1971. An illuminating review of the divergent methods and conclusions of several parties to this dispute appears in W. Baer, H. Geller, J. Grundfest, and K. Possner, *Concentration of Mass Media Ownership: Assessing the State of Current Knowledge*, Rand Report R–1584–NSF (September 1974), pp. 82–92, 167–71.

20. This must at best be a tentative conclusion pending more complete information on the actual rates O&Os charge, as well as on the magnitude of the quantity discounts on five-time rates. Removal of the O&Os from my one-time rates sample (to insure its comparability with the five-time rates) clearly increases the significance of the remaining coefficients in table 5.4, as well as their magnitude in many cases. Had I been able to run the five-time rates with the O&Os in, the significance attributed to nonnetwork groups and in-town newspapers may well have declined. A really definitive statement, then, requires information that I have thus far been unable to secure.

21. See note 18 in this chapter.

positive, whereas with delivered audience in, the sign is negative. Therefore, with TV homes in, network affiliation quite clearly bolsters the value of station prime time for the national nonnetwork (spot) advertiser. That is, the network coefficients tell us how much more any affiliated station can ask for a twenty-second prime spot than a fully comparable independent can, in a *potential* market of any given size. With delivered audience in, the same coefficients become negative and then depict the network system's known competitive superiority in actually reaching prime-time audiences for the national spot advertiser.

How can this apparent mystery be explained? There is no question in regard to one-time rates, that, for several alternative specifications in 1967 (and again, in chapter 6, for 1972), newspaper-owned stations charge rates no higher and no lower, statistically, than nonnewspaper-owned licensees. This holds true, in 1967, for a simple additive model in the present chapter, after taking account of market size, number of competitors, and the station's channel type, network ties, and group owner status. It further holds for 1972, in chapter 6, where I interact the network dummy variable with market size and channel type, and further interact the number of competitors, group-owner and newspaper-owner dummies, also with market size. It is true, finally, even when the station's market share is taken into account.

In contrast, the impact of newspaper ownership on five-time rates *is* statistically significant in 1967, again when either potential or actual delivered audiences are alternatively introduced as control factors. Because the data on five-time rates are more limited than those on one-time rates, we ran one final set of regressions on the latter for a subsample of stations identical to those analyzed for the former. But again, there is no statistically significant impact of newspaper ownership on one-time rates. Although we found no really definitive way to account for this puzzling result, several explanations are possible.

One thesis, more consistent with Peterman than with Owen, is that rates normally reflect delivered audiences in both cases (for one-time and five time rates), but that the chance of *reaching* the average delivered audience is greater where announcements are repeated five times during the week, than where only carried once. Related to this is a second explanation, which follows from two facts. Newspaper-owned stations in 1967 carried more public affairs than nonnewspaper-owned outlets, while advertisers also appear to pay some premium rate to reach audiences that watch informational shows, are better educated, and hence earn more income. Thus the higher five-time rates in table 5.4 may not reflect monopoly power as such. Advertisers may simply place a higher value, per 1,000 homes delivered, on those educated informational audiences the typical newspaper-owned outlet reaches, *plus the greater likelihood of reaching them with five announcements than with one.*

Again, this explanation would reconcile our five-time rate results with those for one-time rates, but make both results more consistent with Peterman than Owen.[22]

Nevertheless, a third and final explanation (in line with Owen), may simply be that the newspaper-owned station feels its five-time rate is more competitive with rates charged by other stations than its one-time rate, given the lower unit cost in accommodating more announcements once the initial transaction is made. By setting its five-time rate higher than that of any nonnewspaper station in the market, the newspaper-owned station may attempt to protect its newspaper parent against rate competition from rival TV stations.

In other words, though the unit costs of handling multiple announcements during a week may be less than the cost of a single announcement, for this very reason competitive five-time rates could elicit more competition from nonnewspaper stations, either those whose five-time rates were higher, or equally, those whose advertising sales more often took the form of one-time spots. On both counts, a newspaper-owned station might favor setting its five-time rates higher than its nonnewspaper rival's, to forestall the kind of competitive response that might *also* erode the newspaper parent's advertising market. In that case, the evidence would indeed imply that the newspaper-owned TV station had more discretionary power than I initially inferred.

The upshot is that short of still more work to test these new hypotheses, the mystery remains! However, the absence of sizable significant newspaper owner impacts on any market economic dependent variable is unmistakable, and this despite limited but significant effects on station ratings. With this one puzzling uncertainty about five-time rates, then, newspaper and nonnewspaper stations do appear to perform comparably from an economic standpoint. I reserve for chapter 6 a more definitive assessment of new station data, and a more refined statistical analysis.

22. That is, for Peterman a rate differential largely reflective of differences in effective audience delivered by stations with and without newspaper (or group) affiliations is not consistent with any hypothesis that affiliated stations have significantly more *market power* than their unaffiliated counterparts. The point is simply that five-time rates data are better *as data* than the one-time rates data.

PART TWO

A Critique
of Current
Policies

Chapter 6

The Policy on

Ownership Diversity

WITHIN the frame of reference developed in the preceding chapters of Part I, the next six chapters will appraise key FCC policies that relate to owner diversity, structural diversity, and network-affiliate relations. The purpose of this chapter is to assess two major policies on owner diversity alone—that is, one relating to cross-media ownership, and the other to nonnetwork group ownership. My plan is to first describe the objectives of these basic licensing policies, and then to assess their effects on a large number of economic and programming variables, at the station and market levels (for 1967). In the following section, a second set of tests examines a few of our main variables with more refined techniques and a larger data base (for 1972). In the next chapter, selective results will then be related to the continuing controversy over strengthening one of these policies—the Newspaper Rule —recent subject of an intensive review by the Federal Communications Commission, and in the courts. Finally, chapter 8 will compare the impact of owner diversity and structural diversity more generally, my objective throughout being to estimate any divergence between the formal goals and the end results of diversified ownership.

My working assumptions are threefold. First, that the FCC does *purport* to further localism, informational service, sources and content diversity, whatever the effective impact of its several licensing-allocation policies. Second, that these stated goals are also desirable as such, as well as for purposes of regulatory assessment in that the industry, the FCC, Congress, the courts, and countless public interest groups, have all paid extensive lip service to such yardsticks in debating regulatory alternatives. But third, that in strict economic welfare terms the goals are not necessarily optimal. Therefore, the most we attempt here or in later chapters is to quantify the costs of each policy goal on the assumption that it is desirable, leaving the many powerful interests which support it free to reexamine their own commitments in light of all social, economic, and programming ramifications.

The Policy to Diversify Station Ownership: Objective versus Results

The policy of promoting diversity in ownership relates (1) to limits imposed on dual station ownership in the same or overlapping markets; (2) to cross-ownership of TV stations by colocated newspapers; and (3) to multiple ownership of TV stations across geographically separate markets.

The Duopoly Rule

Under the first policy—the duopoly rule—no licensee may hold more than one AM, one FM, and one TV station in the same market.[1] The latest embellishment is the prospective ban on joint ownership of colocated TV and AM stations, though common FM-AM ownership remains untouched. The AM duopoly rule was first introduced in 1943, following the Chain Broadcasting Hearings, and at that time forced certain radio licensees to divest themselves of a second AM station they owned in the same market.

The Policy on Cross-Ownership

The policy on colocated cross-media ownership was then instituted following the Newspaper-Radio Hearings, 1941–44. There, a preference was to be given to a nonnewspaper applicant *whether or not* "equal in every other respect" to a competing newspaper applicant. The key point, however, was that the nonnewspaper candidate would win if he was equal in every respect to the newspaper owner. Subsequently, nonnewspapers have long been preferred to equally qualified newspapers, in order to promote diversity. But newspapers with satisfactory technical, legal, and financial qualifications have never been denied licenses on grounds of newspaper ownership alone when they were the sole applicants. Finally, a newspaper has sometimes won on grounds of superior resources and experience. In other cases, locally resident publishers,

1. See FCC Rules and Regulations, 47 CFR pars. 3.35(a), 73.240(1), 73.636(1) (1974).

whom the FCC deemed "civic-minded" and aware of their community needs, were selected, though they would thereby operate the only station in town.[2]

The commission's so-called newspaper policy[3] is one touchstone among many used in granting licenses and permits. Judging from actions since its inception in 1944, the policy's implicit rationale appears to be threefold: first and foremost, to promote the greater program diversity that results from different owners whose outlooks and perspectives differ as individuals. Second, and less important here, to avoid such deliberate abuses of power by joint newspaper-TV enterprises as retarded development of units of a rival medium operated as subsidiaries, use of cross-media ties as a coercive weapon, and, related to point one, the injection of a newspaper parent's editorial position into its TV subsidiary's program content. Third, to induce different media to criticize and assess each other publicly, a process which is more likely to occur when the media are separately owned and competitive. The above benefits are expected to implement the public's right to hear all views, a value in turn desired largely to promote an accurate, fair, balanced, and thorough presentation of facts and commentary, and hence to further a wider range of ends implicit in democratic social-political processes.

Most recently, the commission has explicitly stated the basis for its policy on cross-ownership as follows:

> The premise is that a democratic society cannot function without the clash of divergent views. It is clear to us that the idea of diversity of viewpoints from antagonistic sources is at the heart of the Commission's licensing responsibility. If our democratic society is to function, nothing can be more important than insuring that there is a free flow of information from as many divergent sources as possible. This is not a reflection on the efforts of combination owners in diligently serving the public interest. Rather, it is a recognition that it is unrealistic to expect true diversity from a commonly owned station-newspaper combination. The divergency of their viewpoints cannot be expected to be the same as if they were antagonistically run.[4]

This latest statement seems most in line with our first proposition above, whereas the second point (on abuse), while significant, does not appear to be the basis for the FCC's current posture on cross-ownership.

2. Note, however, that the commission's decisions in this regard are notably arbitrary and inconsistent. See Henry J. Friendly, *The Federal Administrative Agencies* (Cambridge, Mass.: Harvard University Press, 1962), pp. 66–67. Also the actual treatment of newspapers in comparative TV proceedings has been shown to reflect their political orientation as much or more than the factors cited in the decisions themselves. See chapter 1 in this book, notes 20–21 and associated text.

3. See *Newspaper Ownership of Radio Stations*, FCC Notice, 9 Fed. Reg. 702 (1944).

4. FCC, Second Report and Order in Docket No. 18110, 31 January 1975, par. 111.

The Multiple Ownership Rules

The Multiple Ownership Rules [5] limit each broadcast licensee to no more than seven AM, seven FM and seven TV stations (only five of which may operate in the VHF band). The commission itself has recognized that any uncompromising commitment to locally-based and locally-financed broadcast facilities may limit the resources needed for a balanced, widely distributed service. On frequent occasions, therefore, it has overridden this structural criterion to safeguard the continued financial health of network and nonnetwork groups, and of individual licensees. Far less clear is whether the commission also recognizes the possible conflict between the goals of local diversified ownership and competitive business conduct.

The Multiple Ownership Rules are designed in part to insure such conduct in this industry. Groups are sometimes said to enjoy important competitive advantages over single-station owners in regard to (1) obtaining choice network affiliations; (2) the bargains they can strike for premium network time rates, compensation arrangements, and inclusion on the networks' now defunct "must-buy" list; and (3) the terms they can secure in dealing with film syndicators and national spot advertisers.[6]

Being able to bargain for several stations at once, the group owner is deemed able to secure economically more favorable terms for himself in regard to network and nonnetwork program suppliers and advertisers. These advantages are themselves alleged to have led to further acquisitions by TV groups of stations in the leading markets, where profit opportunities are the best. Moreover, the growth of group ownership in television allegedly entails other consequences viewed as undesirable. By buying rather than building most of their stations, and by doing so far more frequently in the lucrative VHF markets than the impoverished UHF band, the group owners are said to subvert ownership diversity as represented by locally based single-owned stations.

Accordingly, group ownership is seen by many not simply to reduce single station ownership, but to reduce program diversity in the process (by carrying programs and viewpoints across all group members), and to pose anticompetitive dangers. Therefore, unless unusual scale economies or innovative contributions to technology or programming can be clearly attributed to the groups, an argument exists for limiting group ownership. Because compensating benefits have not in fact been shown, some critics urge a more rigorous screening of group applicants for new grants, renewal rights, and even transfers.[7] They have also urged that

5. FCC Rules & Regulations, 47 CFR, pars. 73.35, 73.240, 73.646 (1970).
6. House Commerce Committee, *Report on Network Broadcasting* (Washington, D.C.: U.S. Government Printing Office, 1958), pp. 241–46, 564–68, 650–52.
7. See summary assessment of the current state of knowledge in W. Baer, H. Geller, J. Grundfest, and K. Possner, *Concentration of Mass Media Ownership* (Santa Monica, Calif.: Rand Corporation, 1974), R–1584–NSF, especially chapter 4.

special limits be placed on group ownership in the top twenty-five or fifty markets.

One important task is to assess group (or newspaper) owner effects on station viability, since only economically viable stations can perform adequately on the commission's own terms. If group or newspaper owners are more efficient or profitable due to joint ownership, they could in theory cross-subsidize significant amounts of informational, cultural, or local programming, and might indeed do so to offset the FCC's concern over possible editorial control and less diversified owner perspectives. This could weaken the case for divestiture. A second compelling task is to measure group or newspaper owner effects on the actual programming broadcast. Both tasks have to some extent been undertaken in research reported in part in chapter 5 and below.

The Cross-Ownership Policy: An Initial Assessment

In regard to the proposals to reduce cross-ownership, our initial study (for 1967) indicated that they would in no significant way change horizontal diversity across all stations in the market, or diversity per station (table 6.1). This contrasts with clearly significant positive effects of a 1-percent increase in total broadcast hours available, a proxy for the number of commercial stations in the market. The results hold, moreover, even when account is taken of market size, network affiliation, channel type, and network ownership of stations. While the independent variables studied explain 87 percent of the variance in absolute diversity, a 10-point reduction in the newspaper owner proportion implied a loss of 1.57 program types, only .48 percent of the sample mean of 325.5 types, and the coefficient itself was not significant ($t = 1.23$). The impact on diversity of a change in nonnetwork group ownership is even farther from significance (see table 6.1).

True, the analysis of station data for 1967 modifies this picture at several points (table 6.2). However, there too the losses due to divestiture would be small in absolute terms. The sole significant programming loss in 1967 would have occurred in public affairs, but this would actually have deprived the public of at most $(1.557 \times 15)/7$, or 3.3 minutes daily (table 6.2). A token loss in (vertical) program diversity, though statistically significant, would also have been a scant .149 program types daily (ibid.). In short, there would be little effect on program diversity.

With what economic effects would this almost unchanged programming picture have been associated? Holding constant channel type, income, homes, and competitors, a 10-point reduction in the proportion of colocated cross-owned stations had no significant effect on average market revenues or time sales per station (table 6.1), and only the weakest effect on per-station income—namely, $53,240, or 7.2 percent of the sample mean, barely significant at the .10 level.

TABLE 6.1

Estimated Impacts of Selected Policy Variables
on Market Economic and Programming Indicators, 1967*

	Dependent Variables (Marketwide)				
				Equation 4	Equation 5
				Commercial Diversity: Number of Program Types per Market	
Independent Variables	Equation 1 $100,000 Income per Station	Equation 2 $100,000 Revenue per Station	Equation 3 $100,000 Time Sales per Station	Per Commercial Station	Total
Proportion of Stations with:					
In-town newspaper owner	5.324^c	7.657	1.563	2.450	15.729
	(1.7)	(1.3)	(1.5)	(.6)	(1.2)
Nonnetwork group owner	4.037^c	6.581	1.080	−1.078	1.047
	(1.9)	(1.6)	(1.6)	(.2)	(.1)
Adjusted R-square	.764	.855	.744	.435	.872
Sample size	101	101	101	143	143
Sample mean	7.428	26.020	4.917	110.995	325.461

SOURCE: Extracted from the estimating equations for table 5.2. Dependent variables are indicated in column headings to table 6.1. Independent variables, not all reported here, are identical to those in table 5.2, and include: (a) number of 15-minute units of commercial program time on all stations in the markets studied (a proxy for number of stations); (b) TV homes; (c) proportion of stations affiliated with a national network; (d) proportion owned by a TV network, a VHF licensee, an in-town newspaper, an out-of-town newspaper, and a nonnetwork TV group.
*Upper number in cell is a regression coefficient which denotes the absolute change in the dependent variable due to a 100-percentage-point change in the newspaper or nongroup owner proportion. Thus a reduction in the number of stations in any market affiliated with an in-town newspaper by 10 points, will result in a loss of income per station of $532,400 × 10% = $53,240, which is 7.1 percent of the sample mean. Lower number in parentheses is the t-value of the regression coefficient; superscript c indicates statistical significance (two-tailed test), at 10 percent level.

A critical reader may object that any group or newspaper owner impact could merely reflect the licensee's superior judgment in buying or building stations with the technical and economic features that virtually result in premium rates, revenues, ratings, and audiences. Not ownership type but *those* station and market attributes could then be said to produce the apparent economic advantages of group or newspaper affiliation. I return to this matter of causation later (pages 197–99), but here suffice it to note that (1) I have specified a large number of cogent control factors; (2) any residual newspaper or group owner impact clearly reflects something special about type of owner; (3) I know of no other major omitted variable for which my ownership coefficients may be unintended proxies, and the burden of proof rests on those who may contend otherwise. Important though this question is on the merits, finally, it is in one sense irrelevant here. My principal concern is whether

TABLE 6.2
Estimated Impacts of Selected Policy Variables
on Station Economic and Programming Indicators, 1967*
(6 P.M.-11 P.M.)

Dependent Variables	1 In-Town Newspaper	2 Non- network Group	3 Adjusted R-square	4 Sample Mean	5 Sample Size
ADI ratings (%)	1.697[c] (1.8)	1.313[c] (1.7)	.4321	21.1	445
Metro ratings (%)	1.980[a] (2.8)	.470 (.8)	.6362	21.2	408
20-second rates ($)	24.303 (1.1)	17.592 (1.0)	.7694	249.46	452

Vertical diversity: average
    number of program
    types nightly
	.15[b]
	(2.5)
		.01
		(.2)
			.2261	4.2	486

Program types in 15-minute Units

Local	−.629 (.3)	1.166 (.8)	.3934	32.4	486
All nonnetwork	.423 (.3)	2.570[b] (2.3)	.8393	44.8	486
News	.824 (.9)	1.623[b] (2.3)	.3456	18.4	486
Public affairs	1.557[a] (2.7)	.491 (1.1)	.1854	7.5	486
Fine arts	−.131 (.3)	−.230 (.8)	.3024	3.4	486
Mass entertainment	−1.859 (1.2)	−.159 (.1)	.1215	108.4	486
Feature film	−1.920 (1.3)	.350 (.3)	.1578	74.6	486

SOURCE: Extracted from estimating equations for table 5.3. Dependent variables are indicated in row headings in table 6.2. Independent variables, not all reported here, are identical to those in table 5.3, and include: (a) number of commercial stations; (b) TV homes; (c) channel type; (d) network ownership; (e) in-town newspaper owner; (f) out-of-town newspaper owner; (g) nonnetwork group; (h) network affiliation (7 network dummies).
*Upper cell is a regression coefficient which denotes the absolute change in dependent variable due to a switch from nonnewspaper to newspaper ownership (column 1), and from nongroup to group owner (column 2). Lower number in parentheses is a t-value of the coefficient with superscripts indicating statistical significance (two-tailed test): a = 1 percent, b = 5 percent, c = 10 percent.

any policy to diversify ownership (prospectively, or via divestiture), must destroy sizable private equities, and if so, their magnitude. Where losses are not large (as with newspapers), it is academic whether they involve impairment of monopolistic advantage. On the other hand, where losses will be substantial (as with group owners in large markets), even if they do impair excessive market power (and not scale economies or program resources), the commission would still face major practical political obstacles in serious structural change.

Be this as it may, asking if divestiture would lower average market-wide profitability is a very strong hypothesis to test. Market averages, as noted in chapter 5, could mask effects on individual stations. Therefore, an additional analysis of divestiture's impact on *station* economics was also undertaken and did reveal some adverse economic effects. Thus loss of a newspaper tie was found likely to reduce audience ratings 1.7 to 1.98 points on a mean of 21 (table 6.2), whereas, in table 6.3, I also found a loss of as much as $25.40 or $37.80 in discounted five-time spot rates, 13 percent and 20 percent of their respective sample means, depending on whether potential or actual audience was specified.[8] However, my analysis of the larger, more complete sample of undiscounted one-time rates ($N = 426$) revealed no significant impact whatever ($t = 1.2, .85$).

At best, then, the economic effects of divestiture would have been mixed. However, there seems little question that actions by Congress and the commission to diffuse economic and political power would create no economic disaster according to these initial studies. Neither would the public lose (or gain) substantial diversity (so long as the networks remained viable), or witness systematic changes in prime time program composition antithetical to FCC goals. The single exception to the latter point is the moderate loss in public affairs programming.

The Multiple Ownership Rule: An Initial Assessment

What about proposals to reduce the total amount of nonnetwork group ownership across geographically separate centers, especially in the top twenty-five or fifty markets? What likely impact would such action have on diversity? On program composition, or station viability? Is the price in private economic losses worth imposing for the program benefits that result? Or are there better ways to further diversity and merit programming?

Once again, my initial studies have demonstrated that a reduction in group ownership would have no impact on diversity, however measured, so long as network affiliations remain unchanged (table 6.1). Nor, with two limited exceptions, was there any impact on the other program

8. These last two elasticities (PCDVs) may be inflated, as noted in chapter 5, by the lack of data on five-time rates for network-owned stations. Those stations were therefore deliberately excluded from the smaller one-time rates sample to insure comparability with the results for the five-time rates. See Appendix 5A, note 20; also that chapter's text at note 11. On the direction of causation, see pages 197–99, 428–30.

TABLE 6.3

Estimated Impacts of Selected Policy Variables on 20-Second Spot Rates, 1967*
(6 P.M.-11 P.M.)
(station data)

Dependent Variables (A) TV Homes in Equation	In-Town Newspaper Owner	Non-network Group Owner	Adjusted R-square	Sample Mean	Sample Size
20-second one-time rate (1)	$ 24.20 (1.2)	$10.30 (.6)	.8170	$260.70	426
20-second one-time rate (2)	33.20 (1.5)	14.20 (.9)	.6842	228.50	296
20-second five-time rate	37.80[b] (2.5)	20.00[c] (1.7)	.7338	189.00	296
(B) Delivered Audience in Equation					
20-second one-time rate (1)	$-15.60 (.9)	$17.00 (1.2)	.8550	260.70	426
20-second one-time rate (2)	14.90 (.8)	20.00 (1.3)	.7365	228.50	296
20-second five-time rate	25.40[c] (1.9)	23.50[b] (2.3)	.7916	189.00	296

SOURCE: Extracted from estimating equation for table 5.4. Dependent variables are in the row headings to table 6.3. Independent variables, not all reported here, are identical to those in table 5.4, and include: (a) TV homes (for section A results), and (b) audience delivered (for section B results); also, for all results, (c) median family income, (d) a market dummy which weights markets by number of stations therein; (e) channel type; (f) network ownership; (g) in-town newspaper owner; (h) outside newspaper owner; (i) nonnetwork group owner; (j) network affiliation (7 network dummies).
*Upper number in each cell is a regression coefficient that denotes the absolute change in dependent variable due to a switch from nonnewspaper to newspaper owner, or from nongroup to group. Number in parentheses is the t-value of the regression coefficient; superscripts indicate statistical significance (two-tailed test): b = 5 percent; c = 10 percent.

variables studied (table 6.2). Loss of a group tie would have deprived viewers of no more than 3.5 minutes of news daily, and of 5.5 minutes of nonnetwork shows, whereas public affairs, fine arts, and local programming would each have remained unaffected, so that the programming consequences of a tighter policy on group ownership across separate markets would by and large be similar to those of the proposed cross-ownership curbs. Specifically, in virtually no other tests than those just cited (table 6.2), would newspaper and group owner impacts be significant even at the .10 level. There were indeed only three cases where their t-values exceeded 1. Finally, these results were calculated after taking into account the separate impacts of stations, homes, channel type, network ownership, and affiliation.

Economic effects may be more serious. In table 6.1, as with newspaper ownership, a decline in the nonnetwork group owner proportion would significantly reduce overall market averages of income per station (t = 1.9). The decline would be $40,370 for a 10-point decrease, with effects on per-station revenue at least approaching significance (t = 1.6, PCDV = 2.5 percent).[9] Furthermore, loss of a group tie would reduce five-time station rates by as much as $20.00 to $23.50 on a mean of $189, whereas ADI ratings would drop by 1.3 points. Nevertheless, metro ratings would remain unaffected and so would one-time rates, whether analyzed with potential or actual audiences in the equation (tables 6.2, 6.3).[10]

How likely are these factors to impair program composition and diversity? As with cross-ownership curbs, divestiture's direct effects on program composition are small and unlikely to generate other indirect effects due to changes in station rates, revenue, or income. Accordingly, any action to constrain nonnetwork group ownership should not be grounded on any likely affirmative effects on diversity and merit programming. As with cross-ownership curbs, the case must rest on the value of diffusing economic and political power *per se,* a benefit whose assessment lies beyond my quantitative measures. The policy to diversify station ownership in whatever form must be justified largely by the wisdom of being safe rather than sorry. Any potential dangers of opinion manipulation, joint collaborative cross-consultation on editorials, and the like are simply better avoided than sanctioned for want of definitive evidence on abuse.[11]

Finally, owner diversification not only acts to diversify owner perspectives, values, backgrounds, and editorial viewpoints, but also enhances the possibility of new entry by minority groups or other latecomers (at lower purchase prices than hitherto). It might have the latter effect by forcing divestiture of many stations simultaneously. A station might also, after divestiture, be less valuable, due to loss of scale economies (or of limited market power advantages), at least in the hands of a nongroup buyer. But even if the price an ethnic buyer had to pay for a divested station were no lower than the price he would have to pay an operating newspaper owner today, still, under divestiture that owner's noneco-

9. Since the dependent variables here are market averages of income and revenue, not all stations are necessarily affected adversely.

10. On the direction of causation, see citation in note 8.

11. One astute observer argues that cross-media abuses and manipulation may elude conventional social science measurement, but that there is nonetheless a lot of less quantifiable evidence which suggests that they do in fact occur. This underscores the limitations of an *ad hoc* case-by-case approach, and the need for those structural safeguards which diversified ownership provides. (Stephen Barnett, "Cross-Ownership of Mass Media in the Same Community—A Report to the John and Mary Markle Foundation" (Berkeley, Calif.: University of California, 23 September 1974 unprocessed.) For some recent quantitative evidence see William Gormley, *Effects of Newspaper-TV Cross Ownership on News Homogeneity* (Chapel Hill: University of North Carolina Press, 1976).

nomic reasons for refusing to sell would no longer keep the ethnic late-comer out.

In sum, a review of 1967 data suggests that the policy to limit group and newspaper ownership can be applied without serious risk of economic disruption and without substantial public losses in diversity or merit programs.

A More Refined Policy Audit

How do these basic impressions withstand closer scrutiny? Applying more refined techniques to several particularly sensitive economic and programming variables, I have utilized economic data for 1972 as well as 1967. I have also drawn on the commission's newly available questionnaire data on news, public affairs, and other informational programming, (1972), in addition to those I compiled directly from *TV Guide* (1967).

My statistical model is based on the assumption that the hypothesized advantages of newspaper- or group-owned stations may not show up unless other major attributes are considered simultaneously. The model asks such questions as these: Do newspaper or group-owned stations charge higher spot rates (or earn higher revenues or income) than stations without such ties, regardless of whether they are (1) jointly owned by newspaper-group entities; (2) affiliated with a national network; (3) located in the largest markets; (4) among the oldest stations, licensed before 1952; (5) operating on UHF rather than VHF channels? Do the newspaper- or group-owned stations also carry more fine arts, news, public affairs, or other informational programs, considering the same factors as just cited? Are any asymmetries in the economic and programming effects as great here as in the simpler additive model? Do comparable interactions between number of stations and market size markedly alter our simpler initial results? Do they do so in particular when the log form is used for the number of stations variable (market analysis), or for station age (station analysis)? This section will now report my principal findings in selected analyses for the general reader. Those who wish to examine my statistical model and methodology more closely, are referred to appendices I and II.

Economic Assessment

For clarity and convenience my next report is on an extensive regression analysis of spot rates, audiences, ratings, and revenues and, in the next section, of sales prices. In that section I consider evidence on the

relative success of group- or newspaper-owned stations in extracting economic benefits from restrictive licensing; the divergence of buyer expectations from realized sales prices; and the relative prices of stations
bought and sold by joint newspaper-group licensees. Final comments
will then be made on the policy implications of this more refined economic assessment, after which the detailed effects of owner diversity on
program composition and variety will be considered.

Why Alternative Dependent Variables Have Been Utilized. Let us
look first, in table 6.4, at the equation I finally ran after extensive experimentation, on four economic dependent variables. As explained in chapter 5, my analysis of alternative indicators—station rates, audience,
revenues, and ratings—serves two purposes. First, the separate estimation
of group and newspaper impacts with an identical set of control factors permits confirmation of the effects of any single indicator, in the
face of diverse data sources and compilation problems. Second, there are
important conceptual links among the four indicators. Advertisers are
known to pay station rates on the basis of actual audience size and so-
called ratings (percentages of TV viewers in a market tuned in some
designated minutes weekly). But other demographic information is also
relevant, as well as judgments on viewer enthusiasm, and a complete
assessment of economic impact must in any case go beyond rates alone.
Finally, rates are offer prices based on past and expected audience size,
whereas station revenues are the result of past transactions where the
amount of time sold at the offer price is crucial. Here, too, separate
equations are needed to be thorough.

In regard to the basic equations in table 6.4, finally, note that I
have not only specified network affiliation, network ownership, group
ownership, channel type, TV homes, age, and the log of the number of
VHF stations in the market, but have also interacted network, newspaper, and group affiliation dummies with TV homes, and network ties
with channel type.

Stability of Coefficients Across All Four Equations. For all four equations reported in table 6.4, the relative ordering of derived impacts of
the independent variables in table 6.5 is strikingly similar. As expected,
the four most important impacts are associated with network affiliation
(and ownership), estimated conditional upon channel type and TV
homes, large market VHF affiliates being the most affluent licensees today. Then, with two minor exceptions, channel type and age come next
in the ranking of coefficients for all four equations (for reasons noted in
chapters 4 and 5), whereas group and newspaper ownership come last.[12]

12. I list the coefficients in descending order of size as a crude index of relative
importance. However, second-order t-tests are needed to ascertain the *significance* of
differences in their size. Furthermore, there is a question as to how strictly comparable the impacts due to postulated changes in any pair of independent factors are,
except where both factors are dummy variables.

TABLE 6.4

Four Estimating Equations for TV Station Economic Indicators, 387 TV Stations, 1972

Independent Variables	Spot Rate		Audience		Estimated Station Revenue		Metro Rating	
	Coefficient	t-Value	Coefficient	t-Value	Coefficient	t-Value	Coefficient	t-Value
Constant	17.05	3.4	.14	1.8	142.29	2.5	8.65	6.7
Network affiliation*	-14.10	3.3	-.12	1.8	-144.26	3.1	11.21	10.5
Network owner*	65.83	10.0	.13	1.3	497.98	6.8	.95	.6
Nonnetwork group*	-7.65	3.8	-.01	.2	-61.26	2.7	.87	1.7
TV homes	-1.08	3.0	.03	5.8	-6.97	1.7	.19	2.0
Licensed pre-1952*	5.85	2.8	.05	1.5	71.04	3.1	.46	.9
Group owner × TV homes	2.10	6.4	.01	1.3	20.88	5.7	-.18	2.1
Network affiliate × TV homes	7.10	21.9	.14	27.6	76.56	21.4	-.26	3.2
VHF channel*	9.56	2.1	.23	3.3	97.93	1.9	2.66	2.3
Network affiliate × VHF	-2.64	.5	.02	.3	-25.53	.5	4.31	3.4
Log number VHF station (+1)	-12.61	2.2	-.39	4.4	-9.04	.6	-10.42	7.2
Newspaper owner*	.18	.1	.06	1.7	26.22	1.0	.82	1.3
Newspaper owner × TV homes	.05	.2	-.01	1.3	-1.42	.5	-.05	.9
Adj. R²	.904		.971		.939		.722	
Sample size	387		387		387		387	
Sample mean	$33.908		.827		$415.981		17.907	
	(× $10)		(× 1,000,000 homes)		(× $10,000)		(%)	
Mean TV homes (in 1,000s)	610		610		610		610	

SOURCE: The following data were derived from *Broadcasting Yearbook—1973* (Washington, D.C.: Broadcasting Publicatons, Inc., 1974), and *TV Factbook* No. 43, 1973-74 (Washington, D.C.: Television Digest, Inc., 1974): number of VHF stations in market; station channel type, network affiliation, newspaper, group, or network owner status, and age as of 1 August 1972. All rate data derived from Standard Rates and Data Service, *Spot Television Rates and Data* (Skokie, Ill.: Standard Rates and Data Service, 1972, 1973), for selected issues during 1972 and 1973. Rates used were those in effect for longest period during 1972. Statistical methodology is discussed in Appendix II, pp. 469-75. Station revenue estimated as in table 5.1.

*Labeled attribute of dummy variable equals one, zero otherwise.

TABLE 6.5
Estimated Impacts of Selected Policy Variables on Station Economic Indicators, 1972*
(N = 387)
(6 P.M.-11 P.M.)

Station Type	Change in Independent Variable	Equation 1 Spot Rate	Equation 2 Audience	Equation 3 Station Revenue	Equation 4 Metro Rating
	Switch from:				
(1) UHF	Independent to network**	29.23 (7.8)	.71 (12.5)	322.96 (7.9)	9.63 (10.2)
(2) VHF	Independent to network**	26.59 (6.4)	.73 (11.5)	297.43 (6.5)	13.94 (13.2)
(3) Un-restricted	Independent UHF to network VHF**	36.15 (12.2)	.96 (21.3)	395.36 (12.1)	16.60 (22.1)
(4) Network	UHF to VHF	6.92 (2.6)	.25 (6.1)	72.4 (2.4)	6.98 (10.2)
(5) Inde-pendent	UHF to VHF	9.56 (2.1)	.23 (3.3)	97.93 (1.9)	2.66 (2.3)
(6) VHF	Affiliated VHF to network-owned	65.83 (10.0)	.13 (.3)	497.98 (6.8)	.95 (.6)
(7) VHF	Independent VHF to network-owned**	92.42 (12.4)	.86 (7.6)	795.41 (9.7)	14.89 (7.9)
(8) Un-restricted	Nongroup to nonnetwork group**	5.13 (2.9)	.03 (4.0)	66.21 (3.4)	−.20 (.46)
(9) Un-restricted	Nonnewspaper to in-town newspaper**	.48 (.2)	.04 (1.2)	17.56 (.8)	.50 (1.0)
(10) Un-restricted	Licensed post-1952 to pre-1952	5.85 (2.8)	.05 (1.5)	71.04 (3.1)	.46 (.9)
(11) Un-restricted	Add second VHF	−2.22 (2.2)	−.07 (4.4)	−6.88 (.6)	−1.84 (7.2)
(12) Un-restricted	Add third VHF	−1.58 (2.2)	−.05 (4.4)	−4.88 (.6)	−1.30 (7.2)
(13) Un-restricted	Add fourth VHF	−1.22 (2.2)	−.04 (4.4)	−3.78 (.6)	−1.01 (7.2)
	Sample mean	$33.908 (× $10)	.8270 (× 1,000,000 homes)	$415.98 (× $10,000)	17.907 (%)

*The upper number in each cell is a coefficient adjusted (if necessary) to show the estimated impact on the dependent variable (column headings) due to the change specified in the independent variables (row headings). Lower value is the t-value of each derived coefficient. Basic source, notation, computation procedures, and statistical methodology, same as indicated in table 6.4. Station revenue estimated as in table 5.1.

**Denotes that variable is interacted with TV homes at sub-sample mean.

NB. For interpretation of results see analogous commentary in notes to table 4.7, and in Appendix 4A.

Finally, additional VHFs in the market, again as expected, impact negatively and significantly in each equation, added VHFs apparently having a larger impact on audience size and ratings than age, group, or newspaper ownership do, and a larger impact on rates than newspaper ownership.[13]

The relative magnitude of effects due to postulated changes in our policy-related independent variables, then, seems broadly stable across four identical economic equations, and is further apparent in the array of percentages in table 6.6. Those numbers, as in chapter 5, are the absolute impact of each independent factor divided by the equation's sample mean, so-called PCDVs, to give the reader a rough "feel" of the relative magnitude of the impacts of our common independent variables across several separate dependent variables (see Appendix I, pp. 430–32).

In sum, tables 6.5 and 6.6 permit useful conclusions about the impact of newspaper and group ownership across all four equations. At least, ownership effects on rates and estimated revenues are normally confirmed by effects on audience and ratings, notwithstanding the different data sources, compilation problems, and conceptual implications of our four economic measures.

The Focal Point in this Chapter. Given the very high adjusted R-squares in all equations, and general stability of PCDVs, the present chapter will mainly consider the evidence across row 9 (newspaper ownership) and row 8 (nonnetwork group ownership), in tables 6.5 and 6.6. (In chapter 8, on structural diversity, I will mainly return to rows 1 to 7, and 10 to 13, and in chapter 10, on the national networks, again to rows 1 to 5 and row 7). In all cases, I report the estimated impact, a number that expresses it as a percent of the sample mean (PCDV), a significance superscript or t-value, the sample mean, sample size, and adjusted R-square.

Of special import, finally, are additional results in table 6.7 for newspaper, network, and group impacts in the typical largest and smallest TV markets. These are presented separately for each equation reported in table 6.4, where the same coefficients of variables were interacted with TV homes at the sample mean only. For convenience I have calculated the coefficients and PCDVs in table 6.7 at roughly 40 percent and 160 percent of the sample mean of TV homes—namely, at 250,000 and 1,000,000, well within the actual range of homes for these equations. The spread between these two postulated market classes—250,000 and 1,000,000—is just short of one standard deviation of the homes data in our full sample. (A final set of particularly important tests involving comparable impacts on TV station sales prices, will be discussed on pages 181–94.)

Incidence of Group Owner Impact. My first relevant finding is that

13. Ibid.

Table 6.6

Sensitivity of Selected Station Economic Indicators to
Postulated Changes in Major Policy Variables, 1972*

(6 P.M.-11 P.M.) (in percentages)

	Station Type	Change in Independent Variable	Equation 1 Spot Rate	Equation 2 Audience	Equation 3 Station Revenue	Equation 4 Metro Rating
		Switch from:				
(1)	UHF	Independent to network**	86.2[a]	85.6[a]	77.6[a]	53.8[a]
(2)	VHF	Independent to network**	78.4[a]	88.1[a]	71.5[a]	77.9[a]
(3)	Un-restricted	Independent UHF to network VHF**	106.6[a]	115.7[a]	95.0[a]	92.7[a]
(4)	Network	UHF to VHF	20.4[a]	30.1[a]	17.0[b]	39.5[a]
(5)	Inde-pendent	UHF to VHF	28.9[b]	27.8[a]	23.5[c]	14.9[b]
(6)	VHF	Affiliated VHF to network-owned	194.1[a]	15.7	119.7[a]	5.3
(7)	VHF	Independent VHF to network-owned	272.6[a]	103.6[a]	191.2[a]	83.2[a]
(8)	Un-restricted	Nongroup to nonnetwork group	15.1[a]	4.0[a]	15.9[a]	−1.1
(9)	Un-restricted	Nonnewspaper to in-town newspaper	1.4	4.8	4.2	2.8
(10)	Un-restricted	Licensed post-1952 to pre-1952	17.3[a]	6.0	17.1[a]	2.6
(11)	Un-restricted	Add second VHF	−6.6[b]	−8.1[a]	−1.7	−10.3[a]
(12)	Un-restricted	Add third VHF	−4.7[b]	−5.7[a]	−1.2	−7.3[a]
(13)	Un-restricted	Add fourth VHF	−3.6[b]	−4.5[a]	−.9	−5.6[a]
		Sample mean	$33.908 (× $10)	.827 (× 1,000,000 homes)	$415.981 (× $10,000)	17.907 (%)

*The data here are derived from coefficients in table 6.5, by converting absolute impacts into percentage impacts. Specifically, the number in each cell is a response elasticity adjusted (if necessary) to show the unit change in the dependent variables (column headings) as a percent of the sample mean (PCDVs), due to the change specified in the independent variables (row headings). For all variables interacted with TV homes, in equations 1 to 4, each relevant PCDV is calculated at the sample mean of homes (indicated in column heading). The four estimating equations appear in table 6.4. Superscripts indicate statistical significance (two-tailed test) as follows: a = 1 percent, b = 5 percent, c = 10 percent. Basic sources are as indicated for table 6.4.

**Denotes that the effect of the variable is calculated for a market with TV homes at subsample mean.

NB. Interpretation as for table 6.5.

TABLE 6.7

Estimated Impacts of Selected Policy Variables on Station Economic Indicators for Large and Small Markets, 1972—Model I*

(6 P.M.-11 P.M.)

	Independent Variables		Equation 1 Spot Rate		Equation 2 Audience		Equation 3 Station Revenue		Equation 4 Metro Rating	
			250,000 TV Homes	1,000,000 TV Homes	250,000 TV Homes	1,000,000 TV Homes	250,000 TV Homes	1,000,000 TV Homes	250,000 TV Homes	1,000,000 TV Homes
(1) UHF	Independent to network	B	3.655	56.909	.220	1.235	47.149	621.380	10.561	8.622
		t	(.9)	(14.4)	(3.7)	(20.7)	(1.1)	(14.3)	(10.7)	(8.7)
		%	10.8	167.8	26.6	149.4	11.3	149.4	59.0	48.2
(2) VHF	Independent to network	B	1.013	54.267	.241	1.256	21.621	595.850	14.872	12.933
		t	(.2)	(13.4)	(3.5)	(20.5)	(.4)	(13.3)	(12.8)	(12.6)
		%	3.0	160.0	29.2	151.9	5.2	143.2	83.1	72.2
(3) Unrestricted	Independent UHF to network VHF	B	10.572	63.827	.469	1.484	119.548	693.777	17.536	15.597
		t	(3.3)	(19.7)	(9.8)	(30.3)	(3.4)	(19.4)	(21.8)	(19.1)
		%	31.2	188.2	56.8	179.5	28.7	166.8	97.9	87.1
(4) VHF	Affiliated VHF to network-owned	B	66.844	120.1	.369	1.384	519.599	1,093.830	15.822	13.882
		t	(8.7)	(16.2)	(3.2)	(12.4)	(6.2)	(13.4)	(8.2)	(7.4)
		%	197.1	354.2	44.6	167.4	124.9	263.0	88.4	77.5
(5) Unrestricted	Nongroup to non-network group	B	-2.441	13.327	.010	.058	-9.011	147.602	.429	-.886
		t	(-1.5)	(5.2)	(.4)	(1.5)	(-.5)	(5.2)	(1.0)	(-1.4)
		%	-7.2	39.3	1.2	7.0	-2.2	35.5	2.4	-5.0
(6) Unrestricted	Nonnewspaper to in-town newspaper	B	.306	.669	.053	.019	22.674	12.026	.685	.294
		t	(.1)	(.3)	(1.6)	(.6)	(.9)	(.5)	(1.2)	(.5)
		%	.9	2.0	6.4	2.3	5.5	2.9	3.8	1.6
Sample Mean			$33.908 (× $10)		.827 (× 1,000,000 homes)		$415.981 (× $10,000)		17.907 (%)	
Mean TV Homes (in 1,000s)			610		610		610		610	

*The uppermost number in each cell is a coefficient adjusted (if necessary) to show the estimated impact on the dependent variable (column headings) due to the change specified in the independent variable (row headings). The middle number is a t-value for each derived coefficient, whereas the bottom number expresses the coefficient as a percent of the sample mean (PCDV). For all coefficients derived from independent variables interacted with TV homes, we report the results both for markets with 250,000 and 1,000,000 homes, roughly 40% and 160% of the sample mean of homes in each sub-sample analyzed. Basic sources, computation procedures, notation, and statistical methodology same as for tables 6.4, 6.5, and 6.6. Estimating equations for Model I appear in table 6.4. Station revenue estimated as in table 5.1.
NB. Interpretation as for table 6.5.

loss of a group owner link would significantly reduce two of the four economic indicators—rates and revenues—but not audience or ratings.[14] The dollar impact of group ownership, then, while smaller than that of channel type and network tie, is clearly significant and visibly larger than that of adding another VHF.

In table 6.7, on the other hand, we find that loss of a group tie would impose losses in these first two indicators some six to sixteen times greater in the *largest* markets (1,000,000 homes) than in the smallest (250,000). The t-values associated with these impacts are also much larger in the larger markets, whereas in the small markets, only the impact on rates even approaches significance.

Especially noteworthy is the relatively stable rank ordering of PCDVs across both equations where group impact is in fact significant (tables 6.5, 6.6, row 8). Even for audiences and ratings, group impact at least approaches significance so that there, too, in the largest markets especially, the point estimates are worth noting (table 6.7).

So much for my attempt to replicate the 1967 results using improved equations for 1972. Briefly, I continue to find an insignificant group owner impact on metro ratings but now do find significance for the impact on one-time spot rates, in medium-sized and large markets at least, and also substantial effects on station revenues therein. The major new finding, then, is that the most powerful group impact occurs in the largest markets, where aggregate revenue potential is presumably greatest. However, no clear-cut advantage accrues to group licensees in the smallest markets where, as noted, only the impact on rates even approaches significance.[15]

Incidence of Newspaper Owner Impact. For newspaper ownership the results reported in row 9 of tables 6.5 and 6.6 support some of my 1967 findings while qualifying others. For the 1972 data there is no significant or substantial impact on economic variables. For 1967, my simpler additive model reveals a negative impact on metro ratings due to loss of a newspaper tie equal to –9.33 percent of the sample mean (table 6.2), whereas in table 6.6, the more detailed interactive model for 1972 reveals an insignificant impact of only –2.78 percent. Yet additional analysis of audience size itself very weakly supports the 1967 results, in *small* markets at least, where loss of a newspaper tie would now reduce viewers by 6.38 percent of the sample mean, about equal to the decline due to loss of a group tie in the largest markets (table 6.7).

Still more important, however, are the insignificant newspaper owner effects on one-time rates and station revenues regardless of market size.

14. As to whether loss of a group owner tie would actually cause the stated effects, or merely be associated with them, see references in notes 7–8, this chapter.

15. Group and network affiliations would help get advertising revenues from national advertisers, especially in large markets, where competition with other local stations is greatest. In small markets such affiliations are not so important because there is less competition for the advertising dollar.

Those results contrast with clearly significant group owner impacts on the same dollar variables in 1972, in large and medium-sized markets (tables 6.5 and 6.7). They also confirm the absence of newspaper owner impact on one-time rates in 1967 (table 6.3). The newspaper-owned stations, in short, have apparently done far less well economically than nonnetwork group licensees as a class.

Relative Owner Impact in Large and Small Markets: Alternative Equations. The preceding pattern of differential impact for newspaper and group owners in large and small markets prompted me to look further before totally discounting any systematic economic impacts of newspaper ownership. Toward this end I first examined all observations available for each of the four dependent variables, not just the 387 cases where data for all control factors were complete for all four indicators. Although the new results in table 6.8 will on that count be less comparable across equations (than those in tables 6.5, 6.6, 6.7), impacts within any single equation may well be more revealing, given the larger sample size.[16] I next excluded the number of VHFs from my supplemental inquiry so as better to determine whether that variable may in some measure have obscured ownership impacts with borderline significance. (Estimating equations for table 6.8 continue to include market size, further interacted with my newspaper, group, and network dummies.)

Except for having excluded the number of VHFs, then, my common variables in table 6.8 are identical to those reported in tables 6.5, 6.6, and 6.7. That modified specification, together with a bigger sample size, permits a still closer look at owner impact in large and small markets. Now, indeed, newspaper owners do have significantly higher audience size and metro ratings (than nonnewspapers) in small, though not large markets, but again, no advantage in spot rates nor any discernible effects on revenues. Note further that group owners in large markets now, too, have significantly higher audiences than nongroup stations, but also higher rates and revenues. In short, our conclusions in the sections on the incidence of owner impact by size of market, is largely confirmed.

Effects on Sales Price

Turning next to the impact of newspaper or group ownership policies on sales price, it may be recalled in chapter 4 that such prices provided a measure of unintended effects of federal licensing practice. Those prices were seen to capitalize the income-earning expectations of the class of licensee in question. Then, in chapter 5, we saw that restrictive licensing and allocational practice operated to bolster licensee rates, ratings, revenues, and income expectations.

16. Note in table 6.8, that N=541 for rates, N=667 for audience, N=568 for ratings, and N=514 for revenues, compared to 387 observations for all four equations in table 6.4. Marginal t-values using the smaller sample might show significance with the larger samples.

TABLE 6.8

Estimated Impacts of Selected Policy Variables on Station Economic Indicators for Large and Small Markets, 1972—Model II*

(6 P.M.-11 P.M.)

Station Type	Change in Independent Variable		Spot Rate — Market Size		Audience — Market Size		Metro Rating — Market Size		Station Revenue — Market Size	
			250,000 TV Homes	1,000,000 TV Homes	250,000 TV Homes	1,000,000 TV Homes	250,000 TV Homes	1,000,000 TV Homes	250,000 TV Homes	1,000,000 TV Homes
Switch from:										
(1) UHF	Independent to network	B	8.63	56.28	.32	1.38	14.47	12.22	119.65	636.23
		t	3.31	21.67	9.02	35.64	19.25	14.59	4.41	21.07
		%	32.6	212.8	54.4	238.8	87.8	73.3	34.2	181.9
(2) VHF	Independent to network	B	3.74	51.39	.37	1.44	19.07	16.82	146.14	662.71
		t	1.13	15.94	12.16	45.56	29.10	24.80	5.87	26.75
		%	14.1	194.3	64.4	248.7	114.3	100.9	41.8	189.5
(3) Network	UHF to VHF	B	[4.01]		[.13]		[4.42]		[63.85]	
		t	[2.64]		[5.91]		[8.74]		[3.35]	
		%	[15.2]		[21.7]		[26.5]		[18.3]	
(4) Independent	UHF to VHF	B	[8.90]		[.07]		[-.18]		[37.36]	
		t	[3.46]		[.04]		[.23]		[1.31]	
		%	[33.6]		[11.8]		[1.1]		[10.7]	
(5) Unrestricted	Independent UHF to network VHF	B	12.64	60.29	.44	1.51	18.89	16.64	183.50	100.07
		t	5.24	25.51	13.91	42.63	28.25	22.43	7.50	26.15
		%	47.8	227.9	76.2	260.5	113.2	99.8	52.5	200.1
(6) VHF	Independent VHF to network owned	B	65.35	113.01	.78	1.85	22.3	20.0	583.97	1100.55
		t	10.22	19.0	9.35	23.74	12.4	12.1	9.12	18.62
		%	247.1	427.2	135.5	319.9	133.4	119.9	166.9	314.6
(7) Unrestricted	Nongroup to non-network group	B	.32	8.36	.03	.19	.50	.11	6.86	103.05
		t	.27	5.05	1.99	8.06	1.27	.22	.46	5.77
		%	1.2	31.6	5.7	32.1	3.0	.7	1.9	29.5
(8) Unrestricted	Nonnewspaper to in-town newspaper	B	-.38	1.37	.05	.01	1.64	.93	–	–
		t	.23	.72	2.10	.34	2.91	1.57	–	–
		%	-1.4	5.2	9.0	1.6	9.8	5.6	–	–
(9) Unrestricted	Licensed post-1952 to pre-1952	B	[7.82]		[.05]		[-.03]		[92.99]	
		t	[4.40]		[2.08]		[.05]		[4.82]	
		%	[29.6]		[9.2]		[-.2]		[26.6]	
Sample mean			$26.453 (× $10)		.5786 (× 1,000,000 homes)		16.678 (%)		$349.792 (× $10,000)	
Mean TV homes (000s)			527		467		538		583	

*Basic sources, notation, computation procedures, and statistical methodology same as indicated in tables 6.4, 6.5, 6.6, and 6.7. Model II is identical to estimating equations below. All results, except those in brackets, derived after designated coefficients interacted with TV homes at the 250,000 and 1,000,000 homes levels. Bracketed values are not interacted with TV homes. Station revenue estimated as in table 5.1.
B = regression coefficient; t = t-value; % = unit change in dependent variable due to specified change in independent variable, expressed as percent of sample mean (PCDV).
NB. Interpretation as for table 6.5.

Four Estimating Equations for Table 6.8

Dependent Variables

Independent Variables	Spot Rate	Audience	Metro Rating	Estimated Station Revenue
Constant	4.908	−0.047	1.764	23.542
				(1.0)
Network affiliate*	−7.256	−0.041	15.218	−52.537
	(2.6)	(1.1)	(19.6)	(1.9)
Network owner*	61.613	0.343	3.361	400.478
	(11.2)	(4.3)	(2.0)	(6.7)
Nonnetwork group*	−2.359	−0.018	0.629	−25.210
	(1.7)	(1.0)	(1.4)	(.1)
TV homes	−0.300	0.16	0.077	2.614
	(1.6)	(6.8)	(1.5)	(1.4)
Licensed pre-1952*	7.824	0.053	−0.028	92.986
	(4.4)	(2.1)	(.1)	(4.8)
Group owner × TV homes	1.072	0.020	−0.052	12.826
	(5.7)	(8.1)	(1.0)	(6.7)
Network affiliate × TV homes	6.354	0.142	−0.300	68.876
	(31.3)	(52.6)	(5.1)	(32.5)
VHF channel*	8.896	0.068	−0.180	37.363
	(2.6)	(1.8)	(.2)	(1.3)
Network × VHF channels	−4.889	0.058	4.600	26.482
	(1.3)	(1.330)	(5.0)	(.8)
Newspaper owner*	−0.961	0.066	1.876	n.i.
	(.5)	(2.4)	(2.9)	
Newspaper owner × TV homes	0.233	−0.006	−0.094	n.i.
	(1.1)	(1.9)	(1.5)	
Adjusted R²	.9346	.9637	.7748	.9341
Sample size	541	667	568	514
Sample mean	$26.453	.5786	16.678	$349.792
	(× $10)	(× 1,000,000 homes)	(%)	(× $10,000)
Mean TV homes (in 1,000s)	527	467	538	514

*Labeled attribute of dummy variable equals one, zero otherwise.
NOTE: Upper number in each cell is a regression coefficient denoting absolute impact on dependent variable. Lower number in parentheses, is a t-value denoting significance. Station revenue estimated as in table 5.1.

Now in greater detail we consider the degree to which newspaper- and group-owned stations may be better able than their nonaffiliated counterparts to appropriate significantly larger shares of the economic value created by restrictive licensing. If they are, then that evidence would strengthen various earlier conclusions regarding the magnitude and incidence of newspaper and group owner economic impact and their respective implications for regulatory policy.

The Underlying Theory. My refutable hypothesis is that stations with group or newspaper owners may have competitive advantages which yield larger (and more "loyal") audiences and therefore higher sales prices. Their alleged (and rebuttable) advantages may include one or more of the following: (1) institutional prestige, as members of a larger, more affluent, and experienced newspaper chain, and/or TV group enterprise; (2) scale economies, mainly in the management and operation of a TV group, though probably less so for a newspaper-TV enterprise where the evidence is much weaker; (3) cross-promotional advantages, mainly for the newspaper-TV companies in local markets, though possibly for TV groups across geographically separated markets in competing for national advertising; (4) market power which the TV groups are alleged to enjoy in their dealings with national networks (compared to nongroup stations), and the alleged power also of newspaper-TV enterprises in some cases to tie the sale of TV time to that of newspaper space, derived from their dominant share of local advertising going to those media; (5) superior program resources, for both newspaper- and group-owned stations derived in part from the pooling of intracompany talent and in part from the greater financial resources generated by one or more of the above mentioned advantages.

I do not contend that all five advantages are in fact substantial for both types of stations, but only that this assertion is frequently made and in some cases documented with evidence of varying quality.

Tests Are in Part Exploratory. If the above theory were valid, one would expect newspaper- or group-owned stations to enjoy greater competitive advantages than stations without such links, and hence greater success in winning larger, more loyal audiences. I have in fact uncovered at least weak evidence that this may be so for newspaper-owned stations in small markets, and somewhat stronger evidence for group-owned stations, especially in larger markets (tables 6.6, 6.7, 6.8).

Assuming then, as contended and partly confirmed, that group owners do have competitive advantages over nongroup, and newspaper owners possibly over nonnewspaper, I shall next consider three sets of refutable hypotheses. Are the facts consistent with any or all, and if so, what implications follow?

Do Newspaper- (or Group-) Affiliated Buyers Pay More for TV Stations than Buyers Pay without Such Ties? If newspaper- (or group-) owned stations have some or all of the five advantages just cited, one would expect such owners as buyers to pay more for any station than buyers not so linked—regardless of whom they bought it from. This is because an affiliated buyer would expect to do better with a station than any unaffiliated buyer, however that station had performed for its present owner.

Several tests in table 6.9 clearly support this proposition for group-affiliated buyers, though less convincingly for buyers with newspaper links. Thus newspaper-linked buyers who lack group affiliations do not pay significantly more for stations, *cet. par.*, than comparable nonnewspaper buyers (test 2), although the newspaper-linked buyers do pay more when they are also group-affiliated (test 1). Furthermore, buyers with group ties pay more than nongroup buyers do, regardless of whether or not the buyer is also a newspaper affiliate (tests 3, 4).

For reasons stated at the outset, then, my theory leads one to expect group- or newspaper-related buyers to pay more for a TV station than buyers without such ties. The evidence in table 6.9 is consistent with this proposition for group buyers throughout, though consistent for newspaper-linked buyers only when they are also group-affiliated. Hence these tests confirm the existence of some or all of the aforementioned competitive advantages for group-owned stations, but far less clearly for those with newspaper owners.

Do Newspaper- (or Group-) Affiliated Buyers Pay More for Stations with Such Owners than Buyers without Such Links Pay for Stations without Such Owners? If stations with newspaper owners perform better economically than those without newspaper ties, then one would presumably expect the affiliated buyer to pay more for a (better performing) newspaper-owned station, than an unaffiliated buyer would pay for a (worse performing) nonnewspaper-owned station. The same would be expected of group-linked buyers of group-owned stations, compared to nongroup owner transactions.

Are the results in table 6.10 consistent with this hypothesis?

On one hand, in section A, test 6 does confirm the hypothesis. Thus the transfer prices of stations whose buyers and sellers are both joint affiliates of the newspaper plus group enterprises, are significantly greater than those of transfers which lack all four attributes. My hypothesis is also confirmed by section B, test 6, where the transfer prices of stations whose buyers and sellers (that is, traders) are newspaper-affiliated (but not group-affiliated), significantly exceed those of stations whose traders also lack newspaper ties. The hypothesis is confirmed, finally, by section B, test 8. There the transfer prices of stations whose traders are both group affiliates (but not newspaper affiliates), significantly exceed those which also lack group ties. Thus far, the implication is that, under the stated constraints, group- and newspaper-owned stations may both have the alleged competitive advantages as itemized at the outset.

On the other hand, the hypothesis is not supported by section B, tests

Table 6.9

*Estimated Changes in TV Station Sales Price Due to Postulated
Changes in Owner Attributes of Station Buyers Only, 1949-70**

Test Number	Station Type	Switch from: (buyer)	Switch to: (buyer)	Equation 1	Equation 2	Equation 3	Equation 4
(1)	Group buyer	Nonnewspaper	Newspaper	58.03[a] (2.59) 113.6%	59.69[a] (2.80) 116.8%	64.39[a] (2.99) 126.0%	63.40[a] (2.99) 124.1%
(2)	Nongroup buyer	Nonnewspaper	Newspaper	.97 (.05) 1.9%	n.d.	n.d.	n.d.
(3)	Newspaper buyer	Nongroup	Group	74.00[b] (2.51) 144.8%	75.51[a] (3.48) 147.8%	80.81[a] (3.69) 158.1%	78.48[a] (3.64) 153.6%
(4)	Nonnewspaper buyer	Nongroup	Group	16.94[b] (2.31) 33.1%	15.82[b] (2.34) 31.0%	16.42[b] (2.41) 32.1%	15.08[b] (2.25) 29.5%

n.d. = not derivable from equation as specified in table 4.11.

Mean price = $51.1023 (× $100,000)
Sample size = 310

*Dependent variable is a TV station sales price for the designated years, adjusted for inflation as indicated in table 4.11, and drawn from *Television Factbook*, 1973-74. The upper number in each cell is a regression coefficient derived from designated equation in table 4.11. Parenthetical figures are t-values of coefficients, and percentages denote those coefficients divided by sample mean (PCDVs). Superscripts denote significance in two-tailed test—namely, a = .01 confidence level, and b = .05 level.

INTERPRETATION: In test 1, for all 310 stations studied whose buyers were nonnetwork groups, switching from buyers which were *also* nonnewspaper to those that were newspaper owners, would raise price by $5,803,000 (equation 1, table 4.11), significantly greater than zero at the .01 confidence level. This sum is 113.6 percent of the sample mean of prices.

Table 6.10

Estimated Changes in Sales Price Due to Postulated Changes in Owner Attributes of Station Buyers and Sellers, 1949-70*

Mean Price = $51.1023 (X $100,000)   N = 310

	Section A						Section B					
(1)	(2)		(3)		(4)	(5)	(6)		(7)		(8)	(9)
Station Type ("given")	Switch from:		Switch to:		Unit Change in Price	Station Type ("given")	Switch from:		Switch to:		Unit Change in Price	Difference between columns 4 and 8
	Seller	Buyer	Seller	Buyer			Seller	Buyer	Seller	Buyer		
Unrestricted		Nonnewspaper, nongroup	Newspaper, group	Newspaper, group	74.96 (3.3)	Unrestricted		Nonnewspaper, Nongroup	Newspaper, group	Newspaper, group	-14.28 (.8)	**
Group buyer		Nonnewspaper		Newspaper	58.03 (2.6)	Group seller		Nonnewspaper	Newspaper		-26.16 (1.5)	**
Nongroup buyer		Nonnewspaper		Newspaper	.97 (.1)	Nongroup seller		Nonnewspaper	Newspaper		37.51 (1.8)	-36.54 (1.4)
Newspaper buyer		Nongroup		Group	73.99 (2.5)	Newspaper seller		Nongroup	Group		-51.79 (2.7)	**
Nonnewspaper buyer		Nongroup		Group	16.94 (2.3)	Nonnewspaper seller		Nongroup	Group		11.88 (1.8)	5.06 (.5)
Unrestricted	Nonnewspaper, nongroup	Nonnewspaper, nongroup	Newspaper, group	Newspaper, group	60.69 (2.5)	Nongroup seller and buyer		Nonnewspaper	Newspaper		38.48 (1.7)	22.21 (.7)
Unrestricted	Nonnewspaper, nongroup	Nonnewspaper, nongroup	Newspaper, group	Newspaper, group	60.69 (2.5)	Group seller and buyer		Nonnewspaper	Newspaper		31.87 (1.4)	28.82 (3.1)
Unrestricted	Nonnewspaper, nongroup	Nonnewspaper, nongroup	Newspaper, group	Newspaper, group	60.69 (2.5)	Nonnewspaper seller and buyer		Nongroup	Group		28.82 (3.1)	31.87 (1.4)
Unrestricted	Nonnewspaper, nongroup	Nonnewspaper, nongroup	Newspaper, group	Newspaper, group	60.69 (2.5)	Newspaper seller and buyer		Nongroup	Group		22.21 (.7)	38.48 (1.7)

*See table 6.11 for notation and other explanatory information. The estimating equation from which the coefficients here are derived is identical to equation for part A of table 6.11, and appears in Appendix 4A as equation 1. Note that each coefficient reported herein is interacted at the mean value of TV homes for the sample.

**Denotes that no tests undertaken because first order coefficients had different signs, and one or both were also significant.

7 and 9. In test 9, transfer prices for stations whose traders are both group- and newspaper-affiliated, are not significantly higher than those of traders which are newspaper- but not group-linked. In test 7, too, for stations whose traders are both group-linked, a further tie with a colocated newspaper does not appear to raise the transfer price significantly.

How can we reconcile these two sets of findings? Quite clearly, the tests in table 6.10 imply that once a station enjoys the advantages of a newspaper *or* a group tie, adding the *second* tie does not significantly raise expected or realized audience size or earnings, nor the transfer price at which it trades, compared to the price where the traders have only *one* such tie (newspaper *or* group). In test 6 (sec. B), for example, the price difference between a station whose buyer and seller *both* lack newspaper *and* group ties, and one whose traders are newspaper but not group linked, is $3,848,000 (t = 1.7). In sec. A, however, a station whose traders are both newspaper and group owned sells for $6,069,000 more than one with neither link (t = 2.5). Yet the difference between these two price increases ($2,221,000 in column 9) is itself *not* significant (t = .7). In short, there appear first to be increasing and then diminishing returns to scale when stations are traded by entities which have one ownership link (say, group but not newspaper), and then gain the second. (Compare further, sections A and B for tests 6 through 9.)

Do Buyers Jointly Affiliated with Newspapers and Groups Pay More for Stations than Do Those not Jointly Affiliated? Do Jointly Linked Sellers Also Command Higher Prices than Do Sellers without Joint Affiliations? The question here is whether the seemingly buoyant expectations of joint buyers are realized in fact, or whether jointly affiliated stations sell at lower prices than stations without joint affiliations, and if so why? Consider table 6.10, tests 1, 2, and 4. Clearly, buyers with joint newspaper-TV group links do pay significantly more for stations than buyers not jointly affiliated, whereas joint sellers sell for significantly less than those without joint ties. That is, the buoyant expectations of joint buyers are apparently not realized in fact, possibly due to two offsetting factors: (1) diseconomies of joint newspaper-TV group operations leading to station sales under duress; (2) closer public scrutiny of and sensitivity to station ownership by media empires (newspaper chains linked to TV groups), than by more limited interests—further adding to the likelihood of sales under duress.[17]

Do Stations Owned by Newspapers, Groups, or Jointly by Both Derive

17. TV stations owned by groups *or* newspapers but not jointly, may attract less critical public scrutiny, and result in fewer diseconomies, than stations jointly owned by both. For nongroup stations, note in test 3 the statistically comparable impacts on price due to a switch from nonnewspaper to newspaper buyers, and from nonnewspaper to newspaper sellers. Note finally, in test 5, the similar pattern for nonnewspaper stations, clearly confirmed by further tests for the switch from nongroup to group buyers and sellers (see column 9).

Greater Benefits from Restrictive Licensing than Do Stations Not So Affiliated? This takes us next to table 6.11, where our proxy for license limitation is to postulate an increase of 100,000 TV homes in the market, everything else in the equation being held constant. This proxy is valid for two reasons. First, our estimating equation (see table 4.11) holds constant the number of VHF stations in the market, and further interacts that variable with M, a market dummy equal to one if there are three or more VHFs, zero otherwise. Second, signal interference in larger markets is more likely to preclude entry at the margin, because greater population density and economic potential in those markets lead to more potential entrants per square mile than in small markets, and hence to a need for tighter entry control.

On both counts, postulating a rise in TV homes of 100,000 is a convenient and valid proxy for restrictive licensing and allocation. The question that remains is what type of stations benefit more from restrictive licensing, those with or without newspaper or group ties, further linked, or not linked, to a national network company.

Again, following my theory, I should clearly expect the prices of stations traded by newspapers to rise significantly more, *cet. par.*, when TV homes rise by 100,000, than would the transfer prices of stations traded by nonnewspapers. I should also expect the prices of stations traded by groups to rise significantly more than those traded by nongroups, under the same conditions. What this hypothesis implies, then, is that stations with the alleged advantages of ties with a newspaper or group entity, would themselves be in a better position competitively to derive benefits from the tighter market conditions our test postulates, than would stations without such ties.

In effect, my empirical results appear to confirm this hypothesis as it applies to group-owned stations, but not for newspaper-owned stations. This conclusion appears to hold, moreover, regardless of whether either type of station is also network-affiliated, or independent. Therefore we conclude that newspaper-owned stations do not have competitive advantages sufficiently greater than nonnewspaper-owned stations, to benefit significantly more than them from restrictive licensing, whereas the group owned do have sufficient advantages over nongroups to benefit significantly more from restrictive licensing than the latter.

Newspaper-Owned Stations. Thus in test 1, the increase in homes per station raises station prices significantly for stations whose sellers and buyers are both newspaper affiliated, as well as for stations where neither is. However, the difference between these impacts is not itself significant. Neither, in test 2, do the prices of nonnewspaper owned stations respond differently to an increase in homes per station when their buyers are newspaper rather than nonnewspaper. For stations with newspaper attributes, the sole exception to this insignificance appears in test 3,

Table 6.11

Sensitivity of Sales Price to Changes in Market Size for Stations with and without Designated Owner Attributes, 1949-70*

Mean Price: $51.1023 (× $100,000) N = 310

	(1)	(2)	(3)	(4)	(5)
Test	First Type of Sales Transaction	Price Increase Due to Addition of 100,000 TV Homes	Second Type of Sales Transaction	Price Increase Due to Addition of 100,000 TV Homes	Difference between Columns 2 and 4
Part A					
	Seller *Buyer*		*Seller* *Buyer*		
(1)	Newspaper Newspaper	11.55[b] (2.0)	Nonnewspaper Nonnewspaper	5.05[a] (5.7)	6.50 (1.1)
(2)	Nonnewspaper Newspaper	8.51 (1.5)	Nonnewspaper Nonnewspaper	5.05[a] (5.7)	3.48 (.6)
(3)	Newspaper Nonnewspaper	8.08[a] (4.8)	Nonnewspaper Nonnewspaper	5.05[a] (5.7)	3.03 (1.8)
(4)	Nonnewspaper Nonnewspaper	5.05[a] (5.7)	—	—	—
Part B					
	Seller		*Seller*		
(5)	Newspaper, group	11.55[a] (6.5)	Nonnewspaper, nongroup	3.65[a] (4.0)	7.91[a] (4.1)
(6)	Nonnewspaper, group	9.18[a] (7.1)	Nonnewspaper, nongroup	3.65[a] (4.0)	5.54[a] (4.3)
(7)	Newspaper, nongroup	6.02[a] (3.6)	Nonnewspaper, nongroup	3.65[a] (4.0)	2.37 (1.5)
(8)	Nonnewspaper, nongroup	3.65[a] (4.0)	—	—	—

Part C

	Seller	Buyer		Seller	Buyer		
(9)	Newspaper, network	Group, network	10.52ª (6.4)	Nonnewspaper, independent	Nongroup, independent	1.70 (1.6)	8.81ª (4.5)
(10)	Nonnewspaper, network	Group, network	9.44ª (7.8)	Nonnewspaper, network	Nongroup, network	7.40ª (5.7)	2.04ᶜ (1.8)
(11)	Newspaper, network	Nongroup, network	8.48ª (4.5)	Nonnewspaper, network	Nongroup, network	7.40ª (5.7)	1.08 (.7)
(12)	Nonnewspaper, network	Nongroup, network	7.40ª (5.7)	Newspaper, independent	Group, independent	4.82ᵇ (2.5)	2.58 (1.0)
(13)	Newspaper, network	Group, network	10.52ª (6.4)	Nonnewspaper, network	Nongroup, network	7.40ª (5.7)	3.12ᶜ (1.7)
(14)	Newspaper, independent	Group, independent	4.82ᵇ (2.5)	Nonnewspaper, independent	Nongroup, independent	1.70 (1.6)	3.12 (1.7)
(15)	Nonnewspaper, independent	Group, independent	3.74ª (2.7)	Nonnewspaper, independent	Nongroup, independent	1.70 (1.6)	2.04ᶜ (1.8)
(16)	Newspaper, independent	Nongroup, independent	2.78 (1.4)	Nonnewspaper, independent	Nongroup, independent	1.70 (1.6)	1.08 (.7)
(17)	Nonnewspaper, independent	Nongroup, independent	1.70 (1.6)	—	—	—	—

Part D

	Seller Network:		Seller Network:		
(18)	Newspaper, group	12.11ª (6.9)	Nonnewspaper, nongroup**	1.79ᶜ (1.7)	10.29ª (5.1)
(19)	Nonnewspaper, group	10.70ª (8.0)	Nonnewspaper, nongroup	6.75ª (5.2)	3.95ª (2.9)
(20)	Newspaper, nongroup	8.14ª (4.6)	Newspaper, nongroup	6.75ª (5.2)	1.39 (.9)
(21)	Nonnewspaper, nongroup	6.75ª (5.2)	Newspaper, group**	7.16ª (3.3)	-.37 (.1)
(22)	Newspaper, group	12.11ª (6.9)	Nonnewspaper, nongroup	6.75ª (5.2)	5.33ᵇ (2.6)

Table 6.11 (continued)

	(1) First Type of Sales Transaction		(2) Price Increase Due to Addition of 100,000 TV Homes	(3) Second Type of Sales Transaction		(4) Price Increase Due to Addition of 100,000 TV Homes	(5) Difference between Columns 2 4
Test	Seller	Buyer		Seller	Buyer		
	Independent:			*Independent:*			
(23)	Newspaper, group		7.16[a] (3.3)	Nonnewspaper, nongroup		1.79[c] (1.7)	5.33[b] (2.6)
(24)	Nonnewspaper, group		5.73[a] (3.5)	Nonnewspaper, nongroup		1.79[c] (1.7)	3.94[a] (2.9)
(25)	Newspaper, nongroup		3.17[c] (1.7)	Nonnewspaper, nongroup		1.79[c] (1.7)	1.38 (.9)
(26)	Nonnewspaper nongroup		1.79[c] (1.7)	—		—	—

*Dependent variable is a TV station sales price as reported in *Television Factbook*, 1973-74, for the years 1949-70. The upper number in each cell is a derived coefficient that denotes the unit change in price (columns 2 and 4) due to the postulated change in the independent variable (columns 1 and 3). Lower value is the t-value of each coefficient. Comparable numbers in column 5 pertain to the absolute differences between the impacts on price reported in columns 2 and 4, and the t-value of the derived coefficients in column 5. Superscripts indicate statistical significance (two-tailed test) as follows: a = 1 percent, b = 5 percent, and c = 10 percent confidence level.

Column 1 and column 3 attributes are "given" where an attribute is interacted with other variables in the equation. Thus in test 18 the coefficient of 1.79[c] (column 4) denotes that, for stations whose sellers have no newspaper, group or network affiliation, an increase of 100,000 TV homes in market will act to raise price by $1.79 × $100,000, or $179,000, all other specified factors in the equation being taken into account. Furthermore, the t-value of 1.7 indicates that this sum is significantly greater than zero at the .10 confidence level. All price data are in 1958 dollars as adjusted by implicit price deflators for total GNP, 1949-70 (1958 = 100). See January 1972 Economic Report to President, Appendix table B-3. For further discussion of postulated attribute changes in columns 1 and 3, equation specifications, and the calculated coefficients derived from interacted variables, see chapter 4 text and Appendix thereto, also Appendix II. Estimating equations for parts A, B, C, D, above appear in Appendix 4A as equations 1, 2, 3, and 4, respectively. Rounding errors account for minor discrepancies in column 5.

**Denotes that in this case only, the station was an independent.

where the prices of stations with nonnewspaper buyers do rise significantly more (at the .10 level) when sold to them by a newspaper than
by a nonnewspaper seller. This, too, calls into question the alleged advantages of a cross-owner link as hypothesized above.

In no other equation do newspaper-owned stations sell for significantly
more than others when homes per station are assumed to rise by 100,000,
neither when the station is also nongroup owned (test 9), or is sold to a
nongroup buyer who is a network affiliate (test 1), or an independent
(test 16). Nor for nongroup stations generally, do those linked with newspapers (in equation 7) sell for higher prices than those without such links,
again, whether or not the stations sold are also network affiliates (test
20), or independents (test 25). (See column 5.)

One might wonder why, then, a newspaper would want to own a
TV station at all. One explanation is that noneconomic motives have
always been important.[18] A second point is that current newspaper owners may well have expected economies in joint ownership that never
materialized, and that their inability to charge more for their stations
than nonnewspaper sellers simply reflects this. Thirdly, many sales of
newspaper-owned stations have doubtless occurred in a hostile regulatory
climate. Under those conditions the newspaper may have felt pressed
to sell out and been willing to settle for less than otherwise (see discussion associated with tables 6.10 and 6.11).

Group-Owned Stations. For nonnewspaper stations, on the other hand,
those owned by groups do sell for significantly more than those which
are nongroup-owned (test 6), whether or not the stations being compared are also network affiliates (test 19), or independents (test 24).
Indeed, for nonnewspaper stations, those bought by group buyers also
sell for more (when homes per station are assumed to rise) than those
bought by nongroup buyers,[19] whether the stations being compared also
are network affiliates (test 10) or independents (test 15). (See column 5.)

Accordingly, the fact that stations with newspaper and group attributes
sell for significantly more than those with neither attribute (tests 5 to
11 and 13 to 16), quite clearly reflects the presence of a group (not a
newspaper) tie. Nor is the implication that the price of group-owned
(or group-bought) stations respond more to any assumed rise in homes
per station than the prices of newspaper-owned stations, inconsistent
with my conclusion here, namely, that the impact on price is greatest
for stations with all three attributes—group, newspaper, and network;
least for those with none (tests 9 and 18); and probably somewhere in

18. See H. Levin, *Broadcast Regulation and Joint Ownership of Media* (New York:
New York University Press, 1960), chapter 2.

19. The occurrence nonetheless of sales to nongroup buyers may simply reflect
the special limits the FCC has imposed on group ownership in the leading U.S.
markets, or the groups' unwillingness to buy newspaper owned stations for other
reasons—for example, poor spectral location—only partly specified in my equations;
or the groups' sensitivity to being viewed as part of a giant empire of newspaper
chains and cross-owned multiple TV station enterprises.

between for those with two or three attributes rather than one (e.g., tests 10, 13, 19–22).

There is no question, then, that whereas the prices of group-owned stations, other things being equal, rise significantly more than those of nongroup under the postulated conditions, those of the newspaper-owned stations rarely rise significantly more than their nonnewspaper counterparts. Readers may therefore ask why licensees would not prefer ties with a nonnetwork group than any newspaper parent. That is, couldn't the groups bid away choice station properties from single-owner stations with (or without) newspaper ties? And if so, why hasn't this acted to reduce the discrepancy in price between stations with and without group-owner links?

The answer is threefold. First, over time many groups have doubtless acquired single-owner stations with (and without) newspaper ties. But second, the FCC's limits on the number of stations any group may own nationally, necessarily impose a ceiling on the frequency of these acquisitions, especially in the largest markets, where most group-owned stations are now located. True, FCC does not limit the number of groups that may be formed, however, the number of available nongroup-owned network-affiliated (or even independent) VHFs in the top fifty markets which existing (or potential) groups could hypothetically acquire, are very few today.[20] Third, some small single owners, especially those with newspaper ties, simply will not sell out to anyone, for nonpecuniary reasons. This, too, would prevent the group buyers from inducing more single owners to sell out to the groups, in the leading markets.

Policy Implications of Economic Assessment

The policy implications so far are as follows. Reflecting on tables 6.4 to 6.7, the greatest group owner economic advantage is unquestionably in the larger markets, whereas the newspaper owner may have an advantage in small markets, where its impact on audience and ratings (but not revenues or rates) approaches significance. The greatest likely economic loss due to divestiture, or ownership curbs short of that, may therefore be in the largest markets for group owners, and possibly in the smaller markets for newspaper affiliates. These conclusions were confirmed by a further probe which utilized a more complete (though varying) data base for a modified equation, results derived from which were reported in table 6.8.

One possible implication is that, *cet. par.*, divestiture should be limited to those markets where likely economic distress will be the least—namely,

20. I found only thirty-nine nongroup-owned network affiliates in 1972, in markets with four or more stations, only nine of which were also newspaper-owned. I was unable to determine why group buyers had not acquired these nongroup stations too, especially the thirty without newspaper ties. But see preceding footnote.

the smaller markets for group ownership, and the largest for newspaper owners—but there are two problems with this approach.[21]

For Newspaper Ownership. On one hand, newspaper ownership poses the greatest potential danger in those very markets (the small ones) where its economic performance may be relatively strongest, but the number of competing media the smallest.[22] Thus some structural action is clearly needed there, too, to safeguard sources (and hence content) diversity, irrespective of possible economic distress, say, due to divestiture. Furthermore, the degree of likely distress must not be exaggerated, given that the relative strength of newspaper (over nonnewspaper) affiliates in the smaller markets remains uncertain in table 6.7, and that such relative strength anyway extends to audiences and ratings only, and not to dollar impact.

For the dollar impact measures that really count—on rates and revenues—there is no significant newspaper impact in any market class—large, medium, or small—either in tables 6.5 or 6.7, or in our modified results in 6.8. According to those measures, divestiture could probably raise the level of sources diversity (with benefits as just cited), without serious economic distress. Indeed, a final yardstick to which we momentarily turn is the degree to which newspaper affiliates extract disproportionate shares of the economic values created by restrictive licensing. If even the scraps of evidence on the newspaper licensee's possible advantages reflect any such extraction of artificial economic rents, then the loss of these advantages should give the regulator far less pause than were they to reflect significant scale economies. Suffice it to note only that newspaper affiliates, unlike group affiliates, have been normally shown to extract no significant benefits from restrictive licensing greater than those enjoyed by stations without newspaper affiliations.

For Group Ownership. Contrary to most licensees' expectations, steps to reduce group ownership in the smaller markets appear likely to be relatively painless after the fact. Such a strategy would also appear desirable because there are fewer competing voices in smaller than larger markets today. In contrast, the groups' advantages are greatest in the big markets, where alternative station outlets are also most numerous, so that in those very markets where any threat to sources diversity may well be minimal, the economic consequences of steps to diversify ownership appear gravest, whereas divestiture in the smallest markets, where most needed for sources diversity, seems likely to do least harm economically. The upshot for group ownership, then, may well be to limit

21. I assume throughout that the nation is committed to sources diversity (as a vehicle for content diversity)—namely, to a multiplicity of separate media voices on a market basis (see chapter 1). The question addressed in this chapter is how high a price in economic distress must be paid to pursue that goal through a policy of divestiture.

22. See pages 180–81 and also note 29, this chapter.

affiliations more stringently in small than in larger markets, the opposite of my conclusion for newspaper ownership.

Implications of Sales Price Analysis. My exhaustive analysis of station sales prices reveals still further consequences of a divestiture policy, or of curbs short of that. Such changes would inflict less harm where licensees with both affiliations (newspaper and group) are deprived of one, and this is true whether we analyze station seller dummies only, or both seller *and* buyer dummies simultaneously. Furthermore, divestiture or other curbs would deprive newspaper-owned stations of little if any power to appropriate increments to their sales price due to license limitation generally. That is, having had no such power to date, divestiture could clearly not deprive them of it now. In contrast, group owners may have been able to extract rents from their higher prices due to restrictive licensing, and hence might suffer more from divestiture or special curbs than newspaper licensees would.

Nevertheless, it seems quite clear that depriving any newspaper-group joint enterprise of only one of its ties would impose significantly less damage than depriving it of both. For stations having one such tie, gaining the second does not appear to add to their sales price significantly more than stations which lack both at the outset and then gain both, add to their prices.

Accordingly, a prospective ban may be more important than sometimes believed. If in fact the clearly buoyant expectations of joint enterprises do not materialize in higher sales prices, then the alleged diseconomies of coordination, combined with well-known political opposition to joint ownership, may lead to some voluntary dismemberments. However, this by no means implies that prospective rules will suffice; only that they, too, have a role in regulatory reform.

Final Implications. Quite clearly, then, with network status, channel type, visual power, competitors, TV homes, and age of station in the equation, along with newspaper and group dummies, and the interaction of some of the above variables with TV homes and channel type, newspaper-owned stations as a whole will suffer no more than nonnewspaper if deprived of their respective share of benefits due to restrictive licensing. In contrast, group-owned stations would suffer significantly more than nongroup from any such deprivation.

The bearing of these findings on earlier evidence of significant newspaper impacts on ratings, audiences (but not revenues or rates) in smaller markets, and significant group impact in the big markets, must be considered with care. One question there was whether any economic advantages of newspaper or group ownership, wherever they did occur, reflected scale economies, or talent scarcities and restrictive trade practices. All three factors are frequently cited to explain such advantages, but never tested for definitively. Suffice it to say, then, only that the evidence in table 6.11 at least focuses on the economic rents which restrictive licensing creates. The fact that newspapers as a whole, *cet. par.*, are in no better position to share in these rents than nonnewspapers, raises a serious question as to whether any newspaper gains, wherever observed, are indeed rents as normally conceived. By the same token, the opposite holds true for group owners, whose gains clearly are extracted from the restrictive franchise values.

But now let us face squarely the question of causation: does newspaper or group ownership of TV *result in or merely reflect* its observed economic performance, compared to that of a station without such a tie? That is, do the newspaper or group owners build or acquire stations whose technical and market attributes, *cet. par.*, virtually guarantee a stronger economic performance than their unaffiliated counterparts? Or, regardless of those attributes, do the newspaper or group owners do significantly better than stations without such ties? And if the former do excel, does this reflect greater market power, or scale economies, program resources, and managerial ingenuity?

By way of clarification, consider the following interpretation of my evidence. First, group owners quite clearly do have significant economic advantages over nongroup, even after market size, market share, number of VHFs, channel type, and network ties are taken into account, along with selected interactions among these variables. The implication is that this group advantage above nongroup comes from something other than market power (as delineated in the above control factors).[23]

What we can clearly conclude, then, is that the groups do do more with their market position than the nongroups do with theirs. But our inquiry does not reveal which specific factors determine the groups' eco-

23. The structural checks on group power are well-known and further support our interpretation of its estimated impact here. Thus the number of markets where the same groups confront each other (and could thereby better collude on price, market shares, and program scheduling), are very few. Also there are few apparent cases where all or any group-owned stations are affiliated with the same network. This clearly limits the groups' power to exact special concessions for their stations. Finally, the markets where groups operate have more competing stations in them, on the average, than markets where nongroup stations are located (see chapter 9). On all three counts, one must look beyond mere market power differences between group and nongroup to explain any group advantage in economic performance. There is, however, no definitive evidence that the groups enjoy significant or substantial scale economies, which nongroup owners do not. In the absence of detailed regression analysis, reference can be made here to a number of simple cross-tabulations on the percentages of total costs, in 1964, accounted for by technical, sales, programming, and general administrative expenses, for group-owned and single-owned stations. Holding constant station audience size, there is little if any difference between group and nongroup owners for any such cost percentages. Both types of stations tend to experience comparable declines in relative technical, sales, and general administrative expenses as station audience size increases, and comparable increases in relative program expenses. Only where the group-owned station reaches significantly larger audiences than the nongroup are their program expenses a notably smaller fraction (see *The Implications of Limiting Multiple Ownership of Television Stations* [prepared for Council for Television Development by United Research Inc.] filed in October 1966 in FCC Docket No. 16068; see ibid., vol. I, chapter 4, especially Exhibits IV-9, IV-10, IV-11, and IV-12).

nomic success under conditions comparable to those for nongroup owners, that is, whether unique scale economies, entrepreneurial skills, program resources, or talent contracts.

On the other hand, newspaper owners do not have comparable advantages over their nonnewspaper counterparts. True, the newspaper-owned station's five-time spot rates are higher than the nonnewspaper owner's, and this may operate to protect the former's newspaper properties from TV competition generally. Nevertheless, our analysis using 1972 data reveals newspaper ownership to have no significant dollar impact on station revenues or one-time rates in large or small markets, and this despite an improved equation specification. Even in 1967, with a cruder equation, there was no dollar impact on one-time rates, or even on market averages of revenue and time sales per station, regardless of market size.

More important, whatever advantages newspaper owners may enjoy over nonnewspapers, appear to come from their *market position* (in the combined share of newspaper-TV advertising revenues it controls), and not from anything unique about newspaper ownership. That is, any station operating under the same conditions appears likely to do as well. Thus when we exclude the number of VHFs from our 1972 equation as in table 6.8 (and use the fullest available set of station data), newspaper ownership does have a small but significant impact on audience size and metro ratings, in both small and medium-sized markets.[24] (There is never any impact on rates or revenues.) But when we reintroduce the number of VHFs, the newspaper owner impact disappears, again regardless of market size. (We have not reported these modifications of table 6.8 here, but the point is established anyway, by tables 6.5 and 6.7.)

In short, when we do not sufficiently account for the newspaper's economic environment, newspaper ownership becomes an unintended proxy for those basic market factors which actually determine much of its economic performance, whereas as soon as each station's market position is more adequately defined, any effect of newspaper ownership as such generally disappears.

On balance, there is seemingly nothing special about newspaper expertise and ingenuity after all, compared to those of nonnewspaper owners, whereas the group owner's uniqueness seems unquestionable with only its precise character being unclear.

It follows from the preceding *economic* assessment at least that regulators should be less concerned over whether or not any station is newspaper- or group-owned than with its effective market position. That is, once the FCC's licensing-allocation policies operate to limit the competition any given licensee must face, the additional power conferred by enfran-

24. Nor does this reflect the longer-than-average duration of newspaper ownership, for our equations in table 6.4 do indeed take account of each station's age in estimating rates, revenues, audiences, and ratings.

chising any particular class of owner (for example, newspaper or group), is by no means self-evident.

Perhaps the most relevant economic guideline for group ownership, then, is that until we know more about what is actually producing their advantages in rates, revenues, audiences, and sales prices, regulators may best focus on steps to increase structural (not owner) diversity in the largest markets. The existing structural checks on nonnetwork group power there support my position, although the apparent lack of significant scale economies may still qualify it, as does the absence of significant programming contributions discussed in the following section.

In any case, the more definitive absence of scale economies in newspaper-TV joint enterprises, and the well-known nonpecuniary motives that produce many such affiliations,[25] give us far less reason to postpone serious consideration of the kind of widespread divestiture repeatedly proposed by the Justice Department and public interest groups.

Policy Relevance of Effects on Program Composition and Diversity

The final determination of whether to reduce cross-ownership or group ownership relatively more in large or small markets, or at all, depends on associated consequences for program composition. One major issue, anticipated in chapter 5 relates to the degree to which any special economic advantage has further contributed to informational and local programming. No really adequate assessment of serious proposals to diversify station ownership can be undertaken without reference to pertinent programming data.

If, as just seen, a reduction of group ownership would in fact reduce station revenues, audiences, rates and sales prices generally, and particularly in the largest markets, are there likely also to be comparably significant losses in program diversity? In the amount of time devoted to local and informational programming? Or would there be offsetting increases in these variables? Do the largely insignificant economic effects of reduced newspaper ownership on revenues, rates, and sales prices substantially free the regulator's hands to impose tighter constraints? Or would any predictable losses in diversity, local, or informational programming militate against such actions?

In undertaking to replicate my earlier results (now using the commission's own programming data for 1972), I experimented with several new control factors. Eventually I fit the following typical equation on minutes of news carried during prime time, and then on five other pro-

25. See note 18, this chapter. True, such motives include journalistic professionalism which may result in certain qualitative improvements in the very local, informational programs with which FCC is concerned. But effects on quality of other motives (for example, fear of economic competition and desire to hedge against the unknown) are harder to predict. Nor are the advantages of pooling talent from both ends of a joint enterprise unrealizable when these enterprises are separate and independent.

gramming variables (see table 6.12). All major derived results are reported in table 6.13.

New Variable Specifications. By way of improving on my initial studies (1967), I have estimated newspaper and group impact only after taking account of network interactions with channel type, the market's educational composition, age and revenue of stations, and the number of VHFs in the market weighted by a dummy that reflects market size. My assumptions were that (1) revenue is a major determinant of local and informational programming; (2) the audience's educational composition may also affect a station's programming decisions, and those of its potential advertisers; (3) the older the station, the more likely it in the station economic regressions reported earlier in tables 6.4 to 6.7, will be well established and integrated into its community, and hence responsive to local needs and interests relative to news and public affairs coverage. In table 6.13, the significance of most age and revenue coefficients does indeed confirm the validity of assumptions (1) and (3), whereas the significant coefficients for proportions of college graduates in the population in three cases out of six (and near significance in two cases), support assumption (2).

Note the major differences between our typical variable specifications and those in tables 6.12 and 6.13, for programming. Our programming equations (table 6.12) clearly include all the basic variables specified in table 6.4. They also interact network affiliation with channel type on the identical assumption that both variables are major determinants of the resources need to cross-subsidize nonremunerative local and information programming. I chose not to interact owner attributes with market size, however, preferring instead to specify estimated station revenue and revenue squared.

My reasons for including station revenue and revenue squared are these. First, I sought to correct for nonlinearity due to differential resources to fund informational programming in different sized markets, where stations earn different levels of revenue, and where my market dummy (M), the number of VHFs (#VHF), and interacted combination of the two (#VHFM), took me only part way toward accounting for such factors. Second, where I did include revenue and revenue squared, in almost every case I significantly reduced the unexplained variance. Third, in other equations (as in table 10.8), I found that programming's impact on station rates was by no means always significant. Thus the impact of local news and all information was sometimes clearly significant but that of local affairs was never significant. Had all such programming impacts been significant, I would have worried much more about the likelihood of simultaneity bias clouding my results in table 6.13. Furthermore, my owner and market attributes in tables 6.12 and 6.4 do not fully account for station revenue. This too led me to anticipate that the direct

TABLE 6.12

Estimating Equations for Station Time Devoted to Selected Program Categories, Composite Week, 1972 (6 P.M.-11 P.M.)

Independent Variables	Equation 1 All Local (Including entertainment)		Equation 2 All News		Equation 3 Local News		Equation 4 All Public Affairs		Equation 5 Local Public Affairs		Equation 6 All Information	
	Coefficient	t-value	Coefficient	t-value	Coefficient	t-value	Coefficient	t-value	Coefficient	t-value	Coefficient	t-value
Constant	30.131	.4	-99.759	2.1	-27.282	.8	-22.918	.5	-19.222	1.4	-71.914	1.0
VHF channel*	89.971	2.0	86.870	3.0	83.978	3.9	14.189	.6	-6.210	.6	56.515	1.3
Network affiliate*	-32.333	.9	184.760	7.9	49.180	2.8	89.060	4.2	-10.374	1.5	225.091	6.2
In-town newspaper owner*	45.586	2.4	12.869	1.1	9.694	1.1	-2.460	.2	-.518	.1	10.106	.5
Network owner*	-46.054	.9	-12.819	.9	.495	.02	-11.872	.4	-20.826	1.9	-24.495	.5
Nonnetwork group owner*	5.287	.4	-1.184	.1	1.997	.3	-6.536	.8	.179	.1	-7.049	.5
TV homes in market	-2.727	1.8	-.012	.01	-.632	.9	1.167	1.3	.856	3.4	1.121	.7
Percent population 4+ years college	2.667	1.5	2.681	2.3	1.783	2.0	1.511	1.4	.838	2.0	4.174	2.3
Licensed pre-1952*	30.023	1.6	9.803	.8	15.390	1.6	-19.010	1.6	4.943	1.1	2.174	.1
Log number of months on air, 1972	69.399	2.5	50.936	2.8	23.907	1.8	7.088	.4	16.439	2.8	71.625	2.6
Number of VHF stations in market	-6.820	.4	.670	.1	-8.853	1.1	14.711	1.5	2.308	.7	21.311	1.3
Markets with 3+ VHF*	-39.989	.8	-3.979	.1	-52.881	2.1	45.621	1.5	10.214	1.0	50.579	1.0
Number of VHF × market dummy	19.122	.9	.557	.04	20.575	2.1	-20.650	1.7	-4.543	1.0	-23.677	1.2
Network affiliates × VHF channels*	-102.438	2.1	-73.205	2.3	-59.349	2.5	-31.353	1.1	4.032	.4	-74.188	1.5
Estimated Station Revenues	.064	2.6	.068	2.9	.080	4.5	.044	2.1	n.i.		.090	2.5
(Estimated Station Revenues)²	n.i.	n.i.	-.102E-04	1.8	-.128E-04	3.0	-.104E-04	2.0	n.i.		-.158E-04	1.8
Adjusted R²	.1349		.4349		.3648		.0701		.0749		.2794	
Sample size	408		408		408		408		531		408	
Sample mean (minutes)	209.926		249.150		129.605		111.461		24.209		397.708	

SOURCE: The following data were derived from *Broadcasting Yearbook—1973*; and *Television Factbook No. 43, 1973-74*: number of VHF stations in market; station channel type, network affiliation, newspaper, group, or network owner status, and age as of August 1, 1972. Estimated station revenues derived from published FCC financial data for 1972 (by market), and the American Research Bureau's published estimates of each station's share of metropolitan area viewing, Sunday-Saturday, 6 P.M.-11 P.M., during the survey period. See *Television Day—Part Audience Summary*, November 1972. Percent of market population with four or more years of college education from U.S. Bureau of the Census, Census of Population for 1970. All data for estimated program time by program category from FCC's First Annual Programming Report for All Commercial Television Stations, 1973 (published October 8, 1974). The specification of these equations is discussed in Appendix II, pp. 472-75.

*Labeled attribute of dummy variable equals one, zero otherwise.

n.i. = variable not included for design purposes.

TABLE 6.13

Estimated Impacts of Selected Policy Variables on Station Time Devoted to Major Program Categories, 1972*

(6 P.M.-11 P.M.)

Station Type	Change in Independent Variables (Switch from:)		(1) Equation 1 All Local (including entertainment)	(2) t-value	(3) Equation 2 All News	(4) t-value	(5) Equation 3 Local News	(6) t-value	(7) Equation 4 All Public Affairs	(8) t-value	(9) Equation 5 Local Public Affairs	(10) t-value	(11) Equation 6 All Information	(12) t-value
(1) UHF	Independent to network	B	-32.33	.89	184.76	7.85	49.18	2.80	89.06	4.22	-10.37	1.47	225.09	6.21
		%	-15.4		74.2a		37.9a		79.9a		-42.9		56.6a	
(2) VHF	Independent to network	B	-134.77	3.16	111.56	4.04	-10.17	.49	57.71	2.33	-6.34	.71	150.90	3.55
		%	-64.2a		44.8a		-7.9		51.8b		-26.2		37.9a	
(3) Network	UHF to VHF	B	-12.47	.46	13.67	.78	24.63	1.89	-17.16	1.09	-2.18	.41	-17.67	.66
		%	5.9		5.5		19.0c		-15.4		-9.0		-4.4	
(4) Independent	UHF to VHF	B	89.97	2.01	86.87	3.00	83.98	3.89	14.19	.55	-6.21	.64	-56.52	1.27
		%	42.9b		34.9a		64.8a		12.7		-25.7		-14.2	
(5) Unrestricted	Independent UHF to network VHF	B	-44.80	1.36	198.43	9.31	73.81	4.65	71.89	3.77	-12.55	1.89	207.42	6.32
		%	-21.3		79.6a		56.9a		64.5a		-51.9c		52.2a	
(6) VHF	Affiliated VHF to network owner	B	-46.05	.85	-12.82	1.07	.4	.02	-11.87	.38	-20.83	1.92	-24.49	.45
		%	-21.9		-5.1		.49		-10.7		-86.0c		-13.7	
(7) VHF	Independent VHF to network owner	B	-180.82	2.71	98.74	2.24	-9.67	.29	45.84	1.16	-27.17	2.26	126.41	1.87
		%	-86.1a		39.6b		-7.5		41.1		-112.2b		31.8c	
(8) Unrestricted	Nongroup to non-network group	B	5.28	.35	-1.18	.12	1.99	.27	-6.54	.75	.18	.05	-7.05	.47
		%	2.5		-.48		1.5		-5.9		.74		-1.8	
(9) Unrestricted	Nonnewspaper to in-town newspaper	B	45.58	2.44	12.87	1.07	9.69	1.08	-2.46	.23	-.52	.12	10.11	.54
		%	21.7b		5.2		7.5		-2.2		-2.1		2.5	
(10) Unrestricted	Raise college population by 1 percentage point	B	2.67	1.47	2.68	2.29	1.78	2.04	1.51	1.44	.84	2.02	4.17	2.31
		%	1.3		1.1b		1.4b		1.4		3.5		1.0b	
(11) Unrestricted	Increase age by 200%	B	33.11	2.47	24.31	2.81	11.41	1.77	3.38	.44	7.84	2.84	34.18	2.57
		%	15.7b		9.8a		8.8c		3.0		32.4a		8.6b	
(12) Unrestricted	Licensed post-1952 to pre-1952	B	30.02	1.56	9.80	.76	15.39	1.59	-19.01	1.64	4.94	1.11	2.17	.11
		%	14.3		3.9		11.9		-17.1c		20.4		.55	
(13) Unrestricted	Add second VHF	B	-6.82	.40	.67	.06	-8.85	1.09	14.7	1.51	2.31	.65	21.31	1.27
		%	-3.3		.27		-6.8		13.2		9.5		5.4	
(14) Unrestricted	Add third VHF	B	10.56	.53	-1.64	.13	-.01	.001	-1.62	.14	-1.11	.29	.86	.04
		%	5.0		-.66		-.01		-1.5		-4.6		.22	
(15) Unrestricted	Add fourth VHF	B	12.30	1.05	1.23	.16	11.72	2.08	-5.94	.88	-2.24	.84	-2.37	.20
		%	5.9		.5		9.0b		-5.3		-9.2		-.59	
(16) $1 million revenue	Add $500,000	B	3.22	2.58	3.29	2.89	3.85	4.56	2.07	2.04	—	—	4.32	2.48
		%	1.5a		1.3a		2.97a		1.9b		—		1.1b	
(17) $4.09 million revenue	Add $500,000	B	3.22	2.58	2.97	2.92	3.46	4.56	1.75	1.92	—	—	3.84	2.45
		%	1.5a		1.2a		2.7a		1.6c		—		.96b	
(18) $10 million revenue	Add $500,000	B	3.22	2.58	2.37	2.77	2.70	4.24	1.13	1.48	—	—	2.90	2.20
		%	1.5a		.95a		2.1a		1.0		—		.73b	
Sample mean minutes			209.926		249.150		129.605		111.461		24.209		397.708	

SOURCE: The same as for table 6.10. The upper number in columns 1, 3, 5, 7, 9, and 11 are coefficients (B) which denote absolute impact on each dependent variable (column headings) due to postulated changes in independent variables (row headings). Lower number expresses this coefficient as percent of sample mean (PCDV). T-values for each coefficient are reported in columns 2, 4, 6, 8, 10, and 12. Parenthetical attributes are "given" where an attribute is interacted with other variables in the equation. Thus, the coefficient for row 1, column 1 (−32.33) signifies that, for UHF stations, switching from nonnetwork to network status acts to reduce the number of minutes of all local programs (including entertainment) by 32.33 minutes, which is 15.4 percent of the sample mean devoted to such programming, but that this amount is not significantly different from zero at the .10 confidence level (t = .89). Superscripts indicate statistical significance (two-tailed test) as follows: a = 1 percent, b = 5 percent, and c = .10 percent confidence level

inclusion of revenue would help explain more of the variance in our programming dependent variables, which it did in fact do.

What I could not of course know beforehand was how far my coefficients would be distorted by simultaneity bias. But a further analysis of coefficients and t-values reported in table 6.13, as derived from the same equations (but excluding revenue and revenue squared), reveals marked stability across both versions of each equation. In short, I find that my major policy-sensitive variables—newspaper, group, and network affiliation, and possibly the number of VHFs and channel type—are essentially stable, however the equation is specified.

One final consideration in my inclusion of revenue and revenue-squared was this. I know that the least affluent stations, in the smallest markets, though lacking the wherewithal to cross-subsidize nonremunerative informational and local programming, nonetheless incur the lowest opportunity costs in carrying it, due to the paucity of advertisers who would buy commercial time spots there even if associated with popular entertainment shows. I also know that the medium affluent stations have greater wherewithal, but higher opportunity costs in the above terms (that is, far more foregone users of the station time now devoted to low-audience local and informational programming). Finally, the largest stations in the most lucrative markets, with greatest resources, are subject to closest public scrutiny, and may on that score at least be expected to carry more nonremunerative programs notwithstanding their high opportunity costs in so doing. In short, the relative incentives for licensees to run such programs would be smallest in the markets where they have the greatest resources to do so, and greatest where their resources are most meager.

To give full sway to this revenue factor (in line with earlier analysis by Park and others), we specified it in its most suggestive form (by itself, and squared), and also dropped my earlier interactions of owner attributes with TV homes. Our inclusion of revenue and revenue squared in all equations but two, clearly improved total explained variance. Also, the values of my two revenue coefficients in table 6.12, and of the derived revenue results in table 6.13, further indicate that the time devoted to each program category studied first rises rapidly with rising revenue, and then tapers off. In table 6.13—for example, for stations with annual revenues of $1,000,000, $4,090,000, and $10,000,000—an additional $500,000 yields clearly declining increments of news, local news, public affairs, and all information. This presumably reflects, as just noted, the greater relative incentives of low revenue stations (with fewest alternative uses for their program time) to run nonremunerative informational programs, and the lower relative incentives of high revenue stations to do so. The specific form of our power function clearly captures some if not all of these nonlinear effects.

The upshot is that interactions here with TV homes would clearly be redundant given that the economic indicators examined as dependent variables in table 6.4, now figure (through station revenues at least) as major control factors. That is, our task in tables 6.12 and 6.13 is to estimate the relative impact of owner type and station competition (or license limitation) on the amount of time devoted to a few important categories of local and information programming. In so doing, our strategy was to introduce only the most cogent control factors. Station revenue emerged as an eminent candidate here for reasons just given, all the more because the data needed to consider it in our initial studies (for 1967), were not then available.

Another variable introduced for the first time in table 6.12 was the population's educational attainment in each market. After experimenting with several possible forms for such a variable I selected "percentage of population with four or more years of college education." My assumption was that a station's program mix, and in particular the total time it devoted to information, would respond to the educational level of its potential audience.

Once market size, educational composition, and estimated station revenue, were explicitly taken into account (for reasons already given)— along with age of station and channel type—I expected to be able to estimate more accurately the relative impact of owner attributes and structural diversity (competitors) on the several station programming variables. For present purposes, then, the entire focus is on my group and newspaper owner dummies.

I could of course have utilized the log form of number of VHFs in the market, as in table 6.4. However, to minimize avoidable complexities in preliminary runs aimed at exploring the impact of station revenue and college education, I chose instead to use earlier station specifications —namely, the number of VHFs interacted with a dummy variable equal to one for markets with more than two VHF stations, and zero otherwise. My age specification, on the other hand, went beyond the simple break between stations licensed before and after the cessation of all TV licensing between 1948 and 1952. In addition, I also introduced the log of the number of months each station had been on the air by mid-1972, the date of my economic data.[26] That variable, in fact, far better than the simple age dummy, captured the licensee's integration in his community, and greater consequent willingness to carry local and informational programming.

New Derived Results. Bearing in mind this general rationale of the equations in table 6.12, we may now turn to major derived results in table 6.13. The latter reports all basic and interacted coefficients,

26. I used a log of the age of all stations operating in 1972 (instead of a simple linear function) to avoid distorting the relative impact of adding one month to age of a few months, and to age of many months.

PCDVs, and t-values across six major programming variables. Note, finally, that the equations are identical in all but one case—namely, on local public affairs, where revenue is not in fact included. (These results were notably better without revenue in, both for the total variance explained, and the consistency with major coefficients reported in five other equations.)

My new results do in any case merit special attention. Note that the loss of group ties now has no significant programming effect, nor any even approaching significance. However, the loss of a newspaper tie would clearly deprive viewers of 6.5 minutes of local programming daily, as collated by the commission, whereas in 1967, using a different data base (compiled independently), there was no significant impact at all (compare table 6.2). In contrast with 1967, moreover, the new newspaper impact on public affairs in table 6.13 is now unquestionably insignificant ($t = .23$, public affairs; $t = .12$, local public affairs), whereas any loss in news or local news remains speculative ($t = 1.07$, $t = 1.08$).

Implications for Group Ownership. Overall, then, the following conclusions may be drawn. Significant losses in profits, rents, or informational and local service could all operate to strengthen the opposition to tighter curbs on group (or newspaper) ownership of TV stations. Any policy to reduce group owner ties, for one, would mainly impinge on the economic status of stations in the larger markets where significant reductions in profits may well occur. However, because these losses appear to have little effect on public affairs programming, one can still make the change without compromising other important policy goals. Furthermore, those who will oppose almost any regulatory change that imposes significant economic losses on incumbent licensees regardless of programming effects, will be harder pressed to defend their position when the losses are of functionless economic rents rather than of income otherwise earmarked for public service.

In sum, the absence of any significant group owner impact on program composition either year studied frees the regulator to promote sources diversity today. True, the economic losses due to reduced group ownership may still concern some policy makers, but there are at least no other major likely losses in local and informational programming. Nor, in my 1967 market studies, any significant losses in horizontal program diversity either.[27]

The upshot is that steps to limit group ownership generally, and especially in the larger markets, should weigh possible adverse economic consequences—their magnitude, incidence, and proper assessment from the

27. The only slight modification of these conclusions derives from earlier evidence in 1967 (table 6.2), that 3.5 minutes of news, daily, would also be lost. Aside from the small absolute amount of news then in question we have already noted that the equation from which this coefficient is estimated explains less of the variance in news carried by all stations in 1967 (=.3456) than in 1972 (=.4349) when the impact was insignificant. (I have no comparable data for nonnetwork programs in 1972.)

viewpoint of public and private equity. However, *programming* consequences as reflected in my measures simply look too inconsequential to
figure in this decision. True, I have made no attempt to weight programming results by any quality index, but it nevertheless seems clear
that group-owned stations have made no special contribution which
would rank them higher than comparable nongroup stations in local
and informational programming. Nor does this finding vary after a large
number of carefully defined control factors are taken into account.

Implications for Newspaper Ownership. With regard to any reduction
of in-town newspaper ownership, the following additional conclusions
are in order. Such a policy, overall, seems unlikely to impose significant,
let alone substantial, economic losses on licensees, and, in any case, far
less so than similar postulated changes in group ownership. In 1967 I
found significant economic losses due to hypothetical divestiture for both
ownership types in only eight tests out of twenty-four run, divided
equally between them (tables 6.1 to 6.3). However, in 1972 newspaper
ownership was significant only three times in eighteen (16.7 percent),
compared to nine times in seventeen (52.9 percent) for group ownership
(see tables 6.5, 6.7, and 6.8). Only in small markets might reduced newspaper ownership impose any losses at all, and then only in audience and
ratings. That is, impacts on the dollar amount of station revenues and
spot rates were never statistically significant even at the permissive
.10 level, in any market size, with any subsample of data. Nor did
newspaper-owned station sales prices respond significantly to any postulated increase in homes per station more than once in seven tests run, in
contrast with group-owned stations, which respond significantly in all
five cases where they entered the equation. So that the loss of a newspaper tie appears at best unlikely to deprive any licensee of significant
advantages due to license limitation, advantages which they have clearly
not been terribly successful in gleaning anyway.

This mixed evidence on at most limited economic losses due to reduced newspaper ownership leaves the regulator freer than otherwise to
promote sources diversity through divestiture. But would serious additional losses in local and informational programming, or horizontal program diversity, operate as a special constraint nonetheless? Or would
predictable increases in such programming further act to strengthen the
regulator's hand?

The answer is quite clear. Once account is taken of station revenues,
age, educational composition of market (each of which is clearly significant), the losses due, say, to divestiture are notably limited to local programming only (including entertainment—namely, 6.5 minutes daily in
1972. (This contrasts with an insignificant loss in 1967 [where the simpler
additive equation actually had a higher adjusted R-square].) By the
same token, the impact on news was statistically insignificant in both
years studied, which further underscores the likely absence of any such

losses due to divestiture. Finally, the probable 3.3 minute loss in 1967 public affairs, daily, is called into question by a clearly insignificant loss in 1972.

In sum, there is only meager evidence of economic injury (in 1967, on five-time rates and metro ratings, and, in 1972, possibly in small markets, on audience and ratings), and no evidence of substantial or systematic injury. Neither is there evidence of significant losses in absolute diversity (1967), nor, in 1972, in all information, public affairs, news, local news, or local public affairs.

These two inconsistencies between results with my 1967 and 1972 data are not unimportant. However, considering the relative infrequency of significant newspaper impacts on all dependent variables, widespread or substantial changes in program composition or diversity due to divestiture are not really likely. The fact is that significant information or local losses due to divestiture occur in only one test out of nine for 1967, and only one out of six tests for 1972, overall two tests out of 15.

On all counts, then, the minimal likely losses in economic viability and program diversity, informational or local programming suggest that the case for widespread newspaper divestiture remains largely, if not entirely, costless. The positive gains of separating newspaper and television, on the other hand, are manifold, and include: (1) the furtherance of sources diversity and potential latecomer entry as a value *per se;* (2) the reduction of instances of story overlap or common editorial positions, or cessation of all broadcast editorializing for fear it would otherwise extend the parent company's partisan views and elicit public criticism and harsh regulatory action; (3) the further reduction of conditions where a joint enterprise may use its affiliations to coerce rivals on either end of the enterprise,[28] or joint enterprises may act to curb the growth of their electronic subsidiaries so as better to protect their heavier investments in the older print media parents;[29] and (4) furtherance of intermedia criticism by other media in contrast with criticism within the same company only.[30] Still other affirmative benefits of separate ownership include: (1) the reduction of dangers that much harm can be done in opinion manipulation within the limits of tolerable abuse (before the public revolts), because the gap between extreme abuse and the range of bearable dissatisfaction is large; (2) the safeguarding of accuracy and variety that derives from having different owners, editors, and reporters make different mistakes and fail to state what really transpires, at

28. See in particular, Lorain Journal Co. *v.* U.S. (342 U.S. 143 1951) (refusal to deal), and Kansas City Star *v* U.S. (240 F.2d 643 1957) (full line forcing).
29. This is probably more of a danger in markets with only one TV station and one newspaper, since otherwise the effect of curbing the growth of TV might simply allow the growth to be picked up by other TV competitors.
30. See generally, William Gormley, *Effects of Newspaper-TV Cross-Ownership on News Homogeneity* (Chapel Hill; University of North Carolina Press, 1976), and Harvey Levin, *Broadcast Regulation and Joint Ownership of Media* (1960), especially chapters 3 and 5.

different points, with a fuller, more balanced and accurate picture emerging from many versions of the same story; (3) the diversification of the perspectives, outlooks, backgrounds, sex, race, religion, age, as well as occupation—and hence of unconscious biases of owners, editors, and reporters—as still a further safeguard of media accuracy, balance, fairness, and thoroughness; (4) the inducement of salutary adjustments of different media to one another in terms of quality, content, and format.[31]

31. See Levin, *Broadcast Regulation.*

Chapter 7

The Cross-Ownership Proceeding: A Case Study In Factual Deficiencies

SO MUCH, then, for our quantitative assessment of effects of the policy to diversify station ownership. In assessing the efficacy of one part of that policy—a proposed newspaper rule—special attention will now be paid to seven issues: (1) its probable consequences for diversity and program composition, and in particular for cultural, informational, and local service; (2) its further effects on the alleged cross-subsidization of newspaper-owned TV subsidiaries; (3) the use of phased-in divestiture rather than forfeiture via nonrenewal, to minimize licensee distress; (4) the existing adequacy of "multiple voices" in individual communities as an effective safeguard of diversity; (5) the impact of divestiture on localism and absentee group ownership; (6) the developmental role of newspaper pioneers in television; (7) separation as a structural safeguard which renders administrative policing less necessary.

As stated in chapter 6, the affirmative case for owner diversification relates to the diversity of content sources, owner perspectives, editorial viewpoints, and news coverage in the nation's print and broadcast media. It rests also on the inducement of competitive content adjustments of the media to one another. In what follows here, as in chapter 6, I recognize that some readers who accept my empirical conclusions may not accept their logical linkage to this affirmative case for diversification. For them I can only underscore the need to distinguish between my quantitative assessment and the normative judgments I believe consistent with it.[1]

---

1. See, for example, Levin, *Broadcast Regulation and Joint Ownership of Media* (New York: New York University Press, 1960), especially chapters 3 and 5.

Even the severest critic of the policy on cross-ownership must agree that it is now so fundamental a part of regulatory doctrine as to be virtually impregnable. Perhaps the most useful thing a scholarly investigator can therefore do is to quantify the alleged price of this policy in terms of the major stated goals of its many proponents. Even those who rarely question highly esteemed values may elect to reexamine them in the face of definitive evidence on costs and consequences. I have therefore tried to put the major FCC licensing and allocation policies to their severest test for those committed stalwarts. The upshot of my assessment is that the policy stands.

General Issues: Alternative Approaches
to Separating Newspapers and TV Stations

After deliberating for seven years, the FCC acted in 1975 on a proposed newspaper rule [2] that would have ended ownership links between television (or radio) stations and daily newspapers in the same market. The discussion here is limited to newspaper-TV joint enterprises. Specifically, the findings reported in chapter 6 permit us to assess a rule that, as finally adopted, introduced a prospective ban on all new TV grants or transfers to applicants owning daily newspapers in the same market, and required that within five years, by January 1, 1980, all licensees owning the only newspaper *and* the only TV station in a market must divest *one* of these properties.

Actually, the commission's Second Report took far less stringent steps than originally proposed in its Further Notice.[3] The Second Report ordered divestitures in only a handful of cases, those where there was not at least one other unaffiliated daily newspaper or television station operative. This contrasts with the Further Notice, under which a prospective ban on cross-ownership would not only have been enacted, but divestiture would have been applied to all ninety-four colocated newspaper-owned TV stations then operating, not merely the seven cases of local monopoly that the commission finally proscribed (Further Notice, par. 34).[4]

2. Federal Communications Commission, Docket No. 18110, Second Report and Order, 31 January 1975, appendices D, F and G (hereafter called Second Report).

3. Compare Second Report, loc. cit. note 2, with Further Notice of Proposed Rule Making in Docket No. 18110, April 6, 1970 (hereafter called Further Notice).

4. The FCC actually reported ninety-six colocated stations in 1970; the following year, ninety-four; in April 1974, only eighty-three; and by July 1974, seventy-nine (Second Report, par. 112, note 29). But its Further Notice (1970) proposed to divest "all" ninety-four stations, presumably those expected to be operating in 1971.

The assessment below relates to several versions of the newspaper rule; first, to the original proposal (1970) for across-the-board divestitures in all ninety-four cases, as well as to prohibition of all new grants or transfers to newspaper applicants;[5] second, to the far less stringent policy in the Second Report, where divestiture applied only to seven local communications monopolies;[6] and third, to a compromise, where divestiture would apply to all cases of joint enterprises located in so-called "highly concentrated" markets.[7] I reserve for Appendix 7A the bearing of the assessment, here and in chapter 6, on the Supreme Court decision on cross-ownership, handed down after these chapters were largely drafted.

The Arguments and Evidence of Principal Concern

Prior to enacting its Second Report, the FCC had on several occasions recognized the need for "detailed studies . . . [to arrive] at informed decisions" on the wisdom of limiting cross-ownership.[8] Mindful of potential economic hardship in outright divestiture, as well as the inequity of leaving present combinations untouched if future ties are prohibited, information was solicited on: (1) the effects of divestiture on alleged cost savings and cross-subsidization facilitated by cross-ownership, and

5. Further Notice, pars. 33–35.
6. See note 2, this chapter.
7. See dissenting statement of FCC Commissioner Robinson, in Second Report, pp. 22–32. Robinson notes that, under the *Von's Grocery* standard, "undue concentration" could be defined as a market share of 7.5 percent of the combined circulation and audience of any newspaper-TV enterprise in the community of license. In that case, all seventy-nine combinations then existing (January 1975) would be illegal (Robinson Dissent, p. 29). But even when applying the more permissive monopoly standard of *Philadelphia National Bank,* a 30-percent market share would require divestiture of as many as sixty-seven combinations (ibid., p. 30). The National Citizens Committee for Broadcasting (NCCB), following evidence by witness Terrall de Jonckheere, proposed that shares be weighted as 40 points for television, 40 for newspapers, and 20 for radio, and the Philadelphia (30 percent) standard then be applied to determine "undue concentration." A 30-percent market share would constitute prima facie evidence of concentration, with the licensee required to demonstrate otherwise, or to prove compensating public benefits. NCCB was further willing to ignore market shares below 20 percent, unless there were allegations of abuse. See Second Report, par. 41; brief of Justice Department in NCCB v. FCC and USA, pp. 23–27 and appendix thereto, especially at pp. A4–A12. See also W. Baer, H. Geller, and J. Grundfest, *Newspaper-Television Station Cross-Ownership: Options for Federal Action,* (Santa Monica, Calif., Rand Corporation, September 1974), pp. 32–36. Caution is needed, however, in any use of Clayton Act standards, which have varied greatly (as just indicated), a fact that may detract from their usefulness as a reliable benchmark here. Any direct relevance to divestiture as opposed to a prospective ban, may also be questioned in that Clayton Act standards are normally applied to prevent new combinations rather than dismantling old ones, and do not apply to increases in market shares achieved by internal expansion. Nevertheless, the standard for news monopoly may be more stringent than for manufacturing.
8. Order Extending Time for Filing Comments and Reply Comments in Docket No. 18110, 6 July 1970, par. 6.

hence on program diversity and quality; [9] and (2) the possibilities of
phasing in divestiture to minimize disruptive economic and programming
effects.[10]

My own studies in chapter 6 bear on both these issues but not on a
third—namely whether the number of separate media voices today con-
situtes a sufficient safeguard of diversity to obviate the need to end existing cross-media ties; [11] and second, whether far-reaching technological
developments involving CATV, satellites, and other innovations promise
still more numerous voices and hence guarantees against abuse. I return
to both these points later.

The commission rightly observed that if divestiture rendered stations
or newspapers "marginal or unprofitable, compared to a healthier status
when combined, their service to the public would obviously deterio-
rate." [12] However, no published study had ever revealed significant cost
savings in joint ownership, nor any significant impact of radio and television on the viability of unaffiliated newspapers in the same market.[13]
Nor was there such evidence in the public record.

But even if there were some cost savings or cross-subsidization, these
alone would be a poor guarantee of greater diversity or quality (even assuming the latter's desirability for reasons just stated). It would all depend on what the resources were used for. By the same token, diversity
need not suffer if a prohibition of joint ownership induced colocated
newspapers and TV to differentiate their offerings in competition for
audiences and advertiser income.[14] Besides economic studies, therefore,
the commission had to consider evidence on the service that results. Not
until quite late in the proceeding, however, was such evidence forth-
coming, even though it probably represented the single decisive element in evaluating the public consequences of divestiture.

True, diversity of program types is no definitive measure of the public
interest. Yet "it is about the only way we can get any kind of objective
handle on program quality, without . . . making subjective valuations of
programming content. . . ." [15] The question at issue is whether media
concentration poses a sufficient danger to diversity of opinion in local

9. Further Notice of Proposed Rule Making, April 6, 1970, pars. 42–44.
10. Ibid., par. 45.
11. See Motion of National Association of Broadcasters (NAB) in Docket No.
18110 (supported by American Newspaper Publishers Association [ANPA]) December 23, 1970; Order Granting N.A.B. Motion for Further Extension, January 12, 1971,
pars. 1–5; and Memorandum Opinion and Order, March 2, 1971, par. 9.
12. Ibid., par. 43. See also Memorandum Opinion and Order, March 2, 1971,
par. 12.
13. See my earlier analysis in *Broadcast Regulation and Joint Ownership of Media*,
chaps. 4–6.
14. Ibid., chaps. 5–6. Thus the commission quite properly distinguishes between
separating existing stations already in a market (from a newspaper), and encouraging
net new entry which reduces licensee revenues seriously (Memorandum Opinion and
Order, March 2, 1971, par. 12).
15. Robinson Dissent, p. 19.

markets that steps to reduce it are in order regardless of the economic effects of concentration generally.[16] Or whether FCC need do more than demonstrate the existence of a noncompetitive ownership structure, leaving the newspaper licensee to prove that distinctive, overriding public benefits inhere in the status quo.[17] Such benefits might include public service programs, localism, broadcaster continuity, avoidance of local economic dislocations, continued cross-subsidy to marginal stations, and so forth.[18]

In assessing the soundness of any really farreaching newspaper rule, at least seven factual issues must be examined.

1. Would Separation Result in Serious Reductions of Diversity or of Cultural, Informational, or Local Programs in Particular?

In determining the best form for a newspaper rule, special attention must be given the facts on media performance.[19] If newspaper-owned TV stations provide more varied and diversified service than nonnewspaper stations, then even without cost savings or cross-subsidization, the case for owner diversification might have to be reconsidered. By the same token, alleged economic advantages of joint ownership notwithstanding, the ultimate effects on program diversity and local or cultural-informational service must be determinative. It is generally agreed that the public's interest in adequate service must prevail over private industry interests.[20]

Studies prepared for an adversary proceeding are often contradictory and one-sided. Yet to find all twenty-five major inquiries here to be "largely inconclusive," [21] as the commission did, is disquieting to those who undertake extensive social science research to help facilitate difficult public policy decisions. In this case, the commission's findings of inconclusiveness clearly left it free to reach (and defend) a decision rendered on other grounds.

A major question of fact is therefore whether, when relevant factors

16. Ibid., p. 8.
17. Ibid., pp. 20–21. The Appeals Court appeared to endorse Robinson's position, which was that the newspaper parent did indeed have the burden of proof on this issue. See United States Court of Appeals for District of Columbia Circuit, nos. 75–1064 et al. National Citizens Committee for Broadcasting, Petitioner vs. Federal Communications Commission and United States of America et al., Respondent, 1 March 1977, pp. 47–60 (hereafter called Appeals Court Decision).
18. See Second Report, at pars. 62–65, 73–78, 108–09; also Robinson Dissent, pp. 34–38; brief of Justice Department in NCCB v. FCC and USA, pp. 32–44.
19. See especially Reply Comments on CBS in Docket No. 18110, February 27, 1969, pp. 3–4.
20. FCC v. Sanders Brothers Radio Station, 309 U.S.470, 60 S.Ct. 693, 84 L. Ed. 869 (1940).
21. See Appeals Court decision, p. 37; brief for FCC in NCCB v. FCC and USA, p. 9.

are taken into account, newspaper-owned stations contribute significantly more to program diversity, local, and cultural-informational service than nonnewspaper stations.[22] If the newspaper-owned stations contributed more to content diversity, the policy to discourage cross-ownership would be hardest to justify. True, the FCC could still opt to forego some program diversity to diffuse power and reduce centralized media control, the basic purposes of its general policy on owner diversification.[23] However, any decision to diversify ownership (or divest) is much easier if there are no significant differences between newspaper and nonnewspaper stations (the second possibility). No content diversity need then be foregone to diffuse the media's power. So long as newspaper-owned stations do not enhance such diversity, or nonnewspaper stations detract from it, the diffusion of power favors a policy to diversify ownership. True, a third result—that nonnewspaper stations contribute more to diversity and cultural, informational, and local programs—is clearly the most supportive of any stronger rule. For then the commission could simultaneously diffuse power *and* diversify program service, with no need to trade either goal off against the other.[24]

But even short of that, the advocates of cross-ownership and opponents of divestiture must bear a very heavy burden of proof before the commission compromises its traditional commitment to decentralized media control. It is not enough to show that newspaper ownership does no harm to diversity: they must show it has distinct advantages.[25] As of 1979,

22. See chapter 6. For an earlier assessment of ownership impact on media content, see W. Baer, H. Geller, J. Grundfest, and K. Possner, *Concentration of Mass Media Ownership: The State of Current Knowledge* (Santa Monica, Calif.: Rand Corporation, September 1974), pp. 121–43.

23. First Report and Order in Docket No. 18110, 6 April 1970, pars. 16–18.

24. As the commission quite properly notes, power is at issue here and power can be tempered on a structural basis (ibid., par. 20). Nor is it necessary to show improper conduct to act: the effects of joint ownership are at best "so intangible as not to be susceptible of precise definition" (ibid., par. 20). That such effects may be restrictive of the widest range of perspectives, viewpoints, news coverage, and so on nonetheless, has been amply documented elsewhere. See Levin, *Broadcast Regulation and Joint Ownership* pp. 78–88; also W. Gormley, *Effects of Newspaper-TV Cross-Ownership of News Homogeneity* (Chapel Hill: University of North Carolina Press, 1976). The power in question, finally, inheres in the greater relative influence of TV and newspapers than of other media sources of news and comment, especially at the local level (Further Notice, pars. 26–29, 32, 35–36). It inheres further in the well-known facts that (1) the combined effects of reading, hearing, and seeing the same ideas are greater than the sum of separate effects; (2) it is easier to cater to susceptibilities and prejudices than radically to alter them; (3) any media's impact is greater the fewer the views heard; and that (4) even though local monopolists can therefore do little to change any community's views, they may be a strong force in conserving existing vice, prejudices, and opinion (see Levin, *Broadcast Regulation and Joint Ownership of Media*, p. 82).

25. See Levin, *The Policy on Newspaper Ownership of Television: Some Assumptions, Objectives, and Effects*, Comments in Docket No. 18110, April 1971, p. 7. This point was later elaborated in the Robinson Dissent, pp. 20–21, and the Appeals Court decision, pp. 13, 53–55.

there is little evidence that this is so, and my investigation in chapter 6 explicitly challenges those who hold otherwise. I conclude there that steps to diversify and decentralize ownership (by a newspaper rule) would pose no substantial or widespread threat to diversity, localism, cultural or informational programming.[26]

Those analyses of actual program listings offered the kind of objective factual data the commission had invited.[27] Our studies also contrasted with the subjective appraisal of media performance in the so-called Litwin Report, which the commission quite properly rejected as unreliable.[28] This does not mean that no judgment is required to put program logs into a form most suitable for analysis. Nevertheless, subjective ratings of media performance by an unrepresentative group of respondents, aligned with the community's dominant social groups, as in the Litwin Report, are not likely to lead to sound results. Systematic quantification of several hundred separate logs according to widely accepted classificatory principles, and their analysis by multivariate statistical techniques, is at least a more objective way to assess the effects of any new rule.

Stated simply, no convincing basis in fact can be found for the predictions that dire effects on service would flow from any action to keep newspapers and colocated TV stations separate. Yet opponents held that the one-to-a-customer rules are "potentially destructive of a commercial broadcast structure which, through its stability and productivity, [has] served the public interest well." [29] The analysis reported in chapter 6 questions the validity of this statement, at least insofar as newspapers and television go.[30]

The critical bearing of these findings on the issues under scrutiny can be further demonstrated by reference to selected items in the public record. Thus broadcast industry spokesmen have noted:

> No one can say what the actual result of divestiture would be. However, all would agree that the effects of divestiture upon service to the public

---

26. Nor are even possibly affirmative effects on newspaper quality and viability really germane here in that the FCC's jurisdiction is presumably limited to the licensed station only.

27. First Report and Order, 6 April 1970, par. 37.

28. Ibid., pars. 36–40. Also, Memorandum Opinion and Order, March 2, 1971, pars. 22–28 (especially par. 25). See lastly, detailed critique in Barnett, "Cable Television and Media Concentration, Part I," *Stanford Law Review* (January 1970), pp. 260–73. The Litwin Report refers to George H. Litwin and William H. Wroth, *The Effects of Common Ownership on Media Content and Influence* (Washington, D.C.: National Association of Broadcasters, July 1969).

29. NAB Petition for Extension of Time to File Comments as to Further Notice, 17 June 1970, p. 3.

30. Recall my extensive analysis of the probable effects of divestiture on station profitability and sales prices. No evidence was found of significant likely losses in revenues or thirty-second one-time rates (in 1972); or in previous benefits derived from restrictive licensing, 1949–70. However, there might be losses in audience size and ratings, at least in the smaller markets (see, for example, chapter 6, pp. 180–81).

must be our paramount concern and that research which has been conducted to date on that question must be supplemented by more farreaching studies. . . .[31]

My findings bear directly on this contention and are also germane to the kind of evidence which the newspaper publishers' own petition alluded to in part.[32] The results indeed offer some of the "facts" CBS explicitly called for.[33]

Such, finally, is the evidence at issue in the Petition for a Joint Study when it spoke of "the heart of the matter, the quality of service to the public." [34] That petition saw the public interest to lie in establishing

> mass communications media which . . . will . . . constantly impart to the public a greater and greater portion of knowledge and culture which it needs if our people are to enjoy a reasonable measure of happiness and if the complex questions confronting our society are to be resolved through the democratic process.[35]

My studies of economic viability, diversity, and program composition in the previous chapter indicate that the separation of colocated newspapers and TV stations would in no substantial way impair the kind of media performance that the Petition for a Joint Study sought.[36] Other safeguards are also needed, of course. But in view of the above-cited evidence, the several approaches to separation appear more a help than a hindrance to the petition's laudable objectives. With today's "hardware," the "software"—skills, financial incentives, and organizational arrangements—implicit in a local market structure with independent and competing newspaper and TV stations will in no serious way narrow the range of viewer options. Nor would there be more than miniscule losses in informational programming. However, the wider diffusion of economic and political power that results, and the greater concomitant safeguards against potential abuse, remain as net gains. To be sure, some observers see the potential abuses of government action as far more potentially dangerous than the action of any large corporation. My position here, however, is that governmental action to alter business structures poses less public danger in broadcasting than actions that intrude directly on media content.

As noted elsewhere, in any case, the gains of diversified ownership reflect the fact that separate media ownership operates to (a) enhance reportorial accuracy (different reporters and editors make different mis-

31. NAB Petition, cited in note 29 above.
32. ANPA Motion to Extend Time for Preparation and Submission of Comments, June 18, 1970, pp. 2–3.
33. Reply comments of CBS, February 27, 1969, pp. 3–4.
3–4.
34. Petition for Joint Study by Atlass Communications et al., June 11, 1970, pp.
35. Ibid., pp. 4–5.
36. See especially discussion in chapter 6, pp. 194–95, 206–07.

takes); (*b*) reduce the distortion in language symbols and the difficulty of relating them to real world facts (because different people's language distorts reality differently, so that independent reporters, writers, and programmers may produce a more complete picture of what really transpired); (*c*) diversify the outlooks and perspectives of media owners; (*d*) sustain the balance and thoroughness of news coverage; (*e*) minimize common editorial positions, story overlap, avoidance of sensitive issues due to close informal contacts between personnel in a joint enterprise.[37]

This brings us to a further contention that the outlooks and perspectives of media owners are dictated more by their business interests than by any personal predilections, especially in publicly held companies. The very size and resources of modern media may color their outlook in that they are big businesses with "a position and a bias toward a certain system which unconsciously they presuppose is the right one. . . ."[38]

If indeed the business character of commercial broadcasting makes for similar perspectives and viewpoints, does owner diversity really matter? I believe it does, even under these constraints. For even the owners of profit-maximizing TV stations may differ as to race, religion, age, sex, or territorial association, as well as to occupation and economic interest. Racial, religious, or sectional cleavages are known to be as important as differences in income and wealth in shaping individual values and social and political change.[39] Furthermore, the "company interest" is not always clear-cut, and where it is ambiguous, individual decision makers may weigh their own personal beliefs more heavily. And where a newspaper-TV enterprise is part of a larger conglomerate, spinoff may leave at least one of the parts significantly less big-business-oriented. Finally, corporate decisions for TV licensees necessarily occur within the ranges of indeterminacy associated with oligopolistic market structures. At the margin, therefore, even the possibility of small personal differences does matter, especially if structural diversity grows through multichannel cable grids, new UHF, or reduced-space VHF entry.

True, one could justify cross-ownership or group ownership as strength-

37. See Levin, *Broadcast Regulation and Joint Ownership*; W. Gormley, *Effects of Newspaper: TV Cross-Ownership*.

38. Zechariah Chafee, Jr., *Government and Mass Communications*, A Report from the Commission on the Freedom of the Press (Chicago: University of Chicago Press, 1947), p. 614. See also William Ernest Hocking, *Freedom of the Press—A Framework of Principles*, A Report from the Commission on Freedom of the Press (Chicago: University of Chicago Press, 1947), pp. 59–62, 129–30; and for an illuminating recent commentary, Edward Epstein, *News from Nowhere* (New York: Vintage, 1973), chaps. 3, 6, and 7.

39. See Pitirim Sorokin, *Society, Culture, and Personality: Their Structure and Dynamics—A System of General Sociology* (New York: Harper, 1947), chaps. 10–14; Charles Beard, *An Economic Interpretation of the Movement towards the Constitution* (New York: Macmillan, 1948), pp. 52–63, 149–52, 290–91; 324–25; Beard, *Rise of American Civilization* (New York: Macmillan, 1945), vol. I, pp. 315–21, 331–35.

ening the licensee's ability to withstand governmental pique on the sensitive issues that the media air.[40] However, there are many investments besides those in related media through which TV licensees could diversify their revenue sources, granted that the resulting conglomeration of ownership may create problems of its own. Furthermore, to permit licensed TV activities to bolster their economic resources by acquiring unlicensed press activities increases the chances that governmental pressures on the former could operate to constrain the latter too.[41] That is, business interests and outlook create pressures enough, and adding the extra pressure which inheres in government licensing seems like a counterproductive way to strengthen any licensee's ability to undertake greater risks in matters of public controversy.

In sum, the determination of which strategy to use in diffusing media power—accepting this goal as desirable—must be made on grounds other than the unsubstantiated allegations of serious impairment to station viability, continuity, diversity, localism, program quality, and merit service. I have found such alleged impairment to be highly speculative, and at most too minute to weigh seriously. For that very reason, the Appeals Court rejected the commission's conclusion that any broader rule affecting more than the seven "most egregious" cases was unacceptable.[42]

2. Would Separation Seriously Impair Newspaper Cross-Subsidization of TV Subsidiaries at the Expense of Program Diversity and Information?

Newspapers are frequently said to cross-subsidize their TV stations and thus enhance the latter's public service contributions. For such reasons, divestiture has been predicted to produce dire social results.[43] However, nowhere in the record do we find the quantitative evidence on cross-subsidization needed to evaluate these contentions.[44]

To underscore the economic values divestiture allegedly threatened, the newspaper publishers' association (ANPA) filed elaborate estimates of the appraised values of newspaper-owned TV stations, reflective of network affiliation contracts, federal licenses, goodwill, and so on.[45] In the process, ANPA examined recent TV station sales prices. However, it stopped well short of evidence on the existence, let alone magnitude, of cross-subsidization.

40. Epstein, *News from Nowhere*, chap. 2.
41. See discussion associated with notes 88–90, this chapter.
42. See, for example, Second Report, pars. 108–12, and Appeals Court decision, pp. 47–50, and especially pp. 51–59.
43. See, for example, ANPA Comments, April 1971, vol. II, C-22 (Wilcox), D-21 (Udell).
44. This conclusion was explicitly reached in the Appeals Court decision, p. 56, and in the Robinson Dissent, pp. 36–38.
45. ANPA Comments, vol. II, studies A and B.

Such evidence is not easy to produce. However, the ANPA's sales price analysis could have been directed to cross-subsidization problems too, though it chose only to estimate the *private* equities divestiture would impair, not the public ones.

Cross-subsidization could in theory contribute to stated regulatory objectives, and hence provide an argument against separation by fostering greater diversity and public service on newspaper than on nonnewspaper-owned stations, or by sustaining marginal stations that might otherwise go under. As to the first point, the diversity studies already summarized inferentially challenge any contention that newspapers cross-subsidize their TV stations in ways that substantially enhance their relative diversity and public service. The failure of newspaper stations to outproduce nonnewspapers to any great extent in local and informational programming suggests that whatever cross-subsidization may exist simply lacks the claimed effects.

In principle, one can argue that only stations doing *poorly* should be allowed to be owned by newspapers, at least insofar as the parent's cross-subsidies may help keep them afloat, and hence sustain a multivoice media structure that safeguards diversity. By contrast, it is hard to imagine any generalized need for cross-subsidy where newspaper-owned stations earn significantly higher rates, income, revenue and time sales, and sell at higher prices than nonnewspaper stations. Nor are handsome capital gains evidence that prior nonremunerative public service has in any case been internally subsidized. Nor, where newspaper- and nonnewspaper-owned stations sell for statistically *comparable* prices, can one probably infer any more than that the former are in no more, and no less, need of cross-subsidization by their parent companies than are TV stations owned by *non*newspaper interests (such as groups or conglomerates).

In short, my earlier programming studies challenge those who see newspaper ownership as an important source of cross-subsidy enhancing program diversity and public service. With few exceptions, no special program contributions appear to have materialized, a fact which must at the very least give pause to observers who would take assertions about extensive cross-subsidy at face value. Neither do newspaper and non-newspaper station sales prices respond differently to restrictive licensing policies, irrespective of seller or buyer's status as group or nongroup, network affiliate or independent, VHF or UHF, and regardless of market size, age of station, and so forth.

Therefore, newspapers are, other things being equal, no more and no less able to share in the special rents that license limitation creates than their nonnewspaper counterparts. Accordingly, they are in no greater and no lesser need of outside subsidies to stay afloat or to perform in the public interest, a conclusion corroborated by the programming studies mentioned above.[46] The case for diversified ownership nonetheless lies in the positive benefits specified earlier in this and the prior chapter.[47]

3. Would Separation Result in Serious Disruptive Side Effects and Losses in Private Equities? Can or Should TV Licensees Be Cushioned against Such Effects, and If So, How?

During the lengthy cross-ownership proceeding, some observers contended that to deprive newspapers of their TV licenses at renewal would constitute forfeiture.[48] They deemed it unduly harsh to exclude licensees who had violated no law, had originally entered with commission approval, and had long contributed to TV's development, stability, and public service.[49] If publishers were now to be prohibited from owning colocated TV stations, a further question was whether they would continue to play a strong developmental role elsewhere. If too harsh, the proposed divestiture policy might deter their participation in cable television or satellites even before the commission's cross-ownership policies were set definitively therein.

For such reasons, indeed, both the Further Notice and Second Report sought to cushion the impact of any new rule. First and foremost, a five-year period was to be allowed for the necessary divestitures. In addition, special tax treatment would be afforded any losses due to distress sales. Beyond this, even the designation for divestiture of ninety-four colocated entities under the Further Notice would itself have limited the number of required sales, since *out-of-town* newspaper ties would still have been permissible. This too would have acted to reduce the number of distress sales.[50] Under the Second Report, of course, a scant seven colocated entities were affected.

Furthermore, the commission did not intend that "the rules should work a forfeiture . . . [but that] only a sale, not a loss [was] contemplated. . . . Inability to sell the station would be a basis of waiver. Otherwise a refusal to grant a further renewal . . . would work forfeiture; a result contrary to our intent. We would take a similar view if the only sale possible would have to be at an artificially depressed price."[51] Nor was it in any case clear that divestiture would prevent any station from recovering the capital value of its franchise when sold, even assum-

46. See, especially, chapter 6, pp. 194–207, and textual discussion of tables 6.9, 6.10 and 6.11.

47. See notes 24 and 37, this chapter; also chapter 6, notes 11 and 30 and associated text.

48. Further Notice, pars. 10–19.

49. This follows in part from their strong definition of property rights in spectrum which, under present law, they simply do not have.

50. Further Notice, pars. 31, 34, 39–41; Public Notice No. 49811, July 16, 1970 (Issuance of Tax Certificates).

51. Second Report, par. 119.

ing there to be special advantages in newspaper ownership. Colocated owners could, for example, clearly sell to *out-of-town* newspapers. But even if prices did go below market value, as may be likely for newspaper-owned stations with group affiliations,[52] "in most instances the facility will have returned the original investment to the owner several times." [53]

Note, in any case, that the distinction between a phased-in divestiture and outright forfeiture at renewal time recognized business equities in the present structure. The proposed five-year period was indeed longer than that proposed by a National Violence Commission Staff Report in 1969,[54] and longer still than any automatic action at "the next" renewal (as initially proposed by the Justice Department). Thus the Second Report leaned in the direction of allowing more rather than less time to make the needed changes. The only other way to lengthen the period further might have been to make it better approximate the seven years roughly needed to amortize total investments in TV broadcasting. However, there is a basic question of how far any regulatory agency must go to phase in rule changes with a minimum of economic distress to existing licensees.[55]

Three points must be made. First, the status quo is surely not without its own inequities. To safeguard sources diversity, divestiture is needed just because any restructuring through new grants and transfers alone would be too slow and too limited. The market position of existing combinations would actually be strengthened because they would no longer be challenged by new combinations and on that count be even more reluctant to sell out.[56]

Second, in whatever way the commission cushioned its rule changes, at least some economic hardship would occur. In balancing between diversifying media sources, editorial outlooks, ownership perspectives, on one hand, and transitional economic losses and public benefits on the other, virtually *any* rule change at *any* time would impose *some* injury on *someone*. Were the commission strictly guided by such hardship, one wonders if it would ever modify any rule. Admittedly, businessmen enter TV on a set of economic and regulatory assumptions—but the possibility of rule changes is surely one of these. Uncertainties generated by fre-

52. See chapter 6, table 6.10, rows 1, 2 and 4, wherein quite clearly the prices of stations with newspaper and group links sell for lower prices than stations with only one link (or neither). Note also the significance (or near-significance) of these sums at rows 2 and 4.

53. Robinson Dissent, p. 39; also Appeals Court decision, p. 55. The point was raised several years earlier in my Reply Comments, Docket No. 18110, August 1971, p. 19.

54. Robert Baker and Sandra Ball, *Violence and the Media—A Staff Report to the National Commission on the Causes and Prevention of Violence* (Washington, D.C.: U.S. Government Printing Office, 1969), p. 157.

55. Actually it is not the physical assets whose value might be eroded, but the broadcaster's public franchise, an issue to which I shall momentarily return.

56. Further Notice, par. 8.

quent capricious changes might of course have adverse disincentive effects on the inflow of venture capital. However, the long-announced and carefully scrutinized proposal to end cross-ownership was hardly capricious or arbitrary.

Third, it is hard to see how divestiture could be opposed simply because it would injure the joint enterprises if those enterprises in fact enjoyed higher advertising rates on both ends of the enterprise due virtually to their "jointness." To undercut such premium time or space rates can hardly give pause, that is, if significant market power helped produce them in the first place. True, my independent audit of the monopolistic rates issue in Appendix 5A and chapter 6 raised questions about its validity. For present purposes, however, the implications are no different even if the Rosse-Owen-Grey findings cited there are rejected, and NAB's accepted.[57]

Thus, if joint enterprises do not enjoy premium advertising rates due to their jointness, then neither can industry opponents cite the impairment of such rates in the case against divestiture, whereas if the reverse were true, our earlier argument holds and the commission surely need not hesitate to infringe on unfair private advantages to further the public interest in decentralized media control.

To the counterclaim that only the initial grantees of a license capture the rents that government creates, and that nonrenewal or divestiture with or without compensation may therefore be unduly harsh, the following points must be considered. First, it is in no way clear that the initial grantee *is* the only likely recipient of the scarcity rents in TV today (see discussion in chapter 12, note 4). Secondly, insofar as the risk of nonrenewal or divestiture must have been taken into account by entrants at the outset, one might on that count too question the appropriateness of full compensation for any losses imposed. Thirdly, if the government did indeed opt to pay fair market value anyway for the licenses it recovered under forced divestiture, it should then at least sell them to the highest bidder. Only in that way could we be sure that windfall rents were not conferred gratis all over again on the new licensees.

This brings us to another, related question: Did the abundance of nonnewspaper-owned radio and TV stations in most one-newspaper communities virtually obviate the need for divestiture at all, the presumption implicit in the Second Report? Some parties asserted as much because the public already had so many independent alternatives in these markets. A further implication was that these one-newspaper communities could

57. See James Rosse, Bruce Owen, and David Grey, *Economic Issues in the Joint Ownership of Newspaper and Television Media*, May 1970. Comments in Docket No. 18110. See appendix 1, p. 17 (table 1), p. 21 (table 5). Compare A. M. Lago, *A Quantitative Analysis of the Price Effects of Joint Mass Communication Media Ownership*, March 1, 1971 (prepared by Resource Management Corporation for National Association of Broadcasters).

accommodate a cross-media link without seriously narrowing program choice and diversity.

4. Is Any Public Need for Separation Significantly Reduced by the Present Multivoice Local Communications Structure and Further Development of Cable Television and Satellites? Or Is the Contrary True, Given the Preventive Aspect of All Proposed Rules and Far More Numerous Potential Than Actual Cross-Media Links Today?

The multivoice argument has a long and well-known history. It was raised sixteen years ago in Congressman Emmanuel Celler's abortive inquiry into newspaper-TV mergers, and has figured extensively again in the cross-ownership proceeding.[58] Like the ANPA earlier, the NAB has also cited Raymond B. Nixon's work to challenge any need to keep newspapers and television separate to enhance media diversity.[59] More recently, NAB commissioned some original studies of the nation's multimedia communications structure today and over time.[60]

Closely related to safeguards attributed to the present multivoice structure was the further contention that new technology would take care of our problems. By reducing existing entry barriers due to spectrum scarcities or otherwise, new technology was predicted to provide still more structural safeguards of diversity and choice. Let us consider both these aspects of the multivoice argument, in reverse order.

As to the prospects for new cable, satellite, and related technology, I myself have underscored their future importance in providing a framework for greater diversity and choice.[61] Cable technology and broadband circuitry already render obsolete our traditional assumptions about spectrum scarcity. Nevertheless, the commission seemed well-advised to

58. See, for instance, Comments on NBC, August 1, 1968, pp. 3–4, 16–31 (plus appendix tables); Comments of Storer Broadcasting Co., August 1, 1968, pp. 6–7; Comments of ABC, August 1, 1968, pp. 22–23 (and appended tables); Reply Comments of ABC, February 28, 1969, pp. 7–11.

59. See NAB Reply and Supplemental Comments in Opposition to Proposed Rule Making, February 28, 1969, pp. 3–5, and Attachment A (excerpt from Nixon, "Trends in U.S. Newspaper Ownership: Concentration with Competition," published by the ANPA Foundation in January 1969, and in *Gazette* [Netherlands], 1968, pp. 181–93). Compare with Nixon, "Newspaper Ownership and Inter-Media Competition," *Journalism Quarterly*. (Winter 1961), pp. 3–14, cited extensively in *Newspapers-1963*, ANPA Presentation to the House Antitrust Subcommittee, April 1963, pp. 19–25, 28–30.

60. Motion of NAB to Extend Time for Filing Comments, December 23, 1970; M. H. Seiden, *Mass Communications in the United States—1970*, summary volume (Washington, D.C.: National Association of Broadcasters, 1971).

61. Levin, "Competition, Diversity and the TV Group Ownership Rule," *Columbia Law Review* (May 1970), 823–24; Levin, "Broadcast Structure, Technology, and the ABC-ITT Merger Decision," *Law & Contemporary Problems* (Summer 1969), pp. 452–65.

hedge its policy bets, for the future of cable and other broadband media was and still is uncertain. The potential structural relief they offer was, of course, recognized by parties to the cross-ownership proceeding.[62] However, the speed with which such relief would materialize was at best unknown.

The frustrated hopes of those who initially advocated the UHF Allocation Plan twenty-seven years ago, and the FM Allocation Plan even earlier, urge the utmost caution in relying on any "imminent" technological panacea. Nor did it therefore appear necessary or desirable to choose between taking steps to diversify ownership within today's economic structure and technology, and doing nothing, pending the emergence of a new technological base which broadcasters resolutely oppose, and whose uncertain future guarantees for diversity may or may not materialize.

If the separation of print and broadcast media is desirable today to diffuse economic and political power and to widen viewer choices, the fact that new technology may eventually do the same thing is no reason not to act in what could be a protracted interim period. On the contrary, extensive newspaper-TV ties today will needlessly complicate the issues posed by newspaper or TV participation in the cable and satellite systems of tomorrow.

But what about the multiplicity of multivoice communities *already* in existence? Do they constitute sufficient safeguards of diversity in their own right to sanction the status quo? One tenuous assumption here can be dismissed out of hand. If the separation of broadcast and print media is largely consistent with diversity, local and informational programming (as shown in chapter 6), the availability of even a large number of independent voices in markets with joint enterprises constitutes little reason to eschew divestiture, let alone strong preventive action. Even if an existing multivoice structure already helps to safeguard diversity, we could presumably do still better. But the problem, of course, is that the potential number of TV outlets in each market is usually quite small.

The commission had in any case held that there is "no optimum degree of diversification and that [it did] not feel competent to say . . . that any particular number of outlets of expression is 'enough'; and . . . that a proper objective is the maximum diversity of ownership that technology will allow in each area." [63] But even short of that, the multiplicity of multivoice communities in no way militated against that extensive prospective action which the Second Report clearly did take, and the Appeals Court endorsed.[64] Strong preventive steps were quite properly taken to safeguard diversity of owner perspectives, program sources,

62. See, for example, Petition for Joint Study, June 11, 1970, pp. 5–7; Comments of CBS, July 31, 1968, pp. 8–9. This, however, seems particularly incongruous for CBS to argue since, in other proceedings, it has opposed the growth of cable.

63. Memorandum Opinion and Order, March 2, 1971, par. 10.

64. Appeals Court decision, p. 33.

Table 7.1

Intermedia Competition in Daily Newspaper Communities,
1961-68

Communities With	Number of Communities		Number of Enterprises	
	1968	1961	1968	1961
Newspaper enterprises[a]	1500	1461	1578[g]	1555[h]
One-newspaper enterprise	1455[e]	1400[f]	1455	1400
Competing newspaper enterprises	45	61	122	155
Newspaper enterprises with or without broadcast enterprises[b]	1500	1461	5079	3679
Single-media voices[c]	202	355	202	355
Competing media voices[d]	1298	1106	4879	3324

SOURCE: Based on Raymond B. Nixon, "Trends in U.S. Newspaper Ownership: Concentration with Competition," *Gazette* (Netherlands, 1968), pp. 182-93; Raymond B. Nixon and Jean Ward, "Trends in Newspaper Ownership and Inter-Media Competition," *Journalism Quarterly*, (Winter 1961), pp. 3-14.

[a]A newspaper enterprise refers to one or more daily newspapers under a single ownership.

[b]A broadcast enterprise refers to any AM, FM, or TV station under single ownership, or to any combination of those singly owned in the same community.

[c]A media voice refers to a newspaper enterprise or a broadcast enterprise; this includes communities with local monopoly joint enterprises, and communities with one newspaper enterprise but no broadcast enterprise.

[d]Communities with more than one enterprise under separate ownership.

[e]This figure includes 1284 single-newspaper communities and 171 communities with more than one daily where the dailies were under common ownership; there were 342 dailies in these 171 communities.

[f]This figure includes 1222 single-newspaper communities and 178 communities with more than one daily where the dailies were under common ownership; there were 356 dailies in these 178 communities.

[g]Derived by counting the 342 dailies under common ownership in 171 communities as 171 enterprises only; there were actually 1749 dailies on January 1, 1968.

[h]Derived by counting the 356 dailies under common ownership in 178 communities as 178 enterprises only. There were actually 1733 dailies on January 1, 1961.

and contents, just because so many potential cross-ownership situations exist in markets of different sizes. Even the maximum number of conceivable divestitures (ninety-four in the Further Notice) was at best a fraction of the potential cross-media links which preventive action could forestall.[65] So that if the commission looked even to token divestitures to safeguard diversity, it must surely consider also the logically related

65. For example, the 94 colocated newspaper-TV enterprises the commission identified in November 1969 contrasted with 1,253 one-newspaper communities in 1968, which had one or more AM, FM, or TV stations without newspaper links. At that time also there were 189 TV, 394 AM and 245 FM stations with newspaper or magazine ties nationally, in contrast with 4,757 independent newspaper and broadcast enterprises. See tables 7.1 and 7.2.

Table 7.2
*Potential Cross-Ownership Situations in
One-Newspaper Communities, 1961-68*

	Number of Communities		Number of Newspaper and Broadcast Enterprises	
	1968	1961	1968	1961
Communities with one-newspaper enterprise plus one or more independent broadcast enterprises	1253[a]	1045[b]	4757[c]	3169[d]

SOURCE: See table 7.1.

[a]This is derived from table 7.1 by subtracting the 45 communities with competing dailies from the 1298 newspaper communities with competing media voices.

[b]This is derived from table 7.1 by subtracting the 61 communities with competing dailies from the 1106 newspaper communities with competing media voices.

[c]This is derived from table 7.1 by subtracting the 122 dailies located in 45 communities with competing dailies from the 4879 media voices present in 1298 communities with competing media voices.

[d]This is derived from table 7.1 by subtracting the 155 dailies located in 61 communities with competing dailies from the 3324 media voices present in 1106 communities with competing media voices.

step of preventing new grants and transfers to newspaper publishers—an obviously less painful way to proceed. Both the commission's initial proposal and its final enactment did so, and this preventive action was fully consistent with the information in tables 7.1 and 7.2.

5. Would Separation Seriously Aggravate Ownership Concentration and Act Also to Reduce Localism in Television? Would Local Nonnewspaper Interests be Significantly Priced out of the Market?

Some observers predicted a serious upsurge of absentee group ownership because local interests would allegedly lack the means to buy the "high-priced" newspaper-owned stations that would supposedly flood the market.[66] Such a result, they held, would clash with the commission's stated commitment to localism. But even if this were true, the *prospective* ban (as in the latest rule) would operate far more gradually, and clearly pose no such problem.

Unless the capital market were seriously imperfect it is hard to see why high prices need price local entrants out of the market. Furthermore, our analysis in chapter 6 demonstrates that divestiture would often operate to reduce sales prices below normal market levels, and industry studies

66. NAB Comments, pp. 42–43; also ANPA Comments, vol. I, pp. 51–52.

bear this out.[67] Such a general price reduction was also documented at length in an ANPA study which projected the probable loss of property values due to divestiture.[68] Our own estimate is that newspaper-owned stations which were also group-owned would sell for $2,600,000 (t = 1.5) less than otherwise comparable nonnewspaper stations.[69] In that case, clearly, local interests would have a better (not worse) chance to purchase the divested stations. Nor is it in any case self-evident why, if the stations up for sale were such good buys, local entrants could not raise money in the capital market—especially if any distress sale prices were expected to rise again in the future.[70]

In sum, if newspapers were made to divest their stations, those also affiliated with group enterprises would clearly sell at prices significantly lower than their nonnewspaper counterparts, and this is true even though joint newspaper-group buyers paid $7,500,000 more for stations in our sample than buyers with neither attribute.[71] Even newspaper-owned stations sold to newspaper-affiliated buyers would command prices not significantly higher than those where buyer and seller were both nonnewspapers, at least where all stations being compared were also group affiliates.[72] Still more germane to the possibility of local entry through acquisition is the further fact that, for newspaper-owned stations sold to newspaper buyers, the prices for those whose buyers and sellers were also group affiliates are not statistically higher than those where neither sellers nor buyers were members of groups.[73] On both counts, the prospects seem brighter for local entrants who enjoy neither ownership tie.

The commission could in any case institute special safeguards against an undue upsurge in group ownership generally, or against regional concentration in particular.[74] However, group ownership is already limited

67. NAB Comments, pp. 59–62; ANPA Comments, vol. I pp. 46–57; vol II, A-10, A-11.

68. ANPA Comments, vol. I, pp. 36–38; vol. II, studies A and B. For a handy critical assessment of two major ANPA-commissioned studies of sales prices (by Frazier-Gross and First National City Bank), see *Concentration of Mass Media Ownership* (Santa Monica, Calif.: Rand Corporation, 1974), pp. 115–20.

69. See chapter 6, table 6.10, test 2 (column 8). Note further that newspaper affiliates that were also group-owned would sell for $5,179,000 less than newspaper affiliates that were nongroup, whereas group-affiliated nonnewspaper stations would sell for $1,188,000 more than nongroup nonnewspaper stations (ibid., tests 4 and 5). Nevertheless, the pattern does change for nongroup stations which, when also newspaper-affiliated, sell for $3,751,000 more (t=1.7) than when nonnewspaper (test 3).

70. This point, made initially in my Reply Comments, August 1971, pp. 16–17, was subsequently noted in the Robinson Dissent, p. 39, and Appeals Court decision, p. 53. Note further, my preceding new evidence on distress prices that might result from divestiture. See chapter 6, table 6.10, and associated discussion.

71. Ibid., test 1, column 4.

72. Ibid., test 7, column 8.

73. Ibid., test 9, column 8.

74. It must be recognized, however, that removing a newspaper and group tie from any station *simultaneously* would probably hurt it significantly more than removing either tie alone. Thus sales price would decline by $6,069,000 in the former

by special ceilings so that even if the commission did nothing, the influx of group entrants would be checked almost automatically. Furthermore, group ownership has no significant effects on diversity one way or the other once full account is taken of network affiliation and market size. If anything, it may operate to increase viewer choices slightly.

6. Would Separation Seriously Impair the Future Development of TV Broadcasting (and Inflow of Needed Venture Capital) by "Breaking Faith" With Stable Newspaper Pioneers Who Entered Radio and Television at the Outset and Have Steadily Figured in Their Growth over Time?

Whatever the newspapers' pioneer developmental role in broadcasting, the various proposals for separation must be judged on their consequences for diversifying owner perspectives, program sources, and content today. To say that any proposal would break faith with the pioneers and deter new entrants in the future misconstrues the industry's economic history and basic tenets of broadcast regulation.

Before the commission's freeze on new TV grants in 1948–52, some 90 percent of broadcast stations are reported to have been licensed to newspapers or AM radio licensees. Of 108 TV stations operating at that time, 32 were owned by newspapers and 57 by radio stations.[75] The newspaper and radio pioneers have also been stable licensees; 80 percent of newspaper-owned TV stations today remain with their original owners, as do 60 percent of those owned by AM licensees, compared to only 20 percent of those owned by other enterprises.[76] To dispossess the newspaper owners may therefore seem to break faith with those very entities which bore the early developmental losses and risks and have remained steadfast ever since.[77] This is believed likely to stifle future investment in new technology for greater diversity.[78]

Regulators do indeed normally view ownership stability as a virtue insofar as stable owners gain experience and insight into their commu-

---

case, a sum significantly greater than the $2,221,000 to $3,187,000 price decline where one tie only was removed (see table 6.10, tests 9 and 7, column 9). Actually removing either tie *separately* would not affect price significantly (tests 7, 9, column 8).

75. NAB Comments, p. 94.

76. Ibid., pp. 94–95.

77. In a study on "Pioneer AM Radio and Television Broadcast Stations," commissioned by the NAB, Buren Robbins purported to show a greater stability of newspaper than nonnewspaper pioneers. Nevertheless, his data are badly impaired by lack of any comparative analysis (ibid., pp. 17–20), whereas his sparse tabulation (p. 21) leaves us once again with no way of telling whether the differences in so-called "relinquishment rates" as between newspaper and nonnewspaper owners may in fact be due to differences in network tie, group ownership, channel type, market size, or even number of stations in market. Each of these factors (and others) could conceivably affect the relative stability of newspapers as licensees, and the length of time before they sell out.

78. NAB Comments, pp. 95–96.

nity's interests and needs, and are, almost by definition, less likely to sacrifice sustained program quality for quick capital gains.[79] Nevertheless, the pre-1952 VHF stations (in whose development newspapers played a pioneering role) have long ranked among the industry's most lucrative properties.[80] Newspapers would understandably have wanted to retain these valuable privileges, so that at least some of their stability as TV licensees has made very good business sense. Furthermore, the long period of newspaper incumbency must also mean that many early newspaper investments have been recovered many times over by now.[81]

These facts on pre-1952 VHF profitability and long newspaper tenure also leave the breaking faith argument not very convincing. How, for example, could the commission change any rule without breaking faith with at least someone who had entered in reliance on it? Yet even if private equities are given some weight here, surely public equities in sources and content diversity must prevail. Granted, of course, that one should ideally distinguish situations where the security of tenure in private property is so jeopardized as to contribute to a general undermining of the basis on which such property is held, from those where this long-term effect will not occur.

I do not claim to have done so here. However, I do believe that private enterprise is built to assess risks, and that the market does to a point capitalize the risks of regulatory change. True, the sudden discrete jumps of major political events may be harder to predict than the gradual, continuous changes in market trends, tastes, and incomes. Yet the lengthy debates that accompany much of regulatory change probably reduce some of the elements of surprise in the final outcome. Even the market's crude capitalization of the uncertainties of regulatory action, therefore, may provide a pertinent answer to the breaking faith argument. In addition, of course, there is a more familiar contention, namely, that if the commission must never impair economic values that its own policies help create, this wrongly implies that licensees have acquired property rights in spectrum which the law explicitly forbids.[82]

79. See especially Second Report, pars. 108–9; also Robinson Dissent, p. 34, and Appeals Court decision, p. 54.

80. Recall, for example, that in 1972 pre-1952 stations had spot rates $58.50 higher than post-1951 stations (17.3 percent of the sample mean); audiences with 47,000 more viewers (5.7 percent of mean), and station revenues $710,350 higher (17 percent of sample mean). See chapter 6, tables 6.5, 6.6, row 10.

81. This point was cited in the Appeals Court decision, p. 55, and the Robinson Dissent, p. 39. See also similar statement several years prior, in my Reply Comments, August 1971, pp. 19, 21.

82. The legislative requirement that licensees must waive such rights in their frequencies can of course be criticized rather fundamentally as "bad law" and "worse economics." (See Ronald Coase, "The Federal Communications Commission," *Journal of Law and Economics* (October 1960); A. DeVany et al., "A Property System for Market Allocation of the Electromagnetic Spectrum," *Stanford Law Review* (June 1969); also my own critique in *The Invisible Resource* (Baltimore: Johns Hopkins University Press, 1971), chap. 4. Nevertheless, short of a total revamping of spectrum allocation arrangements which the abovementioned economists, among

7. Is Separation a Basic Structural Safeguard Rendering Administrative Policing Less Necessary?

Widespread separation, current or prospective, seems sound policy because it helps preclude situations of potential abuse at little demonstrable cost in foregone diversity and local, cultural, or informational service. Such separation makes the licensee less vulnerable to pressures by government officials sensitive to harsh media criticism. Above all, separation makes less necessary or probable the kind of expensive, cumbersome, periodic audit and administrative policing without which subtle distortions of content may well elude detection.

The commission's critics have held that its initial proposal for widespread separation "[was] not founded on any supposed evils or abuses whatever." That "[t]here [was] no evidence . . . that the present ownership structure does not serve the public interest and has not served [it] well over the years." That "[t]he proposal [had] been made solely on the basis of . . . a striving for some undefined, vague, hypothetical ideal." That "neither the FCC nor any other agency [could] possibly foresee or forestall all possible evils, for anything and everything is possible, and the range of potentiality [could] not even be foreseen." That the commission confronted "enough genuine problems" not to pursue the "will-of-the-wisp of ephemeral possibilities"; [83] and that it already (had) ample safeguards to insure the widest range of conflicting viewpoints—in particular, the Fairness Doctrine and the Red Lion Decision.[84]

Nevertheless, without far more extensive and rigorous policing, neither the Fairness Doctrine nor periodic renewal audits nor prescriptions for equal access by political candidates, necessarily protect what the Supreme Court deems to be the public's right to hear all views (Red Lion v. FCC). For that very reason the commission has normally combined such program policies with the structural safeguard of owner diversity. In addition to periodic regulatory review and professional ethics, that is, there is a strong case to maintain a diversified ownership structure.[85] This is true at least if the diversity of program sources, contents, editorials, and owner perspective are desiderata.

Subtle distortions are difficult to identify, all the more given the meth-

others, have several times proposed, this is where we are today, and my textual point stands.

83. NAB Comments and Arguments in Docket No. 18110, April 1971, pp. 8–9.

84. NAB Comments, p. 37. The Red Lion Decision refers to Red Lion Broadcasting Co. v. FCC (395 U.S. 367, 89 S. Ct. 1794, 23 L. Ed. 2d 371 [1969]).

85. On the need for structural as well as behavioral safeguards, see my Reply Comments, August 1971, pp. 2–4, and paper, "Competition, Diversity, and the TV Group Ownership Rule," *Columbia Law Review* (May 1970), p. 806. The Robinson Dissent subsequently underscored this point, pp. 11–13, 16, further questioning the adequacy of the Fairness Doctrine alone to safeguard more than a "mainstream consensus" and balanced programming. A structural safeguard is deemed essential to provide that "multitude of tongues" which will expose the community "to as many . . . judgments (on controversial issues) as is feasible" (Robinson Dissent, pp. 14–15).

odological limitations of content analysis and the limited FCC resources for any ongoing, comprehensive review of programming. However, the failure to encounter more known abuse does not mean that distortions do not occur under present arrangements; [86] nor that potential abuse does not exist. Sound public policy requires being safe rather than sorry, especially where safety is virtually costless in terms of foregone program diversity, public service, or cross-subsidization. Nor, as already noted several times, is there any dearth of evidence on the affirmative benefits of diversification generally, or of separate newspaper and TV ownership in particular.[87]

The commission's stated preference for even fifty-one rather than fifty voices simply dramatized this case for structural safeguards. Basically, the commission opts to decentralize private power in broadcasting. To the extent it succeeds, this clearly reduces any justification for as much centralized government power for that industry as now exists. The basic question is not whether such steps will increase diversity, but rather: "What loss in diversity and public service will flow from divestiture or preventive action against future cross-media ties?" This loss appears, at most, negligible. Accordingly, the commission's goal of decentralized power can apparently be pursued with no real cost—*in those terms*, at least—and we can, in some ways, have our cake and eat it too. Suffice it to note, finally, that those same owner diversity safeguards that forestall excessive market power may also help forestall program control at the local level.

But there is another reason to support the proposed newspaper rule, and one in the direct interest of rank-and-file broadcasters. A quotation from an interim NAB filing readily illuminates this matter:

> Broadcasting media are now subject to extensive and stringent regulations, limitations, and regulatory burdens. These already constitute a power, and a threat of power, so great as to make all media owners holding broadcasting licenses subject not merely to legal control by the FCC, but . . . to extralegal control by "lifted eyebrow" of both commissioners and staff members. Broadcast licensees simply cannot afford to incur the avoidable displeasure of people that hold such an extensive and drastic power over their economic existence. Consequently, the power of the FCC and its staff is already far greater than any authority that appears in the statute books . . . or decided opinions and precedents. . . . [88]

The point is that by supporting separate ownership, broadcasters can reduce the need for special new administrative policing and annual audits which would pose far more dangerous federal intrusions by lifted eyebrow. For only through really rigorous scrutiny could the commission hope to evaluate the recurrent allegations of opinion manipulation, and,

---

86. FCC First Report and Order in Docket No. 18110, April 6, 1970, par. 20.

87. See notes 24 and 37, this chapter and, in chapter 6, notes 28–31. See also associated text.

88. NAB Comments, p. 64.

like it or not, enough such allegations exist to warrant concern.

In sum, separate ownership helps guard against potential abuses too elusive to ferret out without far more expense and administrative policing than most broadcasters would obviously want.[89] The practical question seems not to be how much added program diversity owner (that is, sources) diversity will provide, but whether the latter will significantly *impair* program diversity or public service. The evidence in chapter 6 demonstrates that new steps to diversify ownership need not sap the broadcaster's wherewithal for content diversity significantly, or seriously alter his program mix, assuming, of course, that content diversity and public service are what we really want.

The argument in the preceding pages is further bolstered by still another important consideration, ably stated by Kenneth Jones of Columbia Law School:

> As long as cross-media ownership exists, arguments as to abuse will recur, not necessarily limited to matters of program content. The FCC will then be called to act. Even if the issue has nothing whatever to do with program content (e.g., the use of combination rates for combined newspaper-television advertising), there is the risk that FCC intervention will be influenced (or will thought to be influenced) by program content. See, for example, the Washington Post's objection to the Justice Department's opposition to renewal of WTOP's television license (alleged by the Washington Post to be a product of its exposures of Watergate matters). It is extremely important that such problems be avoided, and divestiture accomplishes this objective.[90]

In support of my evidence, at any rate, are the independent findings of the Students' FCC Study Group.[91] Drawing on renewal applications of all network affiliates in thirty-three leading markets, the study group examined six vital kinds of public service programming—news, public affairs, other nonentertainment shows, local originations, public service announcements, number and length of commercials. They found no evidence that newspaper-owned network affiliates systematically outproduced nonnewspaper stations in any of these program categories; quite the contrary was often true.

Contending otherwise, to be sure, was an NAB-funded content analysis of local news presentations prepared at Ohio University.[92] That

89. See my Reply Comments, pp. 4–5, and subsequent passing affirmation of the point in Robinson Dissent, p. 13, also, tacitly, in Appeals Court decision, p. 23.

90. This quotation is in a private communication from William K. Jones, November 1977. The *Post* owned WTOP at the time.

91. See Comments of Students' FCC Study Group, filed by Albert H. Kramer, May 1971.

92. See James Anderson, *Broadcast Stations and Newspapers: The Problems of Information Control: A Content Analysis of Local News Presentations* (conducted on behalf of the NAB by the Ohio University Broadcast Research Center) (Washington, D.C.: National Association of Broadcasters, June 1971).

analysis focused on entirely different dimensions of programming—not public service or program type diversity as such, but on the degree of local information control. By asking still other questions and drawing on other data sources, the NAB study may have helped advance the discussion. But even accepting its findings at face value, they constitute no persuasive case against separation. For they reveal no significant difference in correspondence between the news stories carried or broadcast by newspaper-owned and nonnewspaper-owned TV stations and their respective colocated newspapers, in regard to subject matter or treatment. Neither did newspaper and nonnewspaper stations vary significantly in regard to the number of news topics covered, or number and length of stories, though newspaper-owned stations did write more of their own stories.

True, the nonnewspaper stations were deemed to have "more intensive negative attitudes," and to deviate more from objective norms of reporting. But by the same token, the NAB study entirely ignored the relative frequency with which newspaper and nonnewspaper stations *editorialized,* and the degree of correspondence between the broadcast and newspaper editorials. Allegations of opinion manipulation and thought control obviously bring to mind the similarity of editorial positions. In rebutting these, one would like to know how newspaper and nonnewspaper stations varied in this regard, and also how their positions compared with those of the local newspaper. For example, was the broadcaster's frequently criticized timidity on public issues more or less pronounced where the licensee was a local newspaper? Did a newspaper-owned station run editorials very similar in attitude and topic to its parent newspaper's, compared, say, to a competing nonnewspaper-owned station's editorials and those of any unaffiliated local newspaper?

One would also feel easier about any content analysis had more control factors been introduced—for example, number and type of stations in the market, a more refined measure of market size, and the like. In fact, however, the NAB-funded study of local information control used variance analysis exclusively, a far less rigorous technique than my regressions in chapter 6. Anderson's two-variable model is even less persuasive, given the uneven returns to his data questionnaire and his use of loose market definitions.[93] Also, Anderson cross-classified his stations by market size and newspaper ownership only, whereas my regressions consider channel type, network ties, group ties, age, competitors, station revenues, and so on. Accordingly, one cannot tell how far his results may really reflect not newspaper ownership but network affiliation, group links, channel type, or even competitors. Finally, Anderson's uneven returns were drawn from forty-nine television markets, compared to my

93. Ibid., pp. 18 and 21.

data compilations from the bulk of all two hundred TV markets in 1967, and again in 1972.

The main value of the NAB study was probably to illustrate the kind of inquiry the commission itself would have to conduct on an ongoing, comprehensive basis were it entirely to reject the traditional commitment to owner diversity which separation represents. Yet the danger inherent in close administrative policing of program content is exacerbated by the very elusive character of the bias, manipulation, or slanting of news and editorial policies in cross-owned enterprises.[94]

Conclusion

In 1968, FCC Commissioner Lee Loevinger, later NAB special counsel, advised the commission against some proposed limits on TV multiple-station holdings in the fifty leading markets. The criterion in that proceeding, he said, should be the medical maxim of *primum non nocere*: "If you cannot help the patient, at least do not . . . hurt him." [95] However, in matters of local cross-media ownership another maxim seems far more apt: "An ounce of prevention is worth a pound of cure." The several proposed versions of a newspaper rule are mainly valuable, it appears, as prophylactic.[96]

In that regard, my evidence in chapters 6 and 7 has, first and foremost, seriously questioned contentions that any far-reaching curb on co-located newspaper ownership of TV stations (or on nonnetwork group ownership) would in any way significantly reduce (1) program diversity

94. That enough episodes do in fact exist notwithstanding the difficulty of quantifying them was argued at length in Stephen Barnett, "Cross-Ownership of Media in the Same Community—A Report to the John and Mary Markle Foundation" (Berkeley: University of California Law School, September 23, 1974). Barnett's evidence was cited in the Appeals Court decision, pp. 38, 42, and 43. See also the Robinson Dissent, pp. 17–18. Nor are the NAB results in any case consistent with a more recent quantitative study by Gormley which revealed that newspaper-owned stations are more likely than nonnewspaper-owned ones to be located in the same building as the local newspaper, to receive advance copies of the latter's stories, and to have on its news staff a reporter or editor who had worked for the newspaper. Gormley's multiple regression analysis further revealed significantly more news homogeneity for newspaper than nonnewspaper stations (measured as story overlap on the proportion of a TV station's state and local news stories which also appeared in a colocated newspaper). Finally, locally cross-owned stations were significantly less likely to editorialize than those not cross-owned. See William Gormley, *The Effects of Newspaper-Television Cross Ownership on News Homogeneity*, especially chaps. 4–6.

95. Concurring Opinion in Report and Order in FCC Docket No. 16068, February 9, 1968, p. 10.

96. See my Initial Statement in Docket No. 18110, April 1971, p. 31, and modified subsequent affirmation in Robinson Dissent, p. 13.

levels, or (2) the provision of cultural, informational, or local service. Both my broad review of a large number of economic and programming effects and the more refined analysis of a few of the most sensitive policy variables, demonstrate the nonexistence or negligible character of any such adverse side effects. My basic conclusion, therefore, is that if the nation wishes to diffuse private economic and political power by diversifying the perspectives, skills, and viewpoints of media owners as well as the sources of media content, it can do so with no significant price in foregone content diversity, or local, cultural, and informational service on television.

On newspaper-television combinations in particular, my evidence also questions the magnitude of both alleged cross-subsidization of TV subsidiaries, and alleged disruptive economic side effects of any diversification policy. In this regard also we have shown that the commission's safeguards are more than adequate for minimizing any undue private distress caused by its new rule; and that there are indeed limits to any regulatory obligation to mitigate undemonstrated private injuries in cases where the private interests allegedly harmed are themselves a partial result of unfair privileges conferred.[97]

Furthermore, neither the emerging cable and satellite technology nor an existing multivoice communications structure represents persuasive evidence against the initial (let alone final) version of the commission's proposed newspaper rule. On the contrary, the multitude of multivoice communities simply underscores the importance of preventive prospective action, in addition to outright divestitures in the most concentrated markets. Neither, finally, have I found any likelihood that separation would seriously aggravate ownership concentration or act to reduce localism in TV.

One major reality supports owner diversification today. Separate ownership clearly serves as an important structural safeguard which renders any commission reliance on direct administrative policing less justifiable than otherwise, whether in the form of the Fairness Doctrine, periodic renewal audits, or comprehensive studies of program content.

97. If by now the newspaper pioneer's investments have been recouped several times over, one could almost argue that the entire value of the property is an unfair privilege and condemn it outright. Yet this rather extreme conclusion fails to distinguish between the portion of a station's value created by entrepreneurial innovation and creativity, and that by the restrictive entry controls under which he operates. With forced divestiture one presumably loses economic value, part of which reflects "unfairly inflated rates and rents," and part of which was created by the firm. There is at least some reassurance in the fact that not all these losses are of the latter class.

Appendix 7A. Ad Hoc Renewal Proceedings under the Supreme Court Decision on Cross-Ownership *

The United States Supreme Court reviewed the FCC's cross-owner-ship rules in June of 1978 [98] after the research for chapters 5, 6, and 7 was complete. However, our evidence bears on divestiture possibilities under the decision too, as will now be briefly outlined.

The Decision

Essentially, the High Court affirmed the Appeals Court's prior decision in regard to the flat prospective ban against all future newspaper acquisition (or construction) of TV stations in the same (local) market.[99] Affirmed also was the FCC's divestiture of cross-owned enterprises in sixteen egregious cases, where a sole daily newspaper owned the only TV station.[100] In both situations, separate ownership was seemingly justified to safeguard sources diversity as a guarantee of antagonistic views on controversial issues. But in the local monopoly case, divestiture was approved notwithstanding public losses due to alleged economic distress, reduced merit programming, and quality deterioration.[101] The potential abuses of local monopoly were deemed to outweigh the danger of public losses due to outright divestiture, let alone to a prospective ban, with the benefits of sources diversity a net gain.

In contrast, the balance of competing policy considerations was diametrically different in the other sixty-odd cross-owned enterprises—those located in markets with more than one grade-B TV service receivable. Although the narrowing effect on program options of cross-ownership was explicitly recognized, it was deemed less onerous in a context of multi-media voices than in the case of local monopoly. By the same token, the economic dislocation due to divestiture, and possible public losses in local, informational, and other meritorious programming, were cited to justify the FCC's considered decision against divestiture in all situations outside the sixteen egregious ones.[102]

---

* In preparing this appendix, I have benefited much from a recent paper by Charles Firestone, of the UCLA Communications Law Program, and have drawn heavily on my own comments on it for purposes of the FTC Symposium on Media Concentration, Washington, D.C. December 14–15, 1978.

98. Supreme Court of United States, No. 76–1471, June 12, 1978, FCC v. NCCB et al. Cert. to U.S. Court of Appeals D.C. Circuit. (hereafter called Decision) (Slip Opinion).

99. Decision, pp. 1, 15, and 20.

100. Ibid., pp. 1, 10, 15, 25, 26, 36, and 37.

101. Ibid., pp. 36–37.

102. Ibid., pp. 27–32.

The High Court, that is, emphasized the competing considerations the FCC had quite properly weighed—the possible dangers to sources diversity and diverse viewpoints inherent in joint ownership on one hand, against the greater danger to program quality, merit programming, and sustained public service on the other. Where alternative media services are available, in short, the price of divestiture was "too high." As a consequence, some sixty cross-owned TV stations were "grandfathered" to their local daily newspaper owners notwithstanding the flat prospective ban against new affiliations.[103]

Relief in Ad Hoc Renewal Proceedings

Nevertheless, the Supreme Court explicitly left open the possibility that the opponents of cross-ownership might still seek relief at ad hoc renewal proceedings of the grandfathered licensees.[104] The problem with such an avenue for relief, of course, is that petitions to deny any grandfathered cross-owner's license renewal must bear an extremely heavy and costly burden of proof. Essentially, the Supreme Court's approval of the FCC's grandfather provisions (and related reversal of the Appeals Court on this issue), create a heavy presumption for renewal in the absence of evidence of tangible abuse.

Economic Monopolization and Specific Tangible Abuse. As matters now stand, the FCC's sole stated criterion for nonrenewal in any ad hoc renewal proceeding is that of "economic monopolization" and "specific tangible abuse." [105] Should the FCC find economic monopoly in Sherman Act terms (based on structural domination of the market, or behavioral abuse, or both), remedies up to and including outright "forfeiture" of the cross-owner's license have been deemed admissible.[106]

Unless the FCC itself had the needed antitrust expertise to apply such a monopoly standard, however, and were willing to do so, this yardstick offers little hope for petitioners who still oppose cross-ownership. True, the commission might perhaps routinely uncover structural monopoly, or behavioral abuse, and indeed, throw the renewal application into a noncomparative hearing. But if a petitioner himself tried to mount such a case it would be both expensive and difficult. Monopolization is a clearly stringent standard, and the burden of proof on any petitioner of necessity very heavy. This is especially so because the stakes

103. Ibid., pp. 9–15, 25–26.
104. Ibid., note 13 and pp. 31–32.
105. Ibid., note 12.
106. Charles Firestone, "Local Media Concentration: Ad Hoc Challenges to Media Cross-Owners After FCC v. NCCB," prepared for FTC Symposium on Media Concentration, December 14–15, 1978, pp. 22–23. It is unclear whether Firestone, or the Decision, had in mind more a behavioral abuse standard (as, for example, under Standard Oil, 1911), or an Alcoa type of monopolization criterion—that is, a major structural yardstick.

are extremely high. The FCC apparently views the sole admissible penalty to be that of nonrenewal (forfeiture) of the license, a necessarily harsh remedy in light of the very high (if comparable) values of newspaper- *and* nonnewspaper-held TV licenses today. (See chapters 4 and 6.)

Undue Concentration. By way of exploring alternative strategies, two other criteria have been proposed. Those who petition the FCC to deny the renewal of grandfathered licenses, could continue their opposition on an ad hoc basis (as the Supreme Court stated), under standards less stringent than the present yardstick of "monopolization and tangible abuse." Thus the FCC could institute a criterion of "undue concentration." Where the renewal applicant's share exceeded, say, 60 percent of the combined advertising of all printed and electronic media in the market, a renewal hearing might be automatically triggered, on either a noncomparative or comparative basis.[107] That is, commission or petitioner could initiate this hearing by establishing the violation of said market share criterion (no simple matter) as prima facie evidence that the cross-owned enterprise had "undue concentration of control."

The incumbent licensee would then be required to rebut this presumption by presenting detailed evidence on the trade practices, conduct patterns, economic and programming performance of *all* media operating in its local market. Only if FCC deemed this rebuttal inadequate, and the presumption of "undue concentration" remained, would the licensee have to sell its properties. One crucial issue here, of course, is whether the remedy must then be outright forfeiture, or might also include the less harsh option of divestiture, where the station, sold within some designated time period (say three to five years), could recover for itself some of the franchise value too.[108] Given the less stringent character of the standard of undue concentration than of monopolization, the less harsh divestiture remedy is arguably appropriate.[109]

Waiver of the Grandfather Provisions. The third and final option for proposed relief is to consider a petition to deny as a kind of public request for a waiver of the grandfather provisions on cross-ownership.[110] Here the rationale is to grant divestiture where a petitioner has demon-

---

107. Ibid., pp. 23–25.

108. Less clear in Firestone's apt analysis is whether, even failing to rebut a presumptive finding of undue concentration, the incumbent could attempt to demonstrate its reasonableness in Sherman Act terms. This might conceivably be undertaken with reference to the Supreme Court's affirmation of the FCC's presumption that cross-ownership results in (and divestiture reduces the amount of) merit programming, program quality, and economic stability. In either case, the renewal hearing triggered by a presumption of undue concentration as envisioned here, would act to shift some of the burden of proof (and litigation costs) from the normally impoverished petitioner to the more affluent renewal applicant.

109. Firestone, "Local Media Concentration," pp. 23–24. Of crucial importance is that the FCC's grandfather provisions put a tremendous burden of proof on any petitioner. Undue concentration places at least some of that burden back on the renewal applicant's shoulders.

110. This is clearly Firestone's most ingenious suggestion. Ibid., pp. 24–25.

strated that the dual fears, or dual premises of the Supreme Court are not borne out in fact, namely that divestiture as the less harsh remedy need *not* result in serious economic distress to the divested cross-owner, or in program quality deterioration and loss of major meritorious service. On that showing, it might be argued that the basis of grandfathering disappears, that those provisions do not apply to the renewal application in question, and indeed, that divestiture becomes appropriate.

Once again, however, the problem arises from the great cost and difficulty of petitioners mounting enough valid evidence to gain a full and fair evaluation of all stated claims. There is an obvious vicious circle. Until the petition to waive the grandfather provisions actually triggers a renewal hearing, those provisions impose a very heavy burden of proof on the petitioner, and yet, the case for a waiver is also extremely hard to mount. Accordingly, the Supreme Court's invitation for petitioners to seek ad hoc remedies may mean little substantively. At this point reference must be made to the changing "state of knowledge" on the economic and programming consequences of cross-ownership.

Macro-Level Studies and the Emerging State of Knowledge about Cross-Ownership

Clearly, the kind of evidence we have presented (or cited) in the last three chapters offers one conceivable vehicle for equalizing the burden of proof as between petitioner and renewal applicant. Accepting such evidence [111] at face value, for example, TV stations with and without newspaper owners appear to perform comparably, *cet. par.*, in regard to a host of economic and programming indicators. Once full account is taken of market size, competitors, channel type, college education, and other owner attributes, that is, the fact of newspaper ownership results in spot rates, audience size, station revenues, ratings, and air time devoted to local news and local public affairs, not significantly different from nonnewspaper stations. Therefore, divestiture need not result in serious public losses in those terms. At the macro level of knowledge,[112] then, petitioners could argue that, without more specific rebuttal evidence by renewal applicant, divestiture cannot be found to result in the Supreme Court's dual dangers, or dual fears.

111. See earlier textual discussion associated with tables 5.2, 5.3, 6.1–6.6, 6.12, and 6.13, and especially the last section of chapter 6. See also studies by Barnett and Gormley, cited in note 94, this chapter.

112. By macro studies, we refer mainly to those industrywide investigations with statistical relevance (as in chapters 5 and 6). But the Barnett study is also macro evidence in that it obviously does not deal with particular future renewal cases. This macro evidence is part of an emerging state of knowledge, one which petitioners can most clearly draw upon in contesting the incumbent's right of renewal. In short, the post-Decision state of knowledge becomes crucial here because such macro studies will continue to be done, and the cost of mounting a persuasive case is very high.

Equalizing the Burden of Proof

Incumbents would then be induced to divulge more detailed financial and programming evidence in reply, and in the process, the cost and burden of proof would again be shifted somewhat and better equalized between petitioner and applicant. This is no small gain in that confidential station financial data, though filed with FCC, are simply not available to petitioners, and yet, without them, a full and fair assessment is impossible.

Consider the following scenario. Citing the FCC's own programming data, petitioner may contend that a renewal applicant's local and informational programming is significantly lower than that of the national profile of stations with identical attributes (as set forth and discussed below in chapter 13, pp. 370–80, in association with tables 13.4, 13.5, and 13.6). To rebut this contention, applicant must bring forth special evidence of his own. Petitioner may then cite macro evidence to demonstrate the statistical comparability of financial performance of newspaper- and nonnewspaper-owned stations.

Again, incumbent must rebut this prima facie evidence with particular facts on his own economic viability. On both counts, petitioner's use of macro evidence to demonstrate that divestiture need not result in undue economic distress, or serious program deterioration, would force the incumbent to divulge specific private data to the contrary. In the process, the burden of proof is shifted, and a more balanced and fair assessment of the claims of incumbent and petitioner will result.

Chapter 8

Structural Diversity, Owner Diversity, and the Role of Public Television: A Comparative Assessment

THE present chapter will consider the relative impact of structural diversity, owner diversity and, more briefly, public television as alternative (and supplementary) approaches to insure content diversity as herein conceived.

I start by describing the FCC's policy on structural diversity with special reference to new station entry. Then, in the next section, I briefly compare the impact of this policy with that of owner diversity, as examined in chapters 6 and 7. In conclusion, I compare the above with the impact of public television on program composition and diversity.

The Policy toward New Commercial Entry

The policy for promoting new entry has normally taken two forms: first and foremost, proposals to activate unused UHF assignments, and second, proposals to reduce VHF channel spacing and geographic separations.

The commission's posture on UHF is clearly grounded in its hope to achieve diversity through a structural rather than interventionist route. Today, one-half of the top fifty markets have fewer than five stations on the air, yet all VHF channels allocated to these markets are in use. In only twenty-four markets are there more than four stations on the air. Yet if all UHF channels were activated, there could be as many as ten to fourteen stations in each of five markets, fifteen or more in each of three markets, and five to nine stations in as many as forty-one markets. Even in the country at large, most TV stations could potentially be located in markets with five or more stations each—not, as today, in markets with fewer than five.

Among the remedies proposed at one time or another have been: (1) shifting all TV stations into the UHF band, thereby promoting all regulatory objectives simultaneously—competition, wide-area service, localism, and so on—fully activating the UHF frequencies and releasing the twelve VHF channels for other uses; (2) waiving the ceilings on multiple ownership wherever a network or nonnetwork organization sought to purchase or build additional UHF outlets; (3) authorizing low-power (ten kilowatt), low-cost UHF stations geared to share existing channels in reaching ghetto and suburban neighborhoods with tailored programming; (4) tax relief on all-channel receivers to offset higher costs than for VHF-only sets, an action which would lower private but not social costs; (5) limiting VHF signals to the station's retail trading areas so as to prevent the overshadowing of UHF stations in nearby communities.

The first option is now out of fashion; the second may wrongly presume that group owners have relatively greater incentives than other investors to subsidize unprofitable UHFs, or can somehow be induced to do so as the price for expanding their holdings in major markets; the third option ignores the serious handicap low-power UHFs would suffer in a competitive market.

In the end the commission acted through a policy of selective allocational adjustments to de-intermix a number of TV markets.[1] But it looked also to long-run supportive effects of the mandatory All-Channel Receiver Law requiring that all new TV sets be equipped to receive

1. That is, by making homogenous some markets which then had both UHF and VHF stations.

both UHF and VHF signals. Passage of that law rendered academic the earlier proposal of tax relief for all-channel receivers. Indeed the de-intermixture process was suspended, allegedly as part of a price the FCC had to pay to obtain the all-channel legislation. Nor should, in any case, the efficacy or extensiveness of formal de-intermixture proceedings be exaggerated.

Most recently, the FCC has sought to develop an improved, more selective UHF receiver that would permit far closer UHF channel spacing. This could at some point facilitate additional UHF entry into the choicest TV markets. However, there are now unused UHF channels in almost all markets, and the chances for new UHF entrants to succeed is sufficiently bleak to question the efficacy of such an approach. On both counts, the proposal does seem a little bizarre, except for accommodation of more nonbroadcast users.

One other recent proposal is for some form of subsidy for increased power for UHF stations (particularly public TV stations) to make them technically more competitive with VHF. Alternatively, it is suggested that the commission might impose additional requirements on set design (for example, addition of an RF amplifier) to improve UHF reception and thus enhance UHF performance generally.

As for reduced geographic spacing of VHF channels, suffice it merely to note that short-spaced VHF grants in the leading television markets have been proposed by a variety of public groups to accommodate late-comer entrants, minority interests, and public TV stations in markets that now lack them. Given the nonavailability of unused VHF allocations in the largest markets today, the short-spaced grants are favored also to facilitate possible entry of a fourth television network.

On all such counts, reduced VHF spacing has been defended for its potential contribution to the stated or implied goals of localism, competition, and the diversity of sources, content, and owner perspectives.

The FCC's hesitation to authorize any substantial number of such new entrants nonetheless has probably reflected the restrictive technical criteria it still utilizes to protect incumbents against destructive signal interference, and its apparent concern over the economic impact of these new colocated stations on those whose viability is already precarious.

Putting these issues to one side, let us turn next to a more general comparative assessment of structural and owner diversity impact on station viability and program composition. Then, in the last section, I conclude with a similar assessment of public TV.

New Entry versus Ownership Diversification:
A Comparative Assessment

Focusing first on new commercial entry, and leaving for later its comparison with owner diversity and public television, the question at this
point is simply: at the margin, what overall contributions to diversity
and cultural-informational-local programming will another UHF or VHF
station make? With what likely economic consequences?

The Impact of New Station Entry

The brief answer is that promotion of new VHF entry via reduced
geographic spacing makes more economic sense than new UHF entry,
in the near term at least. Any new entrant's principal contribution will
be to horizontal diversity. However, that contribution probably cannot
be realized without inflicting sizable economic losses on newcomer and
incumbent alike, at the time of entry. Therefore, VHF's greater present
relative strength than UHF makes it a more promising vehicle for viable
new entry, and hence greater diversity.

In the longer term, the relative promise of new VHF and UHF entrants may be more comparable. Some of the new short-spaced VHF
stations may have very truncated service areas, causing reduced service
in rural regions. A de-intermixture solution of some additional markets
which now have only one or perhaps two VHFs operating—a kind of
UHF solution—might be more feasible technically, and sounder economically, than hitherto believed.[2] Here, however, I shall focus on near-term
prospects mainly, where VHF's greater relative strength warrants special
weight.

Why Promote VHF Entry in the Near Term? As to whether UHF or
VHF entrants are more promising for increasing diversity and public
service, no answer is now possible on the basis of past programming
impact alone (see chapter 5, table 5.3 and associated text). In 1967,
only in vertical diversity did VHF stations have even a very small
(though significant) advantage over UHF licensees. Offsetting this, however, the UHFs carried significantly less mass entertainment programming than the VHFs. The band in which any postulated "new entry" will
occur therefore seems immaterial for diversity and prime-time program
composition.

Using 1972 data, the results are somewhat mixed but the implications
similar—no substantial or systematic differences in VHF and UHF im-

2. A review of the legislative history of the All-Channel Receiver Law indicates
that the FCC said it would de-intermix no more markets only within a seven-to-ten-
year period that is now over (House Report No. 1559, 87th Congress, 2nd Sess.,
1962, pp. 18–21).

pact on program composition and diversity. Recall, for example, that in table 6.13 network VHFs did carry significantly more news, public affairs, and all information weekly than VHF independents and so, too, for independents, did VHFs carry more local than UHFs. Yet even there, local service on VHF and UHF stations was clearly comparable for network affiliates, and more striking, for the comparison of independent UHFs with network VHFs. Nor for this latter comparison was there more than a very small absolute difference in the respective amounts of their local public affairs service (twelve and one-half minutes weekly), in line with all other comparisons of independents and affiliates, or of UHFs and VHFs, where the difference in local public affairs was insignificant.

Again, there are still other mixed results for network affiliates as a class, the VHF licensees carrying relatively more local news than the UHFs, but only comparable amounts of local and nonlocal public affairs ($t = .41$), all information ($t = .66$), all news ($t = .78$), and all local ($t = .46$). For independents, on the other hand, VHFs carried significantly more local programming, in particular more news and local news, than UHF stations, but only comparable public affairs ($t = .55$) and information generally ($t = 1.27$).

In contrast with this clearly mixed VHF impact on programming, VHF's impact on station audiences and revenues was far more systematic and substantial. Recall the higher VHF audience ratings and prime rates in 1967, and the substantial VHF impact on average market revenues and profitability (tables 5.2, 5.3, 5.4). Recall also my further analysis in chapter 6 of four economic indicators for 1972. The VHF economic strength throughout those tests was clear, however the equation was specified.[3]

True, my statistical analysis is of established stations, while new entrants may be weaker. Nevertheless, a new VHF station does appear more likely to survive today, *cet. par.*, than a new UHF. A policy to promote new VHF entry may therefore make more near-term economic sense than one based on predicting the future prospects of reducing the so-called UHF handicap.[4] On the other hand, a combination of short-

3. See generally chapter 6 above, tables 6.5 and 6.6. See especially results reported at rows 1–5 therein, which involved channel type impact in four different (often interacted) forms. Thus tables 6.5 and 6.6 report four dependent variables. In all twenty tests where channel type is specified, VHF profitability is significantly greater than UHF.

4. Granted that no fourth commercial network built on independent VHF stations alone is likely to be viable in the near term, given the small number of short-spaced assignments likely to be approved under present separation criteria. See especially R. E. Park, *New Television Networks* (Santa Monica, Calif.: Rand Corporation, December 1973), and Stanley Besen and Paul Hanley, "Market Size, VHF Allocations, and the Viability of Television Stations," *Journal of Industrial Economics* (September 1975). Even today, "only (a scant) 33% of TV households could be reached by a fourth network on the VHF band." FCC Network Inquiry Special Staff, *An Analysis of the Network-Affiliate Relation in Television*, October 1979, chapter 1, p. 11.

spaced VHF and UHF stations might reach enough viewers to support a fourth network,[5] the value of whose added viewing options has been estimated as ranging from $1 to $4 billion.[6] The likely viability of these new VHF assignments seems further confirmed by known effects of the commission's past policy to diffuse TV assignments widely. That policy has acted to exclude from big-city markets VHF stations that could otherwise be supported therein, and which narrower spacing could now presumably accommodate.

When the commission instituted its Allocation Table in 1952, the available technology precluded authorization of more stations in the leading urban centers for fear of depriving other medium-sized or smaller communities from having their own outlets. Now, however, with precise frequency offsets, new directional antennas, relaxed ceilings on antenna heights and power, it is deemed technically possible to squeeze in new short-spaced VHF transmitters with far less interference to others than would have occurred twenty-five years ago.[7]

Nevertheless, the net gain in reduced interference over time should not be exaggerated. The facts are still widely debated and the commission has itself contended that, except for some ten or so narrow-spaced channels (out of ninety-six proposed), there would indeed be substantial interference in outlying areas.[8] It comes as no surprise, then, that opponents of these proposed new VHF entrants see in that route a "shoe-horning in" of grants as in AM radio, where the result of all the small amounts of interference caused by each entrant was poor service at night.

New Entry Will Raise Horizontal Diversity but Lower Profitability. Channel type differences to one side, the addition of one more commercial station would clearly reduce per-station income, revenue, time sales, and audience ratings substantially (see tables 5.2, 5.3). It would do so, also, with little or no effect on program composition and with a substantial contribution to horizontal diversity. One more station would raise horizontal diversity by 71.9 program types, or twenty-two percent of

5. See Park, *New Television Networks*, pp. 16–18. However, *early* prospects for a fourth network still seem poor, in that it could reach only 71% of TV households even if existing construction permits (mainly for UHF outlets) were all activated. *An Analysis of the Network-Affiliate Relationship*, chapter 1, pp. 12–13.

6. See Robert Crandall, "The Economic Case for a Fourth Commercial Television Network," *Public Policy* (Fall 1974), 525–30. Even the value of an additional non-network signal, though obviously less than this, would be substantial.

7. See Office of Telecommunications Policy, *Technical Analysis of VHF Television Broadcasting Frequency Assignment Criteria*, October 1973; Office of Telecommunications Policy, *Further Evaluation of Additional VHF-TV Channels That Could be Assigned in the Top 100 Markets*, May 14, 1974; FCC, Notice of Inquiry and Memorandum Opinion and Order in Docket No. 20418 (Proposed VHF Drop-Ins), April 15, 1975.

8. FCC, Memorandum Opinion and Order in Docket No. 20418, March 18, 1977, at pars. 76–91, 101, 107, 207.

the sample mean,[9] reduce vertical diversity a scant 1.2 percent of the mean (in table 5.3), but produce this net gain only with a decline equal to 9 to 11 percent of mean audience ratings, and a fall in market profitability per station of 49.9 percent of the sample mean.[10] Similarly, a reduction of TV homes by 100,000 (roughly equivalent to an added station) [11] would lower vertical diversity a scant .14 percent of its mean, mass entertainment by .17 percent of its own mean, while raising local service by .58 percent of its mean too. Nevertheless, these token changes in programming are again associated with far larger effects on economic performance. The removal of 100,000 TV homes would lower advertising rates 5 to 7 percent of their mean in table 5.4, and per-station income and revenue some 8 to 10 percent of their respective sample mean.[12]

Are these fairly substantial economic losses justified by the small gains in local service and reduced mass entertainment? Or even the large gains in horizontal diversity (hardly offset by the small decline in vertical diversity)? One could of course defend the policy here on strictly competitive (economic efficiency) grounds or, as explicitly stated by FCC, to diffuse economic, social, and political power. Were those in fact the commission's goals, then it should weigh affirmatively the absence of any likely losses in news, public affairs, fine arts; or any large losses in vertical diversity; or any great upsurge of feature film or mass entertainment. Nevertheless, the projected economic losses appear substantial, and program quality could fall.

Indeed, without a tangible measure of "quality" such as I have been unable to devise for this book, the above evidence on gains in local service and diversity may strike some readers as of minor consequence. Yet the comparisons made here constitute a useful place to commence this assessment. Specifically, would the greater horizontal diversity induced by new station entry justify the magnitude of the economic losses that result?

Program Quality Need Not Decline. Several observations must be made. First and foremost, a policy to implement new commercial entry appears likely to increase horizontal diversity a lot without significant offsetting effects on program composition, even if the adverse effects on profits are large.[13] Second, a sizable negative impact of new entry on income does not imply that even large economic losses must seriously impair program capabilities. The new entry might simply reduce the prices that stations pay for programs. I have discovered virtually no

9. Derived from estimating equation for table 5.2.
10. Ibid.
11. See my "Interim Report on Regulatory Effects and Policy Alternatives in Television Broadcasting" (NSF Grant GS–39845), March 1975, vol. II, appendix C, pp. 12–13. (Department of Economics, Hofstra University).
12. Derived from estimating equation for table 5.2.
13. See tables 5.2, 5.3.

significant changes in program composition due to new entry so far, and none counter to FCC goals; however, it must be conceded that I lack any quantitative index of quality change. Third, the significant positive effects of market size on average market income, revenue, and time sales per station (table 5.2) underscore the high returns earned in large markets. New entry could therefore conceivably reduce such supernormal earnings without necessarily impairing the pool of station funds normally devoted to programming. Nevertheless, the two points just made are somewhat qualified by the admittedly small but significant positive impact of station revenues on news, public affairs, local and all informational programming.[14]

In brief, new commercial entry can above all be a potent factor for horizontal diversity (and for diffusion of economic and political power), without significant damage to program composition. Nevertheless, if one sought to bolster the amount of cultural-informational programming affirmatively this appears to require some other policy approach, for example, reduced rate interconnection for merit service, license renewal percentage requirements for designated program types, or an enlarged role for public television.

Structural versus Owner Diversity: A Broad Pattern of Results

Initial Assessment for 1967. We now turn next to an overall comparison of structural and owner diversity as alternative regulatory approaches for which the reader is again directed back to chapter 5, and in particular tables 5.2 and 5.3. The conclusions those results suggest are these: [15]

1.   With one exception, new station entry imposes higher economic losses than a policy of diversifying ownership (though probably not always significantly higher).[16]

14. See table 6.13.

15. The interpretation below follows from a reverse reading of tables 5.2 and 5.3. That is, we reverse the postulated change in each independent variable, as well as change the sign of each elasticity and PCDV therein. Thus in table 5.3, for every station added to (not removed from) the market, ADI ratings decline (not rise) by − 10.58 percent of mean ratings. Likewise, every switch from in-town newspaper to nonnewspaper status reduces (not raises) ADI ratings − 8.06 percent of the mean, and so forth. All postulated changes (and signs) are also reversed in table 5.2, except for the number of commercial units' impact. That is now postulated as a 1 percent increase (not decrease) in the number of fifteen-minute program units available, so it remains as is for the current discussion.

16. In table 5.3, compare mainly the impact of new entry on ADI and metro ratings with that of a switch from in-town newspaper to nonnewspaper station ownership, and from nonnetwork group to nongroup ownership. In table 5.2, the substantial negative economic impact of additional commercial stations contrasts with insignificant effects of newspaper ownership and of group ownership on all but one indicator. Indeed, the significant impact of a 1-percent reduction in the proportion of stations with nonnetwork group ties on average market income is only − .35 percent, of stations with in-town newspaper owners still smaller, compared to a − 1.65 percent for a 1-percent increase in fifteen-minute station program units broadcast.

2.   However, new station entry offers a major contribution to horizontal diversity,[17] whereas steps to limit TV group and cross-ownership offer virtually none (table 5.2).

3.   None of the above policies increases vertical diversity (table 5.3).

4.   The absolute losses in public affairs programming due to curbs on newspaper cross-ownership of stations are very small,[18] as are the absolute losses in news due to curbs on nonnetwork group ownership across separate markets,[19] whereas the policy for new entry leaves news and public affairs untouched while acting to reduce mass entertainment slightly (table 5.3).

5.   Finally, new entry will act to raise nonnetwork programming insignificantly ($t = 1.16$), while a policy of limiting group (not newspaper) ownership would lower it ($t = 2.25$).

These results suggest on balance that the affirmative case for new station entry is stronger on programming grounds alone than the case for owner diversification. However, both policies can probably be rationalized more persuasively as cautionary safeguards against the potential abuse of concentrated power, and affirmatively, to diffuse economic and political power. If that indeed is their ultimate purpose, the commission may take comfort from the evidence that neither policy seems likely to deprive the community of substantial informational or cultural programming and diversity, or seriously to disrupt industry economics, and that entry would enhance horizontal diversity.

Toward a More Refined Policy Assessment. How do these impressions hold up when our dependent variables are subjected to a more refined interactive analysis?

A word first about the more detailed study of policy impacts on three quite different indicators of earnings potential in 1972—spot rates, audiences, and metro ratings.[20] That analysis quite clearly indicates that a new commercial entry will reduce thirty-second one-time spot rates significantly, and not too much less than would loss of a group owner tie, but far more than the statistically insignificant effect of loss of a newspaper tie. On the other hand, the significant negative impact of added VHFs on audience size and metro ratings would now by far exceed the insignificant reductions due to loss of a group tie (metro ratings only) or a newspaper owner tie. In all three equations, finally, the negative impact of added VHFs is significant at the .01 or .05 levels of confidence. But though group owner impact is significant at that level two out of three times, newspaper impact is always insignificant even at the .10 level.

17. In absolute terms, every station added raises program types by 71.86 on a mean of 325.46.

18. In absolute terms they total 23.36/7 = 3.34 minutes, daily.

19. In absolute terms these total 24.35/7 = 3.48 minutes, daily.

20. See tables 6.4 to 6.6. The results for station revenues are mixed, but the value of comparing separate tests on the three other conceptually different economic indicators, each compiled from different data sources, was spelled out in chapter 5, pages 139–40 and 6, page 174.

Nevertheless, even assuming a roughly comparable negative impact of new commercial entry and owner diversity on these indices of earnings potential, what consequences would result for local and informational programming? Are these probable reductions in earnings associated with major changes in program composition?

Review of table 6.13 quite clearly reveals the contrary:

1. There is virtually no significant effect of additional VHFs on local, informational, news, and public affairs programming, with a significant impact by the fourth VHF entrant (not the second or third) on local news only.
2. There is no significant effect on program composition due to any loss of group owner ties.
3. There are no significant effects due to loss of a newspaper tie except for all local programming (including entertainment), of $-45.58/7 = 6\frac{1}{2}$ minutes, daily, or 21.7 percent of the sample mean ($t = 2.44$).

My analysis for 1972, then, quite clearly indicates that a policy of promoting new station entry, and even to curb group ownership, can act to reduce supernormal earnings with no measurable sacrifice in local or informational programs. In contrast, as noted in chapters 6 and 7, the limitation of cross-ownership may result in still more limited economic losses, but again with no significant losses in news, public affairs, or all information, though with small losses in all local (including entertainment).

We are, however, left with the unquestionable contribution to horizontal program diversity of new station entry, while group and newspaper owner diversity has no such effect. Therefore, my earlier conclusions (based on data for 1967) are confirmed—namely that the affirmative case for new station entry seems stronger on programming grounds alone, than the case for owner diversity; but that both policy approaches can be more convincingly defended as cautionary safeguards against the potential abuse of concentrated power. More affirmatively, they also appear to diffuse economic and political power, at the same time diversifying media sources, owner perspectives, editorial and news coverage.

If those were indeed the FCC's ultimate purposes, it could take comfort in the fact that neither approach is likely to deprive the public of substantial local or informational programming, let alone of type diversity. This holds true, finally, regardless of the decline in supernormal earnings which each approach would induce.

The Potential Role of Public Television

To this point I have on balance concluded that neither the commission's policy of limiting entry, nor its permissive posture on cross-media and multiple ownership, has enhanced sources and content diversity, or so-called merit programming, commensurate with the private economic benefits the first policy confers (see chapter 5). Yet the proposals to foster new entry and diversified ownership examined earlier appear likely to effect but limited improvement in most areas, a major exception being in horizontal diversity due to new entry. Accordingly, it seems appropriate to consider other alternatives, such as public television, to whose potential contributions we now turn.

Our major findings here also bear directly on the United Church of Christ's request that a high priority for new narrow-spaced VHF channels be given to public TV licensees in markets which now lack any non-commercial VHF reservation.[21] Just as UCC saw in structural diversity a greater safeguard of program diversity than in owner diversity, so too it expected still greater programming contributions for public television.[22] Nevertheless, the commission dismissed such allocational possibilities out of hand in its drop-in proceeding.[23] My analysis in this section will help assess the relative validity of these conflicting premises, in a general way.

Historical Background

The FCC allocated spectrum for 242 educational TV channels in 1952, eight years before Congress gave the states matching grants-in-aid to build physical facilities, and fifteen years before creation of the Corporation for Public Broadcasting. Yet until recently, fewer stations than that were actually licensed, while the spectrum reserved for hundreds more still lies idle. Clearly, the reservation of spectrum for public television may have deprived the nation of numerous services which alternate users might have provided.

True, all public VHF channels in the top twenty-five markets are occupied today, and the greatest land mobile demand is for spectrum in the geographic region containing most of these markets. Nevertheless, the facts attest that outside the twenty-five largest markets, public broadcasters have activated their VHF and UHF allocations at a notably slower rate than have commercial licensees.[24]

The rationale for public broadcasting has been set forth in numerous legislative and regulatory pronouncements. In 1951, the FCC itself, be-

21. FCC, Docket No. 20418, Memorandum Opinion and Order, March 18, 1977, par. 4.
22. See Petition for Rulemaking by United Church of Christ, et al., RM–2346, 2727, May 7, 1974, especially at pp. 3, 5, 7–10, 19–21.
23. Memorandum Opinion and Order, par. 72.
24. See Levin, *The Invisible Resource* (Baltimore: Johns Hopkins University Press, 1971), p. 354. In contrast, as soon as commercial systems are built in cable TV, there become available ipso facto extra channels for local educators, and for mandatory carriage of local PTV stations. Ibid., pp. 351–56; also Levin, "Television's Second Chance: A Retrospective Look at the Sloan Cable Commission," *Bell Journal* (Spring 1973), 354–55.

fore setting aside spectrum for exclusive noncommercial educational uses, noted that "the need for non-commercial (ETV) stations has been amply documented. . . ." That the proposed channel reservation was "based upon the important contribution which [such] stations can make in educating the people both at school—at all levels—and also the adult public." That "such stations [were] justified [by] the high quality type [of] programming which would be [made] available . . . programming of an entirely different character from that . . . on most commercial stations."[25]

Subsequently, the FCC reiterated this judgment [26] but went still further, noting:

> [T]he justification for [ETV] should not . . . turn simply on account of audience size. The public interest will clearly be served if these stations are used to contribute significantly to the educational process of the nation. The type of programs which . . . the record shows can and would be televised by educators, will provide a valuable complement to commercial programming.[27]

In opting for public television, the commission explicitly discounted the adequacy of precedent in commercial AM broadcasting, where it had sought to safeguard program diversity by defining the public service responsibilities of commercial licensees, and then relying on cooperation between broadcasters and educators. Although that route might have facilitated speedier development of commercial TV years later, FCC chose the slower route, even temporary nonuse of spectrum, to insure more cultural, informational and educational services.[28]

Finally, in reserving special channels for educators, FCC first considered but overrode such counterarguments as: the past financial failure of educational radio stations,[29] the history and promise of cooperation between educators and commercial broadcasters,[30] the availability of free time for educational purposes on commercial stations and the practicality of a new rule to make it mandatory,[31] foundation resources for special interest programs, public service responsibilities of commercial licensees,[32] and so on. Risks that the allocated spectrum might never be activated were viewed as less inimical to the public interest than risks that access would be quickly preempted by commercial interests.[33] Many of the reserved VHF channels would probably have been snapped up quickly if not set aside for the educators.

25. FCC, Third Notice of Further Proposed Rule Making in Docket No. 8736 et al., March 21, 1951, 47 CFR Pt. 3, appendix A, sec. VI, pp. 8–9.
26. FCC, Sixth Report and Order in Docket No. 8736 et al., April 11, 1952, par. 38.
27. Ibid.
28. Ibid., pars. 36–43.
29. Ibid., par. 38.
30. Ibid., pars. 35, 46.
31. Ibid., pars. 47, 49.
32. Ibid., par. 48.
33. Ibid., pars. 37–38, 41–44.

In assessing the proper role of public television, factual answers are urgently needed to several questions. Do public television stations significantly contribute to horizontal diversity across all stations in a market? Are they more or less varied than commercial stations in their own programming? Does their program composition in fact supplement that of commercial licensees? Is there in PTV a vehicle to widen horizontal diversity as well as or better than new commercial entry, and with fewer economic losses for commercial licensees? Is there in PTV also a way to bolster cultural-informational programs, but again, without the adverse economic effects of commission policies on network-affiliate relations?

One would of course ideally want some additional measures of program content, as, for example, whether public TV stations carry more, or less, "controversial" or "in-depth" news and documentary programs than the commercial network affiliates. Or at least, a measure of the degree to which PTV's targeted audiences (say, the aged, the deaf, or the handicapped) do indeed watch a program aimed at them. Such dimensions of programming may well be of greater importance than those my analysis of necessity addresses, but the paucity of quantitative assessment in this field makes my simpler findings useful nonetheless.

What is the Relative Impact of Public Television and Commercial Television on Horizontal Program Type Diversity?

To estimate public television's impact on aggregate market diversity in 1967 I first introduced PTV into my commercial market equations by asking: Other things being equal, what is the relative effect of public and commercial TV on "total diversity" (across all stations in the market, including PTV)? Note, in this regard, that the control factors in table 8.1 other than the amount of PTV program time, are, with one exception (median family income), identical to those in table 5.2 and, indeed, serve a similar function in both cases. Here, at least, they insure that any apparent PTV impact on market diversity, however defined, is in fact due to the presence of PTV and not to the other factors "held constant." Specifically, we assume that market size, family income, and station class (VHF, network, newspaper, group), as well as the number of stations, may all affect program type diversity. To focus more usefully on the relative impact of public and commercial TV, therefore, I have sought to take these other influences into account.

In table 8.1, PTV quite clearly has a much larger impact on total market diversity than on commercial diversity, the latter measured across all commercial stations only and excluding PTV. Thus an increase of 1 percent in minutes of PTV programs causes an increase of a mere .02 percent in commercial diversity, and even a 100 percent rise in PTV minutes (from an average of about 600 to 1,200), would raise commercial diversity by only 2 percent (from about 325 to 332 types in table 8.1). However one interprets these figures, the PTV effect on commer-

TABLE 8.1

Sensitivity of TV Market Income, Net Revenue, and Program Diversity in Relation to Rent-Yielding Market Variables and Presence of Public Television Stations, 1967*

(market data)

Independent Variables	Market Averages per Station			Independent Variables	Number of Program Types per Market	
	Income	Revenue	Time Sales		Commercial Stations Only	Total Commercial Plus PTV Sta.
Number of 15-minute commercial program units[2]	-1.78ᵃ / 2.65	-.97ᵃ / 2.67	-1.45ᵃ / 4.26	Number of commercial program units†	.70ᵃ / 12.42	.65ᵃ / 12.45
Number of 15-minute PTV program units[3]	.19ᵇ / 2.59	.11ᵃ / 2.87	.05 / 1.30	Number of PTV program units§	.02ᵇ / 2.59	.11ᵃ / 19.66
TV homes in market	.77ᵃ / 6.58	.58ᵃ / 9.14	.47ᵃ / 7.89	TV homes	.01 / .45	.002 / .22
Median family income	.29 / .68	.28 / 1.23	.16 / .73	Median family income	n.i.	
Proportion of Stations with:						
Network affiliation	-1.02 / .97	-1.19ᵇ / 2.10	-.82 / 1.53	Number of network affiliates	-.09 / 1.56	-.10ᶜ / 1.86
Commercial VHF license	.28 / 1.51	.28ᵃ / 2.73	.17ᶜ / 1.82	Number of VHF stations	.02 / .85	.01 / .74
Network owner	.22ᵃ / 6.41	.13ᵃ / 6.87	.09ᵃ / 5.31	Number of network-owned stations	-.0002 / .06	.0003 / .09
Nonnetwork group owner	.30 / 1.64	.13 / 1.27	.12 / 1.33	Number of nonnetwork group stations	.004 / .20	.002 / .11
Outside newspaper owner	.02 / .36	.02 / .48	.001 / .02	Number of outside newspaper stations	.01 / 1.36	.01 / 1.62
In-town newspaper owner	.10 / 1.46	.03 / .89	.04 / 1.25	Number of in-town newspaper stations	.01 / 1.47	.01 / 1.19

*Upper number in each cell is an elasticity calculated at the mean: percentage change in the dependent variable per 1-percent change in the independent variable. Lower number is the t-value of the regression coefficient; codings indicate statistical significance (two-tailed test), a = 1 percent, b = 5 percent, c = 10 percent.

†,§ Top two rows of results, respectively, are for the number of 15-minute commercial and PTV program units available in market. That scaling permits us to calculate more informative elasticities than for the actual number of stations. However, in our estimating equations we do report the station coefficients themselves. Scaling differences do not alter the elasticities presented above. Estimating equation for each dependent variable follows.

n.i. = Excluded from equation for design purposes.

Estimating Equations for Table 8.1
(market data)

Independent Variables	Market Averages Per Commercial Station			Independent Variables	Commercial Diversity: No. of Program Types Across Commercial Stations in Market	Total Diversity: Total Prog. Types Across All Comml. Plus PTV Stations in Market
	$100,000's Income	$100,000's Revenue	$100,000's Time Sales			
Constant	12.053	41.842	10.628	Constant	49.995	110.417
Number of commercial stations	-3.990[a]	-7.644[a]	-2.156[a]	Number of commercial stations	75.866[a]	79.296[a]
Number of public TV stations	1.387[b]	2.913[a]	.234	Number of PTV stations	5.193[b]	41.080[a]
100,000's TV homes	.723[a]	1.903[a]	.292[a]	100,000's TV homes	.245	.124
$100's median family income (SMA)	.037	.127	.013	$100's median family income	n.i.	n.i.
Proportion of Stations in Market with:						
Network affiliation	-8.157	-33.31[b]	-4.316	Number of network affiliates in market	-10.808	-13.446[c]
VHF license	2.600	8.903[a]	1.054[c]	Number of VHF stations	2.194	1.980
Network owner	57.612[a]	117.168[a]	16.083[a]	Number of network-owned stations	-.627	.971
Nonnetwork group owner	3.419	5.006	.935	Number of nonnetwork group stations	.615	.347
Outside newspaper owner	1.031	2.615	.019	Number of outside newspaper stations	5.699	7.085
In-town newspaper owner	4.587	5.312	1.323	Number of in-town newspaper stations	6.085	5.101
Adjusted R-square	.777	.867	.745		.880	.937
Sample size	101	101	101		143	143
Sample mean	7.4	26.0	4.9		325.5	363.5

n.i. = Excluded from equation for design purposes.

cial diversity, though statistically significant, is inconsequential in absolute terms, and at this juncture of no policy significance.[34]

In contrast, the elasticity of total diversity with respect to PTV program minutes is both more significant, and about five times larger than, the corresponding elasticity for commercial diversity, as just reported. Thus every 1 percent increase in TV minutes increased total diversity by .11 percent, and doubling the number of PTV minutes would increase total diversity by some 11 percent, from 363 to about 403 program types.[35]

The relative impact of commercial and public TV program minutes can be further described as follows. Each additional commercial fifteen-minute program *unit* yields 79.296/140, or .5664 program types (across all stations in the market), whereas each additional PTV unit yields another 41.080/39, or 1.0533 types.[36] Therefore, at the margin, another fifteen-minute PTV unit adds .4869 (or 86 percent) more program types than does the addition of one fifteen-minute commercial program. The public TV elasticity is smaller, however, because a 1 percent increase in fifteen-minute PTV units is a lot fewer units ($39 \times .01 = .4$), than a 1 percent increase in commercial units (about $420 \times .01 = 4.2$ units). Finally, one more PTV program unit increases commercial diversity by .1332 program types (5.193/39), while each additional commercial unit increases commercial diversity by .5419 types (75.866/140), about four times as much.[37]

---

34. This should come as no surprise, in that only if commercial stations experienced a large diversion of audience to public television's cultural and informational fare would they move to match this competition with more such programs of their own. In that case, public TV's impact on commercial diversity might be greater. It could equally well be argued however, as we do below, that PTV programs are substitutes for commercial diversity, and that their impact should therefore be expected to be negative. (See further discussion on pp. 263–68 in the section dealing with PTV's potential role).

35. Derived from the estimating equation to table 8.1. All these figures assume linear relationships, however, and doubling the number of PTV units is a large change, probably too large for an assumption of linearity to continue to be true. Nor must we in any case forget that there was rarely more than one PTV station in any market in 1967, for if there had been, the diversifying effect of adding still another would have been smaller.

36. In this paragraph I assume that each commercial station in my 143-market sample (all markets with two or more commercial stations), broadcasts during all prime time fifteen-minute periods, 6 to 11 P.M., throughout the sample week. This would total twenty periods, for seven days, or 140 units a week. In contrast, we round off the comparable number of PTV units per PTV station, per market, as 39. The discrepancy between these two numbers mainly reflects (1) the fewer markets in which PTV operated *at all* in 1967; but also (2) its failure even where it did operate to utilize *all* prime-time hours at its disposal; and (3) the sometimes spotty program log listings for public TV stations in *TV Guide*.

37. Derived from the estimating equation to table 8.1. The control factors here are largely the same as those used in the commercial diversity equations. Note further, however, that in regressing diversity on PTV and commercial program "units," we take into account the *number* (not *proportions*) of VHFs, network affiliates, group and newspaper owners, etc. This change permits the kind of convenient impact comparisons just made (and which would have been far more awkward had we used proportions).

As for individual station programming, note in table 8.2 the size, significance, and sign of the dummy variable for noncommercial status (commercial = 1, PTV = 0). Other things being equal, the change in programming due to a switch from commercial to PTV status tells us how much more (or less) of any program category PTV stations will carry than the combined average of PTV plus commercial stations.

I have compared the coefficients of the variable number of stations in equations with and without PTV. With the exception of vertical diversity and news, inclusion of PTV substantially increases the explanatory power of all our equations, as apparent by the larger adjusted R-squares. Furthermore, except for regressions run on news, PTV has the highest elasticity of any independent variables studied, often substantially higher. Only the network elasticities approach PTV's impact.

A PTV station does, at any rate, provide 3.0 times as much fine arts entertainment as the average amount carried by all PTV and commercial stations, and over 4.5 times as much as the average amount on commercial stations only. Similarly, a PTV station provides 1.2 times as much public affairs as the average amount carried by all PTV plus commercial stations, and almost 1.5 times as much as on commercial stations only.

Finally, a PTV station provides less mass entertainment, feature film, news and vertical diversity than do commercial stations, the amount less representing 96 percent, 140 percent, 17 percent, and 11 percent, respectively, of the average of combined PTV and commercial levels of these types. Moreover, the amounts also represent 87 percent, 42 percent, 16 percent, and 11 percent, respectively, of the average levels of these types for commercial stations.[38] Furthermore, the coefficients from which these elasticities are derived are all highly significant (all but news at the 1 percent level).

Finally, public television substantially outproduces commercial broadcasting in regard to public affairs and cultural programming, and also carries significantly less mass entertainment and feature film (than even the commercial network affiliates). PTV's potential role in program enrichment and diversification, as a noncommercial alternative, is qualified only by its "inferiority" in news. Finally, these findings hold after full account is taken of market size, median income, channel type, and various owner affiliations.

38. We may calculate PTV's impact relative to just commercial stations, instead of relative to commercial *and* PTV stations (as in the PCDVs) as follows. Dividing the PTV vs. commercial impact from the estimating equation for table 8.2, by the corresponding sample means from the commercial-only equations related to table 5.3. The difference between a PTV station's performance and a commercial station's, as a percent of the commercial program units broadcast, is as follows:

Fine arts	15.348/3.362 = 456.5 percent
Public affairs	10.964/7.494 = 146.3 percent
Mass entertainment	−93.793/108.366 = −86.5 percent
Feature film	−31.006/74.554 = −41.6 percent
News	−2.974/18.379 = −16.2 percent
Vertical diversity	−.441/4.178 = −10.6 percent

TABLE 8.2

Sensitivity of Individual Station's Prime-Time Program Diversity and Program Composition to Changes in Rent-Yielding Market Variables and Noncommercial Status, 1967*

(N = 545)

Change in Independent Variable	Prime-Time Program Diversity (Vertical)	Type of Prime-Time Programming				
		News	Public Affairs	Entertainment		Feature Film
				Fine Arts	Mass Ent.	
Add 1 commercial	−.88	−.32	−1.47	.96	−.18	1.55
station	1.30	.15	.44	.24	.30	.59
Add 100,000 TV homes	.25[a]	−.03	.82[b]	.73	.17[a]	−.17
	3.00	.13	2.01	1.49	2.38	.54
Switch from PTV to	10.70[a]	17.09[c]	−120.06[a]	−304.06[a]	96.16[a]	140.11[a]
commercial	3.86	1.93	8.79	18.51	39.73	13.09
Switch from UHF to VHF	.96	3.52	1.18	−8.63	.83	−.07
	.69	.79	.17	1.04	.68	.01
Switch nongroup to	−7.19[c]	28.59[b]	2.86	−21.69	−8.60[b]	14.55
network group	1.85	2.30	.15	.94	2.53	.97
nonnetwork group	.04	8.72[b]	4.38	−4.10	−.47	1.54
	.03	2.19	.72	.55	.43	.32
Switch nonnewspaper to						
outside newspaper	−1.11	−4.33	3.58	2.85	1.21	.35
	.64	.78	.42	.27	.79	.05
in-town newspaper	3.41[b]	4.13	14.99[c]	−4.20	−1.90	−8.59
	2.10	.80	1.88	.44	1.34	1.37
Switch independent to						
CBS	10.16[a]	67.27[a]	−35.92[a]	−61.93[a]	6.64[a]	−41.07[a]
	3.86	8.0	2.76	3.96	2.88	4.03
NBC	−1.90	78.89[a]	−77.29[a]	41.25[a]	3.34	−63.05[a]
	.72	9.41	5.96	2.65	1.46	6.20
ABC	−4.70[c]	8.97	−49.26[a]	15.79	14.56[a]	−12.89
	1.79	1.07	3.80	1.01	6.34	1.27
CBS-ABC	8.50[b]	47.88[a]	−40.50[b]	−46.42[b]	11.09[a]	−41.95[a]
	2.54	4.48	2.45	2.34	3.79	3.24
NBC-ABC	−.91	63.18[a]	−67.54[a]	32.81	4.97[c]	−66.43[a]
	.27	5.86	4.06	1.64	1.68	5.09
CBS-NBC	−.41	66.84[a]	−76.59[a]	−33.01	8.62[b]	−56.73[a]
	.09	4.39	3.25	1.17	2.07	3.07
CBS-NBC-ABC	6.07[c]	51.37[a]	−63.62[a]	5.58	9.73[a]	−55.30[a]
	1.70	4.51	3.62	.27	3.12	4.01

*Upper number in each cell denotes percentage change in dependent variable (column heading) due to change specified in independent variable. Lower number is t-value of regression coefficient, with statistical significance (two-tailed test) indicated by superscripts, as follows: a = 1 percent confidence level, b = 5 percent, c = 10 percent. The estimating equation for each dependent variable appears on the next page.

Estimating Equations for Table 8.2

Row		Vertical Diversity: Average No. Program Types Nightly	Type of Prime-Time Programming (in 15-minute units)				
			News	Public Affairs	Fine Arts and Drama	Mass Entertainment	Feature Film
1	Constant	3.662	5.857	22.296	19.314	6.598	1.613
2	Number of commercial stations	−.036	−.055	−.135	.049	−.174	.342
3	100,000's TV homes	.010[a]	.006	.075[b]	.037	.169[a]	−.039
	Dummy Variables:†						
4	Commercial vs. public §	.441[a]	2.974[c]	−10.964[a]	−15.348[a]	93.793[a]	31.006[a]
5	VHF channel	.040	.612	.108	−.435	.813	−.016
6	Network owner	−.296[c]	4.971[b]	.262	−.207	−8.390	3.220
7	Nonnetwork group owner	.002	1.517[b]	.400	−1.095	−.456	.341
8	Outside newspaper owner	−.046	−.753	.327	.144	1.181	.078
9	In-town newspaper owner	.140[b]	.718	1.369[c]	−.212	−1.851	−1.900
10	CBS affiliate	.419[a]	11.698[a]	−3.039[a]	−3.126[a]	6.477[a]	−9.085[a]
11	NBC affiliate	−.078	13.718[a]	−7.058[a]	2.082[a]	3.260	−13.954[a]
12	ABC affiliate	−.194	1.559	−4.498[a]	.797	14.201[a]	−2.853
13	CBS-ABC affiliate	.351[b]	8.326[a]	−3.699[b]	−2.343[b]	10.825[a]	−9.284[a]
14	NBC-ABC affiliate	−.038	10.987[a]	−6.168[a]	1.656	4.850[c]	−14.702[a]
15	CBS-NBC affiliate	−.017	11.623[a]	−6.994[a]	−1.666	8.410[b]	−12.554[a]
16	CBS-NBC-ABC affiliate	.250[c]	8.933[a]	−5.810[a]	.282	9.493[a]	−12.238[a]
	Adjusted R²	.229	.451	.453	.664	.898	.378
	Sample size (station)	545	545	545	545	545	545
	Sample mean	4.1	17.4	9.1	5.0	97.5	22.1

†Labeled attribute of dummy variable equals one, zero otherwise.
§For clarity note that commercial station equals one, public TV equals zero.

These factual findings are probably not too surprising, given the different institutional character and perspectives of educational and commercial TV enterprises. There are, however, a number of important policy implications to be considered below, and in Part III of this book. But here let us first examine more closely the supplementary relation between public TV and commercial TV as suggested in the detailed assessment that follows.

Do Public and Commercial Television Supplement or Imitate Each Other?

There are two hypotheses regarding public TV's potential impact on the program composition and diversity of commercial stations in its markets. The first is that, by relieving commercial licensees of their public service responsibilities, or at least sharing them, public TV inadvertently "frees" the commercial licensee to increase his profits at the expense of merit programming and diversity. The second is that the threat of PTV competition operates to elicit more (unprofitable) merit service from commercial TV, to forestall losses of even limited audiences.

If the first hypothesis held, one would expect commercial and public TV to emphasize quite different program types, particularly when operating in the same markets. One would also expect commercial profits and audiences to be higher in PTV's presence, since a commercial licensee might at least feel freer to focus on the more popular programming. The point is obviously true insofar as any PTV impact on commercial audiences and income in a market implicitly *replaces* that of the commercial entrant who would otherwise operate there instead.

Under the second hypothesis, the opposite would hold. There would be lower commercial profits, greater commercial diversity, and more cultural and informational programming, all in response to public television. If the second hypothesis held, the earlier view of PTV as a catalyst to evoke higher commercial standards would gain support. This pattern would support those who see in public TV a vehicle for raising standards and diversity, but the economic losses would elicit cries of "government competition with private business."

The Factual Evidence in Brief

The factual evidence we have gathered supports the first hypothesis, at least weakly: commercial and public television supplement rather than imitate one another. It suggests also that commercial TV suffers no visible economic losses due to competition from public TV, but rather may be freer to pursue larger profits. However, the very small coefficients, PCDVs, or elasticities calculated, and their generally low significance levels, underscore the distinctly marginal character of any commercial adjustment to public TV, either in program composition or diversity. Indeed, the insignificant impact of PTV programming on commercial station (vertical) diversity (table 8.3), is fully consistent with its small positive impact on market diversity across all commercial stations therein (table 8.1). Furthermore, PTV's apparently positive impact on commercial station economics (tables 8.1, 8.3) is unlikely to evoke opposition to its long-run public funding as "government competition with private business."

The Programming Evidence in Detail

The evidence can best be considered after reformulating in greater detail our first hypothesis, as initially stated earlier in this section. We are actually testing the following propositions:

1. More cultural and informational programming (fine arts, news, public affairs) on public television will result in less of such programming, and in more noncultural and entertainment types (mass entertainment, feature film), on commercial television.
2. Additional cultural and informational programming on public TV will reduce vertical diversity on commercial TV. This is because vertical diversity on commercial TV varies inversely with the number of informational and cultural programs it carries.

Before turning to a summary of findings in table 8.4, let us first consider the coefficients and t-values reported in table 8.3. The forty-eight public TV coefficients reported there are selected from forty-eight regressions specified in the notes to that table. Looking at the thirty-six programming equations only, for each of six dependent variables (commercial mass entertainment, fine arts, news, public affairs, feature film, vertical diversity), we regressed on three market factors (TV homes, competitors, median income), twelve station dummies (channel type, owner affiliations, network ties), and one PTV programming variable. However, each of six different PTV program variables was actually introduced one at a time into all thirty-six regressions run on our six designated commercial program variables.

With the same hypothesis in mind we may now review the results as follows. Note first, that only fourteen of thirty-six PTV coefficients (in the thirty-six programming equations) have t-values greater than 1, and a scant four, t-values greater than 1.645 (10-percent confidence level). For these two sets of coefficients note next that twelve PTV coefficients in the first set are consistent with the two propositions just stated, and two are not, whereas in the second set, four coefficients are consistent and none inconsistent. Because these results are not independent, my nonparametric binomial test may not be as significant as it looks.[39] Yet the pattern is clearly suggestive, the difference between twelve and two in our sample of thirty-six PTV coefficients being statistically

TABLE 8.3

A Summary of Impacts of Public TV Program Types on Commercial Station Economic and Programming Variables, 1967

Public TV Market Data for Selected Independent Variables in 15-Minute Program Units		Commercial Station Data: Dependent Variables			Type of Prime-Time Programming (in 15-minute units)				
		Estimated Station Income	Estimated Station Audience	Average Nightly Program Types	Mass Entertainment	Fine Arts and Drama	Public Affairs	News	Feature Film
All programs	B	.028[a]	.002[d]	−.0003	.021[c]	.0006	−.002	−.0004	.021[d]
	t	2.58	1.45	.76	1.68	.20	.37	.05	1.63
	$\overline{R}^2$	.7473	.5469	.2327	.1473	.3562	.1789	.3548	.1583
Mass entertainment	B	.021	.028[a]	−.006[d]	−.013	.012	.055[d]	−.017	−.019
	t	.29	3.30	1.60	.14	.56	1.56	.29	.21
	$\overline{R}^2$	.7419	.5565	.2362	.1418	.3566	.1832	.3549	.1532
Fine arts and drama	B	.155[a]	.010[c]	−.003[d]	.082[d]	.005	−.0004	.009	.092[d]
	t	3.22	1.71	1.32	1.45	.36	.02	.24	1.58
	$\overline{R}^2$	.7503	.5479	.2347	.1459	.3563	.1787	.3548	.1581
Public affairs	B	.116[a]	.009[b]	−.002	.092[b]	.006	−.002[d]	−.007	.111[a]
	t	2.91	2.05	.97	1.95	.56	1.14	.21	2.29
	$\overline{R}^2$	.7487	.5492	.2334	.1492	.3566	.1811	.3548	.1632
News	B	.215[d]	−.009	−.009[d]	.229[d]	.010	−.047	−.020	.288[c]
	t	1.61	.57	1.38	1.50	.26	.77	.20	1.85
	$\overline{R}^2$	.7440	.5449	.2350	.1462	.3562	.1798	.3548	.1597
Feature film	B	.203[d]	.019	.0003	.148	−.011	.072	−.153[d]	−.198
	t	1.12	.88	.03	.67	.20	.81	1.06	.88
	$\overline{R}^2$	.7429	.5454	.2317	.1427	.3562	.1799	.3564	.1546
Sample size		324	421	453	453	453	453	453	453
Sample mean		9.957	1.347	4.173	108.541	3.329	7.530	18.680	24.777

NOTATION: B = regression coefficient; t = t-value denotes significance of coefficient, further indicated by superscripts (two-tailed test) as follows: a = 1 percent confidence level, b = 5 percent, c = 10 percent, d = t-value exceeds 1 but less than 1.645 at 10 percent level. $\overline{R}^2$ = adjusted $\overline{R}$-square. Notation following certain superscripts indicates consistency of coefficient with hypotheses stated in association with tables 8.4 and 8.7, e.g., d. = coefficient consistent, d.− = coefficient inconsistent.

Form of Estimating Equations Summarized in Table 8.3

Dependent Variable (Commercial Station Data)	Selected Public TV Market Independent Variables	Variables Common to All Equations (not reported)
Station income	All programs,	Constant + TV homes + median city income + (dummy variables):*
Station audience	mass entertainment,	Markets with four or more stations + VHF channel + network owner +
Average nightly program types	fine arts and drama,	nonnetwork group owner + out-of-town newspaper owner + in-town
Mass entertainment	public affairs,	newspaper owner + CBS affiliate + NBC affiliate + ABC affiliate +
Fine arts and drama	news,	CBS-NBC affiliate + CBS-ABC affiliate + NBC-ABC affiliate + CBS-NBC-
Public affairs	feature film	ABC affiliate
News		
Feature film		

*Labeled attribute of dummy variable equals one, zero otherwise.

TABLE 8.4

Public Television's Impact on Commercial TV Programming

Number of Coefficients	PTV Coefficients with t-values Greater than 1		PTV Coefficients with t-values Greater than 1.645	
	Number Consistent with Theory	Number Incon-sistent	Number Consistent with Theory	Number Incon-sistent
significance level in	12	2	4	0
binomial table	.006		.060	

SOURCE: Table 8.3.

significant, at the .006 level.[40] In the second set of coefficients, the difference between four and zero is also statistically significant at the .06 level. In both cases, the frequency of PTV coefficients consistent with the hypotheses constitutes at least weak supportive evidence. For the reader's convenience I report these findings together in table 8.4.

How do public TV stations respond to commercial TV? The discussion so far clearly implies that PTV would put on less cultural-informational (and more of other programs), when commercial TV put on more cultural-informational, whereas PTV would put on more of the latter (and less of others) when commercial TV carries less cultural-informational. The implied relationships can be conveniently stated as three rebuttable propositions:

1. More cultural-informational programming on commercial TV (fine arts, news, public affairs) will result in less of it on public TV, but in more of other programs.
2. Additional cultural-informational programming on commercial TV will raise vertical diversity on public TV. This is because greater diversity there implies the addition of more mass entertainment and film programs to the predominant concentration on cultural-informational service.

39. The character of this test is briefly summarized in a special note below, to which one important qualification must now be mentioned. The binomial test assumes that the various results calculated are independent; here, however, to a considerable extent, they are merely slightly varied treatments of the same underlying data. Therefore, though there is clearly some significance to my results, it is not as great as if completely independent experiments had been performed. I did, however, quantify the existence of a relationship between the variables in question, one which I established for the whole of the data. That is, while I could not determine whether the same relationship exists in many separate data sets, I did reanalyze a single set successively, demonstrating the direction of the relationship between the variables under study.

40. Only six times in a thousand would as many coefficients as this support our hypothesis due to pure chance.

TABLE 8.5

Commercial TV Impact on Public TV Programming

Number of Coefficients	Commercial Program Coefficients with t-values Greater than 1		Commercial Program Coefficients with t-values Greater than 1.671	
	Number Consistent with Theory	Number Incon- sistent	Number Consistent with Theory	Number Incon- sistent
significance level in binomial table	10	6	5	2
		.227		.227

SOURCE: See table 8.6.

3. More horizontal commercial diversity across all commercial stations in the market will produce on public television less cultural-informational programming, more mass entertainment and film, and more vertical diversity. This presumes that greater horizontal commercial diversity reflects added cultural-informational in pre-dominantly mass entertainment and film, whereas greater vertical diversity on PTV reflects additional mass entertainment and film in a predominantly cultural-informational milieu.

In summary table 8.5[41] based on table 8.6, note that my first set of co-efficients include ten consistent with the hypotheses, and six inconsistent. In the second set, five coefficients are consistent and two are not. How-ever, this time the differences between ten and six, and between five and two, are only very weakly significant. The nonparametric binomial test (Appendix Note) indicates that in both cases, differences this large due to pure chance might occur 227 times in 1000. At most, then, we have much weaker evidence than in table 8.4 in support of the general hypotheses.[42]

The evidence thus far reviewed in table 8.3 to table 8.6 must be viewed with great caution. Nevertheless, it at least tentatively supports the hypothesis that PTV and commercial TV respond to one another by differentiating their programming, not by imitation. But any lessening

41. The two sets of equations represented by tables 8.3 and 8.6 represent a system of simultaneous equations. Nonetheless, in this study I have estimated all coefficients by the ordinary least squares method. A review of the results in tables 8.3 and 8.6 suggests that there may be little or no bias associated with the use of ordinary least squares, but confirmation can only be made through the use of a simultaneous equa-tion estimating technique.

42. A partial explanation may be the much smaller sample of stations available for analysis of PTV in table 8.6 than earlier, and the far less detailed specification of station attributes possible for PTV than commercial TV (due to practical data limita-tions). This undoubtedly helps account for the larger residual variance that remains unexplained.

TABLE 8.6

TABLE 8.6

Regression Analysis of Public TV Prime-Time Program Composition and Diversity in Relation to Channel Type, Market Size, and Commercial TV Programming Available, 59 PTV Stations, 1967*

Independent Variable		Vertical Diversity: Average Number of Program Types Nightly on PTV Stations	Prime-Time Public TV Programming (15-minute units)				
			Mass Entertainment	Fine Arts and Drama	Public Affairs	News	Feature Film
Constant		3.743	11.760	23.545	16.525	7.651	1.207
VHF channel dummy[†] (PTV	B	−.369^d	−6.234^a	−.083	4.825^d	−1.240^d	−2.019^d
station)	t	1.56	2.96	.03	1.50	1.16	1.61

Commercial Market Data:

TV homes in	B	.017^d	.063	.186^d	.552^b	.168^b	−.031
100,000's	t	1.08	.44	1.15	2.55	2.33	.37
Median city	B	−.018	−.111^d	−.185^c	−.054	−.00008	.030
income in $100's	t	1.64	1.17	1.72	.40	.00	.52
Number of	B	.010$^{c.}$	.100$^{b.}$	.016	.095$^{d−}$	−.00058	.035$^{d.}$
program types	t	1.81	2.07	.29	1.29	.02	1.20

Commercial Program Units (15 minutes):

Mass entertainment	B	−.008$^{b.}$	−.048$^{d.}$	−.028	−.130$^{b−}$	−.016	.0005
	t	2.22	1.42	.73	2.51	.93	.02
Fine arts and	B	−.003	−.278$^{d−}$	.155	.363	.113	−.204$^{d−}$
drama	t	.10	1.15	.57	.99	.92	1.42
Public affairs	B	−.009	−.053	.024	−.226$^{d.}$	−.060$^{d.}$	.011
	t	.74	.49	.20	1.37	1.09	.18
News	B	−.0002	−.048	.046	.054	.003	−.072$^{c−}$
	t	.03	.79	.67	.58	.09	1.97
Feature film	B	.009$^{d−}$	−.049	.037	.145$^{c.}$	.045$^{d.}$	−.060$^{c.}$
	t	1.58	.91	.61	1.78	1.65	1.89
Adjusted R^2		.1434	.1997	.0349	.1383	.1008	.1400
Sample mean		3.663	8.305	18.932	22.627	6.271	2.169

*Upper number in each cell is a regression coefficient (B), and lower number its t-value, with superscript to indicate statistical significance (two-tailed test) as follows: a = 1 percent confidence level, b = 5 percent, c = 10 percent, d = 30 percent. Notation which follows certain superscripts indicates consistency of coefficient with hypotheses stated in association with table 8.5, for example, d. = coefficient consistent, d− = coefficient inconsistent. Superscripts without suffixes indicate variables not relevant to these hypotheses, though pertinent to analysis in later section, at pp. 270-71.
†For clarity note that the VHF channel dummy equals one for a VHF public TV station, and zero for a public UHF station.

of cultural-informational programming on commercial stations due to PTV (tables 8.3, 8.4) is normally negligible, and hence fully consistent with PTV's small affirmative impact on total commercial diversity in table 8.1.

Indeed this finding is also consistent with the known fact that public TV adds a lot to market diversity by showing programs with limited audience appeal. Hence it would have little effect on commercial profits or, therefore, on commercial program decisions. This may help explain why commercial operators appear largely indifferent to PTV, although the latter clearly does seek to differentiate itself by presenting more cultural and informational programming. Nor can we presume that commercial licensees would, under most conceivable conditions, offer more (nonremunerative) "merit service" to forestall audience diversion to public TV. For any commercial station which tries to meet even token PTV competition in this fashion would presumably risk more serious losses to commercial rivals who chose to capitalize on the lower audience appeal of its merit programs.

Three questions remain. Do commercial stations earn more in the presence of a public television station? This would result if PTV does in fact relieve them of public service responsibilities, leaving them freer to pursue profits and audiences.[43] If public TV's net impact on commercial programming, and commercial TV's impact on public television, are both very small numerically, does PTV necessarily fail as a worthwhile influence for raising program standards and diversity generally? Or, if public TV adds its own program types without affecting the program composition or economic viability of commercial TV, is that not part of the affirmative case for public broadcasting?

The Income Evidence in Detail

The hypothesis tested next is really a corollary to those associated with table 8.4:

> More of any cultural-informational programming on public TV will result in higher commercial audiences and income, whereas more of other programs on PTV will act to reduce commercial audiences and income.

Returning to table 8.4, note that we have reported twelve PTV coefficients which impact on commercial income and audience size, a number of which are then summarized in table 8.7. Note further in table 8.7

---

43. It is probably no longer true that public TV could significantly free commercial licensees to maximize their profits. Public interest groups closely watch such stations, will file petitions to deny if they try to evade their public service responsibilities, especially in regard to minority, informational, local, and children's programming, and the FCC must react to these petitions. For such reasons alone commercial stations would find it hard to use public television as any "out" today, but we shall test the hypothesis to be sure.

TABLE 8.7
Public Television's Programming Impact on
Commercial Station Income and Audiences

	Number of PTV Coefficients with t-values Greater than 1		Number of PTV Coefficients with t-values Greater than 1.671	
	Consistent with Theory	Inconsistent	Consistent with Theory	Inconsistent
significance level in	7	2	5	1
binomial table		.090		.109

SOURCE: Table 8.3.

that seven PTV coefficients in the first set are consistent with the above hypothesis, whereas two are not. A discrepancy this large would occur due to pure chance only 90 times in 1000, insignificant at the .10 level though hardly any strong refutation of the hypothesis in question. In the second set of coefficients, five PTV coefficients are consistent, and one inconsistent, a discrepancy that could be due to chance only 109 times in 1000.

Once again, the coefficients themselves are small and often only very weakly significant. Yet the frequency of their replication is statistically significant and at least mildly supportive of the hypothesis.

Overall, the results in tables 8.3 to 8.7 are consistent with my earlier analysis of market aggregates in table 8.1 and connected material. There I found that adding one hundred commercial program units to the market raises total diversity across all stations (including PTV) by fifty-seven choices ($79.296 \times 100/140$), and commercial diversity by fifty-four ($75.866 \times 100/140$) but not without substantially reducing per station income by $285,000, or 38 percent of the sample mean. On the other hand, adding one hundred PTV units would raise total diversity by eighty-three choices ($41.080 \times 100/49.7$), commercial diversity by ten choices ($5.193 \times 100/49.7$), but with no apparent price in forgone station income. There is indeed a modest positive elasticity of PTV on market income per station,[44] directly in line with the station coefficients

44. In table 8.1, each PTV station adds $1.387 \times $100,000$ income per station, which is $1.387/7.428$ or 18.7 percent of the mean income per station for the sample. Likewise, the elasticity for revenue would be $2.913/26.020$, or 11.2 percent of the sample mean. True, the fact that over half of PTV stations on the air in 1967 were located in the fifty largest markets, and over four-fifths in the one-hundred largest, raises some question as to whether some of PTV's positive impact on commercial income and

reported in table 8.6, and further supportive of both facets of our theory.

This positive PTV effect on commercial station income could well reflect the tacit barrier to new commercial entry which public TV represents (under present allocations), especially when operating on a VHF channel. Surely no public TV station in 1967 posed anywhere near the competitive threat to commercial licensees of any conceivable class of new commercial entrant that would quickly take its place should it for any reason withdraw (and the FCC release its channel for commercial use).

The Residual Case for Public Television

Aside from these limited secondary effects which may improve commercial program composition and commercial diversity, what is the principal case for public TV? This has to some extent already been suggested in the analysis of market level aggregates when the market includes PTV. By that standard at least, PTV's contribution to horizontal program diversity was far greater than that of any other policy option reviewed—new station entry, ownership diversification or steps to strengthen a nonnetwork alternative.

As noted earlier, doubling the number of PTV program units (from forty to eighty) in table 8.1, raised commercial diversity by a mere 2 percent (from 325.5 to 332 choices), but total diversity by a full 11 percent, from 363.5 to about 403. The elasticity of total diversity with respect to PTV units was both more significant and some five times larger than the corresponding elasticity for commercial diversity. Even looking at our full station sample in table 8.2, a PTV station, other things constant, appeared to carry 357 percent more fine arts and 46 percent more public affairs than the respective sample means of those programs on commercial stations, but only 42 percent as much feature film, and 87 percent as much mass entertainment,[45] as their commercial sample means.

More precisely, after accounting for whether a commercial station is independent or affiliated, we find it carries .4 fewer program types nightly than a PTV station, 3 fewer news units, but 11 more public affairs units, 15 more fine arts, 94 fewer mass entertainment, and 31 fewer feature film. This is true taking into account channel type, competitors, market size, and owner affiliations. One would also expect that the difference between PTV and specific types of commercial stations

revenue may not in fact be an inadvertent proxy for market size and advertising potential. Nevertheless, all equations reported in tables 8.3 and 8.6 include TV homes and median city income as control factors. On that count, at least, the PTV impact must be taken at face value, and is less likely to mask any more deep-seated influence of market size.

45. See note 38.

(that is, independent versus affiliated) would be affected in the same direction as the network affiliation coefficients and PCDVs in table 8.2.

In short, PTV's "superiority" over a network affiliate may be even greater than over an independent—in public affairs and fine arts, and so too, its related "inferiority" in mass entertainment and feature film.[46] Thus PTV's major contribution probably remains even when compared to the more affluent, experienced network affiliates. That is, PTV seemingly offers quality and diversity, but mainly through programs that the majority of viewers do not wish to watch, since most people prefer mystery, adventure, sex, violence.

What Weight Shall Be Given to Channel Type and Market Size in Educational Allocations?

To help government spectrum allocators evaluate these results still further, one final question must be considered: in optimizing PTV's role, what weight should be given to channel type and market size? Should that weight differ from the weight appropriate in commercial broadcasting?

The brief answer is: in commercial TV, market size and channel type mainly affect station profitability, not diversity or program composition (tables 5.2, 5.3, 5.4). However, in public television, there is at least weak evidence that these two factors may affect the amount of news, public affairs, and feature film a PTV carries, and its vertical diversity too (table 8.6).

Channel Type. An educational VHF may carry more public affairs than educational UHF, and it does carry less mass entertainment, possibly less feature film, though possibly less news too. Except for channel type's highly significant negative impact on mass entertainment (at the 1 percent level), none of these coefficients passes the 10-percent test. However, the point estimates are still suggestive. Furthermore, all coefficients take into account market size, median income, commercial diversity, and commercial program composition.

By the same token, the fact that a public UHF appears to carry more film than a VHF at least suggests that the resources available for public affairs may be greater where VHF permits access to larger potential audiences, whereas UHF stations, with more meager resources, have to rely more on film.

Market Size. In the larger markets, when account is taken of channel type, PTV provides significantly more public affairs and news than in the smaller markets, and possibly more fine arts too. Indeed the news and public affairs coefficients are quite clearly significant at the 5-percent

46. Public TV's lower vertical diversity in table 8.2 reflects its greater homogeneity and concentration on cultural-informational programming. See discussion above, at pp. 253–57.

level, though the absolute magnitude of the coefficients is very small. Each additional 100,000 TV homes corresponds to eight minutes more public affairs weekly on public television, and three minutes more news. (These estimates are less than 3 percent of the respective sample means.)[47]

Allocating educational channels to the largest markets, then, may facilitate greater resources for news and public affairs irrespective of channel type and available commercial program choices. Similarly, VHF grants to educators, irrespective of market size, may bolster public affairs (but not news), and clearly operate to reduce mass entertainment and possibly feature film.

In commercial TV, on the other hand, size of market (as measured by TV homes) has no comparable effect on news and public affairs, nor indeed on fine arts or feature film. There, license limitation and channel type mainly impact on profitability, whereas program composition responds largely to the network-affiliate relation (tables 5.2, 5.3, 5.4).

One final point relates to vertical diversity. In public television, the estimates (weakly) suggest that an educational UHF provides .369 more program types than an educational VHF, which is .369/3.663, or 10.1 percent of the combined mean of educational VHFs plus UHFs.[48] On the other hand, in commercial broadcasting a VHF station has 3 percent of the sample mean more vertical diversity than a UHF (table 5.3). In PTV, however, as noted previously, greater vertical diversity reflects the inclusion of more *non*informational, *non*cultural programs in an otherwise homogeneous cultural-informational mix, whereas in commercial TV, greater vertical diversity implies a probable addition of cultural-informational programs to the prevailing entertainment types. Therefore, the allocation of VHF channels, in both the commercial and educational segments, appears to produce relatively more cultural-informational programming despite the lower levels of vertical diversity that appear in the latter.

Implications of Our Findings for the Policy toward Public Television

One implication of my findings in this chapter is that bringing a new public TV station into a market without one may be a highly cost-efficient way to promote types diversity, compared, at least, to the number of commercial stations needed to generate an equivalent amount of diversity. Indeed, a more radical conclusion is that taxing commercial TV (or auctioning its licenses to recover commercial rents), and subsidizing public television with these revenues, may do more for diversity than the

47. Citing the unreported sample mean in table 8.6, I calculated the following quasi-elasticities (PCDVs) for news, .16850/6.2711 =2.7 percent, and for public affairs, .55167/22.62711 = 2.4 percent.
48. In table 8.6, the unreported sample mean for vertical diversity is 3.66343.

stated amounts of local and informational programming that commercial licensees can as a practical matter be required to carry, or than the internal cross-subsidies needed for the same purpose.

I return to these questions in subsequent chapters, but here suffice to note simply that the political feasibility of this proposal seems enhanced by (1) commercial TV's apparent success in earning more rather than less in PTV's presence; (2) the consequent absence of evidence that long-run public funding for PTV will constitute government competition with private business; (3) the understandable preference of commercial licensees to compete with PTV than with another commercial station, especially where the former's presence (on a VHF channel) virtually precludes an otherwise certain commercial entrant; (4) the dramatic evidence that PTV adds a lot to program diversity, and a lot more than commercial TV, with no adverse impact on commercial revenues; (5) the further likelihood that for any given dollar, PTV may well have greater incentives to do more for informational and cultural programming (quality-wise) than commercial stations do, for which this is only a side issue.

There are, to be sure, some caveats. Public TV's impact on commercial television may be negligible today because the PTV audience itself is so small. Should that audience grow substantially, then what? Would the government competition argument again be raised? Also, the small absolute audiences for PTV programs necessarily qualify any effective enhancement of program diversity per viewer in the market. That is, very wide hypothetical choices are "real" only for those relatively few viewers who choose to utilize them. Lastly, public broadcasting must be judged not simply by how much diversity it adds to present commercial programming in the face of unused channels reserved for public stations. We must also consider whether PTV adds more diversity than would the commercial service which could be provided (under favorable market conditions), were the reserved channels released for commercial use. Or more significantly, if PTV were switched from VHF to UHF and those VHFs made available to commercial licensees, with the hope of accommodating a fourth national network.[49]

A closely related question, which regulators could usefully explore, is whether a more modest reallocation of public TV channels to commercial use might also make sense in markets now assigned two such channels, one VHF and one UHF, with the UHF dormant. My prior analysis does not permit me to determine how much a second public TV station would in fact add to diversity, only what one such station will contribute. Presumably the second station, when activated, would contribute much less since its program mix, unlike the first's, would necessarily be compared to an existing PTV station as well as to existing commercial sta-

49. See Robert Crandall, "The Economic Case for a Fourth Commercial Television Network," *Public Policy*, Fall 1974, pp. 530–36.

tions. Nonetheless, even a second public TV station (on UHF) could add more to diversity than a new independent commercial UHF station, weak as it will probably be.[50]

Nevertheless, there is probably a limit as to how much FCC can (or ought) directly require from commercial licensees by way of local, informational, or cultural programming. Nor, as we shall see in chapter 13, is the setting of mandatory quantitative renewal requirements any simple matter, or likely to insure more than mere air time for designated program types, as distinct from the resources or incentives needed to do a really first rate job. Therefore, the case for funding public television out of commercial rents continues to merit more serious attention than it has normally received. We return to these issues in chapters 13 and 14.

Conclusions and Policy Guidelines

New entry by commercial stations clearly operates to reduce station earnings but, at the same time, to raise program diversity substantially. Yet such entry offers little or no contribution to cultural-informational programming. Neither does the policy to diversify station ownership offer any certain path to more news, public affairs, or cultural service, or to greater diversity generally. The most one can say is that the policy on newspaper and group ownership poses no serious *threat* to industry economics, to diversity, or to merit programming. In contrast, only public television offers a decisive *contribution* to cultural and informational service without commercial losses.

The policies of promoting new station entry and diversified ownership could each impair economic viability, to a limited degree at least. Therefore, each is bound to encounter some degree of opposition from incumbent stations which would thereby be seriously disadvantaged. This leaves two options for regulation. First, it can recognize any unavoidable economic losses caused by these policies, while defending them anyway for removing the special advantages which regulation conferred upon licensees in the first place (and for diffusing economic and political power and above all, diversifying editorial perspectives). Second, it can adopt other policies with beneficial programming effects and fewer harmful economic ones. Examples of these (to be examined in subsequent chapters) might include quantitative requirements of local and informational programming set by economic class of station; reduced-rate interconnection

50. The key question is how many, if any, markets with two public assignments also have only two commercial assignments, affording the opportunity of adding a third network affiliate on a released public UHF channel, and hence of raising diversity more than a UHF independent would. In those cases the reallocation could make sense.

of public television networks, with uncovered interconnection costs made up by extra charges to private commercial networks; a tax on commercial rents to fund public broadcasting.

Appendix 8A. A Note on Binomial Test for Groups of Coefficients*

In empirical research the researcher frequently encounters a coefficient which lends support to a theory, but which is not of high enough significance to allow a strong conclusion to be drawn. Occasionally, several coefficients of this nature are encountered. If they agree and support a hypothesized theory, a much stronger conclusion can be drawn than would be justified by evaluation of individual coefficients.

In this type of analysis the minimum level of significance is first chosen. The sample is composed of all coefficients, addressing the problem, which have a significance level equal-to or greater-than the chosen minimum level. The coefficients are then categorized as either agreeing or not agreeing with the hypothesized theory. Since the sample is small, made up of nominal data, and has only two categories, a nonparametric test, such as the binomial test, is appropriate.

The binomial test is a simple probability test such as would be applied to a given distribution of heads and tails for a coin. A detailed discussion can be found in any standard text on nonparametric statistics. The general paradigm is succinctly stated by Siegel in *Nonparametric Statistics for the Behavioral Sciences.*[51]

The probability of obtaining x objects in one category and $N - x$ objects in the other category is given by

$$p(x) = \binom{N}{x} P^x Q^{N-x}$$

where

P = proportion of cases expected in one of the categories
$Q = 1 - P$ = proportion of cases expected in the other category

$$\binom{N}{x} = \frac{N!}{x!(N-x)!} \, *$$

*$N!$ is N factorial, which means $N(N-1)(N-2) \ldots (2)(1)$. For example, $4! = (4)(3)(2)(1) = 24$. Table S of the appendix gives factorials for values through 20. Table T of the appendix gives binomial coefficients, $\binom{N}{x}$ for values of N through 20.

* Prepared by Jefferson N. Latham.
51. S. Siegel, *Nonparametric Statistics for the Behavioral Sciences* (New York: McGraw-Hill, 1956), chap. 4, p. 37.

As an example, if the sample size is 14 and the distribution of co-efficients which agree and disagree with the hypothesis is 12 and 2, the probability of such a disproportionate distribution having occurred by chance is 0.006. This is strong support for the hypothesis. With a small sample more cautious conclusions should be drawn even if the distribution in a sample of 4 is 4 and 0. Use of the formula produces a probability of approximately 0.06 which is still good evidence. Although of less significance than the previous example, the researcher can conclude that the 4 coefficients occurred because of a consistent underlying relationship rather than by chance. Such a conclusion could not be drawn if each of the coefficients were looked at as individual items rather than replications of a hypothesis.

Chapter 9

Alleged Bases of National Television Network Power

Background to Present Network Inquiry

NETWORK TELEVISION has from the outset been an oligopoly, with three firms accounting for all network time sales since 1955, and the bulk of network national spot time sales as well. Until recently, two "majors" (CBS and NBC), dominated the third company. Rising time sales and profitability have not however elicited new network entry, in large part because of the scarcity of comparable facilities and economic factors at work in the network-affiliate relation.

Because of limited opportunities for promoting more competition among the national TV networks, the commission has repeatedly sought to insure competition between them and other industry components. Toward that end, a number of trade practices have been checked, altered, or eliminated so as to equalize the competitive position of network and nonnetwork program suppliers, advertisers, stations, and station (spot) advertising representatives. In the 1950s and 1960s, most of these practices were successfully modified, or their alleged impact otherwise shown to be exaggerated, one goal being to sustain a viable nonnetwork alternative to the prevailing network system.[1] Yet the networks have continued to provide their affiliates with a preponderant—and still growing—share of prime-time programs.[2]

---

1. See FCC Report and Order in Docket No. 12782, May 4, 1970, pars. 1–21; Report and Order in Docket No. 19622, January 23, 1974, pars. 8–10.

2. Westinghouse Petition for Inquiry, Rule-Making, and Immediate Temporary Relief in re: Television Network Practices and Their Effects on the Ability of Station

In 1958, the Report on Network Broadcasting (Barrow Report) found little evidence that the networks had exacted from their affiliates disproportionate amounts of aggregate time sales revenue.[3] However, the report did discover that the combined use of preferential rates and compensation arrangements, as well as of option privileges,[4] and the threat of switching affiliates in the larger markets, operated to induce a more frequent airing of network programs than otherwise.[5] Almost twenty years later, in 1976, Westinghouse petitioned for immediate temporary relief from "network domination"[6] on related grounds, contending mainly that network payments to stations since 1964 had risen at a markedly lower rate than network time sales, overall network expenses, and retained income. Not only did station payments grow by only 1.7 percent between 1969 and 1975, when retained network income rose by 124.8 percent, but the payments themselves declined from 23.1 percent of network revenues in 1964 to 13.4 percent in 1975, and from 19.8 percent of station revenues to only 10.7 percent in 1975.[7]

One must, however, bear in mind here that the system of TV advertising has also continued to change over the years in question. Thus national network and nonnetwork spot revenues grew, from 1960 to 1975, by 196 percent and 312 percent, respectively, while local revenues grew by 482 percent. As a consequence, local revenues grew, as a percentage of total TV revenues, from 17.7 percent to 25.4 percent, when national spot fell slightly, from 33.1 percent to 30.9 percent, and national network fell more, from 49.2 percent to 43.7 percent (see chapter 2, table 2.8). Some of the declining portion of station revenues which network affiliates derive from network payments could obviously reflect these basic trends. But the declining portion of network revenues paid to the affiliates must be due to other factors, bound to be debated in the current network inquiry.[8]

Of course affiliates will presumably do better than the independents or they would not remain affiliates, turning instead to syndicators for programming. Therefore one may wonder how justifiable any complaint about the size of affiliate compensation or net earnings will be. Nevertheless, the Westinghouse petition reveals that at least some affiliates want a bigger share of their network's oligopoly gain badly enough to initiate an FCC proceeding toward that end. Nor is there any question that a

Licensees to Operate in the Public Interest, FCC RM:2749, September 3, 1976. See attachment A, charts 1, 7.

3. House Commerce Committee, *Report on Network Broadcasting* (1958), pp. 454–57.

4. The practice is defined in chapter 2, note 8, and associated text.

5. See Levin, "Workable Competition and Regulatory Policy in Television Broadcasting," *Journal of Public Utility and Land Economics* (May 1958), 106–12.

6. Westinghouse Petition for Inquiry.

7. Ibid., pp. 30–40 and attachment A, chart 1.

8. See FCC, Docket No. 21049, Further Notice of Inquiry, October 28, 1978, pars. 8–10, 33–37 (henceforth called Further Notice).

wider diffusion of that gain among more affiliates might put the latter in a better position to carry public service than if the networks alone (not directly licensed) siphoned off much of their rents.[9]

Facing the FCC here, then, are two related but separate issues. If the networks in fact get a large share of oligopoly profits, and their affiliates a small share, the commission, whatever it formally states, might conceivably care because it wants the affiliates to get their fair share of these profits regardless of how they use them. (In fact, the commission denies that this is or should be its proper concern.) Or more likely, the commission may believe that the affiliates, *if* given more revenue, would (or could more easily be asked to) produce more or different merit programming.

Underlying both these issues are the alleged bases of network power, to which we now turn. Then in chapter 10 I shall consider a broad comparative assessment of independent and affiliated stations in economic and programming terms, and in chapter 11, the objectives and consequences of prime-time access.

The issues being raised today are basically similar to those raised fifteen or twenty years ago—the networks' failure to provide adequate information to affiliates beforehand regarding the network programs to be aired; the use of compensation arrangements to induce a high rate of "clearance" (airing), and resultant domination of licensee independence; the erosion of station time and rising clearance rates; allegations of network power derived from network proprietary interests in syndicated program production; the ability of networks to produce their own entertainment; exhibition rights to network reruns; and exclusive rights to new programs.[10]

With the above in mind, let us briefly examine the possible bases of network power in television broadcasting.

An Overview of Network Power

According to some observers, the networks' power vis-à-vis their affiliates is grounded on an ability to reduce the costs of programmers, advertisers, and broadcasters. Noll, Peck, and McGowan have aptly summarized this point:

9. True, there is evidence that the affiliates do not spend their rents on public service as much as independent stations do. However they might spend even less if the networks retained a larger share. Lastly, quantitative requirements (as outlined in chapter 13) must obviously be set lower where the affiliates' residual rents are lower.

10. See FCC, Notice of Inquiry in Docket No. 21049 (RM–2749), January 14, 1977, pars. 13–28 (henceforth called Initial Notice). See also Further Notice, pars. 8–17, 33–42.

First, the networks serve to economize on the costs of arranging for nationwide advertising by employing a single agent to deal with national advertisers and granting him exclusive rights to the sale of prespecified blocks of time. Similarly, by supplying programs that are broadcast nationwide, the network simplifies the guesses advertisers must make about audience size.

Second, further economies can be achieved through centralized program procurement. Without it, the program owner would be required to negotiate with every station separately in order to maximize his return, thus raising transaction costs for both program owners and broadcasters. In addition, concentrating program procurement in three networks unbalances market power, converting a competitive situation into an oligopolistic one favoring broadcasters. By passing some of the gains from market power on to stations, networks provide broadcasters with an incentive not to deal with program producers.[11]

Proceeding further, the authors also note that:

An affiliate will carry a network program if its share in the total advertising revenue generated by the program is greater than the profit from broadcasting a nonnetwork program. Since the total advertising revenue of a program is directly proportional to the size of its audience, the relative attractiveness of a network vis-à-vis a nonnetwork program depends on (1) the size of the audiences of the two programs, and (2) the terms on which the station shares in the advertising revenues of each. These factors interact; the greater the popularity of network programs the smaller the share of revenue required to make them more profitable to the station.[12]

Finally, the authors conclude by emphasizing the special role of network programming. The core of network power, they contend, is the "superior audience appeal of its programming":

Using its economic advantage, a network can offer a program owner more favorable terms than, acting independently, he could obtain from stations. Networks thus acquire, and offer to affiliates, programming more appealing than that available from nonnetwork sources, and do so at prices that afford them a profit representing the value of the scale economies and of their market power. But a potential for profits beyond this amount exists and its magnitude can be influenced by the terms on which networks compensate affiliates for clearing network programs.[13]

Despite the alleged ability of big groups to bargain for preferred compensation arrangements, the Westinghouse petition suggests that they may not in fact be able to cut into the networks' potential for profits beyond the above point. In that regard (and as evidence of

---

11. See Roger Noll, Merton Peck, and John McGowan, *Economic Aspects of Television Regulation* (Washington, D.C.: Brookings Institution, 1973), p. 59.
12. Ibid., p. 60.
13. Ibid., p. 61.

"network domination"), Westinghouse further cited the rising relative share of aggregate industry income going to the networks alone, excluding the network-owned (O&O) stations.[14]

But why should it really matter whether the networks or their O&Os get the net income, given that the money ends up in the same place? One reason, as noted above, may be that this allocation of income will necessarily affect the sums left for the affiliates to spend. Nor is the counterargument that the distribution of network profits is just an accounting convention persuasive. For by downplaying network returns from national advertising, and inflating the apparent income and revenues from O&O time sales, the TV networks could derive bargaining advantages, not only with their affiliates over compensation, but with advertisers who buy O&O time.

A second reason why the allocation of income between the networks and the O&Os matters may be that, lacking an extra margin of income beyond that minimally needed to keep the affiliates from disaffiliating, or otherwise turning to syndicators, station owners may be less able to underwrite the less profitable local and public service programming. True, in some cases the magnitude of VHF-based rents alone may suffice for such cross-subsidy, though more detailed analysis is needed to be sure. For such reasons, among others, the Westinghouse contentions now command careful attention from the FCC and the Justice Department,[15] whereas the networks are quick to challenge them.[16]

The growing competitive advantage has been in part attributed to the dramatic switch from sixty- to thirty-second network announcements over the past decade, and their consequent improved ability to compete with the national spot representatives' cost per thousand viewers delivered.[17] In the following table, note that if the networks had provided *only* the longer sixty-second spot announcements (column 2), their competitive position versus the national spot representative (who has long offered the shorter twenty- or thirty-second spots), would clearly have deteriorated (compare column 2 with column 1). By the same token, the networks' thirty-second spot rates per thousand homes delivered are only half their sixty-second rates, and well below the thirty-second nonnetwork spot rates.

14. Westinghouse petition, p. 30, and chart 2.
15. The current TV Network Inquiry was initially launched in partial response to apparent Justice Department concern. See Letter from Donald I. Baker to Richard E. Wiley, December 3, 1976 re: Westinghouse Petition, and Comments of the United States Department of Justice, RM 2749, November 23, 1976. See also Reply of CBS Inc. to Justice Department Statement, December 23, 1976; Reply Comments of NBC Inc. to comments of Justice Department, December 23, 1976.
16. See especially Statement of CBS Inc. in Opposition, FCC RM–2769, November 23, 1976: Comments on NBC Inc. in Opposition, November 24, 1976; also ABC Opposition to Westinghouse Petition, November 23, 1976.
17. See Westinghouse petition, pp. 12–14.

Cost per Thousand Homes Delivered

	1	2	3
	National Nonnetwork	Network	
	Thirty-second spot rate	Sixty-second spot rate	Thirty-second spot rate
1970	$3.10	$3.61	$1.81
1974	3.21	4.77	2.39

SOURCE: Westinghouse petition, appendix A, chart 5.

Further reflective of the networks' power versus their affiliates, finally, is said to be the continued rise in scheduled network program hours, as a fraction of total available broadcast time, 7 A.M. to 2 A.M.[18]

Let us now turn to specifics.

The Affiliates' Relative Program Cost Savings

Part of the networks' power to bargain with their affiliates on rates and compensation appears to derive from the rising program costs that the former are willing and able to underwrite, costs the affiliates can thereby avoid. In 1976, a half-hour episode of a new prime-time network show cost on the average about $165,000, compared to only $49,000 in 1960, an increase of 235 percent.[19] Total network program expenditures (unseparated from technical) rose comparably, according to FCC annual financial data, from $404,731,000 in 1960 to $1,273,241,000 in 1975, some 215 percent. Even station program expenses reflected this increase,

18. Thus ABC network shows rose from 43 percent to 64 percent of the total program hours ABC affiliates carried, whereas CBS's share rose from 57 percent to 68 percent of total program hours, and NBC's share rose from 63 percent to 68 percent. By the same token, the so-called "station time" which the average affiliate filled itself from local or syndicated sources, fell over 25 percent between 1960 and 1976, as the network schedule grew. Ibid., p. 13.

19. Initial Notice, par. 11. Even deflating by the wholesale price index, real program costs were a full $90,759 in 1976, compared to $51,633 in 1960, an increase of over 75 percent. Over a still longer period, and again adjusting for inflation, a typical film half-hour mystery cost $14,466 in 1952 (1967 dollars) compared to $73,079 for a typical half-hour film drama in 1974, a rise of 405 percent (derived from figures cited in FCC Network Inquiry Special Staff, *The Historical Evolution of the Commercial Network Broadcast System* [preliminary], October 1979, p. 111).

and, excluding the network-owned stations, rose 224 percent, from $196,944,000 to $637,382,000.

But the important question is how much more, if any, did independent stations have to spend on programming than comparable affiliates. Superficially the difference looks considerable. In 1975, the FCC's published financial data permit us to estimate that an average independent VHF station spent $2,200,000 more on programming than the average affiliated VHF, whereas a UHF independent spent $525,731 more than its affiliated counterpart. The proportion of sales revenue which independents spent on programming that year was also notably larger than for the affiliates—47.6 percent and 39.8 percent for an independent VHF and UHF, compared to 31.6 percent and 31.4 percent for comparable affiliates. These proportions must be considered in light of the fact that independents cluster in the fifty largest markets whereas affiliates are distributed more widely.

In sum, affiliation is valuable to the station: the networks do absorb large program costs. But networks could still retain a disproportionate share of net income, one that produces a supernormal return on total investment, which could in turn prevent affiliates from doing as much public service programming as otherwise.[20]

More relevant, actually, are the published NAB estimates for typical station revenue and expenses in 1975.[21] Although NAB's cross-classifications are not entirely comparable to the foregoing, certain conclusions can be drawn. Looking at profitable stations only, for example, we find typical program expenses for a sample of independents earning yearly revenues of $2,000,000 and over to be $1,956,800, or 47.4 percent of their typical sales revenue. In contrast, the average program expenses for comparable profitable affiliates is $1,513,807, or about $450,000 less and only 40.7 percent of the average typical sales revenue. Removing the very largest, most lucrative affiliates from this calculation—those earning more than $10,000,000 revenue—average typical affiliated program expenses drop to $1,204,862, or 39.8 percent of sales revenue, which is about $750,000 less than the typical independent. This latter upperbound figure seems more relevant here in that independents are known to include relatively more UHF stations whose resources and program expenses are both typically lower than for VHF within any broad revenue class.

Whether we estimate the extra program costs incurred by independents to be $0.5 million or $0.75 million, the burden represents roughly 7 percent of typical sales revenue. This figure is remarkably similar,

20. Note, however, that because affiliates must share advertising revenues with the networks, the above comparison with independents may be less meaningful than otherwise. Yet we also know that networks spread their programming costs over numerous stations no one of which needs pay *added* production costs, once a program is produced for a given station, just because it is carried by others.

21. National Association of Broadcasters, *1975 Television Financial Report.*

whether for a UHF independent compared to a UHF affiliate, or for a VHF affiliate compared to a VHF independent.[22] Finally, the comparison pertains only to independents now able to operate at all, almost entirely in the fifty largest markets. Elsewhere only UHF channels remain unoccupied. For them, the combined handicap of meager market potential and inferior signal quality, service range, and click tuning problems would intensify any deterrent to entry due to differential program costs alone.

The affiliate's ready access to network-produced news, public affairs, and sports programs is also well known. The networks virtually doubled their prime-time news and public affairs productions from 1957 to 1968, at the very time when their entertainment production declined by four-fifths (table 9.1). Even the costly network news and public affairs specials literally doubled between 1964 and 1968, while the popular sports specials rose still more (almost three-fold), and popular entertainment specials by one-third (see table 9.2). All of this would at least appear to help the affiliates fulfill their public service responsibilities.

The Alleged Value of "Adjacencies"

A second major advantage often claimed for affiliation with a TV network are the special incremental returns affiliates allegedly enjoy in selling their advertising time for spot announcements. Advertisers are said to prefer network arrangements not only for their convenience, but for the larger audiences they can expect on affiliated stations even for spot announcements in adjacent time slots (that is, "adjacencies").[23] This latter expectation may be grounded less on factual reality than on the advertiser's own perceptions. There is at least crude evidence that audience flow may not be as important a determinant of viewing as is sometimes asserted. More refined inquiry is needed, but the following findings may surprise those who emphasize the importance of audience flow in the valuation of adjacencies. The upshot is that one must look elsewhere for the main value of network affiliation.

I studied all prime-time network programs during the first and last three months of 1974, assigned to twenty-two program categories by

22. The ratio of program expenses to sales revenue in 1975 was 39.8 for a UHF independent, 31.4 for a UHF affiliate, 31.6 for a VHF affiliate and 47.6 for a VHF independent.

23. John Peterman has underscored the value of adjacencies on network-affiliated stations in "The Structure of National Time Rates in the Television Broadcasting Industry," *Journal of Law and Economics* (October 1965), 87–88. B. Owen, J. Beebe, and W. Manning make similar assertions (see their *Television Economics* [Lexington, Mass.: Lexington Books, 1974], pp. 96, 131, 136). So, too, do Noll, Peck, and McGowan, *Economic Aspects of Television Regulation,* p. 131.

TABLE 9.1

Network-Produced Regularly Scheduled Series, 1957-68
(6-11 P.M.)

Type	Number of Hours 1957	1968	Percent Hours 1957	1968
News and public affairs	5.75	9.5	25.3	73.1
Entertainment	17	3.5	74.7	26.9
Total	22.75	13	100.0	100.0

SOURCE: Arthur D. Little, Television Program Production, Procurement, Distribution, and Scheduling (1969), FCC Docket No. 12782, table 3(3).

TABLE 9.2

Special Programs on Networks, 1964-68
(6-11 P.M.)

	1964-65 Shows	Hours	1967-68 Shows	Hours	Percentage of Change in Hours Produced
Entertainment	82	91	112	124	+36.3
Sports	22	25	77	95	+280.0
News and public affairs	129	107	180	215	+101.0
Total	233	223	369	434	+94.6

SOURCE: Arthur D. Little, Television Program Procurement, Distribution, and Scheduling (1969), FCC Docket No. 12782, table 5.

A. C. Nielsen, Inc. Using the Nielsen typology, two questions were asked. Are entertainment shows on any network watched more when programmed against informational (not entertainment) programs on its two rivals, and is the reverse true for informational shows when scheduled against entertainment? Second, does the presence of entertainment or information in a prior time slot on any network further affect the size of the audience that follows? That is, do fewer people watch an entertainment show on, say, ABC when preceded by information (not entertainment), holding constant the type of show on CBS and NBC? Such vertical impact would be evidence of audience flow.[24]

24. I assume throughout that entertainment program classes tend to have higher audiences and ratings than informational categories as a whole. See, generally, notes 26–27 and associated text. Furthermore, while adjacencies often occur within programs, my data permit me to analyze interprogram adjacencies only.

To ensure statistical reliability, adjustments should ideally have been made for distortions due to network market position, time of night, program length, and day of week. Time and resource limitations prevented this. However, in the regression I ran on audience data for most network programs (see table 3.3), taking program types into account, only the internetwork differences appear to be both significant and substantial.

Thus further analysis revealed that the three networks not only had audiences which were substantially different from each other, but these differences were, with few exceptions, significantly greater than the impacts due to day of week, time of night, and program length. The last two factors in particular had very small (though again significant) absolute effects on audience size, ratings, and shares. For present purposes, therefore, any serious distortion in my estimation of audience flow is avoided by limiting my analysis to intranetwork comparisons only. The question asked is simply how any given network performs when faced with pairs of specified program groupings on its rivals.[25]

In fact I found no evidence of vertical impact under those constraints, and the issue is therefore whether the value of adjacencies may not have been improperly attributed to an undocumented, exaggerated assumption of audience flow.

Consider next the nine programming configurations examined in table 9.3. Each of these mainly focuses on one network's audience when (1) its programs are postulated to be entertainment, information, or a news documentary; (2) the prior program in its schedule is entertainment only, or a mix of information and entertainment; (3) its two rivals are postulated to carry entertainment, information, or a documentary, again preceded by entertainment only, or a mix of entertainment and information. The question is whether the presence of prior informational programs, known to have lower circulation, significantly lowers the audiences of entertainment shows that follow, or contrariwise, whether prior entertainment shows will raise the audiences of informational shows that follow. (The program mix on the two other networks is in each case held constant.)

First, note that the data for each network's mean audiences pertain to *entire programs,* and not the larger number of, say, fifteen- or thirty-minute units therein. Therefore, what is being revealed here is audience flow relative to inter-(not intra-) program type adjacencies.

But note next that I use *fifteen-minute units* to measure what two rival networks schedule when I examine the third network's actual pro-

25. I would have preferred to normalize the data first for all factors considered in table 3.3. Nevertheless, the significantly greater impact on viewing of network sources than of any other independent variable supports the procedure in table 9.3. At the very least, intranetwork comparisons rule out the single major distortion that could impair my results.

TABLE 9.3

Analysis of Nielsen Network Audience Data for Entertainment and Informational Programs, 1974

(N = 1558)

CBS

Model	N	Mean Audience (mils)	A	B	C	D	E	F	G	H	I
A	52	12.4		-	x	x	x	x	x	-	x
B	42	12.7	-		-	x	-	x	x	-	x
C	1354	14.9	x	-		x	-	-	x	-	x
D	1530	15.0	x	x	x		-	-	x	-	x
E	72	15.4	x	-	-	-		-	x	-	x
F	66	15.6	x	x	-	-	-		x	-	-
G	22	7.6	x	x	x	x	x	x		x	x
H	13	15.2	-	-	-	-	-	-	x		-
I	14	19.6	x	x	x	x	x	-	x	-	

NBC

Model	Mean Audience (mils)	A	B	C	D	E	F	G	H	I
A	14.0		-	-	-	x	x	-	x	-
B	14.1	-		-	-	x	x	-	x	-
C	13.6	-	-		-	x	x	-	x	-
D	13.7	-	-	-		x	x	x	x	-
E	12.9	x	x	x	x		x	x	x	-
F	10.7	x	x	x	x	x		x	-	-
G	14.2	-	-	-	x	x	x		x	-
H	6.6	x	x	x	x	x	-	x		x
I	11.4	-	-	-	-	-	-	-	x	

ABC

Model	Mean Audience (mils)	A	B	C	D	E	F	G	H	I
A	12.3		-	-	-	-	-	-	-	x
B	12.2	-		-	-	-	-	-	-	x
C	12.2	-	-		-	-	-	-	-	x
D	12.1	-	-	-		-	-	-	-	x
E	12.1	-	-	-	-		-	-	-	x
F	13.7	-	-	-	-	-		-	-	x
G	14.2	-	-	-	-	-	-		x	x
H	14.8	-	-	-	-	-	-	x		x
I	7.5	x	x	x	x	x	x	x	x	

Model	Period	CBS	NBC	ABC
A	#1	+++	+++	+++
	#2	Ent	Ent	Ent
B	#1	Info	Ent	Ent
	#2	Info	Ent	Ent
C	#1	Ent	Ent	Ent
	#2	Ent	Ent	Ent
D	#1	+++	+++	+++
	#2	Ent	Ent	Ent
E	#1	+++	+++	+++
	#2	Ent	Ent	Info
F	#1	+++	+++	+++
	#2	Ent	Info	Ent
G	#1	+++	+++	+++
	#2	NewsDoc	Ent	Ent
H	#1	+++	+++	+++
	#2	Ent	NewsDoc	Ent
I	#1	+++	+++	+++
	#2	Ent	Ent	NewsDoc

SOURCE: Derived from National Nielsen TV Ratings—NTI Reports for January-March and October-December 1974.

LEGEND:

x = denotes statistical significance for scheffe test (at .05 level) of difference between audiences for designated pairs of program configurations from among models A-I; for example, in model A, CBS's informational programs attract mean audiences of 12,414,000 (when ABC and NBC carry entertainment), and this is significantly lower than the 14,881,000 viewers who watch CBS's entertainment programs in model C (when ABC and NBC carry entertainment too).

+ = denotes that period #2 programs (say, starting at 9 P.M.) were selected regardless of prior program types, and that period #1 types (say, starting at 8 P.M.) include entertainment and informational programs.

ent = entertainment programs assigned by A. C. Nielsen, Inc., to one of nineteen categories of entertainment (includes sports events).

info = programs classified by Nielsen as news documentaries, general documentaries, or new sustainers.

NOTE: To maximize the number of cases meeting our specifications, we necessarily started with period #1 programs for 6-7 P.M., and period #2 for 7-8 P.M. By far the bulk of our cases, however, were of programs starting at 8 and 9 P.M., and somewhat fewer, at 9 and 10 P.M. This helps explain the different sample size here (1,558), in table 3.2 (1,358), and again in table 3.3 (about 1,215).

grams. Despite the objection that most programs are actually thirty minutes long, and that the use of fifteen-minute units may therefore distort the results, I believe this procedure to be justifiable. How else could one make the comparison across networks? If this comparison were limited to shows of the same length, starting and ending at the same time, there would doubtless be a drastic loss of observations. Even using only shows which started at the same time, however long, would clearly reduce sample size. Nor do I believe that a thirty-minute program length is as standard as is often asserted. In my Nielsen data base for 1974, the mean length of each network's programs is fifty-three to sixty-four minutes, with a standard deviation ranging from twenty-seven to thirty-eight minutes. Most revealing is a direct search of program length, by network, which summarizes most of my data base as follows:

Program Length (minutes) Number of Programs:	Fifteen	Thirty	Sixty	Ninety
CBS	14	197	247	22
NBC	21	82	208	28
ABC	14	122	204	56
Total	49	401	659	106

NOTE: This search was limited to the data deck analyzed in table 3.3, for the 8-11 P.M. period only. It initially calculated the number of different length programs in 15-minute segments, adjusted here to report the actual number of programs by estimated program length.

It is true, therefore, that there are more thirty-minute than fifteen-minute programs. However, any single unit of length—a minute, an hour, or a half-hour—seems as arbitrary as fifteen minutes. In table 9.3, there is no question that the use of a fifteen-minute program unit for comparisons with the other two networks did indeed produce unique cases where one network ran a fifteen-minute program (sports commentary, news sustainers), while its two rivals ran a thirty-minute (or longer) program which started earlier. Use of the fifteen-minute unit as a kind of common denominator length permitted me to include program type comparisons within (or across) networks that a longer program unit would not.

Returning to my specific configuration, in model A of table 9.3 I searched the full sample for all cases where CBS carried one of the three Nielsen informational program types at the same time ABC and NBC carried one of the nineteen entertainment types, including sports, and each network's *prior* (period #1) program type was permitted to include entertainment and information. I in fact found 52 such observations. In model B, on the other hand, where I restricted the prior (period #1) program type to information only (for CBS), and entertainment only (for ABC and NBC), there were a total of 42 fifteen-minute observations. In model C I found 1354 segments where all three networks carried entertainment preceded by another (period #1) entertainment show, whereas in model D I included all 1530 cases where each network carried an entertainment program regardless of what preceded.

If the audience flow hypothesis were sound, and assuming informational shows to be generally less popular than entertainment, then one might in fact expect smaller informational audiences in period #2 for, say, CBS in model B than model A, and smaller entertainment audiences in model D than model C. Furthermore, we see that CBS's informational audiences in models, A, B, and G are indeed significantly smaller than for its entertainment programs in most of models C, D, E, F and I. Finally in model G, CBS's least popular program type—the news documentary—draws significantly smaller audiences than do any of its entertainment or general informational shows in all other postulated models (A–F, H–I). Therefore, if audience flow were a major determinant of viewing, period #1 programs on CBS, other things being equal, should in fact affect the performance of its period #2 programs. Nevertheless, the difference between CBS's informational audience in models A and B is not statistically significant at the .05 confidence level, and this despite my inclusion of period #1 entertainment shows in model A, and their exclusion from model B. Likewise, the difference between CBS's entertainment audiences in models C and D is insignificant, again, despite the inclusion of informational types in model D and their exclusion from model C.[26]

By the same token, there is no question that NBC's news documentaries (model H) generate significantly smaller audiences than its entertainment programs in all other postulated configurations (models A–G, I), whereas even its general informational programs in model F also draw significantly fewer viewers than such entertainment shows (in models A–E, G–H). Nevertheless, period #1 NBC entertainment shows in model A, and their exclusion from model B, yield no significant difference between the audiences that result. Likewise, inclusion of period #1 informational shows in model D, and their exclusion from model C, again yield only statistically comparable audiences in the two cases. Thus here, too, for NBC as for CBS, the data and the tests are inconsistent with significant audience flow.

26. I considered an alternative approach based on regression analysis. That approach would have dealt with audience levels in a more detailed manner, with up to twenty-three program types, and with many more cases reflecting different program mixes across networks, both within a time slot and across adjacent time slots. In particular, we would have run program audiences on network source and dummy variables for preceding program types and audience size. We would also have considered the type and popularity of programs competitively scheduled against the one we analyzed as dependent variable. However, that alternative approach entailed estimating hundreds of coefficients and conducting thousands of tests of significant differences, which was beyond our means. Nor would it have dealt with the problem of associating homogeneity with lack of significantly different audience sizes. Because I am unable to trace who is watching what without individual diaries, I can comment on homogeneity only where there are significant audience differences (see chapter 3, pages 64–70, text associated with tables 3.3, 3.4, 3.5).

The results for ABC are admittedly different, though once again, ABC's news documentary audiences (in model I) are significantly smaller than its entertainment audiences in all other models. However, unlike the findings for CBS and NBC, ABC's general informational audiences in model E are not significantly different from its entertainment audiences elsewhere. Perhaps the most that we can therefore conclude is that the findings for CBS and NBC are at best qualified by the data for ABC.

In sum, the data in table 9.3 suggest that the less popular information shows need not seriously reduce the audience of programs that follow, and that this may be true whatever the program types scheduled against them. At the very least, the findings question whether the kind of programs which the industry classifies as informational need impair audience flow seriously, and this despite the notably smaller audiences such programs are known to deliver nationally.[27] The question for others to explore is whether the foregone audiences of any nonremunerative informational program mainly appear at the time it is run, and not in any reduced viewing of what follows (which I did not find), nor in any lower resultant value of commercial time spots in between.

For present purposes, then, one must look elsewhere to explain the substantial value of network affiliation. The larger audiences of network entertainment simply do not appear to raise the audiences for adjacent time slots appreciably, nor presumably thereby to elicit higher rates from advertisers, though I have not tested for this directly.

Some readers may want to qualify these findings by underscoring the small number of informational programs under analysis here, given the postulated constraints of competitive scheduling. Thus the difference between models A and B (52 versus 42) reveals only 10 out of 52 prior (period 1) programs in model A to be informational, whereas the difference between models C and D suggests that only 176 of 1530 programs in model D were informational. These informational shows account for a mere 19.2 percent and 11.5 percent of the subsamples in question. Had the number of such shows been larger, the impact might also have been larger.

But such reasoning ignores the fact that these models deal with real-world configurations. The 10 and 176 informational shows are indeed all that the networks ran just prior to their entertainment programs, in face of the postulated rival schedules. Perhaps they were afraid of losing audiences for the programs that follow. Nevertheless, the effective impact in

27. The 18 news documentaries in our sample had average ratings of 11.5 (s = 4.3), audiences of 7,772,000 (s = 2,938,000), and shares of 19.6 (s = 7.3), notably smaller than any other program type studied. Our 20 general documentaries performed better, with average ratings of 16.9 (s = 7.3), audiences of 11,277,500 (s = 4,882,000), and shares of 26.3 (s = 10.3). At the other extreme, 321 situation comedies had average ratings of 21.9 (s = 6.2), audiences of 14,733,000 (s = 4,214,000), and shares of 34.5 (s = 10.1) (s = standard deviation). The latter figures were notably higher than those for other entertainment types, as well as for documentaries of all types. All programs were aired in prime time.

real-world subsamples (of information and entertainment) was clearly too small to register significance. My conclusion therefore stands, namely, that interprogram audience flow may indeed have been exaggerated in the literature, though the tests do not rule out a limited impact.

Alleged Leverage in the Top Markets

A more complete and convincing explanation of why network affiliation continues to be valuable to stations and viewers alike must now consider other factors. Without networks, the public would clearly lose a high-quality expensive type of programming—the documentaries, news, and public affairs specials—which is simply too costly for local stations to produce, let alone acquire from independent packagers. Advertisers, on the other hand, would lose the convenience of a central agency to perform the integrating or brokerage function needed to place a commercial and get it widely aired in prime time. By the same token, station affiliates may presumably have to dissipate some of their time sales revenue in higher negotiation and marketing costs with advertisers (see chapter 11).

The critical question is whether the high clearance rate for network programs really reflects their greater popularity than syndicated programs, or simply the leverage networks derive from power in markets where stations exceed available affiliations. The threat of disaffiliation in those larger markets is real. It may permit the networks to extract a premium from those very profitable affiliates therein who have nowhere to turn so long as the number of markets with more than three stations remains too small to accommodate a fourth network.[28]

Once having extracted this premium in the larger markets, the networks are then in a position to pay premiums to insure the full clearance of even marginal programs by affiliates in the smaller markets. That is, not only do stations in the one-or-two-station markets have greater bargaining power to get favorable compensation, but the networks have the wherewithal and incentives to pay such compensation to insure reliable access to large prime-time audiences nationally.[29] The upshot is that networks may virtually redistribute income from affiliates in the top markets to those in small markets.

For a network's bargaining leverage to be significantly greater in markets with more than three stations, it must have a credible alternative to

28. Robert Crandall develops this point in "FCC Regulation, Monopsony, and Network Television Program Costs," *Bell Journal* (Autumn 1972), 487.
29. Ibid. A similar conclusion is reached in Owen, Beebe, and Manning, *Television Economics*, pp. 97–100.

its present affiliate relationship. The question therefore is whether the independent station in a market with four or more stations would provide access to an audience roughly comparable to what the present affiliate offers. This is unlikely if the independent is a UHF, unless the network affiliates are also UHF in an all-UHF market. Focusing on markets with independent UHFs, and even assuming their comparability to the third VHF affiliate therein, the question is how many such markets exist. Unless they are sufficiently numerous, the Crandall-Owen thesis breaks down.

The data in table 9.4 throw light on the matter. Note first that in markets with four or more stations, independent VHFs have rates, audiences, and estimated revenues some 64 to 82 percent as large as those of VHF affiliates, making those independents possible alternatives for the networks. The discrepancy between independent UHFs and network UHFs is even smaller, those stations presumably operating in all-UHF (or nearly all-UHF) markets. It would therefore appear that, in the markets where our fifty-five independent stations operate, the networks would indeed have the kind of leverage with their present affiliates that Crandall and Owen imply.[30]

But how far would these independents take us in explaining the networks' capacity to pay premium compensation rates in markets with only one or two VHFs? Even limiting this question to the twenty-two independent VHFs (as clearly more affluent than the independent UHFs), reference must next be made to the economic performance of the fifty-four VHF affiliates in two-station markets, and the thirty in one-station markets. Since the rates and audiences of those small-market stations are in fact less than one-fourth of those of network affiliates in the largest markets, any leverage applied to the latter based upon the presence there of comparable VHF independents, would presumably go a lot farther than if VHF affiliates in all size markets were themselves of comparable size.

Short of far more detailed analysis of these data and the above hypothesis, my conclusions must obviously be tentative. Yet it is suggestive that the estimated revenue of VHF affiliates in two-station markets is almost three-fifths that for VHF affiliates in the largest markets, whereas the small market station spot rates and audience size are little more than one-fifth of those in the large markets (see table 9.4). In other words, the estimated mean station revenues in the two-station markets are considerably higher than spot rates and audience size would lead us to expect. This discrepancy is at least consistent with the existence of pre-

30. Supporting evidence of a different sort appears in Wildman's suggestive regression analysis of spot rates, November 1971. See Steven Wildman, "Vertical Integration in Broadcasting: A Study of Network-Owned-and-Operated TV Stations," FTC Symposium on Media Concentration, December 14–15, 1978, Washington, D.C., especially section 4 and commentary at pp. 19–20.

TABLE 9.4

Mean Values for Selected Economic Variables by Class of Station and Market, 1972

Class of Station	Markets with											
	Four or More Stations				Two Stations				One Station			
	Stations	Rates (dollars)	Audience (× 1,000)	Estimated Revenue (× $1,000,000)	Stations	Rates (dollars)	Audience (× 1,000)	Estimated Revenue (× $1,000,000)	Stations	Rates (dollars)	Audience (× 1,000)	Estimated Revenue (× $1,000,000)
Independent												
VHF	22	$302.60	776	$4.1								
UHF	33	74.19	236	1.6								
Network affiliate												
VHF	163	408.06	938	6.4	54	$93.86	209	$3.7	30	$ 77.50	127	$n.a.
UHF	21	93.95	257	1.4	7	87.86	213	1.1	4	103.75	84	n.a.

SOURCE: Spot rates derived from Standard Rates and Data Service—Spot Television (1972). Station revenues estimated from FCC Financial Report for Television Broadcast Service (1972), using procedure outlined in note to table 5.1. Station audience data from American Research Bureau, Day-Part Audience Summary, November 1972.

n.a. = not available from published FCC financial data.

mium compensation payments to network affiliates in the two-station markets, in support of the theory expounded earlier.[31]

Still another advantage in which the affiliates may share derives from the network's efficiency in providing advertisers with information conveniently, from a central point, information they must otherwise seek out in numerous separate negotiations with individual stations. In dealing with a network, the advertiser is essentially spared the uncertainty and cost of predicting total audience delivery.

The Television Networks and the Nonnetwork Groups—Structural Context

One final element in the networks' market power can be illuminated by contrasting their overall position with that of the nonnetwork group owner. Consider first the horizontal network structure, which clearly puts networks in a better position than the nonnetwork groups to collude on advertising rates, prime-time market shares, and even program schedules. Each network faces either or both of its rivals in virtually all TV markets, whether through the stations it owns outright, or the hundreds with which it is affiliated. The networks are thereby intimately aware of each other's programming and pricing decisions.[32]

In contrast, the structural safeguards against nonnetwork group interdependence or collusion are equally clear. First, the average group-owned station in one hundred leading markets confronts as many separate competitors as there are stations in its market, mainly because no group normally faces the same group rival in more than one market. This structural pattern reduces the likelihood of group-owned stations in any market agreeing, overtly or tacitly, to engage in parallel pricing, share markets, or, in the process, gang up on or otherwise constrain their non-group rivals. This likelihood would at least be greater where two or more groups face each other across the whole group, that is, in all their TV markets.

31. After galleys for this chapter were set, seemingly definitive evidence in support of the Crandall-Owen thesis was reported in FCC Network Inquiry Special Staff, *An Analysis of the Network-Affiliate Relationship in Television* [preliminary], October 1979 (Stanley M. Besen and Thomas G. Krattenmaker, Co-Directors). See especially conclusion in chapter 6, pp. 1–3, 8–10, 42. See also derivation of estimating equation and results, ibid., pp. 19–44; and instructive analysis of network-affiliate relationship in chapter 5 generally.

32. See United Research Inc., *The Implications of Limiting Multiple Ownership of Television Stations,* 2 vols. (prepared for the Council for Television Development) filed on October 1, 1966 in FCC Docket No. 16068 (hereafter called *Television Group Ownership Study*). See ibid., at vol. I, chap. 2, pp. 11–15. See also *United Research, Inc., Report of the Proceedings of the Top Fifty Proposed Rulemaking before the Federal Communications Commission (Informal Conference, 1966),* pp. 17–18, 22 (testimony of Paul W. Cook).

Second, only rarely are all of any group's stations affiliated with a single network.[33] This of course means that the groups are less likely than otherwise to derive special advantages over their nongroup rivals in bargaining for premium compensation arrangements and network time rates. By the same token, where the groups are no more able than nongroup licensees to exact special concessions from the networks, they will on that count have less leverage than the latter in their dealings with the non-network system of advertisers, film syndicators, and other program suppliers.

The structural safeguards against vertical restraints are also weaker among the networks than the nonnetwork groups. Paramount in the vertical network structure is the forward contractual link between each network, its owned and operated stations, and the hundreds of affiliates it finances and supplies with programming. But the networks are also linked backward to the market for talent and programs. In addition to their own program production facilities (and long-term talent contracts), as seen in chapter 2, the networks hold proprietary interests in most of the shows they use.[34] By contrast, the nonnetwork groups have no comparable affiliates, and even more limited program production facilities. On the average, they own stations in markets inferior to the networks' key stations. Vertical no less than horizontal structure provides more decisive safeguards against potential restrictive business conduct in the case of the nonnetwork groups than the networks.

Still another widely-cited indication of network power is the so-called NBC-Westinghouse Exchange (1955), wherein NBC virtually compelled Westinghouse, on pain of losing all her NBC affiliations, to agree to trade the then recently acquired Westinghouse radio-TV stations in Philadelphia for NBC's broadcast stations in Cleveland (plus $3,000,000). In paying the Philco Corporation $8.5 million for WPTZ-TV in Philadelphia two years before, Westinghouse had actually valued that station's NBC affiliation at $5 million and therefore viewed with considerable alarm the prospect of disaffiliation across the board (in markets where not all stations could have a network tie).[35] Although the FCC finally ap-

33. Ibid., pp. 17–22 (testimony of Paul W. Cook).

34. Small wonder, then, that program suppliers contend that the networks bargain hard over compensation and program prices, sometimes by threatening to produce their own shows; by forcing producers to use network-owned studios and production facilities; and by recapturing some or all profits from first-run network sales. (See Bruce Owen, "Structural Approaches to the Problem of TV Network Economic Dominance," *Duke Law Journal*, vol. 1979: 191 [February], pt. IV[A]. Prepared for the FTC Symposium on Media Concentration, December 14–15, 1978, Washington, D.C.)

35. *House Antitrust Subcommittee (Subcommittee no. 5) of the House Committee on the Judiciary, Report on the Television Broadcasting Industry, H.R. Rep. No. 607,* 85th Congress, 1st Session 97–108 (1957); and see more generally, "Hearings on Monopoly Problems in Regulated Industries before Antitrust Subcommittee (Subcommittee no. 5) of the House Committee on the Judiciary," 84th Congress, 2nd Session, ser. 22, pt. 2 (Television) at 3109–3205 (1957).

proved these "voluntary" transfers, the Justice Department subsequently brought a civil action against NBC under the Sherman Act.[36]

The absence of comparable instances of overt nongroup coercion by group licensees, or of related exclusionary practices, may be further reflection of still another structural factor. On the average, the group owner faces more competitors in his several markets than single owners do, mainly because of his heavy holdings in our largest, most populous metropolitan centers. These are indeed the very markets which support the most stations (on a per-market basis), the most independents, all the networks' key stations, and many group-owned stations besides. In short, the groups confront larger numbers of rival stations in their markets than the nongroups, and, in the top markets, frequently compete as the sole independents against the network-owned stations or major network affiliates. It therefore follows that the groups' ability to capitalize on groupness at the local level will be narrowly circumscribed.

The Television Allocation Plan

Brief mention must now be made of the allocational constraints on entry imposed in 1952, and still largely in force today. By limiting the number of stations that could technically operate in most TV markets to three, the FCC's allocation plan virtually precludes the existence of more than three national TV networks.[37]

Specifically, problems of signal interference required geographic separation of stations on the same or adjacent frequencies. Therefore most major cities now have only five to ten TV assignments, notwithstanding the eighty-two channels initially allocated to TV broadcasting. Furthermore, very few markets had more than three VHF assignments in 1978. Indeed only one-fifth (49 of 208) of the markets had four or more TV stations *on the air* that year (VHF *and* UHF), and these served only three-fifths of the nation's population.[38]

Without access to the remaining two-fifths of potential U.S. viewers, of course, a fourth network based on those 49 markets would be severely

36. United States v. RCA Inc., Civil No. 21,743 E.D. Pa. filed December 14, 1956.

37. The present Network Inquiry proposes to explore these and other factors which affect the entry of additional advertiser-supported broadcast television networks, and of alternative kinds of national network program delivery (Further Notice, at pars. 43–53). For an argument which assigns even greater weight than we do here to allocational constraints as the major basis of network power, see Bruce Owen, "TV Network Economic Dominance," pt. IV(B).

38. The figures discussed in this section are adapted from Christopher Sterling and Timothy Haight, *The Mass Media: Aspen Institute Guide to Communication Industry Trends* (New York: Praeger, 1978), table 180; and from *Analysis of the Network-Affiliate Relationship*, chapter 1, pp. 3–16, 19.

handicapped. Indeed, in the VHF band alone, a fourth network could have reached only one-third of TV households. On the other hand, over one-half of TV markets that year (135 of 208) had at least three outlets and provided roughly two-thirds of the primary affiliates of all three networks, the remaining third being located in markets with one or two stations only. (This left 116 so-called independent stations without network ties.)

At issue here also is the FCC's longstanding policy on localism. To assign TV outlets to as many communities as possible in 1952, the commission allocated 12 VHF and 70 UHF channels to 1240 communities, for a total of 1875 separate commercial assignments. In 1976, over one-fourth of all U.S. communities could receive ten or more signals (emanating from within or outside their boundaries), but only 1.5 percent (3) of the 208 TV markets had that many stations actually on the air, locally. At the other extreme, over nine-tenths (96 percent) of all communities could receive four or more signals, whereas only one-fourth of all TV markets had four or more local stations operating.

The point here is twofold. First, the local community station goal is by no means realized. There are obviously many communities within all of the top ADI markets (and most others), yet in only 49 of 208 markets is it even possible that as many as four separate communities had their own *local station*. In contrast, almost all U.S. communities could receive four or more *services*, so that the primary goals of wide and diverse service have been achieved, albeit with a three-network system nationally. Indeed almost one-half of all communities could actually receive eight or more services compared to only one-fourth of the ADI markets with even half that number of local stations.

Quite clearly, then, FCC's policy of limiting the number of local stations (in most markets to only three) to limit signal interference to an acceptable level, would alone help explain the three-network triopoly today. However, the intermixture of UHF and VHF channels (again for the sake of local assignments nationally) further contributes to unused channels, and hence to barriers to any fourth network. Even in 1978, for example, 162 UHFs were unoccupied in the top one hundred markets, and 117 UHFs elsewhere, so that markets where a fourth station would be UHF may also impede new network entry.

In short, the structural preconditions for internetwork cooperation and parallelism as sketched earlier (pages 293–94), lie in part at least in the allocational barriers to new station and new network entry just reviewed. So, too, does the aforementioned structural pattern which appears to facilitate leverage for the three networks to exact economic rents from affluent affiliates in the top fifty markets (where strong VHF independents provide credible alternatives for network parents unable to strike an acceptable bargain with their present affiliates).

Conclusion

In sum, the basic allocational structure contributes indirectly to the networks' power in dealing with their advertisers, film syndicators, and other program suppliers. In addition, the networks may well have special leverage versus their affiliates in the nation's leading markets, given the possibility of switching affiliation to the independent stations located there. Under present allocations, there are simply too few markets with four or more VHFs (or UHFs) to make a fourth national network truly viable, but too many to leave the relative bargaining power of networks and affiliates, equal. Nevertheless, I have not been able to test for the differential impact of network power on compensation rates for affiliates in large and small markets.[39]

On the other hand, there is evidence that the frequently alleged incremental value of interprogram time adjacencies may be exaggerated. The true source of economic value of network ties appears to lie in the entry barriers and related power to redistribute station rents from larger to smaller markets, as just mentioned. The value also lies in the popularity of network entertainment and program cost savings which affiliates enjoy per viewer delivered. Both factors doubtless pose a handicap to unaffiliated independents competing in the same market.

Nevertheless, though the networks have, use, and sometimes abuse their market power, the economist's traditional concern with income or profit distribution, and economic efficiency, touches only part of the problem. Of paramount additional importance to the FCC, Congress, and the public is the impact of network power (and network-affiliate relations) on the composition and diversity of TV programming. In particular, we are concerned with effects on information and local programming, as well as on the variety of program types generally. Needless to say, however, this is only part of a larger question involving allegations of the networks' social, cultural, and political power, matters which strictly speaking lie beyond the scope of this book.

39. But see definitive evidence on this power cited earlier in this chapter in note 31.

Chapter 10

The Limits of

Network Regulation

THE present chapter will examine the comparative performance of network affiliates, network-owned (key) stations, and independents. It does so, finally, with an eye on whether the present complex of rules, practices, and industry economics together act to further, or impede, attainment of such goals as localism, competition, and diversity.

In particular, the issues under review are, first, whether network affiliates do indeed earn significantly more than independents when other major factors are taken into account, and, if so, whether superior affiliate earnings result in larger amounts of informational programming, and in greater types diversity generally. Hence my analysis is directly comparable to that in earlier chapters where the same question was raised about newspaper- and group-affiliated stations (chapter 6), and the dual effects of license limitation (chapters 5, 8). With few exceptions, I usually found little or no effect on program diversity and information (of group or newspaper ownership), and this despite the bolstering effects on profitability for group though not newspaper ties. The limitist licensing policy, on the other hand, both sustained station profitability and acted to reduce horizontal type diversity significantly.

The Underlying Theory

The theory examined in those earlier chapters, further tested below, is essentially this: that the higher revenue-generating capabilities of stations with certain ownership affiliations, or located in less competitive markets, provide the financial resources for greater amounts of the less profitable informational programming, though the actual amounts carried of necessity also depend on the licensee's incentive structure. The latter includes the opportunity costs of the informational programming, that is, the net loss of audiences, and revenues due to providing information instead of popular entertainment shows.

Notwithstanding the counterattraction of profit-maximizing entertainment shows, especially in the nation's largest markets, I did find that higher station revenues, *cet. par.*, are associated with larger amounts of time for news, public affairs, and information generally, though at a declining rate (table 6.13).[1] Accordingly, one might expect the classes of stations that earn more revenue to carry more information, in partial response perhaps to pressures from regulators, public interest groups, and opinion leaders. The question here is whether network affiliates (or network-owned stations) do or do not perform in this expected manner, and, if not, what the implications are for public policy.

Do Network Affiliates Carry Relatively More Informational and Cultural Programming Reflective of Greater Economic Resources?

In assessing the performance of network affiliates and independents, let us first consider the comparative record on their actual program composition. In 1967, for example, the independents appear to have allotted significantly more time than the affiliates to local, public affairs, fine arts, drama, and nonnetwork programming generally (table 5.3). However, the affiliates carried significantly more news. For VHF stations in 1972, moreover, independents again carried significantly more of all local programs, and less of all news, but less also of public affairs and all information (table 6.13). On the other hand, the amounts of local news and local public affairs which independents and affiliates carried were statistically indistinguishable. Thus the picture is at best mixed.

For UHF stations, the independents again fell short of the affiliates in all news, all public affairs, and all information, but now in local news as well. However, the amounts of all local and local public affairs on both classes of stations are once more virtually indistinguishable (though with the independents' superiority in the latter nearing significance).

Comparing VHF affiliates with UHF independents, finally, though the amounts of all local programming they carry are again comparable, the independents' margin above the affiliates is at least visible (t = 1.36). Moreover, the independents do carry significantly more local public af-

1. The relation between station profitability and informational programming is further examined in the appendix to this chapter.

fairs, and significantly less of all news, all public affairs, all information, and local news. In short, the upshot is no clearly greater contribution to informational and cultural program time by the nation's network affiliates in 1967 and 1972, though there may be quality variation within given program categories.

As for available economic resources, however, the affiliates' rates, ratings, revenues, and audiences are all significantly and decisively higher than the independents', whatever control factors we specify. This holds true both for 1967 and 1972 (see tables 5.3, 5.4, 10.2). Why, therefore, despite the lip service which the FCC and the industry both pay to public service responsibilities, do the affiliates appear to contribute statistically less, or at least no more than, the independents, to all local, local public affairs, fine arts and drama, and sometimes even to local news? (Table 10.1). Why, indeed, except for CBS, did the network affiliates as a class usually provide significantly less vertical diversity in 1967 than the independents (or at least no more), and this despite the advertiser's apparent willingness to pay more at the margin for access to stations with more diversified programming? (See Appendix to this chapter.)

The answer to these questions is that advertisers may indeed pay more for time on stations with diversified, and in particular informational programming, but will presumably not do so at the expense of substantial reductions in absolute audience size. That is, the premium rates paid for informational audiences may mitigate the revenues foregone in carrying more information (and less entertainment), but there is no question that relatively fewer people watch the informational programs. Affiliates may indeed be profitable just because they carry less diverse or informational service, and, actually, *put on* less such service just to remain profitable. In addition the affiliates may simply not recognize any special legal responsibility to carry informational programming.

Lastly, affiliates may have special incentives to play down local programs generally, local public affairs in particular, and possibly local news as well. Reference has already been made to the networks' practice of setting higher compensation rates in markets with one or two stations (where their leverage is smaller), than in larger markets where stations exceed affiliations. This practice aims to induce affiliates to air more network programs than otherwise, in the smaller markets at least. However, more time for network programs will mean less time for local and nonnetwork, though not necessarily for information as such— that must be determined directly. To assess this hypothesis one must ideally focus on affiliate compensation rates, but without such data I offer instead a crude, indirect look at the relationship between affiliate spot rates on one hand, and the number of local, nonnetwork, and network program clearances on the other.

As to why spot rates should be related to the level of network clearance at all, this would depend on the networks' ability to influence station

TABLE 10.1

Independent Station Margins over Network Affiliates in Prime Time Devoted to Major Program Categories, 1967 and 1972

	1	2	3	4	5	6	7	8	9
	Additional 15-minute Periods Broadcast by Independents Compared with			First Three Columns as Percent of Sample Mean (PCDVs)					
Program Class	CBS Affiliates	NBC Affiliates	ABC Affiliates	Col. 1 ÷ Col. 9	Col. 2 ÷ Col. 9	Col. 3 ÷ Col. 9	Sample Size	Adjusted R-square	Sample Mean (15 minutes)
Part A (1967)									
Source									
Local	+42.409[a]	+42.025[a]	+42.360[a]	+131.03[a]	+142.20[a]	+130.88[a]	486	.3934	32.366
Nonnetwork	+93.490[a]	+100.167[a]	+89.097[a]	+208.63[a]	+223.54[a]	+198.83[a]	486	.8393	44.810
Type									
News	−11.252[a]	−13.254[a]	−1.122	−60.04[a]	−70.73[a]	−5.99	486	.3456	18.379
Public affairs	+4.187[a]	+7.981[a]	+5.385[a]	+55.87[a]	+106.51[a]	+71.86[a]	486	.1854	7.494
Fine arts and drama	+4.288[c]	−.891	+.391	+127.53[a]	−26.50	+11.61	486	.3024	3.362
Mass entertainment	−6.268[b]	−3.053	−14.023[a]	−5.78[b]	−2.82	−12.94[a]	486	.1225	108.366
Feature film	+9.530[a]	+14.404[a]	+3.285	+38.81[a]	+58.66[a]	+13.38	486	.1578	74.554
Vertical diversity	−.301[c]	+.200[b]	+.314[a]	−7.19[a]	+4.79[b]	+7.52[a]	486	.2261	4.178
Part B (1972)									
	No. of Additional Minutes Broadcast by Independents Than by								
Station Type*	Affiliates (UHF only)	Affiliates (VHF only)	VHF Affiliates						(mins.)
All local (entertainment)	+32.33	+134.77[a]	+44.80	+15.4	+64.2[a]	+21.3	408	.1349	209.926
All news	−184.76[a]	−111.56[a]	−198.40[a]	−74.2[a]	−44.8[a]	−79.6[a]	408	.4348	249.150
Local news	−49.18[a]	+10.17	−73.81[a]	−37.9[a]	+7.9	−56.9[a]	408	.3648	129.605
All public affairs	−89.06[a]	−57.71[b]	−71.89[a]	−79.9[a]	−51.8[b]	−64.5[a]	408	.0701	111.461
Local public affairs	+10.37	+6.34	+12.55[c]	−42.9	+26.2	+51.9[c]	531	.0749	24.209
All information	−225.09[a]	−150.90[a]	−207.42[a]	−56.6[a]	−37.9[a]	−52.2[a]	408	.2794	397.708

SOURCE: Part A is adapted from results reported in table 5.3, with basic data sources as stated in table 5.1. Part B is further adapted from table 6.13, with data sources as stated in table 6.12. Statistical significance (two-tailed test) is: a = 1 percent; b = 5 percent; c = 10 percent confidence level.

*UHF only denotes comparison between independent UHF and network UHF; VHF only, between independent VHF and network VHF; VHF affiliates, between independent UHFs and affiliated VHFs.

spot rates, and hence to reward affiliates that clear more network shows, and penalize those that do not.[2] As the National Citizens Committee for Broadcasting states: "It [is] alleged that the networks will manipulate the spot rates in their owned and operated stations . . . to influence national spot rates.[3] Ultimately," NCCB continues, "this has created a situation where instead of a local station being merely an affiliate . . . it has for all practical purposes become a network subsidiary, with the parent company dictating the major financial and programming decisions for its subsidiary operation. . . . Control of advertising rates not only raises anti-competitive questions on their face, it also gives the networks greater financial leverage over local station operators in terms of programming clearances." [4] My own inquiry bears on this contention only indirectly.

The ratio of the margin of O&O rates (above affiliates) to their audiences and ratings, was far greater in 1967 and 1972 than comparable ratios for network affiliates above independents. (See table 10.2.) That is, though audience size is a major determinant of rates (table 5.4), O&Os appear to charge spot rates far above their affiliates', and far higher indeed than their relative audience size and ratings would lead one to expect. All we can tentatively infer here is that any influence of this apparent O&O power on the affiliates' rate levels may help the network clear more programs than local or nonnetwork programmers do.

However, it is by no means clear *how* the networks could influence their affiliates' spot rates. Is there price leadership, or a price umbrella of some sort? Or are the high rates that advertisers pay for prime time on stations that carry more network programming, and less local and nonnetwork programming, mainly reflective of the high audience circulation delivered by popular network programs?

Another factor may be that people simply prefer network affiliates over independents. That is, there may be a kind of brand loyalty at play, such that viewers automatically watch the affiliates on the unverified assumption that the independents' programming is less attractive, though again this should be reflected in audience size. Furthermore, fitting an equation where Program Type = f (number of stations dummy, channel type of station, TV homes, median city income, spot rate), and where the adjusted explained variance ranged from .31 to .41, we found that higher spot rates in 1967 were associated with lower nonnetwork time and higher network program time, whereas higher local and non-

2. See Initial Comments on National Citizens Committee for Broadcasting and National Black Media Coalition on the FCC's Network Inquiry, Docket No. 21049 RM–2749 (submitted by Charles M. Firestone), June 1, 1977, pp. 23–34.

3. Ibid., p. 33.

4. Ibid., p. 34. See also Alan Pearce, *The Economic Consequences of the FCC Prime Time Access Rules* (Washington, D.C.: Federal Communication Commission, September 1973), p. 17.

network time were associated with lower spot rates. However, the likelihood is that the spot rate, and the clearances, were both simultaneously determined, a fact which we had to ignore in our estimations and ask knowledgeable readers to take into account.[5]

How High Are the Relative Returns
Earned by Network-Owned Stations
and of What Public Policy Relevance?

The exceptional profitability of the fifteen network-owned (key) stations doubtless bolsters the average profit margins of the national TV networks as a whole. The key stations' profitability is even further said to enable the networks to raise affiliate compensation rates to induce more program clearances than otherwise, especially in markets with one or two stations.[6]

The implication here is that, in the smaller markets especially, higher compensation rates might keep an affiliate, in borderline cases, from airing a more popular program supplied by another network with which it is also affiliated, by an independent programmer, or by itself. Since available affiliations exceed operating stations in those markets, a station may be tempted to carry the most popular programs regardless of origin, and there are of course no exclusive affiliations today. In principle, therefore, attractive compensation rates can be viewed as a mechanism to induce the compliance of affiliates (at least in markets where they can readily turn elsewere), compliance which was one time mandated by territorial exclusivity and option time.

Although no definitive assessment of this last proposition has been possible here, it is incontestable that the network-owned stations have been

5. On the two-way direction of causation, see chapter 6, notes 7, 8, and the discussion on pages 197–99 and in Appendix 1, pages 428–30. The Network Inquiry Special Staff has actually focused on the dollar amount of station compensation "required" to clear a network program (*Analysis of the Network-Affiliate Relationship* [preliminary], chapter 5, p. 7). However, the higher the value of time slots "adjacent" to network programs (and hence spot rates) an affiliate enjoys, the lower is the compensation it requires to clear any network show (ibid., pp. 7–14). Specifically, an affiliate's "reservation price" for any network program is defined as "that amount which when added to the value of adjacencies just equate the net revenues for a network program with that of its best non-network alternative." Furthermore, "[i]f network compensation is greater than the reservation price, the station will clear the network program (rather than broadcast non-network material)." (ibid., p. 7). Accordingly, higher spot rates would seem to "induce" program clearances indirectly at best, by reducing the minimum level of network compensation affiliates require to clear.

6. See NCCB, Initial Comments, pp. 36–42.

decisively more profitable than network affiliates as a class.[7] This is true, moreover, after taking account of channel type, market size, group and newspaper ties, age of station, and competitors in the market. It is true also when several of these owner attributes are interacted with market size and channel type.

Thus in table 10.2 (section A), the key station's advantage above a VHF affiliate in 1972 was about one-and-a-half to two-and-a-half times as great as the latter's advantage over a VHF independent, both in rates and in revenues ($658 to $266, and $4,979,800 to $2,974,300).[8] Yet the key station's advantage above the VHF affiliate in *audience size* is less than one-fifth as great as the latter's advantage above the VHF independent. That is, for only 18 percent as much advantage in audience (130,000 to 730,000), the key station (O&O) derives about twice the relative monetary benefit.

The evidence on audience ratings (percentages of TV homes in the market tuned in) further underscores the O&O's ability to set its own rates. The fact is that with a ratings advantage above the VHF affiliate of only one-fifteenth of the latter's advantage above VHF independents (.95 to 13.94), the key station still derives twice the monetary advantage.

In other words, the key station's financial benefits are way out of line with its implied impact on audience and ratings, assuming of course that audiences of any given size are of equal value to all advertisers, and assuming further that the relationship of revenue to audience is linear throughout. The validity of the O&O margins in table 10.3 is firmly underscored by the usually high values of the adjusted explained variance in the equations on which the table is based. In five of seven of those equations, including all for 1972, explained variance ranged from .7 to .9, and in the two equations for 1967 ratings, from .4 to .6.

In 1967 I again find the O&O's advantage above an affiliate (as represented by CBS), to be about twice the latter's advantage over an inde-

7. Profitability is inferred from my data on rates, ratings, audience, and estimated station revenues; however, we attempted no *direct* estimation of station *profits* because the individual station income data (derived from the FCC's "grouped" data), with which we had to work, are particularly crude. They permit only uncertain predictions of the profits of stations with postulated characteristics (see R. E. Park, L. L. Johnson, and B. Fishman, *Projecting the Growth of Television Broadcasting: Implications for Spectrum Use* [Santa Monica, Cal.: Rand Corporation, R–1841–FCC, February 1976, pp. 263–87]).

8. Clearly consistent with this evidence of large, significant O&O margins above nonowned affiliates, are suggestive preliminary findings in Wildman, "Vertical Integration in Broadcasting," FTC Symposium on Media Concentration, December 14–15, 1978, Washington, D.C., tables 3–4 and pp. 13–20. In a sample of 105 network affiliates located in the thirty-five largest TV markets (November 1971), *cet. par.*, network-owned stations had significantly higher thirty-second spot rates than network nonowned affiliates. Wildman's reduced form equation specified: (1) each market's TV homes, consumer spendable income and per capita income; and (2) whether a station was (a) located in New York, Los Angeles, or Chicago (where all affiliates were network-owned), (b) was linked to a particular network, (c) competed with an O&O, and (d) with an independent VHF or UHF.

TABLE 10.2

*Margin of Differences in Economic Indicators, for
Network-Owned Stations over Affiliates, and
Network Affiliates over Independents, 1972 and 1967
(6 P.M.-11 P.M.)*

Part A: Coefficients for 1972

	1 Spot Rates (one-time)	2 Audience	3 Estimated Revenue	4 Metro Rating
Network-owned VHF above affiliated VHF stations	$658.30[a]	130,000[a]	$4,979,800[a]	0.95[c]
Network affiliated VHF above independent VHF stations	$265.90[a]	730,000[a]	$2,974,300[a]	13.94[a]

Part B: Coefficients for 1967

	Spot Rates (five-time)	ADI Rating	Metro Rating
Network-owned above affiliated stations	$550.98[a]	5.2[b]	2.2
CBS affiliates above Independent	$273.04[a]	8.2[a]	13.4[a]

SOURCE: Results for 1972 extracted from table 6.5, with data sources as stated in table 10.6 (audience) and table 6.4 (rates). Results for 1967 from coefficients on which the findings in table 5.3 are based, with data for rates and ratings compiled from Standard Rates and Data Service, *Spot Television* (1967 and 1968 issues), and American Research Bureau, Television Day-Part Audience Summary, February/March 1967. Statistical significance (two-tailed test) is: a = 1 percent; b = 5 percent; and c = 10 percent confidence level.

pendent (see table 10.2, section B). Yet the former's advantage in ratings is only two-thirds or one-sixth as great, using ADI and metro ratings respectively, and this confirms the 1972 results.

How the O&Os manage to charge rates relatively so much higher than their audiences and ratings is not entirely clear. Possibly some of this derives from the spread between *ex ante* book rates, and closed transaction prices which reflect special deals. Conceivably such deals may loom larger in the top ten markets (where fourteen of the fifteen O&Os are located), than for network affiliates as a whole, distributed over all two hundred TV markets. Nevertheless, the magnitude of this observed spread hardly seems fully accounted for by such deals. Nor would this explain the advantage as measured by revenues. The results, then, are at the very least consistent with the thesis that O&Os have the economic power to set rates well above the level that their mere audience circulation would warrant.[9] Or with the thesis that something besides net weekly circulation or ADI homes does matter to advertisers.

As to why advertisers do not simply switch to other markets where the deals are better, one conjecture comes to mind. Perhaps the networks provide some service or consideration not due to O&O advertisers (say, special scheduling) and prefer to be compensated for this indirectly, by inflating the apparent price of O&O time. For one thing, this could strengthen the networks' ability to bargain with their affiliates over compensation rates. In striking that bargain the networks would want to play down the revenue they (not the O&Os) had gained from national advertising, and hence the pool of earnings available for the affiliates to share. By the same token, in bargaining with advertisers over O&O time rates, the network would want to play up its apparent O&O time sales revenues, thereby making O&O time appear even more valuable than it really was. We have no direct evidence on this point, but it seems suggestive, and merits exploration by others.[10]

A further question is whether access to 22 percent of U.S. viewers which each network's five key stations potentially provides—including those in the most affluent markets with the highest educational level— operates well beyond the mere number of viewers therein to help explain the O&O's unique value. As noted, the O&Os mainly operate in the ten leading U.S. markets, whereas the network affiliates are dispersed widely throughout all two hundred TV markets. Does this help explain the differences in the relation of rates to audiences, and to ratings, as apparent in columns 1 to 4 of table 10.2?

Unlike network affiliates, the independents are all located in the fifty largest markets. Without adequately normalizing for market size, this could act to narrow the margin of affiliates above independents in regard to audiences, ratings, and rates, and, by the same token, exaggerate the O&O's margin over the affiliates. To ensure against such exaggeration, therefore, I took special pains to account for variations in potential earning power due to market size (see economic equations in table 6.4). Perhaps this was not done sufficiently, especially for differences in wealth inherent in larger markets, regardless of mere numbers of people.

The fact is, in any case, that the top ten markets probably do have more people wanting to advertise there than in smaller markets. It is

9. NCCB urged the FCC to inquire into a number of related questions: "Do the networks use the O&Os to increase their control over [broadcasting]? [D]o the networks insulate their profit margins through the O&Os . . . to manipulate affiliate network compensation rates? Or as Westinghouse, Alan Pearce and others have alleged, do the networks use their O&Os to control alternative program sources particularly with regard to the syndicated market?" (NCCB, Initial Comments, p. 56).

10. This observation was suggested in a private communication from Douglas Ginsburg.

not simply that there are in all markets about the same number of potential advertisers, but that those advertisers are willing to pay more in large than small markets. In fact, many advertisers do not want to advertise in small markets at all because the latter are deemed not to warrant any kind of promotional effort. That is, there may be economies of scale, and a kind of threshold effect, whereby many firms will sell only in markets where the volume warrants setting up distribution, warehousing, and related facilities. (They do not even deliver to some parts of the country.)

Thus we cannot only argue that each potential advertiser is willing to pay more in large markets due to the larger number of people reached, but that there are more advertisers themselves competing for a limited amount of air time. This, too, may lead to higher prices being paid for a given time slot. Finally, although the interaction of various station attributes with TV homes may coincidentally account for some of this nonlinear effect on the largest markets, it is not specifically designed to do so. It will indeed do so only if those attributes are limited to the top (or "nontop") markets exclusively.

The new Network Inquiry will hopefully seek at some point to determine whether, say, the unit pricing of each network's key stations figures in their greater advantage over affiliates than the latter have over independents, in regard both to their respective audiences and ratings (table 10.2). Access to the nation's ten leading markets obviously represents a prize asset. But some other advantage may also be at play here, to gain which O&O spot advertisers are willing to pay rates so much higher than otherwise expected.

In sum, the O&Os' economic strength is indisputable. However, the preceding data alone do not demonstrate conclusively that their market power is sufficient to enable their network parents to control national spot rates generally, or to manipulate affiliate compensation arrangements, so as to induce more prime time program clearances than otherwise. More research and analysis are needed to be sure.

Nor have we yet been able to determine whether the networking operation in some way bolsters O&O profitability (by spreading the national audiences which O&O programs reach far beyond the 22 percent of U.S. population they provide direct access to each network). Or whether, in turn, the exceptional resultant O&O resources and earnings make possible the production and acquisition of sufficiently popular programs to induce the high rate of program clearances achieved. All we really know is that there are separable profits from O&Os and networking, the former being the amount the O&Os would earn if someone else owned the network.[11]

11. The recent Network Inquiry Special Staff Report has also demonstrated, however, that the O&Os clear significantly more network programs than network affiliates as a class (*Analysis of Network-Affiliate Relationship* [preliminary], chapter 6, pp. 8,

Let us suppose that the networks were forced to divest their key stations. The lower bound to which earnings might fall depends on many factors besides those examined here, of course. But it seems proper to consider the affiliates' earnings margin above the independents as a floor toward which any single O&O cut loose from its network parent might fall. At issue, then, is *how much* of the abovementioned margin of a single O&O above a non-O&O affiliate would erode in any hypothetical separation. While cursory review of table 10.2 suggests this erosion might be sizable, it is clear also that the affiliate's position is quite comfortably above the independent's. While considerable, therefore, the losses need not sap overall industry viability.[12] (See table 10.3.) But what, if anything, would be gained?

Do the High Economic Returns of Network-Owned Stations Result in Commensurately More Local, Informational, or Cultural Programs? Of What Policy Relevance Are These Facts?

In 1967, the O&Os carried significantly more news per week than affiliates (90.33/275.69 minutes, or 32.14 percent of the sample mean), more public affairs (35.03/112.41 minutes, or 31.16 percent), and 8.66 percent less mass entertainment (see tables 10.4, 5.3). The O&Os' smaller carriage of nonnetwork programs approaches significance ($t = 1.39$), but their local, feature film, and fine arts were indistinguishable from those of the affiliates. Therefore, the major consequences of divestiture of a single O&O would be a significant (though absolutely small) loss in news, in public affairs, and a significant gain in mass entertainment, at least assuming it does these things because it is an O&O.

Nevertheless, the affiliates themselves carried significantly more news than the independents in 1967 (tables 10.4, 5.3). Therefore, the O&O loss would be less important on that score than otherwise unless, of

---

11, 26, 42–43). Assuming that O&O spot rates reflect the time slots adjacent to network programs, one would expect the O&O's "reservation price" for network programs to be correspondingly lower than their affiliates'. This would then help explain the O&Os' strikingly high clearance rate, reflective also of the networks' greater ability to maximize joint profits with O&Os than with affiliates. (The fact, of course, is that being part of the same overall enterprise, the networks and their O&Os are probably less concerned about the division of total company profits than is true for network affiliates [ibid., chapter 5, pp. 18–21]).

12. Note also, in table 10.3, the four, five, or six to one O&O margin in 1972 over group-owned VHF affiliates (or independents) in rates, audiences, and revenues, but the roughly comparable advantage of group-owned VHF affiliates over nongroup VHF independents.

TABLE 10.3

Mean Value of Economic Variables by Class of Station
in Market with Four or More Stations, 1972

		Mean Value			
Class of Stations	Spot Rate	Audience (homes)	Estimated Revenues	Metro Ratings	Stations
Network-Owned VHF	$2,576.08	5,145,000	$25,010,600	18.0%	14
Nonnetwork Group-Owned					
VHF Affiliate	437.23	981,000	5,251,900	19.7	113
VHF Independent	438.59	1,228,000	5,764,700	5.1	14
Nongroup-Owned					
VHF Affiliate	311.13	800,000	4,365,800	19.9	34
VHF Independent	64.62	154,000	1,556,000	2.7	8

SOURCE: See table 10.2.

course, the networks' news and public affairs production capability were itself severely impaired, or eliminated, by divestiture. Moreover, the O&O loss is of concern just because the affiliates carried significantly less public affairs than the independents in 1967. However, loss of the O&O's significant fine arts contributions (compared to affiliates), but negative non-network carriage, would leave us pretty much where we were before divestiture, namely, with affiliates that carry significantly less local, non-network, fine arts, and feature film than independents. Finally, loss of the O&O's insignificant effect on vertical diversity (–.165 program types nightly, on a mean of 4.2, or –3.96 percent, t = 1.13), simply leaves us with the divergent performance of different classes of affiliates. That is, we refer to the CBS affiliate's significant edge over the independents (7.19 percent), NBC and ABC's negative margin (–4.79 percent, –7.52 percent), and to the insignificant differences between various classes of joint affiliates and the independents (table 5.3).

As for my more refined analysis of FCC data in 1972, the following additional conclusions can be drawn (table 6.13). There would be no significant loss in local service (including entertainment) with O&O divestiture. Nor would the loss in news and public affairs be significant, again compared to the affiliates.

One of my own earlier conclusions is therefore largely confirmed for 1972: there would be no added deterioration in localism when an O&O becomes a nonowned affiliate. Nor would there be any major loss in news or local news with divestiture. Indeed, local public affairs would actually show a slight improvement in that the significant negative margin of an O&O relative to an affiliate would now disappear, while the insignifi-

TABLE 10.4
Network Owner Margin over Nonowned Affiliates, in Prime Time
Devoted to Major Program Categories, 1967 and 1972

Part A (1967)

	Additional 15-Minute Periods Broadcast by Network-Owned Stations than by Affiliates	Percentage of Sample Mean (PCDV)	Sample Size	Adjusted R-Square	Sample Mean (15 minutes)
Source:					
Local	3.479	10.75	486	.393	32.366
Nonnetwork	−5.116	−11.42	486	.839	44.810
Type:					
News	6.022[a]	32.14[a]	486	.346	18.379
Public affairs	2.335[c]	31.16[c]	486	.185	7.494
Fine arts/drama	.360	10.70	486	.302	3.362
Mass entertainment	−9.388[b]	−8.66[b]	486	.122	108.366
Feature film	2.951	12.02	486	.158	74.554
Vertical diversity	−.165	−3.96	486	.226	4.178

Part B (1972)

	Additional Minutes Broadcast by Network-Owned Stations than by Affiliates				(minutes)
All local (including entertainment)	−46.05	−21.9	408	.134	209.926
All news	−12.82	−5.1	408	.434	249.150
Local news	.49	.4	408	.364	129.605
All public affairs	−11.87	−10.7	408	.070	111.461
Local public affairs	−20.83[c]	−86.0[c]	408	.074	24.209
All information	−24.49	−13.7	408	.279	397.708

SOURCE: Results for 1967 extracted from coefficients on which findings in table 5.3 are based, with data sources as stated in table 10.2. Results for 1972 extracted from table 6.13, with basic data sources as reported in table 6.12. Statistical significance (two-tailed test): a = 1 percent; b = 5 percent; and c = 10 percent confidence level. See notation in table 6.13.

cant margin of independents over affiliates would remain. In sum, our evidence questions whether overall program composition need have changed very much in the years studied, *cet. par.*, had a station switched from O&O status to network affiliate.[13]

13. What my data base has not enabled me to consider is the O&O's positive contribution to network programming, especially to news documentaries and public affairs generally. Nor do I reject the possible consequences for greater program quality of the more abundant resources the O&Os can mount for programming. The loss or impairment of such capabilities may be important qualitatively, though not traceable in the evidence reported above.

The Performance of Independent Stations and Its Implications for a Viable Fourth Commercial Network

The lack of a fourth network may have acted to strengthen the present networks' leverage to bargain on affiliate compensation in those markets with more than three stations operating, and to give these networks the resources to pay premium compensation in markets with only one or two stations.[14] Therefore, any barrier to the possible entry of a fourth national network deserves special and continuing attention in the new Network Inquiry. This is particularly true in view of both the affiliates' significantly higher profitability than that of seemingly comparable independents (holding constant channel type, market size, competitors, age, etc.), and of the independents' frequently marginal economic status and higher relative program costs than the network affiliates'. Both facts underscore the incentives of independents to affiliate with some network entity, and the private and public consequences of their being able to do so.

As is well known, the TV allocation table is itself a major impediment to new network entry. According to R. E. Park, there are simply "too few" markets with four or more VHFs to enable a fourth network entrant to reach the needed 90 percent of TV homes to compete with existing networks on an equal footing.[15] Of further interest also is that no fewer than five of Park's ten configurations for a hypothetical fourth network include existing independents. (These options exclude his proposed hook-ups of cable, pay cable, combined broadcast/cable, or satellite systems, and of affiliates divested from the three networks today.)[16]

There is therefore little question that a systematic comparison of independents and affiliates can help throw at least limited light on the kind of economic and programming performance to be expected from a successful fourth network entrant. Without basing any definitive prediction on my several equations (in tables 5.3, 6.4 to 6.8, 6.12, 6.13), it does seem reasonable to expect a new fourth network to perform somewhere between existing network affiliates and existing independents.[17]

14. The reasons that these premiums will be paid are noted earlier in note 5 and in chapter 9, at pages 290–93.

15. See R. E. Park, *New Television Networks* (Santa Monica, Calif.: Rand Corporation, December 1973) at pp. 12–14. Note further that a fourth television network, using existing independent stations plus new UHFs, might be viable if: (a) it could reach all 61,000,000 TV households, and (b) 65 percent of prime viewers tune in, and if we make certain additional assumptions regarding (c) the size of its UHF affiliates' competitive handicap against VHFs, and (d) whether or not short-spaced VHFs are also utilized. Ibid., pp. 16–18. See also discussion in chapter 9, pp. 295–96.

16. Ibid., pp. 12–30.

17. In wresting a place for itself over time, a hypothetical new network entrant's price and programming adjustments may be broadly similar to the ABC network's.

For such reasons it makes sense to compare independents and affiliates in light of my analysis of market data for 1967 and 1972.

An Initial Assessment for 1967

How do the independents perform relative to the regulatory goals of localism and diversity? Relative to the further stated FCC commitment to electorate-informing news, public affairs, and general information? However much air time independents devote to such programming, do they have adequate resources to sustain program quality, compared, at least, to the resources of the nation's network affiliates? On the other hand, is there evidence that any of the affiliates' greater economic capabilities are in fact used for more (relatively less profitable) localism? Station vertical diversity? Informational programming?

Table 10.1 extracts some highly relevant results from a fuller tabulation of PCDVs in table 5.3. These measures quite clearly give high marks to independents for the amount of their local, nonnetwork, public affairs, fine arts and drama programs, compared, for instance, to that of CBS affiliates.[18] This may at least partly help explain the independents' lower relative profitability. But the analysis also reveals that the independents air significantly more feature film. Only in regard to news broadcasts and vertical diversity do they fall significantly behind CBS affiliates.

The economic resources out of which the above programming margins could be funded in 1967 are broadly suggested in table 10.5, wherein, quite clearly, the independent station's ratings and spot rates are significantly lower than those for comparable network affiliates. The sole exception (see table 5.4), is the significantly higher spot rates independents charge for a given delivered (not potential) audience when this is included in the equation, possibly reflective of the networks' competitive superiority therein. This result clearly indicates that cost to the advertiser in reaching 1,000 viewers on an independent station is higher than on a network affiliate.

The most one can say for 1967, then, is that the independents had far less economic wherewithal than the affiliates to infuse into their programming, but in fact carried significantly more of most of the less remunerative program types: local, all nonnetwork, public affairs, fine arts, and drama.[19] (See table 10.1.)

18. The comparison is made to CBS affiliates for convenience only. Any other network or combined network affiliates could have been used. Actually the CBS affiliates' spot rates were highest of all networks in the data studied for 1967.

19. The quality of such programs is of course not judged here and may have been impaired by the independents' more limited resources. I note also that the independents relied more heavily than the affiliates on routine use of feature film; and that they carried significantly less news, whereas their vertical diversity fell short of the CBS affiliates', while exceeding NBC's and ABC's.

TABLE 10.5

Independent Station Margins over Network Affiliates in Major Economic Indicators, 1967 and 1972

Part A (1967) (6 P.M.-11 P.M.)

	1	2	3	4	5	6	7	8	9
	Additional Ratings Points, Dollars, or TV Viewers for Independents Compared with			First Three Columns as Percentage of Sample Mean (PCDVs)			Sample Size	Adjusted R-Square	Sample Mean
	CBS Affiliates	NBC Affiliates	ABC Affiliates	Col. 1 ÷ Col. 9	Col. 2 ÷ Col. 9	Col. 3 ÷ Col. 9			
ADI ratings (%)	−8.243[a]	−7.050[a]	−3.432[c]	−39.14[a]	−33.47[a]	−16.69[c]	445	.4321	21.062
Metro ratings (%)	−13.443[a]	−12.770[a]	−9.259[a]	−63.40[a]	−60.26[a]	−43.67[a]	408	.6362	21.203
20-second 1-time rates ($)	−273.04[a]	−277.85[a]	−249.65[a]	−109.45[a]	−111.38[a]	−100.08[a]	452	.7694	$249.46
Alternate Specifications									
One-time spot rates ($) model #1	−233.50[a]	−228.30[a]	−207.70[a]	−89.58[a]	−87.57[a]	−79.68[a]	426	.8170	$260.70
One-time spot rates* ($) model #2	−166.60[a]	−154.80[a]	−160.50[a]	−72.92[a]	−67.76[a]	−70.25[a]	296	.6842	$228.50
Five-time spot rates ($)	−188.10[a]	−179.90[a]	−177.60[a]	−97.39[a]	−95.14[a]	−93.95[a]	296	.7338	$189.00

Part B (1972) (6 P.M.-11 P.M.)

	A	B	C	4	5	6	7	8	9
30-second 1-time rates (unit = $10s)	−22.02[a]	−19.38[a]	−30.03[a]	−83.2[a]	−73.3[a]	−113.7[a]	541	.9365	$ 26.453
Audience (millions of viewers)	−.55[a]	−.67[a]	−.76[a]	−95.6[a]	−115.5[a]	−131.0[a]	667	.9650	.5786
Station revenue (unit = $10,000)	−196.80[a]	−143.12[a]	−171.71[a]	−56.3[a]	−40.9[a]	−49.1[a]	514	.9422	$349.792
Metro rating (%)	−11.52[a]	−18.13[a]	−18.82[a]	−69.1[a]	−108.7[a]	−112.8[a]	667	.7948	16.678

SOURCE: For 1967, results extracted from table 5.3 with basic data sources as indicated in table 10.2; for 1972, sources as stated in table 10.7 with estimated station revenues derived from (a) FCC, Television Financial Report for 1972, and (b) ARB's estimates of each station's share of metropolitan area viewing for the designated survey period. The latter source is also cited in table 10.7. Statistical significance (two-tailed test) is: a = 1 percent; b = 5 percent; and c = 10 percent confidence level. See notation in table 6.13. A = independents margin over affiliates for UHF stations only; B = independents margin over affiliates for VHF stations only; C = independent UHFs margin over VHF affiliates (unrestricted).
*Model #2 data include only those stations for which both five-time and one-time rates are available.

It is hardly a surprise that independents carry more nonnetwork programming than affiliates do, but as for the other program categories, one or more of several factors could be at play. First, the independents may be more public-spirited than network affiliates as a class. But more likely, with less popular programming than the latter, independent stations simply enjoy less advertiser demand for their time, and hence risk the loss of less time sales revenue when carrying local, cultural, or informational shows. Somewhere in between these first two factors is a third, namely, that facing lower opportunity costs for their air time, the independents can better afford to devote certain periods to local public affairs and news programs which may generate valuable good-will among influential minorities and opinion leaders in the community.[20]

Finally, the independents may simply be less successful as broadcasters than affiliates whose network parents bear many of their entrepreneurial risks. In particular, the independents may be less able than the affiliates to reconcile public service and diversity with commercial success.

There is in any case no question about the relative emphasis in the program composition of independent and affiliated stations generally, granted that there may be offsetting (unmeasurable) quality differences.

Toward a More Refined Audit for 1972

My more refined analysis of 1972 data (compiled from different sources), confirms, qualifies and elaborates on this initial assessment. On the one hand, table 10.1 once more reveals significantly less news (and, with one exception, less local news) on independents than affiliates, regardless of channel type. There is some evidence, also, of more local programming on independents, as expected, though the results are now less clear-cut; and some weakly significant (or near significant) evidence also of more local public affairs. But unlike 1967, there now are significantly fewer public affairs programs generally (including those from nonlocal sources). Finally, I find significantly less "all information" on the independents, a category not examined in 1967.

In sum, though the data and the program categories examined in table 10.1 differ for the two years studied, with a few exceptions the results are at least broadly similar. In both years, the independents carried relatively more local service, but less of all news (and in 1972, of local news). As for public affairs, the independents' strength appears to lay with local rather than nonlocal sources (see tables 10.1, 6.13). "More," however, is not necessarily better, and, while cheaper programs need not be inferior,

20. These groups may include public and cultural leaders' attention to whose activities on local television dignifies and publicizes them. In return, these leaders may favor the independent station with information for news items on a preferred basis, or agree to testify in comparative renewal contests, and so on.

barring any reliable quality index one should probably qualify the above findings by the limited economic resources of independent stations (see tables 10.5, 6.5).

Short of forming a fourth network, then, additional independents can be expected to make definite contributions to local and information programming, and possibly to local public affairs in particular. They will apparently contribute also to fine arts and drama. As already mentioned, their greater relative contribution to certain less remunerative program categories is doubtless due in part to the independents' lower opportunity costs in using their air time this way.[21] Still another factor may be that nationally distributed network shows, whether informational or entertainment, are by definition not produced *locally*, whereas independent stations, without preferred access to the national network feed, choose instead between local origination and syndicated material.

Secondly, any future fourth national television network may be expected to perform somewhere between the present affiliates and present independents, with earnings short of the former's, and programming closer than theirs to the latter's.

Third, since we will always presumably have some independents before they are integrated into a national network, the above pattern may give us a general feel for the composition of their continued future contribution.

Fourth, as network affiliates are freed from alleged network restraints, they too may perform less like present affiliates, and more like present independents, unless, of course, acceptance of network programming even then were to maximize joint profits. It seems fair to say, however, that joint profit maximization is more likely to occur with the network practices than without them, their development and continued existence being grounded on that very goal.

A fifth and last point relates to ABC's experience in equalizing its economic position vis-à-vis CBS and NBC over time. Through the use of counterprogramming ABC is known to have differentiated its offerings from those of its rivals over the entire network schedule. If that experience throws any light on the consequences of a fourth network's likely future attempt to establish itself nationally, it is that a more diversified program mix will result.[22]

21. Note also that cheaper programs on independent stations may literally have to be targeted on distinct audiences because cheaper programs could not compete with costlier programs aimed at the same audience.

22. A related factor derives from table 9.3 (and table 3.11), where we clearly see that, though ABC's entertainment audiences were far larger than its informational ones in 1974, that network also had far less to lose than CBS or NBC in altering its mix of information and entertainment shows (at the margin). This simply follows from ABC's then lower entertainment ratings, shares, and audience size. Since then ABC has emerged as a fully competitive equal to its two rivals. However, during the adjustment period two developments are worth noting. First, the percentage of prime-time shows ABC devoted to information and documentaries, in

Conclusion

So much, then, for an exposition of network structure, power, and performance. Within this framework I turn finally to the objectives and consequences of "prime time access," with passing attention also to certain alternatives to this policy. In making the facts most germane to my discussion there more explicit, a brief summation of findings to this point is now in order.

In chapter 9 I examined the alleged bases of network power and then, in chapter 10, its consequences for station profitability and program composition generally. Of special import have been the public's dual concerns with who gets what share of industry profits, and what is done with it in programming terms. Additional attention has also gone to the comparative performance of independent stations and affiliates in both economic and programming dimensions.

The relative economic strength of all three industry components—key stations, affiliates, and independents—was delineated. The comparative contribution of each component to vertical diversity and informational, local, or cultural programming was less clear-cut. Nonetheless, I was able to comment in a general way on the likely consequences for economic viability and program composition of any proposal either to divest the networks of their key stations or to encourage the entry of new independent stations, prior to the emergence of a fourth national TV network.

In the discussion of FCC requirements for prime-time access in chapter 11, the most pertinent evidence may well be my (albeit rough) comparative assessment of independent and affiliate performance. At the least, prime-time access purports to free the affiliates from preponderant reliance on their network parents for prime-time program service and advertiser income. Of course, even if fully realized, such a goal will by no means eliminate important differences between affiliate and independent station economics and programming. Nevertheless, the direction of change due to the greater prime-time access may be at least tentatively suggested.

---

particular, rose far more rapidly than that of CBS or NBC, 1967–74. Second, ABC was the sole network which supported the Prime-Time Access Rule in the 1970s, and may well have benefited from its adoption afterward. At least displacement of *its* entertainment programs by those of nonnetwork program suppliers hurt it relatively less than the comparable displacement of CBS and NBC's more popular shows necessarily hurt them. (Related issues are reviewed in chapter 11.)

Appendix 10A. Viability of Informational Programming

In this appendix I shall argue that the fact that stations with higher revenues and income are better able than those less affluent to schedule a greater number of relatively less profitable informational programs, does not mean that all such programming is unprofitable absolutely. The fact is that, by facilitating access to the kind of educated higher-income viewers who make likely consumers of the advertised products, stations that carry more information appear to command premium rates from advertisers, at the margin at least.

In table 10.6, for instance, using the FCC's own data for 1972, I regressed spot rates on the percentage of time devoted to major program categories, estimating informational impact conditional first upon audience size, and then upon education. This permitted me to consider possible differences in advertiser interest in reaching better educated audiences as between large and small markets.

Using the equations in table 10.6, I next derived the impact estimates in tests 1–3 of table 10.7, at the mean of the weighting variables (audience size and proportion of viewers with a college education). Those results reveal that rates do indeed rise at the margin, when the percentage of total prime time devoted to information rises at the expense of entertainment. The best support for this proposition is reported in table 10.7, test 2, where I not only control for college education, but also estimate informational impact conditional upon audience size. (See table 10.6, equation 2.) Interaction of information with education instead actually yields poorer results in test 3 (derived from equation 3), where a t-value of 1.56 just falls short of 10 percent significance. The upshot, then, is additional evidence, with a better variable specification, that advertisers place a value on informational programming, at the margin at least, for the reasons just stated.[23]

My principal task in tables 10.6 and 10.7 was to estimate the impact of a relative increase of informational programming on level spot rates. We conclude from both tables that this additional information generally impacts positively, and significantly, on spot rates, but that only when local news is increased at the expense of nonlocal news, does news have similar effects. As for public affairs, only an increase in nonlocal shows

---

23. In tests 4–7 (table 10.7), the results are more mixed when local news and local public affairs are increased, assuming comparable increases in all news and all public affairs. Thus spot rates are significantly higher for stations devoting more of their prime time to local news, at the expense of nonnews programming (movies, sports, public affairs, and so on). See table 10.7, test 4. However, this is not true for stations carrying more nonlocal public affairs at the expense of nonpublic affairs (test 7).

TABLE 10.6

Regression Equations for 30-Second Spot Rates Paid for Time on Stations with Varying Amounts of Informational Programming, 1972
(6 P.M.-11 P.M.)

Dep. Var.	Y-Intercept	Audience Delivered	Percentage of Total Program Time Devoted to					% Population in Market with 4 Years College	Audience × % Information Time	College % × % Information Time
			News	Local News	Public Affairs	Local Public Affairs	All Information			
EQ. 1 *30-Second 1-Time Rate* N = 509 R̄² = .9063 mean = $27.613 (× $10)	B −4.231	40.708	n.i.	n.i.	n.i.	n.i.	16.623	n.i.	10.368	n.i.
	t −1.830	15.040					1.490		1.030	
	sig. .067	0.000					.137		.303	
EQ. 2 *30-Second 1-Time Rate* N = 453 R̄² = .9063 mean = $29.808 (× $10)	B −9.862	41.686	n.i.	n.i.	n.i.	n.i.	16.945	.424	7.156	n.i.
	t −2.810	14.440					.400	2.050	10.700	
	sig. .005	0.000					.163	.041	.503	
EQ. 3 *30-Second 1-Time Rate* N = 453 R̄² = .9071 mean = $29.808 (× $10)	B 5.482	43.525	n.i.	n.i.	n.i.	n.i.	−58.996	−.912	n.i.	6.494
	t .670	63.790					−1.540	−1.400		2.160
	sig. .503	.000					.163	.163		.031
EQ. 4 *30-Second 1-Time Rate* N = 509 R̄² = .9068 mean = $27.613 (× $10)	B −3.812	43.111	−.399	.814	.452	.046	n.i.	n.i.	n.i.	n.i.
	t −1.910	63.200	−1.550	2.120	2.260	.090				
	sig. .057	.000	.122	.034	.024	.925				
EQ. 5 *30-Second 1-Time Rate* N = 453 R̄² = .9067 mean = $29.808 (× $10)	B −8.833	43.316	−.401	.751	.485	−.003	n.i.	.403	n.i.	n.i.
	t −2.740	59.440	−1.410	1.780	2.180	−.010		1.940		
	sig. .006	.000	.158	.075	.030	.996		.053		

SOURCE: Our data sources were as follows. For "audience delivered," we multiplied the American Research Bureau's published station ADI ratings by standard data on TV homes for comparable markets. See ARB, *Television Day–Part Audience Summary*, November 1972; also, *Broadcasting Yearbook–1973*, and *Television Factbook No. 43*, 1973-74. For percent of market population with four or more years of college education, we used U.S. Bureau of the Census, Census of Population for 1970. All data for estimated program time by program type, derived from the FCC's First Annual Programming Report for All Commercial Television Stations, 1973 (published October 8, 1974). All rates data derived from Standard Rates and Data Service, *Spot Television Rates and Data*, for selected issues during 1972 and 1973. Rates used were those in effect for the longest period during 1972.

n.i. = not included in equation for design purposes.

t = t-value; B = regression coefficient.

TABLE 10.7

*The Impact of Selected Informational Program Categories on
TV Station Spot Rates, 1972 (6 P.M.-11 P.M.)*

A Summary of Results

1	2	3		4	5
Test Number	Equation Number	Interactive Test		Results	Levels of Audience or Education at which Column 3 Coefficients were Interacted
1	1	+1% point in % program time devoted to information	B % t	.236 .85 2.26	at mean audience = .668 (× 1,000,000)
2	2	+1% point in % program time devoted to information	B % t	.221 .74 1.94	at mean audience = .722 (× 1,000,000)
3	3	+1% point in % program time devoted to information	B % t	.207 .70 1.56	at mean % population with 4 or more years college = 12.275
4	4	+1% point local news (nonlocal news held constant)	B % t	.415 1.50 1.85	no interaction
5	4	+1% local public affairs (nonlocal public affairs held constant)	B % t	.498 1.80 1.07	no interaction
6	5	+1% local news not coming from nonlocal news	B % t	.350 1.17 1.43	no interaction
7	5	+1% local public affairs not coming from nonlocal public affairs	B % t	.482 1.62 .96	no interaction

SOURCE: Results in column 4 were derived from table 10.6 equations as itemized in column 2. Data sources as stated in table 10.6.

NOTATION: B = regression coefficient; % = unit change in dependent variable due to designated change in dependent variable as percent of sample mean (PCDV); t = t-value.

at the expense of nonpublic affairs programs will have significant effects on rates.[24]

24. These significant impacts on spot rates of more time devoted to local news and local public affairs assume constancy of all news and all public affairs. Therefore any increases in such local programming must come from less such nonlocal programs. Accordingly, more local news (at the expense of nonlocal news), does impact significantly on spot rates, whereas more local public affairs (at the expense of nonlocal) does not. By the same token, more nonlocal news (read off the all news coefficients with local news in the equation) does not impact significantly on spot rates, whereas more nonlocal public affairs does so impact under comparable assumptions (see equations 4–5 in table 10.6).

There is also other evidence that informational programming may not be as unprofitable as often asserted. Thus Robert Crandall has argued that the TV networks do not lose money on their news and public affairs once program costs are taken into account.[25] It is indeed widely assumed that network affiliates as a class make as much as 40 to 60 percent of their revenue from advertising on their local news shows.[26] Both local news and local public affairs shows are usually very low-cost, so that the revenues earned will add relatively more to net income than were those program costs the same as costs for comparable network programs, or for network entertainment shows more generally.

Some readers may object that the causation runs the other way: profitable stations command higher spot rates and then respond with more informational programming to satisfy the FCC. Informational programs would then be the result, not the cause, of higher rates. Otherwise, it is asked, why would the stations not simply continue to raise the proportion of time devoted to information until any rate premium declined to zero?

In considering this issue, I must refer to table 6.13, where I estimated the impacts on local and informational programming of postulated increments in station revenue levels. Thus another $500,000 in revenue is associated with 4.3, 3.8, and 2.9 minutes more information weekly, for stations earning $1 million, $4 million, and $10 million, respectively. This means that the additional information declines as a percent of the sample mean from 1.1 percent, to .96 percent, to .73 percent. That is, the analysis of revenue data alone, even without reference to program costs, provides at most qualified support for the thesis that profitable stations command higher rates and then carry informational programs to satisfy the FCC. At this stage perhaps the most we can say is that neither inference is entirely rejected—advertisers may indeed pay premium rates to reach informational viewers, but profitable stations may also put on extra informational service.

That is, the causation goes both ways. Stations may respond to price and profits, in the face of FCC's expectations about informational programming, but advertisers may *also* pay more to reach informational audiences as attractive customers for the products they advertise. Possible distortions due to simultaneity bias have not been analyzed, but should not be exaggerated in this instance. (See Appendix I, pages 428–30.)

Nevertheless, it still seems fallacious to argue that stations will continue to raise the proportion of air time they devote to information until any rate premium declines to zero. Bear in mind first that advertisers aim to maximize audience adjusted for quality, that is, for its potential responsiveness to advertised products. However, it is inconceivable that

25. Robert Crandall, "Regulation of Television Broadcasting," *Regulation* (January/February 1978), 31–39.
26. *Broadcasting* (August 28, 1978), 38.

informational programming, with its relatively smaller absolute audiences, will be added indefinitely at the expense of entertainment programs (given the fixed amount of air time). True, for any thousand viewers, *cet. par.*, a marginal increment of informational service may raise spot rates. However, the far greater magnitude of the entertainment audiences (and associated revenues) will obviously swamp such informational effects. At most, therefore, our informational coefficients are valid only within a narrowly circumscribed "threshold of reasonableness." [27]

Furthermore, the ultimate sales effectiveness of any particular advertising campaign is a closely guarded secret. Therefore, the possibly greater value to advertisers of access to informational audiences for selected programs (reflected in higher spot rates), may simply not be known by all stations. The larger, better established, and more profitable stations may be better able to hire marketing consultants to make their own estimates of sales effectiveness, and hence to bargain more effectively than the smaller stations which lack this information. The point, however, is that the premium rate could well be a profit-maximizing rate once sales effectiveness relative to the informational viewer is fully taken into account. Supportive of this point in table 10.6 are my significant positive coefficients for college education in equations 2, 3, 5, and the reduced significance and magnitude of informational impact in the presence of the college variable in those equations.

Note next that my estimates are of informational impact on marginal revenue not marginal profit, given that we do not know the cost effects of any increased informational proportion. Nor does the linear equation consider diminishing returns to successive increments of the informational proportion, or changes in the station's program mix. For these reasons, too, it by no means follows from the significant positive informational impact on spot rates, that one should expect a licensee to continue to raise his informational proportion indefinitely.

Finally, my data for station rates are mean prime rates, only the crudest composite of the host of specific per-program rates which make it up. If I could have analyzed all rates (for interprogram *and* intraprogram adjacencies), and all related audiences, for informational (and entertainment) programs, the premium the advertiser appears to pay in his average station spot rate might well be consistent with a profit-maximizing position. But lacking these per-program rates, the data could not yield that kind of determination directly.

In sum, the results appear to be consistent with other recent evidence that informational programming is remunerative in general, given

27. Under conditions of constrained profit maximization, as here, with fixed air time one would expect the marginal impacts on revenue and hence rates of additional program time devoted to each program type to be equal, *cet. par.*, assuming comparable programs costs. Even if costs are not the same, moreover, we would still expect significant positive impacts for all program types.

the kind of audience to which it facilitates access. However, this in no way qualifies the greater *relative* profitability of entertainment programs as a whole, and the strong incentives of licensees therefore to maximize their circulation and net income by scheduling them. Nor do my findings distinguish informational types which may in fact be unprofitable, absolutely. Nor, finally, do the findings refute the further hypothesis that stations with higher revenues and income are better able than those less affluent to schedule more of the relatively less profitable informational programs (as apparent in table 6.13).

Chapter 11

Objectives versus Consequences in Prime-Time Access

Introduction

AT THE OUTSET of chapter 9, mention was made of the pivotal importance FCC has for many years given prime-time access to the network system by nonnetwork program suppliers and advertisers. We saw there that the network affiliates' preponderant airing of evening network shows was better explained by the program cost savings they thereby enjoy, and possible leverage the networks derive in the largest markets, where stations exceed networks, than by the value of adjacent time slots to advertisers. Prime-time access is a much debated mechanism through which regulators have purported to delimit, and eventually pare back, the blanketing by networks of massive nighttime television audiences. But can such an approach succeed and, if so, with what economic consequences and costs in foregone program resources and quality?

The current Prime-Time Access Rule has four ostensible objectives: to reduce network dominance over TV program decisions; to increase market opportunities for creative new talent which the networks are presumed to exclude and, concomitantly, to reestablish local control of those program decisions; and finally, to increase the supply of first-run syndicated programming.

By now the FCC's stated commitment to each of these goals should be clear. But what do the proponents of prime-time access hope to achieve through this policy? First, the three-network oligopoly and its alleged power to induce a pervasive airing of programs over its many affiliates are said to have operated to the competitive disadvantage of nonnetwork program suppliers or advertisers seeking to deal directly

with these affiliates. The upshot has been deemed a heightened economic disparity between network affiliates and independents. Safeguards
of prime-time access are expected by their advocates to help rectify
such trends.

Meanwhile, a small number of major decision makers determine
prime-time program composition and scheduling today. This is particularly true for local news, public affairs, documentaries, and other informational and educational programming.

On all three counts the FCC has looked to prime-time access to enhance program diversity, localism, first-run syndication, and generally to
reduce "network dominance." Finally, the future emergence of a few
major access time brokers, and of growing public interest group pressures,
could conceivably produce new network-type entities which might help
diversify programming in their own right. ABC's apparent success, as
third network entrant, in improving its national position through a strategy of counterprogramming is at least mildly suggestive in that regard.
So, too, as noted in the previous chapter, is that network's sole support
of prime-time access.

A Chronology of the Prime-Time Access Rule

In 1970 an initial version of the Prime-Time Access Rule (PTAR–I)[1]
prohibited network affiliates in the top fifty markets from carrying more
than three hours of network programs during prime time nightly.[2] The
goal was to make available an hour of top-rated evening time for competition among present and potential nonnetwork program sources for
further diversity.[3] This was essentially to open up time outside the
network funnel for nonnetwork suppliers of first-run syndicated programs. Nor, as also in today's rule, could the time cleared of network
programs be filled with off-network reruns, or feature films shown in
the market during the previous two years.[4] Nevertheless, exemptions
were made for network news coverage and political broadcasts.[5] Of
special note, finally, this initial version did not clear any particular hour
of network and off-network (reruns) and feature films, was reduced to
P.M., Eastern Standard and Pacific Time, and 6–7 P.M., Central and
Mountain Time.

1. See Report and Order in FCC Docket No. 12782, May 1970, cited in Report
and Order in FCC Docket No. 19622, January 23, 1974. References in this chapter
are to the later document (1974).
2. Ibid., par. 1; sec. 73.658(k).
3. Ibid., par. 17.
4. Ibid., pars. 1, 21.
5. Ibid., pars. 1, 23.

The second version of the rule (PTAR–II), effective September 1, 1974, instituted several changes. The access period now to be "cleared" of network and off-network (reruns) and feature films, was reduced to six half-hour periods between 7:30 and 8:00 P.M., Eastern and Pacific Time, and 6:30 to 7:00 P.M., Central and Mountain Time, Monday through Saturday only. The networks regained all of Sunday, plus six of the weekly half-hours from which they had initially been excluded. Exemptions were made where networks offered documentaries, public affairs, news specials, and now, children's programs. (Actually, the waivers on these counts granted under the initial rule [PTAR–I] were now largely codified.) Furthermore, the precise access period was specified, unlike the earlier general requirement.

Today's version, PTAR–III, has returned largely to the original version. Again, it provides that no network-owned or affiliated station in the fifty largest markets may carry more than three hours of network or off-network programs (network reruns), including movies previously shown on a network, during the four hours of prime time. In addition, it singles out certain program types which are not to be counted toward this three-hour limitation, exemptions which largely codify program types granted waivers under the initial rule in 1970. Such exemptions include: (1) network or off-network shows designed for children, public affairs, or documentary programs; (2) special news programs dealing with fast-breaking news events, or on-the-spot coverage of news events; (3) political broadcasts by legally qualified candidates for public office; (4) regular half-hour network news programs when immediately adjacent to a full hour of locally produced news or public affairs; (5) sports runovers, where a network telecast was reasonably scheduled to conclude before the scheduled nonnetwork program in prime time; (6) simultaneous sports or other live broadcasts where time zone differences were involved.[6]

Unlike PTAR–II, PTAR–III returns to the initial *general* requirements for access time, leaving to the network the specific hours actually to be cleared. Finally, the networks are once more to be excluded from a full hour of prime time daily (not a half hour), Sunday included.

Today, then, not every network affiliate in the top fifty markets need have the same access period; the access period could be staggered, though as a practical matter it is not.

The interim shift in PTAR–II reflected some concern over the kind of programming which started to replace network entertainment as well as the loss of network specials, documentaries, and children's programs. However, the final version (PTAR–III) assumes that a compromise could better be struck through the policy on exemptions than, as under

6. FCC, Second Report and Order in Docket No. 19622 (Prime-Time Access), January 17, 1975, pars. 1–2, 14–18.

PTAR–II, by reducing by half the amount of time from which the networks would be excluded, Monday through Saturday, or by opening up Sunday to them again.

Objectives of Prime-Time Access

The FCC has been criticized for the basic contradiction in its latest formulation (PTAR–III). On one hand, the commission purports to provide licensees with enough nonnetwork programs to insure them "more than a nominal choice of material," freeing them to broadcast programs they deem "most responsive to the needs, interests, and tastes of their communities."[7] However, the commission denied intending to "smooth the path for existing syndicators or [for] . . . any particular type of programs. . . ." "[T]he types and cost levels of programs which will develop," it observed, "must be the result of competition which will develop."[8]

On the other hand, the FCC evidenced concern over the rising criticism of low-cost, low-quality access programs after 1971. As a partial response, it took the aforementioned steps to insure the continued availability of preferred network programs types (children's, public affairs, documentaries) during the access period too.[9]

Although the rule has by no means yet "caused the wasteland to breed lilacs,"[10] it does appear an admittedly clumsy attempt to reconcile the potential conflict between quality and public service on one hand, and sources diversity (or maximum opportunities for programmer entry), on the other.[11] This is true at least insofar as: (1) the threat of mandatory exclusion from access time induces the networks to put on more informational programs to retain their own access, and to use their abundant resources therein; (2) the modified rule acts to widen the affiliates' choice from one among nonnetwork access programs alone, to one which also includes special network originations. The rule implies, then, that sources diversity per se is good (for social and political reasons), almost regardless of effects on quality and types diversity. However, any greater resultant diversity from a consumer viewpoint is also good, though this may take time to emerge. Finally, the Rule implies that the networks'

7. Ibid., par. 14.
8. Ibid.
9. Ibid., pars. 28–39.
10. Ibid., Dissenting Statement of Commissioner Glen O. Robinson, p. 4.
11. Presumably the main thing not fully reconciled is allowing networks or stations to provide those entertainment programs preferred by the largest audience groups—which are not news, public affairs, or the like.

unique national capabilities in providing special programs of widely recognized merit can and should be retained, even spurred.[12] A more balanced program mix would thereby hopefully result.

The Consequences of Prime-Time Access

The questions of major concern appear to be these: in reducing network dominance over prime-time access, will the access rule seriously reduce economic efficiency and program resources by proliferating the number of independent transactions between program suppliers and station owners? That is, will there be smaller residual total net revenues due to the higher transactions costs? Or will this be more than offset by the much larger share of revenues retained by licensees from access than from network shows?

Will the public interest groups in any case meet less resistance from station owners than where they must induce them to preempt a lucrative network entertainment show? That is, with lower opportunity costs, will local licensees have much less to lose in responding to the public groups, and therefore greater incentives to carry the programming these groups want? Will the access entertainment itself diversify the network mix—insofar as it excludes new network shows or network reruns? On the other hand, are significant welfare losses also incurred by viewers who would have preferred the network entertainment and now switch to the independents, or to access shows they do not like as well? Or, unless total viewing declines (doubtful), can we really presume that welfare *is* lost? Indeed, if total viewing eventually rises after the program supply adjusts to an access rule over time, can we even presume out of hand *any* significant decline in *diversity?* (See chapter 3.)

The Issue of Network Dominance

The concept of network dominance cuts two ways, relating, on the one hand, to the networks' recognized ability to induce affiliates to clear nine-tenths of prime time for network shows, and on the other hand, to the fact that hundreds of program suppliers must deal with only three national network broker-buyers. Accepting this concept for present purposes, we saw in chapter 9 that such dominance in some measure arose from FCC's allocational constraints and the fact that a fourth network in the VHF band could at best reach only 33 percent of TV households. Net-

12. Second Report, par. 33.

work dominance is allegedly due also to the fact that programs which enjoy less than national exposure cannot readily compete with those on the networks. Where program distribution is less than nationwide, that is, program budgets will allegedly have to be much smaller per dollar advertising generated.[13]

The fact is that the networks are no mere brokers of station time, but also investors in the programs they carry. Hundreds of local affiliates are committed beforehand to a given program series. The program supplier is thereby assured of some minimum payment well before the broadcast. In this way the network is able to justify a programmer investment of $250,000 or more for each hour of entertainment the network carries, a budget which might represent too great a risk without this prior selling of station time.[14]

The Higher Transactions Cost of Prime-Time Access. A related problem must be considered at this point. Under prime-time access today significant energies and resources are dissipated in a distribution process where numerous program suppliers deal directly with local stations, offering them a variety of seemingly low-cost, low-quality programs without an intervening broker. The high resultant transactions and negotiations costs are, it is feared, likely to divert substantial revenues away from potential program budgets even if a few large access time program brokers emerged nationally.[15] Even if such brokers could operate more efficiently in access time, there is the additional question of how different the resultant access programming would be, given the fewness of viewer options therein. Just as the present network oligopoly has been attributed to allocational constraints and distributional scale economies, suppose that similar factors could produce a small number of national access period brokers—another triopoly. Would program suppliers be likely to sell markedly different programs to the three new access brokers than they would to three national network buyers today? Even looking beyond the access period to prime time more generally, would the resulting program mix be much different with six national brokers than with three? The opponents of prime-time access say "no." [16]

Indeterminacy of the Program Mix under Oligopoly. But is this necessarily so? The proposition that the number of viewing options will uniquely determine the program mix that results is probably an overstatement for oligopoly markets, where options (and program brokers) are so few. What the opponents of prime-time access fail to see is that there are ranges of indeterminacy under oligopoly wherein personal, or-

13. Robinson Dissent, p. 11.

14. Ibid., p. 12.

15. Ibid., pp. 12–13. This point is more fully and explicitly developed in Robert Crandall, "The Economic Effect of Television-Network Program 'Ownership'," *Journal of Law and Economics* (October 1971), 406–08.

16. Robinson Dissent, pp. 14–15, and the important analysis in Crandall, "Television-Network Program 'Ownership'," note 15, 393–408.

ganizational, and institutional differences may very well matter.[17] That is, price, output, and product characteristics are not uniquely determined by the underlying market structure.

Nor is it clear what will happen over time as syndicator capabilities grow, and public interest groups negotiate for more minority, women's, children's, public affairs, and documentary programs. The networks clearly fear access encroachments if they do not offer such programs, and station licensees fear renewal contests and petitions to deny if they resist. Furthermore, such programs have opportunity costs in foregone audiences that are much lower when scheduled against access entertainment than against the more popular network series.[18]

Since the very outset of regulation, under the public trustee concept each licensee is expected to forego some audiences and revenues to bring nonremunerative informational, cultural, and educational programs to minority as well as majority taste groups. In one sense, access time simply gives the minority groups a better chance to bargain with licensees toward this end. Although it is admittedly too early to know the likely result,[19] the main lines of impact may soon emerge.[20]

Bargaining by the Public Interest Groups: Reduced Opportunity Costs for Specialized Programming under the Access Rule. To retain their permissible corner of the access period, the networks may conceivably offer those public affairs, documentary, and children's programs now exempted from the Rule. Licensees who can no longer choose lucrative network entertainment shows would then have lower opportunity costs in running minority, women's, ethnic, as well as children's, and documentary programs generally.[21] Where affiliates do in fact carry such programming, or less popular syndicated entertainment, their rival independent stations would also enjoy lower opportunity costs in trying something new, or in adding to their informational service. The fact that this may not

17. Oligopolistic indeterminacy is nothing new in economic literature. For a lucid exposition of all major aspects, see Fritz Machlup, *Economics of Sellers' Competition* (Baltimore: Johns Hopkins University Press, 1952), chap. 13 generally, and in particular, note 3. See also chap. 14, pp. 456–61. See further the classic shorter statement in K. W. Rothschild, "Price Theory and Oligopoly," *Economic Journal*, vol. LVII (1947), 299–320, reprinted in Stigler and Boulding (eds.) *AEA Readings in Price Theory* (Homewood, Ill.: Richard D. Irwin, 1952), pp. 440–64.

18. A similar point is made more generally by Roger Noll, Merton Peck, and John McGowan, *Economic Aspects of Television Regulation* (Washington, D.C.: Brookings Institution, 1973), pp. 80–82, where they address the economic impediments to diversity and informational programming on the national television networks.

19. See Second Report and Order, appendix C, par. C-1.

20. There is already evidence of relevant planning for such programming. See ibid., pars. C-3, C-4, C-5, C-8.

21. Nor are present network organizations the only potential sources of such programs. There is, for instance, evidence that the networks have systematically opposed their own delivery of "freelance" (nonnetwork) documentaries, and further, that the producers of same are already a promising new source of program supply. (See Mark Neubauer, "The Networks' Policy Against Freelance Documentaries: A Proposal for Commission Action," *FCC Law Journal*, vol. 30, no. 2 [Summer 1978], 117–33).

yet have happened doesn't mean that incentives for it are not emerging. It is all part of a dynamic bargaining, negotiating process wherein each station's program mix is determined within the outer bounds of oligopolistic constraints. Nor, as syndicator capabilities develop, is it inconceivable that new, yet unknown program types may appear.

The Issue of Diversity and Quality

The data we have so far seen do not indicate whether the critics are right about lack of diversity and low quality being inevitable under prime-time access.[22] There has simply been no adequate test. Aside from uncertainties about the rule's permanence the alleged economic obstacles to quality and diversity have not yet been decisively assessed.[23] Nor, according to FCC, is the present menu as tedious as many critics assert. True, there are innumerable game shows, but also nature programs and musical variety (looking at syndicated material alone), and a good deal of local news.[24]

Propriety of Value Judgments on Access Shows. Can we in any case judge the quality of Welk or Hee Haw out of hand? The commission seems bent on leaving the door open to those offerings as well as to the special network public service categories. The exempted nonremunerative nonentertainment network programs appear to be in a special class all their own, of widely recognized social merit.[25] FCC is in contrast far less willing to make value judgments about the new access entertainment programs. "[The] types and cost levels of programs which will develop," it holds, "must be the result of competition which will develop."[26] Aside from whether the FCC can in fact establish rules to prevent duplicative programming, the commission's comment on the "value" of game shows is telling: "[A]ssuming that 65.6% of access entertainment time devoted to game shows is undesirable, what about 41.2% of network prime-time devoted to crime-drama shows of various types? If we look at the concentration of game shows in certain markets such as Cincinnati or Albany, must we not look also at three network crime-drama shows opposite each other on Wednesdays at 10 P.M.?[27] "

How can the commission reconcile its endorsement and exemption of network specials, documentaries, and children's programs on one hand, with its reluctance to question, let alone alter, the replacement of prior

22. The commission's data were for 1972 or 1973, and my own for 1972, a date that does not constitute enough time to assess the efficacy of prime-time access.

23. Second Report and Order, par. 18, and in appendix C, par. C-62. See also January 1974 Decision in Docket 19622, pars. 89–91, 44 FCC 2d 1081, 1137–38.

24. Second Report and Order, par. 19, and appendix C, pars. C-5, C-52, C-55; also appendix D.

25. Ibid., pars. 44, 47, 48.

26. Ibid., par. 14.

27. Ibid, par. 20.

network entertainment programs by game shows, Hee Haw, and Welk?

First Amendment Aspects. In First Amendment terms, the commission simply asserts that its rule was designed to reduce station carriage of network or off-network entertainment shows so that "the voices of other persons might be heard." [28] It would ostensibly restrain *some* licensees in order to reduce restraints imposed by the networks. Licensees would be prevented from choosing present or former network programs so that new program sources may arise and be seen by the public.

At the same time, the initial version of the rule apparently drove other important program types off the air. Because in that sense the commission was itself responsible for a reduction of special network documentaries, children's programs, and so on, it deemed reasonable its subsequent exemption of such programs from the rule. Such exemptions were at least consistent with the widely recognized importance of electorate-informing and children's programming.[29] Nor do these exemptions violate the First Amendment insofar as they only consider general program formats and kinds of programs.[30]

Nonetheless, the commission majority and minority both appear to make subjective value judgments here. On one hand, the majority rates the relative merits of network programs and nonnetwork access shows in codifying past waivers for network public affairs, documentaries, and children's programs, On the other hand, the minority openly deplores the low cost and low quality of Hee Haw, Lawrence Welk, and game shows.

Perhaps the most one can say is that the commission has elsewhere stated its commitment to electorate-informing and children's programs, and that the unique importance of such program types is at least acknowledged widely. In contrast, nowhere in the access proceeding (or elsewhere) does the FCC endorse "quality entertainment" as strongly as informational programs, nor spell out the former's social function as persuasively. For that reason at least, the commission's direct intrusions into day-by-day entertainment decisions under the access rule seems particularly hard to justify.

Sources Diversity, Options Diversity, and Types Diversity. A more persuasive assessment of access time can be grounded on the concept of diversity. If it is indeed proper to assess prime-time access relative to the commission's diversity goal, we must presumably draw a further distinction between sources diversity and resultant program diversity.[31] One might of course ask what good the former is without the latter. But

---

28. Ibid., par. 46.
29. Ibid.
30. Ibid., par. 45.
31. Commissioner Kenneth Cox did indeed draw this line. See Report and Order in Docket No. 12782, May 1970, 23 FCC 2d 416, 419.

sources diversity is really a political and social value in its own right and only time will tell (when the program supply side has fully adjusted) what kind of program diversity will result.

Some experts appear to imply that virtually every program is potentially unique in the viewer's eyes.[32] Short of that, others deplore television's insufficient variety within major entertainment categories.[33] Probably the only way to estimate even very roughly the magnitude of viewer welfare losses imposed by prime-time access would be to undertake empirical estimates along lines illustrated in chapter 3. Such estimates are necessarily very crude, given that the level of viewing is not synonymous with viewer welfare. But observers have already asked whether total access viewing has gone significantly up, or down, other things being equal, since the rule was instituted. It would indeed be helpful to know what has happened, market by market, to the level of network affiliate viewing, independent viewing, and total viewing (including new viewers).

In short, First Amendment dangers notwithstanding, if we are willing to consider any diversity measure at all (relative to types, options, sources), then it is by no means clear that all access programs are (or must inevitably be) the same as one another or as customary network entertainment, from a consumer viewpoint.

If access time should coincide for all three networks, horizontal diversity might not change very much, especially if only nonnetwork (rather than exempted network) access programs were actually run. However, vertical diversity would presumably increase even then, whereas any more substantial contribution to horizontal diversity might require a mandatory staggering of access periods for all networks, giving them each a pick of preferred times on alternate dates. The objective would be to prevent the same access time, horizontally, from being occupied by the same type of program.

Badly overdue here is an analysis of the possible ways in which an objective appraisal could be undertaken of variety within and across program types, as evaluated by members of the audience. Assuming one could assemble a representative panel, the task would be, first, to determine proper phrasing of questions about their program preferences; second, to motivate "correct" answers; and third, to devise techniques to use the latter to define optimal programming.[34]

Access Time and the Power to Influence the Program Mix. Valid or not, recall that the theory implicit in prime-time access is that providing a piece of coveted prime time to nonnetwork suppliers will eventually stimulate the demand for it. What is not yet clear, but certainly possi-

32. See chapter 3 in this book, notes 1–7 and associated text.
33. Noll, Peck, and McGowan, *Economic Aspects of Television Regulation,* pp. 1–2, 267–70. See also chapter 1 in this book, notes 24–26, and associated text.
34. This suggestion appears in private communications from William S. Vickrey.

ble, is that independents and affiliates may both innovate and risk more
in face of the lower audience appeal of network-provided access entertainment. The question is how much slack the economics of prime-time
TV program distribution leaves for the public interest groups to bargain
in. Above all, for what can women's, children's, and minority ethnic or
other public interest groups more effectively negotiate with station
owners under oligopolistic indeterminacy when, in addition to renewal
contests and petitions to deny, they are also helped to gain access to a
small portion of prime time free of network domination? Only time will
tell what kinds of programs these groups can secure from individual stations with which they negotiate over how much local revenues the licensee should use for the kind of programs those minority groups want
and the commission sees as meritorious public service. Herein lies the
true answer as to whether access time and *sources* diversity will eventually produce a diversity of options and types.

Local Programming Responsibilities

Just as the commission views program diversity as "a hope, rather than
one of [the rule's] primary objectives," [35] so too it recognizes increased
localism as a coincidental side-benefit. "[It is] clearly erroneous to
claim," the commission observed, "that we cannot consider an obvious
public benefit from the rule [that is, localism] even though it was not
one of the main reasons for its adoption." [36]

The observed increase of local service in access time could well reflect
the licensee's greater willingness to schedule its local programs against
two other access time programs than to preempt a popular network show
opposite two other popular network broadcasts.[37] The likely loss of audience resulting from a switch to a local public service broadcast would
then be smaller than without the access rule. That is, by acting to reduce
the opportunity costs of any time licensees may devote to local public
affairs, local news, and local information generally, the disincentives to
carry each such program will be smaller.[38] In addition, the extra hurdle
of having to preempt network entertainment shows for far less attractive
local ones is directly eliminated.

Admittedly, there may be better ways to reconcile local responsibility

35. Second Report and Order in Docket No. 19622, par. 14.
36. Ibid., par. 15 and especially note 16.
37. Ibid., par. 15; especially appendix C, par. C-3, C-4, C-5, C-50. The point is
made more generally with reference to all nonnetwork programs (including syndica-
tions) in *Analysis of Network-Affiliate Relationship* (preliminary), chapter 5, p. 36.
In contrast, network affiliates now replace less than 10 percent of the prime-time network programs they *pre-empt* with local shows (ibid., chapter 4, p. 5).
38. On the lowering of opportunity costs even in this special sense of "viable"
entertainment or nonentertainment programming, see suggestive treatment in Noll,
Peck, and McGowan, *Economic Aspects of Television Regulation*, pp. 80–82.

with an efficient high-quality system of program production and distribution. (One such mechanism, reviewed in chapter 13, is that of quantitative license renewal requirements.) Nevertheless, access time (with the specified exemptions) is a pragmatic compromise to insure a more balanced program mix [39] than would result from network and station profit maximization alone. Even if the networks should qualify their pursuit of profits, by definition they rarely generate *local* programs (except on their own stations). In contrast, the access rule does reinstate more local service on the affiliates, opens up time for possible minority interest programs, and gives the independents a better chance to compete. At the same time, the FCC grants waivers to retain the networks' own special merit programs.

The FCC may have substituted its own preferences for public choice in television by excluding network entertainment. But a maximum opportunity for new program suppliers to enter is a fairly objective and widely accepted value whose pursuit, I saw, has led some observers to defend access time (and its diversifying effects on program sources) regardless of consequences for quality and types diversity. Furthermore, diversity in the mix of local and network service almost necessarily imposes some price in foregone viewers, though that price can of course be reexamined from time to time (in this instance after programming has more fully adjusted on the supply side). Nor is the alleged linkage between low-cost and low-quality shows really self-evident. Yet there is no "free lunch," and if localism is desired (by the FCC), it is bound to cost something.

An apparent side-benefit of the rule, greater localism may partially offset the low-quality service opponents of prime-time access attribute to it. However, it misconceives the process to imply that low-quality access programs are sought "in order" to promote localism, or "in order" to give independents windfall gains.[40] The fact seems rather that stronger independents and more local and informational programming are simply unexpected side results of a prime-time access rule whose direct ostensible purpose is sources diversity per se.

39. That is, a schedule with informational and cultural as well as entertainment shows, local and nonnetwork as well as network originations, and so forth.
40. Commissioner Glen Robinson implies otherwise, in his dissenting statement in Docket 19622, p. 26. His critique does, however, seem consistent with the analysis here which argues that the reduced opportunity costs of local or informational programming under prime-time access are an unintended side-effect, but that resultant increases in such programming are still benefits in terms of stated or implied FCC objectives.

Conclusions

There is no question that excluding the networks from access time has now operated to reduce their dominance of prime time,[41] though not without loss of important national distributional benefits. True, the emergence of a few big access brokers could help us retain such benefits. However, there would then be no significant increase in the number of separate program suppliers and programs.

The question is not simply whether we can reduce network dominance, create new program ideas and creative energies, and encourage more localism, all without sacrificing the efficiency and resources needed for program quality. We must also recognize the value of maximum opportunity and sources diversity in their own right. Nor can we dismiss out of hand that there may be an unsatisfied demand for such shows as Welk and Hee Haw, the very kind that access programmers supply. In this, the latter may help meet the viewers' desire for variety within as well as across the standard entertainment types. Recall, finally, that longer-term adjustments on the supply side could well alter the program mix if public interest group pressures should intensify, within an otherwise indeterminate decisional context.

To give excessive weight to the inefficiencies of proliferating separate transactions among a multitude of program suppliers and station owners in access time, fails to consider the minority group's potential role in shaping the local program mix. Or it assumes that one can ignore the value of minority access as such. True, higher transactions costs may reduce the total net revenue pie available. However, licensees will also retain a much larger share of total access revenues than they now do of network revenues. Finally, public groups will presumably, meet less resistance from any station owner in access time than where they must induce him to *preempt* lucrative network entertainment shows.

Alternatives to Prime-Time Access

In his perceptive dissent on prime-time access, Commissioner Glen Robinson proposed to split the broadcast day into several separate but equal segments. This, he said, was better able than the access rule to reduce network dominance without affecting program decisions or net-

41. The latest estimate is that the access rule has reduced the prime-time network programming carried by affiliates "by more than ten percent." *Analysis of Network-Affiliate Relationship* (preliminary), chapter 7, p. 7; see also chapter 5, pp. 34–35, and table III–1 therein.

work control over program prices or advertising messages.[42] In his own words:

> The Commission is beginning such a division [of the broadcast day] with the access rule, but it is not striving for equality in the segments. This seems to betray less than a full conviction in the logic of its decision. If we really want to cut the prime time market into separate segments, why not divide prime time into two equal two-hour periods, allowing an individual network broker to program only one of these segments? Or—indeed— why not extend the division into other day parts so as perhaps to create three or four sets of brokers during different program hours? Of course, such a division would literally increase the number of network organizations and, thus, reduce "network dominance" but it would have little other effect. . . . [T]he number of programming hours and the economics of program selection would be unchanged. . . . It is important, however, that the division of the broadcast day be effected in such a manner as to give each network a fairly large number of weekly program hours. The problem with the access rule is that seven weekly hours are so few as to create the possibility of serious scale diseconomies in carrying out network functions. There may be economies which are not exhausted until the entire broadcast day is brokered by a single organization for one station in each market, but the diseconomies inherent in dividing this day into two unequal segments would be avoided by giving each firm at least 14 weekly prime viewing hours.[43]

Robinson's final conclusion was gloomy because he still feared that the above approach would arbitrarily reduce network circulation and hence dissipate the revenue potential for relatively profitable merit programming into higher transactions costs. " . . . [T]his trade-off cannot be considered favorable," he observed, "especially if it is only achieved after a long transition period during which audiences are afforded only cheap game shows in the access period." [44] Bruce Owen has expounded a partly related form of "temporal monopoly" wherein there may be "as many temporal monopolists as there are time periods in the time span." [45] Owen then goes on to observe that under his model's conditions

> . . . [T]he institutional structure of temporal monopoly provides an economic incentive to producers to lessen both competitive duplication and monopolistic production of common-denominator programming. Such a structure is not at all far-fetched. One might give many networks each successive one-hour blocks throughout the day, allowing each network in turn to program all three channels. Or one might allow each network one evening, rotating networks in succession, as discussed earlier. Note that there is no limit to the total number of possible networks, so that this approach could also be used to increase the number of viewpoints, and thus serve First Amendment objectives.[46]

42. Robinson Dissent, p. 30.
43. Ibid., pp. 30–31.
44. Ibid., p. 32.
45. Owen, Beebe, and Manning, *Television Economics* (Lexington, Mass.: Lexington Books, 1974), p. 133.
46. Ibid., p. 136.

Because Owen did not consider the comparability of distributional economies under the present network triopoly, it was not clear whether his proposal could meet Robinson's objections, and hence, indeed, better reconcile than the commission's own rule the apparent conflicts among diversity, localism, efficiency, and adequate program resources.

Recently Owen has rectified the foregoing omissions, though he has not yet attempted any empirical evaluation of testable hypotheses derived from his full theoretical model.[47] Briefly, he now distinguishes between "geographic disintegration" (closest to the situation under prime-time access), "temporal disintegration," and "temporal monopoly." [48] By geographic disintegration he refers to any regulation which limits the degree to which an existing national network can exploit economies of scale in distributing its programming. This could be achieved by, say, limiting the number of stations any network may affiliate with, or, at the extreme, excluding network programming from a designated time slot (as under prime-time access).

Insofar as access program audiences are smaller than network audiences, distribution and marketing costs will be higher for syndicated programs. If distributional economies are indeed largely absent, the stations will broadcast local-oriented programs which maximize audience size.[49] However, this necessarily comes at the expense of higher distribution and advertising costs, the sole question being whether the smaller net revenue for programming, and the higher programming costs, must reduce program quality commensurately. For want of any adequate quality index, investigators often use program expenditures as a proxy for quality. But as noted earlier,[50] there is no necessary relation between program costs and program quality. In some cases at least, cheaper programs may well have to represent higher quality for the specific groups to which they are aimed if they are to compete effectively against the more elaborate, better advertised, and more costly network shows.[51] Under prime-time access, greater sources diversity may in any case reduce the networks' political power to some extent.

In contrast with prime-time access and other forms of geographical disintegration, Owen argues that so-called *temporal* disintegration "achieves many of the same benefits (localism, reduced political power of networks, greater sources diversity), without sacrificing economies of audience size." Instead, temporal distintegration "sacrifices whatever economies exist across programs." At the extreme, he contends that the

47. The first Owen proposal was set in strictly theoretical terms. Owen, et al., *Television Economics*, pp. 130–37. Nevertheless, I want to underscore its importance here, especially in light of experience under British commercial television, which has certain analogous structural features. Owen's latest arguments are considered below.
48. See Bruce Owen, "Structural Approaches to the Problem of Network Dominance," *Duke Law Journal*, vol. 1979: 191 (Feb. 1979), especially sec. V.
49. Ibid.
50. See chapter 10, note 21.
51. Compare with Owen, "Problem of Network Dominance," p. 233.

FCC could "prohibit any licensee from affiliating with any network that broadcasts more frequently than one day per week." Assuming three local stations, and hence three networks, per market, this would produce twenty-one networks over a seven-day week, "though still only three at one time." [52]

Once again there would be considerably more national TV network sources diversity than at present, and hence reduced political power of any single firm. However, the number of stations, and hence viewing options per market, would remain unchanged. By the same token, some, perhaps most, of networking economies are alleged to be preserved if the designated time slots for any single network were long enough to "overcome the various fixed costs of establishing the network . . . and . . . to take advantage of whatever economies of scale there are across programs." [53]

As with prime-time access, then, under temporal distintegration there is more network sources diversity than today, less network political power, but no change in options diversity. Unlike prime-time access, however, there may be as much program quality as today (given distributional scale economies), though less localism.

Temporal monopoly, finally, would modify temporal disintegration by placing control of, say, all three channels in each market with each of the twenty-one networks Owen hypothesized under temporal distintegration. Each of those firms is envisioned as being assigned to a particular time segment (morning, afternoon, evening), on a particular day of the week, but controlling all channels in each market on that occasion. Owen contends that this will combine the best elements of competition and monopoly. While temporal monopoly does not add to options diversity (channels per market are constant), it does operate to raise the broadcaster's "propensity . . . to cater to minority taste audiences, . . . and to that extent may increase program quality in the eyes of some viewers. Each firm would in effect try to maximize audience size by appealing to as great a range of interests as the number of channels under its control allowed." [54]

In sum, there is no question that these structural alternatives are more fundamental than prime-time access as mechanisms to reconcile greater diversity of program sources, options, and probably types on the one hand, with distributional or networking economies, program quality, and possibly specialized minority programming, on the other. However, prime-time access is a better route to localism, while at least conducive to reduced political power, and greater diversity of sources and contents. Furthermore, temporal monopoly or temporal disintegration necessarily requires far more extensive institutional changes than prime-time access,

52. Ibid., p. 235.
53. Ibid. On the latter score, we have argued to the contrary, namely, that audience flow, and hence interprogram scale economies, may well be smaller than frequently asserted. See chapter 9, table 9.3, and related discussion at pp. 283–89.
54. Ibid., p. 240.

or even than divestiture of network-owned stations (chapter 10). For such practical considerations alone, the recognized political and social value of greater sources diversity need by no means warrant total rejection of prime-time access. The obstacles to institutional change may well prevail notwithstanding the clear conceptual superiority of the other two structural alternatives.

Conclusion

Short of something akin to these structural changes, or to Robinson's more limited conception of splitting prime time in half for the existing network and some new access brokers, we are left with renewed attention to what I have in chapters 6 and 8 called "owner diversity" and "structural diversity." However, those policies offer certain success only in regard to the diversity of program *sources,* granted that sufficient independent sources may also diversify program types horizontally (chapters 5 and 8).

By the same token, prime-time access offers an additional if limited vehicle for sources diversity, and eventually types diversity (albeit not without losses in program quality and resources). More time and analysis are needed to be sure of these conclusions, and much depends on the success of public interest groups in negotiating with individual stations and networks.

Furthermore, to experiment with ways to make access time a more effective vehicle for diversity, we probably do want it to be uniform with respect to the particular time slots from which the networks would in the first instance be excluded (as in PTAR–II). Otherwise stations carrying access programs might be overwhelmed by network entertainment shows on one or both rivals, at the expense of horizontal diversity. True, this would not necessarily make viewers worse off. However, it obviously would impair the development of possibly new program sources to the point where they could effectively meet network competition. Finally, uniform access periods will doubtless give rise to more access brokers of significant size.

Nevertheless, even leaving any required access period voluntary as today, it would probably end up (as now) the same as when mandatory under PTAR–II (in 1974). A more satisfactory mechanism to divert rents into diversity, localism, and public affairs, may indeed have to take us well beyond existing policies into, say, the development of quantitative program requirements under which the networks' production and distribution economies would remain intact, but where each station must carry specified minima of news, public affairs, and local services (chapter 13). Under the access rule, the indirectly related provision is that a network could remain in the access time from which it would otherwise be barred only if it offered the aforementioned merit programming—documentaries, public affairs, and children's.

Other promising approaches may be recent proposals to collect licensee rents via taxes or auctions, making them then available for local public affairs or other informational programs through the vehicle of a broadcast trust fund, or, less directly, through grants-in-aid to public television. I turn to those issues later, in chapter 14.

PART THREE

Assessment of Selected Alternatives

Chapter 12

A Note on the Regulatory Implications of Scarcity Rents in Television

THE EVIDENCE so far expounded strongly suggests that FCC licensing and allocation policies have more often operated to bolster industry profits and rents than to channel them into local, cultural, or informational service. These divergent effects call into question whether regulation has been able to induce broadcasters to invest more in less remunerative (merit) programming than otherwise, as a *quid pro quo* for the valuable privileges they enjoy.

The rents which licensing and allocation policies have created, that is, appear to have remained with commercial licensees as a group, whereas their distribution is shaped by the pattern of market trading in broadcast facilities over time (chapter 4). In contrast, restrictive licensing has so far had only very small effects on prime-time program composition, and actually negative effects on the market diversity of programming, and possibly on local service too (chapter 5). Nor have the policies on owner diversity had decisive effects one way or the other on station franchise values, public affairs, or diversity (chapters 6 and 7).

The choice for public policy is therefore either to structure broadcasting so that monopolistic competition will dissipate more of the rents, or else try to redirect them into greater diversity and merit service. The further question is how far we can plan for the latter in well-designed *ex ante* rules, to avoid difficult *ex post* actions later. This all assumes, as in this chapter and those that follow, that we do indeed aim to collect and redirect the rents rather than simply dissipate them.

The Dissipation of Rents through Competition

It is not in any case entirely clear how monopolistic competition could "eliminate" the scarcity rents in broadcasting. Under the current restrictive licensing and allocation system, even market-clearing prices for TV advertising time will probably generate sizable revenues whose very existence indicates that rents have not been funneled into public purposes. Therefore, the proposals to dissipate the rents may well try to solve the regulatory problem by evading it. That is, "eliminating" the rents really entails their transfer from a present recipient, the licensee, to other industry components (say, talent agencies, networks, programmers, advertisers), or to the public generally.

One such proposal would entail marginal adjustments in the system, as, for example, greater prime-time access to network affiliate time by non-network programmers and advertisers (chapter 11). Another such adjustment might be the proposed accommodation of narrow-spaced VHF stations (chapter 8).[1] In both cases, we have seen that rents and profits would decline as a consequence, but with less clearly predictable effects on program diversity and merit service.

At some point, the sheer proliferation of stations, with or without new networks, could significantly increase talent and program costs (chapter 11). As a consequence, station rents may decline sharply while those of program suppliers and talent increase. As rents are increasingly captured by the latter, conceivably fewer types of programs might lie within the economic reach of stations. Therefore, with revenues constant, possibly less talent-intensive and hence less diverse program types might be aired. Nevertheless, the significant positive impact of new station entry on horizontal diversity in chapter 5 appears to qualify the above tendency.

A second approach might entail more extensive modifications of the present organizational framework of television. A far-reaching restructuring of the network triopoly could, as noted earlier, produce as many as twenty-one separate "seminetworks" operating on different days of the week (chapter 11). The question there, as with prime-time access, is how far one could go before the rents now potentially available for informational-cultural service are largely dissipated in higher interfirm transactions and distributional costs.

Under a related version, conduit could be separated from content, as has long been true in Great Britain. There, all transmitters and studios

1. Additional related proposals include steps to: (1) activate the UHF band (de-intermixture, click tuning, improved UHF receivers); (2) promote a new fourth commercial TV network in part by utilizing unused public television channels for that purpose; (3) switch the entire commercial TV system to the UHF band, or, more recently, to the VHF band by (4) allocating six VHF channels to each of 204 TV markets nationally.

are actually owned by a public corporation, the Independent Television Authority, with limited renewable operating rights then periodically negotiated with competing private programmers. One safeguard against impairment of public service in any such arrangement might be a more rigorous enforcement of program service standards. With physical facilities publicly owned and fewer private equities to worry about on that account, regulators might be more willing to define such responsibilities explicitly, and licensees to take them seriously. Should divorcement simply redistribute the rents, however, and the operator-programmer end up with none, while the public conduit owner retains all, programmers would hardly underwrite more public service. If such a scheme is to reduce rents without impairing program standards, conduit charges must be designed carefully.

Assuming, then, that we have decided to collect rather than dissipate the scarcity rents, the major near-to-mid-term strategies for so doing include techniques to: (1) induce the commercial station itself to spend the rents more meritoriously (as via quantitative program requirements); (2) collect and transfer the rents from commercial stations and networks to an alternate programming entity; and (3) cross-subsidize such an alternate entity through reduced network interconnection rates. In the longer term, there is (4) a further possibility of supporting socially desirable programming on multitudes of cable transmission systems, themselves interconnected by microwave or satellite links.

Quantitative Program Requirements

The next chapter—on quantitative programming requirements—will deal at length with the first of these four strategies. So, in another sense, has much of the evidence reviewed throughout Part II, in the chapters on structural diversity, owner diversity, and network-affiliate relations.

The proposal for quantitative requirements in effect aims to divert the rents directly into public service and diversity, sidestepping the stage of actually recapturing them first. A major problem there is one of quality control and, if the commission deals forcefully with that, there may be First Amendment issues.

The Use of Scarcity Rents
to Fund Public Broadcasting

In my final chapter I propose to deal mainly with the second option—
the collection and transfer of rents to public broadcasting. Following
that, however, I shall touch more briefly on the third—reduced-rate access to TV network interconnection facilities such as those provided by
AT&T. Before considering either of those alternatives, moreover, I shall
first review the legal-administrative possibility of recovering the rents
under the government's standard fee-setting criteria today.

This leaves two final options, one of which, the policy toward cable
television (the preceding option 4), is not considered in this book—not
because I question its highly promising potential contribution to program
diversity [2] but because of time and space limitations. The menu of policies
under review is already sufficiently large, and a line had to be drawn
somewhere. The last option has already been alluded to in passing in
chapter 4, that is, the direct control of station sales price in a context of
comparative transfer proceedings. That option will now be briefly discussed, given that current legislative proposals make it once more a real
possibility.

The Direct Control of Sales Price
in Comparative Transfer Proceedings

As noted earlier, the direct control of sales price would probably not
eliminate rents entirely. If the control were really rigorous, then licensees
would be induced to sell shares of stock to numerous separate individuals or companies. True, we might characterize the dividends paid
on those shares as a distribution of rents and subject that to recapture.
However, no direct sales of stations would take place: there would just
be a lock-in effect, together with the circumvention just mentioned.

One could clearly not eliminate the rents if the licensee just refused to
sell at a controlled price which did not cover all or most of these rents.
He would simply continue to "collect" them in salaries and dividends on
his own stock. If the licensee also performed poorly programwise, regulators would be hard pressed by the public to recover the rents in kind,
and might do so more effectively than today. Under price control, licensees would have far less chance to sell out at a profit and, on that
account at least, be less willing (than without price control) to sell at
all, even if saddled with substantial public service requirements.

It may of course be argued that corporate licensees in television con-
tinually sell shares in themselves at prices which fully capitalize the

2. Even the contention that cable's continued growth must erode local broadcast
service has been increasingly qualified in light of deficient empirical knowledge. See,
for example, Paul W. MacAvoy (ed.), *Deregulation of Cable Television* (Washington, D.C.: American Enterprise Institute, 1977), pp. 33–39 (MacAvoy) and 68–87
(Besen et al.).

associated income stream. But that does not mean that no rents accrue to the buyer. The fact is that, even assuming a more perfect capital market exists than some observers contend, buyers of stock, or stations, simply cannot anticipate how much regulatory change there will eventually be, or when it will occur. Therefore, though they initially pay a price that includes some risk premium for regulatory change generally, they will also fight hard to prevent such change from getting out of hand. Thereby they try to minimize the danger that the realized risk of regulatory change will exceed the *ex ante* risk. Their opposition would be no less adamant, for example, when such change proposes to accommodate the entry of cable television, pay television, or satellite broadcasting.

Observation seems to indicate that markets are poorer at predicting political than economic events such as innovations. If technical advances are marginal, moreover, they will pose few large risks, whereas even major advances will be phased in gradually over time. In contrast, big regulatory changes (like the decisions on domestic satellites, specialized carriers, and cable rules, let alone the outcome of the proposed Communications Act of 1978), are much harder to predict. The unanticipated event which occurs after a purchase of stock (or a station), explains why all the rents are not recaptured when an initial grantee sells stock to the public.

Under price regulation, then, the licensee's rents may be tapped for a time by regulatory pressure for greater public service. Yet with no chance to reap sizable capital gains later by selling the station outright, and hence to capitalize his rents, a potential newcomer may be unwilling to risk any venture capital at all. The flow of capital into the industry could therefore decline, and with it, the resources needed for balanced and diversified programming.

Direct price control in a context of comparative transfer proceedings might be a somewhat more promising way to divert rents into public service and diversity. True, a progenitor of this proposal, in force between 1946 and 1949, was finally dropped as unworkable.[3] Under that version, would-be transferors had to advertise the first bona fide bid they received from a "qualified" prospective buyer, and other potential buyers could then apply for the station at the announced price. The FCC would finally select the "best" of the qualified bidders, until the 1952 amendments of the Communications Act explicitly prohibited this.

Because the Communications Act of 1978 (HR 13015) has indeed proposed to authorize comparative transfer proceedings once again, it is well to consider the lessons to be learned from this earlier attempt. In that abortive experience, the expense and delays of comparative proceedings apparently scared off some of the smaller unaffiliated buyers who were then trying to enter television through the transfer route. The sheer

3. Levin, *Broadcast Regulation and Joint Ownership of Media,* (New York: New York University Press, 1960), pp. 188–90, and associated footnotes.

complexity of the sales (few of which were 100 percent sales, or sales for cash only), may also explain why no more than six competitive applications were filed among the one thousand received by the commission, over the entire period of the experiment.[4]

Under the new conception today, the FCC could once more consider a transferee *other than* the initial applicant. However, judging from this past experience, licensees must be required by law to sell the whole station or nothing at all, and to stipulate the price in cash terms. But even then, the procedure would not work unless the first acceptable price-bid the commission approved was at the going market level, or better still, below it. Otherwise most potential buyers would be excluded.[5]

Should the FCC set the transfer price below the market-clearing level, a larger number of applicants would presumably come forth, possibly including small, unaffiliated local or minority ethnic candidates. Buyers would at any rate be prevented from bidding well above predicted equilibrium price just to forestall competing applications from such candidates (whom the commission might otherwise favor). There would thus be less of a danger, too, that buyers would get in "over their head" by paying prices that impaired their subsequent ability to fulfill their program service promises. Therefore the buyers would be under less pressure, too, to cut corners on program quality so as to amortize an inflated capital cost more rapidly. Accordingly, the commission would have less difficulty in monitoring the transferee's program performance in general.

True, if the FCC really established a merit standard in concrete terms, it could in theory hold any transferee to that standard on grounds that transferee had bought the station in full knowledge of the standard. Nevertheless, the buyer would presumably gamble on how likely the commission could effectively monitor his program performance in detail. The higher the sales price, the greater the inducement to gamble versus effective enforcement, and the more difficult the commission's monitoring problems.

So much, then, for the general regulatory implications of scarcity rents in television broadcasting. Within that context we will now take a closer look at two policy options in particular, namely, quantitative local and informational program requirements in chapter 13, and in chapter 14, mainly the use of scarcity rents to fund public broadcasting and diversity.

4. Ibid., p. 189.

5. See HR 13015, sec. 433(b). Influential public interest groups already predict that this provision may facilitate immediate approval of a proposed sale "to a joint venture applicant comprised of *all* the groups which seek the right to buy." These groups note further: "Purchasers with strong local ties and free of other media interests could compete for licenses . . . against multiple owners . . . [an important possibility] . . . given that there are far more station transfers than new facilities today." (Telecommunications Consumer Coalition, *A Preliminary Legal Analysis of HR 13015,* July 31, 1978, p. 28).

Chapter 13

Quantitative Program Requirements

THE RASH of renewal contests and petitions to deny which followed the commission's failure to renew the license of station WHDH in 1969 has posed a difficult administrative task: to devise procedures that reconcile the stimulus of potential challenges with the industry stability essential to adequate informational and diversified programming generally.[1] It is within this context that the proposal for quantitative requirements must be carefully assessed.

In its 1970 Comparative Renewal Policy Statement, the commission stipulated that a demonstration of "substantial" service would insure renewal in the face of a competing contestant. Only if such demonstration failed would the challenger be heard in full, with incumbent then bearing a heavy burden of proof. The U.S. Court of Appeals (D.C. Circuit) remanded in Citizens Communications Center v. FCC (1971), holding invalid the summary procedure in this two-stage hearing. Additionally, it saw the yardstick for presumptive renewal in any case to be "superior" (not "substantial") service. By way of further response, the commission then inquired (in Docket 19154) into specific quantitative yardsticks to help it more persuasively identify those cases where a summary procedure would in fact be defensible.

The dilemma is striking. Some modicum of economic stability and continuity for incumbents is essential for improved program service and diversity, but so too is the competitive spur of potential challenges. Within this context, we will examine quantitative program requirements as a technique to divert broadcaster rents into local and informational programming, and greater diversity generally. A key question is how far

1. For an excellent background source on the delicate issues laid out in the first half of this chapter, see Henry Geller, *The Comparative Renewal Process in Television: Problems and Suggested Solutions* (Santa Monica, Calif.: Rand Corporation, P-5253, August 1974).

one can press such requirements without seriously impairing the incentive or capacity for such service.

First the background of this proposal will be described, with special reference to the commission's Policy Statement on Comparative Renewals (1970), its subsequent License Renewal Proceeding (Docket No. 19154), and its response to the Appeals Court decision in Citizens Communications Center v. FCC. The major obstacles to introducing any quantitative standard will be noted in passing, as well as the principal reasons this proposal was rejected in 1977, and the proceeding terminated.

The next section will then consider the economic rationale of quantitative renewal requirements both in terms of the FCC's stated commitment to electorate-informing local and informational programming, and the economic incentives which work against its carriage by commercial licensees.

In light of these obstacles, the third section will ponder the ingredients of a usable methodology to set equitable requirements in broad local and informational terms. However, I shall deal only indirectly with the commission's concept of substantial service in a comparative renewal context, focusing instead on the implications of a more basic programming requirement applied to all licensees, annually. Furthermore, this method could, in principle, be applied also to a far more detailed set of program categories, though there are special problems in doing so.

Following this methodological discussion, the next three sections present some illustrative models and results based on real-world economic and programming data. At this stage I can only illustrate the pitfalls and promise of this approach, leaving to others, and in particular to governmental agencies, the task of ironing out future practical yardsticks.

My basic conclusions are these: First, there is no question that the development of such yardsticks poses extremely difficult measurement tasks. That would be so even if we accept the FCC's data as valid and meaningful. Nevertheless, a quantitative yardstick can be developed and introduced, second, without serious economic harm or inequity. Third, though the alleged dangers for First Amendment guarantees could pose problems outside the scope of this volume, the most I can do here is to consider the kind of requirements (broad program categories) that seem most free from those dangers.

Background of the Proposal

Because property rights in spectrum were not defined and enforced at the outset of radio communication in the 1920s, or private rights left freely transferable in a spectrum market, a centralized nonprice licensing and allocation system virtually had to be utilized to contain the costly and far-flung signal interference that would otherwise have resulted. Leaving open the question of whether this centralized system of direct entry control was in any sense inevitable, once we adopted it the potential entrants had to be selected by a central authority empowered to do so.[2]

To be sure, that choice of licensees could have been made automatically, by auctioning off predetermined rights to the highest qualified bidder, or by lot. Nor did auction bids necessarily have to take the form of large lump-sum payments—annual rental charges or royalties could have been collected from the winner during his license term. Instead Congress adopted a public trustee approach, instructing the regulatory authority to choose those applicants most likely to serve the public interest, and to develop licensing-allocation criteria toward that end.

Initial grants were in practice made first for six months, then yearly, and finally triennially (with periodic renewals), to applicants who had met a public interest standard that Congress never explicitly defined. Since 1934 the Federal Communications Commission has sought to spell out that standard mainly in separate licensing decisions, case-by-case, but with occasional attempts also to codify and rationalize the criteria it often applies inconsistently.

As stated in chapter 1, two sets of standards have emerged to date—minimum and maximum, with the latter applied in comparative proceedings to choose between otherwise minimally qualified candidates. However, the choice between competing newcomers for rights to build and operate stations not yet on the air is one thing. It is quite different and more difficult to choose between an incumbent, with a record of past performance and sizable capital investments in broadcast facilities, and a newcomer seeking the latter's license on the basis of largely "paper promises" to do better.

In this latter regard, the Communications Act permits new parties to demonstrate that they will better serve the public interest than a renewal applicant at the end of a limited license term. However, there are deemed also to be "legitimate renewal expectancies implicit in the structure of the Act" which imply that "meritorious stations . . . should [not] be deprived of broadcasting privileges . . . unless clear and sound reasons of public policy demand such action."[3] Yet the maintenance of a com-

---

2. The technical and economic obstacles to creating a full-fledged market for property rights in spectrum are well known, as are also the possible alternatives to that approach here. See H. Levin, "Spectrum Allocation Without Markets," *American Economic Review Papers & Proceedings* (May 1970), 209–18, and more recently, Levin, "Externalities, Common Property Pricing, and the Management of TV Broadcast Rents," in Trebing (ed.) *New Dimensions in Public Utility Pricing* (East Lansing, Mich.: MSU Press, 1976), especially pp. 85–92. For a more extensive general review of these issues, see my *The Invisible Resource* (Baltimore: Johns Hopkins University Press, 1971), chaps. 4–5.

3. FCC, Report and Order in Docket No. 19154 (Renewal Requirements), April 7, 1977, par. 3.

petitive spur (inherent in the mere possibility of a challenge) must be reconciled with the stability and predictability deemed needed for costly broadcast operations to yield a meritorious program service.[4] Basically, excessive renewal uncertainty is feared likely to induce the "opportunist" to maximize short-term profits (to amortize his large capital investment in station facilities), all at the expense of diversified and meritorious service to the public.[5]

In a comparative renewal situation, then, the minimal performer should not expect renewal. If he has chosen to render minimally sufficient service, and if his rival will do significantly more, the public interest is served by granting the newcomer his application. This is the statutory spur—the incumbent will never know if or when he will be challenged, but this mere possibility forces him to render more than minimal public service. Yet the incumbent cannot be treated as a newcomer.

From the very outset the commission has tried to develop standards to balance between "a competitive spur to solid service," and "the need for reasonable stability."[6] Yet the FCC failed to strike that balance in one crucial decision in 1951 (the WBAL renewal), opting instead for stability alone. There it chose the incumbent simply because he was one, and even allowed him to upgrade his service during the protracted proceeding.[7]

At the other extreme, almost twenty years after, in WHDH the commission was alleged to undermine reasonable stability by denying renewal to an (albeit unique) incumbent because the newcomer was preferable on grounds of integrated and diversified ownership. Atypical though this comparative renewal was, "the result was nonetheless unsettling."[8]

The Policy Statement on Comparative Renewals (1970)

Within this context the commission, in 1970, adopted a policy of presumptive renewal for incumbents who could demonstrate, in a contest with any competing newcomer, that their program service during the prior three years had been "substantially attuned to meeting the needs and interests of [their potential audience]."[9] This assumed also that their operations were not otherwise marred by "serious deficiencies."

Given that said incumbent had met the statutory goal of "substantial service," the requirement of predictability and stability would ipso facto

4. Ibid., pars. 3–4.
5. Ibid., also see Public Notice, Policy Statement on Comparative Hearings Involving Regular Renewal Applicants, January 15, 1970, p. 2 (FCC mimeo 70–62 40869).
6. Geller, *The Comparative Renewal Process*, p. vi.
7. Ibid, pp. vi, 9–11.
8. Ibid., pp. vi, 13–18.
9. Policy Statement on Comparative Renewal Hearings, January 15, 1970, p. 2.

justify renewal. If, however, an incumbent had not rendered substantial service, he would obtain no controlling preference. On the contrary, the challenger who could demonstrate that he would render such service would be preferred over any incumbent who, given that opportunity, had failed.[10]

Because the 1970 policy, and the standard set forth there, lacked mathematical precision,[11] substantiality of service was to be developed within the factual circumstances of each case. Substantial service implied only that that service was solid, strong, or ample, rather than minimal or lowest permissible. Application of the standard would be left for the hearing process itself, where incumbent and challenger could both support their claims with the testimony of community leaders and analysis of program logs.[12] On the other hand, any upgrading of service after a competing application was filed (to ward off a full hearing), would be disregarded in that if incumbents were allowed to obtain favorable consideration by increasing their public service at the last moment, the statutory competitive spur would be undermined. Substantial service must be continuous, and no belated spurts must be given weight.[13]

The commission did however recognize that more competent potential challengers might be less likely to unseat incumbents who had rendered a substantial yet lower level of service than they were willing to promise. Yet the higher the level of service, the less the likelihood that a new applicant would file against the incumbent at renewal. Therefore, the incumbent would hopefully have a special incentive to provide substantial service as a kind of insurance policy.[14]

License Renewal Proceeding—Notice of Inquiry (1971)

In short, an incumbent who had demonstrated "substantial service" without substantial defects would be preferred over any newcomer. But there remained the question of whether substantiality could be practically or appropriately quantified for purposes of comparative assessment. The two areas of greatest import were "local programming and programming designed to contribute to an informed electorate, specifically news and public affairs programming." [15] Percentage ranges were proposed for local programming (10–15 percent of prime time), for news (8–10 percent for network affiliates, and 5 percent for independents), and for public affairs (3–5 percent). Station profitability, annual revenues,

10. Ibid., p. 3.
11. Ibid.
12. Ibid., p. 4.
13. Ibid., pp. 4–5.
14. Ibid., p. 7.
15. FCC, Notice of Inquiry in Docket No. 19154 (Renewal Requirements), February 23, 1971, pars. 3–4.

and market size were to determine where, generally, within this range any particular station's requirements would be set.[16]

The guidelines were in any case not automatically definitive, or dispositive. Incumbent or challenger could still argue and assert other issues both in regard to programming and nonprogram matters—for example, qualitative efforts in both, equitable service to the community, and compliance with other FCC policies such as the fairness doctrine, the anti-discrimination rules, and overcommercialization. Finally, the guidelines would only be "prima facie indicators of substantial service." [17]

Citizens Communication Center v. FCC

In June 1971 the U.S. Court of Appeals (D.C. Circuit) invalidated the commission's 1970 policy statement which gave the incumbent renewal applicant a controlling preference over the mutually exclusive application of his challenger if he could demonstrate substantial past performance without serious deficiencies.[18] In passing, the court cited the WBAL case as illustrative of earlier FCC policy and decisions in this area, reflecting a bias in favor of the past record of incumbent licensees, "coupled with the unavoidable uncertainty" implicit in the challenger's paper promises. But it then added that "in the very controversial WHDH case, the FCC for the first time in its history, in applying comparative criteria in a renewal proceeding, deposed the incumbent and awarded the frequency to a challenger." [19] That, observed the court, seemed to indicate a swing away from the incumbent bias. The FCC stated its intention to insure that "the foundations for determining the best practical service, as between renewal and new applicants, [were] more nearly equal at their outset." [20]

This controversial decision, said the court, led to the introduction of an industry-supported bill (Pastore bill) in the Senate that would have required a two-stage hearing wherein the renewal issue would be determined prior to and exclusive of any evaluation of the competing application. The incumbent was to be granted renewal if he had served the public interest. This bill came under strong attack from citizen groups and its progress was measurably slowed. Then, without any formal rule-making proceedings, the court went on, the FCC suddenly issued its own policy statement (1970) and the Senate bill was deferred in response to this FCC "compromise." [21]

Incumbents, the court ruled, should be judged primarily on their past

16. Ibid., pars. 4–5, and appended tables 1–4; also Report and Order, ibid., April 7, 1977, par. 5.
17. Notice of Inquiry, ibid., par. 6; Report and Order, ibid., par. 6.
18. Citizens Communications Center v. FCC (U.S. Ct. of Appeals, D.C. Circuit), 447 F. 2d 1201, 1203–05 (1971).
19. Ibid., p. 1208.
20. Ibid.
21. Ibid., p. 1210. See also Geller, The Comparative Renewal Process, pp. 18–23.

performance: "Insubstantial past performance should preclude renewal of a license. The licensee having been given the chance and failed, should be through. At the same time, *superior* performance should be a plus of major significance in renewal proceedings." [22] Even though the *Ashbacker* decision guarantees the challenger the right to a full comparative showing, the court continued, that decision admits that he is under a greater burden to "make the comparative showing necessary to displace an established licensee."

The public, that is, would itself suffer if incumbents could not reasonably expect renewal when they had rendered superior service. Nevertheless, the decision went on, the FCC should strive in rule-making proceedings to clarify, in both quantitative and qualitative terms, what constitutes superior service, so the licensee could know where he stands.[23] Specifically, along "with the elimination of excessive and loud advertising and delivery of quality programs, one test of superior performance should certainly be whether and to what extent the incumbent has reinvested the profit on his license to the service of the viewing and listening public." [24]

Judicial review, the decision noted, would protect the licensee from the unlikely contingency that the FCC might abuse the renewal procedure so as to inhibit and chill First Amendment interests in free speech.[25] In fact, if the FCC considers ownership diversification in the renewal context, diversity of ideas and expression in accordance with the First Amendment will be promoted. Therefore, diversification of ownership is a factor properly to be weighed along with past performance records at the renewal hearing.

The broadcast licensee, in sum, should be a public trustee. The decision purported to attempt to restore healthy competition by repudiating an FCC policy which had struck its balance too far toward stability and rigor mortis at the expense of the statutory competitive spur, and the public interest.[26]

In the commission's own words, the court had found that

> . . . superior, rather than substantial, performance should be the standard in a comparative renewal situation and that all relevant factors, such as the diversification of ownership of mass media, independence from governmental influence . . . , the elimination of excessive and loud adver-

22. CCC v. FCC, p. 1213.

23. Ibid., note 35.

24. Ibid., note 35; also CCC v. FCC (petition for clarification granted) at 463 F. 2d 822, 823 (1972).

25. CCC v. FCC, p. 1214.

26. Fears of instability seemed groundless. In the year following WHDH, only eight out of two hundred and fifty (or 3 percent) renewal applications were challenged. In the year after the policy statement was adopted, not one single comparative renewal challenge was filed. Ibid., p. 1214 and note 37. Nor has the apparent increase in competing renewal applications since then been large. See H. Geller, *The Comparative Renewal Process*, p. 18.

tising, the delivery of quality programs, and the extent to which the
incumbent has reinvested the profit of its license to [serve the] . . . public,
should be considered in determining whether the renewal applicant had
rendered a superior service entitling it to a "plus of major significance." [27]

But the commission also concluded that the above decision actually "rein-
forced rather than obviated, the need to seek out and quantify . . . a
past performance entitling the comparative renewal applicant to a 'plus
of major significance.' " [28] What mainly counted, said the commission,
were "the guidelines actually adopted to indicate the 'plus of major
significance'—the type of service which, if achieved, [was] of such a nature that one [could] . . . 'reasonably expect renewal.' " [29] In addition
to the narrow question of whether "any quantitative standards should
be established to define substantial service," the commission proposed to
look further into such practical matters as "the categories of programming
selected, [their] precise definitions . . . , the relative merit of exact percentages or percentage ranges to reflect substantial service, and the ap-
plicability of the suggested standards to various groups of stations." [30]
That is, however the selected program categories were quantified,
should the percentage levels be applied uniformly, across-the-board? Or
should they be varied, say, according to region, market size, station
revenue, profitability, affiliation status, or channel type? [31]

The License Renewal Proceeding—Report and Order (1977)

After assessing a voluminous record, the commission concluded on
March 9, 1977, that no quantitative standard should be introduced, and
the proceeding was terminated.[32] Its reasons were basically these. It
found, first, that the proposed quantitative standards of substantiality
would in fact become the licensee's "own minimum standards." This
would thereby "artificially increase the time . . . [devoted] to local,
news, and public affairs programming . . . , not [the commission's] purpose. . . ." [33] The resultant limitation on licensee discretion was de-
plored "in the absence of clear and substantial public interest benefits."
Reasonable amounts of local and informational programming were one
thing, but the imposition by government of "a national standard of performance in place of independent programming decisions attuned to particular [community] needs," something quite different, and patently
undesirable.[34]

27. Report and Order, April 7, 1977, par. 7; CCC v. FCC, p. 1210.
28. Report and Order, par. 8.
29. Ibid.
30. Ibid., par. 9.
31. The doctrinal aftermath of CCC and WHDH is ably reviewed in Geller, *The
Comparative Renewal Process*, pp. 18–34.
32. Report and Order (1977), pars. 22, 26.
33. Ibid., pars. 15, 20.
34. Ibid., par. 20.

Nor were "mere quantitative increases" in local and informational programs evidence of significant public benefits. Account must also be taken of "the resources committed to [their] production and [their] relation to audience needs and interests." [35] If a station's resources were spread thinner, program quality might be impaired. Nor should the licensee's broad discretion to serve its public be in any way restrained unless there were "clear and substantial benefits accompanying [this]."

Still another reason for rejecting the quantitative standard was the conclusion that equity would require no single standard applied uniformly to all licensees, but as noted rather a range of percentages, modified in light of differences in station ownership attributes, economic status, and market characteristics. However, this necessary flexibility was deemed inevitably to "reintroduce . . . much of the uncertainty [the commission] sought to avoid in the first place." [36] Thus the competing applicants would in fact dispute over which precise requirements, within which specified ranges, should be applied. Applicants would indeed further dispute over whether "other factors overcame the *prima facie* showing of substantial or insubstantial service," even if a station's sub-par or above-par performance could be determined.[37] That is, quantitative percentages would at best not obviate the need for qualitative judgments in determining substantiality or adequacy of past programming.

Given that the proposed standards would neither "simplify the hearing process . . . [nor] offer a licensee any real assurance of renewal," they were explicitly rejected. Instead, the inherent deficiencies of the comparative renewal process were referred to Congress for more basic remedies.[38] Pending such reform the commission proposed to continue to determine an incumbent's "legitimate renewal expectancy" case by case, without the help of quantitative standards, on the basis of its overall record. That record, it concluded, "should be measured by the degree to which the licensee's program performance was sound, favorable, and substantially above a level of mediocre service which might just minimally warrant renewal." [39]

The Minority Statement

For similar reasons in part, Commissioners Hooks and Fogarty concurred with the commission majority in rejecting quantitative standards. On one hand, they questioned whether "[any] licensee's overall obligations [could] be measured solely by the raw time it has devoted to three rather narrow programming categories," namely, local, news, and pub-

35. Ibid., par. 16.
36. Ibid., par. 18.
37. Ibid.
38. Ibid., pars. 22–23.
39. Ibid., par. 24.

lic affairs.[40] They then further questioned both the crudity of program type air time as any measure of the public interest, and the qualitative judgments entailed in categorizing the programs. "[A]ny such qualitative analysis," the minority concluded, may "run afoul of a broadcaster's First Amendment rights. . . ." [41]

Like the majority, moreover, they saw any quantitative requirement as "likely [to] escalate into a potentially ad absurdam inflation of the regnant norm, . . . quickly convert[ing] the 'superior' into de rigueur." [42]

Nevertheless, rather than urge legislative review they proposed instead to devise a far more detailed checklist of the elements in any definitive comparative appraisal.[43] Essentially, each comparative renewal applicant would be assessed *relative to the average station in its class,* and hence the objective, the minority concluded, would be "to make our *ad hoc* decisions more predictable, orderly and reasonable." [44]

The Major Objections Restated

The preceding review underscores several points.

First, there is repeated concern that minimal program requirements may inevitably lead to an escalation in the amount of local and informational air time. It would do so by inducing licensees to program *above* the minimum so as to insure winning a significant plus for substantiality. But this would then operate to raise the official minimum requirement (derived from each class of licensee's actual performance), next time around.

Second, program time alone is deemed no adequate measure of the public interest. Further assessment of program quality is seen as also necessary, as is that of the economic resources any licensee utilizes therein. Yet such assessments are themselves feared to pose a serious First Amendment problem, just as would the mere designation of appropriate program categories alleged to impair licensee discretion in program scheduling.

Third, equity requires that any quantitative standard of substantiality be applied flexibly, not uniformly across the board. Account must be taken of station economics, affiliation status, other owner attributes, and market characteristics. Yet such attempts to ensure equity would allegedly create those same uncertainties about renewal to eliminate which the quantitative approach was introduced at the outset.

40. Separate statement of Commissioners Benjamin Hooks and Joseph Fogarty, ibid., p. 5.
41. Ibid.
42. Ibid.
43. Ibid., pp. 7–10 and "Hypothetical TV Renewal Check List" appended there.
44. Ibid., p. 10.

The Focal Point Below

In what follows I shall consider a methodology for devising quantitative standards that do in fact take account of at least some of these problems and criticisms. Fully mindful that the issue is now at least temporarily closed, I proceed in the spirit of constructive review in the event—for example, that a quantitative approach should one day be reconsidered.[45] I do so fully aware also of the continuing dispute over First Amendment aspects, an issue that lies beyond my present scope.

I shall focus mainly on techniques to define and introduce an equitable quantitative standard responsive to differences in licensee economic status, owner attributes, and market characteristics, and on the related possibility of reducing the uncertainty associated with percentage ranges. Nor may I properly ignore licensee resources. For if program requirements were to impose an excessive economic burden, the station's wherewithal might be spread too thin, and the quality of increased local or informational service impaired. (This may not be a serious problem in large markets.)

Note, however, that my analysis will not directly focus on substantiality in a comparative renewal context, but rather on the economic and programming consequences of minimal local-informational program time requirements for all stations annually, during prime time.

I do not predict any early adoption of such requirements nationally. Indeed, the objections against a quantitative standard of substantial service could be raised also against this more basic requirement. Nevertheless, my review will serve at least two purposes. Public interest groups may find here the analysis and evidence on which to explore the costs, benefits, and political strategy for introducing this proposal in fact. Also, the opponents of quantitative standards may find in this assessment good reason to support alternative approaches of, say, a structural or ownership diversity of sorts. To the extent that my analysis and evidence underscore the conceivability and practicality of quantitative standards, that is, critics would be harder pressed to demonstrate the superiority of some alternate policy approach to diversity, localism, and informational service.

---

45. The latest Appeals Court decision of Cowles Broadcast Co. (WESH-TV) does indeed once again underscore the need for a quantitative yardstick. (See U.S. Court of Appeals for D.C. Circuit, No. 76–172, Central Florida Enterprises, Inc. v. FCC, Cowles Broadcasting Inc., September 25, 1978, especially pp. 19–38). In response, the commission has apparently begun to consider a new proceeding to establish such a standard. (*Broadcasting Magazine*, November 6, 1978, pp. 24, 90; November 13, 1978, p. 26). Pertinent here, finally, is a petition to the FCC from the National Telecommunications and Information Administration. See NTIA, *Petition to Issue Policy Statement on Comparative Television Renewal, or to Initiate Rule Making, and to Initiate Inquiry to Formulate General Percentage Guidelines for Such Renewals*, October 31, 1978.

Economic Rationale of Quantitative Requirements

The rationale of quantitative requirements is grounded in the commission's allocations policy. Having allocated so much valuable spectrum to broadcasting for local and informational service, against the counterclaims of nonbroadcast and government users, the commission cannot then ignore the end result. Once having imposed such large spectrum costs to provide for an informed electorate, the commission must insure that this goal is reasonably met.[46] Nor in so doing may it ignore the current economic incentives for networks to carry entertainment rather than the more "serious" informational program types.

There is, for example, no question that informational programming is less popular, and hence less remunerative, than entertainment generally, or that stations and networks will therefore favor the latter. To ensure a balanced mix would thus require some willingness by licensees to qualify their profit maximization voluntarily, or in response to explicit regulation.

Table 9.3, for instance, shows that in 1974 CBS and NBC's informational programs (when competing with entertainment on each of their two rivals) usually attracted significantly smaller audiences than their entertainment programs when the two rivals carried entertainment *or* information. This was true regardless of what preceded the entertainment shows and, though not reported in that table, it was true also for program ratings and audience shares. Indeed, ABC was the sole apparent exception to this pattern in 1974, a fact consistent with my earlier evidence that its entertainment shows commanded significantly smaller audiences, ratings, and shares than CBS or NBC, but that its documentaries and news sustainers came closer in each case to those of at least one of its rival's (tables 9.3, 3.11).

The upshot is that CBS and NBC each had significantly more to lose in 1974 than had ABC by replacing entertainment with information, or, in particular, by replacing their most popular entertainment types with their least popular news documentaries. Profit incentives would therefore have appeared to operate less strongly on ABC than on its rivals to substitute entertainment for information. The classic problem of economic incentives which favor entertainment at the expense of information was most apparent on CBS and NBC. Yet there is still other evidence that on ABC, too, entertainment shows drew far more viewers than its news documentaries (when CBS and NBC carried entertainment), and far more indeed also than the CBS or NBC documentaries (see table 9.3).

46. This argument was examined in passing, in Levin, *The Invisible Resource*, pp. 350–56, and more explicitly, in Geller, *The Comparative Renewal Process*, pp. 41, 47, 48, and especially in his illustrative Draft Report and Order, ibid., pp. 53–54. Nor need such implementation necessarily impair First Amendment guarantees (ibid., pp. 47–49, 55–66).

Since 1974, ABC has progressed swiftly in audience size, ratings, and shares for entertainment shows. It has clearly emerged as a fully competitive equal in the network triopoly. In future years, therefore, on the assumption that ABC no longer ranks as third, and unless the third-ranking network is as subordinate a company as was ABC in past years (unlikely), my hypothesis here would seem to be largely confirmed. In substituting documentaries or other informational programs for entertainment, that is, all three networks would appear likely to have more to lose in the future than ABC lost in 1974, and are therefore less likely than was ABC to run the information shows.

In sum, the networks' economic incentives for carrying relatively more entertainment than information seem incontestable. The questions are how much information is "enough" to meet regulatory expectations, and whether quantitative requirements are a useful device to induce even small changes.

So much for the incentive structure under which commercial licensees operate and which constitutes the basic justification of renewal requirements of *some* sort,[47] granted the difficulty of setting them optimally. Before turning to a possible technique for introducing such requirements, I must consider two related preliminary issues.

Do Advertisers Pay Premium Rates to Reach Informational Audiences and Are They a Mitigating Factor Here?

As noted in chapter 10 (pp. 317–22) advertisers do appear to pay premium rates, per viewer delivered, to stations that carry relatively more informational programming. This suggested that the kind of viewers watching such programs, instead of entertainment, are more likely to be attractive customers for the advertised products in terms of buyer affluence, education, and tastes. Now we must further recognize that such premium rates could, at the margin, act to reduce the need for licensees to cross-subsidize informational programs, or for new quantitative renewal requirements toward that end. But such mitigating effects do not even remotely offset the decisive economic appeal to stations and networks of mass entertainment program and audiences.[48]

Tables 10.6 and 10.7 show that a one percentage point increase in total program time devoted to information raises thirty-second spot rates

47. One might of course ask whether commercial licensees would voluntarily carry any information unless there were diminishing marginal utility or marginal revenue from entertainment programs. But this simply underscores the case for governmental requirements of some sort, assuming, at least, that informational programming has important and inappropriable external benefits in any democratic political-social system.

48. Another interpretation of the premium rate is simply that stations with more informational programming attract smaller audiences and hence must charge higher costs-per-thousand, to their competitive disadvantage. If so, the need to cross-subsidize the information clearly remains.

significantly, per viewer delivered. This was true taking into account the viewer's educational level (equation 2), and even estimating conditional upon the percent of information carried (equation 3).[49] Informational impact on rates remained significant, finally, when interacted with audience size (equation 1). Also we found that the amount of local news not coming from nonlocal sources may impact positively and significantly on rates when the educational level is not specified,[50] and at least approaches significance when it *is* specified.[51]

There was, in short, at least some evidence in chapter 10 for the notion that advertisers may pay more per one thousand viewers to reach audiences that watch informational programs. Nevertheless, we were still left with the far greater economic incentives favoring large-audience entertainment shows over small-audience informational programs. Any premium rate for access to informational audiences would clearly have had to be much larger than in tables 10.6 and 10.7 to offset the incontestable numerical superiority of entertainment audiences today.[52] The tacit case for quantitative requirements therefore remains, and I return to it later in this chapter, where a variety of methodological hurdles are identified.

A Second Preliminary Issue—Station Revenue As Determinant of Local and Informational Programming

Economic wherewithal is a widely cited determinant of any station's less remunerative local and informational programming. To the extent that this is the case, proponents of quantitative program requirements will be harder pressed to guard against imposing program standards that, by impairing station viability, might be counterproductive. The need to keep program standards consciously consistent with station viability will assume paramount importance.

Note therefore that in table 6.13, station revenue was indeed significantly associated with (if not a demonstrated determinant of) the amount of news, local news, public affairs, all information, and all local

49. It is hard to see why "viewer's educational level" should be considered endogenous in this equation. But even if it were, the issue is not whether endogenous variables can be put on the right hand (determinants) side of the equation, but whether we are using good judgment in placing them there in this case, without a simultaneous equation estimator. As noted in Appendix I, section 8, pages 428–30, this was a matter of resources, and our judgment was that it was still better to show OLS estimates of these admittedly simultaneous equations, than to attempt nothing. Another issue, indeed, is why account for education at all. The answer is that rates are apt to respond both to changes in programming and to changes in educational levels, and we are simply trying to avoid confusing the impacts of these two factors.
50. See tables 10.6, 10.7, equation 4, t=1.85.
51. Ibid., equation 5, t=1.43.
52. See, for example, tables 3.2, 3.3, 3.4, and 3.11. See also table 9.3.

programs in 1972.[53] Except for local public affairs and all local, I also found that the inclusion of revenue-squared in the equation (our power function), added explanatory power. The implication is that licensees with the greatest resources to fund nonremunerative programming in the largest TV markets also incurred the greatest opportunity costs in so doing, given the intense demand for their limited air time by alternative commercial users. In contrast, the least affluent stations, in the smallest markets, forego far less income by carrying information and local service.[54] If direct informational programming costs are no higher (indeed probably lower) than those for entertainment shows, the small market stations could in fact carry more such information on that count at least.

It follows from table 6.13, then, that any reduction of station revenue can be expected, *cet. par.*, to reduce the amount of, say, news, local news, and indeed public affairs, all information, and all local carried. This pattern is further confirmed by unreported impacts of station income, revenue, or spot rates on the amount of news carried in 1967. Finally, an improved equation, run on the commission's own data for 1972, again revealed significant positive effects of spot rates on news, public affairs, and information.

What these unreported findings do not, however, indicate is whether the reduction of, say, news time when station resources decline is in any economic sense inevitable. That is, could some minimum number or percentage of minutes be required of all licensees without seriously impairing their viability? These questions must be answered regardless of whether advertisers put any premium on reaching informational audiences.

With the above two preliminary considerations in mind, let us now consider a possible methodology for developing quantitative annual program requirements for selected categories of informational programming.

53. It is true that station revenue, news, public affairs, and information are all endogenous variables. But it is hard to conceive of any such variable that is not also a determinant of another such variable. That is, endogenous variables always have exogenous attributes, and yet are still used in policy analysis. Any system of equations will have endogenous variables on the right hand side, unless put into a so-called reduced form, which I have been unable to undertake here (see preceding note 49).

54. I basically identify two opposing forces that affect the station's decision to fund less remunerative informational programming. Revenues affect the capacity to broadcast uneconomic programming. Therefore, one can conjecture that revenues have a positive effect on information programming in a supply equation. However, the same conditions that may cause a station to have large revenues imply a higher opportunity cost from broadcasting nonremunerative programming. I am not able to separate these opposing forces, but do have an estimate of the net effect.

Toward a Usable Methodology for Setting Quantitative Program Standards [55]

In regard to quantitative requirements, the FCC had proposed to define as substantial service one where (1) 10 to 15 percent of prime time is devoted to local service; (2) 8 to 10 percent and 5 percent of prime time, respectively, are devoted to news by network affiliates and independent VHF stations; (3) 3 percent of prime time is devoted to public affairs.[56] Such guidelines would establish presumptions for or against renewal but alone would not suffice to determine it. In setting the standards, one must actually explore two sets of relationships.

One set would help us estimate the potential programming performance of a station, against which we would then compare its actual programming performance. Using actual performance data, we would ask: how many minutes or how large a percentage of air time does any station devote to particular program types, and how does this vary with its advertising rates, net income, revenue, audience size?

A second set of equations would then examine economic performance and in particular help us determine the economic effects of increases in air time devoted to particular program types. These second type equations would enable us to delimit the effective range within which any standard of performance for renewal can be imposed without undue risk to economic viability. The objective is to devise an economically comfortable requirement for any year based on the actual performance of different types of stations, in the sample years. Once a renewal applicant is fully identified in regard to all specified independent variables, the calculated regression parameters of the two types of equations would help us arrive at such a requirement. Specifically, the first set of equations would establish a norm based on actual performance, and the second set, how far above or below this norm the standard should be set in the light of economic constraints.

Both types of equation should help advise regulators on how best to use renewal percentages to induce greater (but viable) public service and diversity. Once a station is fully identified with regard to station and market characteristics, the first equation tells us if it actually realizes its potential program performance as estimated from the actual past performance of stations with its several attributes. The second equation

---

55. The methodology outlined and illustrated in the next two sections was developed in close collaboration with Jacob Merriwether. In particular, the empirical analysis and assessment reported thereafter drew extensively on several of his detailed memoranda.

56. See earlier citations in footnotes 15 and 16.

would then tell us how much more of any program type the station *could* have carried without eliminating all (or some postulated portion) of its excess profit margin, conservatively estimated. Note, however, that the maximum level of, say, informational or local air time consistent with a competitive rate of return need not be imposed on commercial licensees. Yet even crude estimates of that maximum could help us ascertain the reasonableness of alternative performance requirements.

One promising dimension of such a study would be to compare the relative impact of renewal requirements (set at various hypothetical levels) with the economic and programming effects attributable to the policies to promote new station entry, to limit in-town newspaper ownership and/or nonnetwork group ownership of TV stations, and, lastly, to modify the network-affiliate relation.

Any overall inquiry should quantify and compare the relative impact of each commercial TV policy studied on programming and profitability. It should also compare any problems posed by the more certain effects of direct administrative fiat (renewal requirements), and the less certain results of an indirect structural approach (new entry, diversified ownership).

Form of the Needed Equations

Let us specify the first set of ("supply") equations as follows:

1.   Program
      Time in   = F   (economic   competitive   supply
      Minutes   variable,   , factors, e.g., , factors,
                        e.g., spot   number of   e.g., owner
                        rate   stations   affiliations)
                                        market size

In contrast, the second set of ("demand") equations, is of a different form:

2.   Economic
      Result of   (competitive   viewer
      Demand,   factors, e.g., , attributes   , program
      e.g., Spot   number of   influencing   time in
      rate   stations,   demand, e.g.,   minutes)
                        market size   family income,
                                        college education

Let us refer to these in what follows as type-1 and type-2 equations, respectively. The objectives in developing these equations would be twofold.

First, type-1 (supply) equations would be used to determine industry standards against which to measure the actual performance of a given station. Typically, we would use these equations to determine the expected number of minutes of each program type particular stations with given attributes (independent variables), would broadcast. In other words, we compare the actual number of program minutes carried by a station from within or outside the sample with its predicted value from the equation. If the actual minutes fall below the predicted value, the performance is said to be substandard. The farther below it falls, the more substandard, and the greater the case for remedial action.

In this first stage, note that the number of minutes designated as the requirement for any station would be the expected number of minutes for any station. This would be derived from knowledge of the actual performance of all stations in my sample in light of all control factors included in the equation. One could also work with percentages, as the commission did. But the main difference is that my proposed method has a logical basis from which to derive the minimal requirements. Where any actual performance level fell significantly below this predicted level, the short-fall would provide a measure of how much additional programming of that type is needed.

Second, type-2 (demand) equations would help determine the economic impact of requiring a station to change its programming as a result of the analysis in type-1. In other words, given that a station lacks, for example, thirty minutes of news programming to reach the standard given by a type-1 equation, I would use type-2 to estimate the economic impact of such a change in programming. If the estimated economic impact were too severe, the regulator could compromise and reduce the required change, bringing the station only part way up to the norm for its type. The objective would be to avoid any serious impairment of the station's economic viability.

Note here that the absence of significant adverse economic effect due to a required increase in local or informational service bears at least indirectly on the economic capacity of the licensee to provide such.

We cannot be sure whether the licensee has devoted significantly more program resources to the increased local/informational service, or has simply spread the same program resources thin. Nevertheless, we do know that (1) he has not lost so much audience and advertising revenue as to reduce station revenues significantly; and (2) he therefore at least had no less capacity to fund his nonremunerative programming after than before the postulated increase. That is, finally, (3) the chances of any licensee spreading his program resources thin are obviously smaller if an increase in local and informational service does not further reduce his audiences or advertising revenues.

Methodological Impediments. Let us next consider a number of impediments to developing such equations and to using them as just outlined. These problems are not insurmountable but do give pause to a quantitative requirement approach criticized on other grounds. My discussion here, in any case, is about the economic method used to set such standards, their rationale, and the conceivable consequences for economic and programming performance. I make no attempt to assess their administrative viability or consistency with First Amendment guarantees. Nor do I explicitly assess the validity of their rejection by the FCC in 1977. Rather do I spell out the analytic and economic measurement problems that would confront any future attempt to reconsider this approach.

Development of Type-1 (Supply) Equations

Although there is relatively less difficulty in using type-1 than type-2 equations, the former do represent a new use here of the station equations reported in earlier chapters. Three problems arise, none of which, however, is really insurmountable, assuming adequate time and resources for estimation.

The Effect on Average Station Performance of Raising Subpar Performers. First, any policy aimed at raising all subpar performances (those below the mean), will simultaneously raise the mean. In other words, this process of raising all submean values to the prior mean value is endless, unless all stations performed exactly at the mean.

Nevertheless, the use of regression analysis to establish standards against which to measure actual performance is quite common in cost accounting. Furthermore, if the outlined procedure worked so well as to create this problem of endless escalation, in some sense that procedure will have dramatically succeeded. Our problem would then become one of preventing too much of a good thing, a more congenial task from the regulator's viewpoint. Finally, stations with substantially above-standard performance may themselves begin to substitute more profitable entertainment programming for less profitable information. Any such pattern of change will to some extent operate to offset the tendency of renewal requirements to raise the standard itself.

The Problem of Low Explained Variance. A number of the regression equations in earlier chapters were marked by low measures of explained variance. Although this was a source of some frustration, it has not been too big a problem so far. In particular, I have not hesitated to interpret significant coefficients in those equations or to draw policy implications from them. That has been a valid procedure so long as the *ceteris paribus* conditions were satisfied.

But now we are talking about interpreting the predicted value of the dependent variable, in particular its level. The predicted level (for example, the "standard" number of news minutes from a station with given values for its independent variables) involves using all coefficients in the equation.

The upshot is that a station whose actual number of news minutes is well below the standard given by type-1 equations, may *not* be significantly below in a statistical sense. We have used the t-test to determine if a coefficient is significantly different from zero, or in modified form, if the coefficient of one independent variable is significantly different from that of another such variable. In a similar way, I can determine if a station's actual performance is significantly different from the industry norm for its given characteristics.

But to generate useful results, the *regulator's* equations must have higher explained variances, and hence smaller error terms than many of ours here. Presumably these problems of low variance could in some measure be corrected by allocating adequate resources for estimation purposes.

Development of Type-2 (Demand) Equations

As difficult as type-1 equations may be to use, type-2 equations are even more so.

Overall Lack of Significance of Program Type. In type-2 equations programming coefficients must be used to measure the economic impact of changes in the level of merit programming. We cannot do that if these coefficients are not significant. Income and spot rates generally are significant as independent variables in the type-1 equations here, but the program type variables generally are not significant when included as control factors in the income and spot rate equations. Even when the program variables are significant, there is the further problem of simultaneity bias.

Nevertheless, like the problem of low variance, so too the distortions due to simultaneity bias may warrant allocating more resources than I have been able to do to the estimation procedure. Admittedly, these criticisms may qualify the interpretation of my sample results (on pages 370–80). However, they will not apply as much to the results that could be obtained from a full-fledged, properly financed data gathering and parameter estimation program such as one which the government could obviously mount.[57]

Total Programming Must Sum to a Constant. Suppose, then, that we could in fact produce reliable coefficients for the programming variables in type-2 equations, and that we proceeded to utilize them to estimate the economic impact of, say, increasing the news offered by some stations by thirty minutes. The fact is that a station cannot increase its news by thirty minutes without reducing some other offering by thirty minutes, and the impact of this latter reduction must also be considered.

In my case studies below, I could make some statements on the basis of one of the other programming types used in my own type-2 equations. If I am using seven program types, for example, as in table 5.3, I could estimate the size of different economic impacts of the thirty-minute increase in news, depending on which of the six other types is reduced by thirty minutes. In principle, if I split the thirty minutes among fifteen-minute reductions in two other program types, I would have to consider as many as thirty possible estimates of the impact of thirty minutes more news.

Part of the problem here, in any case, is that the coefficients represent

57. See also explanatory comments earlier in footnotes 49 and 53.

average impacts of changes in program units for the sample of stations under the given *ceteris paribus* conditions. On the other hand, I am talking about using these average impacts as estimates of impacts for specific, individual stations. When we talk about an individual station, we have to ask what programming types will be reduced in order to increase some merit programming. The average impact over all stations in the sample (some of which offer more news instead of cartoons, others more news than movies, and so on) is not well suited for predicting the impact for a particular station when we have this constraint on the total number of programming minutes offered. One way to do this may be to consider the coefficients more in terms of their implied *ranking* of impact than their specific dollar impact.

Let us in any case assume that the preceding problems can be manageable and, further, that a set of usable equations are derived, illustrated below in table 13.1. We can then proceed to consider these illustrative results in some detail, in order to make explicit the methodological risks as well as the promise of a quantitative standards approach.

Some Illustrative Equations and Statistical Results

With regard to type-2 (demand) equations, we find in tables 13.1 and 13.2 that programming impacts on economic indicators permit the following conclusions: (1) Whatever the justification for requiring a station to increase informational programming, these results suggest the impact on that station's economic viability will at most be modest, and possibly favorable. (2) The only suggestion of an adverse effect is from the increase in nonlocal news, where we find a resultant loss of revenue equal to 1.5 percent of the mean revenue for all stations in the sample. But even this result is somewhat suspicious, given the total lack of significance in the effect on audience of a fifteen-minute increase in nonlocal news (table 13.2). On the other hand, local news has, if anything, a positive impact on audience and revenue, whereas public affairs and other programming do not seem to significantly affect either audience or revenue (table 13.2).

With regard to type-1 (supply) equations, on the other hand, a number of other points are at issue. My first concern must be whether these equations (for example, tables 13.3 and 6.12, 6.13) can be used to develop useful industry standards, a standard being really an adjusted industry average, where we have compensated for the various station attributes included as independent variables. That is, can we properly introduce as independent factors in these equations specific values for a real or hypothetical station's variables, multiply each by its estimated coefficient, and sum together with the intercept? Will the result then be a predicted or

TABLE 13.1
Estimating Equations for Station Audience and Estimated Revenue with Special Reference to Informational Programming, 1972*
(6 P.M.-11 P.M.)

Independent Variables	Equation 1 Audience: Average Quarter-Hour Homes	Equation 2 Estimated Revenue	Equation 3 Audience: Average Quarter-Hour Homes	Equation 4 Estimated Revenue
Constant	0.119[c]	118.272[b]	−0.119[b]	95.961[a]
	(1.710)	(2.400)	(−2.330)	(2.670)
Log (no. of VHF stations + 1)	−0.349[a]	−24.718	n.i.	n.i.
	(−4.660)	(−0.470)		
TV homes in market	.033[a]	−3.765	0.033[a]	−4.010
	(6.420)	(−1.050)	(6.390)	(−1.090)
Minutes of all news	0.0000527	0.323[b]	0.000424[a]	0.175[b]
	(0.230)	(−2.010)	(3.500)	(2.060)
Minutes of local news	0.000744[a]	0.888[a]	n.i.	n.i.
	(2.730)	(4.590)		
Minutes of information	−0.000146	−0.081	n.i.	n.i.
	(−1.580)	(−1.240)		
Dummy Variables†:				
VHF channel	0.184[a]	42.017	0.167[b]	69.967
	(2.800)	(0.900)	(2.520)	(1.500)
Network affiliate	−0.136[a]	−104.280[b]	−0.070	−152.370[a]
	(−2.150)	(−2.320)	(−1.210)	(−3.750)
Network owner	0.086	410.151[a]	0.097	438.449[a]
	(0.920)	(6.230)	(1.020)	(6.550)
Nonnetwork group owner	−0.001	−54.933[a]	0.015	−52.236[a]
	(−0.040)	(−2.800)	(0.510)	(−2.620)
Licensed before 1952	0.046	63.062[a]	0.060[b]	75.417[a]
	(1.590)	(3.060)	(2.010)	(3.600)
Interacted Variables:				
Group owner × TV homes	0.003	17.100[a]	0.001	17.452[a]
	(0.640)	(5.130)	(0.240)	(5.170)
Network affiliates × TV homes	0.134[a]	73.612[a]	0.131[a]	73.784[a]
	(29.430)	(22.880)	(28.310)	(22.690)
Network affiliates × channel type	0.046	15.707	−0.039	−9.469
	(0.650)	(0.310)	(−0.550)	(−0.190)
Adjusted R^2	.9696	.9399	.9676	.9371
Sample size (stations)	445	445	445	445
Mean dependent variable	.782	$390.894	.782	$390.894
	(× 100,000)	(× 10,000)	(× 100,000)	(× 10,000)

SOURCE: The following data were derived from *Broadcasting Yearbook, 1973*, and *Television Factbook No. 43*, 1973-74: number of VHF stations within the American Research Bureau's Area of Dominant Influence markets, by channel type and network affiliation; by whether newspaper, group, or network owned, and whether licensed before 1952. Estimated station revenue derived from published FCC financial data for 1972 (by market), and the ARB's published estimates of each station's share of metropolitan area viewing, Sunday to Saturday, 6 P.M.-11 P.M., during the survey period. See ARB, *Television Day-Part Audience Summary*, November 1972. Audience data also compiled from *Audience Summary.*

*Upper number in each cell is a regression coefficient, lower number (in parentheses), a t-value denoting statistical significance further indicated by superscripts (two-tailed test) as follows: a = 1 percent confidence level; b = 5 percent level; c = 10 percent level.

†Labeled attribute of each dummy variable equals one, zero otherwise.

n.i. = not included in equation for design purposes.

TABLE 13.2

*Sensitivity of Station Audience and Estimated Revenue to
Changes in News and Public Affairs Programming, 1972*
(6 P.M.-11 P.M.)

Postulated Change in Independent Variables		Equation 1 Audience	Equation 3 Audience	Equation 2 Estimated Revenue	Equation 4 Estimated Revenue
			Dependent Variables		
Change in All News	B		.000424^a		.175^b
	t		(3.50)		(2.06)
Change in dependent variable due to increase of:					
1 minute	E$_1$		.054%		.045%
15 minutes	E$_{15}$		.813%		.672%
Change in Local News	B	.0006507^a		.4832^a	
	B	(4.212)		(4.416)	
Change in dependent variable due to increase of:	t				
1 minute	E$_1$	.08327%		.1236%	
15 minutes	E$_{15}$	1.249%		1.854%	
Change in Nonlocal News	B	.0000936		−.4043^a	
	t	(−.4465)		(−2.721)	
Change in dependent variable due to increase of:					
1 minute	E$_1$	.01198%		−.1034%	
15 minutes	E$_{15}$	−.1797%		−1.551%	
Change in public affairs and other	B	−.000146		−.081	
	t	(−1.58)		(−1.24)	
Change in dependent variable due to increase of:					
1 minute	E$_1$	−.0187%		−.021%	
15 minutes	E$_{15}$	−.2805%		−.315%	

SOURCE: Derived from results reported in table 13.1. Basic source materials, sample size, mean of dependent variables, and adjusted R-square, all identical to those in table 13.1.

NOTATION: B = regression coefficient; t = t-value, that is, coefficient divided by its standard error. Statistical significance (two-tailed test) is: a = 1 percent; b = 5 percent; c = 10 percent confidence level. E$_1$(E$_{15}$) = denotes estimated percentage change in station audience or revenue due to an increase of 1 minute (15 minutes) in news or public affairs carried.

expected value of the dependent variable, where the expectation is based on the information contained in the entire sample and embodied in the estimated coefficients?

In the next two sections, I shall further illustrate the use of these supply equations in determining and identifying subpar performance. I also consider the degree to which my corresponding demand equations suggest that rectification of subpar performance in information-type programming will not seriously impair station economic viability and may even be beneficial.

Let us first consider the amount of local news we can expect to be carried by stations with postulated attributes in 1972. We shall do so with the help of an intermediate tabulation that characterizes twenty-five hypothetical classes of stations.

TABLE 13.3

Factors Affecting Station Time Devoted to
Local News Broadcasts, Composite Week, 1972
(6 P.M.-11 P.M.)

	Regression Coefficient	t-value
Constant	−27.282	−0.78
Channel type	83.978[a]	3.89
Network affiliation	49.180[a]	2.80
In-town newspaper	9.694	1.08
Network owner	0.495	0.02
Nonnetwork group owner	1.997	0.27
TV homes in market	−0.632	−0.85
Percentage of population with 4+ years college	1.783[b]	2.04
Licensed before 1952	15.390	1.59
Log number months on air, 1972	23.907[c]	1.77
Number of VHF stations in market	−8.853	−1.09
Market dummy (1 = 3+ VHF, 0 = other)	−52.881[b]	−2.14
Number of VHF × market dummy	20.575[b]	−2.08
Network affiliation × channel type	−59.349[a]	−2.48
Estimated station revenue	0.080[a]	4.54
(Estimated station revenue × revenue)	−0.0000128[a]	−3.02
Adjusted R-square	.3648	
Sample size (stations)	408	
Sample mean (minutes local news)	129.605	

SOURCE: Same basic source materials as in table 13.1. In addition, percent of market population with four or more years of college education from U.S. Bureau of the Census, Census of Population for 1970. Estimated local news minutes from FCC's First Annual Programming Report for All Commercial Television Stations, 1973 (published October 8, 1974). For comments on statistical methodology, see Appendices I and II, at end of book. Statistical significance (two-tailed test) is: a = 1 percent; b = 5 percent; and c = 10 percent confidence level.

Some Illustrative Predictions of the Amount of Local News That Should Be Carried on Stations with Postulated Attributes, 1972

The amount of local news one would hypothetically expect on stations with attributes like those designated in table 13.4 is reported in table 13.5. In column 5 of table 13.5, I have derived the expected amount of local news for each of the twenty-five classes of stations identified in table 13.4, by simply substituting, in the equation reported in table 13.3,

TABLE 13.4

Hypothetical Attributes of Twenty-Five Stations Whose Local News Time Will Be Predicted, 1972 (6 P.M.–11 P.M.)

Station Attributes	VHF Affiliates Licensed Pre-1952				VHF Affiliates Licensed Post-1951				UHF Affiliates							VHF Independent					UHF Independent				
	1	2	3	4	5	6	7	8	9	10	11	12	13	14	15	16	17	18	19	20	21	22	23	24	25
Network affiliates*	1	1	1	1	1	1	1	1	1	1	1	1	1	1	1	0	0	0	0	0	0	0	0	0	0
VHF license*	1	1	1	1	1	1	1	1	0	0	0	0	0	0	0	1	1	1	1	1	0	0	0	0	0
Network owner*	0	0	0	0	0	0	0	0	0	0	0	0	0	0	0	0	0	0	0	0	0	0	0	0	0
Nonnetwork group owner*	1	1	0	0	0	0	0	1	0	0	1	0	0	0	1	1	1	0	0	1	1	0	0	1	0
In-town newspaper owner*	1	0	1	0	0	1	0	1	0	1	0	0	0	1	0	0	1	1	1	0	0	1	1	0	0
Licensed before 1952*	1	1	1	1	0	0	0	1	0	1	0	0	0	1	0	1	0	1	1	1	0	0	1	0	0
Number of VHF in market	4	4	4	4	1	1	1	1	1	1	1	1	1	1	1	4	4	4	4	3	3	3	3	3	3
TV homes in market (millions)	1	1	1	1	.25	.25	.25	.25	.5	.5	.5	.5	.5	.5	.5	1	1	1	1	1	1	1	1	1	1
Percentage of population with 4+ years college	18	18	18	18	12	12	12	12	12	12	12	12	12	12	12	18	18	18	18	12	12	12	12	12	12
Years on air by mid-1972	22	22	22	22	8	8	8	8	8	8	8	8	8	8	8	18	18	18	18	12	12	12	12	12	12
Estimated station revenue ($ millions)	10	10	10	10	2	2	2	2	2	2	2	2	2	2	2	8	8	8	8	2	2	2	2	2	2

SOURCE: Basic data sources same as for table 13.1.

NOTE: Hypothetical values were assigned to each of eleven station attributes for five classes of stations. All values assigned in light of the real world mean values and range for all cross-classified station subsamples in our 1972 data deck. These hypothetical values were inserted into the equation reported in table 13.3, to generate the results in table 13.5.

NOTATION: 1 = dummy variable with value of 1; 0 = dummy variable equal to 0.

*Labeled attribute equals one, zero otherwise.

the hypothetical values for each independent variable, for each station class. We then record in table 13.5 (columns 4–6), the amount by which any particular station must deviate from its expected level to be significantly different at the 10 percent, the 5 percent, and the 1 percent confidence levels, respectively.

Bear in mind that these results are illustrative only, although my twenty-five hypothetical stations do span the reasonable real world ranges and combinations of my several independent variables.

Hypothetical Divergence between Expected and Actual Amounts of Local News Carried on Stations with Designated Attributes

Suppose we have a station whose attributes are exactly those of station 1 in table 13.4. That station is actually broadcasting a level of local news which for the moment I shall leave unspecified. If in table 13.5 this level of local news is more than 30 minutes less than 218.7 minutes, it is significantly less than the expected amount, at the 1 percent confidence level. Likewise, if the station actually broadcasts 30 minutes more than 218.7 minutes, then it broadcasts significantly *more* at the 1 percent confidence level (see figure 13.1).

FIGURE 13.1

A Generalized Picture of Confidence Bands around Expected Amounts of Local News for Type-1 Television Stations

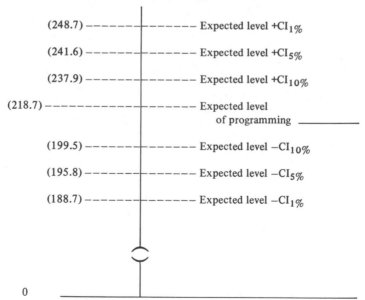

NOTE: Numbers in parentheses correspond to type-1 stations, as postulated in table 13.4, in line with confidence bands (of permissible deviations) reported in table 13.5.
CI = denotes confidence band or interval.

TABLE 13.5

Confidence Bands around Expected Minutes of Local News for Twenty-Five Hypothetical TV Stations, 1972

6 P.M.-11 P.M.)

1 Station #	2 Expected Local News	3 Standard Error	4 CI* 10%	5 CI* 5%	6 CI* 1%
1	218.7	11.66	19.2	22.9	30.0
2	209.0	10.97	18.0	21.5	28.3
3	216.7	13.10	21.5	25.7	33.7
4	207.0	12.94	21.3	25.4	33.3
5	120.4	12.98	21.4	25.4	33.4
6	130.1	15.11	24.9	29.6	38.9
7	122.4	12.68	20.9	24.9	32.7
8	132.1	15.28	25.1	29.9	39.4
9	94.2	9.53	15.7	18.7	24.5
10	103.9	12.20	20.1	23.9	31.4
11	96.2	9.26	15.2	18.1	23.9
12	94.2	9.53	15.7	18.7	24.5
13	79.8	12.28	20.2	24.1	31.6
14	89.5	14.93	24.6	29.3	38.5
15	81.8	13.21	21.7	25.9	34.0
16	195.8	22.63	37.2	44.4	58.3
17	186.1	20.96	34.5	41.1	54.0
18	193.8	23.57	38.8	46.2	60.7
19	184.1	21.17	34.8	41.5	54.5
20	46.9	16.31	26.8	32.0	42.0
21	39.2	13.38	22.0	26.2	34.5
22	37.2	14.70	24.2	28.8	37.9
23	28.3	15.70	25.8	30.8	40.4
24	20.6	13.34	21.9	26.1	34.4
25	18.6	13.35	22.0	26.2	34.4

*CI = confidence band at designated significance level.

NOTE: The interpretation is best illustrated with an example. Take station 1, whose postulated owner and market attributes are indicated in table 13.4. Introducing these values into our estimating equation for local news (table 13.3), we calculate the expected amount of local news as 218.7 minutes. Judging from the performance of all 408 stations analyzed in fitting the equation in table 13.3, a station with attributes equivalent to those specified for station 1 (in 13.4), would be expected to carry 218.7 minutes of local news in prime time, per week.

But how far above or below that level would any station have to perform before being singled out as significantly above or below par? These confidence bands are designated in columns 4-6, which report the calculated range in minutes around the expected value of 218.7. A station would have to carry 218.7 − 30 = 188.7 minutes before being called sub par at the 1 percent confidence level, but only 218.7 − 19.2 = 199.5 minutes to be so classified at the less demanding 10 percent confidence level.

The confidence bands themselves are derived by use of standard econometric methods as, for example, in J. Johnston, *Econometric Methods* (New York: McGraw-Hill, 1972), pp. 152-55. We simply compute the standard error of the forecasted or predicted level of local news minutes. For large samples, any value more than 2.576 standard errors from the expected value is deemed to differ from the latter by a significant amount at the 1 percent level. Hence we use a 2.576 factor in determining a confidence band (CI) for the 1 percent level (as reported in column 6). Likewise comparable use of a 1.960 and 1.645 factor estimates "CI" at the 5 percent and 10 percent significance level.

In table 13.5, for station 1, the predicted amount of local news is 218.7 minutes, and the computed standard error of that value is 11.66 minutes (in column 3). Multiplying the latter by 2.576 generates a confidence level of thirty minutes at the .01 level. That is, any station carrying less than fifteen minutes more local news than the 218.7 minutes predicted would not be significantly above expectation. Nor would any station carrying less than fifteen minutes of local news under the predicted amount, fall significantly below par, at the 1 percent confidence level.

If the station's expected local news is between 22.9 and 30 minutes below or above 218.7 minutes, then it is still significantly different from the expected level, but now the significance is at the 5 percent level, and so forth. Finally, if local news is within 19.2 minutes of 218.7 minutes, then its level is *not* significantly different from that expected for a station with its particular attributes, even at the 10 percent confidence level.

In sum, $\pm CI_1$ percent defines bands of acceptance around the expected value at the 1 percent level, and any station with the same attributes whose programming falls outside these bands is statistically worse if below, or significantly better if above, the expected level. Similarly, $\pm CI_5$ percent and $\pm CI_{10}$ percent define acceptance bands at the 5 percent and the 10 percent confidence levels. Clearly, then, to be significantly different at a higher significance level, the station must differ from the expected by a greater amount.

By the same token, any station whose actual programming falls *within* the bands at some level of significance, carries an amount, say, of local news that is not significantly different in the statistical sense from the one we would expect for that station, in light of its attributes.

Restatement of Procedure to Set Hypothetical Program Requirements

By way of implementing this concept in actual practice, one would presumably start by first defining the particular station under analysis, "measuring" the actual values of the independent variables for it, as well as its level of local news programming. Then one would use the specified equation to estimate the expected level of news programming and corresponding statistics. Finally, one would evaluate the station in light of whether its actual programming were within or outside the bands determined for it. If above the bands, its performance would be rated "exemplary," whereas if within the bands, it would be rated "as expected." If below the bands, its performance would be deemed "below par" for a station with its attributes.

This commentary should permit the reader to analyze each of the twenty-five hypothetical stations in tables 13.4 and 13.5. For some stations, such as class 16, the statistics are not discriminating, and a station's actual offering must differ from its expected value by a large amount (± 60 at 1 percent) to be significantly better or worse than expected. On the other hand, station 9 would face a rather stringent test. It only has to be 24.5 minutes below the predicted level (which itself is low) to be singled out as below par at the 1 percent confidence level.

If my equations were estimated without error, of course, it might appear that the station would have no leeway at all. However, there is nothing sacred about the existing expected level for a given station (where that level is determined entirely from current performance of all stations via the regression, and where said level reflects no social welfare judgments as to what the level *should* be). Expected levels are simply useful, in the absence of a welfare maximization approach, for highlighting performances that are unusually good or bad, as compared with the rest of the industry, after accounting for the factors incorporated in my equation.

Further Comments and Avenues for Analysis

Several observations are now in order. Note first that my range of expected values, 18.6 to 218.7, lies within the range of real-world values in my sample of 408 stations, which was from 0.0 to 350 minutes. This is therefore a reasonable comparison.[58] Note also that there are two stations, 24 and 25, whose level of expected programming is not significantly different from zero, and a third station, 23, that differs from zero only at the 10 percent level. Thus one could say that the range of expected values is really from 0.0 to 218.7 minutes.

Strictly speaking, of course, we should specify what other type of programming is to be reduced were we to require a below-par station to increase its local news programming. Changing the time allocated to a particular type of programming is necessarily a "zero-sum game," and, as noted earlier, there has to be an offsetting change elsewhere.

To this point, I have presented a limited demonstration of what might be done with really adequate resources for estimation. Judging from the equation in table 13.3, at least, it seems clear that the method will work better with some types of stations than with others. Nor should we in any case be too concerned here about the particular equation we have used. If the FCC or some other body should adopt this technique at some point, it must allocate sufficient resources to obtain the best data possible and a fully specified equation. The illustrative equation in table 13.3 has not had the kind of intensive attention needed to meet the challenges it would receive from licensees told to increase their local news programming.

So much, then, for this proposed methodology. Let us conclude by applying the method to a small number of stations drawn from the full sample. Any exhaustive evaluation by examining the entire sample clearly transcends my resources. Therefore I will simply undertake a more intensive demonstration by selecting a few stations at random from the five station classes subsumed in my estimating equation (table 13.3).

58. Recall that it is quite possible to come up with hypothetical stations whose expected performance falls outside the range of actual performance. I cite the fact that my hypotheticals are within the actual range to point out that they are not unreasonable mixes of independent values.

Actual versus Expected Local News Performance for Twenty-Three Stations, 1972

In selecting a random sample of twenty-three stations from my full sample, I drew them from the five general classes of stations represented in table 13.4. These include: network VHF affiliates licensed before and after 1952; network UHF affiliates; independent VHF; independent UHF.

Actually the purpose of this analysis was not to compare these groups of stations. If my equation is well estimated, we will find both good and bad stations within each category. By selecting about five stations from each group, I expect to find some above average and some below.

For each station studied, table 13.6 reports its expected minutes of local news, as predicted from the equation in table 13.3; the station's actual amount of local news as reported to FCC in 1972; the numerical difference between the two, its standard error and computed t-value. (The latter denotes the statistical significance of the difference between actual and predicted values of local news.)

Of special interest to the reader in reviewing table 13.6 will be the actual values of the sixteen independent variables used to define each station's attributes for purposes of the prediction. These appear at the end of the chapter, in table 13.7. I note in table 13.6 that fifteen of twenty-three stations had expected amounts of local news significantly different from their actual values. Furthermore, three stations—KBMA, KBFF, and WUTV—have expected levels of news that are not significantly different from "no news at all." Rather than work with negative expected levels of news, a meaningless quantity, we recalculated the statistics for the three stations using zero as the expected level.[59] The summary statistics shown at the bottom of table 13.6 reflect the zero-expectation versions for those three stations.

Using the estimating equation in table 13.3, I can identify two stations with inexplicably poor performance—WKZO and WCIX—both significantly below that expected of stations with their attributes at the 1 percent level. The other station singled out for criticism is KZAZ, which is significantly below par at the 5 percent level.

On the other hand, a fourth group—KPLR, KZAZ, and WCIX—does not appear to be randomly distributed around their expected levels of news programming.[60] This probably reflects a lack of explanatory power of the equation with respect to these VHF-only stations. Finally, the large

59. That is, deviations from expectations were based on zero expectations rather than negative expectations.

60. These stations are defined as a group simply because they are all more than two standard deviations below expectation. However, note in table 13.6 and related discussion that they are also a group because they are the only independent VHFs in the sample. As a group defined on the latter basis, they are not randomly distributed.

TABLE 13.6

Deviations from Expected Minutes of Local News for
Twenty-Three Actual Television Stations Selected at Random, 1972

Stations	Expected Local News	Actual Local News	Difference	Standard Error	t
WEWS	126.88	100	−26.88	15.88	−1.69
WFAA	133.15	243	+109.85	14.96	7.34
WMAL	161.56	279	+117.44	18.03	6.52
WTOP	160.83	251	+90.17	18.06	4.99
WWJO	135.37	293	+157.63	16.44	9.59
WBRC	118.21	108	−10.21	14.02	−0.73
WDSU	132.86	241	+108.14	12.92	8.37
WKZO	118.83	82	−36.83	12.62	−2.92
WLWC	150.25	163	+12.75	15.20	0.84
WTNH	127.60	141	+13.40	14.32	0.94
KFSN	95.00	134	+39.00	11.87	3.29
WANE	96.51	137	+40.49	11.86	3.41
WCCB	107.71	102	−5.71	16.75	−0.34
WNEP	87.78	120	+32.22	12.60	2.56
WRAU	95.36	115	+19.64	11.90	1.65
KPLR	115.22	78	−37.22	18.22	−2.04
KZAZ	119.88	75	−44.88	20.49	−2.19
WCIX	106.41	24	−82.41	19.12	−4.31
KBMA	0.08	5	+4.92	14.41	0.34
WBFF	−9.48	44	+53.48	16.32	3.28
WGNO	23.57	28	+4.43	14.37	0.31
WLTV	30.92	235	+204.08	14.77	13.82
WUTV	−5.74	36	+41.74	15.17	2.75
KBMA*	0.00	5	5.00	14.41	0.35
KBFF*	0.00	44	44.00	16.32	2.70
WUTV*	0.00	36	36.00	15.17	2.37

SOURCE: Basic reference materials same as for table 13.1. For each station selected at random for the analysis reported above, the actual values of all its owner and market attributes appear in table 13.7 at end of this chapter.
*See comment below.

Summary of Station Performance

(using results of the three alternative tests denoted by * for KBMA, KBFF, and WUTV, where expected local news is not significantly different from zero, and where it was therefore reported for the analysis as zero to avoid dealing with negative estimates)

Number of Stations:	Number of Stations:
below expected = 7	above at 10% significance = 1
above expected = 16	below at 10% significance = 1
	above at 5% significance = 2
not significantly below = 2	below at 5% significance = 2
not significantly above = 4	above at 1% significance = 9
	below at 1% significance = 2

number of deviations with strong positive significance cannot be typical of the entire sample, and may reflect my groupings and choices within those groups.

As mentioned several times, were the government to adopt the methodology I have expounded, it must undertake an intensive study to develop a "best" equation as the basis for these tests. What I have shown is that such an undertaking would single out stations in terms of relative performance, complete with ranking from worst to best. The government's case would obviously be strongest with the most significantly negative performances and weaker as the significance decreases below 10 percent. On the other hand, the stations in question would presumably present evidence that the equation used does not adequately reflect the circumstances in which they operate.

In sum, these results mainly serve to illustrate a methodology which might be useful for policy makers and enforcers. However, the results can be used to single out and identify the poor performers only if the policy maker is prepared to make a case that his equation is the best obtainable for the purpose, a case I have not tried to establish here.

An Alternative Approach

In laying out the methodology to set quantitative standards, I have considered the incentive structure within which they would operate, but not the incentives they might *create*. Aside from methodological obstacles, a central problem arises from the licensee's temptation to cut corners on the quality of his informational programming. It arises also from the cost, inconvenience, and possible First Amendment issues posed by comprehensive monitoring arrangements. The ultimate efficacy of such a scheme will necessarily depend on the regulator's ability to manage these troublesome problems.

The proposal this chapter considers would clearly permit the broadcaster to meet an annual requirement for informational programming in terms of allocated air time only. No provision is made for quality safeguards, or resource dedication. The licensee may conceivably attempt to circumvent the intent of the designated requirements through compliance at lowest possible cost.

Today, without quantitative requirements, such circumvention of FCC's less precise expectations takes the form of scheduling informational programming on Sundays, and early or late on weekdays. With the advent of quantitative requirements, on the other hand, a danger arises that minimal program resources will be invested in whatever air time *is* devoted to information. Nevertheless, it might take fairly complex, detailed regulations and close surveillance to prevent this from happening.

For this very reason, in Citizens Communications Center v. FCC, the Court of Appeals cited, among other yardsticks of superior service, "the extent to which the incumbent has reinvested the profit from his license to the service of the viewing the listening public." [61] However, several problems arise here. Can a regulatory agency set profit reinvestment quotas without classifying "eligible" programs for the accounting in such detail as to impair First Amendment guarantees? What would the appropriate percentages be? Are we to favor out of hand, as between two stations with comparable revenues and programming, the one whose expenses are higher, due perhaps to marketing inefficiencies? Shall we penalize the one that innovates low-cost but high-quality public affairs shows?[62] While such problems are not insoluble, the use of profit reinvestment quotas to forestall quality deterioration would appear to raise a number of difficult issues. Perhaps the most we can hope to do at this juncture is to "develop expertise . . . by examining the matter in *ad hoc* hearings. . . ." [63]

An alternate approach might instead require that some designated minimum audience circulation be generated through specified informational program categories every week or month. The licensee could then be left free to decide on the means, the percentage of profits so reinvested, or conceivably, in a modified version, even when during the day, week, or month he carried such programming. It would also be possible to permit the licensee to utilize even fringe time for his required circulation, provided he used enough air time and enough resources to attain the prescribed target. That is, the broadcaster could be left free to meet his circulation requirement by using high-quality prime-time programming or much more fringe-time low-quality programming.

Richard Schiro has presented the strongest case for the latter approach. Because nonentertainment diversity programming lacks mass appeal, he writes, mandatory information air time requirements may have a "possibly devastating impact of [financial] loss" [64] and may, in any case, yield no major benefits "because there is no guarantee that audiences are watching the programs." [65] To promote First Amendment diversity, Schiro holds that program balance "must foster diversity in the eyes of the viewer, in what the viewer sees rather than merely what the licensee broadcasts." [66] A so-called average audience distribution (AAD) proposal does this, he contends, by "[shifting] the focus for measuring program

61. CCC v. FCC, 463 F.2d 822, 823 (1973), pars. 3, 4; also see 447 F.2d 1201 (1971), note 35.

62. See Geller, *The Comparative Renewal Process*, pp. 73–74.

63. Ibid., p. 74.

64. Richard Schiro, "Diversity in Television's Speech: Balancing Programs in the Eyes of the Viewer," *Case Western Reserve Law Review*, vol. 27 (1976), 356.

65. Ibid., 360.

66. Ibid., 355.

balance from percentages of the licensee's broadcast time to percentages of the viewer's viewing time." [67] Finally, Schiro argues that, by permitting a licensee to decide when to schedule his informational requirement, it is possible that "the requisite number of viewer hours . . . [may] be accumulated quickly, thereby freeing other portions of the broadcast schedule for profit-maximizing entertainment programs." [68]

This approach does appear consistent with the evidence developed in chapter 3 that horizontal and vertical types diversity impact positively on TV viewing (tables 3.6, 3.9, 3.10) and therefore presumably on station profitability. Second, the economic viability of an audience circulation target is further suggested by the premium rates advertisers apparently pay to reach informational audiences (tables 10.7, 10.8). On the other hand, the contention that quantitative air time requirements must impose serious financial losses seems not borne out by the facts. At the margin, we have seen that the proportion of time devoted to news, public affairs, and all information could probably be raised substantially without demonstrably serious economic losses (tables 13.1, 13.2).

Accordingly, the choice between quantitative air time requirements and any required informational audience circulation does not rest on their respective economic viability. Even an audience circulation approach will deprive the licensee of revenues he could have earned from entertainment programming. The key difference is one between diversity as the licensee *offers* it, and diversity as the viewer *perceives* it. Nevertheless, quality deterioration is possible under either approach, under air time requirements for reasons stated earlier, but under the audience circulation approach, too, on still other counts. It is quite clear that low-cost informational programs, geared to sensational or superficial contents, could operate to generate any required circulation more quickly and more profitably than high-cost, high-quality informational service. In short, the same incentives for corner cutting or quality debasement exist under both approaches.

It is therefore hard to see how either approach could avoid the danger of quality deterioration or the resultant need for explicit quality safeguards. Clearly, an audience circulation approach also must entail governmental surveillance of the monetary resources licensees dedicate to the informational service with which they generate their required circulation. Without such surveillance, still more objectionable steps (for example, to devise quality weights) may be unavoidable. Without safeguards of some sort licensees may simply decide to limit their losses on profit reinvestment for information and diversity regardless of the audience circulation reached, because reinvestment of the same profits on entertainment would yield still greater circulation (and profits).

67. Ibid., 356.
68. Ibid., 357; also 361.

Conclusions and Policy Implications

The upshot of this chapter is to suggest that quantitative program requirements may be more practical than many critics believe. As a consequence their opponents will be harder pressed to demonstrate the superiority of *alternative* approaches to program diversity, localism, and information, for example, than those of owner diversity or structural diversity. Public interest groups, on the other hand, will find here encouragement for further cost-benefit analysis and for developing a political strategy to *introduce* quantitative requirements. However, more resources alone will not solve all the problems of estimation and interpretation.

My earlier analysis in chapters 6 and 7 questions the relative efficacy of owner diversity to reconcile program diversity with station viability. Owner diversity offers little if any contribution to type diversity or merit programming, though it admittedly safeguards diversity of sources, viewpoints, owner and reporter perspectives, news coverage, and so forth. Structural diversity, as seen in chapter 8, may contribute significantly to horizontal (but not vertical) type diversity. However, it will do so only at the expense of station profitability, granted that this may well be of supernormal profits.

Program requirements, in contrast, seem fully consistent with network scale economies as considered in chapters 2, 9 and 11. At the same time, they appear better able to divert rents into public service, localism, and type diversity than the policy to diversify ownership. Finally, quantitative requirements appear to be more finely tuned, potentially, to diverting rents into diversity, localism, and merit service than the policies to promote new station entry. What structural diversity clearly does much better than program requirements is to diversify content without the threat of direct governmental intrusions. But here, too, the proper (broad) definition of quantifiable program categories can help minimize such recognized dangers.

Conceivably, then, economic resistance to new station entry may make it harder to promote horizontal diversity structurally than for direct program policies to promote type diversity vertically. However, indirect structural incentives seem less likely to pose the threat of direct federal intrusions into program content.

The question regulatory strategists may ultimately have to confront, therefore, is whether influential groups in society are *more* sensitive to the public consequences for First Amendment guarantees of explicit quantitative requirements. What, in any case, are the potential comparative contributions of either approach to type diversity, merit service, and localism? And for any resultant increment to local and informational programming, which approach will impose the least economic distress on commercial licensees, with the smallest likelihood of specifying program contents so narrowly as to pose unwarranted threats to free expression?

TABLE 13.7

Actual Values of Sixteen Attributes Used to Predict the Amount of Local News Expected on Twenty-Three Television Stations, 1972

(6 P.M.-11 P.M.)

Station	V	N	P	O	G	H	College	#V	Log Age	Age Dum	#V × M	VN	M	Rev	Rev²	Local News
WEWS	1	1	1	0	1	13.04	10.9	3	2.459	1	3	1	1	12.50	156.25	100
WFAA	1	1	1	0	1	9.92	13.8	3	2.427	1	3	1	1	11.25	126.56	243
WMAL	1	1	1	0	1	1.84	23.4	4	2.462	1	4	1	1	10.52	110.67	279
WTOP	1	1	1	0	1	11.84	23.4	4	2.439	1	4	1	1	8.27	68.39	251
WWJO	1	1	0	0	1	15.30	9.5	4	2.473	1	4	1	1	17.05	290.70	293
WBRC	1	1	0	0	1	3.70	8.9	2	2.430	1	0	1	0	4.73	22.37	108
WDSU	1	1	0	0	1	4.31	10.6	4	2.441	1	4	1	1	4.98	24.80	241
WKZO	1	1	0	0	1	4.21	9.7	3	2.412	1	3	1	1	4.12	16.97	82
WLWC	1	1	0	0	1	4.70	14.0	5	2.435	1	5	1	1	4.94	24.40	163
WTNH	1	1	0	0	1	6.22	14.8	2	2.450	1	0	1	0	4.45	19.80	141
KFSN	0	1	0	0	1	2.49	10.2	0	2.271	0	0	0	0	2.44	5.95	134
WANE	0	1	0	0	1	1.72	10.2	0	2.316	0	0	0	0	1.85	3.42	137
WCCB	0	1	0	0	1	4.70	14.0	5	2.334	0	5	0	1	3.70	13.69	102
WNEP	0	1	0	0	1	3.71	5.5	0	2.354	0	0	0	0	1.85	3.42	120
WRAU	0	1	0	0	1	1.85	9.3	4	2.338	0	0	0	0	1.99	3.96	115
KPLR	1	0	0	0	0	9.15	10.1	4	2.180	0	4	0	1	1.80	3.24	78
KZAZ	1	0	0	0	0	1.55	15.1	4	1.763	0	4	0	1	0.19	0.04	75
WCIX	1	0	0	0	0	7.32	10.9	4	1.708	0	4	0	1	0.85	0.72	24
KBMA	0	0	0	0	0	6.06	11.6	3	1.176	0	3	0	1	1.32	1.74	5
WBFF	0	0	0	0	0	7.08	10.3	3	0.903	0	3	0	1	0.48	0.23	44
WGNO	0	0	0	0	0	4.31	10.6	4	1.699	0	4	0	1	0.62	0.38	28
WLTV	0	0	0	0	0	7.32	10.9	4	2.057	0	4	0	1	2.55	6.50	235
WUTV	0	0	0	0	0	5.95	9.6	3	1.079	0	3	0	1	1.25	1.56	36
Mean Value						5.67	12.18		2.225					3.694	47.69	128.17

SOURCE: All values of each owner and market attribute reported in table 13.7 (for the twenty-three stations selected at random for tests reported in table 13.6) are as recorded in the data deck compiled from *Broadcasting Yearbook–1973*, *Television Factbook No. 43*, 1973-74, Television Audience-Day Part Summary, November 1972 (ARB), and U.S. Bureau of the Census, as identified in notes to table 13.3.

NOTATION:

Age Dum = age dummy, 1 = licensed before 1952, 0 = licensed after 1951.
#V × M = number of VHF stations in market times market dummy.
M = market dummy, 1 = 3 or more VHF in market, 0 = other.
VN = network affiliation times channel type.
Rev = estimated station revenue in millions of dollars.
Rev² = square of estimated station revenues in millions of dollars.
Local News = minutes of prime-time local news.
O = network owner.

V = channel type, 1 = VHF, 0 = UHF.
N = network affiliation, 1 = affiliated, 0 = independent.
P = newspaper owned, 1 = in-town newspaper tie, 0 = other.
G = nonnetwork group owned, 1 = group owned, 0 = other (excludes network owned).
H = TV homes in market, in 100,000s.
College = percent of population in market with four or more years college education.
#V = number of VHF stations in market.
Log Age = log number of months on air as of August 1, 1972.

Chapter 14

The Use of Scarcity Rents to Fund Public Broadcasting

IN this final chapter I shall mainly consider alternative techniques for recapturing television's scarcity rents to fund public broadcasting. This proposal has had a long and checkered history. In one form it has now been incorporated in Title IV of the proposed Communications Act of 1978 (HR 13015), and is a central component of the recent Carnegie Commission Report on the Future of Public Broadcasting. Both the proposal's history, and its latest version will be examined in the second section, after which I consider a less promising but timely version (involving internal cross-subsidy) to illustrate the problems and pitfalls of another approach. There I largely focus on two early techniques to divert rents into merit service and diversity internal to the firm. One pertains to reduced-rate access to TV network interconnection facilities as now provided by AT&T; the other, to a somewhat related internal pricing arrangement proposed by the Ford Foundation in 1966.

Before examining either of these approaches, however, I will look first at the government's present fee-setting standard. That preliminary analysis is crucial to ascertain the legal-administrative feasibility of recovering scarcity rents under the law today.

This chapter could of course have been organized differently. One might have considered ways to recoup industry rents for the general treasury and then focused separately on funding alternatives for public television. But this would have obscured the special role of rents-financed public TV to reconcile the divergent objectives and results of TV regulation generally.

It is not the funding of public television as such that mainly concerns me, so much as the *relative promise* of a rents-financed public TV for diverting *commercial rents* into merit programs and diversity. A comparison of rents-financed public TV, quantitative program requirements, owner diversity, and structural diversity constitutes the core of my assessment in this book. Any contributions to program balance and diversity of present or future FCC policies toward ownership or market structure (or to network-affiliate relations) can best be delineated by contrasting them with the more fundamental reforms outlined in chapters 13 and 14.

Current Guideposts for Pricing Government Services and Property with Special Reference to Television

Administrative agencies perform many vital functions that sometimes benefit the public to the exclusion of specific private parties. At other times the regulated entity may itself derive special private advantages— for example, where regulation insulates it from market competition. Passage of Title V of the Independent Office Appropriations ·Act of 1952 (31 USC 484a) tacitly reflects congressional concern that such private benefits may indeed flow from public regulation administered at public expense. It was a temporary measure designed to bring all regulatory fees into conformity until individual laws could be passed. Under Title V, agencies such as the FCC could collect fees for any work, services, benefits, or items of value they provide private recipients, and the fees were to be based upon (1) the direct and indirect cost of such services to the government, (2) their value to the recipient, and (3) the public interest or policy served.[1]

Scarcity rents as assessed in this book are obvious indicators of franchise value to any license holder. However, that by no means implies, under the narrow confines of Title V or with the Supreme Court's recent emphasis on value to recipient in regulatory fee setting, that that standard does indeed permit recovery of all or most of the scarcity rents in television today.

Cost to Government, Value to Recipient and Public Policy Served

It is easy to see why, starting in 1953, the Bureau of the Budget (now Office of Management and Budget) further clarified Title V by outlining a policy of recouping full costs for special services rendered to identifiable recipients, where such services provided special benefits above and

1. The major statement under review here appears in Bureau of the Budget (BOB) Circular No. A–25 (User Charges), September 25, 1959, sec. 31(a) (1).

beyond those accruing to the public at large.[2] In other words, the full cost, separable and overhead, of providing special services to private recipients sets the ceiling on the fee assessed (and hence rents recovered), whereas "value of recipient" apparently figures in the equitable apportionment of total fee assessments. Even loosely conceived, the total burden could never exceed total budgeted agency appropriations, although the true opportunity costs of regulation may exceed regulatory costs as more narrowly defined. In effect, neither Title V, nor the Budget Bureau, appeared to recognize that licenses can have greater value than costs, so they set charges based on the cost of the regulatory services rendered, not on the value the license entitled the recipient to enjoy.

Regulatory Cost versus Value of a Resource

Consider this anomaly. In fiscal 1977 the whole proposed FCC budget was about $57 million, of which only some $10 million was spent on television and radio regulation. This includes all commission activities affecting television and radio—for example, policy and rule making, new grants, hearings, enforcement, international, network study. It also includes not only Broadcast Bureau activity but also the Administrative Law Judges, Review Board, Opinions and Reviews, Docket Branch, and Data Automation Division. (Presumably cable TV regulation may contribute to the magnitude of TV rents by an unknown degree, but even adding the Cable Bureau's regulatory costs of $2.4 million to the costs of TV regulation proper does not alter our discussion significantly.)

Yet in chapter 4 we saw that aggregate VHF rents for television ranged between $300 and $400 million. The rents were thus some thirty to forty times the size of total regulatory costs and no less than six to eight times the cost of regulating all communications industries. Indeed under the current law, only that portion of the $10 million regulatory cost which generated this "private value to recipient" would have been recoverable in annual license fees.[3] Otherwise, TV station owners would have been "improperly" made to pay either for benefits that regulation mainly provided the public at large, or for the cost of regulating other (nonbroadcast) services and entities.

There is, however, one important qualification to this limitation on recovering scarcity rents today. Budget Bureau Circular A–25 further provides that "where a federally-owned resource or property" is sold or leased, the agency should aim to recover fair market value.[4] In that case, the charges need obviously not be limited to cost recovery alone but could also generate net revenues beyond regulatory costs. Add to this the presumption that, under the Federal Property Act, all government-owned

2. Ibid., sec. 5(b).
3. Our proxy for "value to recipient" in this book is aggregate TV rents.
4. Circular A–25, sec. 3(b).

property be sold at fair market value except for overriding reasons to the contrary, and the pivotal importance of how TV licenses are conceived should be perfectly apparent.[5]

One observer sees this confusion clarified once a distinction is drawn between cost-related fees for widely dispersed regulatory services, and benefit-related fees for entitlements conferred by licenses, franchises, or permits. David Colander writes:

> Fees for products and services [should] be based on the marginal cost of the service; fees for entitlement [should] be based on the marginal benefits derived from the license or entitlement. . . . To an economist, [the cost of providing a regulation] should hardly be considered. The scarcity value . . . of the entitlement granted by the license is the important cost; therefore, if prices are to be used to efficiently allocate the spectrum, the costs which reflect scarcity or rental value must be charged. The difference between benefit-related fees and cost-related fees . . . is the opportunity cost of the license, but it is a cost that is only defined by calculating marginal benefits.[6]

Essentially, such entitlement fees would aim not to raise revenue but to "promote long-run equity and efficiency" by pricing "the social cost of the activity."[7]

Under Colander's distinction, as with my own characterization of the radio spectrum resource (under Circular A–25), the anomaly I have just cited would vanish, the bounds of Title V be breached, and the larger issues stated at the outset finally faced. Shall an excess profits tax be imposed on broadcasting and, if so, how shall the receipts be disposed of? Shall they be used to support public TV programming, to offset reduced interconnection rates, or be returned to the general treasury?

One must not of course exaggerate the importance of Circular A–25 or of Title V. The FCC could surely have designed its own basis for fees as other agencies have done. Having taken such pains to establish the public character of the spectrum resource in communications legislation fifty years ago, it is hard to see how Congress could with consistency limit regulatory fees to the mere cost of regulation, rather than the value conferred upon spectrum users. Nevertheless, the language of the documents cited provides a convenient point of departure for this discussion, all the more given the courts' pivotal reference to them in major decisions.

5. Federal Property and Administrative Services Act of 1949, Ch. 288 Pub. 152, sec. 302 (c) (1) (2); sec. 303. "Property" as defined therein excludes "the public domain and lands . . . dedicated for national forests or national park purposes" (sec. 3[d]). Public domain for commercial purposes would be let competitively under other legislation (as with oil and gas leases on the Outer Continental Shelf, or timber rights in national forests), or at negotiated prices (as with grazing rights generally).

6. David Colander, "On Cost and Benefit-Related Fees" (unpublished paper, May 16, 1978, Brookings Institution), pp. 2–3.

7. Ibid., p. 3.

Within this context, four long-neglected questions demand attention:

1. Are TV licenses de facto quasi-property rights to use a valuable public resource, legal waivers to the contrary notwithstanding?
2. If so, does BOB A-25 imply a presumption to recover their "fair market value," except for overriding public policy considerations that deem otherwise?
3. Would extensive use of franchise values by commercial licensees to fund merit programming and diversity constitute such "overriding considerations"?
4. Are estimated franchise values in any case a valid proxy for fair market value of the licenses in question?

Without exhaustive analysis of these issues we are left with the anomaly that leases to use a valuable national resource—the radio spectrum —worth hundreds of millions of dollars annually—are provided to profit-making commercial licensees at a tiny fraction of that value. What, above all, is needed is to distinguish between recovery of aggregate scarcity rents as a measure of the market value of a spectrum *resource,* and rents as a mere guide to apportioning a predetermined level of regulatory *costs* equitably among all spectrum users.

Developments in FCC Fee-Setting Criteria to 1974

Not until 1963 did the FCC announce its first fee schedule, subsequently upheld in Aeronautical Radio v. U.S. (335 F. 2d 304, 7th Circ., 1964, cert. den., 379 U.S. 96631965). Then on February 18, 1970, in Docket No. 18802, the commission looked toward the upward revision of those fees in line with congressional sentiment that agency activities should be more nearly self-sustaining. In the new schedule proposed at the time, the commission would have recovered its entire budgetary request for fiscal 1971—namely, $25 million.

On that occasion, explicit recognition was given "in appropriately varying degrees, to the 'value to the recipient' of the privileges granted, as well as the public interest served and the direct and indirect cost to the Government" (21 FCC 2d at 503–04, 1970). Thus, the proposed fees were to be related to the value of the authorization. First, the commission proposed annual operating fees (instead of triennial renewal fees) amounting to "24 times a radio station's highest single one-minute spot announcement rate, but never less than $52, and 12 times a television station's highest 30-second spot rate, but not less than $144." Second, a broadcast assignment and transfer fee was set at 2 percent of the price paid for the station sold.[8]

On July 21, 1972, the Court of Appeals upheld the 2 percent transfer fee as reasonably in line with the "value of the benefit conferred." In

8. FCC, Schedule of Fees, 35 Fed. Reg. 10988, July 10, 1970, at 10996-10997. See discussion at pars. 14–27.

approving this formula, the court cited favorably the FCC's distinction between new grants that "simply authorize a new station of undetermined profitability," and station transfers that "are insulated from competition and concern a going business whose profitability is reflected [in an agreed-upon] price to be paid." [9]

In regard to the annual license fee, the Court of Appeals further found that the FCC need neither prorate its broadcast licensing costs nor set up the cost of each service as the outer perimeter of any fee. The language of Budget Bureau Circular A–25 which states that the "maximum fee for a special service will be governed by its total cost and not by value of service to recipient," did not require any such precise cost proration. Nor is such precision necessarily possible.[10]

The FCC's two-stage method of fee determination was described as follows. First, the direct and indirect cost of regulating television broadcasting was estimated at $9,661,000, about 38.8 percent of the proposed FCC budget for 1971 and less than .3 percent of $3.5 billion of gross broadcast revenues in 1968. Then a broadcast fee schedule was derived in light of public policy considerations and value to recipient to generate the preceding sum.[11]

In exchange for this payment, broadcasters were said to enjoy "an exclusive right to operate for a profit on the public's electromagnetic spectrum." The FCC's regulation was further deemed to provide individual licensees with "continuing protection from technical interference as is consistent with the public interest." The FCC also "maintain[ed] a market structure which makes it possible for commercial broadcasting to operate at a profit." On both counts the court found reasonable and fair the imposition of annual fees as "part of a schedule calculated to fully recover the direct and indirect cost of [regulating the broadcast industry]." [12]

Two Supreme Court Decisions—NCTA, New England Power

In 1974 the Supreme Court reviewed one lower court decision on the reasonableness of the FCC fee schedule for cable television[13] and another regarding the fairness of the Federal Power Commission's license fees. In NCTA v. FCC,[14] the High Court questioned the reasonableness of the FCC fee schedule under Title V. It rejected the lower court's findings that those fees were reasonable in the level of revenue generated, and that FCC's maintenance of a profit-yielding market structure

9. U.S. Court of Appeals for the Fifth Circuit, Clay Broadcasting Co. v. FCC and USA, No. 71-1621, et al., July 21, 1972, at p. 10.

10. Ibid., p. 7.

11. Ibid., p. 8.

12. Ibid.

13. The FCC fee schedule in question was derived in Docket No. 18802.

14. U.S. Supreme Court, National Cable Television Association Inc. v. USA and FCC, cert. to U.S. Court of Appeals for Fifth Circuit, No. 72–948, March 4, 1974. (slip opinion).

was a sufficient private benefit to justify imposition of a fee. In New England Power,[15] on the other hand, the Supreme Court confirmed a lower court's finding that an agency policy designed to benefit an industry as a whole was not the type of benefit for which fees could be imposed under Title V.

In NCTA v. FCC, then, the High Court dealt with factors that govern the level and incidence of fees, whereas in FPC v. New England Power it considered the activities for which a fee may be imposed and the necessary beneficiaries of such activities. The lower court was found correct, then, for holding that whole industries were not a category that could properly be assessed a fee, and also that an agency could only impose specific charges, for specific services, to specific individuals or companies.

The Supreme Court appears to reason as follows: (1) Title V authorizes fees only, and not taxes; (2) the fee concept presupposes that an application is actually made; (3) BOB Circular A–25 indicates that a "reasonable charge should be made to each identifiable recipient for a measurable unit of service from the government," but that (4) no charge should be assessed if the ultimate beneficiary is obscure and the service can be primarily considered as broadly benefiting the general public; (5) the term identifiable recipient of a unit of service does not describe members of an industry who do not ask for or receive agency service during the year.[16]

Nor may an agency assess fees that totally recoup regulatory costs, for private beneficiaries would then be paying for benefits rendered the public, too. In that case the assessment could in part be deemed a tax (also because regulated firms would be charged for benefits they did not receive). Value to recipient was held to be the proper standard for fee setting, to preserve the concept that a fee and not a tax was being imposed. The phrase "public policy or interest served" was deemed not relevant, as implying both a taxing power not delegated by Title V and "a search for revenues beyond the agency's normal pursuits." [17]

We are ostensibly left with two considerations. First, what portion of total agency costs is demonstrably incurred to provide net private benefits? Second, how can those costs be fairly and equitably apportioned? On the first determination, an agency is apparently limited to "value to recipient" alone, recoverable agency costs being only those incurred to produce net private value. Unclear, however, are the principles by which the properly recoverable costs may then be apportioned.

In NCTA the Supreme Court found this apportionment could be achieved within the framework of value to recipient. Yet this is surely

15. U.S. Supreme Court, Federal Power Commission v. New England Power Co., et al., cert. to U.S. Court of Appeals for D.C. Circuit, No. 72–1162, March 4, 1974 (slip opinion).
16. NCTA v. FCC, pp. 1–8.
17. Ibid., pp. 4–8.

not so where such private value exceeds total (recoverable) regulatory cost, let alone that portion incurred to generate net private benefits. The direct and indirect cost to government for said benefits appears to set a ceiling on fee assessments, a conclusion clearly consistent with the concurring opinion in NCTA and New England Power. That opinion held that an agency should be free to use all the statutory language, so long as consistent with the criterion of special benefit to identifiable recipients. It was indeed deemed unrealistic to determine how much of value to recipient can be included in any fee unless other factors are also looked to—namely, cost to government, public policy, and so on.[18]

Conclusions on Title V

Very much called for in the above context today, then, is a reliable measure of scarcity rents created by government licensing, allocation, and spectrum developing R&D. For those rents most accurately and least ambiguously measure the net private benefits enjoyed by "identifiable recipient[s] [of] a measurable unit of service from the government." (This of course refers to net economic rents, excluding those plowed back into public service, entertainment, or technical improvements.)

One important future consequence of these Supreme Court holdings over the long haul may be to encourage a more intensive effort to develop such measures of spectrum value to any and all users. Under Title V, as noted, these measures would mainly help determine an equitable apportionment of fees assessed to support a predetermined level of regulatory expenditures. Should the bounds of Title V now be breached, as suggested by Title IV of the proposed Communications Act of 1978, the larger issues stated at the outset of this section may well have to be faced.[19] To some of these issues I shall now turn.

Collecting and Transferring
the Rents to Public Broadcasting [20]

Numerous proposals have by now sought to collect rents and divert the proceeds into merit programs. The most far-reaching legislative expression of such schemes was indeed recently incorporated into section

18. Concurring Opinion of Justices Marshall and Brennan, ibid., 72–948, 72–1164, March 4, 1978, p. 9.

19. I presented these issues publicly at a plenary session of the Sixth Annual Conference on Telecommunications Policy Research, Airlie, Va., May 13, 1978. See especially preceding discussion of "Regulatory Cost . . . ," pp. 387–88.

20. Parts of this and the next section are adapted from my earlier paper on franchise values and policy options in television broadcasting. See R. Caves and M. Roberts (eds.), *Regulating the Product* (1975), especially sec. 3, pp. 133–40.

413 of the proposed Communications Act of 1978. Another closely related version is central to the recent Carnegie Commission Report.[21] In what follows I argue that these rents can and ought to be recaptured and devoted to public purposes on both equity and administrative grounds. Because there is no single technique for doing so, moreover, a combined approach is best. I shall then consider whether there are advantages to linking the rents with specific public services within a single entity instead of relating them across separate decision-making units.

My analysis is clearly reminiscent of major portions of the Van Deerlin-Frey bill, HR 13015, June 6, 1978, also of the focus in FCC's Notice of Inquiry in Gen. Docket No. 78–316 (Fee Refunds and Future Fees), Oct. 6, 1978, at pars. 82–110. However, my distinctions and formulations were developed separately from and well before both those documents or, indeed, the preparatory work for them.[22]

Readers in principle opposed to the linkage of user charges and specific public activities may approach the rest of the chapter with skepticism. For them, the main defense of earmarked or "dedicated" taxes or fees could be called investment efficiency. That is, dedication is supposed to ensure that the "correct" amount of the activity is supplied. To accomplish this, however, the payees must be the ultimate beneficiaries. Specifically, those who pay higher prices for products advertised on television must be the ones who will mainly benefit from more merit programs on commercial stations or from expanded public broadcasting. Otherwise, the recaptured rents are deemed more properly returnable to society at large, via the general treasury. This is said to be underscored, too, by the fact that television rents arise from a spectrum scarcity attributed to nature.

Purists will oppose dedicated (earmarked) levies at all costs, fearing the evasion of public accountability and, above all, that public activities that could not otherwise command as much support politically will somehow secure it on false pretenses.

Nevertheless, the purist position is not the only one. One can argue in reply that the validity of linking user fees to public broadcasting, or of dedicated taxes more generally, depends upon the political context as much as on economic principles. Some political mechanisms may be so imperfect that we must turn to a dedicated tax in last resort.

Proponents of this latter position see general budget making as less

21. *The Public Trust*, Report of the Carnegie Commission on the Future of Public Broadcasting (Bantam Books, 1979); Les Brown, "Carnegie II—A New Blueprint for Tomorrow's System," *New York Times* Arts and Leisure Section, February 11, 1979, pp. 1, 33.

22. See my paper on franchise values and policy options (note 20); also my "Federal Control of Entry in the Broadcast Industry," *Journal of Law & Economics*, (October 1962), 57–67; "Regulatory Efficiency, Reform and the FCC," *Georgetown Law Journal* (Fall 1961), 22–45; and especially, "TV *Can* Be Better," *Challenge* (May 1962), reprinted in *Congressional Record*. (June 27, 1962), and *Chubu Reports* (Japan Broadcasting Corp.).

consistent and rational in the United States than, for example, in a parliamentary system like Canada's or Great Britain's. For them, specific dedication is "bad" only if *general* expenditure decisions are politically rational; otherwise not. In the final judgment, political sociology and equity are deemed to loom large.

Such issues certainly cannot be resolved here. Suffice it to say that proponents of any dedicated tax to recapture scarcity rents must face these issues head-on.

1. Scarcity Rents, License Fees, and Public Trust Funds—The Rationale of External Linkage

The Advent of HR 13015. The proposed Communications Act of 1978 has now explicitly recognized the linkage between scarcity rents and public purpose. On the one hand, it would authorize a new Communications Regulatory Commission to assess a license fee for all spectrum users (including the common carrier and nonbroadcast services), taking into account both processing costs and scarcity value of the spectrum being assigned, unless that value is minimal or the user is a public or governmental entity, in which case this factor may be waived. Such fees would be phased in over a ten-year period, after which users would pay sums equal to the added cost of processing their licenses, plus the full scarcity value of their rights.[23]

On the other hand, all such fees (and scarcity rents) would be deposited in a telecommunications fund administered by the Secretary of Treasury. The fee monies would then be used first to reimburse the general fund of the Treasury for all regulatory costs under the act, with the remaining sums to fund public broadcast programming, rural telecommunications development, and minority ownership of stations, "in amounts equal to fixed percentages established by Congress."[24]

Such proposals are by no means new.[25] What is new is that they have now been sponsored in the most influential legislative circles, after exhaustive preparatory staff work and hearings over a twenty-month period. The latest proposals occurred also at a time when the public broadcast system—barely in its infancy when the earliest versions were publicly announced almost twenty years ago—was far more fully developed, with federal funding for physical facilities and programming very much a fact of life.

At this important crossroads in regulatory history, it is well to recall the broad contours of analogous mechanisms proposed earlier.

23. See Communications Act of 1978, HR 13015, June 6, 1978, sec. 413(c) (1) (2).
24. Ibid., sec. 413 (d) (2), pt. B of Title VI, and secs. 708–09.
25. I examined several at length over fifteen years ago, as just cited in note 22.

The Fischer Plan in 1959. In part reminiscent of the latest conception, the so-called Fischer Plan proposed that the FCC be authorized to charge all broadcast licensees for their channel space, and then plow back the funds annually (at the rate of $500 to $800 millions by 1976) into public service on a modified system of *commercial* stations.[26] In the face of an infant public broadcast capability, Fischer looked to the dominant commercial segment to bear the main burden both of the spectrum user charges and of the cultural and informational features that the Van Deerlin-Frey bill proposed to fund over public broadcast stations.

The Reuss Bill in 1960. A similar scheme, with still other modifications, was introduced by Congressman Henry Reuss in 1960.[27] Like the Van Deerlin-Frey bill today, the Reuss bill would have eliminated comparative proceedings (at least in part)—not, however, through "random selection" but through public auctions. Also, as today, Reuss further proposed to link scarcity rents and public broadcast programming.[28]

Broadcast licenses would be auctioned to the highest bidder after all applicants were first classified according to three priorities, first priority going to local applicants unaffiliated with other media, second priority going to local applicants with other media holdings, and third priority to all others. Sole applicants in the top priority would be enfranchised forthwith if otherwise qualified; but where two or more applicants fell into the same high category, FCC would invite competitive bids (in cash, public service, or both) and select the winner after proper weighting of all bids.[29]

The contests between competing applicants within the aforementioned priorities would be resolved by cash bids, promises of public service, or both [30] but with "public service" explicitly defined.[31] The sums paid by successful bidders would be deposited in a special Educational and Cultural TV and Radio Fund, from which FCC, on advice of an advisory board on education and culture, could make "loans or grants to non-profit . . . stations or organizations" to further cultural-informational-educational programming.

Subsequent Developments. Since then the linkage of scarcity rents and public service has had a lengthy history which need not be recounted.

26. See John Fischer, "Television and Its Critics," *Harper's Magazine* (July 1959), pp. 10–14, and his testimony in FCC Docket No. 12782, vol. 13, Tr. pp. 865–1008 (1960).

27. See HR 9549, 86th Cong., 2nd Sess. (1960), and comments in *Congressional Record*, January 12, 1960, pp. 317–19.

28. See HR 9549, p. 7, lines 11–15.

29. On the replacement of comparative hearings by public auctions with specified safeguards, see my "Regulatory Efficiency, Reform and the FCC," 24–33. See also Commissioner Glen O. Robinson's illuminating Dissent to the Commission's Decision in Re: Applications of Cowles Florida Broadcasting Co., et al., 60 FCC Reports 2d, July 20, 1976, pp. 443–48 (contrast of auctions and lotteries).

30. HR 9549, p. 6, lines 15–25; p. 7, lines 11–16.

31. Ibid., p. 5.

Suffice it to note only that since the proposal's initial conception two decades ago, its two principal elements—the auction and the fund—have developed separately.[32]

On the one hand, various (albeit token) license fees have been imposed on spectrum users generally, broadcast and nonbroadcast alike, geared to recover varying portions of the annual FCC budget and hence limited to a tiny fraction of gross communications revenues and even of estimated television rents. On the other hand, the emergence of the Corporation for Public Broadcasting and the Public Broadcast System Network, backed by growing federal, foundation, industry, and membership support of public broadcast stations and programming, has proceeded on a parallel route. However, not until the latest proposal (HR 13015) have policy makers once again publicly linked these two strands.[33]

So much for the explicit external linkage of scarcity rents and public service in broadcasting. In earlier chapters I have indeed argued that the rationale for such linkage in some measure derives from the government's decisive role in creating those rents [34] and from FCC's longstanding commitment (still unrealized) to negotiating back commensurate merit service and diversity.[35]

At present there is no guarantee that the rents will be used for public purposes. Their ultimate disposition has normally been determined by informal bilateral negotiation between an agency much influenced by its licensees, and a powerful, influential industry with its own notions about public service. In contrast, the more automatic diversion of rents to public broadcasting might facilitate a more reliable response. Such linkage would ensure, for example, that any reduction of public service on commercial television would be offset by more such service on public television, although the taxed rents could also be diverted into a trust fund that underwrote merit programs on commercial TV.

I recognize, of course, that long-run efficiency requires a lowering of licensee rents (ideally to zero), a reduction that will act to weaken the

---

32. There were actually three components in the Reuss Plan—a Broadcast Trust Fund, a license charge set by auction, and a nonpartisan Presidential Advisory Board to administer the fund for public service programming. All three features also appeared separately in other legislative proposals at that time. See citations in Levin, "Regulatory Efficiency," note 73.

33. The idea itself, however, has never been entirely lost from view. See, for example, *Public Television—A Program for Action,* Report of the Carnegie Commission on Educational Television (1967), Concurring Opinion of Commissioner Joseph J. McConnell, p. 72. See also *Report of the Task Force on the Long-Range Financing of Public Broadcasting,* Washington, D.C., September 1973, especially appendix F. One long-time observer further proposed a dedicated franchise tax of 6 percent on all broadcast and common carrier revenues to raise $1.2 billion annually for public broadcasting (letter to *New York Times,* January 14, 1978, from Sydney W. Dean).

34. See especially, chapter 1, note 35, and associated text.

35. See, for example, chapter 13, footnote 46, and chapter 5 generally.

political forces against deregulation and thereby enhance the chances for entry-opening technological change in the form of cable television, pay-TV, and satellite broadcasting (see chapters 4, 12). Nevertheless, with a few exceptions I have found little evidence that owner diversity or structural diversity will contribute significantly to content diversity, let alone to merit service generally. Therefore, the equity issue does appear more compelling here than efficiency considerations alone.

Such a conclusion must in any case be drawn from this discussion of the latest legislative initiatives in linking scarcity rents with public service.

In the remainder of this section I shall examine two techniques for recovering the rents—auctions and taxation. After that I turn to the possibility of diverting the rents into public service through internal linkage—that is, within a single communications entity.

Auctioning Of New Grants and Renewal Rights

The auctioning of broadcast licenses to qualified bidders would end the current give-away and induce more efficient spectrum utilization. One possibility here is to create perpetual rights (as proposed in section 431[b][2] of the Communications Act of 1978). Such a stipulation might indeed make far more defensible than otherwise the kind of once-and-for-all-auction (to levy a lump-sum tax on rents) that economists often favor on economic efficiency grounds.[36] In this case, to be sure, a lump-sum charge may entail too big a gamble for the licensee to work. Broadcasters may later sue, for example, to prevent the FCC from changing any rules of the game; that is, they may assert legal claims on the right to stop new entry and technological change.

A second possibility would be to "reauction" TV licenses for limited renewable terms. This would collect more of the franchise value than the auctioning of new limited-term grants, without requiring the perpetual enfranchisement stipulated by HR 13015. Furthermore, the public interest groups' desire to hold open the possibility of latecomer entry, especially by minority owners, could be met more readily than under any system of perpetual rights. Nevertheless, the periodic resale of renewable licenses would be subject to other objections almost as serious as the auctioning of perpetual rights.

Like the latter, if the reauctioning scheme worked effectively it might recapture too much—all the franchise value—and thus act to reduce the amount of merit programming on commercial stations unless the FCC were willing to disqualify owners who had failed to meet more explicitly defined program service responsibilities. Furthermore, renewal applicants might be demoralized if their incumbent status were entirely disregarded

36. See Richard Musgrave, *The Theory of Public Finance* (New York: McGraw-Hill, 1959), pp. 137–44.

in periodic reauction proceedings. This is clearly apparent in their growing anxiety over renewal contests, and their persistent pressure to extend the license term. Nor are limited renewable license terms likely to be sufficiently long to induce broadcasters to make risky long-term program investments.

Finally, any periodic auctioning of renewal rights at the end of, say, successive three-year terms might require that FCC be authorized to (1) set a price on all physical station assets equal to their scrap value plus allowable good will; (2) forbid potential buyers to pay less; and (3) invite competitive bids for all licenses at renewal time. Otherwise incumbents would run the risk of losing not only their licenses (and franchise value) but also the values they themselves had created (capitalized as good will). If an incumbent lost his rights to another bidder, for example, the winner, as by far the most suitable user of the physical facilities in their present form, need pay a price no greater than their scrap value, well below replacement costs, plus good will today (with risks of nonrenewal virtually zero).

Accordingly, fear of a similar loss might induce the new licensee to try to augment his own circulation through debased program service before the next auction three years later, clearly counterproductive to the end in view.

Were these safeguards imposed, on the other hand, a mandated price equal to estimated scrap value plus allowable good will might well be lower, perhaps very much lower, than the prices at which stations would otherwise sell even on a triennial basis. Many private traders heretofore outbid might now come forth to compete for the license alone. The premium above scrap value otherwise paid to the seller would now go to the commission instead. Nor, under the stated assumptions, would the total prices of stations plus licenses be any greater than they are today, when the seller gets both payments, and risks of nonrenewal are nil. Indeed, the reauctioning of rights every three (or even five or seven) years would certainly reduce the licensee's effective time horizon from what it is today, and would reduce as well the resulting price of station plus license.

The key question is whether longstanding legislative reluctance to legitimize property rights in spectrum may now be significantly altered. The recent provision for "indefinite" (perpetual) rights in television and radio ten years hence (HR 13015, section 431) suggests as much. So, too, does the proposal that FCC be prohibited, in the interim, from considering competing applications in determining whether to renew any existing license or to revoke one thereafter (HR 13015, section 437[a]).

However, one must not forget the dramatic defeat some years ago of two massive campaigns to protect incumbents against challengers. The so-called Whitehead Bill had unsuccessfully sought to extend the license term to five years, as well as raise major barriers to renewal contests. A comparable campaign three years earlier also culminated in the defeat of Senator John O. Pastore's proposal (S. 2004) for similar protection against challengers.[37]

It is still too early to know just how far the longstanding tradition against property rights may now be eased. But even at this writing, the public interest groups have taken a strong position against such easing.[38] Furthermore, any proposal that FCC be empowered to set a price of the replacement value of physical TV assets runs directly counter to the conception of broadcasting as a nonpublic utility. Nor does it seem politically realistic in light of Congress's longstanding hostility to setting direct controls on broadcast sales prices.[39]

Accordingly, a more workable approach may be to collect only part of the rents beforehand, by auctioning off new broadcast grants. Then some of the residual rents could be recaptured by an annual user charge on spectrum access (say, a gross receipts tax on TV licensees). The need for some such combined attack flows in large part from the unique problems just described.[40]

In regard to new grants, to be sure, auctions would simply divert to FCC sums that applicants would otherwise have paid to buy existing licenses or to utilize (or circumvent) complex procedures to get a new license gratis. Therefore the auction itself need raise neither the buyer's capital charges, nor the station's supply price, nor, if total demand for and supply of stations remain constant, the demand price. Quite the contrary, as noted, the price may well be lower than today, insofar as a triennial auction would drastically alter the present conferral of virtually unlimited de facto rights.

Accordingly, station prices as a whole would hardly be higher today had new grants been auctioned publicly from the outset for, say, three- or five-year terms than they now are after decades of almost unregulated private trading. Nor, on that score, or with proper safeguards, would the pressures toward ownership and area concentration have been intensified or service standards worsened; yet millions of dollars of franchise values might have been recaptured.

In sum, the difference between today's market for stations (and licenses) and the proposal to auction off at least new grants lies mainly

37. Those struggles are vividly described in Fred Friendly, "The Campaign to Politicize Broadcasting," *Columbia Journalism Review* (March/April 1973), 8–18, and reported frequently in the trade press at that time.

38. See *Broadcasting* (June 12, 1978), 41; *Wall Street Journal* (June 8, 1978).

39. See, for example, chapter 4, pages 108–9. Notable also is the absence of any such proposal anywhere in the relevant provisions of HR 13015. See HR 13015, sec. 414 (license requirements), sec. 433 (assignments and transfer), sec. 437 (renewals, petitions to deny).

40. The latest legislative proposal is heavily grounded in the latter user charge route. See HR 13015, sec. 413 (a)–(c). However, competing applications for new grants are to be handled by random selection (a lottery) and not by auctions to the highest qualified bidder (Sec. 414[c]). Compare also the FCC's own extended concern with formulae to estimate spectrum value (Docket No. 78–316, pars. 86–110), and its much briefer attention to auctions (ibid., pars. 92, 111).

in the ultimate disposition of the sizable rents at stake and in the question of long-run efficiency. Today TV transfers redistribute those rents among the participating buyers and sellers over time, except for token amounts converted into merit service and diversity. An auction scheme would at least permit a separate decision to redirect more of the rents directly into public service.

A Dedicated Gross Receipts Tax on Television Licensees

As an alternative (or supplement) to auctions, a gross receipts tax for spectrum use offers a number of special attractions as a way to fund public merit programming. Shiftable only in part, its three-way incidence offers a seemingly equitable apportionment of needed tax support for public television. Insofar as shifted forward, the tax raises the price of advertised products and is thereby widely diffused among the public. Hence it will actually fall on public TV's principal beneficiaries, given that even nonviewers benefit from its contribution to expanded political discussion, an informed electorate, the resolution of group conflict, and improved education and cultural values generally.

To the extent that television rates do not rise, moreover, backward shifting would mean that the network companies, the talent, and the programmers who now benefit directly from the licensee's quasi-monopolistic position would have to share in some of his obligations, too, through reduced income. Nevertheless, the licensees themselves will probably have to pay something out of rents in return for their privileged access to the spectrum.

In short, while offering many equity advantages of an excess profits or net income tax, the tax on gross receipts would be no more regressive than a household TV license fee or an excise on TV sets. Equally important, the partial shiftability of a gross receipts charge could reduce the opposition of vested interests toward a tax on rents alone. Finally, the size, the growth rate, and the stability of the former's tax base may permit a lower tax rate for any desired level of funding than would tax on rents. Indeed, such advantages could well outweigh the adverse effects of special taxes on relative prices and economic efficiency.

General versus Special Levies

Use of general revenue is the obvious alternative to the specialized taxes just mentioned. For merit programming, however, the traditional, normally attractive case for a general levy seems less persuasive than otherwise. True, the presumed progressive character of federal general revenue funding would still cause it to rate high on equity grounds, all the more because we cannot identify (and hence charge) the precise consumers of merit programs. Nor does general taxation distort relative prices of, or efficiency in producing, TV-related goods and services. (It presumably does impair efficiency by distorting the relative prices of leisure and income-producing activities, as is true of all taxes except lump-sum [head] taxes.)

By not imposing special burdens, moreover, use of the general revenue may also forestall the kind of powerful group opposition that could plague dedicated funding. By distributing general revenue funds by statutory formula, with predetermined appropriations, the public broadcaster might even be insulated, to a degree, against periodic governmental intrusions (in the normal appropriations process) into their program decision making.

Yet the ease of such insulation must not be exaggerated. The repeated failures of earlier proposals for ten-, five-, or even two-year general appropriations give pause, despite the latest White House endorsement of a major $1 billion five-year funding scheme.[41] In contrast, a dedicated tax is more insulated. It requires a major congressional effort to alter its use, and its vulnerability to industry lobbies must not be exaggerated. Once the initial decision to collect scarcity rents is made, it is hard to see why the taxed industry would lobby more strenuously simply because the tax take was earmarked for public broadcasting, rather than deposited in the general Treasury.

The really central question is whether recovery of rents—justified as it is not simply for general equity but because of the spectrum's unique characteristics and government's vital role in developing it—is an appropriate basis for determining the level of support for public broadcasting. While I by no means suggest the adequacy of commercial rents for that purpose, I do recognize their appropriate contribution to PTV's aggregate funding requirements.[42]

Nevertheless, one final set of questions not directly researched in this book must be explored before instituting any definitive fee schedule. These pertain to the longstanding hostility to even token fees by commercial broadcasters (and at one time many regulators and legislators as well).[43] Fees are indeed still opposed for allegedly impairing the industry's incentives and capabilities for diversity. With fee levels under the proposed new Federal Communications Act approaching even $350 or $400 million for all spectrum users,[44] a high research priority must

41. President Carter's Message to Congress on Public Broadcasting, October 6, 1977, especially p. 3.

42. See earlier notes 34 and 35 and associated text.

43. Compare past hostility and reticence (as noted in my *Invisible Resource,* pp. 104–15), with the detailed investigation now proposed in FCC, Docket No. 78–316, October 6, 1978, especially pars. 86–111.

44. This includes charges on common carriers and other nonbroadcast users as well as broadcasters, but the bulk of the estimated levy appears to be aimed at television. See *Broadcasting* (June 19, 1978), 28; and (June 12, 1978), 29.

go to the consistency of fee requirements and public service on commercial television.

Illustrative of the issues needing examination are these: (1) At what point would an attempt to recover aggregate scarcity rents impair the commercial provision of cultural-informational programming? (2) If such programs were to decline with rising fee levels, were the fees in fact being collected out of scarcity rents in the first place? (3) Could we not in any case assess a low fee first and raise it gradually over time, instead of, say, a lump-sum auction charge from the start? [45] (4) If so, would such gradualism help minimize any incentives to cut back on public service?

So much, then, for alternative techniques to recover the scarcity rents and divert them into public service. The discussion has so far focused on the principle of external linkage where rents are recaptured from a private entity and transferred to a public one, in a separate visible public decision. Because of political tensions and concerted commercial opposition generated by such proposals in the past, still other techniques merit review, in particular those that aim to convert rents into public service through internal linkage (within a single communications entity). Although far more limited sums are doubtless recoverable using such devices, they do permit us to explore devices at once dedicated, automatic, and possibly less vulnerable to the aforementioned tensions under external linkage.

Two such mechanisms to which I now turn are the so-called Ford satellite proposal and reduced-rate interconnection for public television. I do not, however, intend to imply that there are no other funding options for public television, or that rents-financed public TV cannot be combined with other techniques in a diverse package of options. On the contrary, there is good reason to diversify those options both because scarcity rents may dry up as new entry-opening technologies develop, and because the FCC and public broadcasters may block such technologies to prevent this from happening. Including rents funding as one among several options may help forestall these counterproductive tendencies.

45. HR 13015 does indeed propose to phase in the fees (sec. 413[c] [2]). However, its conception is somewhat different from that presented here. Thus in exchange for their scarcity rents, licensees are to be granted indefinite license terms (sec. 431), revocable only for gross abuse (sec. 417, 437) and additionally relieved of certain specified programming responsibilities (secs. 434, 439). Any impairment of informational or local programming due to the fee assessment would presumably be minimized by monitoring (sec. 434[a] [1] [2]) and/or offset by diverting the rents into public broadcasting, rural facilities development and loans for minority station owners (sec. 413[d]). It is, however, worth noting that the current FCC Notice of Inquiry into Fee Refunds and Future Fees does not inquire explicitly into issues of program impairment. The sole veiled reference to it appears in Notice of Inquiry in Docket No. 78–316, par. 110 (sec. k).

Cross-Subsidy for Merit Programming
within a Single Entity

But why bother with examples of internal linkage able to generate at most a small fraction of the scarcity rents of a dedicated gross receipts tax, or public auctions? And why, finally, review the specifics of these schemes in detail here?

The answer is threefold. First, the automaticity of internal linkage is clearly greater than that of the prevailing proposals for a dedicated spectrum user charge (HR 13015, sec. 413) and, indeed, than external linkage more generally. On that score alone their conspicuous absence from the latest legislative proposals makes a fuller discussion here both timely and appropriate.

Second, whatever the near-term disposition of external linkage, the internal schemes merit ongoing consideration in the future on the closely related ground of insulating public TV funding from federal intrusions. Automaticity is of course tantamount to insulation. But here the lower visibility of the rents which internal linkage diverts is an important extra advantage in particularly sensitive programming areas.

This brings us to a third and last reason for examining the illustrative details of internal linkage. The small annual sums involved ($7–$21 million, or 2–7 percent of estimated VHF rents in 1975) further ensure low visibility. However, the possibility (and the merits) of earmarking even such a small sum to the most sensitive programming areas of public television warrant considered debate.

A previous administration not only sought to reduce or even to eliminate public TV's public affairs and documentary function, but also seriously to impair development of the whole system.[46] Nor is the future recurrence of such blatant pressure under another administration beyond the realm of possibility.

On the face of it, these bits of regulatory history may appear to contribute little to the current dialogue over legislative reform. Before relegating them to the archives of past experiments, however, readers may want to sift through their mechanics to determine what the impediments were, what the possibilities might have been, and what future adaptations are conceivable and useful.

46. See text associated with preceding note 41. The Nixon Administration saw, in the "liberal" thrust of a centralized, federally funded public broadcast system, a political threat it could not sanction. This basic antagonism may help explain the repeated failure of even the most modest proposals for long-term funding throughout the 1970s.

The Ford Satellite Proposal

As conceived by the Ford Foundation in 1966, all television networks would buy interconnection from a newly created Broadcasters Nonprofit Satellite Corporation licensed to own and operate the sole domestic television satellite system.[47] Funding for public television would be derived as follows. The corporation (BNSC) would charge commercial networks less for interconnection than their then available next-best land alternative, but more than the cost of providing the circuits (1) on a nonprofit basis, or (2) via a multipurpose satellite that also served nonbroadcast (general) users, or (3) via a TV network joint venture that served its parent companies direct. In this way BNSC would not only generate resources to interconnect a public network gratis, but also to support the latter's nonremunerative merit programs, at least in part.

Recapturing the Incremental Value of Space Satellite Spectrum. Viewed as just described, the Ford proposal was really not, as then reputed, a tax to recover the government's past investment in space satellite technology. Rather would it essentially have recaptured for educational purposes some of the increments to spectrum value (that is, rents) due to new satellite technology. Those rent increments would tend to equal the difference between the commercial networks' annual interconnection costs through AT&T landlines, and the cost of comparable interconnection through relay satellites.

The assumption behind this approach was that the communications industries should not be permitted to appropriate all the increased rents created by the government's development of satellite technology. In this case the latter had raised the economic value of those microwave frequencies that the existing land carriers (especially AT&T) and the new space satellite service would in some regions both share.[48] Beyond that, the Ford brief argued that, in any conventional common carrier-operated satellite system, the cost savings would be absorbed and passed on to users "in amounts too small to be noticed," with cost reductions for TV "largely lost in the shuffle." However, the nation had a right to "tangible, identifiable returns for its huge investments in space technology." [49] The difficulty of eliminating such rents, say, via rate base regulation, simply underscored the need to recover them direct.

With no incentives for TV stations to use the larger rents derived from satellite cost savings for merit service, we are implicitly confronted with this hard choice: either to devise new techniques (such as quantitative program requirements) to induce licensees to use their rents for

47. The Ford Satellite plan was originally filed in FCC Docket No. 16495, Comments of Ford Foundation, vol. 1, August 1, 1966, pp. 7–23; Reply Comments, vol. 1, December 12, 1966, pp. 1–11, 48–59.

48. See Levin, *The Invisible Resource*, pp. 168–69, 237–39, 275.

49. Reply Comments of Ford Foundation in Docket No. 16495, December 12, 1966, vol. I, pp. 27–33; Supplemental Comments, vol. I, April 3, 1967, pp. 49–50.

more merit service *ex post,* or to adopt something like the Ford plan to divert any new rents at the source, *ex ante.*[50] It is true, however, that such a plan could operate to raise the price of using the satellite facility above its marginal cost, and thus impair the efficiency of resource allocation.

In short, the Ford plan appears to proceed from the view that any lowering of interconnection charges to commercial networks would have less effect on program diversity (via new network entry or internal subsidies by those who enjoy the larger rents) than would a scheme to divert the cost savings into public television directly.[51] However, the low elasticity of the networks' demand for interconnection could imply that the efficiency cost would be small.[52]

Automaticity. The relative automaticity of the plan was one of its major virtues. This would keep it relatively freer than the proposals in the previous section from political pressures and the strains of an external linkage of fund sources to fund users. Nevertheless, the plan withered on the vine, in part because the industry objected to being implicitly taxed, as they saw it, to support public TV, and in part also because the predicted satellite economies were simply "too small."[53]

Uncertainty of Funds. Nor is the appropriateness of satellite cost savings as a source of funding for a public service of such importance entirely clear. Such income could well be uncertain, because the level of AT&T land line or microwave charges would limit the spread between satellite circuit costs and the prices charged the commercial networks. If technological improvements continued to reduce land circuit costs, as they had in the past, the income recovered could well decline, perhaps substantially. In the final analysis, the FCC might be pressured to

50. See especially J. Dirlam and A. Kahn, "The Merits of Reserving the Cost-Savings from Communications Satellites for Support of Educational Television," *Yale Law Journal* (January 1968), 494, 502–13.

51. This point is well demonstrated in Dirlam and Kahn, "Support of Educational Television," note 4. Lower-level interconnection charges alone would not facilitate new network entry: AT&T's rate structure must also offer special charges to part-time specialized users, a possibility long impeded by FCC rate regulatory practice (ibid., pp. 502, 511–13; House Commerce Committee, *Report on Network Broadcasting* (Washington, D.C.: U.S. Government Printing Office, 1958), pp. 198–204, 541–46, 552). Nor was it in any case clear that lower interconnection costs would in the first instance induce existing networks to supply more programming to more families, by affiliating with more stations and otherwise achieving more program clearances (Dirlam and Kahn, pp. 504–10). Without such additional effects, economic rents would presumably swell at the station level (ibid.). See additional evidence also in chapter 8, on the relative impact on type diversity of new commercial and public TV entry.

52. "Even a tax of as much as 40 percent on satellite service is unlikely to deter their use," whereas the "amount of a tax could be as high as $25 to $30 million without making satellites more expensive than [terrestrial] . . . interconnection" (Noll, Peck and McGowan, *Economic Aspects of Television Regulation* (Washington, D.C.: Brookings Institution, 1973), p. 232.

53. See critique of Ford plan in Comments of AT&T in Docket No. 16495, December 15, 1966, attachments 1 and 3.

slow down technical advances in microwave or cable transmission merely to protect this funding source.

Aggregate Funds Expected. Today only some $21 million annually could be generated under such a proposal, since each network's costs could just be lowered from $20 million to $13 million.[54] Yet such a sum would have covered almost all of the Corporation for Public Broadcasting's outlays for both interconnection and programming in 1971 (albeit only 13 percent of total expenditures by all public TV licensees that year). Obviously also, by not charging quite so much, some of the cost savings could be returned to the commercial system (as under the Reuss plan), in hopes for better programming from that source, too.

Other Analogous Schemes. Once we recognize that some relatively automatic diversion of funds, especially for highly sensitive news and public affairs programming, is both feasible and needed,[55] there is no reason to stop with satellite interconnection. The linkage of rents and public service could be located within the current AT&T-Bell complex by means of differentiated (dual) interconnection rates for public and private networks. As with the Ford proposal, this arrangement also could recapture the rents *ex ante* and avoid difficult problems in acting *ex post*. Presumably the higher charges for commercial interconnection would be partly passed on to advertisers (and hence consumers), partly shifted backward to networks and programmers, and partly borne by TV licensees.

Reduced-Rate Interconnection for Public Television

Reduced-rate interconnection for public networks could indeed be realized by setting rates near long-run incremental costs as presently calculated. Because this calculation excluded spectrum costs, it would permit public television to enjoy the economic rents associated with the frequencies used to serve it. Let us further assume the existence of a single dedicated and self-sustaining interconnection facility, which all public and private networks utilize. AT&T would then have to charge the private commercial users for the common costs of servicing the public users too, so that these commercial users would pay more than the fully distributed cost of servicing them alone. The subsidy implicit in the rates set at current long-run marginal nonspectrum costs of servicing the public users, would be paid out of rents the carriers collect by charging commercial users for their access to the spectrum.

54. The estimates cited in this paragraph and the next appear in Noll, Peck, and McGowan, pp. 231–32, 249–51.

55. This point was driven home in testimony before the Senate Commerce Committee, *Hearings on S. 1160—The Public Television Act of 1967,* 90th Cong. 1st sess. (1967), pp. 173–76 (Fred Friendly). An automatic diversion of BNSC cost savings was viewed as guaranteeing even more insulation than would dedicated tax revenues in a federal trust fund.

Current Significance of the Proposal. The sums at stake in reduced-rate interconnection are admittedly small. In 1971, CPB budgeted only $7 million for "interconnection grants" administered by its networking subsidiary, the Public Broadcasting System (PBS), compared with almost $18 million for "programming grants." PBS in turn paid Bell $2 million (annual charges raised to $4 million by 1975). This was for network hook-ups worth roughly $15 million at commercial rates. Therefore, even if this whole interconnection bill were reduced to zero, CPB's high programming costs would obviously still make the going tough.

Nevertheless, there are good reasons to examine this policy alternative. First of all, interconnection costs for a full-fledged public network are no small matter given that service's financial plight. Although the $61 million commercial interconnection bill in 1971 was only 5.6 percent of network broadcast expenses, the comparable costs for CPB loom much larger in *its* budget. If it were indeed to cost $13 million to interconnect a fully equivalent PTV system in 1980 (at commercial rates), CPB's bill would run about 13 percent of its projected budget.

Furthermore, AT&T's sensitivity to reduced rates may well reflect still other concerns. Preferential rates here could confuse delicate negotiations and decisions elsewhere, in regard, for example, to commercial program transmission, "telpak," press rates, the "hi-lo" tariff, and so on. These wide-ranging ramifications are also of obvious concern to the FCC.

Lastly, there is the matter of recurrent governmental pressures on PTV's program acquisition and scheduling decisions in the annual appropriations process. Some observers therefore want to strengthen PTV's independence in program production and distribution. Guaranteed reduced-rate (or free) access to a $20 million or eventually $13 million interconnection service, they contend, is a step in the right direction.

Issues of Fact and Policy. Several sets of issues merit special attention in the continuous dialogue over interconnection rates.

The first set relates to costs and benefits. If public TV interconnection is in fact priced below levels for an equivalent commercial system, who will primarily bear the costs, and who ultimately would use the program service or otherwise benefit? How much of the higher commercial rates, that is, would broadcasters pass on to their advertisers (and thence to general consumers)? How much would they shift backward to program suppliers, talent agencies, equipment companies, et cetera? How much would they themselves pay out of economic rents? Finally, would the availability of private, specialized, or land line systems (or satellite alternatives) virtually guarantee that broadcaster rents remain intact, and force the general telephone user to bear a lion's share of the burden?

A second set of questions pertains to another closely related issue. Rates that deviate from strict economic principles must presumably be set with reference to the "benefit externalities" that result. But can such benefits be measured accurately enough to permit regulators to set economically rational charges below the relevant incremental cost? Would such reduced rates enable certain viewers to see programs that they value, for example, but are not otherwise available? Would still other programs appear that some viewers may want to be available for themselves (or for others), even though few may choose to watch them? Does this latter merit justification of reduced rates go to the heart of the matter insofar as diversity could also be provided by pay-TV, sufficient new station entry, and other technical or policy options? Finally, does a unique case for preferential pricing not appropriate elsewhere follow here from the political dangers of more conventional funding alternatives?

A third set of issues transcends such considerations and asks whether a persuasive case for totally free access can be mounted on sheer grounds of administrative convenience. That is, do the complexity of joint cost allocations, and the negligible and widely diffused cost effects of zero rates on the general telephone user, imply as much?

Fourth and last, if an insulated funding source for CPB's program distribution subsidiary (PBS) really makes political or administrative sense, the practicality of differentiated interconnection rates for commercial and public television networks seems at least worth exploring. It is of interest, for example, that in 1971 a 10 percent increase in Bell's commercial rates, if other things had remained constant, would have yielded enough revenues to cover almost all of the $7 million PBS network budget. By the same token, commercial TV network revenues would have declined by only .56 percent and total network costs risen by a scant .59 percent.

Economics of Reduced Interconnection Rates. "Reduced" rates must be defined relative to some specific cost standard. Under one approach, rates below average costs (so-called fully distributed costs) of serving the "favored" user alone would be considered a reduced or preferential rate. With constrained efficiency pricing, however, customers with less elastic demand get charged more, and those with more elastic demand get charged less. Those constrained efficiency prices, determined in part by relative demand elasticities, then, may be greater than, equal to, or less than the distributed average cost of relevant-run incremental costs of serving the user in question.

According to the fully distributed cost standard, a reduced rate is any rate below fully distributed costs, which cannot be determined until the shape of the user's demand curve for the service is known, along with, inferentially, the cost and availability of his next-best alternatives. Nor would a rational monopolist in any case ever price below relevant marginal cost.

There is, furthermore, a possible limit to the cross-subsidy implicit in reduced interconnection rates. As the level of cross-subsidy rises, so does the cost of resource misallocation, so long as price exceeds marginal cost in the old markets. At the extreme, new customer charges would be set at marginal cost, the difference between marginal cost and fully distributed cost being one measure of the cross-subsidy.

At some price the demand for interconnection from the commercial networks will become sufficiently elastic that marginal revenues exceed marginal cost,[56] so that further price increases would actually diminish the subsidy funds available. That level will depend upon the value of simultaneity to the networks and upon the value and costs of various interconnection alternatives (see generally chapter 2, pages 31–33, and Appendix 2A). Two questions here are: What would the so-called bicycling of videotapes or delayed program transmission cost, and what audiences and advertising revenue be lost in the process? What are the comparative costs of other major TV network interconnection alternatives, such as various private, joint network, or specialized carriers?

Finally, a number of unwanted side effects might flow from the preclusive consequences of reduced rates on possible entry into the interconnection business. There is evidence that even today AT&T is pricing television interconnection and other services to deter potential entry.[57] Cross-subsidized AT&T interconnection rates for public television would probably make it harder still for, say, specialized common carrier entrants to get the public television business. Even new entry into the commercial interconnection segment could well become less attractive if, as seems likely, FCC had to keep the allowable commercial rates of such new entrants higher than otherwise to ensure continued cross-subsidy to the public network.

Some possible consequences of this rate differentiation proposal are actually suggested by Microwave Communications Inc.'s abortive plan for a special nonprofit interconnection system (EDUCOM). ETV stations were to be permitted to hang their own radio transmission equipment gratis on microwave towers operated for other purposes by CATV systems or specialized carriers. The initial annualized comparative costs estimated for EDUCOM were considerably lower than even for Bell's then newly proposed part-time, daytime rates for ETV stations.[58] How-

56. For some evidence that the networks have considered turning elsewhere, if only as a useful bargaining strategy in dealing with Bell and FCC, see Docket no. 18684, Networks Ex. no. P10, May 28, 1971, Proposed Testimony of David M. Blank on Behalf of ABC, CBS, and NBC, and Attachment A thereto—Joint Statement of ABC, CBS, and NBC in Docket no. 16495, March 29, 1971.

57. Melody, "Market Structure and Public Policy in Communications," unpublished paper presented at 82d Annual Meetings of American Economic Association, December 28, 1969, pp. 7–18; Roger Noll and Lewis Rivlin, "Regulating Prices in Competitive Markets," *Yale Law Journal*, vol. 82 (June 1973), 1426–34. There is some evidence that the television tariff adjustments Bell has offered are generally consistent with a strategy of precluding new system entry. See *Hearings on S.1160*, pp. 411–15.

58. See FCC, RM–1418, Microwave Communications Inc., a Proposal to the Corporation for Public Broadcasting and the Interuniversity Communications Council (EDUCOM), December 13, 1968, transmitted as petition to FCC; letter from Goeken, MCI, to Waple, FCC, March 10, 1969 (RM 1418) and attached Report, MCI's Proposal to Establish a Nationwide Network to Interconnect Non-Commercial Educational Broadcast Stations, February 10, 1969 (RM–1).

ever, Bell subsequently set rates interconnecting a 110-point CPB network still lower, down near the then estimate of long-run incremental cost, and the MCI plan doubtless suffered as a consequence.[59] After all, similarly specialized carriers like United Video and Western Telecommunications have for some time interconnected local CATV systems by terrestrial microwave hook-ups, and the American Broadcasting Companies still operate their own private system for partial interconnection of certain affiliates.

The structural side effects and regulatory burden of the dual rates proposal may by no means be trivial. Are they worth incurring for the admittedly small absolute amounts of money in question? Or are we faced here with a tail-wagging-the-dog syndrome?

Specifically, even granting the unique character of legalized benefit externalities of public television, will the problem of rigorous definition and measurement be so insurmountable as to question almost any departure from long-run incremental cost or fully distributed cost? Does the dual rate proposal at best require value judgments beyond the economist's competence to make *qua* economist? In short, are the proposal's risks so great, and its benefits so speculative, as to make it less attractive than pursuing progress in the traditional measurement of incremental cost and demand elasticities, the refinement of cost avoidance concepts, and the analysis of market structure strategies? Or could we devise useful ways to combine reduced interconnection rates with other funding options in arriving at an adequate and reliable level of public broadcasting?

Conclusion

This brief review of alternative techniques to recover and redirect the scarcity rents in broadcasting suggests several conclusions.

The rate differentiation proposals to support public broadcasting will clearly generate far less revenue than the auction-tax-user charge approach. The former proposals also pose not insignificant structural problems and in particular require considerable regulatory monitoring to avoid raising still higher entry barriers to specialized carriers.

By way of compensation, the internal linkage of dual rates with public broadcast funding may avoid the political problems posed by external linkage. In the latter case, the recapture of far larger rents from a private

59. During the long negotiating period with CPB, Bell did successively reduce its public TV offer to 50 percent of commercial rates (letter from Emerson, AT&T to FCC Chairman Hyde, April 29, 1969) to 40 percent (letter from Kelley, AT&T to Griffith, FCC, September 25, 1969), and then to 33 percent (FCC Memorandum and Order in Docket no. 18316, June 3, 1971, pars. 4, 6–7, 18–19).

commercial entity than under dual rates, and their redirection to a public one, in a separate visible decision, could well create greater tensions and political opposition.

Four guideposts for future action follow.

First, a combined approach seems to make greatest conceptual and practical sense, all the more because even under external linkage there is no single ideal technique to recapture scarcity rents (recall the pros and cons of several possible taxes, auctions, reauctions, etc.).

Second, the limited revenue derivable from the dual rates proposal should be specially and explicitly earmarked for the highly sensitive news and public affairs service. A relatively automatic diversion of even limited funds here, operating without fanfare, could still contribute importantly to any realistic mix of policies. The small sums involved and the uncertain structural consequences, then, both advise against heavy reliance on internal linkage.

Third, estimation of the level and incidence of aggregate scarcity rents by station class should be given the highest priority in future governmental efforts at fee setting.

Fourth and last, the organizational framework in which rents will be redistributed among public (or conceivably commercial) users is another research priority of the highest order. It would be desirable, for example, to design at least some modicum of automaticity in collection and redistribution of the rents (external linkage). As with dual rates (internal linkage), some such automaticity seems essential to prevent administrative or political tensions among the several participating governmental and private entities, which could impair the whole process.

Appendix I

Basic Methodological

Issues*

THE PURPOSE of this appendix is to describe how we handled ten methodological issues that influenced the character of our investigation. Special reference will be made to (1) the basic criteria guiding our variable specifications; (2) our early testing for multicollinearity; (3) the obscuring effects of overspecification; (4) the use of interactive as well as simple additive estimation; (5) the use of logarithmic variables and (6) quadratic forms; (7) problems of heteroskedasticity and (8) simultaneity bias; (9) the use of "quasi-elasticities" based on the full sample mean; and (10) the rejection of beta weights. Thus, whereas Appendix II reviews our principal estimating equations directly, in chronological order, Appendix I supplements that commentary with a more detailed explanation of basic methodological assumptions and decisions.

1. Our General Criteria for Equation Specification

We essentially utilized six criteria in developing our variable specifications: economic relevance, hypothesis testing, limited experimentation, simplicity of interpretation, avoidance of multicollinearity and stability of coefficients, and total explanatory power.

(a) *Economic Relevance.* Our equations had to make economic sense. That is, they were expected to reflect notions of causality represented in our investigatory model. This criterion helped us define a large set of possible specifications rather than to identify *a priori* any single preferred one. It did constitute a necessary condition for acceptance of any

---

*This appendix was distilled from a number of separate memoranda prepared in accordance with the author's specifications, by senior project consultant Jacob D. Merriwether.

equation but often facilitated the choice among specifications equivalent in how they met other criteria.

(b) *Hypothesis Testing.* All equations had to facilitate hypothesis testing. This criterion further narrowed the set of possible equations and, in our research, led us to fit specific groups of dependent variables to the same set of independent variables. The coefficients and elasticities from these equations were thereby made more comparable by having the same set of factors held constant, or taken into account.

(c) *Limited Experimentation.* Only a few equations could be estimated for any single portion of our overall model. There was no hard rule on the number of specifications to be investigated. However, the fact that much of our research was a "first pass" at model estimation, and that the project investigated a broad range of issues, generally precluded our going into great depth in specifying any single equation. As a result, many alternative specifications could not be explored. With a few important exceptions, for example, the large number of possible nonlinear transformations was simply not investigated. We do not argue that our simple additive model was optimal; but, given our time constraints, broad research objectives, and the generally good results from that model,[1] we feel it was in fact the best use of limited investigatory resources. No matter how many formulations are fitted, moreover, one could always be criticized for not having tried another.

(d) *Simplicity of Interpretation.* We attempted to specify equations simple enough to facilitate their interpretation by nontechnical readers. While this was no overriding consideration, a drawback of many nonlinear specifications is that their interpretation in terms of meaningful units and elasticities often involves mathematical manipulations that would leave the untrained reader unwilling even to consider the results. The additive model, with its frequent use of (o, 1) dummy variables, permitted us to derive meaningful conclusions without extensive manipulation of the estimated coefficients.

(e) *Avoidance of Multicollinearity and of Unstable Coefficients.* In adding variables to any particular equation, we tried to avoid the accumulation of multicollinearity that would render insignificant coefficients that might otherwise retain significance. This was done in two ways. First, as a basic equation was modified by respecification of included variables (such as by changing the number of fields of a dummy variable) or by addition of new variables, the behavior of the existing coefficients was carefully monitored. Stability of coefficients of variables common to several equations was viewed as an indication of their worth. The second approach was to check statistically for multicollinearity by regressing each independent variable on all others and analyzing the

1. One major refinement was the extensive specification of interactive dummy variables.

results. The generally large sizes of our samples prevented multicollinearity from affecting our results to any significant degree.

(f) *Total Explanatory Power.* Other things equal, a higher adjusted R-square and a higher t-ratio were preferred to the opposite. R-squares are of course not comparable in equations with different dependent variables (a problem that requires the choice among various nonlinear specifications be made on other grounds than maximizing R^2). However, where many specifications of equations with the same dependent variable were tried, the equation with the highest, or near-highest, adjusted R-square would ordinarily be chosen. Likewise, more emphasis was given to the interpretation of significant coefficients than to insignificant point estimates. Indeed the existence of significance in the face of extensive multicollinearity was further evidence of acceptable specifications.

So much then for these six guiding principles. Depending on circumstances, different criteria might dominate in the specification of variables in particular equations. In all cases a good deal of personal judgment and knowledge of the industry and of earlier research played important roles.

2. Testing for Multicollinearity

The preference for a common and rather complete specification of independent variables for an entire group of dependent variables (criterion 2) implied that some equations might have a number of insignificant coefficients. Multicollinearity had to be checked to determine whether those coefficients were really insignificant or simply rendered so by our having included so many independent variables.

Besides being alert for coefficients that were especially sensitive to minor changes in equation specification, there were several occasions when a more direct "test" for multicollinearity was carried out. Our station sales equations (table 4.11) and the market equations (5.2, 8.1) are two such cases. For those equations each independent variable was regressed on all other independent variables and the resulting R^2 statistics evaluated. In almost all instances the variables with high R^2 (indicating a high degree of collinearity with other variables in the equation) had significant coefficients. That is, the evidence of multicollinearity was not of sufficient magnitude to render insignificant most coefficients in the model. For this we can thank the large samples being used.

Of equal importance, there was little evidence that our *insignificant* coefficients were so rendered by *multicollinearity*. For example, the newspaper coefficients were of particular interest in this research, and they were generally insignificant. The multicollinearity tests support our conclusion that they are truly insignificant and not simply rendered so by multicollinearity due to the large number of independent variables.

3. Effects of Overspecification

In regard to cases where we may have overspecified equations by including insignificant variables, the following should be noted. We incur no bias in our estimates by including variables that are not statistically significant (at an arbitrary level). "Too many" variables can reduce the number of degrees of freedom so as to make the achievement of statistical significance an impossibility. However, our large sample size tended to forestall such an eventuality, as well as comparable results of multicollinearity (as has been seen). Nor does multicollinearity in any case bias our coefficients. Finally, we base the conclusions in this study heavily on coefficients that *are* significant.

A further basic point is that by including all the variables, and still getting significance for many of them, we are sure that the coefficients, significant and insignificant, do not reflect the impact of factors omitted from the model.[2] For many purposes we wish to compare the impact of a given independent variable on several different dependent variables. How, for example, does newspaper affiliation impact on local programming compared with its impact on news programming? (tables 5.3, 6.12). To do this reliably, we want the *ceteris paribus* conditions to be the same for the two estimates of the newspaper coefficient. Therefore, it would be an error to drop insignificant variables from the local programming equation if those variables were significant in the news equation, and vice versa.

In short, one reason not to drop the insignificant coefficients is to ensure comparability among equations for the purpose of making meaningful comparisons of coefficients in those equations.

4. Additive versus Interactive Estimation

At the outset of our inquiry we focused exclusively on first order, or independent effects (see tables 5.2 to 5.4, 8.1, 8.2). That limitation, imposed for simplicity, permitted us to proceed with other issues in the face of limited resources. In only a few cases did we anticipate much benefit from investigating the many types of nonlinear equation specifications involving logarithms and power functions (see sections 5 and 6). Nevertheless, we did investigate many additional interdependencies through the use of interactive dummies, at least in the more interesting and potentially useful cases. However, again, no thorough investigation was practical of all the interactions conceivable in equations with as many independent variables as ours.

2. See Wonnacott and Wonnacott, *Econometrics* (New York: Wiley, 1970), pp. 309–12; J. Murphy, *Introductory Econometrics* (Homewood, Ill.: Richard D. Irwin, 1973), pp. 258–66.

(a) *The Additive Model.* We recognize that all regressions in this study are additive, in the sense at least that we assume each dependent variable can be estimated from the sum of the products of coefficients and variables. They are additive also insofar as estimated changes in dependent variables can be determined from summing the product of coefficients and changes in variables.

(b) *The Interactive Model.* Nevertheless, our interactive model is further distinguished by the fact that some of the variables in an additive (linear) model are themselves products of other variables. These special variables, which we call interactive variables, have special properties by virtue of the transformations that created them, not because the computer treats them differently in estimation. They are just another variable in a linear regression. They do differ in their definition, their interpretation, and in the interpretation of their corresponding coefficients.

When we regress Y on variables P_1, P_2, and P_3, we are fitting the additive, linear model between Y and the three variables. The fact that P_3 might be defined as P_1 times P_2 is incidental so far as the computer is concerned. The fact that P_3 is merely P_1 times P_2, however, makes a big difference in how the estimated coefficients are interpreted.

(c) *Key Distinction.* The key distinction, then, is between equations involving variables none of which is related to (constructed from) other variables, compared with other equations involving variables some of which are related to or constructed from other variables. Rather than distinguishing between additive and interactive models, we could better contrast our models as simple additive versus interactive additive, or just simple linear versus interacted linear. Essentially, our initial equations and derived results (as reported especially in chapters 5 and 8) utilized the simple additive or simple linear model. The more refined specifications in chapters 3, 6, 10, and 13, on the other hand, used our interacted additive model.

(d) *Attributes of Interactive Analysis:* i. *Generality and Flexibility;* At the minimum, an interacted model, incorporating variables that are products of other variables in the equation, helped us arrive at a more general and flexible specification. In such equations, if the least square (best) set of coefficients happened to be those with the interacted variables' coefficients all equaling zero, then it would be identical to the corresponding, noninteracted equation.

Suppose $P_3 = P_1 * P_2$.

The simple model is $Y = a + bP_1 + cP_2$.

The corresponding, more general interactive model is

$Y = a + bP_1 + cP_2 + d(P_1 * P_2)$.

But suppose the least squares estimate of the second version has a coefficient of zero for P_3. Then the equation is effectively the same as the first equation. Assuming P_3 contributes to the explanation of Y over and above that assumed by P_1 and P_2, then the second form is better and more general, and P_3 will have a nonzero coefficient.

Therefore, the interacted form is more general or less restrictive than the corresponding simple form.

ii. *Estimation of Conditional Impacts;* The interactive form permits the decomposition of the impact of a variable into a series of conditional impacts, which differ among themselves by the values assumed for other variables in the equation. Therefore, except where we had reason to expect the impact of one variable to be dependent on the levels of other variables, there was no value in such decomposition. If, however, the impact, say, of being network rather than independent were itself believed to depend upon market size, it would make sense to try to measure separate impacts of the network attribute, each measured for a different market size. That is the main motivation for using interactive variables: to permit the measurement of impacts of one variable that are themselves functions of the values of other variables.

iii. *Added Complexity;* One byproduct of such interactions is added complexity. In effect, we gain flexibility by not forcing the impact of, say, the network attribute to be the same for all market sizes. However, in exchange we must now analyze several impacts (one for each market size), instead of only one. Of course, if none of these impacts from the interactive model were significantly different from each other, then it would be pointless to interact the network attribute with market size. Nothing would be gained by the complexity, and something would probably be lost.

One further inconvenience is that the impacts of interacted variables can no longer be read off the estimating equation directly, as with the simpler noninteractive OLS model used in chapter 5. Nor can we even too readily predict beforehand, from the significance or the insignificance of separate components of any interactive variable, what the *global* impact—and significance—will be when all components are considered together. Flexibility and generality of interpretation are clearly not costless.

iv. *Simulated Subsample Analysis;* One way to view the added detail resulting from our interactions is to consider the result as analogous to that obtained from dividing the sample of data into separate subsamples, each homogeneous with respect to one of the variables. We could, for example, have divided our station rates sample into two groups, VHF and UHF stations, and further' estimated the impact of the network attribute for both these samples (table 6.4).

While most people can more readily see how the two-sample technique could give us the separate network impacts for VHF and UHF stations from the two network coefficients, we can get comparable if not identical results from a single sample by adding the interactive variable for network × VHF channel type. The primary gain is that we can more easily test for the significance of the difference between the network impacts for VHF and UHF stations when estimated from interaction, than when we use separate subsamples. Indeed, for some applications a particular subsample is often too small to yield reliable estimates, whereas their impacts can be separated out using interactive variables and the full sample.

(e) *Differences in Ceteris Paribus Conditions.* Perhaps the most difficult distinction to grasp here is the differing *ceteris paribus* statements for the simple versus the interactive model. In table 5.3, for example, we estimate a simple linear equation without any interactive variables. How do we interpret the coefficient, say, of being a CBS affiliate in such an equation? The CBS coefficient is the impact of being that network's affiliate versus being independent, after purging the dependent variable of the effects of the other variables in the equation through a linear (additive) combination of those other variables. We are not holding constant those other variables. That could be done by subsampling or by interaction. Instead, we are saying that, "after accounting for" the variation in the dependent variable caused by these other factors, the impact the network attribute is "x."

The basic objective of any regression, then, is to assign to an attribute only that explanatory power it truly deserves and to separate out the influences of other attributes. We prefer to have no variables acting both as measures of an attribute of interest and as "proxies" for other factors omitted from the equation. Such variables would make it difficult to conclude that the measured impacts are to be attributed to the specific attribute alone.

When we utilize interaction, on the other hand, we develop a series of impacts for the attribute, each of which is for a particular level of one or more of the other variables in the equation. We can no longer look at one coefficient when we deal with interaction, but must compute impacts using several coefficients. These impacts can be thought of as coefficients, but strictly speaking they are not. They are functions of several coefficients.

Suppose we now interact network with channel type by including the product of the two ($N \times V$) in the equation (see table 6.4, equation 1). In a sense we are breaking the sample into UHF and VHF subsamples, at least in regard to estimating the network impact. Because we are saying here that the impact of being network is itself dependent on whether the station is also VHF or UHF, we must estimate *two* impacts for network. Those impacts now have a different *ceteris paribus* statement than where we had no interaction (in table 5.3). Each impact of network (for VHFs and for UHFs) is estimated "after accounting for the variation in the dependent variable caused by the other variables in the equation." We are now holding constant the channel type attribute (at VHF or

UHF), and then purging the dependent variable of the effects of other variables, before measuring the impact of being network.

(f) *Why Not Interact Everything?* If interactive analysis leads to a more general and flexible specification, why not interact all variables with each other? The simple answer is that the number of combinations becomes unmanageable very quickly, and so does the number of variables.

Therefore, we use our own judgment to determine which variables interaction makes sense for, at least at the exploratory stage, and we investigate those variables only. A frequent effect of extensive interaction, especially if a few variables are common to most of the interactions, is multicollinearity. Because interaction is pointless unless the resulting stratification of impacts is significant, we limit our interactions to the minimum consistent with what theory suggests we try and with the realities of multicollinearity.

(g) *Illustrative Examples.* As an example of the limitations of our initial simple additive equations, recognize that those dummy specifications did not permit us to determine whether, say, a colocated newspaper impact on dependent variables was itself influenced by whether the station was also group owned (table 5.3). The impact of newspaper affiliation was initially assumed to be independent of group ownership. We therefore added interactive dummy variables to our initial equations and thus were able, say, to determine whether the impact of a newspaper tie *was itself* influenced by group ownership, and if so, by how much (table 4.11). Essentially this required separate dummies for newspaper and group ownership and an interaction of the two.

The same type of investigation was also undertaken for network affiliation and channel-type interactions (see tables 4.11, 6.4). Our initial simple additive equations assumed that the impact of network affiliation was independent of channel type. This may, in fact, have been the case but could only be determined by specifying the appropriate interactive dummies. Thus the independent variables have impacts on the dependent variables that are themselves dependent on the level of other variables.

As already noted, we often allowed for the fact that the effect of being a VHF station (instead of UHF) was itself dependent on whether the station in question was a network affiliate or an independent. Theoretically, however, we could have made the VHF impact conditional upon many more factors, and presented an entire array of VHF impacts, each conditional upon a specific set of conditions of the other variables in (and perhaps outside of) the equation. Time constraints, multicollinearity, and a desire to examine special cases of other independent variables, inevitably forced us to limit the amount of interaction, compared to the seemingly infinite number of possibilities.

A somewhat different kind of interaction, also represented in table 6.12, is used in many of our equations. This is the treatment of number of VHF stations in the market. There are three variables involved, and they are identified by the following variable names in table 6.12: #VHF, M, #VHF(M). They are defined as follows:

#VHF	= the number of VHF stations in the market
M	= 1 if #VHF is equal to 3 or more
	= 0 if #VHF is equal to 0, 1 or 2
#VHF(M)	= Product of #VHF × M
	= #VHF if M = 1; that is, if #VHF is 3 or more
	= 0 if M or #VHF = 0; that is, if #VHF = 0, 1 or 2

Depending on the signs and the magnitudes of the coefficients of these three variables, a variety of nonlinear impacts of additional stations can be reflected in the equation. It should be intuitively clear that the formulation will be able to reflect certain changes in impacts, depending on whether there are more or less than three stations in the market when an additional station is added. Assuming the coefficients of #VHF and #VHF(M) are both positive, this equation is able to reflect any of the representative kinds of impacts depicted below.

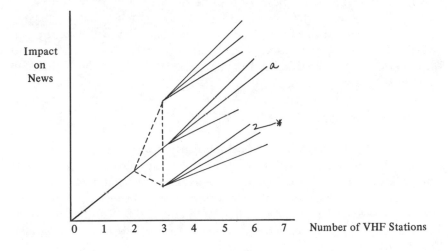

There are three different zones reflected in this formulation. Within each zone, the impact of adding a VHF station is the same. The zones are: first and second station, third station, fourth and all additional stations. Note from table 6.12 that the coefficients of the three relevant variables are:

#VHF	: 0.67
M	: −3.98
#VHF(M)	: 0.56

The following table computes the estimated impacts of additional VHF stations starting with the first.

Added Station	Corresponding Change in			Resulting Impact		
	#VHF	M	#VHF(M)			
1st	+1	0	0	+1 × 0.67	=	0.67
2nd	+1	0	0	+1 × 0.67	=	0.67
3rd	+1	+1	+3	1 × .67 + 1 × (−3.98) + 3 × .56	=	1.63
4th	+1	0	+1	1 × .67 + 1 × .56	=	1.21
more	+1	0	+1	1 × .67 + 1 × .56	=	1.21

As always, the only coefficients involved in computing a given impact are those whose corresponding variables are affected by the change being examined. The variable M only changes on the addition of a third station, and therefore its coefficient, −3.98, enters into the estimation only for the case of the third station. The variable #VHF(M) does not enter into the computation until the third station is added, since M effectively eliminates its influence until at least the third station is added.

So much, then, for this brief contrast of the logical and statistical properties of our simple and interactive additive models. The character and value of interactive analysis is further illustrated in specific estimating equations, in Appendix II.

5. Use of Logarithmic Variables

This investigation was much too broad to permit more than a modest investigation of nonlinearities in any given area. Nevertheless, aside from *interaction* of variables (nonlinear in the sense that some variables consist of the products of other variables), we did investigate a quadratic formulation of station revenue (as in table 6.12) and logarithmic formulations of number of stations in market equations (as in table 3.6). Finally, we utilized the log form in treating the age of stations.

A common logarithmic formulation is to simply replace each variable by its logarithm. It can be shown that the equation

$$LnY = Ln(a) + b(LnX) + c(LnZ)$$

is equivalent to $Y = aX^bZ^c$, where X, Y, and Z are variables, and a, b, and c are parameters (coefficients). This multiplicative form is frequently found in econometric studies but was not suitable for our purposes. It has the convenient property that the coefficients (b and c) are also the elasticities associated with X and Z.

One problem with the double-log form was the presence of zero values of one or more independent variables. The equation implies that if any independent variable is zero, then the dependent variable is also zero. In our market equations (table 5.2), if we had a newspaper proportion of zero, the dependent variable in that equation would be zero for that market. (This relation is reflected in the fact that we would not be able to take the log of zero and would have to doctor up the data to include that market in the sample.) In time series data (as with sales price in chapter 4), the occurrence of zero values of independent variables is often not likely. In cross-section studies, especially of our type, it is much more likely (even without the use of dummies, as in the preceding newspaper proportion example).

In much of this investigation we did not have an obvious case for use of the double-log form. We either had dummy variables as in our station decks, or proportions, as in the 1967 market deck, some of which can be zero. Even if we could computationally handle zero proportions in log form, in many cases we would be opposed to the assumption that, if one independent variable is zero, then the dependent variable must also be zero. In addition, we had no theoretical basis to expect a multiplicative form to be appropriate and no theoretical argument for constant elasticities.

Rather than use the preceding (double-log) formulation, therefore, we selectively used the logarithm of certain variables only. Thus we did use logarithms to take advantage of the ability of the transformation to represent diminishing impact as the level of activity increases. In other words, with logs we could better represent decaying impacts (assumed, for example, with the age variable) and the notion of saturation (see tables 4.11, 6.4, and 6.12). Both of these relationships can also be represented through dummy variables, with interaction, but the logarithmic form requires our estimation of fewer parameters and leads to a smoother functional relationship. See the following figures for an indication of how the two approaches can be considered approximations of each other.

Our most intensive use of logarithms was in estimating the impact of the number of stations of different types on dependent variables utilizing the television market data (chapter 3). One example here is the equation estimated in table 3.6 where we attempted to estimate the interacted logarithmic impact of the number of stations, where the interaction was with the number of TV homes in the market. We anticipated a diminishing effect of additional stations of each type, as more and more were added in the market. This hypothesis suggested the use of logarithms. We also wanted to interact this impact with TV homes, on the assumption that the impact of adding a station to a market—for example, the third network VHF station—was itself dependent on size of market.

We could have achieved a similar functional relationship by using in-

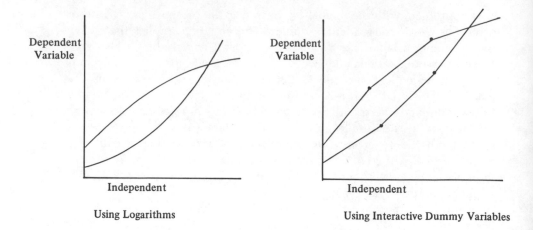

Using Logarithms   Using Interactive Dummy Variables

teracted dummy variables, as in the earlier example (#VHF, M, #VHF[M]), but that would have required us to estimate more coefficients, even without interaction with TV homes. Therefore, we investigated the use of logarithms and, in comparison with simple linear formulations, determined that the former added significantly to our equation's explanatory power.

To illustrate the interpretation of coefficients of logarithmic variables, we will examine the estimated impacts of additional network VHF stations on quarter-hour viewing, as reported in tables 3.6 and 3.9. We leave it to the interested reader to combine the concepts discussed here with those dealt with in our discussion of interactions, in order to compute the impacts for the other station types, which were interacted with TV homes.

Since the logarithm of zero is infinitely negative, and since we had markets with zero stations of a given type in our sample, we added one to the number of stations of each type, prior to taking the logarithm of the variable In determining impacts of added stations, we had to take this "+1" factor into account. To facilitate the following discussion, we list below the logarithms [3] of the integers from 1 to 5.

X	LnX
1	0.0000
2	0.3010
3	0.4771
4	0.6021
5	0.6990

From table 3.6 we find the coefficient of the log of the number of network VHF stations plus 1 was +12.802. Given this information, we can

3. We use log to the base 10, since that is the form used by the computer regression package.

now compute the estimated impact on viewing of adding the third network VHF station in a market. We use the notation NV to represent the number of network VHF stations in the market, so our illustrative example will be to determine the effect of changing NV from 2 to 3. If NV increases (or differs) from 2 to 3, then $NV + 1$ increases from 3 to 4. We must determine what is the change in the $Ln(4) - Ln(3)$, or .6021 − .4771, or 0.1250. Therefore, in comparing two markets, with all factors the same but that one has three network VHF stations, while the other has two network VHF stations, our equation differs only in the $Ln(NV + 1)$, which differs by 0.1250. The estimated impact is simply the coefficient times the change in the associated variable, or 12.802 × .1250, or 1.6003 as reported in table 3.6.[4]

By a similar exercise, the impact of adding a second network VHF is 12.802 × (.4771 − .3010) or 2.2544. Had we been using a simple linear regression, we would have estimated the same impact when adding the second as when adding the third station (unless interactions were used as in our earlier example). We see that the use of logarithms has resulted in a diminishing impact as more stations are added. The second station corresponded to an increase in audience of 2.544, while the third station corresponded to an increase of only 1.6003.

The t-ratios for these impacts are the same as for the coefficients themselves (when no interactions are involved).

6. Use of Quadratic Forms

There was one instance in this investigation where we utilized another form of nonlinear estimation. We refer to the inclusion of Revenue-squared as well as Revenue in the programming equations of tables 6.12 and 6.13. The rationale of this approach is discussed in chapter 6, pages 202–3.

Our purpose here is to explain how such a formulation can be interpreted. The two variables and their coefficients are shown (from table 6.12):

Variable	Coefficient
Revenue	0.068
Revenue Squared	−0.0000102

Note first that if the estimation process should yield a coefficient of zero for Revenue-squared, then the data have told us that the relationship is really linear, as would be the case if we included only the Revenue

4. For further discussion, see chapter 3, Appendix 3B on computation procedure.

variable, and omitted Revenue-squared. Thus, as with the interacted form of number of stations in the market (#VHF, M, #VHF[M]), while we specify a fairly general class of nonlinear relationships when we use this quadratic form, we still have the opportunity to conclude that the relationship is actually simple and linear. That is precisely what happened in equation 1 of table 6.13, where Revenue-squared was eliminated, and we report a linear effect of changes in revenue.

One property of the quadratic form is that the rate of change of the dependent variable with respect to changes in the independent variable (Revenue) is itself a linear function of the independent variable (Revenue). That is, the sensitivity of all news to revenue, in equation 2, was itself a linear function of the *level* of revenue. Remember that the impact of changes in logarithmic variables was different for different *levels* of the independent variable (refer to the previous discussion of logarithm forms). Similarly, the impact of changes in variables represented in the quadratic form was dependent on the *level* of that variable. In our example, an increase in one unit of revenue would result in a change in all news of

$$.068 - .0000204 \times \text{Revenue}$$

where "Revenue" is the *level* of revenue from which the postulated increase of one unit originates.[5]

For these equations, Revenue was scaled in units of $10,000. Therefore, a level of $1 million revenue was equivalent to Revenue = 100, and the postulated change of $500,000 equivalent to a change in revenue of +50. The preceding equation indicates that at a *level* of $1 million, each additional $10,000 in revenue resulted in an increase in all news of .068 − .0000204 × 100, or .0659. That is, a $10,000 increase in revenue, when revenue was already at a level of $1 million, resulted in an increase in all news of .0659 units. Our postulated $500,000 increase in revenue was 50 times as much, or 50 × .0659, or 3.29 news units. This is the impact shown in table 6.13.

Similarly, this same equation can be used to determine the incremental effect of another $10,000 revenue at revenue levels of $4.09 million and $10 million. The resulting figures, when multiplied by 50, would yield the corresponding impacts of $500,000 additional revenue, starting at the respective levels.

As an aside, we should indicate that the same results could have been derived by simply computing the change in Revenue-squared associated with going from a revenue of $1 million to a revenue of $1,500,000, and using the estimated coefficients directly. The methodology always reduces to that of multiplying each change in variable by the associated coefficient, and summing.

5. Reference to a basic calculus text will show that the slope of the curve $Y = aX + bX^2$ is $= a + 2bX$.

7. Problems of Heteroskedasticity

The problem of heteroskedasticity, being a property of the residuals of the equation, necessarily involves the behavior of both the dependent and the independent variable. For a dependent variable that assumes a wide range of values, the achievement of a constant residual variance is more difficult generally than for a dependent variable with limited range. However, the important matter remains how well the independent variables, however specified, explain the behavior of the dependent variable over the latter's range of values. Sometimes a nonlinear form of the equation is required to achieve a constant variance. For reasons of simplicity, however, we stuck to the linear form; and in those cases where one or more of the independent variables have variations similar to the dependent variable, the heteroskedasticity in the resulting equations may be considerably diminished but not eliminated. In our case we have both independent variables with similar variance and, in addition, a non-linear formulation.

Thus TV homes were a wide-ranging independent variable, but in those cases where the dependent variable was also far-ranging, we had a better chance of achieving satisfactory linearity even without the in-teractions in the equation. That is, the fact that quarter-hour viewing was also wide ranging made it more likely that the impact of homes (even without homes interaction) was approximately linear over the en-tire range of homes. In addition, however, we interacted homes with number of program types and with three variables representing numbers of stations. Since the number of stations was generally correlated posi-tively with number of homes, we had built-in nonlinearity in the specifi-cation of homes that should compensate for any inherent nonlinearity between homes and audience.

As a practical matter, to correct for heteroskedasticity requires a lot of experimentation to determine which of an infinite number of possible causal patterns (variables and functional forms must be chosen) may be assumed the culprit. Procedures are extremely ad hoc and subject to much discussion. One correction procedure involves dividing all vari-ables, including the dependent and the vector of 1's used to estimate the intercept, by a function, possibly nonlinear, of one of the independent variables. However, the reader and many analysts will lose the intuitive feel for what the equation is doing, after it has been transformed. This means even more must be accepted on faith.

Heteroskedasticity does not in any case bias coefficients, although it does bias the estimated standard errors and therefore the t-statistics.[6] We felt that only our marginal t-ratios might be significantly affected by

---

6. Almost any econometrics textbook will state (and generally prove) that the co-efficients under heteroskedasticity are still unbiased and consistent. For example, see Jan Kmenta, *Elements of Econometrics* (New York: Macmillan, 1971), pp. 249–69.

the problem. Actually few authors undertake extensive testing for the problem with corrective action, and we believed it even rarer to do so when undertaking an investigation as broad as ours.

In sum, while the knowledgeable reader may question the validity of ordinary least squares estimates due to possible heteroskedasticity problems, we preferred to allocate our resources over a broader range of issues than possible had we examined those problems in the necessary detail.

8. Problems of Simultaneity Bias

Simultaneous equation bias is caused by correlation between one or more independent variables and the error term (residuals) in the particular equation under consideration.

This correlation is rarely grasped by the casual observer. Most of us can see how variables can be correlated with one another (including options [# stations] and types diversity), but it is not always possible to see how a variable can be correlated with an error term. Yet the latter is the basic ingredient of simultaneous equation bias.

Now, one way to suggest that there is such a problem is to show (argue) that there is another equation (different causal/functional relationship) in which the independent and the dependent variable roles are reversed. If such another equation exists, then one can show through suitable mathematical manipulations that in each equation the independent endogenous variable is likely to be correlated with the error term in the equation where it appears as independent variable.

Consider, for example, an equation of the form:

Equation 1 Audience = f (Options, Diversity, other variables) + error term (residuals)

(This is similar to what was specified in table 3.6.) It does not matter that Options and Diversity are themselves correlated (related by another equation, where for example diversity is a dependent variable, and options is independent). Such correlations among independent variables (multicollinearity) does not cause any bias.

What *would* matter would be that, should we estimate an equation (equation 2) Options = f (Audience, other variables), or an equation (3) Diversity = f (Audience, other variables), and get significant coefficients for audience, we would have some (admittedly crude) evidence that we had a problem of simultaneous equation bias in equation 1. However, just the possible rationale for such equations as the two shown here does not mean that, if they were estimated, we would find significance— or even if we found significance, that the bias in equation 1 would be meaningful in terms of deviations from our ordinary least squares (OLS) estimates.

Consider further these two additional types of equation (similar to those specified in chapter 13):

1. Economic Variable = f (Market Size, Amount of Programming by Type)
2. Amount of Programming of a particular type = f (Market Size, Station Type, Economic Variable)

We can interpret equation 1 as essentially reflecting the demand function for programming, noting also that we have several market size variables and many programming type variables, so that equation 1 has a lot more than just two independent variables.

We can interpret equation 2 as essentially reflecting the supply function for programming. Station type is really our whole set of dummies for network affiliation, newspaper ties, et cetera. The economic variable is included to reflect a "source of funds" hypothesis—namely, that because some types of programming require more costly inputs, only stations with the required financial resources can afford to air those programs.

Assuming there are no time lags involved (as there might be in the demand equation, where the economic benefits may not be realized until after the programming has been aired), these two equations represent the classic simultaneous system of equations. We have two *different* relationships between the amount of programming and the economic variables.

How do we estimate the parameters of the two equations? One of the assumptions we make in order to claim unbiased estimates from ordinary least squares regressions is that the independent variables are not correlated with the error term (or residuals) in the equation. It can be shown that each of the programming types in equation 1 is correlated with the residuals from that equation, and that the economic variable in equation 2 is correlated with the residuals from equation 2. The only way we can safely conclude that the estimated coefficients from OLS are not biased in equation 1, for example, would be to show that the coefficient of the economic variable in equation 2 is not significantly different from zero. But in order to do that, we must use something other than the OLS of equation 2.

Assuming we have a good hypothesis that equations 1 and 2 are the correct specifications, we cannot get unbiased estimates of the coefficients from either equation with OLS but must use one of several possible techniques for estimating coefficients in simultaneous systems of equations. Essentially these methods make use of all the variables in the system in estimating the coefficients of a particular equation in that system. In other words, the station type variables from equation 2 would be used in estimating the coefficients for equation 1.

Without using some simultaneous estimating technique, we are not able to make a precise statement as to how poor our OLS estimates of these equations are. We can argue that the coefficients of the options and types variables in the first, and the coefficient of the audience variable in the second, will be biased upward (assuming we think those coefficients would be positive if properly estimated). We do not know, however, if the bias is large enough to affect our conclusions. (Just as we can have statistically significant coefficients that are trivially small in terms of policy implications, we can have *biases* that are also trivially small in those terms.) Finally, it is not uncommon in the reporting of econometric results to find OLS estimates giving substantially the same, and sometimes better, results than more sophisticated simultaneous estimators.[7]

The point is that while we should ideally use a simultaneous estimator for equations 1 and 2, the same criticism can be made of many conceptually related published studies. The needed techniques are hard to use, hard to interpret, and not yet available to many researchers.[8]

For investigatory purposes, then, as with possible heteroskedasticity problems, so with possible simultaneity bias, we preferred to use our limited resources over a much wider range of issues, variables, and original compilations than we could have had we analyzed those statistical problems in depth. We simply ask the knowledgeable reader to take this into account in his or her assessment.

9. "Quasi-Elasticities" Based on Full Sample Mean

At many points in this study we express our estimated coefficients, or absolute impacts, as percentages of the full sample mean. The acronym we have created for such measures is that of the PCDV, or "unit change in dependent variable due to postulated change in independent variable, expressed as percentage of sample mean."

Such measures are most useful when comparing impacts across different dependent variables for a given independent variable. For example, what are the relative impacts of an additional station on rates, ratings, revenues, and programming? To avoid a comparison of apples and melons, we normalize the impacts to simple percentages. These percentages or PCDVs are of course not the same as the standard type of elasticity which is meaningless for a dummy variable, where there is a complete change of state.

One could of course discuss all impacts in absolute terms, with no

7. See for example, Kmenta, *Elements of Economics*, pp. 581–82; Potlury Rao and Roger Leroy Miller, *Applied Econometrics* (Belmont, Calif.: Wadsworth, 1971), p. 195; Karl Fox, *Intermediate Economic Statistics* (New York: Wiley, 1968), pp. 401–2; Edward Kane, *Economic Statistics and Econometrics* (New York: Harper & Row, 1968), pp. 316–18.

8. Simultaneous estimators are more difficult to interpret and therefore more difficult to explain than OLS estimators. For example, the R^2 statistic is invalid for simultaneous estimators. Also, the usual test statistics, such as t-ratios, are no longer unbiased for finite samples. There is a variety of formulas available for computing t-ratios, each giving different results. Finally, the specification of the equation is not straightforward and involves much more judgment. In addition to specifying the variables in a particular equation, we must specify the instrumental variables from the other equations in the system which are to be used by the simultaneous estimator.

elasticities or PCDVs at all. We mainly use the latter to compare impacts across equations or one set of results with another. However, the choice of a base for the percentage change in dependent variable is entirely arbitrary, provided the same base is being used for all impacts represented in the equation. If one impact is twice another variable's impact, then its PCDV will also be twice that of the other variable, provided the same base is used in calculating the PCDV.

When one sees a coefficient or computed impact in dimensioned form (dollars, rating units, et cetera), it may not be apparent to the reader whether this impact is big or small in terms of the usual level of the dependent variable. Relating it to the sample mean, via the quasi-elasticity or PCDV, simply expresses the dimensioned absolute impact in an alternate form where its magnitude is shown relative to an understandable standard.

Some readers may contend that the sample mean of dependent variable is not the best base to use. They may propose that the base should depend upon the particular impact being measured. We agree with this criticism in part and disagree in part.

In table 6.11 (Part C, test 9), for example, note that after an increase of 100,000 homes, a group buyer will pay $1,052,000 more than before for a newspaper-owned network affiliate. In suggesting how important this sum is to the station in question, we might best compare the price increase to the mean price of stations with the designated attributes. After all, our test focuses on those stations. But consider next an independent station that a nonnewspaper owner sells to a nongroup buyer. This time the price rises by only $170,000 with an additional 100,000 homes. Yet this smaller impact on the price of the second station may be relatively greater than the $1,052,000 impact on the former's price.

An argument can therefore be made for selecting a different base for each impact, determined by the subsample as it stands before any variable in the test is changed. The correct base would be not the full sample mean, but each individual subsample mean before postulating a change in any independent variable.

Nevertheless, there are good reasons for not using subsample means this way. Subsamples may not even be available for the initial condition of a particular test. Nor were we to use subsample means, could many second order tests be presented at all in PCDV form. Suppose that the subsamples for the two impacts being compared are mutually exclusive, as in the test just discussed where the difference in impacts is $1.1 million and $.2 million, or about $.9 million (table 6.11, Part C, test 9). What base do we use to express this relative to some average level of sales price? No single station can satisfy both subsample bases used in the two first order tests run; indeed, many stations lie outside of both subsamples used here. It is hard to know what we could properly use.

An even simpler example is in table 4.9 which compares a switch from

UHF to VHF for independent stations, with a switch from independent
to network for VHF stations. The base for the former's PCDV would
be the mean sales price of independent UHF stations (before the postulated switch occurred), but the base for the latter's PCDV, would be the
mean sales price for independent VHFs. A station would have to be
UHF and VHF at the same time to satisfy both subsamples, and it is
hard to see what the correct base for any PCDV would be.

On balance, then, we decided not to use subsample means in this
study, in order to avoid complexities which would not only require
sizable resources just to explain, but would also divert readers from our
substantive findings.

10. The Decision Not to Use Beta Weights

Beta coefficients are essentially regression coefficients where variables
are expressed in standardized form, that is, where the raw variables are
replaced by their deviation from their own mean, divided by their standard deviation. Therefore, the beta coefficient for variable X is interpreted as the number of standard deviations the dependent variable increases for each standard deviation change in X. For the analysis here we
found this not to be useful.

In this study many of our variables are dummies, and beta weights are
not comparable to relative amounts of variation in the dependent variable
explained by the independent variable. To use a beta weight to make
such a statement, one must first weight the beta by the correlation of its
variable with the dependent variable. Even that measure is only a measure of relative variance explained if the independent variables are perfectly uncorrelated with each other and normally distributed.

Yet our television data were certainly not uncorrelated, and dummy
variables are not normally distributed. We therefore concluded that nothing useful could be said about beta weights (standardized regression coefficients) that could not be refuted on both grounds just cited.[9] Nor
would anything really be lost by ignoring the beta weights. The most
interesting conclusions, especially those germane to policy assessment,
were derived from careful interpretation of regular regression coefficients.
It is more useful and meaningful for the reader, for example, to predict
by how much a dependent variable (say, diversity) will change due to
an additional PTV station versus another commercial station, than to express the same impact in terms of standard deviations.

9. See Aigner, *Basic Econometrics* (Englewood Cliffs, N.J.: Prentice-Hall, 1971),
pp. 75, 101–2; Ezekiel and Fox, *Methods of Correlation and Regression Analysis* (New
York: Wiley, 3rd ed., 1970 printing), p. 535.

Appendix II

Principal Estimating Equations*

---

* This appendix was prepared with extensive help from senior project consultant Jacob D. Merriwether. Of special value throughout were his numerous advisory memoranda written in response to the author's analytical statements and detailed requests. For the reader's convenience we have reproduced all estimating equations under review here, however the initial tabulations, additional derived results, and major policy assessment appear in the designated text chapters.

B. Group Two Equations: Interactive Additive Model

At the outset of this investigation we chose between two statistical approaches: an analysis of principal components, and what might be termed a consistency approach. We chose the latter for convenience in the extensive experimentation needed given the crudeness of our data, the large number of issues (hence equations), and the limited time and resources at each stage of analysis. The equations we initially specified included variables (1) of known importance from other published work; (2) of obvious importance judging from general knowledge of industry structure and performance; (3) whose impact, while debatable or insignificant, was germane to the testing of policy-related hypotheses and therefore included for reporting purposes; (4) introduced entirely as exogenous control factors to enhance the reliability of other measured policy impacts.

If our model were viable, it should apply across a variety of dependent variables, with or without any minor changes needed to adapt it to the requirements of those variables. In short, we sought the most comprehensive model, starting essentially with a simple linear or additive form and later exploring interactive interdependencies among our independent variables and, in special cases, certain nonlinear forms as well. This followed from the unusual data compilation requirements that plagued us at the outset.

Our approach was in a basic sense cost-effective. Severe practical constraints forced us to choose between (1) in-depth experimentation with almost endless alternatives in functional form for a few major variables and equations, and (2) the great variety of issues and measures germane to overriding policy concerns. We recognize that greater attention to functional form might have improved particular specifications. Nevertheless, our broad-brush approach achieved results that would otherwise not have been possible. In short, our initial use of a simple linear additive regression model well suited the fundamental task of broad regulatory assessment in the face of limited time and resources.

1. Extensive Compilation Requirements

For several reasons we had to compile and organize extensive original data decks. First, a perfectly adequate set of program logs had been generated in 1968 by an industry-commissioned study of TV program diversity and transmitted at that time to President Johnson's (Rostow) Task Force on Communications Policy.[1] Although an NAB officer permitted me to use these data, its contractor retained proprietary rights and imposed prohibitive charges which blocked access. Nor at that time would the National Archives or, later, the Lyndon Baines Johnson Library at the University of Texas release the data for which it was subsequent repository. All such Rostow Task Force background materials were to be released much later simultaneously with all other presidential papers. In fact we were never able to gain access to these important data and soon had to commence our own extremely time-consuming, costly compilations over an eighteen-month period.[2]

A second, similar constraint was the reported disappearance of John Peterman's excellent data base for 1968 spot rates.[3] This unfortunate loss once again forced us (with Peterman's painstaking assistance) to under-

1. Herman W. Land Associates, *Television and the Wired City* (Washington, D.C.: National Association of Broadcasters, 1968).
2. Some of those early data decks were preliminarily examined in H. Levin, "Program Duplication, Diversity, and Effective Viewer Choices: Some Empirical Findings," May 1971 Proceedings of the American Economic Association, pp. 81–88.
3. See John Peterman, "Concentration of Control and the Price of Television Time," May 1971 Proceedings of the American Economic Association, pp. 74–80. See also appendix to chapter 5 in this book.

take an extremely complex and time-consuming collection and coding of spot rates.

A third barrier arose from our inability to gain access to the FCC's confidential financial records for individual TV stations. This required that we not only compile rates but also analyze the commission's published grouped financial data on a market-wide basis (see chapter 5).

A fourth problem arose from the failure of earlier studies of TV station sales prices (over time) to report their independent control variables as of the year of each sale. Coding all control variables at the time of sale for a new regression analysis, in addition to expanding our data deck, was obviously no small task.

In sum, the state of available data when we began simply did not permit us to analyze, in depth, a single ideal economic dependent variable. Furthermore, once we had to commit substantial resources to a basic compilation effort, the incremental costs of updating some of the data sets from 1967 to 1972 (rates), extending other sets over time, from 1949–65 to 1970 (sales price), seemed less than the statistical benefits from replicating our results for different years, with a far larger sample size than ordinarily available to investigators. (The latter advantage, though costly in time and money, subsequently provided safeguards against multicollinearity obscuring the significance of policy-sensitive coefficients even with imperfect variable specifications.)

2. The Diversity of Data Sources and Dependent Variables

There were at least three good reasons for examining the numerous dependent variables (and hence estimating equations) in this investigation. First, the diversity of compilation sources (and of sample sizes) put a premium on corroborative tests across several indicators rather than just one. Our objective there was confirmation and reliability. Second, our several economic indicators were by no means entirely duplicative conceptually. Third, there were special advantages for confirmation of policy-sensitive results in their replication at different points in time.

Note, for example, that the most readily available economic data for TV stations when we began were so-called audience ratings, percentages of TV homes tuned in. Those data provided important information that advertisers take into account in their expenditure decisions. However, the ratings alone did not indicate station revenue earned, let alone profit before or after tax. Indeed, we found the ratings data to have equal or greater value for our assessment of viewer behavior (in chapter 3), than in our analysis of economic performance (say, in chapters 5 and 6). Spot rates, on the other hand, were strictly speaking list prices and no measure of actual closed transactions. Together our impact estimates of several station and market variables, which are influenced by regulation, on audience size, ratings, and rates did provide a basis for economically relevant assessment. Beyond this we sought still other important measures—namely, of the dollar flows that finally resulted from all estimated effects on rates and audience size. For that we turned to the market averages of income, revenue, and time sales, and to the effective sales price of television stations.

To replicate our station results at different points in time (using alternative equations in part), we developed separate data sets for 1967 and 1972, for a number of economic indicators: ratings, rates, audience size, estimated revenue. Then for programming, a unique set of program listings was initially compiled from all seventy-nine regional issues of *TV Guide* for the week of 25 February 1967. These permitted us to create new measures of horizontal program type diversity across all stations in the market, and of vertical program diversity on individual stations (see chapter 3). Furthermore, the *TV Guide* listings enabled us to calculate the number of quarter-hour units of air time devoted to major types of programming—namely, news, public affairs, fine arts, mass entertainment, feature film. Personal judgment necessarily played an important role in allocating those listings among major program categories, and this notwithstanding our use of explicit allocational criteria. Therefore, it seemed prudent to replicate initial statistical results with an entirely different data base, from a different source—namely, the first annual programming report (for 1972–73) of the FCC's own questionnaire survey of informational and local program service.

It should now be clear why this book presents such a large number of equations and derived results. Briefly, there is no single algorithm on which each estimating equation in any chapter is based; practical constraints and the plethora of dependent variables simply prevented us from optimizing in this fashion.

We started instead with a single basic economic equation (on sales price) specified out of past work and policy relevance (see pages 456–57 and citations in footnote 6). This equation was then modified and expanded experimentally until it took the form reported in table II.2. With large sample sizes, we were frequently able to generate significant impacts for many or all independent variables there (and in tables II.3 and II.4, among others) notwithstanding multicollinearity. With few if any modifications of our initial equation, we would simply run it across a whole set of dependent variables, using a simple linear additive model. We followed this same procedure later, as we developed more detailed and refined specifications, using interactive terms and logarithmic variables.

The remainder of this appendix will present the high points of two major groups of equations. Our presentation is roughly chronological so as to delineate more clearly the principal prior steps and experience drawn on to develop newer variable specifications as the study evolved.

Partial List of Principal Equations Discussed in Appendix II *
(by order of reference)

---

* The numbers in parentheses are those of the identical tables in earlier chapters,
which may be located by consulting the list of tables in the front of this book.

A. Group One Equations: Simple Additive Model

1. Dual Effects of Restrictive Licensing

Equations in tables II.1 and II.2 (pages 442–43) best illustrate our starting point. The initial hypotheses related to dual effects of restrictive licensing and allocation policies on the economic viability of TV stations, and their program diversity and composition as well. The most readily available station economic data were for the aforementioned audience ratings, or proportions of tuned-in households (ARB). Ratings figure importantly in advertiser decisions though do not uniquely determine station rates, revenues, or income. A priori, station profitability was assumed to vary directly with market size and inversely with the number of commercial stations. In addition, a VHF channel and network tie were also believed to significantly effect economic viability. More debatable was the likely impact of ownership by a colocated daily newspaper or nonnetwork group enterprise. Those owner attributes were of a clearly different character than market size, network tie, channel type, and number of stations. However, their inclusion for reporting purposes was imperative, given our desire to assess proposals to reduce or eliminate the frequency of such links in certain situations. Indeed, our fully specified station attributes initially distinguished further between in-town and out-of-town newspaper owners, while knowledge of the industry required a final distinction between network-owned stations (the most powerful and lucrative component) and nonnetwork group ownership.

TABLE II.1 (5.2)
Estimating Equations for Table 5.2
(coefficients)

Independent Variable	Dependent Variables			Commercial Diversity Number of Program Types per Market	
	$100,000s Income per Station	$100,000s Revenue per Station	$100,000s Time Sales per Station	Per Commercial Station	Total
Constant	14.862	50.386	11.509	121.962	138.68
Number of commercial stations in market*	-3.696[b]	-6.986[b]	-2.114[a]	-11.760[a]	71.862[a]
100,000s TV homes	.774[a]	2.014[a]	.301[a]	.406[a]	.536
Proportion of stations with:					
Network affiliation	-9.996	-37.512[b]	-4.675	21.644[b]	-43.749
VHF license	3.217[c]	10.093[a]	1.144[b]	1.092	4.463
Network owner	58.511[a]	120.412[a]	16.429[a]	2.968	14.385
Nonnetwork group owner	4.037[c]	6.581	1.080	-1.078	1.047
Outside newspaper owner	1.207	3.703	.151	2.184	14.821
In-town newspaper owner	5.324[c]	7.657	1.563	2.450	15.729

Superscripts denote statistical significance (two-tailed test) as follows: a = 1 percent confidence level, b = 5 percent, c = 10 percent.

Adjusted R^2	.764	.855	.744	.435	.872
Sample size (markets)	101	101	101	143	143
Sample mean	7.4	26.0	4.9	111.0	325.5

*Results report the number of fifteen-minute commercial program units. This scaling permits us to calculate more informative elasticities in chapter 5 than with the actual number of stations. However, in the estimating equations here we report station coefficients proper.

2. Network Affiliation Dummy

Special attention was given to the form of a network affiliation dummy. Published FCC financial data distinguished only between network and independent status, whereas initial experiments separated out major affiliations (CBS or NBC), major-minor ties (CBS or NBC plus ABC, or all three), and an ABC-only link. Early experiments revealed significant effects of these dummy variables as late as 1967. However, a more detailed set of network dummies was finally utilized—namely, CBS, NBC, ABC, CBS-ABC, NBC-ABC, CBS-NBC, CBS-NBC-ABC (see table II.2). This not only permitted us to distinguish between the separate impact of each existing network tie (or combined ties), but also better controlled for network affiliation in estimating the impacts of all other independent variables.

TABLE II.2 (5.3)

Estimating Equations for Table 5.3

(coefficients)

Independent Variables	Station's Share of Viewers		20-second Prime Rate ($)	Average Number of Program Types Nightly	Type of Prime-Time Programming (in 15-minute units)						
	ADI Ratings (%)	Metro Ratings (%)			Local	All Non-network	News	Public Affairs	Fine Arts and Drama	Mass Entertainment	Feature Film
Constant	16.094	10.950	−386.14	3.364	98.089	123.912	5.723	16.084	7.548	92.831	88.258
Number of commercial stations	−2.229a	−1.838a	32.619a	−.049c	.954	.769	−.027	−.095	−.095	−.004	.528
TV homes (in 100,000s)	−.035	−.039	22.802a	.006c	−.187c	−.112	−.050	−.001	−.005	.181b	−.053
*Dummy variables:**											
VHF Channel	4.502a	5.057a	118.371a	.123b	−1.060	.200	−.981	−.876	−.577	3.379b	.899
Network group owner	5.244b	2.246	550.983a	−.165	3.479	−5.116	6.022a	2.335c	.360	9.388b	2.951
Nonnetwork group owner	1.313c	.470	17.592	.008	1.166	2.570b	1.623b	.491	−.230	−.159	.350
Outside newspaper owner	−.102	−.309	−12.762	−.050	−1.772	−.436	−.755	.291	.085	1.263	.108
In-town newspaper owner	1.697c	1.980a	24.303	.149b	−.629	.423	.824	1.557a	−.131	1.859	−1.920
CBS affiliation	8.243a	13.443a	273.040a	.301a	−42.409a	−93.490a	11.252a	−4.187a	−4.288a	6.268b	−9.530a
NBC affiliation	7.050a	12.777a	277.852a	−.200b	−46.025a	−100.167a	13.254a	−7.981a	.891	3.053	−14.404a
ABC affiliation	3.432c	9.259a	249.652a	−.314a	−42.360a	−89.097a	1.122	−5.385a	−.391	4.023a	−3.285
CBS-ABC affiliation	12.724a	18.468a	245.636a	.190	−43.104a	−98.451a	7.676a	−4.445a	−3.328a	7.945a	−10.544a
NBC-ABC affiliation	10.358a	15.806a	216.687a	−.185	−45.489a	−101.170a	10.447a	−7.107a	.265	4.630	−15.069a
CBS-NBC affiliation	8.558a	13.918a	215.688a	13.918	−39.413a	−94.814a	11.187a	−7.758a	−2.946b	8.140c	−12.859a
CBS-NBC-ABC affiliation	15.908a	16.880a	252.708a	16.880	−47.664a	−101.547a	8.380a	−6.973a	−1.288	9.702a	−12.394a
Adjusted R^2	.432	.636	.769	.226	.393	.839	.346	.185	.302	.122	.158
Sample size (stations)	445	408	452	486	486	486	486	486	486	486	486
Sample mean	21.1	21.2	249.5	4.2	32.4	44.8	18.4	7.5	3.4	108.4	74.6

Superscripts denote statistical significance (two-tailed test) as follows: a = 1 percent confidence level, b = 5 percent, c = 10 percent.

*Labeled attribute equals one, zero otherwise.

3. Proper Specification of Dummy Variables

Attention next went to the initial specification and interpretation of dummy variables for Group One equations. The qualitative attributes of any economic entity are expressed here as one or more binary variables which generally take on the value of one if the attribute is present, zero otherwise, though in fact the scaling is arbitrary.[4] In this system it is not acceptable to specify one dummy variable with more than two possible values, since to do so would prejudge their relative impact.

4. Initial Programming Equations

The impacts of our major independent variables on economic indicators were sufficiently robust (in table II.2), and total explained variance sufficiently high (.432 to .636), to lead us next to apply the same equation across a whole set of programming variables. To generate data for the latter, we had to compile air time estimates for a set of thirty-five program categories (later collapsed to twenty) applied, as noted, to prime-time program listings reported in *TV Guide*, week of 25 February 1967, for all codable stations therein (some 545, including public TV).

5. Initial Estimation of Advertising Rates and Other Economic Indicators

Note that table II.2 also includes runs on prime advertising rates. However, those data resulted from subsequent studies and can better be discussed in light of table II.3, where suspected nonlinearity of relationships between number of stations and rates led us to specify the former variable as a commercial market dummy equal to one for markets with four or more stations, zero otherwise.

A word next, however, about table II.1 where we examine market averages of per-station income, revenue, and time sales on one hand, and horizontal program type diversity across all commercial stations in the market, on the other. Our task here was twofold. First, we sought additional economic variables to test a major initial hypothesis—namely, that restrictive licensing had divergent impacts on industry viability and program diversity. Second, a market equation was clearly needed to examine our measure of *horizontal* diversity, conceived as the number of different program types across all stations in the market during each fifteen-minute period in prime time for the sample week. In addition, as noted, we had to rely on the FCC's grouped financial statistics for individual markets because of the strictly confidential nature of economic data for individual stations.

4. See J. Johnston, *Econometric Methods* (New York: McGraw-Hill, 1972), pp. 176–86; or Jan Kmenta, *Elements of Econometrics* (New York: Macmillan, 1971), pp. 409–28.

TABLE II.3 (5.4)
Estimating Equations for Table 5.4
(coefficients)

Independent Variables	Dependent Variables					
	TV Homes in Equation			Audience Delivered in Equation		
	20-second One-time Rate ($100s)	20-second One-time Rate ($100s)	20-second Five-time Rate ($100s)	20-second One-time Rate ($100s)	20-second One-time Rate ($100s)	20-second Five-time Rate ($100s)
Constant	−4.152	−0.690	−1.221	0.111	1.209	−7.869
TV homes in market (100,000s)	.193[a]	.134[a]	.097[a]	n.i.	n.i.	n.i.
100,000's TV homes "delivered"	n.i.	n.i.	n.i.	1.543[a]	1.259[a]	.978[a]
Median city income in ($100s)	.013	.004	.004	.014	.002	.004
*Dummy variables**						
4+ more stations in market	2.847[a]	3.117[a]	3.368[a]	2.554[a]	2.693[a]	2.709[a]
VHF channel	.756[a]	.656[a]	.581[a]	.235	.463[b]	.445[a]
Network owner	5.034[a]	n.i.	n.a.	3.416[a]	n.i.	n.a.
Nonnetwork group owner	.103	.142	.200[c]	.170	.200	.235[b]
Outside newspaper owner	−.085	.015	−.014	−.344[c]	−.315	−.257[c]
In-town newspaper owner	.242	.332	.378[b]	−.156	.149	.254[c]
CBS affiliation	2.335[a]	1.666[a]	.184[a]	−1.101[a]	−1.399[a]	−.461[b]
NBC affiliation	2.283[a]	1.548[a]	1.799[a]	−.965[a]	−1.334[a]	−.373[c]
ABC affiliation	2.077[a]	1.605[a]	1.776[a]	−.979[a]	−1.236[a]	−.343
CBS-ABC affiliation	2.026[a]	1.152[b]	1.215[a]	−1.166[a]	−1.830[a]	−1.013[a]
NBC-ABC affiliation	1.911[a]	1.170[b]	1.324[a]	−1.467[a]	−2.100	−1.148[a]
CBS-NBC affiliation	1.995[a]	1.252[c]	1.441[a]	−1.676[a]	−2.555[a]	−1.458[a]
CBS-NBC-ABC affiliation	1.910[a]	1.116[b]	1.247[a]	−1.253[a]	−1.668[a]	−.828[a]

Superscripts denote statistical significance (two-tailed test) as follows: a = 1 percent confidence level, b = 5 percent, c = 10 percent.

Adjusted R^2	.817	.684	.734	.855	.737	.792
Sample size (stations)	426	296	294	426	296	296
Sample mean	2.607	2.285	1.890	2.607	2.285	1.890

*Labeled attribute equals one, zero otherwise.
n.i. = Not included in equation for design purposes.
n.a. = Data not available.

Note, however, the broad similarity of our two sets of independent factors in tables II.1 and II.2. Once again in table II.1 we include the two major factors that influence industry economics—namely, market size and number of competing stations. We further take account of channel type and principal owner attributes. However, we specified the number of different kinds of stations in the market as "proportions of stations" with a VHF license, a network affiliation, a network owner, a group owner, etc., rather than as a market dummy variable where, say, markets with 90 percent or more VHFs equal one, zero otherwise, et cetera. There were three good reasons for this. First, the critical levels by which markets should be distinguished (in terms of the number or proportion of network affiliates, of VHF licensees, of newspaper owners, et cetera) were by no means self-evident; and second, the potential number of market dummies could become large. Direct inclusion of the actual proportion of stations with such attributes seemed a far simpler way to proceed. Finally, the proportions data included more complete and useful information than market class dummy variables.

6. Divergent Effects of Economic and Programming Variables

Once again the coefficients of most principal variables (number of stations, TV homes, VHF license, network ownership) were robust, and the explained variance was substantial (.744 to .855). Applying the same equation (the same set of independent variables) across all three economic measures and two measures of horizontal types diversity permitted a broad assessment of the restrictive licensing hypothesis. License limitation did in fact appear to have divergent impacts on industry viability and diversity. The results in tables II.1 and II.2 were clearly consistent with this hypothesis. A good deal of effort was expended to assess (as illustrated there) the consistency of various station and market equations, of different economic equations with one another, and of dummy variable equations and proportion variable equations.

7. Assessment of Public Television

Early efforts were made also to broaden our programming data base to include public TV stations and, having done so, to modify our initial commercial equations to apply them to public television, too. Again, the consistency of public TV equations with each other as well as with commercial equations was carefully examined. That analysis, mainly discussed in chapter 8, entailed the specification of equations in tables II.4 to II.7.

(a) *Modified Market Equations.* In our modified market equations (table II.4) there were two minor changes in the economic regressions. First, to the identical commercial equations run on market averages of income, revenue, and time sales per station (table II.1), we added "the

TABLE II.4 (8.1)

Estimating Equations for Table 8.1

Independent Variables	Market Averages Per Commercial Station			Independent Variables	Commercial Diversity: Number of Program Types across Commercial Stations in Market	Total Diversity: Total Program Types across All Commercial plus PTY Stations in Market
	Income ($100,000s)	Revenue ($100,000s)	Time Sales ($100,000s)			
Constant	12.053	41.842	10.628	Constant	49.995	110.417
Number of commercial stations*	−3.990[a]	−7.644[a]	−2.156[a]	Number of commercial stations	75.866[a]	79.296[a]
Number of public TV stations*	1.387[b]	2.913[a]	.234	Number of PTV stations	5.193[b]	41.080[a]
TV homes (100,000s)	.723[a]	1.903[a]	.292[a]	100,000s TV homes	.245	.124
Median family income (SMA) ($100s)†	.037	.127	.013	$100s median family income	n.i.	n.i.
Proportion of Stations in Market With:						
Network affiliation	−8.157	−33.331[b]	−4.316	Number of network affiliates in market	−10.808	−13.446[c]
VHF license	2.600	8.903[a]	1.054[c]	Number of VHF stations	2.194	1.980
Network owner	57.612[a]	117.168[a]	16.083[a]	Number of network-owned stations	−.627	.971
Nonnetwork group owner	3.419	5.006	.935	Number of nonnetwork group stations	.615	.347
Outside newspaper owner	1.031	2.615	.019	Number of outside newspaper stations	5.699	7.085
In-town newspaper owner	4.587	5.312	1.323	Number of in-town newspaper stations	6.085	5.101
Adjusted R^2	.777	.867	.745		.880	.937
Sample size	101	101	101		143	143
Sample mean	7.4	26.0	4.9		325.5	363.5

Superscripts denote statistical significance (two-tailed test) as follows: a = 1 percent confidence level, b = 5 percent, c = 10 percent.

*The top two rows of results are, respectively, for the number of fifteen-minute commercial and PTV program units available in market. That scaling permits us to calculate more informative elasticities than for the actual number of stations. However, in our estimating equations, we do report the station coefficients themselves. Scaling differences do not alter the elasticities presented in chapter 8.

†Standard Metropolitan Area.

n.i. = Not included in equation for design purposes.

number of fifteen-minute public TV program units available." This permitted us to test the hypothesis that average commercial market income was higher in the presence of public TV, a thesis that those results support (as shown in chapter 8). For completeness we also added median family income to the previous commercial market equations (table II.1). As a consequence, our explained variance (in table II.4) rose slightly over that in table II.1, whereas the coefficients and the elasticities common to both sets of equations were strikingly stable.

Such stability further underscored the reliability of our PTV elasticity, as consistent with the thesis that the presence of PTV significantly bolsters commercial profitability, *cet. par.*, in part perhaps by relieving commercial stations of public service responsibilities, but more likely by often precluding additional commercial VHF entry. The Television Allocation Plan assigned only a limited number of VHF channels to any market, and allocations to PTV necessarily reduced the number of VHFs allocated to commercial TV. To be doubly sure that the presence of PTV was no simple proxy for market affluence,[5] our economic equation also included median family income. The evidence was unmistakable (see chapter 8, pages 253–63, 268–69).

A further change in our programming equations must also be mentioned. Note that, besides adding the number of PTV stations in the market (in terms of 15-minute program units), we changed our station proportion variables, into additional "number of station" variables. Thus, instead of taking account of the *proportions*-of-stations with network affiliations, VHF licenses, network owners, et cetera, we now controlled for the *number* of network affiliates, VHF stations, network-owned stations, et cetera. These numbers of stations, too, were expressed as fifteen-minute program units supplied. The scaling adjustment was even more important here than in table II.1 because PTV stations varied widely in the number of evening hours they broadcast in 1967, in different markets. In both tables II.4 and II.1 expressing the number of stations in fifteen-minute program units facilitated the calculation of true elasticities; that is, the essentially discrete number-of-stations variable was transformed into an equivalent continuous variable. One final reason for converting our proportion-of-stations variables to number-of-stations variables (in fifteen-minute units) was that it enabled us to make direct comparisons of the relative impact on diversity, not only of the number of PTV and commercial stations, but of the latter when subdivided into five major classes (VHF, network affiliates, etc.). The impact on diversity—say, of another network affiliate, another newspaper owned station, et cetera—was more straightforward than working with proportions-

---

5. PTV has often been criticized for being elitist and mainly tailored to the needs of better-educated, more affluent viewers. Only if market income and/or TV homes is taken into account can we isolate out the impact of PTV itself on market averages of income and revenue per commercial station.

of-stations, though in the final analysis this generated few significant coefficients.

Note also that median income was excluded from the equations for programming for two reasons. In early experiments this variable added little to explained variance adjusted for degrees of freedom (adjusted R^2). It registered insignificant (with a low t-value) in the economic equations, where, a priori, one might have expected impact. Because TV homes rather than median income was the clearly more powerful determinant of commercial TV income and revenues, TV homes alone should better explain diversity. Considering, however, that PTV stations have been criticized as being elitist and might therefore have greater impact in markets with higher median income, the ideal procedure would have been to interact PTV with percentage of families earning $10,000 and over. Unfortunately we could not readily compile such information at that stage, and without those more detailed data there seemed little to be gained from specifying median income alone, at the cost of losing degrees of freedom. Therefore, median income was excluded from the equations for programming.

There is yet another consideration here. Our economic dependent variables in table 8.1, as market data divided by the number of stations, require a per station methodology. Proportions-of-stations in the market with designated attributes are appropriate for those dependent variables. We were testing to determine whether license limitation bolsters market viability per station, or whether such viability is sensitive to PTV's presence. Other owner attributes are control factors only; and since a station can only have or *not* have any single dichotomous attribute in market-wide analysis, we chose to cast the attribute as the *proportion* of stations having it, rather than as the number of stations that had it. The main focus, in any case, was on the relative impact of commercial and PTV stations on commercial income.

As for commercial diversity and total diversity, those dependent variables are not divided by number of stations. Here we are dealing with absolute levels (not per station averages), levels that go up with the number of stations. In estimating changes in these levels, we must include the number of different classes of stations in the market, rather than the assortment or mix of stations therein. This is essentially why we specified proportions of stations for our economic equations, and number of stations for our equations for programming.

(b) *Modified Station Equations.* Turning next to table II.5, that specification differs from table II.2 in only one respect. We had introduced a public TV dummy equal to one if the station were commercial, and zero if PTV. Note also that the sample size for table II.5 is 545, compared to 484 for the commercial-only equations (table II.2), because table II.5 includes 61 PTV stations. The coefficients and t-values common to tables II.2 and II.5 are essentially stable, the PTV (versus commercial) dummy

TABLE II.5 (8.2)

Estimating Equations for Table 8.2

		Prime Time Programming					
		Vertical Diversity:	Number of 15-Minute Units of:				
Row	Independent Variables	Average Number of Program Types Nightly	News	Public Affairs	Fine Arts and Drama	Mass Entertainment	Feature Film
1	Constant	3.662	5.857	22.296	19.314	6.598	1.613
2	Number of commercial stations	−.036	−.055	−.135	.049	−.174	.342
3	TV homes (100,000s)	.010[a]	.006	.075[b]	.037	.169[a]	−.039
	*Dummy Variables:**						
4	Commercial vs. public TV†	.441[a]	2.974[c]	−10.964[a]	−15.348[a]	93.793[a]	31.006[a]
5	VHF channel	.040	.612	.108	−.435	.813	−.016
6	Network owner	−.296[c]	4.971[b]	.262	−.207	−8.390	3.220
7	Nonnetwork group owner	.002	1.517[b]	.400	−1.095	−.456	.341
8	Outside newspaper owner	−.046	−.753	.327	.144	1.181	.078
9	In-town newspaper owner	.140[b]	.718	1.369[c]	−.212	−1.851	−1.900
10	CBS affiliate	.419[a]	11.698[a]	−3.039[a]	−3.126[a]	6.477[a]	−9.085[a]
11	NBC affiliate	−.078	13.718[a]	−7.058[a]	2.082[a]	3.260	−13.954[a]
12	ABC affiliate	−.194	1.559	−4.498[a]	.797	14.201[a]	−2.853
13	CBS-ABC affiliate	.351[b]	8.326[a]	−3.699[b]	−2.343[b]	10.825[a]	−9.284[a]
14	NBC-ABC affiliate	−.038	10.987[a]	−6.168[a]	1.656	4.850[c]	−14.702[a]
15	CBS-NBC affiliate	−.017	11.623[a]	−6.994[a]	−1.666	8.410[b]	−12.554[a]
16	CBS-NBC-ABC affiliate	.250[c]	8.933[a]	−5.810[a]	.282	9.493[a]	−12.238[a]
	Adjusted R^2	.229	.451	.453	.664	.898	.378
	Sample size (station)	545	545	545	545	545	545
	Sample mean	4.1	17.4	9.1	5.0	97.5	22.1

Superscripts denote statistical significance (two-tailed test) as follows: a = 1 percent confidence level, b = 5 percent, c = 10 percent.

*Labeled attribute of dummy variable equals one, zero otherwise.

†For clarity note that commercial station equals one, public TV equals zero.

variable is usually highly significant, and its coefficient is substantial. Inclusion of the PTV dummy also, in many equations, raised adjusted R^2 considerably. In all, the implications of tables II.4 and II.5 regarding PTV impact on TV performance are basically consistent. Reliability of that measure is confirmed by the general stability of coefficients common to both the commercial-only and PTV-inclusive equations.

(c) *Impact of Public TV on Commercial Economics and Programming.* The several hypotheses being tested in tables II.6 and II.7 are amply expounded in chapter 8. Here suffice it to note only that table II.6 reflects a further modification of earlier commercial-only station regressions. Essentially we used a single set of common explanatory variables (augmented by one of six PTV variables) run on eight designated dependent variables. This produced our forty-eight equations. The objective was to determine whether the presence of particular types and amounts of programming on PTV stations in any TV markets impacted significantly on the income, audiences, diversity, and program composition of commercial stations therein. In each case a single common set of independent variables was included—namely, those we finally introduced in table II.3. To test for PTV impact, however, we also introduced, in each of six equations run on each of eight dependent variables characterizing commercial stations, a different PTV programming variable—namely, all PTV program time, mass entertainment on PTV, fine arts on PTV, public affairs on PTV, and so forth. A profile of PTV impact on commercial television's economic and programming performance was thereby generated. Its consistency with a variety of specific hypotheses on such impact was examined in chapter 8.

(d) *Impact on Public TV of Commercial Program Composition and Diversity.* A comparable analysis of the diversity and composition of programming on fifty-nine of our PTV stations was then undertaken in table II.7. For each of six measures of public TV programming, we ran an identical equation that included two measures of commercial (and implicitly PTV) market size—namely, TV homes, median city income. The equation also specified a measure of horizontal program diversity across all commercial stations in the market, and the amount of each of five groupings of commercial programs available in each market. The basic question was the obverse of that in table II.6. There we sought to estimate the impact of PTV's presence on *commercial* station economic and programming performance. In table II.7, we wanted to estimate the impact on the magnitude of different PTV program categories (and on its vertical diversity), of commercial horizontal types diversity, and of the amount of time devoted to different commercial program categories.

For policy purposes, finally, we included the channel type of our fifty-nine PTV stations. In this way, we hoped to correct for differences in PTV program performance that might be due to the greater potential audiences (and hence public, state, or other support) for VHF trans-

TABLE II.6 (8.3)

A Summary of Impacts of Public TV Program Types on Commercial Station Economic and Programming Variables, 1967

Public TV Market Data for Selected Independent Variables in 15-Minute Program Units		Commercial Station Data: Dependent Variables			Type of Prime-Time Programming (in 15-minute units)				
		Estimated Station Income	Estimated Station Audience	Average Nightly Program Types	Mass Entertainment	Fine Arts and Drama	Public Affairs	News	Feature Film
All programs	B	.028[a]	.002[d]	−.0003	.021[c]	.0006	−.002	−.0004	.021[d]
	t	2.58	1.45	.76	1.68	.20	.37	.05	1.63
	$\bar{R}^2$	.7473	.5469	.2327	.1473	.3562	.1789	.3548	.1583
Mass entertainment	B	.021	.028[a−]	−.006[d]	−.013	.012	.055[d]	−.017	−.019
	t	.29	3.30	1.60	.14	.56	1.56	.29	.21
	$\bar{R}^2$	.7419	.5565	.2362	.1418	.3566	.1832	.3549	.1532
Fine arts and drama	B	.155[a]	.010[c]	−.003[d]	.082[d]	.005	−.0004	.009	.092[d]
	t	3.22	1.71	1.32	1.45	.36	.02	.24	1.58
	$\bar{R}^2$	.7503	.5479	.2347	.1459	.3563	.1787	.3548	.1581
Public affairs	B	.116[a]	.009[b]	−.002	.092[b]	.006	−.002[d]	−.007	.111[a]
	t	2.91	2.05	.97	1.95	.56	1.14	.21	2.29
	$\bar{R}^2$	.7487	.5492	.2334	.1492	.3566	.1811	.3548	.1632
News	B	.215[d]	−.009	−.009[d]	.229[d]	.010	−.047	−.020	.288[c]
	t	1.61	.57	1.38	1.50	.26	.77	.20	1.85
	$\bar{R}^2$	.7440	.5449	.2350	.1462	.3562	.1798	.3548	.1597
Feature film	B	.203[d−]	.019	.0003	.148	−.011	.072	−.153[d]	−.198
	t	1.12	.88	.03	.67	.20	.81	1.06	.88
	$\bar{R}^2$	.7429	.5454	.2317	.1427	.3562	.1799	.3564	.1546
Sample size		324	421	453	453	453	453	453	453
Sample mean		9.957	1.347	4.173	108.541	3.329	7.530	18.680	24.777

NOTATION: B = regression coefficient; t = t-value denotes significance of coefficient, further indicated by superscripts (two-tailed test) as follows: a = 1 percent confidence level, b = 5 percent, c = 10 percent, d = t-value exceeds 1 but less than 1.645 at 10 percent level. R^2 = Coefficient of multiple determination (or total explained variance) adjusted for degrees of freedom. Notation following certain superscripts indicates consistency of coefficient with hypotheses stated in association with tables 8.4 and 8.7, e.g., d = coefficient consistent, d− = coefficient inconsistent.

Form of Estimating Equations Summarized in Table 8.3

Dependent Variable (Commercial Station Data)	Selected Public TV Market Independent Variables	Variables Common to All Equations (not reported)
Station income	All programs,	Constant + TV homes + median city
Station audience	mass entertainment,	income + (dummy variables):*
Average nightly program types	fine arts and drama,	Markets with four or more stations +
Mass entertainment	public affairs,	VHF channel + network owner +
Fine arts and drama	news,	Nonnetwork group owner +
Public affairs	feature film	Out-of-town newspaper owner +
News		In-town newspaper owner +
Feature film		CBS affiliate + NBC affiliate + ABC affiliate + CBS-NBC affiliate + CBS-ABC affiliate + NBC-ABC affiliate + CBS-NBC-ABC affiliate

*Labeled attribute of dummy variable equals one, zero otherwise.

mitters generally. In addition, this channel type dummy permitted some tentative conclusions as to recommended allocation policy for PTV.

(e) *Conclusion.* In brief, tables II.6 and II.7 represent a tentative first look at the mutual impacts of commercial TV and PTV on one another. Both sets of equations, though clearly more for table II.6, are derived from our earlier commercial-only regressions, in particular as specified in table II.3. In chapter 8, the mass of regression results are then summarized broadly in terms of stated hypotheses by applying the binomial test of nonparametric estimation (see chapter 8, pages 264–74). Only the most modest conclusions are drawn, but the pattern of revealed impacts is suggestive.

B. Group Two Equations: Interactive Additive Model

Building on Group One equations with their simple additive model and 1967 data base, our Group Two equations incorporate the results of extensive experimentation with interactive dummy variables and selected use of logarithmic and quadratic forms (see Appendix I, pages 422–26). The Group Two equations are also generally run on a new data base, from different sources, for the year 1972.

This new stage of investigation initially focused in greatest detail on the estimation of TV station sales prices from 1949 to 1970. The starting point there was in my earlier published studies (cited in footnote 6). Using those results, we experimented systematically with major modifications of variable specifications which had essentially included TV homes, number of VHF stations in market, age of station, network affiliation, nonnetwork group and in-town newspaper ownership. One further development was to explore major interactions of owner attributes with TV homes, number of stations with TV homes, and owner attributes with channel type. A second development was to explore the log form for age of station and to interact that with an age variable dummy that captured the FCC's cessation of all TV licensing between 1948 and 1952.

Our sales price specification (in chapter 4) constitutes the largest single investment in arriving at any estimating equation here. Because of that, and the related fact that all other station equations (as reported in chapter 6) built on the extensive experience garnered with the sales price specification, we intend to summarize the latter's high points in some detail. Following that we shall consider the main additional modifications in specifying station equations for a number of other economic and programming indicators (see tables II.9, II.10, 6.8). Then we turn to equations in Tables II.11 and II.13 (for quarter-hour viewing) whose derived results appear in chapter 3. Even these latter market equations

TABLE II.7 (8.6)

Regression Analysis of Public TV Prime-Time Program Composition and Diversity in Relation to Channel Type, Market Size, and Commercial TV Programming Available, Fifty-nine PTV Stations, 1967*

Independent Variable		Vertical Diversity: Average Number Program Types Nightly on PTV Stations	Prime-Time Public TV Programming (15-minute units)				
			Mass Entertainment	Fine Arts and Drama	Public Affairs	News	Feature Film
Constant		3.743	11.760	23.545	16.525	7.651	1.207
VHF channel²	B	-.369^d	-6.234^a	-.083	4.825^d	-1.240^d	-2.019^d
(PTV stations)	t	1.56	2.96	.03	1.50	1.16	1.61
Commercial Market Data:							
TV homes (100,000s)	B	.017^d	.063	.186^d	.552^b	.168^b	-.031
	t	1.08	.44	1.15	2.55	2.33	.37
Median city income ($100s)	B	-.018	-.111^d	-.185^c	-.054	-.00008	.030
	t	1.64	1.17	1.72	.40	.00	.52
Number of program types	B	.010^c	.100^b	.016	.095^{d-}	-.0058	.035^d.
	t	1.81	2.07	.29	1.29	.02	1.20
Commercial Program Units (15-minutes):							
Mass entertainment	B	-.008^b	-.048^d.	-.028	-.130^{b-}	-.016	.0005
	t	2.22	1.42	.73	2.51	.93	.02
Fine arts and drama	B	-.003	-.278^{d-}	.155	.363	.113	-.204^{d-}
	t	.10	1.15	.57	.99	.92	1.42
Public affairs	B	-.009	-.053	.024	-.226^d.	-.060^d.	.011
	t	.74	.49	.20	1.37	1.09	.18
News	B	-.0002	-.048	.046	.054	.003	-.072^c
	t	.03	.79	.67	.58	.09	1.97
Feature film	B	.009^{d-}	-.049	.037	.145^c.	.045^d.	-.060^c.
	t	1.58	.91	.61	1.78	1.65	1.89
Adjusted R²		.1434	.1997	.0349	.1383	.1008	.1400
Sample mean		3.663	8.305	18.932	22.627	6.271	2.169

*Upper number in each cell is a regression coefficient (B), and lower number its t-value, with superscript to indicate statistical significance (two-tailed test) as follows: a = 1 percent confidence level, b = 5 percent, c = 10 percent, d = 30 percent. Notation following certain superscripts indicates consistency of coefficient with hypotheses stated in association with table 8.5—for example, d. = coefficient consistent, d— = coefficient inconsistent. Superscripts without suffixes indicate variables not relevant to these hypotheses, though pertinent to analysis on pages 270-71.

†For clarity note that the VHF channel dummy equals one for a VHF public TV station, and zero for a public UHF station.

benefited from our experience with interactive estimation of sales price. In addition, the specification of variables to test the thesis that options and types diversity each impact significantly on aggregate TV viewing drew on knowledge gathered from still earlier, related noninteractive market equations (tables II.1 and II.4) for quite different dependent variables. The final specifications in tables II.11 and II.13 naturally benefited also from unreported experiments with the same dependent variable, aggregate viewing, but without interactive or logarithmic variables.

In the bulk of what follows, then, we shall review our variable specifications for estimating sales price (section 1), followed by further consideration of interactive estimation of other station economic and programming performance indicators (section 2) and, finally, of comparable estimation of aggregate level TV audiences, and proportions of tuned-in households, with special reference to options and types diversity (section 3).

1. Interactive Estimation of Sales Price, 1949–70

For convenience, let us consider some major problems faced from the outset, posed largely by the time series character of our sales price data, by the staggering number of conceivable interactive variable combinations, and by the consequent need for considerable judgment in all experiments. For convenience also we directly append our four final estimating equations (table II.8), along with a summary of the notation used in specifying them and later equations.

(a) *Initial Hypothesis.* As noted, we developed this equation from my earlier work [6] where the hypothesis was that the level of TV sales prices over time varied both with a station's market conditions and its position therein. Presumably price would rise, *cet. par.*, the more TV homes in the market and the fewer the rivals that compete to reach them. Presumably also the commission's licensing and allocation policies would affect both factors. On one hand, the FCC may refuse to permit entry into markets of varying size; and, on the other, it may impose limits on the number of sellers who compete.

That earlier hypothesis was of continued interest for chapter 4 and, using other cross-sectional economic indicators (station rates, revenues, audiences, ratings), for other chapters, too. Nevertheless, I deliberately broadened my inquiry in this book to look more closely at network ties and, not hitherto attempted, at newspaper and group owner ties as well.

6. The best revised equation in that work appears in *The Invisible Resource* (Baltimore: Johns Hopkins University Press, 1971), at p. 397, and includes these independent variables: TV homes, age dummy, network affiliation, number of stations, signal power, original cost of assets, and average daily circulation. Other references are "Economic Effects of Broadcast Licensing," *Journal of Political Economy* (April 1964), and advisory analysis of sales price for United Research Inc. (URI), *The Implications of Limiting Multiple Ownership of Television Stations* (2 vols.), filed on 1 October 1966, in FCC Docket No. 16068.

In particular, I sought to determine whether sales price (and other economic variables) varied significantly, *cet. par.*, with a station's link with a colocated daily newspaper, a nonnetwork group enterprise operating stations in geographically separate markets, and a national TV network. At the same time I retained most of my earlier common variables—namely, TV homes, video power, number of VHFs in market.

To maximize our sample size, we built on the 198 sales examined by United Research Inc. (URI), 1949–65, and those in addition coded by Checchi and Co., 1956–59 (see *The Invisible Resource*). By scouring *TV Factbook* listings, commission dockets, and doctoral studies over the whole period 1949–72, we created a special data deck of 310 usable cases (expressed in equivalent dollar sums and complete with all control variables). Our control factors were indeed far more numerous than URI's, and our final data base was one-third again as large.

To ensure greatest flexibility in exploring hypotheses raised by other work, we coded as of the time of each sale: all key owner attributes (newspaper, group, network), channel type, number of VHF and UHF stations in market, TV homes in market, age in months, video power, aural power, highest hourly rate. In addition, we introduced from other sources information on "class of sale"—namely, whether 100 percent cash sale, or majority interest projected to 100 percent, or combined cash plus securities projected to 100 percent, or combined radio-TV-newspaper sales. Note, finally, that for the first time to my knowledge, we also classified each sale by owner attributes before and after the sale—that is, by class of seller and *buyer*.

(b) *Adjusting the Price Data for Inflation.* Like United Research, Inc., we were compelled to draw on observations for a wide range of years, thus foregoing the advantage of the limited time period (1956–59) of my two earliest studies. Apparently no other investigator had adjusted the price data for inflation, a failure that would cause little problem if the time period were sufficiently short, but *would* cause distortions with a period long enough to increase sample size substantially.

There is, for example, no question that the impact of station age at the time of sale could well be affected by inflation and in particular by general market growth. We used two corrections for this: first, a GNP implicit price deflator to adjust all sales data (and hourly rates) to a 1958 base; and second, as noted, the compilation of all independent variables at the time of sale. Coding TV homes in particular in this manner would additionally ensure against any serious influence of changing market potential over time on particular sales prices. Together, therefore, our adjustments for inflation and specification of market size at time of sale would capture most influence of time as an explicit variable. (We would ideally have preferred to introduce changing real per capita income over time to normalize for market growth, but our resources did not permit this.)

Finally, our interaction of ownership buyer and seller dummies with
TV homes went farther than any earlier study in holding constant a station's market potential as an influence on its sales price (or, in chapter
6, its advertising rate, estimated revenue, audience size, or audience
ratings).

(c) *Specification of Station Age.* Age of station could on several counts
be expected to enhance earning power and likely sales price. The older
the station, *cet. par.*, the more likely it will have solidified preferred links
with network companies, advertising agencies, and sources of talent. Age
could also be expected to be a proxy for station experience, knowhow,
audience loyalties, and possibly for real per capita income in the market.

For such reasons investigators consider age in months at the time of
sale as a cogent determinant of sale price. In adding this variable to our
earliest specifications, we cast it in a logarithmic form. Our assumption
was that after some time additional experience or the advantages of
early linkage with talent-network-advertiser organizations would diminish in value. Stated otherwise, younger rivals will, after a point, better
match the advantages that an older rival enjoys from its early start.

A second form for our age variable, also used in my earlier work, was
an age dummy equal to one if a station were licensed before 1952,
and zero otherwise. The break at 1952 reflects the well-known cessation
of all TV grants during the three and a half years ending May 1952
when the FCC instituted its new Television Allocation Plan. The 108
stations licensed before 1952 enjoyed considerable protection against new
entry into their markets and gained time to entrench themselves with
preferred advertiser-network-talent contracts. In addition, those VHF
pioneers were located in the leading United States markets and operated
on the low VHF channels (table 4.6) whose clarity and range were superior to the high VHFs or UHF channels. But after 1952 the new grants
did indeed go to those higher VHF channels and to UHF stations. They
also went to stations more likely to be in medium-sized and small markets.

(d) *Impact of Station Age on Adjusted and Unadjusted Prices.* The
importance of inflation became clear in early experiments with age as a
variable. Thus, log of age at time of sale had a sizable and significant
impact on the *un*adjusted price data but literally no impact on *adjusted*
data. What this suggests is that, with time series data at least, the older
the station, the more important general inflation (and possibly basic
market growth) will be in influencing its price, regardless of other control factors. Adjustment for inflation, on the other hand, effectively re-
moves the variations log of age had explained, and that variable therefore
loses significance.

In contrast, our age *dummy* picks up significance after the adjustment
for inflation. Thus, its impact before adjustment was 80 percent of the
unadjusted mean price of stations in the sample, but after adjustment

it was 90 percent of the adjusted mean price. In both equations the variable's t-values were consistently greater than three, with rather complete *ceteris paribus* conditions. In comparable experiments run on each station's highest network hourly rate at the time of sale, once again the impact of the age dummy was 55 percent of the unadjusted mean rate and 67 percent of the adjusted mean rate.

A third dimension of our age specification entailed experiments to interact the age dummy, of unquestionable significance in all early equations, with log of age (of little or no significance alone). Perhaps the unique advantages of the pre-1952 licensees might enhance the value of age more generally. The way to find out was to interact the dummy (A) with log of age. Those experiments further showed that, when both variables were in the equation together, the age dummy lost its significance but the interactive variable (A × log of age) was even more significant than the age dummy or log of age alone. Apparently, A alone and A × log age were too highly correlated as variables for us to measure separate impacts given the small number of sales of stations licensed before 1952 (44 out of 310), and the small range of log age for those sales. Two final criteria for adding the interactive variable were that its inclusion did not cause unstable coefficients elsewhere in any equation but did in fact raise total explained variance more than a random variable would.

Even though log of age lost significance with adjustment for inflation, we kept it in the equation in part because its t-value persistently exceeded 1.0, suggesting some of the stated advantages of older stations. Second, it really did make a difference, after including log of age, whether the station was licensed before 1952. That impact was positive, highly significant, and of large magnitude.

(e) *Highest Hourly Rate as Predictor of Sales Price.* At an early stage we considered introducing highest hourly rate at the time of sale as a predictor of sales price. I had actually used spot rate in my initial JPE study, and average daily circulation in 1972, both to good effect. We also noted Blau's specification of net broadcast revenue as a major predictor.[7] We nevertheless excluded highest hourly rates on the following counts:

1.   We found considerable evidence in early runs of two-stage causality with our fundamental owner, market, and policy-related variables significantly impacting on rates, and rates in turn impacting on sales price.
2.   The following variables were significant in sales price equations only when rates were excluded: TV homes; video power; age dummy; newspaper seller dummy; two of seven network affiliation dummies, those for CBS-ABC and for CBS-NBC-ABC joint affiliations.

7. See R. Blau, R. Johnson, and K. Ksobiech, *The Determinants of Television Station Sales Prices, 1968–73*, Institute for Communication Research, Indiana University, May 1975.

(Only the newspaper and group buyer coefficients lost significance when rates were excluded, the newspaper seller dummy gained in significance.)

3.   Furthermore, TV homes, newspaper owner, video power, and age all also impact significantly on the highest hourly rate at time of sale. Indeed those variables impact more significantly and sizably on rates than on sales price direct.

4.   These two sets of significant impacts—on rates and sales price— constituted a kind of test of multicollinearity of our fundamental policy variables and rates. It also underscored the need for caution about interpreting in any literal way the lack of significance (due to multicollinearity) of the policy variables in those sales price equations which contained highest hourly rate.

In sum, although we found evidence of two-stage linkage, we chose not to make separate estimates of each but instead to focus on the jump from stage-1 policy-related variables directly to the impact on sales price.[8]

(f) *Some Complexities in Specifying Interactive Variables.* As explained in Appendix I, pages 416–21, use of interactive terms makes variable specification a lot more complex, and that complexity explains why so much judgment is essential throughout all interactive specifications. The extensive details we next present on sales price will help illustrate the strategy followed in specifying other equations too, many of whose interactive terms and basic variables were identical or very similar to those here.

Among the criteria guiding our variable specifications were four in particular. We asked:

1.   How stable are the other unrelated coefficients in an equation (not included in the interaction) when we introduce any new variable or interactive term?

2.   Does the new variable raise total explained variance more than a random variable would?

3.   Do one or two basic variables, significant before their interaction, remain significant in the presence of the new interactive term? If not, does the interactive term's impact and significance exceed those of the basic variable before the former is introduced?

4.   Is the distribution of both components of our interactive variable such that multicollinearity would preclude significant impacts of either? Or do we have sufficient observations for each interactive term along with the kind of impact needed to get significance notwithstanding the multicollinearity?

With these considerations in mind, let us now summarize the remaining steps in specifying four estimating equations for sales price (table

8. The alternative assessment, say, of the question—by how much does newspaper ownership raise rates, *cet. par.*, and through higher rates in turn raise sales price?— would have been extremely awkward. In addition to other considerations, moreover, hourly rate is no really adequate or accurate proxy for recent absolute profits, the most germane determinant of sales price.

II.8). Brief reference will be made to number of stations in market and to several sets of dummy variables [9] and their interactions with channel type and market size.

(g) *Specifying the Number of Stations in the Market.* At the outset we specified the stations variable as "total number of commercial stations." That form provided a convenient benchmark in our simple noninteractive additive model, extensively utilized in chapters 5 and 8. However, we learned from this early estimation that the number of stations could be usefully cast to capture its nonlinear character. Thus, as stations in the market rise from one to eight (1967), or one to twelve (1972), in units of one, the rate of increase obviously declines. We also confirmed important expected differences in our noninteractive additive OLS model between the earning power of stations classified by network status and channel type (tables II.2 and II.3).

As the work proceeded, then, we used two additional specifications. First in chapter 4 and again in chapter 6 (with equations run on other station dependent variables), we experimented mainly with the number of VHF stations only, interacted with a dummy variable equal to one for markets with three or more VHFs, and zero otherwise.[10]

Our market dummy variable in the sales price equation was derived after examining plots of price data and cross-tabulations which clearly showed a dramatic break in the data when a third VHF station entered. Specifically, sales prices were much higher in markets with three or more VHFs than they were elsewhere.

What appeared to be happening was that, with only one or two VHFs in the market, those stations were necessarily *joint* affiliates of two or three networks. Hence the distinguishing characteristic of going from two to three VHFs is going from a market with joint affiliates to one with exclusive or primary affiliates each of a single network. Apparently the single affiliate stations are worth more than those with joint affiliations. The network company presumably feels a bigger stake where it alone fills the station's network time. However, this notion seems harder to accept when the station being sold was an independent. Why should it, too, be more valuable as a competitor of a single affiliate? We concluded that the answer might lie in the fact that in markets with one or two VHFs, the station sold *had* to be an affiliate, possibly unless UHF. In fact, the reason the average sales price fell when we went to four VHFs is that the fourth VHF must be an independent. (See table II.2 for a seven-way breakdown of network affiliates—namely, single affiliates of CBS, NBC, and ABC and joint affiliates of CBS-ABC, NBC-ABC, CBS-NBC, and CBS-NBC-ABC.)

9. Specifically, to newspaper, group, and network affiliations, and the buyer and seller attributes of all stations traded.

10. In chapter 6 this approach worked well enough for our programming equations. However, we explored the log form for our economic equations, drawing in part on related experience in chapter 3. See discussion on pages 470–72.

TABLE II.8 (4.11)

Four Estimating Equations for Television Station Sales Prices, 1949-70

		Equation 1		Equation 2		Equation 3		Equation 4	
		Sales Price Coefficient	t-value	Sales Price Coefficient	t-value	Sales Price Coefficient	t-value	Sales Price Coefficient	t-value
H	Constant	-104.950	1.99	-83.158	1.63	-59.745	1.18	-55.471	1.11
	TV homes in market	5.053	5.70	3.647	3.96	1.704	1.57	1.798	1.70
G	Nonnetwork group seller	11.878	1.77	-5.856	.76	12.403	1.92	-.545	.07
P	In-town newspaper seller	25.939	1.68	31.509	2.11	29.843	2.03	32.583	2.22
Gb	Nonnetwork group buyer	16.934	2.31	16.419	2.41	8.021	1.02	15.079	2.25
Pb	In-town newspaper buyer	-12.354	.50	n.i.		n.i.		n.i.	
#VHF	Number of VHF stations in market	.413	.06	.501	.07	-.191	.03	.107	.01
Vis Pwr	Visual power	.566	2.18	.493	1.96	.418	1.67	.427	1.72
N	Network affiliate	73.205	2.69	54.965	2.05	23.048	.79	17.034	.59
V	VHF channel	68.291	2.59	45.698	1.76	41.711	1.61	33.074	1.28
M	Markets with 3+ VHF	129.425	5.27	112.875	4.72	80.139	3.10	78.319	3.06
logAge	Log number months on air when sold	9.538	1.84	11.618	1.49	11.644	1.50	13.475	1.76
#VHFM	Number of VHF × market dummy	-33.080	3.36	-28.866	3.03	-19.346	1.95	-18.922	1.93
HP	Newspaper seller × TV homes	3.023	1.81	2.371	1.47	1.078	.65	1.384	.86
PG	Newspaper-group seller	-63.669	3.08	-76.552	3.80	-64.282	3.24	-76.083	3.84
NV	Network affiliate × VHF channel	-62.177	2.15	-39.350	1.39	-32.952	1.17	-24.612	.87
HPb	Newspaper buyer × TV homes	3.480	.61	n.i.		n.i.		n.i.	
PG[b]	Newspaper-group buyer	57.062	1.88	64.392	2.99	59.681	2.80	63.399	2.99
A logAge	Age dummy × log age	21.646	4.25	19.903	4.04	19.249	3.93	18.818	3.88
HG	Group seller × TV homes	n.i.		5.534	4.27	n.i.		3.945	2.91
HGb	Group buyer × TV homes	n.i.		n.i.		2.038	1.80	n.i.	
HN	Network affiliate × TV homes	n.i.		n.i.		5.693	3.93	4.961	3.38
	Adjusted R^2	.3890		.4264		.4364		.4461	
	Sample size	310		310		310		310	
	Sample mean (\$100,000s)	51.1023		51.1023		51.1023		51.1023	

SOURCE: For data sources and compilation procedures, see Appendix I.

n.i. = Excluded from equation for design purposes.

Notation	Variable Definition
K	Constant
H	TV homes—namely, number of homes with one or more TV sets with market areas of dominant influence (ADI) as defined by the American Research Bureau, in thousands.
G or Gs	For nonnetwork group *seller* = 1, 0 otherwise (not network-owned).
P or Ps	For co-located newspaper *seller* = 1, 0 otherwise.
Gb	For nonnetwork group buyer = 1, 0 otherwise (not network-owned).
Pb	For co-located newspaper buyer = 1, 0 otherwise.
#VHF	Number of VHF stations in metropolitan area market.
Vis. Pwr.	Visual (video) power in hundreds of kilowatts.
N	For network-affiliated seller = 1, 0 otherwise.
O	For network owner = 1, 0 otherwise.
V	For VHF channel = 1, UHF = 0.
M	Market dummy, 1 = 3 or more VHF stations in market, 0 otherwise.
logAge	Log of station's age in months at time of sale.
A	Age dummy, 1 = licensed 1951 or before, 0 = licensed 1952 or after.
A × logAge	Age dummy × logAge: for stations licensed before 1952-logAge, 0 otherwise.
#VHFM	Number of VHFs in market × market dummy: for markets with 3 or more VHF = #VHF, 0 otherwise.
HP	Newspaper seller dummy × TV homes: for newspaper seller = H, 0 otherwise.
PG	For newspaper-group seller = 1, 0 otherwise.
NV	For network affiliated VHF seller = 1, 0 otherwise.
HPb	Newspaper buyer dummy × TV homes: for newspaper buyer = H, 0 otherwise.
PG[b]	For newspaper-group buyer = 1, 0 otherwise.
HG	Group seller dummy × TV homes: group seller = H, 0 otherwise.
HN	Network affiliate dummy × TV homes: for network affiliate = H, 0 otherwise.
HGb	Group buyer dummy × TV homes: for group buyer = H, 0 otherwise.
$\bar{R}^2$	Total explained variance adjusted for degrees of freedom.
$\bar{Y}$	Mean of dependent variable.

Actually this improved market dummy modified an earlier one specified a priori for an expected break in our 1967 rates data, when the
first independent station entered. That specification worked pretty well in
estimating twenty-second one-time rates in 1967 (table 5.4), for which
purpose we still report it in chapter 5. However, our revised market
dummy was better grounded empirically, and when further interacted
with number of VHFs, all three elements in that specification (#VHFs,
M, #VHF × M) appeared better able to capture the nonlinearity of the
relationship between those elements and our economic dependent variables.[11] Briefly, larger markets, with more advertising potential, had relatively more stations but substantially higher advertising potential per
station, too, in view of heightened technical entry barriers in urban areas
(with their higher population density and greater intensity of signal
interference per TV household).[12]

Our first experiments in deriving the equations in table II.8 were with
the number of VHF stations (#VHFs), the VHF market dummy (M),
the interactive term #VHFs × M, and the number of UHFs (#UHFSs).
That specification offered the most inclusive set of possible impacts in the
most general form among the alternatives we explored. Using our interactive term, our coefficient for #VHFs would give us the impact of the
first and second VHF station, the coefficients of #VHFs plus #VHFs × M
would give us the fourth and fifth impacts, and the coefficient of #UHFs
any added UHF impact.[13] However, we soon dropped #UHFs since it
was unimportant competitively, and we could ill afford the loss in degrees
of freedom.

Inclusion of #VHFs × M, our interactive term, along with #VHFs and
M as basic variables, often raised adjusted R-squared substantially and
also increased the significance of TV homes and our age coefficients.
Hence our early sales price equations looked much better, overall, when
#VHFs was interacted with M, in the continued presence of those two
basic variables.

Our final coefficients for M and #VHFs × M were actually each significant across all four estimating equations, at the 5 percent confidence level
or better. The coefficient for #VHFs was not itself significant, however,
its impact being dominated by the interactive variable. Nonetheless, we

11. In developing this specification we had first considered such alternatives as
total commercial stations, number of VHF and UHF outlets separately, and a commercial market dummy equal to one for markets with four or more stations, zero
otherwise. However, we were unable to explore the further distinction between the
number of low-band VHF and high-band VHF stations (see table II.3). Nor did we
deem fruitful any simple distinction between the number of network affiliates and of
independents. Because an added independent always appears in markets that already
have three affiliates, that specification would contribute no more than our initial commercial market dummy, leaving us with the same kind of discontinuity when a fourth
station enters, with linearity before and after that point.

12. See chapter 5, note 9.

13. This is because, where M is zero, the M and #VHF × M variables fall out.

retained it, too, for a more comprehensive estimation of station impact across different-sized markets, having noted no major instability in other coefficients as a consequence.

(h) *Specifying the Interactive Dummies for Newspaper and Group Ownership, and for Network Affiliation.* The next task was to consider whether the impact of any one of these owner attributes—newspaper, group, or network—was conditional upon either or both of the others or on channel type.[14] Of major importance also was whether any interactive impact was further conditional upon market size.

(1) *Newspaper Ownership;* Our first experiments focused on the interaction of channel type (V), newspaper ownership (P), and network affiliation (N). But in our first sample of 268 cases, some 29 of 30 newspaper-owned affiliates were VHF (VP = 29), 28 out of 30 were also network (PN = 28), whereas 27 of 30 were both VHF *and* network (VPN = 27). While it was possible for these variables to have significant impacts when considered simultaneously, this required far more substantial effect (than we had here) of the two independents relative to 28 network affiliates, and of the one UHF relative to 29 VHFs.

One way to deal with this small number of unique stations and with the extreme related multicollinearity was to delete each interactive term selectively from the equation. However, given our special interest in the newspaper owner impact policywise, we opted first to interact P with just one other variable. This ultimately enabled us to retain P, the basic newspaper variable, HP, its interaction with TV homes, and PG, its interaction with group ownership. (The latter was highly significant throughout all experiments, a fact that did not appear traceable to any intermediate impact of PG on rates and through rates on sales price.)

We actually specified equation 1 for sales price (in table II.8) through experiments which early on revealed that, in the presence of the VPN interactive, P alone was insignificant, whereas without VPN, P was quite significant. We were equally convinced that the results would have been identical had we also included PV and PN, separately or together, in the equation with P. While we could not claim there was no global impact from P jointly with the above interactives, P itself was clearly not significant in this particular sample. Thus, we had the classic example of insufficient independent observations for each interactive term, along with the needed impact, to get significance notwithstanding collinearity among our interacted variables.

In other experiments, however, P revealed significance in the presence of PG and HP, suggesting that newspaper owner impacts were in fact conditional upon simultaneous group ownership and possibly also upon market size.

(2) *Network Affiliation and Channel Type;* As for group and network

14. Channel type was indeed too strongly linked with these interactions to be worth analyzing by itself.

impacts, we had similar problems of multicollinearity as with newspaper ties. Thus, 255 of the 310 stations in our final sample were network *and* VHF, and only 26 network and UHF. By the same token, there were 23 independent VHFs and 6 independent UHFs. Presumably each basic variable, N and V, could be significant when introduced singly but insignificant when brought in simultaneously. However, that was not in fact the case. The separate impacts of each component—V and N—were sufficient to overcome the collinearity, and we therefore successfully introduced N and VN at the same time. This then permitted a more accurate estimation of network tie with and without the VHF attribute present. Early on we were therefore able to introduce N, V, and VN simultaneously and to measure the impacts of N and V, the two most powerful basic determinants of economic performance, conditional upon each other.

(3) *Nonnetwork Group Ownership;* [15] In regard to group impact (G), the collinearity among G, V, and VP prevented G, VG, or VPG from impacting significantly on sales price. Excluding those two interactive terms (or VPN), however, G was generally significant and especially so with PG present. In other words, the coefficient of basic variable, G, alone, was our best measure of group impact. This was true even though we had good reason to expect the positive interaction among group ownership, VHF channel type, or a national network affiliation also to heighten that impact. The statistical properties of our sample simply did not permit us to make that more refined determination here.

(4) *Interactions with Market Size;* As for interactions with market size, these specifications improved markedly once we limited them to interactions between one basic owner variable (P, G, or N) and TV homes alone. Thus, once HV and HVP were removed (due to collinearity with H, V, and P), H and HP were consistently significant. Also, the magnitude of the H and HP coefficients was relatively insensitive to the specification of the rest of the equation. Only at a much later stage, after we had attempted to specify "buyer dummies" for G and P (see pages 468–69), did we conclude that we could not simultaneously introduce HP, HG, and NG into a single equation.

This raises the further and final question of our rationale in specifying "buyer dummies" for G and P, remembering however that our major emphasis throughout is on the seller side. Buyer dummies were of course arguably appropriate only for sales price equations. Yet we coded none for network affiliates or network owners, since we expected to find very few such transactions in our data base. Only for group and newspaper-owned stations did our special policy interest in owner diversity warrant specification of buyer dummies.

(5) *Specification of Dummy Variables Denoting That Station Was Sold*

15. From this point on the reader may want to consult frequently our list of variable definitions at page 463.

to Nonnetwork Group or In-Town Newspaper Buyer ("Buyer Dummies"); Our hypothesis here was simply that the price of a station will vary, *cet. par.,* with the buyer's expectation of subsequent income; that is, if a newspaper or group affiliated buyer correctly anticipated substantial scale economies or unique market power in running a TV station, this could well show up in the maximum price he is willing to pay at the outset. Whether he will be *compelled* to pay any extra margin for a TV station would depend upon the seller's characteristics, on market size, and on market structure.

In short, we attempted to decompose sales price into two components. The first component reflected a station's past economic performance, probably best captured by some measure of absolute dollar profits, perhaps averaged over the most recent years. The second component related to any unique attributes of the buyer that might explain why he would be willing to pay a premium price.

As noted, we treated this first component (past station performance) indirectly, by specifying those basic ownership and structural factors that determine station profits, rather than rates (as a proxy for profits) directly as an independent variable. This made sense insofar as some of the basic factors were policy variables, of obviously greater concern to us than any intermediate variables (like rates) that transmitted that impact. Rates were indeed a price per unit of product, not an absolute revenue variable, and did not even suggest profit per unit let alone recent absolute profits, in that costs were ignored. (In television, as elsewhere, there are doubtless instances where high rates and low profits go hand in hand.)

The second component of sales price was deemed to reflect the characteristics of each station's buyers which may cause them to pay a price that reflects more than just past economic performance. Here would be included also the extent to which buyers thought *their* unique attributes (say, derived from special ownership ties), could enhance their future economic performance.[16] We handled this second component (buyer expectations) with the so-called buyer dummy variables we shall now describe.

i. *Jointly Specified Equations Including Both Buyer and Seller Dummies.* The addition of buyer dummies repeatedly improved our selleronly equations. Thus an adjusted R-square of .366 for one characteristic equation rose, with the addition of buyer dummies, to .381 or .389. Indeed, the jointly specified equation most similar to our main seller-only equation (in that it specified the buyer dummies precisely as the seller dummies were) had the highest adjusted R-square of all such jointly specified equations.

---

16. Presumably there could also be buyer characteristics that *reduced* their future profit expectations. Yet if the price were low enough, this might still be a profitable purchase in terms of return on investment.

(1) *Emphasis on Newspaper-Affiliated Buyers;* Of the buyer dummies, HPb, VGb, and PNb never came close to significance (see partial list of variable definitions on page 463). Of these, VGb and PNb had been dropped from the seller-only equations earlier, so it was not surprising that they did not perform well either when representing buyers. While we kept HPb in our seller equations, it was only significant at the 10 percent level; however, it retained that significance when buyer dummies were added. Yet the buyer version of HPb was not significant.

Gb and PbGb were the only buyer dummies that appeared to be useful additions to the previous seller equations. Thus, the buyer Pb variable came close to significance ($t = 1.624$), but only when we omitted all other newspaper buyer dummies and then at the expense of no significance in the buyer G variable.

We were also interested in what happened to the coefficients and t-ratios in the original seller equation to which we had added these buyer dummies. In terms of significance, we found seller Pb and seller Gb each dropped from 5 percent to 10 percent significance, whereas log of age increased to the point where it became significant at 10 percent. All other original coefficients in the seller-only equations retained their same levels of significance when the buyer dummies were added.

On the basis of these initial observations, we decided to drop the buyer dummies HPb, VGb, and PbNb from further equations that retained the seller dummies. Among the jointly specified equations, we nevertheless finally included, for reporting purposes, HPb and Pb (in table II.8, equation 1), given their policy relevance and that they did not adversely affect the other results.

(2) *Buyer Dummy-Only Equations (Exclude Seller Dummies);* Our buyer dummy variables clearly appeared to add enough unique independent information to favor their inclusion along with the seller dummies, as specified earlier. True, we gained some isolated significance in buyer-only equations, but that was out of increasing the significance of already significant coefficients. In contrast, the jointly specified equations had substantially higher adjusted R-squares than did the buyer-only equations.

(3) *Emphasis on Group Ownership, Network Ties, and Related Interactions;* In the third phase of this analysis we dropped all three-level interactives, such as VGH, VHN, and VGN, in that each of these had a simple correlation greater than .9 with, say, HG, HN, and GN, respectively. It was normally hard to obtain significance in such cases.

That left us with: Seller (HG, HN, GN) and Buyer (HGb, GNb). However it would be hard to add more than one more "H"-related seller variable at a time without multicollinearity clouding the results. Note also that we had 140 group-owned stations in our seller equations deck, 130 of which were also network affiliates and, in all but 13 cases, at the same time VHFs. There was a limit to the mileage we could get out of this much overlap, and it was hard to predict the outcome of various experiments beforehand. There was also a question as to what type equation to start with—whether seller-only, buyer-only, or jointly specified.

Eventually our buyer experiments led to the conclusion that with only one buyer dummy of even 10 percent significance (PG[b], Gb) we could not improve our equation very much by adding others.[17]

The final set of experiments from which we subsequently selected sales price equations 2–4 (in table II.8), were as follows. First, we selected our "best" jointly specified equation to that point, the one that focused on newspaper ownership (subsequently called equation 1)—namely, SP = H + G + P + Gb + Pb + #VHF + Vis Pwr + N + V + M + LogAge + (#VHF × M) + HP + PG + VN + PG[b] + (A × logAge). To this we added sequentially each of the following combinations of interactive terms, mainly focusing on G, N, and H:

(1) HG, HGb; (2) HG, NGb; (3) HN, HGb; (4) HN, NGb; (5) HG; HGb; (6) HG; NGb; (7) HG; (8) HN; (9) NG; (10) HBb; (11) NGb; (12) Pb; (13) none of the above; (14) HG, NG, HGb; (15) HG, HN, NGb; (16) HG, HN.

Although we could not introduce *all* major types of interactions into any single equation simultaneously, we were nonetheless able to add information beyond that captured by equation 1. We did so once again by using the criteria outlined earlier (page 462), selecting as equation 2, option 7 in the list above; as equation 3, option 3; and as equation 4, option 16. In each case the value of adjusted R-square rose visibly, with only limited instability in the variables common to all equations.[18]

2. The Estimation of Station Economic and Programming Indicators, 1972

In regard to our station economic regressions for 1972 (table II.9), we have noted elsewhere the mutually supplementary and nonduplicative character of our four dependent variables—namely, spot rates, audience, station revenues, and metro rating. Compiled as they were from three quite different data sources (Standard Rates and Data Service, American

17. The only other interactive buyer dummy of potential value further emerged as HGb which, in sales price equation 3, had a t-value of 1.8.

18. All four equations appear in table II.8. The coefficients of equations 2–4 were generally closer to one another than to equation 1. However, there was basic stability across all four equations in a number of coefficients—logAge, age dummy (A), A × logAge, Pb, PG, #VHF × market dummy (M), M, Visual Power, Gb, P. Differences in some other coefficients (for example, N, V, and VN) appear associated with the presence of HG, or HGb, and HN simultaneously. This suggests simply that the V and VN impact is too widely diffused (among too many variables) to reveal significance. Nevertheless, while the added interactions among N and V may have rendered their impacts less precise in equations 2–4, interactions among P and G (for PG, PG[b]) may well have enhanced theirs.

Research Bureau, and FCC grouped financial data), their further corroborative character was particularly valuable. This was all the more so in view of our necessarily crude estimates of station revenue, derived as (1) a station share of tuned-in households multiplied by (2) its market's total net broadcast revenues.

(a) *The Economic Equations.* The procedure for table II.9, in effect, was first to estimate spot rates, drawing on our prior detailed analysis of TV station sales prices. Indeed, the alternate regressions we ran there on highest hourly rate (using a similar set of independent variables), as well as our simple additive estimation (table II.3) of twenty-second one-time and five-time spot rates in 1967 (with and without delivered audience in the equation), gave us a good starting point.

Drawing heavily on the preceding results, our initial task was to introduce as many of our principal interactive variables as multicollinearity would permit. Recalling the difficulty of introducing HN, HG and HP simultaneously in any single equation on sales price, with or without each basic variable specified too, our first experiments here were also on various combinations of those interactions.

After some initial analysis we started with the fullest variable specification for rates and then selectively dropped various interactive variables. Our initial specification was RATES = $H + G + O + P + S + N + V + \#VHF \times M + HP + HG + NV + HN + LogAge + M \times LogAge + PG$. ($S$ = station's share of tuned-in homes.) The variables underlined in table II.9 actually remained as a common base throughout our experiments. However, we also ran various combinations of the variables not underlined as well as three equations with HO added.

In developing a suitable specification, three major criteria were once again applied. In particular we considered (1) the significance of each basic variable and its interactive term, before and after the latter was removed (singly or in combinations of interactions); (2) stability of all other coefficients after each marginal change in the specification; (3) the effects of each modified specification on adjusted R-square.

The upshot of these experiments was that HN was without doubt the most potent of the three network variables, N, VN, and HN. All in all, we had strong evidence for including HN and N and mixed evidence for VN. Furthermore, network ownership (O) was also consistently significant and positive in its impact on rates, with t-ratios around ten. Finally, age had no impact for post-1952 stations, and the impact from pre-1952 seemed to hinge more on the age dummy (pre-1952 attribute) than on log of age itself. This suggested that we include only the age dummy here and not the age variable.

On the other hand, the surprising absolute insignificance of our stations specification throughout—$\#VHF$, M, $\#VHF \times M$—and of channel type (V) too, and the opposite signs of G and HG (and hence likely insignificance of our G attribute), raised the possibility that we may

TABLE II.9 (6.4)

Four Estimating Equations for TV Station Economic Indicators, 387 TV Stations, 1972

Independent Variables	Spot Rate		Audience		Estimated Station Revenue		Metro Rating	
	Coefficient	t-value	Coefficient	t-value	Coefficient	t-value	Coefficient	t-value
Constant	17.05	3.4	.14	1.8	142.29	2.5	8.65	6.7
Network affiliation*	−14.10	3.3	−.12	1.8	−144.26	3.1	11.21	10.5
Network owner*	65.83	10.0	.13	1.3	497.98	6.8	.95	.6
Nonnetwork group*	−7.65	3.8	−.01	.2	−61.26	2.7	.87	1.7
TV homes	−1.08	3.0	.03	5.8	−6.97	1.7	.19	2.0
Licensed pre-1952*	5.85	2.8	.05	1.5	71.04	3.1	.46	.9
Group owner × TV homes	2.10	6.4	.01	1.3	20.88	5.7	−.18	2.1
Network affiliation × TV homes	7.10	21.9	.14	27.6	76.56	21.4	−.26	3.2
VHF channel*	9.56	2.1	.23	3.3	97.93	1.9	2.66	2.3
Network affiliate × VHF	−2.64	.5	.02	.3	−25.53	.5	4.31	3.4
Log number VHF station (+1)	−12.61	2.2	−.39	4.4	−9.04	.6	−10.42	7.2
Newspaper owner*	.18	.1	.06	1.7	26.22	1.0	.82	1.3
Newspaper owner × TV homes	.05	.2	−.01	1.3	−1.42	.5	−.05	.9
Adjusted R^2	.904		.971		.939		.722	
Sample size	387		387		387		387	
Sample mean	$33.908 (× $10)		.827 (× 1,000,000)		$415.981 (× 10,000)		17.907 (%)	
Mean TV homes (× 1,000)	610		610		610		610	

SOURCE: The following data were derived from *Broadcasting Yearbook—1973*, and *TV Factbook No. 43*, 1973-74: number of VHF stations in market, station channel type, network affiliation, newspaper, group, or network owner status, and age as of August 1, 1972. All rates data derived from Standard Rates and Data Service, *Spot Television Rates and Data* for selected issues during 1972 and 1973. Rates used were those in effect for longest period during 1972.

have included "too many" variables in our common set for these experiments. For that reason we really could not tell how much of this insignificance (as well as for P and HP) may have been due to multicollinearity.

Accordingly, we planned additional experiments, starting with only our statistically significant variables from these initial runs—A, G, N, HN, H, O, HG. To this common set we then added various combinations of V, #VHF, VN and, given the poor performance of our interactive market dummy—#VHF, M, #VHFM—now log (#VHF + 1). (Actually the log form for #VHF had been quite useful in our new market equations on aggregate quarter-hour viewing. Here, too, at least three of our dependent economic variables—rates, audience, revenues—were far-ranging. Following the lessons learned in table II.11, therefore we opted to cast #VHFs in a log form, to control for market size and to further interact a number of owner attributes each separately with TV homes.)[19]

Our final specification for spot rate was clearly much improved, with all but three variables significant. Actually P and HP, both insignificant (as also in many interim experiments), were retained for reporting purposes and comparative assessment. VN itself was also insignificant, the main network impact being reflected in HN and, additionally, in N. By this time we concluded that, for ease of interpretation and explanation, we should generally include a separate term for each variable involved with any interaction coefficient even if not statistically significant (as here). This is because synergistic effects captured by the interactive terms are greater than the sum of the separate effects of each of the interacted variables.

Once having specified this spot rate equation, we also ran (for corroborative and reporting purposes) our other three economic indicators—audience, ratings, and estimated revenues—on the same variables. The stability of coefficients and PCDVs[20] across all four equations was moderate to high, and sufficient to confirm the general profile for economic effects of major licensing policies, as laid out in chapter 6, in the derived impacts in tables 6.5 and 6.6 and, in 6.7, as between large and small markets.

(b) *The Programming Equations.* As for our equations for programming table II.10 clearly, experimentation took a somewhat different form. There we initially focused on all news, the variable whose earlier non-interactive additive equation had the highest R-square, and the most numerous significant owner impacts.

i. *Initial Specification;* Building on our accumulated experience with several economic variables (including sales price), we started with a

---

19. Subsequently the often highly significant negative coefficient of log of number of VHFs revealed that the changed specification may have helped make a marked improvement. The three significant t-values were 2.2, 4.4, and 7.2.

20. Unit changes in dependent variable as percent of sample mean.

TABLE II.10 (6.12)

Estimating Equations for Station Time Devoted to Selected Program Categories, Composite Week, 1972
(6 P.M.–11 P.M.)

Independent Variables		Equation 1 All Local (Including Entertainment)		Equation 2 All News		Equation 3 Local News		Equation 4 All Public Affairs		Equation 5 Local Public Affairs		Equation 6 All Info.	
		Coefficient	t-value	Coefficient	t-value	Coefficient	t-value	Coefficient	t-value	Coefficient	t-value	Coefficient	t-value
	Constant	30.131	.4	−99.759	2.1	−27.282	.8	−22.918	.5	−19.222	1.4	−71.914	1.0
V	VHF channel*	89.971	2.0	86.870	3.0	83.978	3.9	14.189	.6	−6.210	.6	56.515	1.3
N	Network affiliate*	−32.333	.9	184.760	7.9	49.180	2.8	89.060	4.2	−10.374	1.5	225.091	6.2
P	In-town newspaper owner*	45.586	2.4	12.869	1.1	9.694	1.1	−2.460	.2	−.518	.1	10.106	.5
O	Network owner*	−46.054	.9	−12.819	.4	.495	.02	−11.872	.4	−20.826	1.9	−24.495	.5
G	Nonnetwork group owner*	5.287	.4	−1.184	.1	1.997	.3	−6.536	.8	.179	.1	−7.049	.5
H	TV homes in market	−2.727	1.8	−.012	.01	−.632	.9	1.167	1.3	.856	3.4	1.121	.7
COLL	Percent population 4+ years college	2.667	1.5	2.681	2.3	1.783	2.0	1.511	1.4	.838	2.0	4.174	2.3
A	Licensed pre-1952*	30.023	1.6	9.803	.8	15.390	1.6	−19.010	1.6	4.943	1.1	2.174	.1
L-AGE	Log number of months on air 1972	69.399	2.5	50.936	2.8	23.907	1.8	7.088	.4	16.439	2.8	71.625	2.6
#VHF	Number of VHF stations in market	−6.820	.4	.670	.1	−8.853	1.1	14.711	1.5	2.308	.7	21.311	1.3
M	Markets with 3+ VHF*	−39.989	.8	−3.979	.1	−52.881	2.1	45.621	1.5	10.214	1.0	50.579	1.0
#VHFM	Number of VHF x market dummy	19.122	.9	.557	.04	20.575	2.1	−20.650	1.7	−4.543	1.0	−23.677	1.2
NV	Network affiliate x VHF channels*	−102.438	2.1	−73.205	2.3	−59.349	2.5	−31.353	1.1	4.032	.4	−74.188	1.5
REV	Estimated station revenue	.064	2.6	.068	2.9	.080	4.5	.044	2.1	n.i.		.090	2.5
(REV)²	(Estimated station revenue)²	n.i.	n.i.	−1.102E-04	1.8	−.128E-04	3.0	−.104E-04	2.0	n.i.		−.158E-04	1.8
	Adjusted R²	.1349		.4349		.3648		.0701		.0749		.2794	
	Sample size	408		408		408		408		531		408	
	Sample mean (minutes)	209.926		249.150		129.605		111.461		24.209		397.708	

SOURCE: The following data were derived from *Broadcasting Yearbook*, 1973; and *Television Factbook No. 43*, 1973-74: number of VHF stations in market; station channel type, network affiliation, newspaper, group, or network owner status, and age as of August 1, 1972. Estimated station revenues derived from published FCC financial data for 1972 (by market), and the American Research Bureau's published estimates of each station's share of metropolitan area viewing, Sunday-Saturday, 6 P.M.-11 P.M., during the survey period. See *Television Day–Part Audience Summary*, November 1972. Percent of market population with four or more years of college education from U.S. Bureau of the Census, Census of Population for 1970. All data for estimated program time by program category from FCC's First Annual Programming Report for All Commercial Television Stations, 1973 (published October 8, 1974).

*Labeled attribute of dummy variable equals one, zero otherwise.
n.i. = variable not included in equation for design purposes.

rather full specification—namely, NEWS = V + N + P + O + G + H + #VHF + M + #VHF × M + LogAge + VN + A. Our assumption was that informational or local programming, reputed to be nonremunerative, could well require greater economic wherewithal for its transmission. There were two ways to explore this. First, we could include those same owner and structural variables that had repeatedly been shown to impact significantly on economic variables. A priori, on a supply of funds theory, those very economic effects could of course have further consequences for programming. Second, we could specify station revenue itself as a direct determinant of informational programming, in line with earlier work by Park and others. Actually we proceeded in both directions, subsequently running our fully specified equation both with and without station revenue (and revenue squared).

However, we first focused further on the interactive market variable, #VHF × M, given that numerous experiments did not register significance for #VHF, M, or #VHFM. Exclusion of #VHFM did not, however, improve these results, and, for reporting purposes, we left all three elements in our final equations. (Recall that we had included Pb in sales price equation 1 for the sake of added convenience, although it was never significant) (see table II.8, page 462).

ii. *Interactive Market Dummy;* Furthermore, the coefficients and t-values of #VHF, M, and #VHFM were quite stable over our experimental equations, though not quite significant. However, it appeared that any other specification would have given us similar results. Another reason we stayed with the now standard stations specification, was that it offered a simple interpretation and left us free to focus on two new variables of possibly considerable importance—namely, on the percentage of a market's population with four or more years of college education (COLLEGE), and estimated station revenue (and revenue squared).

iii. *College Education;* A priori an audience's college education appeared to be a reasonable determinant of any station's informational program mix. We introduced college education, however, more as a control factor strengthening the reliability of other independent variables. College education did indeed have a consistently positive and significant impact on news, at least when it was not interacted with other variables. However, none of the interactions of college with owner types, market size, or other variables was significant. Hence the basic variable alone was included, with statistical significance, but with a small absolute impact being expected.

iv. *Station Age;* In specifying age we found a continuously significant and sizable impact of log of age on news and later on other programming variables. This probably reflected the better integration into the community of older stations in 1972. Older stations may have been more responsive to public issues on that score and also have had time to develop news-gathering organizations and contacts. Neither the age dummy, however, nor the interacted age variable added significance either singly or jointly. Since they made practically identical contributions to adjusted R-square, we retained the age dummy for ease of interpretation and to fill out our *ceteris paribus* conditions. This acted to enhance the reliability of policy-related variables most relevant to our assessment—namely, of several owner attributes and number of stations in the market. Indeed, all those variables (P, G, #VHF, M, #VHFM) were retained for reporting purposes, notwithstanding frequent insignificance in alternative specifications.

v. *Inclusion of Station Revenue and Revenue Squared;* One final distinction between this new specification for programming and that for economic indicators was our inclusion of estimated station revenue and revenue squared. This took us back to our second option in explaining the supply of funds theory of informational programming (see pages 202–04). The precise reasons for their inclusion are spelled out in chapter 6. Here suffice it to note we sought thereby to correct for nonlinearity due to differential capacity to fund informational service in different sized markets, where stations earn different level revenues, and where our interacted stations specification (V, M, #VHFM) could account for such factors only in part. Because owner and market attributes did not fully account for station revenue, moreover, we believed that direct inclusion of revenue would help explain more of the total variance in programming variables, which was in fact the case.

Running our final equation with and without revenue and revenue squared further confirmed the marked stability of our major policy sensitive variables—P, N, and G—and guarded against distortions due to simultaneity bias. To give full sway to the revenue factor for additional reasons stated in chapter 6, we dropped all earlier interactions of those variables with TV homes. Such interactions would have been redundant here insofar as the economic dependent variables estimated in table II.9 (by equations using those interactions) would themselves now figure as major control factors (in table II.10), via station revenue at least.

In sum, once having derived our best estimating equation for news (adjusted R^2 = .4349), we ran it across all six programming dependent variables. The identical *ceteris paribus* conditions provided useful contrasts, comparisons, and corroboration for major policy-sensitive independent variables retained for reporting purposes even when insignificant. In that regard, our principal concern was with the reliability of those coefficients. Therefore, the significance of such control factors as college education, age, and station revenue was particularly reassuring.

3. The Analysis of Influences on Average Quarter-Hour Viewing and Proportions of Tuned-in Households with Special Reference to Program Diverstiy

Our principal hypothesis in estimating aggregate viewing (in table II.11, page 473), was that, other cogent influences being held constant (or taken into account), the number both of program options and of program types across all stations in the market had significant effects. Program type differences were coded in terms of a standard twenty-category industry typology. The validity of such typologies was indeed further confirmed by an exhaustive regression analysis of some 1300 network programs whose delivered audiences were reported by A. C. Nielson, in a similar typology, weekly (see chapter 3, tables 3.2, 3.3, and 3.4). Those results clearly suggested that type differences of this sort were not only perceived as such on the producer side (by station owners, advertisers, and network companies) but also by viewers generally. However, there was evidence, too, that type diversity was only one of many attributes that explained viewer behavior, and that day-of-week differences, network origin, time of night, and program length accounted for only a small part of the unexplained variance (see table 3.3, page 64).[21]

To pick up more of these other factors, we explored the further impact of the sheer number of program options (regardless of type) as potentially reflective of additional influences. However, in so doing we considered the differences between VHF and UHF attributes and between network and independent. Essentially a four-way breakdown of stations —NV, NU, IV, IU—served as a useful way to allow for variations in resources available for programming. At the very least, the program mix on network and independent stations was known to be quite different, as were the resources with which either ordinarily had to work. The further distinction between VHF and UHF was also known to have major economic ramifications.

The reason we proposed to examine options and types impacts on aggregate viewing was simply to determine whether additional types or additional options were at the margin distinguishable by the viewer and, in any sense, offered him or her a chance to discover preferred programs not hitherto available. If such marginal increments did in fact provide the chance to discover preferred programs, *cet. par.*, aggregate viewing should rise.

To ensure the reliability of any types or options measures we finally used, considerable care must first be given to the further specification of major control factors. There we reviewed a detailed Nielsen survey—*The*

21. Together the variables in that estimating equation explained 23 percent of total variance. However, more detailed analysis revealed that network tie and program type differences alone contributed by far most of the explanatory power (see detailed discussion in chapter 3, pages 63–65).

TABLE II.11 (3.6)

Estimating Equation for Aggregate Quarter-Hour
Viewing in 133 Television Markets, 1967
(Sample mean = 21.804 [X 10,000] Average Quarter-Hour Homes)

Independent Variables	Regression Coefficient	t-value
Constant	−0.375	
Percentage of homes with less than $3,000 income	+0.777[d]	1.390
January mean temperature	−0.086[a]	2.510
Percentage of multiset homes	+20.350[a]	3.430
Central time zone dummy	+2.376[a]	3.620
Number of program types in market	−0.037[a]	3.530
Program types X TV homes in market	+0.002[a]	34.380
Log (number of network VHF stations +1)	+12.802[b]	2.270
Log (number of network UHF stations +1)	+14.339[b]	2.160
Log (number of independent VHF +1)	+26.415[a]	5.040
Log (number of independent UHF +1)	+12.700[b]	2.030
Log (number of network UHF +1) X (TV homes)	−0.384[b]	2.260
Log (number of independent VHF +1) X (TV homes)	−0.600[a]	15.650
Log (number of independent UHF +1) X (TV homes)	−0.411[a]	8.030

Adjusted R^2 = .9922

SOURCE: The following data were derived from *Broadcasting Yearbook, 1973*, and *Television Factbook No. 43*, 1973-74: number of stations within the American Research Bureau's Area of Dominant Influence markets, by channel type and network tie; percentage of homes with more than one TV set; time zone location of each market. Additional sources include: U.S. Bureau of the Census, Population Reports for 1967, for percentage of families earning less than $3,000 income; Statistical Abstract of the U.S. (1967), for January mean temperature of market. Number of program types derived from *TV Guide*, February 25-March 3, 1967, and Broadcast Measurement Bureau, Series, Serials, and Packages—A Film Source Book, Vol. 6, Issue 2 (1965-66) and Issue 2S (Fall 1966). Statistical significance (two-tailed test) is: a = 1 percent; b = 5 percent; c = 10 percent; d = t-value exceeds 1 but less than 1.645, the 10 percent confidence level.

Television Audience, 1971 (unpublished). The task was to select meaningful exogenous variables, factors that influenced TV viewing but were not themselves either a function or determinants of our policy-related variables—namely, options and types. The Nielsen survey permitted a passing review of the possible impact on viewing of such exogenous factors (and combinations of factors) as sex, age, income level, persons per household, multiset households, and season. Time zone differences and of course market size could also explain differences in quarter-hour viewing; and these, too, must be carefully examined.

The ultimate objective, then, was to estimate variations in the level of quarter-hour viewing, with key exogenous factors taken into account, of postulated changes in the number of program options and program types across all stations in the market. Subsidiary issues we explored to an intermediate point were the related question of: how many more (or less) dollars advertisers would spend in the market, *cet. par.*, in response

TABLE II.12 (3.7)

Estimating Equation for Table 3.7A

Independent Variables	Regression Coefficient	t-value
Constant	0.251	5.9
Percentage of homes with less than $3,000 income	0.008	0.7
January mean temperature	−0.001	1.6
Percent multiset in market	0.255	2.1
Central time zone dummy	0.036	2.7
Number of program types in market	0.001	2.8
Program types × TV homes	*	
Number of TV homes in market	−0.002	0.5
Log (number of network VHF stations +1) in market	0.128	1.1
Log (number of network UHF stations +1)	0.100	0.8
Log (number of independent VHF stations +1)	−0.145	1.4
Log (number of independent UHF stations +1)	−0.030	0.2
Log (number of network VHF +1) × (TV homes)	*	
Log (number of network UHF +1) × (TV homes)	−0.059	1.7
Log (number of independent VHF +1) × (TV homes)	0.033	0.5
Log (number of independent UHF +1) × (TV homes)	−0.005	0.6

Adjusted R^2 = .408.
Sample size (ADI markets) = 133.
Sample mean = 0.5396 (× 100).
Dependent variable = percentage of TV homes that tune in some designated amount
of time weekly, as estimated by the American Research
Bureau for its "Areas of Dominant Influence."
SOURCE: All data sources as for Table II.11.
*Not calculable due to collinearity.

to an additional program type or program option. This would permit some crude valuation of additional types or options at the margin within current institutional and financial arrangements.

There were essentially three steps in our specification for table II.11 (page 477), as further modified in table II.12: selection of the exogenous control factors, specification of options and types, analysis of interactions between options, types and other control factors.

(a) *Exogenous Variables.*

i. *Temperature, Rainfall;* The Nielsen survey revealed a big seasonal difference in viewing, "Summer prime time (viewing) levels (being) roughly two-thirds Winter prime time levels" (Nielsen, pp. 164–71). The longer it stays light outside, and the less likely people remain indoors generally, *cet. par.*, the lower the expected level of viewing. Two factors that might pick up this length-of-day-life-style influence are temperature and rainfall.[22] Subsequent analysis repeatedly showed

22. We did indeed specify those factors explicitly to capitalize on the suggestive results of the Nielsen survey, even though they are both subsumed under each market's longitude and latitude (an alternative combined variable).

negative significance for January mean temperature (as expected), but no significance for rainfall, with or without temperature in the equation. Conceivably rainfall levels did not vary inversely with temperature, and the latter better reflected life-style-length-of-day as an influence on viewing. Therefore we retained January mean temperature of the market in our final estimating equations, with its expected negative significance (tables II.11, II.12).

ii. *Persons per Household, Multiset Families;* The Nielsen survey further reveals that average household viewing per week was much more influenced by whether there were three or more persons in a household, than by the number of sets or even the number of stations.

Number of Stations Receivable	Percentage Change in Hours per Week for Households with Three or More Viewers to Those with Two Viewers or One
1-4	25%
5-8	38%
9 or more	67%

SOURCE: A. C. Nielsen Co., *The Television Audience* (New York: A. C. Nielsen Co., 1971), p. 153.

In other words, in markets with from five to eight stations, households with three or more viewers view about 38 percent more hours per week than do households with one or two viewers.

We considered specifying some measure of persons per household in our equation. However, the only such measure we could conveniently muster was the market average which did not in fact pick up enough of this influence to provide significant explanatory power. Most of the impact occurs at a discrete jump from two to three persons per household, a break in the data which our market average variables simply could not capture. That average hid the split between one- and two-person families, and three- and more-person families, and in addition evidenced little variability, having by far the smallest ratio of standard deviation to mean (only 7 percent) of all the independent variables run in early experiments. A "percentage of households with three or more persons" variable might have performed better; however, we could not readily calculate that.

Therefore we experimented further, and with much better results, with the percentage of multiset families. True, the impact of moving from single-to-multiset families appeared far smaller than that of any comparable switch from two to three persons per household.

Number of Stations Receivable	Percentage Change in Viewing Hours per Week for Households with Two or More Sets Compared with Households for One Set
1-6	4%
7 or more	8.5%

SOURCE: A. C. Nielsen, Inc., *The Television Audience*, 1971, p. 155.

Nevertheless, since it was reasonable to assume that households with multiple sets will watch more hours than will single-set households, it made sense to experiment with a multiset variable. Not only would one expect households with more persons to have more sets *cet. par.*, but a "percentage of households with more than one set" variable was in fact readily calculable from trade statistics and more sensitive to variation among markets than any market average figure. On both counts, excluding consideration of a host of social factors, a multiset family variable might reflect the likelihood of more viewing due to more persons per household (or in multiperson households generally).

This was indeed true in our final estimating equations where the percentage of multiset families had a t-value of 3.430 and a large percentage change in dependent variable (PCDV) as defined in Appendix I (pages 430–31). Furthermore this variable contributed to explanatory power even after the number of stations was taken into account.

iii. *Family Income;* A third exogenous factor was that of family income, either as median level or as percentage of families earning above or below some critical level. The Nielsen survey quite clearly revealed that, for adult males only, viewing tends to decrease with rising income, with one minor exception. For men both above and below fifty years of age, in both the 7:30–9 P.M. and 9–11 P.M. time slots, maximum viewing occurs with one minor exception, in families earning less than $5,000. The same holds true for female adults, except in the 9–11 P.M. time slot for women over fifty where the results are inconclusive. In contrast, viewing for the total household (including children) rises in both time slots from the below $5,000 to the $15,000 income class, above which it drops noticeably.

Presumably, then, children (below eighteen) coming from higher-income homes watch more television than those from lower-income homes. They do so, moreover, in sufficient numbers to dominate total household viewing up to the $15,000 income class, and notwithstanding directly contrary influences of adult male and female viewing behavior. Above $15,000 income, the substantial fall in adult viewing of either sex, especially in the 9–11 P.M. slot, appears to dominate any influence of children's income sensitivity, with household level results consistent with those for adults.

Considering income level only, we explored the impact of census data closest to a relevant Nielsen cut-off point—namely, percentage of households earning below $3,000. The Nielsen survey suggested that this class might have watched least. However, the variation in hours viewed with income was not pronounced for households as a whole, the maximum being only about 9 percent greater than the minimum in the 7:30–9 P.M. slot, and some 17 percent greater in the 9–11 P.M. slot. However, the corresponding percentages for adult male and female viewing, by age groups, ranged all the way up to 64 percent. Given the opposite impacts of children and adult viewing, then, there would be much less variation over income levels when examined in the aggregate than when examined in detail.

Nevertheless, the income class below $3,000 was the most relevant discriminant we could readily muster from census data. At the upper end the percentage of families earning $10,000 or more was not sufficiently refined to capture the drop in viewing clearly apparent above $15,000. Indeed some early experiments with the $10,000 and above income class revealed no impact whatever on aggregate viewing in the market. For that reason, too, we preferred to include the below-$3,000 income variable in our later equations. Its t-value was always greater than 1.2 in all prior experiments, sometimes rising as high as 2.0 or more and always greater than for median family income (a variable more likely to hide variations among markets).

On the other hand, the *positive* impact of the below-$3,000 income class variable suggested that *adult* viewing, perhaps in the eighteen to forty-nine-year age group, may have dominated children's viewing in 1967, the year of our assessment (table II.11, page 477). In our final equation, at any rate, the variable's impact was insignificant at the 10-percent level, but with a t-value of 1.390. We retained it, then, as a third exogenous control factor, with our principal interest remaining in the number of program options and program types across all stations in the market.

iv. *Age Composition of Population;* Mention should next be made of our inability to capture the effect of age on viewing. The Nielsen survey showed that male viewing rose from 38 percent of men in the eighteen-to-forty-nine age group who watch prime time television, compared with 47 percent for those above fifty. The comparable figures for women were 45 percent (below fifty) and 51 percent (above fifty). These measures clearly indicate that, to the extent that markets vary in composition of persons over and under fifty years of age, that factor will influence the variation in audience among markets. This conclusion was also verified by data broken down by sex, income, age, and the time slots just cited. There it was clear that age and hours of viewing are correlated positively in all cases—except for women in the 9–11 P.M. slot, where we found two positive and two negative effects.

Nevertheless, in many early experiments with *ceteris paribus* conditions fully specified, our age composition variable was persistently insignificant; and, indeed, its t-value never even approached 1.0. To be doubly sure, we also specified the variable as percentage of population above sixty-five years of age, the standard census classification; but here, too, the impact was far from significant. Apparently there was insufficient variation in these proportions among markets to be meaningful in market equations.

v. *Central Time Zone Dummy;* A fifth exogenous variable explored to ensure the reliability of our principal coefficients—those for options and types diversity—was that of a suitable time zone dummy. The only persistently significant dummy variable in our earliest experiments was equal to one if the market were located in the Central Time Zone, and zero otherwise. Similar dummy variables for the Eastern and Pacific Time zones had no comparable impact. As expected, then, the significance of CTZD reflected the different times the East Coast and West Coast programs were received in the central states. Thus prime-time programming starts at 6:30 P.M. in the Central Time Zone instead of 7:30 P.M. as elsewhere. Following our experiments with all three time zone dummies (for four time zones), then, we confirmed the validity of Robert Crandall's sole inclusion of CTZD in his regressions on alternate measures of marketwide viewing in *Public Policy* (Fall 1974). In our own estimating equation (table II.11, page 477), the variable had a t-value of 3.620, significant at the 1 percent confidence level.

vi. *TV Homes;* One last exogenous factor necessary to the analysis was TV homes in the market. Our assumption here was that the greater the number of potential viewers in the market (TV homes, multiset families), *cet. par.,* the higher the probable level of *actual* quarter-hour viewing. Or contrariwise, taking homes into account along with other exogenous variables, variations in level aggregate viewing will necessarily reflect postulated changes in the number of program options and program types.

Be this as it may, TV homes was consistently the strongest independent variable in all early experiments run on average quarter-hour viewing. This was true with or without multiset families in the equation. The more searching questions were whether TV homes should properly be cast into logarithmic (or some other nonlinear) form, and whether to interact it with the number of program options and program types. In regard to the first point, our numerous experiments with linear and log homes underscored the need to stay with the linear form even if there were some theoretical justification for nonlinear. Not only was adjusted R-squared adversely affected by any log transformation of homes, but the latter's own significance also fell dramatically. The many individual comparisons of separate pairs of equations which differed in the specification of homes without question showed that any small gains due to the log transformation were far outweighed by losses.

(b) *Specifying the Number of Stations (Options Diversity).* Our basic hypothesis here was that, exogenous factors constant, options diversity and types diversity each impact significantly on aggregate viewing. Our proxy for the number of program options available across all stations in the market was indeed the total number of such stations. Adding a station to the market clearly increases the number of different programs receivable by viewers in that market, and hence the chances of finding an option preferable to those available with fewer programs. If viewing levels rose significantly, *cet. par.,* with added stations (hence options) available, one could argue that new viewers entered the market and/or previous viewers found more of interest to watch.

i. *Four-Way versus Two-Way Classification of Stations;* Was there, however, any reason to specify stations in some more refined way? We know, for example, that channel type and network affiliation both impact substantially on station economic performance (tables II.1, II.2, and 6.4–6.7). Indeed, there is considerable evidence that they impact significantly on program composition too (tables II.10 and 6.13). There is some earlier evidence finally that they may even impact on vertical program diversity. Accordingly, there was good reason in testing the hypothesis that options diversity (number of stations) significantly affected viewing, to distinguish not only between the number of VHF and UHF stations but further among numbers of network VHFs, network UHFs, independent VHFs, and independent UHFs. At least, this four-way breakdown of stations would distinguish between the major sources of *programs,* noted for the resources they can bring to bear and the composition of what results. This more detailed specification of stations was tantamount to a two-dimensional weight for each program source (in terms of economic resources available and likely program mix), and increased the chances for program options to show significance.

ii. *Logarithmic Form;* The next questions were whether to cast stations in log form and then whether to interact with market size. One advantage of the log form here over our use of the interactive market dummy (as in the sales price equation) relates to the greater simplicity in handling our four-way breakdown. Thus only four separate variables are needed, each possibly (though not necessarily) interacted with TV homes.

With market dummies, on the other hand, we would need first the four separate stations variables, then four different market dummies, and finally four new interactive terms. Nor need the use of logs of variables (or of variables + 1 to account for the presence of zero values) prevent us from distinguishing between the different impacts of additional stations of any type. As with the sales price interactive market dummy, we would have not a single impact but a table of impacts depending on initial conditions.

With linear equations, to be sure, the reader can go directly from tabulated coefficients to the impacts on dependent variables or to differences in impact, whereas with logs we not only have separate impacts depending on initial conditions but can no longer easily see how our conclusions follow from tabulated coefficients. Yet on balance we felt that the log form was preferable to more cumbersome multiple-market dummy interactives.

In addition, the log of stations is highly correlated with (and a proxy for) log TV homes which we do not specify here. Actually, as noted below, experiments with log TV homes explained far less of total variance than those with linear homes. Also, the log form for number of stations, as seen in Appendix I (pages 422–25), best captures the declining percentage increment in stations which each additional station represents.

iii. *Interactions with TV Homes;* Mention should next be made of interactions with TV homes. The hypothesis was that the number of options as well as of programs types will have different effects on viewing in markets of different sizes. There could be several reasons for this. Market size is a known influence, *cet. par.*, on station economic resources and hence on the quality of (or investment in) particular programs or program groupings. Secondly, market size is correlated with a host of qualitative factors sometimes characterized as degree of urbanization, or life style, which are likely to influence viewing behavior. On both counts interactions of stations or program types with number of TV homes seemed reasonable, though even without such interactions the specification of TV homes alone would of course take some account of these life-style influences.

To sum up so far, the four-way breakdown of stations was preferable to a one- or two-way division on the basis of our knowledge of economic resources and program composition of different kinds of station. In experiments to compare the performance of the two-way and four-way linear specifications, moreover, the evidence did on balance favor the four-way split. In addition to improved explained variance, several exogenous variables showed increased significance with the four-way split, while two of the four-way variables (but neither of the two-way) were significant.[23] Furthermore, the types impact remained significant at the 10 percent level whichever form was used, or retained positive significance in its interacted form.

(c). *A Ranking of Best Equations by Adjusted Explained Variances.* A ranking of the adjusted R-squares of the fourteen best of twenty-two equations run as final experiments, revealed the following.

1. The unique characteristic common to the seven best equations was the significance of the interaction of linear TV homes with program types and with number of stations (options). However, the main contributions to explained variance came principally from the former (types) interactions.

23. The "four-way" variables refer to number of network VHF, network UHF, independent VHF, and independent UHF stations, whereas the "two-way" split refers to the number of VHFs and UHFs only.

2. There was no real advantage in specifying the log of types versus linear types, but there was perhaps a slight gain in significance from the linear form.

3. Equations that had an interaction between the log of TV homes and other variables do not appear in the ranked list until the next to last equation. Indeed, equations that do not interact TV homes at all have higher adjusted R-squares than those in which the interaction is with log of TV homes.

4. Equations that specify the four-way breakdown for stations have higher R-squares than those that specify the two-way split in log form, which were in turn superior to linear two-way.

In sum, there was a gain from interacting TV homes with the number of stations however specified, and with the number of program types as well. However, the additional contributions to explanatory power came mainly from the former interactions.

(d) *Toward a Final Estimating Equation.* Our final estimating equation reflects the preceding findings. Following points 1 and 3, we specified linear homes and also interacted it with stations (options) and types. Following point 2, we kept types linear. These interactions reflected our assumption that options and types could well impact differently in markets of different sizes, for reasons already suggested. Our specification of linear homes and linear types reflected our further assumption that deviations from linearity should be made only for strong reasons, which were lacking here.

Following point 4, we next specified stations by network class and channel type—namely, the four-way breakdown. However, here too there was an important additional reason to do so—namely, the demonstrable impact of these interacted network and channel type attributes as factors influencing the economic resources available for (and hence probable quality of) individual program options. Further supportive of our final specification was the impact of those attributes also on program composition generally. Specifying stations in this detailed manner would optimize the chances for additional stations and hence programs from each source to impact on viewing. The further decision to cast stations in a log form + 1, followed only in part from the superiority of that form over linear for our two-way breakdown. More important, as explained earlier, was the inherent nonlinear character of the stations variable and the greater awkwardness in capturing this with a set of interactive market dummies, where a four-way breakdown is used.

Inclusion of the strongest exogenous variables has already been explained—temperature, multiset families, families earning less than $3,000 income, a Central Time Zone dummy, and TV homes.

Our final estimating equation appears in table II.11 (page 477) (run for average quarter-hour homes), and again in table II.12 (page 478) (run for proportions of tuned-in households). Results derived from each equation are further reported in chapter 3, table 3.7A and 3.9.

TABLE II-13 (3.8)
Estimating Equations for Proportions of Tuned-In Households, 1967
(Based on Station Data)

Independent Variables	ADI Rating	Metro Rating	Metro Share
Constant	1.267	.178	.305
	(5.8)	(5.2)	(5.7)
Average number of program types daily	.290	.028	.043
	(3.8)	(5.0)	(4.9)
TV homes	.008	*	*
	(2.0)		
Network dummy**	.108	.114	.164
	(.4)	(6.3)	(5.8)
VHF dummy**	−.630	.017	.028
	(2.2)	(.9)	(.9)
Log (number of station +1) in market	−3.81	−.359	−.594
	(10.8)	(11.0)	(11.4)
Network dummy × VHF dummy	1.111	.029	.052
	(3.7)	(1.4)	(1.6)
Network dummy × TV homes	−.001	−.0001	−.0002
	(.5)	(1.5)	(1.8)
Number of program types × TV homes	−.001	−.0001	−.0002
	(1.6)	(3.4)	(3.8)
Log (number of station +1) × TV homes	*	.001	.001
		(4.2)	(4.6)
Adjusted R^2	.428	.616	.622
Sample size (stations)	466	399	399
Sample mean (%)	2.102	.214	.330
	(× 10)	(× 100)	(× 100)

NOTE: "Ratings" are percentages of TV homes in market that tune in designated stations specified amounts of time weekly, as estimated by the American Research Bureau (ARB). "Shares" are percentages of tuned in audiences in each market that watch designated stations. ADI markets are "areas of dominant influence" as defined by ARB, whereas metro areas (narrower than ADI markets) are core metropolitan market areas therein.

The upper number in each cell is a regression coefficient, and the lower number in parentheses is a t-value denoting statistical significance.

*Variable rejected by computer program possibly due to collinearity.

**Labeled attribute equals one, zero otherwise.

A final word is in order on the specification of three equations reported in table II.13, geared to replicate our market-level results at the station level. In those equations we regressed proportions and shares of homes tuning in to a large sample of stations during prime time, on the average number of program types carried nightly (vertical diversity). To correct for additional factors that could influence station audience size (and hence obscure our analysis of the impact of diversity on viewing), we also controlled for differences in market size and the number of competing stations.

In addition to normalizing for these factors, we specified two other variables—network affiliation and VHF channel type—which earlier analysis showed to impact substantially on ratings and rates in somewhat similar equations (tables II.2, and II.3). This admittedly crude specification was improved by interacting TV homes with diversity, number of stations, and network ties, and network tie also with VHF channel. The equation was in any case the best we could manage given our inability at an advanced stage of research to introduce the exogenous factors we had specified in our market equation earlier (tables II.11 and II.12).

4. Estimation of Spot Rates with Special Reference to Informational Programming

(a) *Initial Hypotheses.* The specification of our equations to estimate advertiser valuation of informational programming and audiences (table II.14, page 490) was initially developed to explore such assertions as the following: (1) If advertisers place a higher value per viewer on specialized than on mass audiences, the effect on program composition is equivalent to that which would flow from a less skewed distribution of viewer preferences than actually exists. That is, the effective disparity between the sizes of different viewing groups, is said to be reduced by any premium the advertiser places on reaching, say, cultural-informational audiences. Under these assumptions, program duplication will be less likely to occur under competition *or* monopoly.[24] (2) On the other hand, if mass audiences are worth more than specialized audiences per viewer in the advertising market,[25] this will act to reduce diversity and increase program duplication. (3) The "groups worth more to advertisers will more likely get their preferred choice, not viewers in general, but only groups worth more to advertisers."[26]

(b) *Preliminary Equations.* To explore such propositions as these, we first modified our initial, fully specified equation for spot rates (tables II.2, II.3). From the latter specification for 1967, we retained the following common variables: a commercial market dummy equal to one for markets with four or more stations, and zero otherwise; channel type; delivered audience; median city income. These were our original structural factors, many of which significantly influenced twenty-second one-time and five-time spot rates in 1967.

In chapter 5 (table II.3, page 445), however, with these *ceteris paribus* conditions, we had focused principally on three major sets of policy sensitive owner attributes—namely, stations affiliated with newspaper, group, or network companies, the latter affiliations being subdivided into seven zero-one dummies reflective of the full range of single and multi-

24. Owen, Beebe, and Manning, *Television Economics*, pp. 76–77.
25. Ibid., p. 77.
26. Ibid.

ple affiliations that year. The results of this simple additive model were good, with major significance of key structural conditions (channel type, market dummy, delivered audience) and, at points, of all owner attributes.

(c) *Inclusion of Station Programming and Diversity as Independent Variables.* Adapting that equation for present purposes required, in addition to the common market structural factors, inclusion of data on different kinds of programming as well as vertical type diversity. These programming factors were indeed clearly associated with the owner attributes specified in table II.1 (page 442)—almost identical to those in table II.2 (page 443). To permit the programming variables to pick up a maximum of effects on rates directly, we excluded the owner attributes from our first experiments on advertiser valuation. Thus were we able to examine the impact—for example, of fine arts programming, public affairs, news, and vertical diversity generally—directly on rates.

Regardless of the basic determinants of program composition and diversity, that is, we wanted to determine whether, even with an admittedly crude variable specification, advertisers appeared ready to pay some premium to reach the kind of people who watched cultural-informational programming.

(d) *Major Experiments.* In a set of twelve experimental equations run on twenty-second one-time and five-time spot rates in 1967 (N = 426, 296, respectively), the following pattern of results was at least tentatively consistent with the existence of the advertiser's willingness to pay extra for certain programming patterns:

Adjusted R-squared	=	ranged between .6936 and .8021 for equations for one-time rates (N = 426) and from .4696 to .6625 five-time rates (N = 296).
Market dummy	=	positive significance in all twelve equations at 1 percent level.
TV homes	=	positive significance in all six equations where specified, at 1 percent level.
Audience delivered	=	positive significance at 1 percent level, in all six equations where specified.
Median income	=	positive significance in all six equations where specified for one-time rates, at 5 percent or 10 percent levels; positive significance at 10 percent level in two equations for five-time rates, and t-values exceeding 1.0 in four other equations.
Vertical division	=	positive significance at 5 percent level in two of four equations where specified; otherwise t-value below 1.0.
Fine arts	=	positive significance at 10 percent, 5 percent, and 1 percent levels, in five out of seven equations where specified.
Public affairs	=	positive significance at 10 percent level in one out of eight equations where specified, and in two equations with t-values greater than 1.0.
Local news	=	positive significance at 1 percent level in three out

of eight equations where specified, a fourth equation at the 5 percent level, and a fifth equation where t-values exceed 1.0.

Feature film = positive significance at 1 percent level in three out of eight equations where specified, twice more at 5 percent level, and once negative significant at 1 percent level.

Mass entertainment = all negative signs, twice significant at 1 percent level.

The upshot, then, was at least crude evidence that advertisers might indeed be willing to pay a premium to reach audiences who watch cultural-informational programs in prime time (given their tastes, affluence, and education).

(e) *Modified Variable Specification.* However, more detailed analysis was needed. Furthermore, our rates variable was not for individual *program-related* rates but rather a single estimated prime-time spot rate for each station, overall. Be this as it may, we proceeded to verify and refine our variable specification using (1) the FCC's new informational programming data base for 1972; (2) our own further compilations of thirty-second one-time rates also for 1972; and (3) our college education variable as specified for the programming equations in table II.10.[27]

(f) *Further Interactive Analysis.* To improve the estimate of the impact of informational programming on rates, we experimented with several interactions between audience-delivered, college education, and the amount of informational programming. As reported in table II.14, we finally specified five categories of informational programming as percentages of total prime time for each station studied. The question was whether an increase in the percentage of such information time, *cet. par.*, acted to raise spot rates significantly, The single most powerful control factor in this analysis was delivered audience, which we had already confirmed to be a major predictor of spot rates generally.

(g) *Final Estimating Equations.* To minimize distortions due to collinearity between different components of the many relevant interactive terms, we introduced only two interactive variables, one at a time, in equations where we had focused on percentage of time devoted to information. (These interactions were between information time and audience size, or college education.) Interacting with information time this way, we allowed for different informational impact in markets with different educational composition and audiences of different sizes.

Two final equations are reported where, instead of all information, we specified the percentages of time for news, local news, and local public affairs. There the question was simpler than where we had interacted information time. Per one thousand homes delivered did advertisers pay

27. Our assumption in specifying college education was that advertisers would be more likely to pay higher rates, per one thousand audience delivered, in markets with better-educated people. Our basic noninteracted college variable was indeed significant in both equations where it appeared.

TABLE II.14 (10.6)

Regression Equations for 30-Second Spot Rates Paid for Time on Stations with Varying Amounts of Informational Programming, 1978 (6 P.M.-11 P.M.)

Dep. Var.		Y-Intercept	Audience Delivered	Percentage of Total Program Time Devoted To					Percentage of Population in Market with 4 or More Years College	Audience × Percentage of Information Time	Percentage College × Percentage of Information Time
				News	Local News	Public Affairs	Local Public Affairs	All Information			
EQ. 1 *30-Sec. 1-Time Rate* N = 509 R̄² = .9063 mean = $27.613 (× 10)	B t sig.	-4.231 -1.830 .067	40.708 15.040 0.000	n.i.	n.i.	n.i.	n.i.	16.623 1.490 .137	n.i.	10.368 1.030 .303	n.i.
EQ. 2 *30-Sec. 1-Time Rate* N = 453 R̄² = .9063 mean = $29.808 (× 10)	B t sig.	-9.862 -2.810 .005	41.686 14.440 0.000	n.i.	n.i.	n.i.	n.i.	16.945 .400 .163	.424 2.050 .041	7.156 10.700 .503	n.i.
EQ. 3 *30-Sec. 1-Time Rate* N = 453 R̄² = .9071 mean = $29.808 (× 10)	B t sig.	5.482 .670 .503	43.525 63.790 .000	n.i.	n.i.	n.i.	n.i.	-58.996 -1.540 .163	-.912 -1.400 .163	n.i.	6.494 2.160 .031
EQ. 4 *30-Sec. 1-Time Rate* N = 509 R̄² = .9068 mean = $27.613 (× 10)	B t sig.	-3.812 -1.910 .057	43.111 63.200 .000	-.399 -1.550 .122	.814 2.120 .034	.452 2.260 .024	.046 .090 .925	n.i.	n.i.	n.i.	n.i.
EQ. 5 *30-Sec. 1-Time Rate* N = 453 R̄² = .9067 mean = $29.808 (× 10)	B t sig.	-8.833 -2.740 .006	43.316 59.440 .000	-.401 -1.410 .158	.751 1.780 .075	.485 2.180 .030	-.003 -.010 .996	n.i.	.403 1.940 .053	n.i.	n.i.

SOURCE: Our data sources were as follows. For "audience delivered," we multiplied the American Research Bureau's published station ADI "ratings" by standard data on TV homes for comparable markets. See ARB, *Television Day–Part Audience Summary*, November 1972; also, *Broadcasting Yearbook–1973*, and *Television Factbook No. 43*, 1973-74. For "percent of market population with four or more years of college education," we used U.S. Bureau of the Census, *Census of Population for 1970*. All data for estimated program time by program type, derived from the FCC's First Annual Programming Report for All Commercial Television Stations, 1973 (published October 8, 1974). All rates data derived from Standard Rates and Data Service, *Spot Television Rates and Data*, for selected issues during 1972 and 1973. Rates used were those in effect for the longest period during 1972.

n.i. = not included in equation for design purposes.

B = regression coefficient; t = t-value.

higher rates to reach stations that carried relatively more of news or public affairs, local or total? Did they do so even taking into account the market's educational composition?

So much for this brief account of how we arrived at our estimating equations in table II.14. The results derived from this (in table 10.7) are further discussed in chapter 10. Note, finally, the substantial value of adjusted R-squared, .9063, which suggests that the equation (with delivered audience specified) did indeed account for the bulk of total variance.

5. Estimation of Station Audience and Revenues with Special Reference to Informational Programming, 1972

The two sets of equations that underlie our discussion of quantitative license requirements will now be briefly explicated.

The first equation (table II.15, page 492), addresses this question: would any marginal increment of news or public affairs that a station was required to carry, significantly impair its economic viability? In contrast, the second equation (table II.16, page 493), estimated the amount of station time devoted to local news by way of illustrating the impact, *cet. par.*, on the amount of informational programming of such economic factors as station revenue, competition, market size, and fully specified owner attributes.

(a) *Estimating the Amount of Informational Programming Stations with Particular Attributes Could Be Expected to Carry.* This second equation (table II.16), suggested how one might construct industry standards against which to measure a given station's actual performance. The task was to determine the amount of informational programming any station with particular attributes (our specified independent variables) would be predicted to broadcast. If this station's actual performance fell significantly below its predicted level, we presumably have a case for remedial policy to provide required informational programming, with no quality loss.

(b) *Estimating the Economic Effects of Requiring Stations to Alter Their Program Mix.* The first equation (table II.15), on the other hand, attempted to estimate the economic consequences of requiring any station to alter its program mix in light of "deficiencies" revealed by the second equation (table II.16). Presumably, if economic effects were excessive, the required change in programming could be reduced to ensure the station's continued viability, and hence capacity, to provide required informational programming, with no quality loss.

(c) *An Illustrative Local News Equation.* In regard to the second equation (table II.16), finally, we simply used the fully specified programming equations developed mainly in table II.10 (page 473). Our selection of the local news equation for illustrative purposes reflects the high degree of FCC (and public) interest in this variable. However, any other

TABLE II.15 (13.1)

*Estimating Equations for Station Audience and Estimated Revenue with
Special Reference to Informational Programming, 1972**

(6 P.M.-11 P.M.)

	Independent Variables	Equation 1 Audience: Average Quarter-Hour Homes	Equation 2 Estimated Revenue	Equation 3 Audience Average Quarter-Hour Homes	Equation 4 Estimated Revenue
	Constant	0.119^c	118.272^b	-0.119^b	95.961^a
		(1.710)	(2.400)	(−2.330)	(2.670)
L(#V + 1)	Log (number of VHF stations +1)	-0.349^a	−24.718	n.i.	n.i.
		(−4.660)	(−0.470)		
H	TV homes in market	$.033^a$	−3.765	0.033^a	−4.010
		(6.420)	(−1.050)	(6.390)	(−1.090)
NEWS	Minutes of all news	0.0000527	0.323^b	0.000424^a	0.175^b
		(0.230)	(−2.010)	(3.500)	(2.060)
LOCNEWS	Minutes of local news	0.000744^a	0.888^a	n.i.	n.i.
		(2.730)	(4.590)		
INFO	Minutes of information	−0.000146	−0.081	n.i.	n.i.
		(−1.580)	(−1.240)		
	Dummy Variables:†				
V	VHF channel	0.184^a	42.017	0.167^b	69.967
		(2.800)	(0.900)	(2.520)	(1.500)
N	Network affiliate	-0.136^a	-104.280^b	−0.070	-152.370^a
		(−2.150)	(−2.320)	(−1.210)	(−3.750)
O	Network owner	0.086	410.151^a	0.097	438.449^a
		(0.920)	(6.230)	(1.020)	(6.550)
G	Nonnetwork group owner	−0.001	-54.933^a	0.015	-52.236^a
		(−0.040)	(−2.800)	(0.510)	(−2.620)
A	Licensed before 1952	0.046	63.062^a	0.060^b	75.417^a
		(1.590)	(3.060)	(2.010)	(3.600)
	Interacted Variables:				
HG	Group owner × TV homes	0.003	17.100^a	0.001	17.452^a
		(0.640)	(5.130)	(0.240)	(5.170)
HN	Network affiliation × TV homes	0.134^a	73.612^a	0.131^a	73.784^a
		(29.430)	(22.880)	(28.310)	(22.690)
NV	Network affiliation × channel type	0.046	15.707	−0.039	−9.469
		(0.650)	(0.310)	(−0.550)	(−0.190)
	Adjusted R²	.9696	.9399	.9676	.9371
	Sample size (stations)	445	445	445	445
	Mean dependent variable	.782	$390.894	.782	$390.894
		(× 100,000)	(× 10,000)	(× 100,000)	(× 10,000)

SOURCE: The following data were derived from *Broadcasting Yearbook–1973*, and *Television Factbook No. 43*, 1973-74: number of VHF stations within the American Research Bureau's Area of Dominant Influence markets, by channel type and network affiliation, by whether newspaper-, group-, or network-owned, and by whether licensed before 1952. Estimated station revenue derived from Published FCC financial data for 1972 (by market), and the ARB's published estimates of each station's share of metropolitan area viewing, Sunday-Saturday, 6 P.M.-11 P.M., during the survey period. See ARB, *Television Day–Part Audience Summary*, November 1972. Audience data also compiled from the same source.

*Upper number in each cell is a regression coefficient, lower number (in parentheses) is a T-value denoting statistical significance further indicated by superscripts (two-tailed test) as follows: a = 1 percent confidence level; b = 5 percent level; c = 10 percent level.

†Labeled attribute of each dummy variable equals one, zero otherwise.

TABLE II.16 (13.3)

Factors Affecting Station Time Devoted to Local News Broadcasts,
Composite Week, 1972, (6 P.M.-11 P.M.)

		Regression Coefficient	t-value
	Constant	−27.282	−0.78
V	Channel type	83.978[a]	3.89
N	Network affiliation	49.180[a]	2.80
P	In-town newspaper	9.694	1.08
O	Network owner	0.495	0.02
G	Nonnetwork group owner	1.997	0.27
H	TV homes in market	−0.632	−0.85
COLL	Percentage of population with 4+ years college	1.783[b]	2.04
A	Licensed before 1952	15.390	1.59
LogAge	Log number months on air, 1972	23.907[c]	1.77
#VHF	Number of VHF stations in market	−8.853	−1.09
M	Market dummy (1 = 3+ VHF, 0 = other)	−52.881[b]	−2.14
#VHFM	Number of VHF × market dummy	20.575[b]	−2.08
NV	Network affiliation × channel type	−59.349[a]	−2.48
REV	Estimated station revenue	0.080[a]	4.54
(REV)²	(Estimated station revenue)²	−0.0000128[a]	−3.02

Adjusted R-square	.3648
Sample size (stations)	408
Sample mean (minutes local news)	129.605

SOURCE: Same basic source materials as in table 13.1. In addition, percentage of market population with four or more years of college education from U.S. Bureau of the Census, Census of Population for 1970. Estimated local news minutes from FCC's First Annual Programming Report for All Commercial Television Stations, 1973 (published October 8, 1974). Statistical significance (two-tailed test) is: a = 1 percent; b = 5 percent; and c = 10 percent confidence level.

informational category could have been used instead, provided that its explained variance were substantial (in table II.10 this probably limits us to all news, local news, and all information).

Given the origin of our equation for programming, then, there is no need to comment further on its specification here. Suffice it to note only that the divergence between expected and actual amounts of local news carried on stations with designated attributes is calculated by a procedure spelled out in chapter 13 proper (pages 372–80).

(d) *Specification of Informational Programming in Equations for Audience Size and Station Revenue.* In regard to table II.15, on the other hand, the final estimation of audience size and station revenue with reference to minutes of informational programming must be examined briefly. First and foremost, the major ingredients of that variable specification were derived from our experience in estimating these same economic dependent variables as well as spot rates and ratings (table II.9), though without reference to any programming variables. We also drew on our experience with the sales prices equations (table II.8), in particular equations 2–4. (Our exclusion in table II.15 of P and HP reflects their poor performance both in table II.9 and in sales price. However, table II.15 could be further modified to round out our assessment to include the newspaper attribute, too.)

It is clear that our inclusion, in addition to most of the same common variables as in tables II.9 and II.8, of minutes of news, local news, and information only, reflects the higher explained variance of the related equations for programming in table II.10. We would of course equally well have liked to estimate the impact in table II.15, of increased public affairs, local public affairs, and all local (including entertainment). However, the low explained variance of the equations for these program types (in table II.10), raised a serious question as to whether we could effectively introduce those program categories as independent variables in our economic equations (in table II.15).[28]

To estimate a maximum impact of *some* informational category on station economics, we reran equations 1 and 2 in table II.15 *without* local news *or* all information, retaining only *all news* whose own estimating equation had the highest explained variance of any (in table II.10). With few exceptions, most coefficients and t-values in table II.15 were stable across both sets of equations specified, though with a few sign changes in coefficients with low t-values. In dropping local news and all information (and log #VHF + 1), for example, the impact of all news on quarter-hour viewing reached a positive significance level but switched from a negative to a positive influence at 5 percent significance for estimated station revenue. At the same time, the adjusted R-square fell only negligibly. Our removal of log (#VHF + 1) stations reflects earlier experience with sales price equations where inclusion of a comparable stations specification—#VHF stations, market dummy (M), and #VHF × M —at one point made it difficult to include a number of other owner attributes and interactions simultaneously.

The final results derived from table II.15 are reported in table 13.2 and discussed there briefly in the text (pages 367–70). Suffice it here to note that the contrary signs of significant all news and local news impact on economic performance in table II.15, equation 2, wash away when all news alone is specified. In equations 3 and 4 the impact is then significant positive on both audience size and station revenue but extremely small in absolute terms.

28. Since in a system of simultaneous equations (as here) poor predictors will not work, there was of course a problem in introducing some of these programming variables on the right-hand side of our equations in table II.15. Yet too accurate a direct prediction of any dependent programming variable would also have impaired its usefulness as an independent factor due to collinearity.

Name Index

Subject Index

ABC, 223n, 281n, 287, 289; affiliates of, 312n; competitive success of, 30, 30n, 311n, 315, 315n, 316n; entertainment and informational programs on, 360–61; interconnection facilities used by, 410; live programming on, 31–32; merger of, with ITT, 30n; Monday Night Football on, 91–98; opposition of, to Westinghouse Petition, 280n. *See also* National network companies, the

Adjacencies, 42, 46n; alleged value of, 283–90

Adventure programs, 61, 69, 71

Advertisers: FCC's influence on, 44; growth of spot and local, 39; and the NAB Television Code, 45n; and the national networks, 28–29; rates paid by, for informational audiences, 361–62, 382; and rates set by newspaper licensees, 156–60; role of, in program production, 34–35, 39–43; small, 35n; and station ownership, 20, 151, 154; weakening control of, 46. *See also* Commercial announcements; Spot announcements

Affiliates, 27; and economic rents, 125–30; and the function of national networks, 28 (*see also* National network companies, the); news programming carried by, 299–302; profitability of, 140, 155–56; relative program costs of, 281–83; and syndicators, 38; top market leverage of, 290–93

Aged, the, 253

Aggregate viewing, impact of diversity on, 60–61, 62–85

Air transport, 19

All-Channel Receiver Law, 242

Allocation. *See* Licensing and allocation policies; Television Allocation Plan

American Newspaper Publishers Association (ANPA): on cross-ownership issues, 212n, 215, 216n, 218, 218n, 223, 227, 227n; divestiture study by, 227

American Telephone and Telegraph Company (AT&T), 25, 28, 33, 48; and the Bell complex, 406; deterrence by, of potential entry, 409; and the Ford Satellite Proposal, 404–6; reduced-rate access to interconnection facilities of, 385, 405–11

Analysis of the Network Affiliate Relationship in Television, An, 30n, 245n, 246n, 293n, 295n, 303n, 333n

Antidiscrimination rules, 354

Appeals Court decisions. *See* U.S. Court of Appeals (D.C. Circuit)

Ashbacker decision, 355

Atlass Communications, 216n

Auctions of broadcast licenses, 340, 394–400, 410

Audience flow, ·30, 43, 43n; and simultaneous transmission, 34; and the value of adjacencies, 283

Audiences: and advertising rates, 159; evaluating the response of, 25; for informational programming, 300, 360–62, 382; predicting, 33–34; program type impact on size of, 63–73; targeted by public television, 253; of VHF stations, 149–50. *See also* Audience flow

Average audience distribution (AAD) proposal, 381–82

Award ceremonies, 69

Barrow Report (House Commerce Committee *Report on Network Broadcasting*), 29n, 38n, 39n, 44n, 59, 277, 277n

Bell complex, 406–7, 409–10

Bicycled tape networks, 33, 47–50, 409

Block-booking, 29, 39n

British television, 43, 344–45

Broadcasters Nonprofit Satellite Corporation, 404

Broadcast regulation. *See* Federal Communications Commission (FCC); Licensing and allocation procedures; Television

Broadcast rents. *See* Economic rents; Scarcity rents

Broadcast trust fund, 340

Bureau of the Budget Circular No. A–25 (User Charges), 386, 386n, 387–91

Cable television systems, 345, 346n, 347; and cross-ownership issues, 223–24, 235; and deregulation, 397; impediments to, 103; presumable regulatory cost of, 387

Report on Chain Broadcasting (FCC), 29*n*
Report on Network Broadcasting (Barrow Report), 29*n*, 38*n*, 39*n*, 44*n*, 59, 277, 277*n*
Reruns, 324–25
Reuss Bill, 395, 396*n*, 406
Robinson, Glen O.: on contrast of auctions and lotteries, 395*n*; on the Cowles Florida Broadcasting decision, 395*n*; on cross-ownership issues, 211*n*, 212*n*, 213*n*, 214*n*, 218*n*, 221*n*, 227*n*, 229*n*, 230*n*, 232*n*, 234*n*; on prime-time access, 37, 37*n*, 326*n*, 328*n*, 334*n*, 335–36, 336*n*, 337–39
Rural area service, 7, 45, 109

Satellite technology, 7, 19*n*, 345, 347; and cross-ownership issues, 223–24, 235; and deregulation, 397; Ford Foundation proposal to utilize, 404–6; as guarantee against abuse, 212; impediments to, 103
Scarcity rents: control of, 346–48; dissipation of, through competition, 344–45; diversion of, into public service, 345–46 (*see also* Quantitative program requirements); external linkage of, with public services, 394–97, 411; internal linkage of, with public service, 403–11; regulatory implications of, 342–48; use of, to fund public television, 385–86, 392–411. *See also* Economic rents
Science fiction, 69, 71
Second Report and Order in Docket No. 18110 (FCC), 10*n*, 11*n*, 218*n*, 220–22, 229*n*
Second Report and Order in Docket No. 19622 (FCC), 37*n*, 325*n*, 333*n*
Sets, 28, 242–43
Sherman Act, 29, 295
Signal interference, 6, 104–5, 246; and the licensing and allocation system, 351; and the Television Allocation Plan, 295
Signal quality, 25
Simultaneous transmission: costs of, 31–34, 38, 47–50; and the time zones, 31*n*
Situation comedy, 55, 57*n*, 61, 69, 71
Sixth Report and Order (FCC), 7, 7*n*, 144*n*. *See also* Television Allocation Plan
Soap operas, 92
Social attitudes, 45*n*
Source diversity, 57, 57*n*, 58, 61; and prime-time access issues, 331–40
"Sources of Economic Legislation," 17*n*

Space utilization. *See* Satellite technology
Spectrum congestion, 106–7
Spectrum rights, 105. *See also* Entry controls; Property rights in spectrum
Sponsorship. *See* Advertisers; Commercial announcements; Spot announcements
Sports programming, 31, 31*n*, 69; Monday Night Football, 91–98; and prime-time access, 325
Spot announcements, 26, 38, 42; growth of, 39; impact of informational programming on rates for, 317–22; network, 280, 283–90; rates for, 300, 302, 317–22; twenty-second, 159, 280; thirty-second, 35*n*. *See also* Advertisers; Commercial announcements
Station editorials, 11, 209, 217
Station ownership. *See* Ownership
Structural diversity, 248–50
Students' FCC Study Group, 232
Symposium on Media Concentration (FTC), 291*n*, 294*n*, 304
Syndication, 26, 38, 166

Talent unions, 102
Telecommunications Consumer Coalition, 348*n*
Television: British, 43, 344–45; cable, 28, 103 (*see also* Cable transmission); competition in, 9–11, 276 (*see also* Competition); educational, 25–26, 329 (*see also* Educational television); function of affiliation in, 290–93 (*see also* Affiliates); government R&D expenditures in, 19, 19*n* (*see also* U.S. government); interconnection facilities for, 406–11 (*see also* Interconnection facilities); licensing procedures in, 102–10 (*see also* Licensing and allocation policies); live, 31–34 (*see also* Live transmission); local, 330, 333–34 (*see also* Localism); magazine format for, 4, 46; methods for studying licensing of, 3–21; national network operations in, 28–30 (*see also* National network companies, the); objectives versus results in regulatory assessment of, 4–8 (*see also* FCC); program diversity in, 59–87, 331–40 (*see also* Diversity); programming biases in, 9*n* (*see also* Programming); proposed indefinite licenses for, 20*n*; public, 269–70, 340 (*see also* Public television); regulatory criteria as standards for evaluation of, 8–17
Television Allocation Plan, 26, 148, 150, 246, 295–96; and economic rents, 125–26. *See also* Sixth Report and Order